OUR PEOPLE'S WAR

OUR PEOPLE'S WAR

HOME INTELLIGENCE REPORTS AND THE MONITORING OF BRITISH MORALE, JUNE 1941–DECEMBER 1944

Edited by Jeremy A. Crang

BLOOMSBURY ACADEMIC
LONDON • NEW YORK • OXFORD • NEW DELHI • SYDNEY

BLOOMSBURY ACADEMIC
Bloomsbury Publishing Plc
50 Bedford Square, London, WC1B 3DP, UK
1385 Broadway, New York, NY 10018, USA
29 Earlsfort Terrace, Dublin 2, Ireland

BLOOMSBURY, BLOOMSBURY ACADEMIC and the Diana logo are
trademarks of Bloomsbury Publishing Plc

First published in Great Britain 2024

Cover design by Grace Ridge
Cover image: Michael Ford, 'War Weapons Week in a Country Town'
(1941) © Imperial War Museum (Art.IWM ART LD 1291)

A catalogue record for this book is available from the British Library.

A catalog record for this book is available from the Library of Congress.

ISBN: HB: 978-1-3503-3502-8
        ePDF: 978-1-3503-3504-2
       eBook: 978-1-3503-3503-5

Typeset by Integra Software Services Pvt. Ltd.

To find out more about our authors and books visit www.bloomsbury.com
and sign up for our newsletters.

For Fiona and Emily
and
in memory of
Paul Addison (1943–2020)

CONTENTS

LIST OF FIGURES

ACKNOWLEDGEMENTS

In compiling this volume, I have accumulated a number of debts. First and foremost, I am grateful to Andrew Gordon at David Higham and to Emily Drewe at Bloomsbury Academic for their indispensable support for the project. Thanks are also due to the staff of the National Archives at Kew for their unfailing courtesy and helpfulness, to Lucy Metzger, Anne Halliday and Amanda Speake for their invaluable assistance in preparing the Home Intelligence reports for publication, to Megan Harris, Paige Harris, Grace Ridge, Peter Stafford and Geoff Reynolds for seeing the book through the press with such skill and conviviality, and to Magda Kowalczuk and Alistair Gaeta in the School of History, Classics and Archaeology at the University of Edinburgh for their expert help with the administration of the project. I am also indebted to colleagues and friends who provided advice and support along the way: Martin Alexander, Rosalie Alexander, Joan Cole, Terry Cole, Mark Connelly, Owen Dudley Edwards, Trevor Griffiths, Emma Hunter, Lisa Kendall, Paul MacKenzie, Paul Norris, Richard Overy, Sarah Prescott, Rachael Quirk, Sabine Rolle, Gary Sheffield, Edward Spiers, Peter Stanley, Wendy Ugolini and David White. I am especially grateful to Richard Toye for providing helpful comments on the manuscript (and to the anonymous referees for Bloomsbury Academic who did likewise). All errors of fact and interpretation are of course my own. The Home Intelligence reports are published here under the Open Government Licence.

I owe a deep debt of gratitude to my late colleague and friend Paul Addison. This is the third volume of a trilogy of Home Intelligence volumes that we had planned and, like the previous two (which were published in 2010 and 2020 respectively), it would have been co-edited with Paul but for his untimely passing. This book is thus a product of our close collaboration over many years and, in many ways, as much his as it is mine. In this respect, I must pay special tribute to Rosy Addison and Michael Addison for their support in enabling me to complete the volume. I am further grateful to Charles Taylor for sharing memories of his father, Dr Stephen Taylor (later Lord Taylor), who was director of Home Intelligence during the period covered by this book. My last word of thanks goes to my wife Fiona and our daughter Emily, for their unstinting love and forbearance.

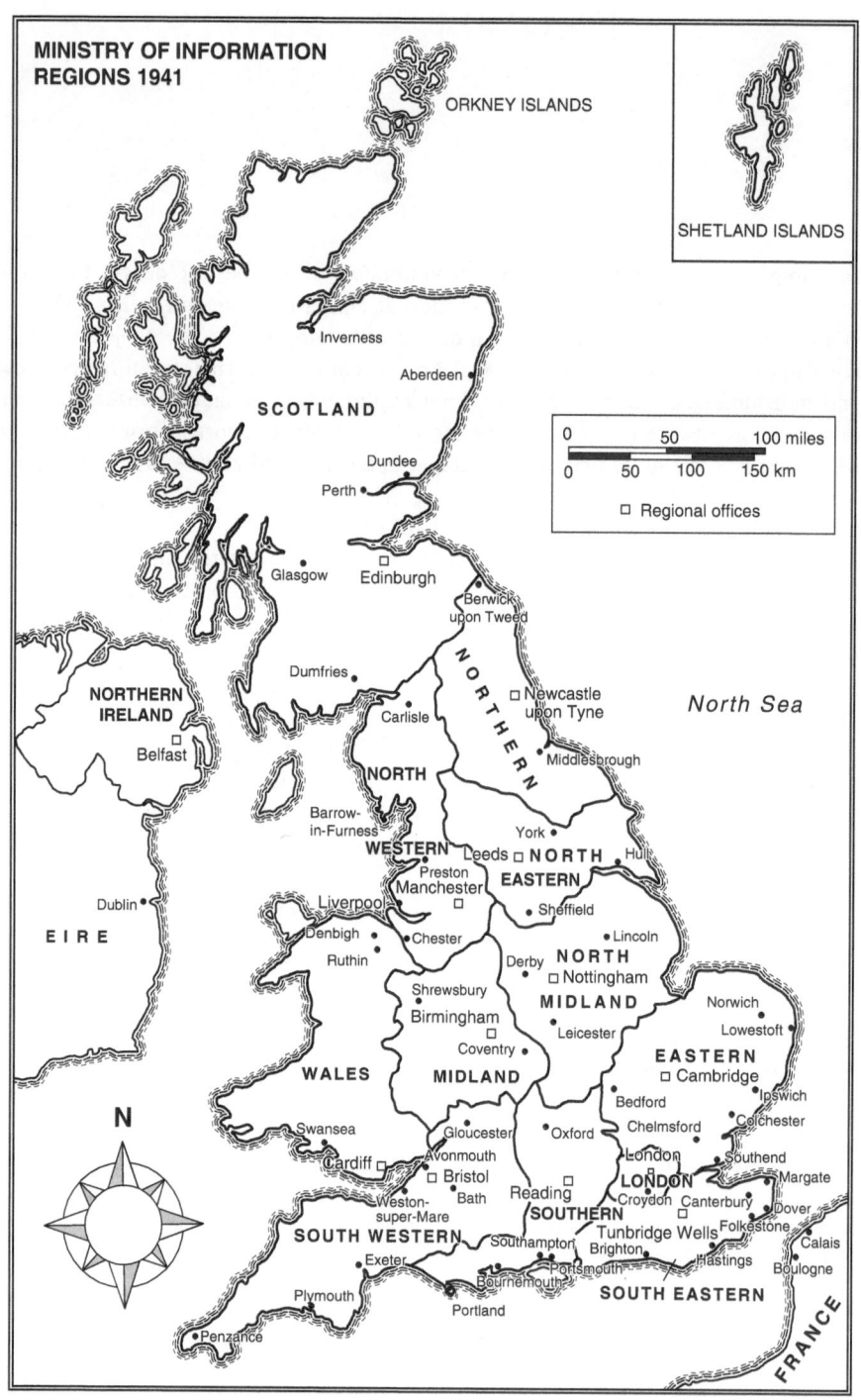

MAP: Ministry of Information Regions, 1941.

INTRODUCTION

During the Second World War the British government undertook a unique experiment in the monitoring of public opinion. This was organized by Home Intelligence (HI), a unit of the Ministry of Information (MOI) that kept a close watch on popular attitudes on the home front. Intelligence from a range of sources and from all regions of the United Kingdom was sifted by a small team of officials, based at the Senate House of the University of London, who compiled secret reports on the state of public morale. These came to be circulated both within the ministry and across Whitehall. From May to September 1940, they were issued every day (Sundays excepted), after which they were presented as weekly reports until Home Intelligence was closed down in December 1944. This collection of documents offers us a remarkable insight into the mindset of the British people at a time when the fate of the nation depended, among other things, on their willingness to support the war effort. It is also worth remembering that the British public, like those who collated the reports, did not know what was going to happen next and had none of the historical hindsight that we now possess. The reports thus give us a vivid sense of living through an unfolding drama.[1]

In *Listening to Britain: Home Intelligence Reports on Britain's Finest Hour, May to September 1940* (The Bodley Head, 2010), Paul Addison and I published a complete set of the HI reports covering the period of the Dunkirk evacuation, the Battle of Britain and the early weeks of the Blitz. In a sequel, *The Spirit of the Blitz: Home Intelligence and British Morale, September 1940–June 1941* (Oxford University Press, 2020), we published an unabridged set of the HI reports covering the full Blitz period. This volume completes a trilogy and covers the period from June 1941 to December 1944, when the HI reports ceased. These were the years when the Soviet Union and the United States became Britain's allies, the military tide of the war gradually turned against the Axis powers after their victories in Europe, North Africa and the Asia Pacific theatre, and thoughts turned increasingly to reconstruction and the post-war world.

Our People's War, however, differs from the previous two volumes in that it incorporates a selection of the weekly HI reports (and selected appendices) from June 1941 to December 1944, rather than the complete series; to do otherwise would have made the book unmanageable for the reader given the number of reports produced over this period. The reports are supplemented by a selection of 'special' reports that HI conducted for government departments from December 1941 onwards. The aim has been to ensure a spread of reports across the three-and-a-half-years of the war they encompass, but with some allowance for clustering around key wartime events. An endeavour has also been made to incorporate reports that illustrate the range of topics and themes covered by HI, as well as the fluctuations of public opinion.

On the outbreak of war, an MOI was created in Britain to help maintain morale on the home front. It was, however, realized that in order to influence public opinion the ministry needed its own independent source of intelligence on popular attitudes to provide a rapid and effective means of monitoring the nation's mood. An HI unit was thus established in December 1939 to 'provide an assessment of home morale' and the story of this enterprise resembles an Evelyn Waugh novel with its cast of colourful and unconventional characters.[2] The unit was run initially by Mary Adams. Adams was one of the many temporary wartime civil servants drafted into government who brought an unorthodox element to the Whitehall establishment. A graduate in botany from University College Cardiff, she had been a research scholar and extra-mural lecturer at Cambridge in the 1920s and published papers on cytology. In 1930 she had joined the staff of the BBC as an adult education officer and gone on to make radio programmes for the Talks Department. In 1937 she had become the corporation's first female producer for its infant television service.[3] Although married to the Conservative member of parliament, Vyvyan Adams, she herself, in the words of her daughter, was 'a socialist, a romantic communist ... a fervent atheist and advocate of humanism and common sense'.[4] One of Adam's early recruits to HI was the artist Nicolas Bentley, who had drawn illustrations for the books of humorous authors such as J. B. Morton ('Beachcomber') of the *Daily Express*.[5] Another Adams recruit was the poet and writer Winifred Holmes, who was part of a literary circle that included T. S. Eliot, W. H. Auden, Edith Sitwell and Christopher Isherwood.[6] However, in order, perhaps, to counterbalance the artistic talents of Bentley and Holmes with a more scientific perspective, she also recruited Dr Stephen Taylor. He was a psychiatrist who as a young doctor had been keen to get his voice on the airwaves and had broadcast for Adams when she was at the BBC. In 1938 he had published a study of 'suburban neurosis', which delineated the symptoms of loneliness, boredom and anxiety among housewives who presented at the outpatient departments of London hospitals. By 1940 he had turned his attention to the investigation of 'mental illness as a clue to normality'. During the early months of the war, Taylor was serving in the Royal Navy Volunteer Reserve as a neuropsychiatric specialist at Barrow Gurney naval hospital near Bristol; but Adams persuaded the First Lord of the Admiralty, A. V. Alexander, to release him. He joined HI in May 1940.[7]

Adams set to work on constructing the machinery of intelligence from which HI's morale reports would be compiled. The assumption was that no single source could be relied upon as an authoritative indicator of popular morale, and thus a range of sources were drawn on. These included intelligence from the MOI's own regional information officers (RIOs) in the thirteen MOI regions across the United Kingdom; from the MOI's Wartime Social Survey, which undertook quantitative studies using market research techniques (initially for HI but then restricted to other government departments); from the postal censors who monitored outgoing mail from the UK as well as from vulnerable areas within the country; from the police duty room reports of Chief Constables; and from the BBC Listener Research department.[8]

HI also placed much reliance on Mass Observation (MO) at this time. MO was an independent social research organization run by the brilliant but maverick self-taught social anthropologist, Tom Harrisson, who had been another of Adams's broadcasters during her time at the BBC. It had at its disposal a nationwide panel of volunteers who responded by post to requests for their own observations and opinions, but it also employed a team of paid observers who conducted interviews in the street, watched people's behaviour, eavesdropped on their conversations and recorded their unguarded remarks. Pushing the line that MO could bridge the gulf between the leaders and the led, Harrisson was commissioned by HI to provide it with regular summaries of morale.[9] The first of HI's reports was issued on 18 May 1940, and over the following year Adams's unit closely monitored the public mood as the three acts of Britain's 'finest hour' – the evacuation from Dunkirk, the Battle of Britain and the Blitz – played out. Yet HI's articulation of popular complaints against the authorities in its reports made it enemies among those in government who were sensitive to criticism. Tensions arose, in particular, with the Home Office, and Adams found herself increasingly frustrated and isolated as the decision was taken to restrict her reports to circulation within the MOI and deny them to other home front ministries, such as Food, Labour or Health, whose interactions with the public were important influences on morale. In April 1941 she departed the MOI, a casualty of the 'turf wars' and internal politics of Whitehall. She went on to a job in the North American service of the BBC.[10]

Stephen Taylor took over the running of HI from Adams.[11] Taylor was far more at home in the male-dominated corridors of power than his predecessor. 'To look at,' wrote Nicolas Bentley, who became his deputy, 'he was tall, with good strong features – what Dornford Yates would have called an open countenance, though at times it could close up in an expression of strong disapproval – and large blue-grey eyes, which, besides their traditional association of innocence, could occasionally take on a look of stone-cold cunning.' Taylor was also, Bentley continued, 'very tough indeed … he knew as a rule exactly what he wanted to do, why he wanted to do it and how it should be done'.[12] No doubt his professional standing as a psychiatrist, and his ability to explain the psychological concepts that lay behind the assessment of popular morale in common-sense terms, gave him a certain authority within government circles. But he could also be disarming in his dealings with civil servants. Bentley recounted that at meetings he had a habit of chewing his handkerchief as though it was a lettuce and that this quirk was exploited by Taylor to skilful effect to deflate the more obstructive type of official: 'There's nothing like a mouthful of handkerchief to disconcert a higher civil servant who, having asked a question wittily barbed, awaits your answer.'[13] Like Adams, Taylor was a socialist, and he combined his work for HI with discreet lobbying for a national health service through the pages of the *Lancet* (of which he had briefly been an assistant editor in 1939) and the *Spectator*.[14] He was also strongly patriotic, with a distrust of the progressive intelligentsia. Before the war he had been a regular guest at Friday night cocktail parties held at the Adams's flat in London, overlooking Regent's Park, where such figures tended to congregate. There he had 'met any number of "progressive" people, with whom I found I had almost nothing in common'.[15]

Taylor reorganized HI's intelligence-gathering machinery. He significantly boosted the MOI's own regional intelligence apparatus. From the summer of 1941, regional intelligence officers were added to the staffs of the RIOs. These intelligence officers (or senior assistant officers, as they were known, to avoid any implication of spying on individuals) were tasked with compiling weekly reports for HI on public opinion in their individual regions. To this end they were to create panels of regional 'contacts' (an MOI version of the MO panel) to provide the raw material from which their reports could be compiled. This was a system that had been organized by HI in the London region during the summer of 1940 and was now rolled out across the country. These contacts were to be recruited within each region, on a ratio of one to every 10,000 head of population, from among men and women who were regarded as 'sensible' and 'level-headed'; who were able to 'understand the nature of the work, and ... appreciate its value'; and who were in occupations that came 'into contact with a large number of people each day'. The types of contacts suggested were doctors, parsons, shopkeepers, publicans, librarians, teachers, foremen, trade union officials, bank managers, factory welfare workers, billeting officers and local journalists. Contacts in a region were to be asked to report – by letter, by telephone or in person – on the spontaneous attitudes of people they met on a range of home front issues. A list of suggested subjects for comment included general matters, such as the state of public confidence and reaction to the news, as well more specialized topics that affected people's lives, such as food, fuel and transport. The guidance emphasized that this process was not about 'snooping' on the public but observing and relating what people 'thought' and 'said'. The contacts were further instructed that they should relay the opinion of others rather than 'what they themselves feel'. They were also expected, when necessary, to pass back to those with whom they were in touch 'correct information on subjects about which they are seriously misinformed'. In compiling the reports, the intelligence officers could, in addition, draw upon their local information committees. These had been established early in the war to assist RIOs in sustaining local public morale and were composed of representatives of the political parties, businesses, local authorities, voluntary bodies and other interest groups. Further material could be gleaned from the MOI staff at the regional offices, such as films officers, who came into regular contact with the public. Any pressing concerns that came to light in the reports, and which could be resolved at a local level, were to be taken up with the regional offices of the relevant government departments. Those matters unlikely to be settled locally were to be identified to HI, which maintained close contacts with the headquarters of these departments. By April 1942 intelligence officers had recruited between 200 and 400 contacts in each of the MOI regions. Not all of these contacts were called upon each week, so as to reduce the demands on them and avoid staleness; but it was reckoned that a minimum of thirty of them, and often a good many more, contributed to each regional report. RIOs were expected to vet and approve these weekly assessments.[16]

The thirteen weekly regional intelligence reports were sent to the headquarters of HI in London, which in the spring of 1942 housed about a dozen staff in total.[17] There, they were cross-referenced and synthesized for the consolidated HI national report. The material was divided up between 'general' and 'special' comments, although the division was not always clear cut. The compilers included statements only if there was considerable regional evidence to support them. In this respect, the space devoted to each subject, and order in which they were placed, came to be roughly indicative of the degree of public interest a subject was generating. The intelligence from the regions was further scrutinized against, and supplemented by, other available sources such as the Wartime Social Survey, BBC Listener Research, the postal censors and police duty room reports.[18] The Gallup polls of the British Institute of Public Opinion also became a regular feature of the appendices. MO was, however, sidelined. Taylor had apparently met the buccaneering Harrisson at one of Adams's parties before the war and was unimpressed. 'I did not take to him', he recounted, 'if only because he seemed to be a journalist masquerading as a scientist.'[19] He was also sceptical about the reliability of MO's intelligence. He suspected that Harrisson interpreted his results 'with greater enthusiasm than accuracy' and found his reports alarmist and tendentious. Although MO continued to receive ad hoc commissions from HI, Harrisson would be forced to look outside the MOI for future patronage.[20]

The HI reports were drafted and edited by Taylor and his staff. This involved checking for clarity and style; for objectivity (such phrases as 'it is surprising to find' or 'contrary to what one might expect' were omitted); for policy considerations (so that 'where personalities were involved' there was 'a true picture without being gratuitously offensive'); and for even-handedness (to ensure 'an honest balance as existing in the minds of the public'). From 28 May 1942, the weekly reports were issued on a Thursday. This came to be regarded as the optimal day in order to allow the regional intelligence officers the maximum time to compile and despatch their individual reports, whilst also giving the HI staff in London (who began drafting at 9.30 on a Wednesday morning) enough time to prepare the consolidated report and circulate it on a Friday. Meanwhile, government departments commissioned HI to produce 'special' reports on subjects in which they were particularly interested.[21] The earliest is dated 5 December 1941, and some sixty survive in the archives.[22]

Taylor judiciously restored the circulation of HI's reports to interested parties outside the MOI. By 1943 the weekly external circulation list had grown to 148 copies.[23] The recipients came to include other Whitehall departments, the War Cabinet Offices, 10 Downing Street, Buckingham Palace and the US Embassy (a sign of how integrated into the British establishment the US ambassador, John Winant, had become). They were also despatched to the British ambassador in Moscow (and later to those in Paris and Rome) and British ministers of state in Cairo, Algiers and West Africa.[24] Given the circulation of the reports to Downing Street, it was inevitable that they would come to the attention of prime minister Winston Churchill. Indeed, in April 1942 he sent a dismissive minute to the Minister of Information, Brendan Bracken, who he had appointed the previous year:

> There is hardly anything in this which could not have been written by a man sitting in a London office and imagining the echoes in the country to the London Press.

I doubt very much whether this survey is worth its trouble. How many people are engaged upon it, and how much does it cost?[25]

This was an ominous intervention. But Taylor had cultivated the support of the prime minister's personal assistant, Major Desmond Morton, as well as his doctor, Sir Charles Wilson (later Lord Moran), in order to 'protect us from the wrath of the mighty'.[26] The MOI hierarchy also backed him. Cyril Radcliffe, the MOI Director-General, prepared a briefing document for Bracken in which he explained the careful process by which the reports were constructed and advised that it would be a mistake to end them:

> they are extremely useful pointers, and I think accurate ones, to trends of feeling and to phases of feeling in which trouble lies or is beginning to be felt ... I think that it was said of Jeremiah 'This man is worthy of death for he hath prophesied against the city.' I should deprecate the same remedy being applied to the Home Intelligence Reports.[27]

Bracken, one of Churchill's most trusted Conservative allies and confidants,[28] took Radcliffe's advice and in his response to the prime minister affirmed their value:

> I agree that a plausible weekly intelligence report could be compiled by one man sitting in a London office and using his imagination. The important thing is the fact that the reports are not written in this way ... .
>
> ... the final summary report does in fact proceed from the genuine collection of views and opinions from a very large number of independent non-official people all over the country.[29]

Churchill indicated his agreement and HI was allowed to continue its business.[30] In fact, from June to November 1942, at a time when there was a good deal of concern in government circles about the state of public morale, Bracken submitted periodic summaries of 'home opinion' to the War Cabinet which were based on the weekly HI reports.[31] In August 1943 the prime minister even directed that a verbatim extract from the report for 20–27 July, which featured an assessment of public attitudes to the Allied bombing of Rome, should be included among the War Cabinet papers.[32]

As historical sources, the documents presented here need to be read with a critical eye. In an explanatory cover sheet for recipients, HI drew attention to some of the methodological issues to be kept in mind when scrutinizing the reports. For example, they deal in perceptions of public opinion rather than verified facts: 'The aim of this Report is to present an impartial assessment of public feeling about the war and the war effort. It is not a record of *fact*, except in so far as public opinion is itself a fact.'[33] They also tend to foreground aspects of discontent over those of satisfaction: 'The public is more prone to criticise than to praise. Good work or efficiency is usually taken for granted. An accurate record of expressed feeling will, therefore, tend to be critical rather than laudatory.'[34] Furthermore, they were not intended to be seen in isolation from one another: 'In assessing the state of public feeling there are no absolutes. Findings can only be comparative. Each issue of this Report must therefore be read as part of a continuous series. Unless the series is seen as a whole, the significance of fluctuations in feeling cannot be appreciated.'[35] All of this was sometimes difficult for harassed government officials to appreciate when their departments came under attack in the reports. Taylor had to work hard to convince them that 'the recording of a public misapprehension did not imply its endorsement'.[36]

There are questions, too, around how effectively the intelligence machinery was able to excavate all strata of popular opinion. It is likely, for instance, that working-class attitudes were often reported second-hand through middle-class panels of regional contacts, and that aspects of wartime experience were therefore lost in transmission.[37] In the spring of 1944, an MOI conference concluded that, with the exception of the Northern and North Midland regions, working-class opinion was not proportionately represented in the coverage of contacts.[38] The RIO for the Midland region admitted that the 'Intelligence Officer and I are still haunted by the suspicion, which every week more nearly approaches a conviction, that our operative field does not really represent working class opinion on the war and its problems, in so far as there may be such a thing'.[39] This difficulty was compounded by the expectations of regional contacts. As James Hinton has argued, in asking them to report on the views of other people's opinions, but not their own, there was a danger that many would generalize on the basis of their personal experiences. What was more, by encouraging the contacts to correct misinformation among the people they met, they were acting as influencers for the MOI, rather than simply reporters of opinion, and thus potentially compromising their impartiality.[40] Meanwhile, some regional intelligence officers were more rigorous than others. In the South-Western region, it was disclosed that instead of arranging for her weekly quota of contacts to communicate their assessments of opinion to her just before writing the report so that it was as up to date as possible, as happened elsewhere, the intelligence officer preferred to receive staggered feedback throughout the week so she was not overwhelmed. This meant that her reports suffered from 'bittiness and lack of solidity'. She was persuaded to come into line with the general practice.[41]

There is a further consideration related to the assessment of morale. Paul Addison characterized this term as 'the woolliest and most muddled concept of the war', and although it was frequently on the lips of government officials and commentators no one knew quite how to define or measure it.[42] Taylor tried to bring some intellectual clarity to the task. He defined good morale as the public's willingness to 'go through with the war to final victory, whatever the cost to the individual or the group' and categorized it as being determined by a mixture of mental and material factors, and primarily reflected in behaviours rather than states of opinion: 'Morale must therefore ultimately be measured, not by what a person thinks or says, but by what he does and how he does it. This distinction is particularly important in dealing with the British public in whom admirable behaviour is often coupled with a veritable wail of grumbles.'[43] But it can be surmised that HI was better equipped to report on popular opinion than behaviour. It is probable that the Ministry of Labour, for example, would have known more about the incidence of industrial disputes than HI; the Ministry of Production more about levels of output; the Ministry of Food more about the extent of the black market; and the Ministry of Home Security more about participation in civil defence duties. HI's knowledge of these matters probably derived mainly from the indirect reporting of chatter among patients in the doctor's surgery or among workers in the factory canteen. As an accurate measurement of morale, as defined by Taylor, the HI reports are thus more likely to be indicative rather than conclusive.[44]

Nonetheless, with these provisos, the weekly HI reports are an invaluable resource for historians of the home front. They are methodical and systematic in their compilation, presented in a standard format, indicative of the most important public issues of the moment, cover all parts of the United Kingdom, and draw on an impressive range of sources supplemented by a full reference apparatus. Taylor believed that the reports were 'a surprisingly accurate statement of British public opinion' and convincing evidence of their validity was the 'high degree of agreement which is usually found between the thirteen different regional intelligence reports', reinforced by the fact that 'the Intelligence Officers have no possibility of collaborating'.[45] He likened them to 'a weekly barometer reading of public feeling'.[46] In this regard, they offer us a unique record of the contemporaneous thoughts and sentiments of the British people, as well as the ebbs and flows of popular opinion.[47] Collectively, they read like the war diary of a nation.[48]

Readers will come to their own judgements on the reports, and interpretations will undoubtedly diverge. But the documents reproduced in this volume provide a compelling 'real time' window into public reactions to the major military events of the period. These include the German invasion of the Soviet Union, the Japanese attack on Pearl Harbor, the fall of Singapore, the surrender of Tobruk, the defence of Stalingrad, the victory at El Alamein, the defeat of Italy, the strategic bombing of Germany and the Normandy landings. They also offer us much valuable information on the continuing stresses and strains of life on the home front such as the blackout, rationing, fuel economy, public transport, billeting, income tax and industrial relations – not to mention the V-weapon attacks of 1944 which brought back the terrors of the Blitz. Prominent too are commentaries on broadcasting and presentation of the news, juvenile delinquency, anti-Semitism and relations with US servicemen. Running alongside this, popular hopes and fears about the post-war world come to feature strongly and HI carefully monitored attitudes to the Beveridge report, as well as other aspects of reconstruction. Reading and re-reading the reports, one repeatedly discovers some new aspect previously overlooked and we can regard them as indispensable in understanding both the unity and the diversity of wartime Britain, as well as the many-sided experience of living through the 'people's war'. We also catch glimpses of public emotion at moments of high drama. The report for 31 May to 7 June 1944 covered the first reactions to D-Day:

'At last ... Thank God it's started!' sums up the general feeling of profound relief from the tension and the strain of waiting.

Many were surprised when the news first broke, having expected a more sensational start, more 'fuss' and dislocation of civilian life; some cheered; some wept hysterically; some felt 'flattened out' ... 'sick in the stomach'. The great majority, however, are described as confident, calm and steady, and excitement – even when intense – is usually restrained ... There is, too, much anxiety for the safety of those taking part, relatives – and especially women – being particularly fearful....

... many find it 'too big to talk about'.[49]

The selected HI special reports amplify themes raised in the weekly reports. The most extensive of the special reports included here is on 'Public Feeling on Post-War Reconstruction'. This was commissioned in June 1942 by Sir William Jowitt – a Labour minister in the coalition government who was serving as Paymaster General with responsibility for reconstruction matters.[50] The inquiry took HI into the contested territory of party politics, and there were rumblings from Conservative party central office about local information committees being dragged into discussion of political problems.[51] The report was nevertheless completed in November 1942 and incorporated a series of progressive ideals across a range of social, economic and industrial policy areas. Although Taylor privately found the contents of the report 'on the dull side – perhaps a very good thing',[52] Jowitt was delighted. He commended it to Brendan Bracken as 'an extraordinarily valuable document'.[53] Another Labour minister, Hugh Dalton, President of the Board of Trade, was equally taken with it when he obtained a copy.[54] Mindful no doubt of its value in strengthening the hand of the Labour party in lobbying for the social reforms incorporated in the Beveridge report, which had been published to public acclaim on 1 December 1942, he wrote to Jowitt on 6 December:

> This is a most interesting and encouraging document, which should stimulate us all, Ministers and officials alike, to quicken our steps and to leap over obstacles placed in our path by timid, short-sighted, or sinister persons. I would like to suggest that copies should be circulated to all our colleagues who are concerned with Reconstruction problems, and to their principal official advisors. This document is too good to keep within a narrow circle. For my part, I would like to publish it as a White Paper.[55]

Jowitt agreed to distribute the report to the ministers and officials concerned.[56] Bracken, however, resisted its transformation into a government publication:

> I am afraid that I don't think it would do at all to publish the Survey as a White Paper. The work done by the Home Intelligence Division depends on their keeping out of the public eye and it would be a most dangerous precedent to publish any of the documents they prepare. Besides, there is scarcely the material in this particular report to warrant such a course.[57]

It was of course important that HI's reports were deemed to be of value by their readers across Whitehall. In September 1943, Cyril Radcliffe wrote to 142 recipients on the external circulation list and asked them for a 'candid opinion as to the utility of this report in its present form and whether you feel that its withdrawal would deprive you of a useful service'.[58] The response was encouraging. Over the following month, MOI received 114 replies from those it approached, of whom 102 wished for the reports to continue, eight did not, and four were indeterminate.[59]

While many of the recipients wrote in general terms of the usefulness of the reports in keeping them in touch with trends of public opinion, a number indicated that they were of practical utility in their work. The Assistant Chief of the Air Staff at the Air Ministry, for example, regarded them as 'extremely useful' in assessing public reactions to the air offensive.[60] The Public Relations Officer at the Ministry of War Transport recorded that they 'kept us closely, and I think accurately informed' about attitudes towards the taking of holidays.[61] The Assistant Secretary at the Board of Trade revealed that the references to shortages of torch and cycle lamp batteries 'helped us considerably'.[62] The Leather Controller at the Ministry of Supply found it 'of real value' to discover that footwear was a major source of complaint.[63] The Chief Medical Officer at the Ministry of Health acknowledged that the comments about the VD campaign had 'been of great help' in developing the department's publicity on the subject.[64] The Private Secretary to the Minister of Fuel and Power disclosed that he frequently came across items which 'I think are worth bringing before my Minister'.[65] US Ambassador Winant appreciated the attention paid to relations with US forces and thought the findings had 'been of great usefulness to us in correcting certain situations'.[66] From her perspective as a BBC governor, Lady Violet Bonham Carter believed that the weekly report was 'an extraordinarily sane and accurate assessment of public opinion ... . My constant reflection when reading it is: "How I hope that all members of the Government receive and study this Report!"'[67] Likewise, the Director of BBC Listener Research, Robert Silvey, stressed 'how valuable I find this document' and confirmed that 'there is nothing of a comparable kind available in this country'.[68] Taylor described the responses as 'overwhelmingly favourable'.[69] Bracken scrawled on an MOI minute: 'The business of feeling the public pulse is more popular than I judged. Let it go on.'[70]

In the event, HI was shut down in December 1944.[71] The fact that victory in Europe was in sight, and morale was evidently not going to collapse, were no doubt considerations in its demise. But Taylor hinted that an important factor was the sensitivities involved in the MOI monitoring domestic public opinion while the political parties jockeyed for position as the coalition came under strain and a post-war election loomed. 'With the return of party politics', he recorded, 'the service was discontinued.'[72] The Wartime Social Survey did, however, survive and in 1946 became part of a Central Office of Information.[73] As for Taylor, he was elected Labour MP for Barnet in the 1945 general election and went on to serve in the Attlee administration as Parliamentary Private Secretary to the Lord President of the Council, Herbert Morrison. After losing his seat in 1950, he held positions on various public bodies, including the Harlow New Town Development Corporation and the Harlow Industrial Health Service. He was made a life peer in 1958 (Lord Taylor of Harlow) and returned briefly to office as Under-Secretary of State for Commonwealth Relations and the Colonies in Wilson's first government. In 1967 he took up the post of President and Vice-Chancellor of the Memorial University of Newfoundland in Canada. There he helped to establish a medical school.[74]

The work of HI represented a bold and imaginative attempt to bridge the divide between the machinery of government and the people.[75] The construction of a rapid and effective method of monitoring popular opinion placed at the disposal of Whitehall a means of testing the public reaction to aspects of government policy and determining what levers of power needed to be pulled in order to maintain the nation's confidence. As Taylor explained:

Those who built up the organisation believed that public opinion was something which should be constantly in the minds of the administrators – not because the administrators ought to follow public opinion – but because only with full public co-operation could the wartime machinery of controls, affecting every aspect of civilian life, be made to operate efficiently. Their studies suggested that, provided the public really understood *what* was proposed, and appreciated *why* it was proposed, and provided also they were satisfied it was both essential and equitable, they were prepared to put up with whatever difficulties and discomforts were necessary for winning the war.[76]

The introduction of something like a science of public opinion into the apparatus of government could also be regarded as an enhancement of the workings of democracy. Taylor elaborated on this in a wartime article for *Public Administration* (although he was careful not to mention HI by name):

Those of us who believe that the future must belong to the democratic society, rather than to any form of oligarchy or dictatorship, must be on the alert to find new ways of making democracy more effective, and of removing its obvious faults. The new social science of public opinion study is probably as important a step forward as the introduction of the secret ballot.[77]

A few words of explanation are required on the editing of the documents. The selected weekly reports (and appendices) published here are extracted from the files of original documents in the National Archives at Kew under the reference INF 1/292. The selected special reports are taken from INF 1/293 (with the exception of the report on 'Public Feelings on Post-War Reconstruction', which is located at CAB 117/209).[78] Mistakes in spelling, punctuation and numeration have been corrected, some headings excluded where they seem superfluous, and other minor editorial changes made to enhance the readability of the documents and create a more uniform house style. From the summer of 1941, HI included a regular section at the end of the weekly reports on 'constant complaints'. These sections (which evolved into a 'monthly summary of constant topics' in list form) have been omitted to reduce unnecessary repetition. The reference apparatus has also been largely removed to enhance the flow of the reports; but, for the purposes of illustration, it has been retained in one sample weekly report for January 1943. In all other respects, the documents are reproduced in their original form. It should be noted that they embody the values and prejudices of the time. As a result, some of the language or approaches used might be regarded as offensive. For the convenience of readers, the weekly reports have been divided into four periods, with brief introductory timelines. The special reports appear in a separate section. A list of abbreviations is appended, as well as a glossary which identifies, as appropriate, individuals and terms referred to in the text.[79]

Jeremy A. Crang
Edinburgh and Dundee

NOTES

In the preparation of this introduction, I am deeply indebted to the late Paul Addison. Many of the ideas presented here were generated in close collaboration with him during our work together in co-editing the previous two Home Intelligence volumes and in contemplating this third volume. In many ways this is a co-production. All errors of fact and interpretation are of course mine alone.

1. P. Addison and J. A. Crang, 'Home Intelligence, the Blitz and the British' in Addison and Crang (eds), *The Spirit of the Blitz: Home Intelligence and British Morale, September 1940–June 1941* (Oxford: Oxford University Press, 2020), xi; P. Addison and J. A. Crang, 'Introduction' to Addison and Crang (eds), *Listening to Britain: Home Intelligence Reports on Britain's Finest Hour, May–September 1940* (London: The Bodley Head, 2010), xvii.

2. D. Welch, *Persuading the People: British Propaganda and World War II* (London: British Library, 2016), 12–13; I. McLaine, *Ministry of Morale: Home Front Morale and the Ministry of Information in World War II* (London: George Allen & Unwin, 1979), 1, 22, 49–51; The National Archives, Kew, London, Ministry of Information papers (TNA INF) 1/47, 'Note on the Functions of Home Intelligence', by Mary Adams, 9 February 1940; TNA INF 1/290, 'The Work of Home Intelligence Division 1939–44', 1, 6. This short history of HI is unsigned and undated but almost certainly the work of Stephen Taylor. The Evelyn Waugh novel that immediately comes to mind is the satirization of the Ministry of Information in *Put Out More Flags* (1942).

3. S. Adams, 'Adams [née Campin], Mary Grace Agnes', *Oxford Dictionary of National Biography* (online edition, 2004); K. Murphy, '"In on the Ground Floor": Women and the Early BBC Television Service, 1932–1939', *Critical Studies in Television*, vol. 17, no. 3 (2022): 240–1, 249–51.

4. Adams, *ODNB*.

5. R. McLean, 'Bentley, Nicolas Clerihew', *ODNB* (online edition, 2012).

6. 'Winifred Homes', *The Times*, 20 September 1995, 18.

7. G. Rivett, 'Taylor, Stephen James Lake, Baron Taylor', *ONDB* (online edition, 2011); Lord Taylor of Harlow, *A Natural History of Everyday Life: A Biographical Guide for Would-Be Doctors of Society* (London: British Medical Journal/The Memoir Club, 1988), 71–2, 146–8, 259–61; J. Hinton, *The Mass Observers: A History, 1937–1949* (Oxford: Oxford University Press, 2013), 180; S. Taylor, 'The Suburban Neurosis', *The Lancet*, 26 March 1938, 759–61; S. Taylor, 'Mental Illness as a Clue to Normality', *The Lancet*, 13 April 1940, 677–80, and 20 April 1940, 730–5; Addison and Crang, 'Home Intelligence, the Blitz and the British', xvi–xvii.

8. TNA INF 1/296, Mr. Rhodes to Mr. Balfour, 11 June 1940; TNA INF 1/47, 'Home Intelligence Machinery', memorandum by Home Intelligence, 16 July 1940; Mass Observation Archive, the Keep, Brighton, Mary Adams papers SxMOA4/1/1, 'Weekly Report by Home Intelligence: Special Report on Methods of Compilation', memorandum by Home Intelligence, undated; McLaine, *Ministry of Morale*, 87; The National Archives, Kew, London, Ministry of Defence papers 1/333, 'History of the Postal and Telegraph Censorship Department 1938–1946', vol. 1, Home Office, 1952, 50–1, 272–5.

9. TNA INF 1/290, 'The Work of Home Intelligence Division 1939–44', 2; J. M. Heimann, 'Harrisson, Tom Harnett', *ODNB* (online edition, 2010); J. M. Heimann, *The Most Offending Soul Alive: Tom Harrisson and His Remarkable Life* (Honolulu: University of Hawaii Press, 1999), 38–9, 118; Hinton, *The Mass Observers*, 33, 128–34, 152–62, 166–7, 260–78. For a fuller discussion of the early period of HI, see Addison and Crang, 'Introduction', xi–xix.

10. For a more in-depth examination of these events, see Addison and Crang, 'Home Intelligence, the Blitz and the British', xi–xxvii.

11. TNA INF 1/944, office circular no. 73, by DBW, 9 April 1941. Taylor established HI as a separate division within the MOI. Previously, it had come under the purview of R. H. Parker as head of the MOI Home Division. See TNA INF 1/944, 'Intelligence Division, Proposals', by Stephen Taylor, 5 January 1942; Taylor, *A Natural History of Everyday Life*, 261.

12. N. Bentley, *A Version of the Truth* (London: Andre Deutsch, 1960), 197–8.

13. Ibid., 198.

14. Taylor, *A Natural History of Everyday Life*, 73, 147, 216, 265–71, 283.

15. Ibid., 260. Also see Addison and Crang, 'Home Intelligence, the Blitz and the British', xxii.

16. TNA INF 1/290, 'The Work of Home Intelligence Division 1939–44', 3, 5, 6, 21–9; TNA INF 1/287, 'Instructions for Specialist Officers', MOI, 17 September 1941; TNA INF 1/291, confidential report, appendix 'M', 29 September 1944; TNA INF 1/282, 'Home Intelligence Division: How the Weekly Report is Made', no author (but almost certainly S. Taylor), 6 April 1942, 2–3; TNA INF 1/282, Director-General to Minister, 9 April 1942; McLaine, *Ministry of Morale*, 46; Hinton, *The Mass Observers*, 278–81.

17. TNA INF 1/282, L. C. Nash to Mr. Woodburn, 8 April 1942. Taylor indicated that half-a-dozen were directly involved in compiling the weekly reports. See TNA INF 1/290, 'The Work of Home Intelligence Division 1939–44', 12. In 1943 the offices of the London and South-Eastern Regions were amalgamated under the London Regional Office, with a district office in Tunbridge Wells.

18. TNA INF 1/290, 'The Work of Home Intelligence Division 1939–44', 6–7, 10–15; TNA INF 1/282, 'Home Intelligence Division: How the Weekly Report is made', 4; TNA INF 1/282, Director-General to Minister, 9 April 1942; TNA INF 1/698, 'A Note on Regional Weekly Intelligence Reports', by Home Intelligence Division, 15 May 1942; TNA INF 1/292, cover sheet to weekly report no. 95, 21–28 July 1942. Also see the list of source references attached to the original reports. These include the Wartime Social Survey.

19. Taylor, *A Natural History of Everyday Life*, 260.

20. Ibid., 260–261; TNA INF 1/290, 'The Work of Home Intelligence Division 1939–44', 2–3; Hinton, *The Mass Observers*, 180–1, 190, 212–15.

21. TNA INF 1/290, 'The Work of Home Intelligence Division 1939–44', 11–12, 15–20.

22. The earliest extant special report, a study of recruitment for the Royal Navy, is for some reason not marked no. 1.

23. TNA INF 1/282, Dr. Taylor to Mr. Gates, 24 February 1943.

24. TNA INF 1/285, 'Report on Director General's Enquiry into Value of Home Intelligence Weekly Report', Home Intelligence, 12 October 1943; TNA INF 1/290, 'The Work of Home Intelligence Division 1939–44', 9–10.

25. TNA INF 1/282, WSC to Minister of Information, 4 April 1942. Churchill read the press in great depth. See R. Toye, *Winston Churchill: A Life in the News* (Oxford: Oxford University Press, 2000), 3. I am grateful to Professor Toye for bringing this to my attention.

26. Taylor, *A Natural History of Everyday Life*, 275.

27. TNA INF 1/282, Director-General to Minister, 9 April 1942.

28. J. Tomes, 'Bracken, Brendan Rendall, Viscount Bracken', *ODNB* (online edition, 2008).

29. TNA INF 1/282, BB to Prime Minister, 13 April 1942.

30. TNA INF 1/282, J. H. Peck to A. S. Hodge, 15 April 1942.

31. The National Archives, Kew, London, War Cabinet papers (TNA CAB) 66/23/35, 'Propaganda at Home', by Minister of Information, WP(42)155, 10 April 1942; TNA CAB 65/26/10, conclusions of a meeting of the War Cabinet, WM(42) 49th conclusions, 15 April 1942; TNA CAB 66/25/30, 'Report on Public Feeling', by Minister of Information, WP(42)250, 10 June 1942; TNA CAB 66/26/28, 'Report on Home Opinion', by Minister of Information, WP(42)298, 17 July 1942; TNA CAB 66/28/15, 'Report on Home Opinion', by Minister of Information, WP(42)385, 28 August 1942; TNA CAB 66/29/34, 'Report on Home Opinion', by Minister of Information, WP(42)454, 9 October 1942; TNA CAB 66/31/28, 'The Assessment of Public Feeling at Home', by Minister of Information, WP(42)548, 25 November 1942; TNA CAB 66/31/30, 'Report on Home Opinion', by Minister of Information, WP(42)550, 27 November 1942.

32. TNA CAB 66/40/14, 'The Bombing of Rome', by E. E. Bridges, WP(43)364, 9 August 1943.

33. See, for example, TNA INF 1/292, cover sheet to weekly report no. 95, 21–28 July 1942.

34. Ibid.

35. Ibid.

36. S. Taylor, letter to the Editor, *The Times*, 5 October 1945, 5. Also see Taylor, *A Natural History of Everyday Life*, 274–5, and Hinton, *The Mass Observers*, 200–1.

37. Addison and Crang, 'Home Intelligence, the Blitz and the British', xxvii.

38. TNA INF 1/287, Home Controller to Regional Information Officer 1, 2, 3, 5, 9, 10, 11, 5 June 1944.

39. TNA INF 1/287, Regional Information Officer, Midland Region no. 9, to Home Controller, 7 June 1944.

40. Hinton, *The Mass Observers*, 280–1. In relation to the instruction that contacts were to report the views of those they met, rather than their own opinions, HI recognised that

'in practice many will fail to do this'. See TNA INF 1/287, 'Instructions for Specialist Officers'.

41. TNA INF 1/287, Mrs. Pearsall to Dr. Taylor and Mr. Archibald, 10 June 1944.

42. P. Addison, *The Road to 1945: British Politics and the Second World War* (London: Quartet Books, 1977), 121.

43. TNA INF 1/292, 'Home Morale and Public Opinion', by Stephen Taylor, 1 October 1941, 1, appendix to weekly report no. 52, 24 September–1 October 1941.

44. I owe these observations to Paul Addison. Among the last documents produced by HI is a graph representing the fluctuations in public feeling between March 1941 and December 1944 scaled against the military events of the war. It is, however, difficult to know what to make of it beyond the conclusion that defeats depressed the British people while victories cheered them up. See TNA INF 1/291, 'Graph Showing Fluctuations in Public Feeling during the Past Three Years and Ten Months', Home Intelligence, 29 December 1944.

45. TNA INF 1/282, Dr. Taylor to Mr. S. G. Gates, 28 March 1942; TNA INF 1/282, 'Home Intelligence Division: How the Weekly Report is Made', 4.

46. TNA INF 1/285, Dr. Taylor to Mr. Gates, 24 August 1943.

47. It is, however, regrettable that, apart from a small sample (in TNA INF 1/291), the intelligence reports from the regions do not seem to have been preserved in the National Archives. This might have afforded the opportunity to construct a regional history of the home front.

48. Addison and Crang, 'Home Intelligence, the Blitz and the British', xi.

49. TNA INF 1/292, weekly report no. 192, 31 May–7 June 1944, 1.

50. T. S. Legg and M.-L. Legg, 'Jowitt, William Allen, Earl Jowitt', *ODNB* (online edition, 2011).

51. The National Archives, Kew, London, Home Office papers (TNA HO) 262/16, Sir Robert Topping, Conservative and Unionist Central Office, to R. H. Parker, 15 October 1942.

52. TNA HO 262/16, Stephen Taylor to Mr. Parker, 19 October 1942.

53. TNA HO 262/16, William Jowitt to Brendan Bracken, 20 November 1942.

54. B. Pimlott, 'Dalton, (Edward) Hugh Neale, Baron Dalton', *ODNB* (online edition, 2011).

55. TNA CAB 117/209, Hugh Dalton to Sir William Jowitt, 6 December 1942. I am again grateful to Paul Addison for his insights here.

56. TNA HO 262/16, William Jowitt to Brendan Bracken, 9 December 1942.

57. TNA CAB 117/209, BB to Sir William Jowitt, 15 December 1942.

58. TNA INF 1/285, 'Report on Director General's Enquiry into Value of Home Intelligence Weekly Report', by Home Intelligence, 12 October 1943.

59. Ibid.

60. Ibid., 'An Analysis of Actual Letters, with Extracts of Points Made', 6.

61. Ibid., 25.

62. Ibid., 7. The Assistant Secretary was Richard Pares, who later became Professor of History at the University of Edinburgh.

63. TNA INF 1/285, Leather Controller, Ministry of Supply, to C. J. Radcliffe, 11 September 1943.

64. TNA INF 1/285, 'An Analysis of Actual Letters, with Extracts of Points Made', 20.

65. Ibid., 19.

66. Ibid., 28.

67. Ibid., 10; TNA INF 1/285, Violet Bonham Carter to C. J. Radcliffe, 14 September 1943.

68. TNA INF 1/285, 'An Analysis of Actual Letters, with Extracts of Points Made', 10; TNA INF 1/285, R. J. Silvey to C. J. Radcliffe, 15 September 1943.

69. TNA INF 1/944, Dr. Taylor to Mr. Nash, 27 September 1943.

70. TNA INF 1/285, BCS to Minister, 26/1. Further discussion of the survey of recipients, as well as other aspects of the history of HI featured in this introduction, can be found in P. Addison and J. Crang, 'Monitoring Morale: the History of Home Intelligence 1939–1944', Open History Society website: https://openhistorysociety. org (accessed 10 April 2023).

71. TNA INF 1/288, 'Closing Down of Home Intelligence', by E. St. J. Bamford, 23 October 1944. No formal MOI record of the reasons for this decision seems to have been kept.

72. S. Taylor, letter to the Editor, *The Times*, 5 October 1945, 5; also see Taylor, *A Natural History of Everyday Life*, 274.

73. L. Moss, *The Government Social Survey: A History* (London: HMSO, 1991), 14–16. 'Wartime' was dropped from the title.

74. Rivett, 'Taylor, Stephen James Lake, Baron Taylor', *ONDB*; Taylor, *A Natural History of Everyday Life*, 148–53. Taylor retired to Glyn Ceiriog in North Wales and passed away in 1988. He was married to Lady Charity Taylor, also a doctor, who served as the first female governor of Holloway women's prison.

75. Addison and Crang, 'Home Intelligence, the Blitz and the British', xiii.

76. TNA INF 1/290, 'The Work of Home Intelligence Division 1939–44', 6.

77. S. Taylor, 'The Study of Public Opinion: An Aid to Administrative Action', *Public Administration*, vol. 21, issue 3 (October 1943): 109.

78. In 2019, HI's daily and weekly morale reports, as well as its special reports, were made available to the public in a fully searchable online format by the MOI digital project team at the University of London: https://moidigital.ac.uk/reports/home-intelligence-reports/ (accessed 10 April 2023).

79. Place names used in the timelines and the glossary generally conform to the contemporary British wartime spellings and forms, rather than current practices.

FIGURE 1: The Senate House, University of London, where the Home Intelligence unit was based. (© Mary Evans Picture Library)

FIGURE 2: Mary Adams, Director of Home Intelligence, 1939–41. (© BBC Photo Archive)

FIGURE 3: Stephen Taylor, Director of Home Intelligence from 1941. (© National
Portrait Gallery, London)

FIGURE 4: Nicolas Bentley, Taylor's deputy at Home Intelligence. (© National Portrait Gallery, London)

June to December 1941

22 JUNE Hitler launches Operation Barbarossa, the German invasion of the Soviet Union. After large-scale early victories, German forces advance deep into Soviet territory.

26 JULY The British and American governments freeze Japanese assets in response to Japan's advance into southern Indochina.

8 SEPTEMBER The German siege of Leningrad in north-west Russia begins.

19 SEPTEMBER German forces capture Kiev, the capital of Ukraine.

18 NOVEMBER British and Commonwealth troops of the Eighth Army mount an offensive against Axis forces in Libya. Rommel withdraws towards western Cyrenaica.

29 NOVEMBER Soviet forces retake Rostov in southern Russia, the German Army's first major reverse in the campaign against the Soviet Union. A week later the Red Army launches a counter-offensive to relieve pressure around Moscow.

7 DECEMBER Japanese carrier-based aircraft attack the US naval base at Pearl Harbor in Hawaii. The US Pacific Fleet suffers significant damage and 2,403 Americans are killed. Across the Pacific, Japanese forces attack Malaya, Hong Kong and the Philippines.

8 DECEMBER In an address to the United States Congress, Roosevelt describes 7 December 1941 as 'a date which will live in infamy'. The United States and Great Britain declare war on Japan.

10 DECEMBER The Royal Navy battleship HMS *Prince of Wales* and battlecruiser HMS *Repulse* are sunk off the east coast of Malaya by Japanese land-based aircraft. In all, 840 sailors are lost.

11 DECEMBER Germany and Italy declare war on the United States. In response, Roosevelt signs declarations of war against them.

25 DECEMBER Hong Kong surrenders to Japanese forces.

NO. 38: WEDNESDAY 18 JUNE TO
WEDNESDAY 25 JUNE 1941

I. GENERAL COMMENTS

1. GENERAL STATE OF CONFIDENCE AND REACTION TO NEWS

In the earlier part of the week there was again a slight rise in general confidence. The factors making for greater cheerfulness were, in the main, the same as those of last week: the freedom from heavy raids, increased hope of American aid, and the absence of any obvious impending disaster. Added to these there was the fresh tale of RAF successes (in daylight sweeps, night raids on Germany, and against enemy night bombers) and the fact that the announcement of radiolocation was taken by many people as a proof of our growing superiority in the air. In this connection, the RIO North-Western Region reports that 'press prominence given to radiolocation, coinciding with Mr. Bevin's statement about the conquest of night bombing and the lull in raids, has produced an unfortunate reaction. There is a widespread tendency to infer that night bombing is now likely to disappear. It is said that relief in some cases is as great as if people had been told the war was over. This attitude is felt to be bad for morale, as optimism is likely to deteriorate when the next heavy night raids are experienced.' Though the attack on the Sollum area was considered a failure in some quarters 'in spite of official reassuring statements', RIOs report that on the whole 'the operations in the Western Desert caused satisfaction'; and our withdrawal at their close 'was not accompanied by cynical comment such as has marked the reception of this kind of news in the past; this is probably because we took the initiative in attacking the enemy'. It is also reported that 'the allied progress in Syria is contributing to the rise in confidence, though there is considerable anxiety that we should hurry'. Yet another factor making for cheerfulness was 'President Roosevelt's action in closing the German Consulates and agencies in the USA; this is welcomed as further evidence that America means business'.

On the other hand, there were still 'some residues of the Cretan agitation, chiefly in the form of a conviction that we do not appear able to beat the Germans on land'; distrust in our Higher Command; grave concern about the state of industry; and in the background a fear summed up by the feeling, 'Hitler is saving up for something.' A new cause of anxiety this week was 'the signing of the pact between Germany and Turkey, which was regarded as a further serious diplomatic setback'. There has been comment on the Government's apparent anxiety to find every excuse for the Turks, and to 'play down the significance of the pact'. But on balance, before the announcement of the German attack on Russia, it was said that morale was 'rather higher than it had been for some time'.

The reception of the news that Germany and Russia were at war has been reported as 'jubilant, with a strong under-current of caution', and as having a further 'tonic effect on the morale of those who had previously shown signs of war-weariness and apathy'.

Reactions so far seem mainly to be:

(1) A belief that Germany has been forced into this attack, since the time chosen – before the harvest – is generally regarded as unpropitious.
(2) A feeling of relief that Hitler, engaged in the East, 'will not have much time for us, and will lose equipment and men, while we strengthen our resources'.
(3) Satisfaction at what is called 'a final demonstration to the world of the complete worthlessness of any pact into which Germany may enter'. It is added that 'the public have been told many times that no agreement with the present rulers of Germany will ever be possible, but the latest development has brought that fact home with a force which no other means could have achieved'.

The disinclination to believe in good news, recorded last week, seems to be responsible for a certain amount of vague foreboding which has been expressed. Actual reasons given for regretting the news were:

(1) An unprovoked attack must be taken as 'a mark of German strength'. Hitler's 'cheek' in attacking Russia while we are still unconquered is commented on.
(2) 'Hitler has always known what he was doing up till now.'
(3) Our position would be adversely affected if the German onslaught were successful, 'since the enemy would then have much larger resources to draw on, which would do much to offset American aid to Britain'.

There is little confidence in Russia's military capacity, which is judged by her performance against Finland, and a large section of the public feel that the most that can be hoped for is that she will be able to hold out long enough to give us some real advantage. It is accepted by many people that the true object of the attack is not the Ukraine and its riches, but Hitler's desire 'to make 100% sure that he would not be stabbed in the back while attacking England'. There is eagerness that we ourselves should, in some way, 'strike now, while the Nazis are tied up, before it is too late for us to strike at all'. Unless we do this, it is feared we may have to 'sit down for defence when we are still more savagely attacked'.

Mr. Churchill's pledge, on the part of the country, to give aid to Russia has been 'generally accepted as both a practical and logical move', and it is felt that he 'discharged a difficult task well when he spoke of our support for Russia, after he had for many years voiced his contempt, and at times his abhorrence, for the Bolshevik regime'. His speech was greatly admired, and has more than offset the recent fear that his touch was not quite so sure as it had been.

2. PUBLIC OPINION ON RUSSIA BEFORE THE NAZI ATTACK

Two months ago, the British Institute of Public Opinion put the following question to a sample of 2,200 people:

'Would you like to see Great Britain and Soviet Russia being more friendly to each other?'

The results were as follows:

	Yes	No	Don't know
Total:	70%	13%	17%
Men:	76%	13%	11%
Women:	63%	14%	23%
Economic groups:			
Higher:	61%	26%	13%
Middle:	69%	15%	16%
Lower:	70%	12%	18%

The question is admittedly so worded that it carries a slight bias in favour of friendship with Russia. However, an analysis of the spontaneous comments shows that definite reasons were usually advanced for the opinions held:

44% of spontaneous comments followed these lines:

> 'It would help us ... Russia is powerful ... The more friends we have, the better ... Better for us than against us ... It would be one in the eye for Hitler.'

Frank self-interest is the keynote of this group.

19% followed these lines:

> 'It's our own fault it hasn't happened before ... They're progressive, or go-ahead, or socialist.'

These are the rather more ideological comments.

18% were antipathetic:

> 'Don't like Russia ... Don't trust them ... They were never any good ... No truck with communism.'

19% were miscellaneous noncommittal comments:

> 'Don't know anything about Russia ... I'm not interested in politics ... I would agree if they kept communism out of it.'

3. PUBLIC FEELING ON INVASION PROSPECTS

There is still much discussion of possible points for enemy landings. In the South-Western Region, fear is reported that the overcrowding of the coastal districts with evacuees and summer visitors might considerably hamper military efforts in the event of invasion from the west. In Wales anxiety about our defences is again expressed, especially in connection with the defence of aerodromes. It is thought also that there may be 'successful landings from Eire by airborne forces strong enough to establish themselves'; and that invasion of Wales from Eire is not unlikely. In this connection, although Eire's desire for neutrality seems to have been strengthened by the bombing of Dublin, the feeling that 'the time has come for action' appears to be increasing both in England and among pro-British elements in Eire. 'Unless we can be sure the Hun won't get the ports, we should take them now' ... 'If you knew how we (Southern Irish) despise you for not taking them!' A report, quoted by RIO Northern Ireland, says, 'There is a growing opinion that America could save us by occupying the Eire ports, as Eire would not (and could not) fight her own kith and kin'.

4. SYRIA

There is now some disappointment that our progress is not 'overwhelming and rapid, in the grand German manner'. Two theories are widely held to explain its slowness:

(1) That Britain is not hitting as hard as she might for fear of offending French susceptibilities.
(2) That the strength of the Vichy resistance is greater than had been expected.

The daily repetition of the news that we were nearing Damascus resulted in 'people becoming a little impatient, with no capacity for enjoying the final occupation of the city'. The statements that 'some captured French soldiers were not aware of German penetration, and did not know against whom they were fighting' is held to be a reflection on our propaganda.

5. PRESENTATION OF NEWS

'Pungent criticism about the nature and quality of official news is still prevalent', but there is 'some appreciation of the lack of "frills" of which there were formerly many complaints'. The public is as insistent as ever on hearing 'the whole truth as far as war news is concerned', in so far as this will not 'give the enemy any actual advantage'. It is frequently reported that public confidence mounts 'when plain facts are plainly expressed, even though the news may not be wholly encouraging'. There are again comments that the 10 a.m. European news bulletins in English are much better than the Home News bulletins. From those who listen to our foreign broadcasts, there are suggestions that the compilers of the Home News have much to learn from the 'Les Français parlent aux Français' service.

Vernon Bartlett's Sunday *Postscript* (standing very high in popularity compared with those of Mr. Herbert and others) has been eclipsed in general appreciation by Mr. W. J. Brown's *Postscript* on the Polish slave in Germany. This is described as 'the most consummate piece of defensive oratory yet heard'.

6. THE BATTLE OF THE ATLANTIC

The Prime Minister's insistence that the debate on shipping must be held in secret was considered 'a bad omen', coming at a time when public confidence in our war effort as a whole was still 'considerably shaken by our losses in Crete'. Much anxiety was felt, especially after the postponement of the announcement, lest our Atlantic losses for the month should prove to be appalling. Due partly to the fact that they were lower than was feared, and partly, it is thought, to the general improvement in spirits, there is now some belief that secrecy was necessary 'because of the increasing success of our counter-measures'.

7. WAR-WEARINESS

Reports of apathy in industry continue to come in, but there are also reports of some apathy among other sections of the general public. 'Indifference, and reluctance to discuss the war', are alleged. 'People are not listening so closely to BBC bulletins, and confess to being fed up with eternal speculation' ... 'In some districts indifference to war news is associated with a growing fear that the war will last much longer than earlier estimates indicated' ... 'This lack of interest, and the absenteeism and slackening of effort which is widely thought to prevail in factories' seem, to some people, 'to indicate a degree of war-weariness' in the whole country. It is added, however, that 'it may be attributable in part to the excessively long hours of work, and the need for recreation and holidays'.

8. RUMOUR

Russian soldiers are already reported to have landed at Dover; and from Wales come rumours of 'suspicious characters in British uniforms, who speak poor English and wear no distinctive badges'. It is also said that 'Jehovah's Witnesses' are suspected of encouraging conscientious objectors, and are on the staff of the Ministry of Food at Colwyn Bay.

II. SPECIAL COMMENTS

9. BILLETING DIFFICULTIES

Although billeting systems are much the same in all areas, they operate less efficiently in some places than in others. One of the chief difficulties is the frequent reluctance of the billeting officer (who may be the Town Clerk, the Sanitary Inspector, or some other local official) to enforce his powers. If he himself lives in the neighbourhood, he may fear the annoyance of other residents, particularly if they have 'influence' which may prejudice his position with the local council. If the council is a supine body, he may hesitate to take steps in which it may not give him adequate support.

The responsibility for the reception of evacuees is vested in local authorities, to whom the Ministry of Health has delegated its powers in this matter. Complaints about billeting must, therefore, be made to local authorities, and only if they remain inactive can a direct appeal be made to the Ministry of Health. But sometimes when such an appeal has been made, the Ministry is said to have been reluctant to override the decision of the local authority.

Although there is a fairly general feeling 'that billeting should not be left in the hands of the local agents' (this is very strongly felt in some areas), there is no agreement as to what might be a better arrangement. Some think the power to appoint billeting officers should be transferred from local authorities to the county councils. Others think that they should be responsible to, and appointed by, a Government department.

It is frequently suggested that the owners of large country houses are shirking their billeting responsibilities. This is said to be the 'cause of perpetual minor grievances in many districts'. Stories are told of billeting officers who say: 'If this goes on, I shall have to start on some of the big houses.' In another case the officer is alleged to have discouraged a man who was anxious to take evacuees by telling him that, in doing so, he would be 'letting down' owners of other large houses in the neighbourhood.

Complaints, however, are by no means confined to large houses. Enquiries in one area suggest that 'there is far more persistent difficulty and resentment regarding the 5–7 bedroom type of house, where the occupant is a person of some local consequence whom the billeting officer or local council do not wish to offend'. A reliable report states that, in one area, out of twelve billeting officers, 'only two would face up to the occupant who was unwilling to accept evacuees'.

The following is a summary of complaints mentioned in recent reports from the London, Eastern, Southern, South-Western, Welsh and North-Western Regions, and also from Northern Ireland, and other sources. Districts mentioned by name include: Cornwall, Cheshire, Lancashire, Cumberland, mid-Wales, north Bucks, the Thames Valley, Horsham, Welwyn and Budleigh Salterton.

1. Many large country houses are already used as hospitals, hostels etc., or are earmarked for future use as such by one of the Services or the Red Cross, etc. In one area the bigger houses are said to have been reserved for the Air Ministry for 18 months and the bulk of them are still unoccupied.

2. In some cases old houses have inadequate water and sanitary arrangements for the number of available rooms.

3. Householders, though obliged to provide water and sanitary arrangements, are not required to give cooking facilities and may prevent the local authority from putting in cooking stoves and heating arrangements, etc., by objecting to structural alterations. There are said to be cases of evacuees being 'frozen out of country houses through lack of comfort'.

4. The hostility of owners who do not refuse evacuees, but who make them feel unwelcome. The case is quoted of a house in the Thames Valley which 'has repeatedly had evacuees pumped into it; they have regularly retired, beaten by the unsympathetic attitude of the owner and his wife'.

5. The difficulty of accommodating children in houses where an elderly couple have been looked after by two or three maids, and who are

now reduced to making do with one. Cases are known of old servants threatening to leave, and actually doing so, on the arrival of evacuees.

6. Problems also arise from the billeting of war workers; e.g. the shift system, which dislocates the domestic time-table of a household.
7. Responsibility is sometimes said to be evaded by securing exemption on medical grounds.
8. Some householders have taken the precaution of filling the house with relatives and friends, not necessarily from bombed areas, so as to leave no room for evacuees.
9. The isolated position of some houses, remote from urban amenities, such as fried fish shops, cinemas, and public houses, is such that many evacuees will not remain in them.

10. EVACUATION

There are still reports, particularly from the Bristol Region, of evacuated children being brought back to blitzed areas. Various reasons are suggested:

1. A wave of optimism caused by the radiolocation announcement, and the resulting confidence, felt among certain sections of the public, that night bombing will have been overcome by the winter.
2. The extra cost of keeping children's clothes mended and repaired.
3. The distance separating children and parents – particularly in the case of Bristol evacuees in Cornwall.
4. Children's homesickness, or local billeting maladjustments.

11. FOOD

BLACK MARKETS AND ILLICIT TRADING: Although the existence of black markets seems to be taken for granted by a large section of the population, evidence that they do exist is scanty and unreliable; and it is thought that talk about them is in most cases little more than an emotional outlet, and that they are a scapegoat for difficulties in obtaining goods. Few people, however, seem to doubt that illicit trading is extensively practised, and there is a 'strong undercurrent of public resentment at all manifestations of the food racket'. This discontent tends to link up with feeling about the war effort as a whole. It is pointed out that 'people are ready to accept the "guns before butter" system of rationing, but object to being swindled either by profiteers or by those who can pay any price'. This feeling is expressed by the remark 'We all know you can get plenty of butter in the West End, if you like to pay for it'; but criticism is somewhat vitiated by the 'fact that so many people appear to have no moral scruples if the chance to get a little extra comes their way'.

There is said to be a good deal of trafficking in eggs by motorists visiting outlying farms, and one case is mentioned of a dealer getting 60 dozen eggs a week in this way, by paying a slightly higher price. There appears to be a certain amount of 'bartering'. People in agricultural and rural districts feel certain shortages, and have little opportunity to shop in the towns, and they are glad to barter eggs or pigs or rabbits for tinned produce which may be unobtainable in the shops. The practice of illegal slaughter is said to 'obtain throughout the Region', according to the Bristol RIO, the meat being distributed to various butchers.

A certain amount of illegal retail trading is admitted, and is excused on the grounds that if a shop-keeper were to adhere strictly to the law he would go out of business. Thus, a greengrocer maintains that, unless he is prepared to pay enhanced prices at Spitalfields and Stratford, he could not supply his customers. In Manchester recently, on the day when the maximum price for gooseberries was announced as 5d per lb, the greengrocers complained that they could only buy them in the market at 1/8d. There is some feeling that the wholesalers are often responsible, but that the retailer is blamed.

The public appear to welcome any signs of action being taken to stop illicit trading and to punish profiteering. Great satisfaction is said to have been expressed in Leeds at the magistrate's decision in sending a man and wife to prison for a month for profiteering in eggs and jam, and there is a wide hope that Lord Woolton will be able to carry out his promise to stop food racketeering.

There is thought to be a certain amount of trafficking in cigarettes. People ask how it is that hotels often have such large supplies. Some tobacco wholesalers are said to be selling all their supplies retail, and a man on duty at a shelter, largely used by Jews from Bow and Poplar, said that he was offered practically anything he wanted, including 500 Player's.

EGG DISTRIBUTION SCHEME: Criticism still tends to come more from the country than from the town, though in both it is from the 'small man'. The fact that a shop must have a minimum of 50 registered customers before it can sell eggs is taken in some quarters as 'further evidence of Lord Woolton's supposed animosity towards small traders'. People with a small flock of hens are said to resent the scheme 'as being a kind of encroachment on their personal liberty'; and to regard the taking of their eggs as being 'like taking the cabbages out of their garden'.

There have been complaints of misleading information in the press. An article in the *Daily Sketch* of June 14th is said to have given the impression that people need not register for eggs, as the scheme had been shelved.

QUEUES: The position appears to be unchanged. Queues for unrationed goods, mostly cooked meats, sausages, tinned goods, biscuits and cigarettes, and even green groceries, are still reported from a number of towns. There continues to be strong criticism against the responsible authorities for not taking sufficient account of the 'influx and deflux of population caused by war emergencies'. It is suggested that the billeting of servicemen and women has not been allowed for in the population figures. Shops are still blamed for encouraging queues for advertising purposes.

GENERAL FOOD MATTERS: There appears to be no lessening of the demand from dockers and other heavy manual workers for an increase in rations. Miners are still said to be very 'dissatisfied with the amount of foodstuffs available for taking down the pits', and railway men 'continue to grumble because so little is available for sandwich meals which they need when out working long journeys, etc.'.

There is a feeling that the sedentary worker does not need as much as the physical worker.

The beer shortage appears to be on the increase, and consternation is reported at the closing of public houses in some towns for certain periods. In Rugby three out of four 'pubs' are said to close one night a week. It is suggested that, psychologically, this shortage appears to have more effect upon the factory workers than any naval disasters; they 'interpret this shortage to mean that we are in a worse position than is being disclosed'. Shortage of coal, labour and transport are suggested as causes of the beer shortage.

Before the new announcement about sugar for home jam-making, there was still widespread dissatisfaction about the jam scheme, and most housewives were said to be 'saving their sugar so that they will be able to make their own jam with their own fruit'; those without sugar were said to be preparing to bottle their fruit. This possibility, and the dubious prospects of the fruit harvest, might, it was feared, make something of a fiasco of the scheme. There was also the feeling that much fruit would be wasted because of transport difficulties and the 'impossibility of running to the jam centre with each few pounds of fruit as it ripens'.

BRITISH RESTAURANTS: There is continued praise for British Restaurants, and a demand for even more of them. It is hoped that they will be better advertised because it is often very difficult to find them. There is some talk of local authorities, with suitable buildings commandeered, and anxious to begin, being held up by endless correspondence and delay until given the permission to start. The question is raised as to how British Restaurants can get enough supplies to have a meat meal every day, while some factory canteens are only allowed enough for one meat meal a week.

12. COAL

That the coal shortage is causing less comment this week is said to be due to the warm weather, but it continues to be reported from several places and is still said to 'agitate every part of the Midland Region'. It is continually urged that there are not sufficient stocks to enable people to lay in supplies for the winter. There are still protests against 'draining manpower from the mining industry for munitions work and the armed forces, especially in view of the serious coal shortage'. The miners themselves are said to be 'very upset at the use being made of the figures for absenteeism, pointing out that this is common in every industry and that it is unfair to make use of this against men who are as patriotic as any'. The attendance bonus proposal is reported to be meeting with strong criticism from the miners and their organisation, and to be regarded as a slur on them.

13. TRANSPORT AND HOLIDAYS

Feeling about so-called 'joy-riding' seems to be growing, and the Government's appeal to people not to travel long distances during the holidays has led to increased resentment at the amount of pleasure motoring, particularly in connection with the recent race meeting at Newmarket. In the Midland Region, 'holidays at home' is said to be 'honoured more in the breach than the observance'. At one holiday resort, resentment is apparently felt at so many young people taking more than two weeks' holiday and using their cars so much. Strong criticism has been made lately of people who drive out of Bristol every night to sleep in the country, thus taking advantage of those who have no cars or who are too patriotic to use petrol in this way. This contrasts with the reports of crowded conditions in trains and buses and the 'inadequate transport facilities for war workers'. Criticism continues of people who motor round the countryside looking for eggs.

Resentment at the 'bad and selfish driving' which is said to 'characterise the officers and men of the army' has not been altogether allayed by the recent War Office statement on the subject. In a 'heavily militarised region', where 'few people have not had unpleasant adventures owing to the rottenness of khaki-clad drivers', the statement is described as 'the sort of thing which discredits official "hand-outs"'.

NO. 41: WEDNESDAY 9 JULY TO WEDNESDAY 16 JULY 1941

I. GENERAL COMMENTS

1. GENERAL STATE OF CONFIDENCE AND REACTION TO NEWS

Public confidence – in some cases complacency – remains on the same high level as last week. This once more appears to be due mainly to Russia's continued resistance, and to the RAF's offensive action over Germany and the occupied territories. Three weeks had fixed itself in the minds of many people as the probable limit of Russia's resistance. This period now having passed, the fact that the Russians are still giving a good account of themselves leads to a hope that 'the beginning of winter will find the Germans still heavily engaged in Russia'. Particular satisfaction is caused by the realisation 'that the headlong rush of German mechanised divisions *can* be stopped'.

The Anglo-Russian Agreement has met with 'general acceptance and modulated approval', though among the 'cautious and elderly' a certain uneasiness is reported in case 'we may be committing ourselves in advance with respect to peace treaty terms'. There is also anxiety about the possible contamination of our political ideals. Though there is some mistrust of Russia (and still more of communism) there is, on the whole, 'an appreciation that our complete understanding with Russia is a natural development of the present situation'. Communists seem now to be supporting the war effort, though they continue to demand that the ban on the *Daily Worker* should be lifted. The BBC's artful compromise on the question of playing the 'Internationale' was greeted with some ironic comments. There is a feeling that 'those in authority show an unworthy desire to sit on the fence'.

The belief that our assistance to Russia has so far been confined to the RAF's western offensive has caused 'substantial disappointment', and there is lively impatience for more adventurous manoeuvres to be undertaken. Some sections of the public are 'all agog to hear of the landing of the BEF on the Continent'. Newsreels of the Prime Minister inspecting invasion exercises seem to have encouraged this. There is also some indication that the desire for action is shared by certain army units, notably by Canadian and Welsh regiments.

The end of the campaign in Syria has been greeted everywhere with relief. The situation is described as 'the end of a combat almost as unnatural as civil war'.

The American occupation of Iceland has been 'received with acclamation and has increased and in some cases restored confidence in America'. The majority hopes it will lead to further action; a few seem nervous of any 'fresh encroachment by America in Europe.'

For the past few weeks there has been a progressive rise in public spirits. This improvement is related in most incoming reports to a growing sense of complacency. There appears to be a hopeful but often imperfect interpretation of recent happenings. It is suggested that the situation is not being presented in such a way as to enable the public to get a realistic idea of conditions in any particular sphere of the war. If, for example, more facts and publicity were given about the Battle of the Atlantic, and if these were related more precisely to particular food shortages, it is thought that there would be not only a diminution of grumbling, but a growth of realisation and responsibility about this subject.

Among other reasons given for increasing complacency are:

(1) 'The prominence given by the newspapers to the more encouraging claims of the Soviet communiqués.'

(2) The belief, produced by the radiolocation announcements, that 'large-scale air attacks by night are a thing of the past', is maintained. Evacuees are still returning to target areas, and there are even reports of people taking down their blackout fixtures. People are talking as though we had experienced our last raid, and 'predictions of the victorious end of the war at no very distant date' are said to be common.

(3) The infectiousness of the apathy and *laissez-faire* which are widely believed to exist in industry.

(4) Astrological prophecies that the war will end on the 22nd or 25th July (our report last week gave an indication of the reliance placed on such belief); and one based on the Pyramids that it will finish in September.

(It should be noted that these reports were received before the Prime Minister's recent speeches on Civil Defence and Industrial Production.)

In spite of complacency and optimism there are still strong undercurrents of anxiety and discontent, chiefly on the subjects of food and industry. 'From many quarters reports continue to be received of a growing spirit of restlessness among the workers.' There are 'signs of dissatisfaction with the general conduct of the war and with much that the Government is doing; and there is criticism, not only of the Government departments, but also of certain Ministers'. There is still 'much discussion about the alleged waste of time in factories engaged in war work', and in this respect the debate on production is said to have 'confirmed what was already known to exist'. Criticism is made of the 'lack of firm policy, rather than of absenteeism or of individual self-interest', and it is repeatedly asked: 'Why should it be necessary to call up extra men and women for industry when those already in it appear to be wasting half their time?' That the debate failed to induce the Government to take any drastic action was a keen disappointment to many workers, who are said to be calling for a 'thorough clean-up', and to be hoping for 'another Lloyd George to arise'. Some are asking 'why the Government does not use the emergency powers which were so freely granted to it?' And it is suggested that all war production should be 'put on a military footing and discipline, with corresponding ranks and pay'. Those in contact with the industrial population are confident that, 'given leadership on propaganda and production, nothing will hold them'.

Although criticism of industry tends to come mostly from the workers themselves, there is 'no doubt that this sort of talk is exercising a bad effect on public feeling generally'.

2. LONG-TERM OPINIONS

Some four weeks ago (15th June 1941) the British Institute of Public Opinion made a series of enquiries which yielded the following results. (The sample in each case consisted of about 2,200 people.)

(a) 'What do you think we are fighting for?'

The following are the chief headings into which answers fell:

46% said: 'Freedom, liberty and democracy', or analogous expressions.

14% said: 'To stop Fascism, Hitlerism, Nazism, aggression.' This was more strongly marked among upper- and lower-income groups than in middle-income groups. There was not, however, a difference of more than 6 or 7 points.

8% said: 'It is Britain v. Germany; we are fighting to keep what we've got; it's them or us.' This was slightly more emphasised in the lower-income group than in others.

7% said: 'For a better post-war world; for lasting peace.'

5% said: 'For our existence, our lives.'

4% said: 'For capitalism; power for a few; for imperialism.'

2% said: 'Freeing the small nations; to fulfil our pledges.'

1% said: 'Not what we're told – so-called democracy.'

6% made miscellaneous comments, and 7% had no opinion.

(b) Are we going about it the right way?

> Some of the headings in the previous questions were grouped so that percentages expressing agreement or disagreement with question (b) could be estimated.
>
> (1) Of those believing that we were fighting for 'freedom, liberty and democracy; a better post-war world; to free the small nations':
>
> > 73% said we were going about it in the right way;
> >
> > 27% said we were not.
>
> (2) Of those saying it was 'Britain versus Germany'; 'We are fighting to keep what we've got'; 'It's them or us'; 'For our existence, our lives':
>
> > 54% said we were going about it in the right way;
> >
> > 46% said we were not.
>
> (3) Of those saying: 'To stop Fascism, Hitlerism, Nazism, aggression':
>
> > 69% said we were going about it in the right way;
> >
> > 31% said we were not.

It will be seen that those with a more idealistic conception of our war aims (Groups 1 and 3) are least critical of our present efforts, while those with a more materialistic approach (Group 2) were most critical.

(c) Do you think the Germans will try an invasion during this year?   Do you think they would be defeated if they came?

	Yes	No	Don't Know	Yes	No	Don't Know
Total	39%	40%	21%	82%	4%	14%
Men:	37%	45%	18%	83%	4%	13%
Women:	42%	35%	23%	82%	4%	14%
Economic Groups:						
Higher:	41%	38%	21%	90%	3%	7%
Middle:	43%	37%	20%	80%	5%	15%
Lower:	38%	41%	21%	82%	4%	14%

The first part of this question was also asked in February this year. The total results were then:

Yes: 62%   No: 21%   Don't Know: 17%

Analysis of results from the present enquiry indicate a reduction of 27% among men who expect invasion, among women a reduction of only 18%.

In upper-income groups there is a decrease of 17% among those expecting invasion; among lower-income groups the decrease is 23%; and, as is shown by the 'economic' percentages above, the lower-income groups are also less confident than the upper in our ability to resist invasion effectively.

3. IRISH NEUTRALITY

There are few signs that Eire's desire to stay out of the war has been affected by the Russian development, although the belief that 'Britain is already beaten', and 'it is only a question of months', which was widely held early this year, seems to be far less prevalent now. The final, overwhelming proof that neutrality is no protection against German invasion seems to have been more-or-less cancelled out, as an incentive to helping England, by the religious tendency to believe that no good can come of an alliance with Russia. There is, however, considerable evidence from Postal Censorship that opinion in Eire is increasingly in favour of giving up or leasing the ports to Britain or, preferably, to America. The majority of writers are still against this measure, in the proportions of 57% against and 43% in favour; but this is in itself a notable change from the comparable figures for last month, which were 65% against and 35% in favour. Typical views stated on both sides are: 'We Irish think they (the British Government) should just take the ports, and no more about it ... nearly everyone wants Britain to win. But without our help if possible.' And 'Of course we know we are of vital importance to England, but what did we get from her in the days gone by? Do you think she would treat us differently if we gave up our ports? She might while the war is raging, but after the war it is not known how we would be treated.'

4. RUMOURS

Current gossip in Salisbury contends that the Krupps works at Essen and the synthetic oil works at Leuna are not attacked by the RAF with the frequency which their importance merits, on account of the 'vested interests of European financiers'.

In Cornwall there is a revival of the idea that this part of the country would be undefended in the event of invasion; this is attributed to the withdrawal from West Cornwall of considerable numbers of troops, and also to the demolition of concrete road blocks.

It is believed in Falmouth that captured British planes were used in a recent raid on that locality, and that because of confusion deliberately caused in this way, some of our own fighters were fired on by the anti-aircraft guns.

From Fishguard comes a persistent rumour that the *Queen Mary* has been sunk.

II. SPECIAL COMMENTS

5. WASTE

Public discussion of waste as it affects industry – i.e. in men, material, time and enthusiasm – has followed the tone of the Parliamentary debate on war production. This in turn seems to have directed attention in detail to various other forms of waste. Where, as a rule, complaints deal with alleged unfairness in rationing or distribution, this week they are concentrated on every form of loss which it is felt might be avoided by better organisation.

6. FOOD

There is great indignation about rumours of vegetables and fruit being destroyed, so that prices shall be kept up. In some places the pea crop is said to have been incompletely gathered because of the lack of pickers. Elsewhere there are tales of tomatoes being allowed to rot because dealers consider that price-control will not allow them enough profit to warrant the trouble of marketing. Although there has been some response to Lord Woolton's appeal to give the egg scheme a fair trial, there are bitter complaints that, so far, 'all it does is to ensure that the eggs are stale when distributed'. Canadian eggs are reported to have been sent to the south of England, where many were found to have gone bad through delays in transit; while in Liverpool, where they were unloaded, there was a serious scarcity of eggs at the time. According to another report, Irish eggs, 'mostly bad', have been received 'in the heart of an egg-producing area in the west of England'; yet in the same area farmers had eggs which had been awaiting collection for nearly a fortnight.

Army canteens are accused of throwing away 'pounds and pounds worth of food'. Among the WAAFs, the girls themselves are said to be 'horrified by the waste' of being given 'much more than anyone could eat'.

7. PETROL

In many parts of the country, notably in the Cardiff and Bristol areas, and in several northern districts, bus services are now curtailed for lack of petrol, or if running normally, they are unequal to the increase in passengers where factories, camps, etc., have been opened in the locality. In the circumstances the sight of 'hundreds and hundreds of private cars, obviously used for pleasure' is arousing more and more irritation and the demand is steadily growing that the basic ration should be cut still further, 'despite the vested interests involved'.

8. CALL-UP OF MINERS, ETC.

The refusal of the military authorities to release miners from the army is thought to be 'inexplicable, since they should never have been called up'. But in spite of their repeated requests that compulsion should be introduced, the public shows no signs of interest or satisfaction now that the Government has decided to compel miners to return to the mines. The Regional Information Officer, Northern Region, states that 'a strong feeling remains that miners are still underpaid, and that great difficulty may be expected in drawing them back from better-paid, less arduous and more secure work in industry'. There are also protests against the 'wastefulness' of calling up trained and experienced wardens – 'men who know their job and also their locality, both of which are essential' – in order that they may, in the public's opinion, 'do nothing for months' in the army.

NO. 42: WEDNESDAY 16 JULY TO
WEDNESDAY 23 JULY 1941

I. GENERAL COMMENTS

1. GENERAL STATE OF CONFIDENCE AND REACTION TO NEWS

No essential change in public feeling has been reported this week. The predominant note is still one of confidence, ranging from 'quiet hopefulness' with reservations, to excessive optimism. The main causes for this are the same as for the past three weeks: Russia's resistance, the RAF offensive, the collapse of the French in Syria, and the country's comparative freedom from heavy raids.

Among the most optimistic sections of the public, it is said, complacency about the war is still 'far too prevalent', and it appears to be increasing. There are reports of 'a growing belief that the war will not last much longer', and the view that 'at any rate the bombing is over' continues to be expressed. Expectations as to 'when the war will end' are variously given as – this month, in September, before Christmas, or at any rate this year. Some people are 'ridiculing the idea of having to spend another winter in the shelters' and are talking of taking down their blackout curtains. The return of evacuees still continues. Fire-watchers are stated to be 'very slack'. There is no evidence that the severe raid on Hull on July 18 has had any sobering influence on the country, though it came as a shock to the people of Hull; for this 'the cheerful official predictions that night-bombing would shortly lose most of its terrors' are held partly responsible. This feeling of complacency has been further increased by the belief that the 'V' campaign, and press statements of a split between Hitler and Goering, indicate an 'impending revolt in Europe, and the imminent collapse of German morale'. A recent remark by Field Marshal Lord Ironside that the war might be over 'a good deal more quickly than many of us imagine' has had a similar effect. In view of this, the warning note in the recent speeches of the Prime Minister, and of the First Lord of the Admiralty, has been welcomed as likely to check over-optimistic tendencies. But, in spite of so many disappointments, the public still has the habit of treasuring optimistic prophecies and forgetting more realistic utterances, so that the latter tend to be submerged by the former.

RUSSIA: The fact that the Germans are still making such slow headway in Russia is the cause of rising spirits. The slow retreat of the Soviet armies is felt to be more in the nature of a deliberate withdrawal – which may have the effect of 'luring the Germans onwards to their doom' – than of a rout. Every day the Russians continue to hold out adds to the general satisfaction.

People are still unwilling to put much trust in communiqués from the Eastern front, though the Russian claims are felt to be considerably more reliable than the German. There is, however, much uncertainty, not only over the fluctuations of the campaign – which are described as bewildering and on which more authoritative information would be welcomed – but over the whole question of Russian resources and potentialities. There is some feeling that in the past the public has been misled on the subject of Russia. There are comments on the fact that 'in Godless Russia' thousands of people crowded the churches to pray for victory. People are noticing that 'an ill-fed, ill-equipped rabble, whose best officers have all been shot', and whose tanks were so summarily handled by the 'gallant little Finns', has succeeded in 'putting up a better show than we did'. Russian propaganda to the Germans is considered to be admirable and 'far superior to any we have produced'.

A feeling of distrust of the Soviets still persists in many quarters, both on religious and political grounds. On the other hand, a latent working-class sympathy for the 'workers' republic' has also become manifest among more conventional followers of Labour. However, both extremes find general agreement in the realisation that 'Russia is fighting, not only for her own existence, but also for ours'. There is general approval of the Prime Minister's 'forthright declaration' that our agreement with Russia is an alliance; and general condemnation of the failure to play her national anthem. Suggestions that the ban on the *Daily Worker* might be lifted now come from a rather wider circle than adherents of the Communist Party.

From almost all regions, there are reports of strong wishes and hopes that the RAF's offensive may be implemented by land and sea operations, even if these are to be no more than raids on the French and Belgian coasts. The belief continues that we have a 'golden opportunity' at present, and there are some sarcastic comments to the effect 'that we shall start something when Russia is on the point of collapse, and then it will be too late'. In this connection, the 'V' campaign 'mystery date' of July 20th was seized upon by a large number of people as the day for the invasion by us of northern France. There is also a growing hope that we may soon take the offensive in North Africa.

THE NATIONAL WAR EFFORT: Criticism of the Government and administration has been less vocal this week, but demands for greater efficiency in industrial organisation, together with 'sterner measures' and less of the 'pampering policy', continue. It is suggested that some of the criticisms of industrial inefficiency, unbacked by definite facts, are doing severe harm.

2. BROADCASTING AND NEWS PRESENTATION

There is little criticism of news presentation this week. People are grateful for the fuller details of the results of RAF raids, in particular for the aerial photographs of bomb damage. There is still, however, a considerable demand for more information on the Battle of the Atlantic. It is widely believed that a report of submarine sinkings, divorced from dates and localities, could safely be given without revealing information to the enemy.

Cassandra's *Postscript* was 'received with disgust', as a 'futile and vindictive piece of scurrility', by some of the more articulate sections of the community; the susceptibilities of the less articulate were not so upset; but 'all condemn Wodehouse'. There has been considerable praise for Mr. Swing, and there is continued appreciation for Mr. W. J. Brown for his 'hair-raising description of the conditions that Hitler was planning to impose on us'.

There have been criticisms of the *Kitchen Front* programmes, on the grounds that they are showing signs of 'padding' and 'staleness', that they take for granted stores of food which do not exist in poor people's larders, and that what Mr. Grisewood calls 'lunch' is, for most people, dinner.

3. THE 'V' CAMPAIGN

The campaign has captured the imagination of a large section of the public. Its extensive use in this country by shopkeepers, publicans, and writers on walls and public utility vehicles is widely commented on. It is mentioned by two RIOs as 'probably being responsible for a rise in public confidence'. More thoughtful people feel that it is 'admirable for occupied countries, rather than at home'; they fear it may 'become meaningless unless some definite post-war aim is agreed upon'. The effect of the campaign in producing belief in imminent invasion of France or rebellion in the occupied territories has already been noted. There is no connection in the public mind between the campaign and the Ministry of Information.

4. RUMOURS

Once again, rumours have not been numerous. A variant of the 'Rumanian oil wells' rumour alleges that the immunity from air attack of a concentration of industrial objectives, which includes an ICI factory at Hayle in West Cornwall, is due to some mutual arrangement with the opposite number of ICI in Germany.

In peace time the Orangemen of Northern Ireland hold processions and light bonfires in the streets on July 12th. From Belfast a rumour is reported that 'this year the Luftwaffe would light their bonfires for them'.

A Stirling bomber crashed in Northampton on July 15th. It is rumoured to have been returning from Germany, and still to have had a number of bombs on board.

Other rumours are that the casualties at Hull were higher than those at Coventry; and that soap is to be rationed.

II. SPECIAL COMMENTS

5. FOOD

EGGS: Criticism of the egg situation has now reached 'bitter dimensions'. Although grumbling about other shortages continues, none of them has provoked such widespread resentment. From almost all regions, there are complaints along the following lines:

1. Eggs are still in short supply in many parts, and distribution is patchy.
2. Retailers in egg-producing areas complain angrily that they are asked to handle Canadian and Irish eggs, many of which are bad.
3. Producers complain that arrangements for the collection of eggs and their delivery to packing stations are 'woefully inadequate', so that they have eggs left on their hands.

The mildest report received on this subject (from the Northern Region) refers to 'some lack of enthusiasm about the quality of many of the eggs'.

QUEUES: These continue to be a major problem which, it is suggested, 'is affecting, or may soon affect, public morale. Charges of greed and favouritism are bandied about.' Two complaints of 'peace talk being fostered in queues' are mentioned by the RIO Midland Region, while several other RIOs refer once again to the fact that working women cannot compete in queueing with the idle, a situation which is causing 'growing anger'. Queues are also said to be 'hot-beds of anti-Semitism' because of the belief, very generally held, that Jews 'always manage to get hold of more food than other people'. 'Opinion is steadily forming, especially in urban districts, that queues are an unhealthy symptom, and inconsistent with the underlying principles of rationing'; and, moreover, that 'they are unnecessary', and 'make it appear to the world that we are starving to death, and our people are lining up for a crust'.

One example of queueing, quoted by a Manchester report, is of a four-hour wait by people at Smithfield Market, with four police officers needed to control the crowd. Police efforts to abolish queueing, reported in many parts of the country, appear to have met with little success. Harrogate people, for instance, are said to 'queue by instinct', in spite of the efforts of the police; and women at Ilkley to have 'the habit of stopping at every queue they see, on the principle that there must be something worth getting at the other end'.

RATION BOOKS: There has been grumbling about what are thought to be 'the complex operations necessary to fill in the new ration books', a task which is 'rapidly becoming one of the abstruse sciences'. It is suggested that directions published in the press were far from clear. 'No wonder the Food Offices are kept busy correcting mistakes' sums up the general attitude.

The RIO South-Eastern Region reports: 'If a ration book is lost the owner can go to her Local Food Office, make a statement to the effect that she has not used any of her margarine coupons for the purchase of clothing, and have the whole 26 coupons replaced. In due course this dodge will become generally known, and there are many who will take advantage of it.'

6. PETROL AND PARAFFIN

Cars bearing labels such as 'ARP', 'Doctor', 'Urgent Medical Supplies', parked outside shops and roadhouses, are said to be adding considerably to the suspicion that a revision of the supplementary petrol allowance is as urgently needed as a further cut in the basic ration. It is still possible to hire a car for holiday purposes; one instance is given of a man hiring a car to take his family to Devonshire and receiving petrol coupons for 750 miles. On the other hand, there are recurrent reports that tradesmen and businessmen, on urgent national work which yet cannot be scheduled as war work, are in serious difficulty owing to lack of petrol. It is believed that, where supplementary rations are granted, inadequate effort is made to discover why the recipient must go by car rather than by train. It is also said that insufficient check is kept as to the purpose to which the petrol is put – logs being 'easy to cook'; no solution is, however, offered.

In country districts, a large section of the populace depends wholly on paraffin for cooking. Considerable hardship has been caused by the recent scarcity. In some places, supplies have been reduced to 25% of the individual's former consumption; in others it is unobtainable for several weeks at a time. Bearing in mind the threatened coal shortage, many people regard the winter prospect as extremely serious, if oil stoves cannot be used to supplement fires for warmth as well as for cooking. It is urged in some quarters that paraffin should take precedence over the basic petrol ration for shipping space. 'A few of the more intelligent' suspect that 'the Treasury may be at the back of the retention of the basic petrol ration'. They are said to feel that 'the unnecessary consumption of imported fuel in order to raise revenue has no justification in a war economy'.

7. DAY NURSERIES

The difficulty of providing for their young children continues to be one of the two main reasons put forward by women for not volunteering for industry. (The other, referred to in previous reports, is the shopping problem, when factory and shopping hours coincide.) Reports in favour of more nurseries attached to factories, or in workers' residential districts, have come in from many parts of the country. In some, women are said to be 'clamouring for them', and the Ministry of Health's new War Nursery Scheme is described as 'merely scratching the surface of the trouble'. (It is proposed, in this scheme, to add 83 whole-time and 35 part-time nurseries to the 117 – mostly part-time – which are already in being, in order to accommodate a maximum of 9,000 children.)

8. SERVICE PAY AND ALLOWANCES

'More and more ill-feeling' is alleged on the part of relatives of men in the Forces, at the discrepancy between their pay and the amount earned by their contemporaries in reserved occupations. In this connection, it is often said that 'everyone of service age should have been conscripted, and those wanted for industry should have been drafted into the factories, at the same rates of pay'.

The inadequacy of their marriage allowance is given as the reason for the 'flocking back to town' of many soldiers' wives, with their evacuated children. The loss of the 3/6d a week 'London Rent Allowance', if they live elsewhere, is a very bitter grievance. Social workers report that 'When families are evacuated from London it is almost impossible for them to find storage for their furniture if they give up their rooms.' They realise, also, that after the war, supply will not equal demand, and they want to be sure of a home when they return. 'They take our men and they take our money, and then they try to make us give up our homes' is a point which is frequently made. Widowed mothers, drawing 'dependent's allowances', are often deeply resentful of their treatment. If they are able to earn a little money, their allowance is withdrawn should their income reach 25/- a week after payment of rent and rates.

9. ANTI-SEMITIC FEELING

A slight increase in anti-Semitic feeling is associated with the present increase in food difficulties. Few specific instances of anti-social behaviour are brought forward against individual Jews, but general allegations suggest that 'Jews always have money to burn; they crowd out the evacuation areas' and 'seem to think of no-one but themselves'. The following incident is informative:

> 'A Jewish women evacuee buying fish in a small town was told that the price was high. She insisted on having it. This was quoted as evidence of Jews having 'money to burn'. To anyone acquainted with orthodox Jewish practices, however, the explanation was that the women, being unable to obtain Kosher food, had to buy fish whatever the price.'

NO. 44: WEDNESDAY 30 JULY TO WEDNESDAY 6 AUGUST 1941

I. GENERAL COMMENTS

1. GENERAL STATE OF CONFIDENCE AND REACTION TO NEWS

The balance of public feeling appears to be unchanged, and optimism in regard to the Russo-German conflict remains unaltered. At the same time, our situation vis-à-vis Japan has introduced in some quarters a more sober note of speculation than was noticeable last week. Her actions in Indo-China seem now to have brought her rather more vividly into the minds of most people. Great satisfaction has been expressed in many reports at the firm attitude taken by Britain and America, and it is a common belief that Japan's entry into the war would automatically bring in America too. The tone of most comments on this possibility is – 'The sooner the better.' There appear to be no doubts about the ability of the US to deal effectively with Japan in the Pacific. Apprehension appears to be divided between a belief that if Japan attacks Russia, our ally's difficulties will be greatly increased, and a fear that if America is forced to take up arms, our war supplies from the US will consequently be cut down.

There is now 'a belief that Russia's successful resistance is due to a deep-laid plan, long conceived', and that having held out for more than six weeks, she will now be able to fight on till September. (This six-week period seems to have been arbitrarily chosen by the public as a second crucial testing time after the first three weeks were safely over.) The idea is widespread that 'if September is reached with Russia still on her feet, all will be well'. Comparisons, unfavourable to us, continue to be made between our own propaganda and that of Russia. Particular approval is still expressed of the personal message broadcast to the wife of a German soldier killed at the front.

With confidence in Russia's strength maintained there has also been noted a lessening of the scepticism which greeted Russian communiqués at the beginning of hostilities. It has been pointed out, however, that 'if Russian news had not been ridiculed at the time of the Finnish campaign, it might have been better received today'.

Factors which have tended to increase public confidence during the past week include:

(a) This country's comparative freedom from air raids.
(b) The RAF's continued assault on Germany and the occupied territories, and especially last week's raid on Berlin. For the first time, however, our losses in planes and crews are being considered with some misgiving.
(c) Belief in America's power and will to help. Mr. Harry Hopkins' speech, repeating the promises of President Roosevelt, has been warmly welcomed, although there is still a tendency to feel that Americans 'talk too much and do too little'.

Factors tending to lessen public confidence during the past week have been:

(a) Continued disappointment that we have made no move on land to aid Russia.
(b) Fear that silence about the Battle of the Atlantic is maintained in order to hide the seriousness of our losses.
(c) A feeling that 'many people know of too many flies in the ointment' to be much reassured by the Prime Minister's statement in the recent debate on Production.
(d) Lack of confidence in our leaders, both in the army and in public affairs.

A belief that 'we have much to learn from Russia in military strategy' appears to be growing; and so does dissatisfaction about discrepancies and contradictions in the statements of various Ministers. 'Public confusion' is said to have resulted from the 'difference between the optimism attributed to Lord Halifax, and the sterner realities indicated by Mr. Herbert Morrison', the cheerful statements of Mr. Bevin about radiolocation, and the Prime Minister's recent warning of renewed raids.

There are still reports that 'a dangerous degree of complacency' exists in many parts of the country. Expectations that the war will soon be over – 'in September', 'this winter', or at least 'by next spring' – seem to be gaining new support. Various reasons are put forward for supposing that 'the end is well in sight'. The most usual are that it is 'thanks to Russia', 'thanks to America', and occasionally, 'thanks to air ascendancy'. It is said that 'the reports of Udet's suicide, and of the disgrace and even replacement of Goering, which have appeared in the newspapers, have gained general credence, and have been taken as real indication of the beginning of a German collapse'.

2. EXPECTATION OF AIR RAIDS

There are so many variations of opinion, and so many qualifying circumstances, in the public's attitude towards the prospect of raids, that it is impossible to generalise on the subject. Very few people seem to believe there will be no raids at all, though places like Oxford and Exeter, which have so far escaped, still expect to be immune. Many people, however, are said to anticipate a renewal of heavy bombing in industrial areas as soon as the nights begin to get longer. In London, where a good deal of wishful thinking on the subject has been noted, official warnings are said to have been less effective than the raid on July 27th, in bringing home a realisation of what may be in store. Nevertheless, evacuees continue to return to target areas; the number of children who are being brought back is said to be causing 'alarm and concern among the less complacent sections of the public'. In Belfast, though there is said to be an expectation of further raids, less than 2,000 people out of five thousand registered for priority evacuation have availed themselves of the opportunity to leave the city.

Opinion varies considerably as to the probable intensity of raids. Some two hundred Londoners in five different districts were asked their views on the subject. 70% thought there would again be heavy raids; 10% held the opposite view; and 20% were undecided. Other reports show varying expectation of their intensity. Reasons put forward to support the belief that they might be lighter include:

(a) Russia's continued resistance, which is thought likely to absorb the Luftwaffe's strength on the Eastern front. (Russia certainly seems to be the deciding factor in most minds; if she should collapse before the winter, prolonged and savage attacks on this country would then be expected.)

(b) 'The optimistic attitude which certain members of the War Cabinet have adopted in their speeches.'

(c) Publicity given to radiolocation; the superiority of our night fighters; and the speed-up of American output.

(d) An idea that the Germans will not be able to use their bases in northern France because of the sweeps made by the RAF.

3. PARLIAMENTARY DEBATE ON PRODUCTION

In spite of its lukewarm reception by the press, the debate seems to have had a somewhat reassuring effect on the public. The Prime Minister's 'emphatic denial of wholesale muddle has helped to restore a proper sense of proportion' and is said to have 'given great encouragement to factory workers'. There is a tendency, however, to regard his 'masterly array of facts' as being intended primarily 'for overseas consumption'. 'A fear that we are not turning our industrial resources to the best advantage' is still reported, as are alleged instances of idleness in munition factories caused by shortages of materials, of which, however, the workers are given no explanation.

Mr. Bevin's 'wages doctrine' has given rise to some criticism among 'men of maturer age'. There are apprehensive speculations about 'what will happen after the war to youths between 18 and 21, who are now on work of national importance and enjoying a fat basic wage, as well as overtime, for what is often little better than common labouring'.

4. BROADCASTING

Following 'Cassandra's' *Postscript* on P. G. Wodehouse (15th July 1941) a brief survey of opinion was carried out by Listener Research. From their panel of honorary local correspondents, fifty-five of the most reliable were asked for their views. The report points out that: 'Although because of its urgency the enquiry had to be confined to a small number of correspondents, the quality of their replies is very high. It can confidently be stated that had the number been very much greater, it is very doubtful if the results would have been materially different.'

Most of the correspondents emphasized that the *Postscript* was widely listened to, and that considerable spontaneous comment was forthcoming.

The general tenor of their reports was that the close-up predominant attitude towards the *Postscript* was one of approval, for which various reasons were stated or implied.

The *Postscript* has been commended because the use of Wodehouse by the Germans was regarded as an example of the most insidious form of propaganda – ostensibly innocent and harmless. It was held to be entirely salutary that a clear warning, by example, should be given to those who, whether through weakness, simplicity, or simple treachery, were inclined to help the enemy in any way.

Though there were few comments on the manner and delivery of the speaker, most of these were favourable.

Criticism of the matter of the broadcast was also small in volume. Moral objections emphasized that the full facts of the case could not be known; though, even if they were, and there were no moral objections against broadcasting them, 'it was, nevertheless, inexpedient to draw too much attention to enemy broadcasts'.

Only a very few correspondents were inclined to condemn the broadcast on the grounds that it constituted a breach of good taste.

The report goes on to state: 'Quite clearly, the majority of correspondents are, during war, concerned less with questions of good taste than with the effectiveness of propaganda as part of the war effort. And there is no reason to suppose that these correspondents are not representative of the general public in this respect.'

5. 'V' CAMPAIGN

It is thought that in this country interest in the campaign has passed its zenith, although the notable response of the public ('taking it perhaps more seriously than it deserves') suggests that inarticulate sections of the people have welcomed a simple sign by which they may express their feeling of national unity. It is to be noted also that there appears to be an increasing use of the 'V' sign in commercial advertising. On the other hand, there is a good deal of annoyance at what is thought 'the childishness of the whole thing over here' and impatience with people who will not realise that 'the war is not to be won with chalk and tar'.

6. RUMOUR

For the next few weeks, we are paying special attention to rumours. The number mentioned, therefore, should not be taken as an indication that rumours are actually more plentiful than usual. This week, the quantity is about normal.

From widely separated parts of the country, and with local variations, comes a story about a gipsy to whom a farmer showed kindness; she is said to have warned him to move his cattle from one field to another for no apparent reason. He did so, and the following night the field they had left was bombed. (Alternatively, he derided the suggestion and the cattle were killed.) Asked how she knew what would happen, the gipsy made some suitably occult reply, and added that the war would be over by a certain specific date (usually some time in October).

The belief that Hess is back in Germany is said to be spreading.

There are the usual exaggerations of casualties in recent raids, the figures for Hull, for instance, being given as 'over 1,000'.

It is freely said that the Government will not honour its obligations after the war to repay National Savings Certificates and 3% Defence Bonds, should such payments prove to be too heavy.

Arrangements to stop mutual bombing are supposed to have been made between Germany and Britain, with both sides 'keeping up occasional raids for the sake of appearances'.

Military raids on the Continent, on the Lofoten scale, are rumoured to be occurring everywhere, from the Baltic to the Mediterranean.

Almost all articles not yet rationed are mentioned as 'next on the list'.

II. SPECIAL COMMENTS

7. FOOD

There have been fewer complaints about food; several RIOs' reports do not mention the subject at all. There appears to be little uneasiness concerning the general food situation, and the large majority still feels that on the whole it is 'getting a fair deal'. As the following comments indicate, it is rather on the 'day-to-day difficulties of getting domestic supplies' that dissatisfaction continues.

1. EGGS: Although only three RIOs refer to eggs, they report criticism on familiar lines. In the South-Western Region there are complaints that new-laid eggs are sent to other parts of the country, while imported eggs are provided in their place. In the Midland Region the volume of complaints during the last week is 'as great as in any week since control began', and the demand for cancellation of the scheme is said to be growing. When eggs are available in industrial districts, they are described as 'often stale and frequently bad'.

2. DISTRIBUTION: The allegation is still made that the distribution of un-rationed food does not make allowance for the large numbers of men in the Services who are stationed in various parts of the country. The 'imposition of a shopping ban on troops, particularly in connection with confectionery, restaurants and eating-houses, and tobacco' is suggested.

3. AGRICULTURAL WORKERS: There are more requests for additional food for harvesters; in some cases farm workers are said to be provided with 'little more than bread and jam for their dinner baskets'. There is general welcome for the farmers' canteens which are to be opened in villages by the WVS and Women's Institutes during August and September.

4. HOLIDAY CATERING: There is reported to be some difficulty in catering for 'holiday-makers who, while not going out of the Region, visit holiday resorts near home for long week-ends'. This problem has been greatly aggravated by the Bank Holiday rush.

5. MILK: There have been complaints that shops may not turn sour milk into cheese, and that farmers who occasionally produce more milk than is required by their registered customers, may not distribute it; yet if they make it into butter, they may not sell it. A good deal of milk is said to be wasted in this way, and there are reports of 'bitterness and sarcasm on the subject of Government schemes'.

6. QUEUES: Although in the Northern Region queues are said to be decreasing, the general situation appears to be unchanged; and some anxiety is expressed about the effect on health that may be expected when winter sets in. There is some evidence that people are becoming 'queue-minded'. Besides the 'oft-told story of shoppers who wait their turn without knowing what is for sale, and turn away from the counter without making purchases', there are cases of 'queues for tomatoes on one side of the road while shops on the other side have tomatoes and no queues'. Durham now has the prize for the earliest queue, starting at 6 a.m.

Tradespeople are thought to be much to blame in advertising certain times of day when various goods will be released; but in some cases shopkeepers complain that official broadcasts, stating that a certain commodity is to be released, sometimes even naming areas, naturally send shoppers swarming hopefully to the shops.

On the whole the feeling seems to be that queues are 'undesirable and dispensable', and that the time has come to act in the matter; but 'although criticism is on the whole constructive, people appear to expect the solution to be found for them'.

Police action is generally welcomed, but at Kettering, where queues have been banned, 'people now form themselves into groups and hang about in the vicinity of the shop and make a rush the moment it is opened'. The most widespread suggestion is that cards should be issued unofficially to regular customers by the individual retailers themselves. This experiment is actually being made by a Sunderland confectioner, who has issued priority cards to 660 of his regular customers, undertaking to supply each with 3/6d worth of cakes a week; unregistered customers are not supplied until after 2.30. Since introducing this system he has had no more queues, though they are a daily occurrence at the other local confectioners. Shopping cards are particularly demanded as a solution to the factory workers' shopping problems, together with free shopping periods for people with domestic responsibilities.

8. WOMEN IN INDUSTRY

There have been fewer comments on this subject during the past week. Dealing with factors which are said to have an adverse effect on recruiting, one report mentions the following matters:

(1) Complaints of inefficient medical services in connection with Royal Ordnance and other war factories. An illness in which the skin turns green is reported in some places.

(2) Preference for home life, rather than life in a hostel (even at the cost of 'weary hours spent travelling').

(3) Maternal anxiety for the girls, and 'greedy concern on the mothers' part for a continued participation in their daughters' earnings'.

(4) The prejudice in 'better' social circles against factory girls. It is suggested that this 'stigma' might be removed by more flattering references in the press to 'young ladies on war work'.

Feeling is again reported, in connection with appeals for more women to enter industry, that 'the Government might well do more ordering and less asking'. It is thought that 'the biggest number of slackers is to be found among the women of the 30–40 age group'.

9. HOLIDAYS

The evident lack of response to the Government's appeal not to travel during the August Bank Holiday has led to a good deal of criticism of the Government's policy in this matter. The wisdom of relying solely upon exhortation is frequently questioned, especially by those who consider that 'it must be known that appeals will be completely ignored'. The campaign for 'holidays at home' is described as having 'developed into a broad farce'. Opinion seems to be divided on whether munition workers and the inhabitants of blitzed towns should take a sea-side holiday. Many reports suggest that 'it is asking too much to expect people to spend their few moments of leisure in work-a-day surroundings, particularly in blitzed areas'. The railways are blamed for facilitating travel by running extra trains (particularly when the coal shortage is said to be so serious); and 'in view of the fact that the holiday resorts are not receiving any extra food rations, it is futile to encourage the public to begin journeys which are bound to have an unsatisfactory conclusion'.

NO. 52: WEDNESDAY 24 SEPTEMBER TO WEDNESDAY 1 OCTOBER 1941

I. GENERAL COMMENTS

1. GENERAL STATE OF CONFIDENCE AND REACTION TO NEWS

Public spirits have recovered a little from the depression which followed the fall of Kiev. Although 'the general attitude of the people remains serious and rather grim', the lack of any further outstanding German successes on the Eastern front – particularly round Leningrad and Odessa – has lessened the fear that a Russian crack-up is imminent. On the whole, confidence appears to be slightly higher than it was last week, but lower than for some weeks previous to that.

The fear of an eventual Russian collapse, perhaps before winter, remains at the back of many people's minds, finding expression in vehement demands that greater aid should be given to our allies 'while British and American material might still be effective, in filling the gaps made in Russian industrial output'. Concern is still said to be growing 'about our policy of inaction on land', and the comment is reported once more: 'If we can't do anything now, with 90% of the German army fully engaged, and the occupied countries seething, how can we ever hope to do anything?' The dispatch of RAF men and material to Russia, though welcomed, is considered as yet an 'inadequate response to the seriousness of the situation'.

Five RIOs' reports speak of the connection in the public mind between what is considered 'the smallness and slowness of our help to Russia', and 'distrust' of certain elements in the Government. Criticism of 'those at the top' is more widely reported this week than for some time past; there is still said to be 'suspicion that some Ministers are not too enthusiastic about collaboration with Russia'. In general it is thought that the Prime Minister is 'far ahead of his cabinet'. There seems to be a fairly widespread feeling that the Government is 'unable to act swiftly and effectively, through clogging machinery, and that it is on the wrong tack in trying to persuade people to co-operate, when compulsion following a frank presentation of facts would be more welcome'.

The main reactions to 'Tanks for Russia Week' have been:

(1) among the simple majority, pleasure at the figures of increased production,
(2) among the more sophisticated, the suggestion that if production could suddenly jump by 20% there must be something wrong with our normal working methods,
(3) fear that this appeal will be made the basis of many similar drives; it is said that the workers have reached satiation point with appeals and Government campaigns.

From a number of areas, there are reports of 'a feeling of unreality' about the war. This is attributed to the difficulty which people experience in visualising the gigantic scale of the distant struggle on the Eastern front, to the improvements in the food situation, and to the continued absence of serious raiding.

The unpopularity of the army with the civilian population continues to cause concern. Resentment is felt on the home front that 'key-men are still being called up to do nothing in uniform', and 'the immobility of the army causes comment to the effect that industry is being starved in the interests of a huge army which is not adequately used now, and which must soon be difficult to equip unless industry gets more men'. It is suggested that to counteract this criticism, more publicity should be given to the size of the forces we are maintaining overseas.

There is 'a tendency to wonder whether the RAF offensive sweeps over France and Germany are too expensive for the comparatively small results claimed'.

2. AMERICA

There is 'little recorded comment on the present position regarding the Neutrality Act'. People seem to be taking it almost for granted that it will be repealed, and in fact, to regard US entry into the war as only a matter of time.

3. ITALY

It is said that 'people are critical of our failure to strike at Italy; there is much talk of low morale there', and there are suggestions of 'a hand behind the scene, holding back our maximum effort, probably on religious grounds'. It is said that 'air attacks on Genoa, Turin and Sicily cut no ice, as a belief persists that to bomb the capital would have a great psychological effect'.

4. THE INTER-ALLIED CONFERENCE

Although there is now a pronounced tendency to 'discount speeches of all kinds – we have heard too many', considerable importance has been attached to this meeting, and 'there has been little tendency to decry its pronouncements as empty assertions'; in particular 'America's request to be kept informed of plans for post-war relief in Europe is taken as indicating that she accepts a certain responsibility for European reconstruction', and Russia's adherence to the Atlantic Charter is felt to give 'greater hope for post-war Europe'.

5. FASCIST CAMP DISTURBANCES

Though it is regarded as of minor importance, public reaction to the disturbance by internees in the Isle of Man has been unanimously in favour of stronger disciplinary action. The following are typical of all RIOs' reports: 'There is great indignation at the advantage taken by these enemies of the state of the fact that they are in British hands. They must know that in Germany, Italy or Russia they would certainly be shot' ... 'It is felt that the authorities have been too lenient with them, and stern measures should be taken to make an example of the offenders' ... 'We had to show we are not Nazis', but 'there must be no more velvet-gloved handling of such people'. 'There can be no doubt that the public would support the Government in the most rigorous action to suppress disturbances of this kind.'

6. BROADCASTING

It is said that 'scarcity of real news in the Russian bulletins, and our own, is causing more people to turn to enemy broadcasters to know what is happening on the Eastern front', and more reliance is being placed on enemy bulletins. It is thought to be most damaging to our own news services when 'a German claim is followed by BBC protests that it is unconfirmed, suggesting that the German news agency has falsified a statement; and then follows the Russian admission of its truth'.

7. 'OXFORD GROUP' AND 'BRITISH ISRAELITES'

Considerable criticism has been reported recently by several RIOs of what is regarded as 'unfair efforts of the Buchmanites to avoid being called up in their respective age-groups'. Two RIOs this week mention intensified attempts to mobilise public opinion in support of their exemption, through newspaper and other channels; they draw attention to the report that 'a letter to the press in their favour, signed by a number of clergymen, is not a document compiled by those over whose signature it appears, but is a copy of a circular sent out by the Secretariat of the Oxford Group'.

It is deplored that 'some measure of credence' is given to 'prophecies put about by the British Israelites that the war will be over by the spring, as a result of a German defeat in the Middle East. This defeat, which is to follow decisive German successes in Russia, will bring about Germany's complete collapse.' It is suggested that such prophecies may lead to slackening of effort.

8. RUMOURS

Rumours are few this week, and of a miscellaneous character; but income tax is cropping up increasingly – that 'it is to be 18/- in the £', and that 'very soon they are going to take two years in one: in other words, they are going to tax us on income we haven't yet earned'.

Other rumours include:

The Italian royal family are 'getting out of Italy whilst they can' and have left for America.

Food 'to the value of £10,000' has been looted from convoys arriving at Liverpool from the States.

A BEF has landed in Russia.

'The aerodromes in France are absolutely empty: there are no planes anywhere'. (This comes from a contact whose brother-in-law is a pilot, who 'has been over France a lot recently'.)

There is a practice now in 'some of the big shops, of making up lengths of crepe-de-chine into sheets for wealthy ladies to buy coupon-free'.

II. SPECIAL COMMENTS

9. INDUSTRY

Apart from the 'Tanks for Russia' drive, the main public comments about industrial matters have been along the following lines:

1. Criticism of the drafting of skilled men from industry into the Services. This is thought to be particularly undesirable when production for Russia is regarded as our most important task.
2. Complaints about reduction in overtime work. Workers are unwilling to recognise that a decrease in overtime work may lead to an increase in production, as it certainly leads to a decrease in time-work wages.
3. Complaints that men are transferred from jobs where they have been working hard to new jobs where they are comparatively idle.
4. Allegations that 'cost plus percentage' is leading in many cases to employment of more workers than is really necessary; two RIOs and Postal Censorship report stories of foremen telling their men to 'take it easy'.
5. Renewed requests that managements should give explanations to the men, whenever hold-ups of supplies occur; and reports of successful results when this has been done.

The closing down of a number of tinplate and sheet metal works in the Neath area (Glamorganshire) is reported to have caused considerable dissatisfaction; and the 'compulsory removal' from the area of large numbers of skilled workpeople is much criticised, especially because it is thought that they are being sent to England to do ordinary unskilled labourer's work. The spirits of the people in this area are said to be adversely affected and there is reported to be a strong feeling that, since 'all the usual industrial necessities' (labour, coal, water, buildings, etc.) already exist, the present factories could be adapted for war production, thereby avoiding the 'hardships and inconveniences' of compulsory migration.

10. REGISTRATION OF WOMEN

There is little to add to our last report on this subject; latest information received confirms what was said then. It appears to be 'increasingly felt that single women should be conscripted for suitable work in industry and the Services, and that opportunities for local work should be afforded to married women with no children'. The news that younger shop girls are to be called up does not seem to have caused any stir; it is felt that 'definite action of this type is welcomed, instead of patriotic, sentimental or other appeals', but the question is asked, 'What happens if a healthy young woman of 20 just says she won't work?'

It is said, in the case of the Services, that the smallness of dependants' allowances holds back many volunteers, because 'so many of these girls contribute a considerable proportion of their earnings towards the home'.

11. FOOD

GENERAL: Again this week there are 'few complaints of major importance' about the food situation; and, according to most of the RIOs and Postal Censorship, satisfaction far outweighs criticism. The reduced price of bread, the control of the price of sweets, the distribution of oranges and the falling-off of queues all receive praise. Scarcity of fruit and eggs is reported from some Regions, and also queues for cakes and, in some cases, for bread. Thus, in Coventry, many bakers are reported to shut for long periods, as they say it is not worth while opening when they have bread only, as they make their money in cakes. As a result, there are queues for bread and cakes even when there is plenty of bread, and this waste of their time is particularly resented by women workers.

'Trouble is reported to be brewing again over the milk problem', and considerable apprehension and some annoyance is reported at the prospect of milk control on October 10th. Some sections of the public are complaining of having been 'misled, as the impression created by Lord Woolton's last pronouncement was that there would be no rationing for some months'.

The suggestions that neighbouring families should 'cook their meals on a communal system', and that the oven should only be used once a week, are described by many housewives as 'ridiculous', although they admit the need to economise fuel.

Praise for British Restaurants continues.

BLACK MARKETS: There is a strong feeling that severe penalties should be imposed for black market offences. In the case of major offences, and the sale of spurious food substitutes, 'the tide of public indignation is rapidly rising'. Sentences should be far more severe, it is felt, and should consist of imprisonment as well as heavy fines. It is even suggested 'in some people's serious judgment, that the gang-leaders should be shot as guilty of "worse than desertion from the ranks"'.

More than one RIO reports the connection in the public mind between the Jews and the black markets, chiefly as instigators, but also as customers 'willing to pay any price to get things they want'. There is 'unquestionably a feeling about that Jews in big business are behind the black markets', and the recent disclosures are said to have intensified 'acute and bitter anti-Jewish feeling' which exists in some quarters.

12. CIVIL DEFENCE

Reports that the bulk of those registering for compulsory fire-watching (in the case of Salford, as high as 75%) have applied for exemption has increased the desire that women should be conscripted for the Fire Guard. Still more is it felt 'that soldiers ought to share this duty, which at present falls most heavily on the elderly and less fit male population, many of whom carry increasingly heavy burdens in their daily work'. There is some criticism that 'volunteer ARP "key-men" are not reserved except in their own individual occupation. One town reports having to lose two Sub-Controllers, who were trained through active service last winter, and who are considered almost irreplaceable.'

Instances of ill-feeling are reported as a result of the changes in the Fire Service under the new arrangements. There is 'adverse criticism of the high salaries being paid to the officers in the new Fire Force'.

13. PAPER SHORTAGE

It is suggested that, in view of the paper shortage, 'steps should be taken to forbid the publication of a considerable number of wretched little magazines and other publications of no public value'. It is asked why collectors should have to save paper to make up the shortage, 'when unnecessary publications are issued to a public that does not need them, or even want them'.

14. TRANSPORT

'Various reports again stress the need for re-organisation of transport services for workers', and there is considerable apprehension in country districts as to the probable effects on health during the winter of waiting for buses in inclement weather. The difficulties of country people are particularly acute because they are often unable to board buses en route as they are filled at the starting place. According to one RIO, people waiting at bus stops 'express themselves very heatedly at the number of cars whizzing along'. It is suggested that there should be another campaign to encourage motorists to give lifts to foot passengers, as this practice seems to be dying out of late; and unless people are in uniform they cannot usually succeed in making motorists stop.

Though the public as a whole does not regret the cut in the petrol ration, among private motorists there is a 'good deal of talk concerning the new petrol allowance which operates after the first of October. The feeling seems to be that the allowance is so small that if a motorist pays tax and insurance and receives only a basic allowance and no supplementary allowance, he is either mad or breaking the law by getting petrol illegally.'

15. INCOME TAX AND WAGES

There is still a good deal of comment on the high wages paid to unskilled workers. It is even alleged that the workers themselves sometimes complain about being paid high wages for insufficient work. Farmers complain that they cannot 'compete with the contractor who offers the village "ne'er-do-well" £5 a week as a labourer on Government work; and farm hands who are tied to their work feel angered by a situation they can do nothing to remedy'. Considerable concern is expressed about youths earning large amounts on temporary work such as demolition, where income tax is not deducted at source, because they are boasting that by the time they are called up they will owe the Government large sums. As most of these lads are minors, the debt will fall on their parents, and there are already cases of people defaulting in their rent because they are having to pay off debts for sons in the army. What is described as 'an impossible situation' is being created, as the parents have no control over their boys and are yet responsible for their debts.

There is reported to be 'much discontent among British workmen at aerodromes in the Kettering district because the wages of Irish labourers are not subject to income tax deductions in the same way as their own. It is understood that until a man has been in employment for six months in this country, he is not liable for tax; and the suggestion is made that when the six months are up some of these men go back to Ireland to seek other employment.'

It is suggested that explanatory talks should be given over the radio both on income tax and War Damage Insurance, on both of which considerable misunderstanding is still reported.

16. EVACUATION

Reports of children in great numbers returning to the target areas continue to come from even the worst-hit towns. There is now considerable difference of opinion as to whether parents should be permitted to jeopardise their children's lives in this manner, although even those in favour of compulsory evacuation admit the difficulties in the way of such a policy. In view of the great public expense involved in evacuating and re-evacuating the same children (in some cases as many as 5 times) 'a half-way solution' has been suggested:

(1) A definite order that any child evacuated under Government auspices cannot be re-evacuated if the parents have brought the child home, except in special circumstances approved by the authorities.

(2) Refusal of any financial aid (for travelling) to parents who withdraw officially evacuated children from reception areas, except in special circumstances.

17. CLOTHES RATIONING

Shoreditch stretcher parties are said to be 'in a fury' at having to surrender 18 coupons for their uniforms, especially as WVS uniforms are coupon-free. There are also complaints from men in the Home Guard who have to buy special articles of clothing, when promoted to commissions, without extra coupons.

There is still a 'lot of irritation' over the delay in the issue of forms for obtaining coupons when books have been lost, with the usual corollary that 'plans should not be announced in the press before a scheme is complete'.

Enquiries about arrangements for growing children are said to be 'constant'.

Complaints are reported about the difficulties of obtaining replacement coupons for clothes not delivered (for various reasons, such as theft, garments too small, etc.), although coupons have been surrendered. The purchaser is left minus coupons and clothes.

APPENDIX TO WEEKLY REPORT NO. 52

HOME MORALE AND PUBLIC OPINION

1 OCTOBER 1941

A review of some conclusions arising out of a year of Home Intelligence Weekly Reports.

1. SOME DEFINITIONS

MORALE is the 'state of conduct and behaviour of an individual or a group'. Morale must therefore ultimately be measured, not by what a person thinks or says, but by what he does and how he does it. This distinction is particularly important in dealing with the British public in whom admirable behaviour is often coupled with a veritable wail of grumbles. Indeed, the constitutional pessimist is often the most reliable soldier, while the constitutional optimist is the least reliable.

GOOD WAR MORALE of the British public is 'conduct and behaviour indicating that they are prepared to go through with the war to final victory, whatever the cost to the individual or the group'. Indices of good morale which may be mentioned are:

a. The ready acceptance of the compulsory fire-watching order.
b. The demand before the last budget for an increase in income tax.
c. The present demand for the exercise of the Ministry of Labour's compulsory powers to conscript women.
d. The complaints, both by workers and by managements, that they are not yet working 'all out'.

PUBLIC OPINION is 'the integrated result of expressed private opinion'. It is not a simple summation, since opposite opinions do not cancel out, but persist. From public opinion, it is often possible to assess the probable state of morale. But such assessments must be made with great care. The relationship between the two is seldom a direct one. Thus, when the war as a whole appears to be going well, grumbles are often loudest, while when things are going badly, grumbles are silenced.

2. THE FACTORS ON WHICH MORALE DEPENDS

These factors are of two kinds: Material and Mental. Since most British people are, on the whole, practical and unimaginative, the material factors appear to be more important than the mental ones. This generalisation is subject to one proviso. Certain of the mental factors are so strongly ingrained in the average British man and woman that they are not shaken by the ordinary processes of argument and reason. If, in some as yet unforeseen situation, they *were* shaken, the results might well be more disastrous than the most dire material upset. So far, even the most calamitous events have been turned to a mental profit by the British public. Thus, the collapse of France was treated along these lines: 'At last, we're on our own and there's no-one else to let us down; now we've really got to get on with the job.' Again, the blitz was converted from a thing of terror to a symbol of pride and toughness: 'Our blitz was worse than yours – and look at us.'

The MATERIAL factors affecting morale are:

1. FOOD. Starvation, particularly starvation of children, is a probable breaking-point. In severely blitzed populations, *hot* food has been found to be of great importance in morale. As minor irritations in non-blitz times, inequalities of distribution, and wastage and profiteering, have proved to be the main foci of feeling.

2. WARMTH. Heat, like food, has assumed a particular importance in blitzed areas. Lack of either accentuates the need for the other. The problem has three aspects: warm clothing; the heating of rooms; and cooking. The danger points here are: the coal situation; the paraffin situation in rural areas; and the post-blitz situation where gas, electricity and fuel transport may be dislocated.

3. WORK. The demoralizing effects of lack of work are obvious. Less obvious, but no less important, is the fatigue which follows overwork. Not only does it lower output, but further it reduces vitality and resistance to disease. The uneconomical effect of excessive overtime is fully recognised officially, but employees, welcoming overtime pay, and employers, working on the 'cost plus 10%' basis, in some cases still need convincing.

    The failure to explain to the workers the reasons for lack of work (shortage of materials, changes of design etc.) creates a feeling of inefficiency and futility, which may combine dangerously with the other effects of idleness.

4. LEISURE, REST AND SLEEP. The importance of rest is a natural corollary to the dangers of overwork. With regard to sleep, the continuous aerial bombardment of London demonstrated the self-assertiveness of nature. People who were determined to remain awake in all raids finally fell asleep, and a combination of physical fatigue and 'growing used to raids' redressed the balance of enforced insomnia.

5. A SECURE BASE. The need for a secure base for the fighter in Civil Defence has been demonstrated most clearly in the medium-sized provincial towns which have been repeatedly blitzed. Unless, after his spell of duty or danger, the civilian can have 'time off' in a place which he believes to be safe, he returns to the battle less vigorous, and consequently less efficient and less determined.

    In the medium-sized provincial towns, there was no part which could be regarded as outside the target area, and when heavy aerial attacks were made on successive nights, their effect on civilian morale was in geometric rather than arithmetic progression. A suitable secure base, in which the civilian fighter may get his 'second wind', may be a billet outside the town or a shelter of such a kind that he believes it to be safe. The secure base has not arisen as a serious problem in large cities, as so far there have always been large areas of houses escaping unscathed.

6. SAFETY AND SECURITY FOR DEPENDANTS. Evacuation, and the nightly trek from the blitzed cities, are the organised and unorganised answers to the problem of safety for dependants in blitzed areas. The official answers to the problems of security for dependants are the various pension arrangements for Service and civilian casualties, and the systems of Service dependants' allowances. The fact that the Forces' dependants now constitute the poorest section of an industrial community in which wages have risen rapidly, has not passed unnoticed by the public.

Turning now to the main MENTAL FACTORS which affect morale, the following stand out:

1. BELIEF THAT VICTORY IS POSSIBLE. This is not synonymous with belief that defeat is impossible, which must be regarded as a slightly less satisfactory morale state. All the evidence points to confidence, on the part of the great majority of the public, that victory is not only possible but certain. Six months ago, questioning voices were asking how victory could be won. Events in Russia have now silenced these enquiries, though should another period of apparent stalemate arise, these questions will probably spring up again.

2. BELIEF IN EQUALITY OF SACRIFICE. The ubiquity of the bomber and the income tax have done more than anything else to silence doubts on this score. With the recent improvements in the food situation, the complaints about the unrationed rich in restaurants have declined. The main doubt now in the public mind is over the profits accruing to the controllers of industry, and there is need for further explanation of the working of the Excess Profits Tax.

3. BELIEF IN THE EFFICIENCY AND INTEGRITY OF LEADERSHIP. This includes national, local, industrial, and Forces leadership. Efficiency is, perhaps, rated higher in the public mind than integrity. Particular exception is taken to anything which can possibly be regarded as 'kid-glove' handling of our enemies. It is for the absence of 'kid-gloves', as well as for many other qualities, that the public particularly admires and respects the leadership of the Prime Minister.

   Least confidence in leadership is expressed in the industrial and military spheres. The absence of opportunity which has hampered the army in showing its paces is not fully appreciated. And the need for more explanations to workers of the often cogent reasons which produce industrial hold-ups has been repeatedly stressed.

4. BELIEF THAT THE WAR IS A NECESSITY AND OUR CAUSE JUST. The combination of the propaganda of events, and a large volume of direct and indirect public education on this subject, have succeeded in convincing the great bulk of the public on both these points. The 'What have I got to lose'

school is steadily diminishing, though in another period of stalemate they
may again raise their heads.

3. THE FACTORS ON WHICH PUBLIC OPINION DEPENDS

Public opinion is notoriously fickle. Yet when in possession of the relevant facts, it
is surprisingly sound. It respects 'security reasons' for reticence, provided it can be
satisfied of their validity. It always spots if it is being 'talked down to', and it is most
suspicious of the 'high-falutin''. The factors which influence it are as follows:

1. PERSONAL EXPERIENCE. For the British public, this is the most
   important of all. Seeing, for them, is believing. Air raids, food shortages,
   shopping difficulties, queues, factory conditions, evacuees and hosts, these
   are the things about which the British public thinks and feels most. A
   good example of this 'out of sight, out of mind' attitude is provided by the
   income tax. Deduction at source has greatly reduced the volume of criticism
   with which the regular payers usually meet their demand notes; though the
   new classes, who are paying for the first time, are less silent.
       It is a common custom of the public to argue from the particular to the
   general, from the single instance which has touched them personally to
   the problems of the country as a whole. Thus misconceptions requiring
   correction are constantly arising.
2. CONVERSATION. Conversation consists largely of magnified and
   distorted experience at second-hand, or material culled from the radio or
   press treated in similar ways. Its most important end-products are rumours,
   gossip, and idle talk. It is, perhaps, the least important factor in forming
   public opinion.
3. THE PRESS. The press claims for itself a double function, that it both
   forms and reflects public opinion. Since it does not discriminate as to which
   it is doing at any one time, its reflection of public opinion is, at times,
   inaccurate. As a creator of public opinion, its activities fall into two parts:
   (a) FOREIGN AFFAIRS. On all matters outside Britain it exercises
       considerable influence on opinion, as the public as a whole has no
       means of cross-checking by personal experience. On such matters,
       press feeling and public feeling often go hand in hand, with an
       occasional lag behind on the part of the public when faced with a
       press campaign.
   (b) HOME AFFAIRS. On matters at Home, the press is a far less
       powerful formative agent. The public often makes up its mind on
       its own experiences before the press knows anything about it. Then
       the press 'clocks in' on a pre-existing discontent and may claim the
       credit for any Governmental action. (A similar process, on a smaller
       scale, was formerly the regular practice of the Communist Party.) As
       a reflection of public discontents, the press is handicapped in two
       ways: press investigations of discontents must be 'good stories', and
       as a result, public indignation is over-played, and often the reporter's

indignation is projected on to the public; further, long-standing troubles soon cease to be 'news', while they still continue to bulk large in the public mind.

A distinction must be drawn between the national press and the provincial and more particularly the local press. The local weekly newspaper is a much more accurate reflection of public opinion than the big national dailies, for two reasons. First, its staff are members of their local community and not of a coterie of other journalists. Secondly, it devotes a much greater proportion of its space to the local happenings which are, in themselves, the main creators of public opinion.

The sifting of public feeling from national press influence is complicated by certain special wartime factors:

(a) Political proprietor bias has largely disappeared, as a result of all-party Government.
(b) The limited supplies of paper and advertising have done much to reduce news bias on behalf of advertisers, if such there was.

It may be noted that the public has shown no signs of regret at the reduction in size of the newspapers.

One aspect of public opinion the national press does reflect. It gives a fairly accurate index of the national taste of the different social groups.

4. THE RADIO. Next to personal experience, the radio is the most powerful agent in forming public opinion. It has a degree of universality not possessed by any group of newspapers. On affairs outside Britain, it is a powerful corrective to the press. It is regarded as having no axes to grind. Its honesty is thought to be unimpeachable. Its errors are regarded as being due to ineptitude rather than knavery. Though an intelligent and vocal minority protest when the radio drops its 'kid-gloves', the public as a whole appreciate vigour rather than good taste. Any inconsistency, woolly speaking, or obscurity of meaning is quickly detected and proclaimed.

4. SOME GENERALISATIONS AND CONCLUSIONS

The following generalisations have many exceptions. But their essential validity has become obvious during the past year's work on Home Intelligence Weekly Reports:

1. The British public as a whole shows a very high degree of common-sense. Given the relevant facts, it will listen to and accept explanations when it will not accept exhortations.
2. Its taste is as low as its common-sense is high. In England, the main exception to this is in the matter of the spoken word. The English appreciate fine oratory – but it must be rich in the meat of common-sense. In Wales, the main exceptions are in the matter of music and poetry.

3. The British public are pragmatic. They are little influenced by immaterial, ethical or theoretical considerations. To this, there are three main exceptions:

    (a) A determination not to be 'put upon' or 'messed about' except by their own consent. In fact, a deep-rooted belief in the liberty of the subject.

    (b) A determination not to allow others to be 'put upon' similarly, *provided* the 'others' concerned are reasonably near the British Isles geographically, or in the British Empire. Thus, the butchering of a thousand Chinese creates far less indignation than the shooting of twenty Belgians.

    (c) A sense of 'fair play' inside our own team. Outside 'the public school' classes, 'dirty tricks' on the enemy are, however, regarded as most desirable and very funny.

4. The British public has a basic stability of temperament, with a slightly gloomy tinge. Arising apparently from this are:

    (a) A tendency to smell out and voice grumbles loudly. The volume of grumbling varies inversely with the severity of the war situation.

    (b) A distrust of excessive enthusiasm, and a delight in 'knowing the worst'. With this is coupled a strange anxiety about not being told 'the worst'.

    (c) A tendency to doubt rather than believe any new information, unless gloomy, and particularly, a suspicion of 'newspaper talk'.

5. The public has a great capacity for righteous indignation when things go wrong. For disasters, the tendency is not to blame the enemy, but to blame some section of those in authority. In this process, it is usual for the public to get hold of the wrong end of the stick. Thus, when the news is bad, it blames the press, the radio, and above all, the Ministry of Information.

6. Gratitude is rarely exhibited. It is usual rather to examine the actions of benefactors to discover what personal benefit they obtain from their actions.

7. A fundamental tenet of the British public's creed is that all in authority, above all 'officials', are inefficient.

8. The public is unimaginative. It is unable and has, apparently, no great wish to picture the details of the post-war world. It speculates relatively little about the end of the war. And the possibility of defeat is neither imagined, nor imaginable.

9. The English public is basically lazy, with, in consequence, a very large reserve and capacity for effort on the rare occasions when it considers this vitally necessary. This does not apply to Scotland, Wales or Northern Ireland. This innate laziness leads secondarily to a high degree of tolerance, coupled with an apparent indifference to unpleasant environments.

10. The public, as a whole, is happier since the war than it was in the peace, for the following reasons:

  (a) The uncertain fear of the unknown has gone. The predicted picture of war on the home front was fortunately far more terrible than the real thing turned out to be.

  (b) Schisms and party distinctions have largely disappeared. In their place there is a new sense of purpose in life with a clear-cut objective in view – winning the war. Class distinctions among men have also greatly declined.

  (c) Thanks to air raids, rationing, war industrialisation, and Civil Defence, everyone has some sense of personal participation in the work of the country.

  (d) Many gross inequalities of income have been 'ironed out'.

  (e) Thanks to dispersal by evacuation, higher wages for the undernourished, rationing for the overnourished, and milk for children, general health has, on the whole, improved rather than deteriorated.

The only large groups who have suffered seriously are:

  (a) Those who have lost members of their families.

  (b) Dependants of servicemen.

  (c) Pensioners and others with fixed incomes.

11. There is, at present, no evidence to suggest that it is possible to defeat the people of Britain by any means other than extermination.

STEPHEN TAYLOR MD, MRCP
HOME INTELLIGENCE

NO. 60: MONDAY 17 NOVEMBER TO MONDAY 24 NOVEMBER 1941

I. GENERAL COMMENTS

1. GENERAL STATE OF CONFIDENCE AND REACTION TO NEWS

(a) LIBYA

Spirits have risen sharply this week with the opening of the Libyan campaign. For the first time for several months, there has been no mention in any report of apathy or war-weariness. The point around which most comment has centred is the Prime Minister's extreme confidence in the outcome of this offensive, as expressed by him in the House of Commons. His reference to meeting the enemy on equal terms at last is thought to 'commit us to victory' so thoroughly that we are believed to have reason for very considerable optimism in this theatre of war; and 'the public is in a state of elated expectancy'. It is pointed out that 'Britain's War Asset No. 1', as Mr. Churchill is now called, has never been given to boasting, and would not have spoken as he did if there were serious doubts about the issue. 'But even those who have claimed to detect, in his recent utterances, an undercurrent of special optimism, have been surprised by the completeness of our preparations, and the sweeping character of the attack.' There is thought, however, to be little 'expectation of the rapid successes of the former campaign; chasing Italians last winter was one thing, but this is a different matter – the first real trial of strength between German and British troops'. Several RIOs have commented on the 'general satisfaction' expressed by the public that it is the Germans we are now meeting, and that 'Britain is in the war again. We have been out of the fighting too long.'

Two aspects of the campaign which are giving much pleasure are:

(a) alleviation of 'the uneasy feeling that we are always following the German lead, and always too late';
(b) removal of 'some of the doubts about our production, it having been so often asked: "If we have air parity at last, why cannot we strike harder at Germany?"'

This offensive is taken as answering that question satisfactorily, although in some quarters it is emphasised that 'there is no tendency to regard the desert campaign as opening the second front to which M. Stalin referred'; it is still assumed, apparently, that this must be in Europe.

(b) RUSSIA

Although it is widely said that the war on the Eastern front has been overshadowed for the moment by the North African offensive, 'this in no way implies a lessening of interest or of anxiety' about the situation in Russia. There is said to be 'no disposition to minimise the seriousness of our ally's position, and the desire that we should rush all aid to her remains unabated. The news that British tanks have been in action on the Eastern front was welcomed.' But despite grave concern over the threat to Moscow and the situation at Rostov, the absence of further 'spectacular German gains in Russia causes growing confidence in the ability of our ally to hold the Nazi onslaught. Hitler's hopes are felt to have received a serious setback' by Moscow and Leningrad being still in Russian hands, though winter has already begun. It is said that 'his disregard of losses, his renewed ferocity in attack, and the uncertain tone of his propaganda are all taken as indications that the Germans are beginning to get desperate'. There is 'much discussion' (although, apparently, few definite opinions) as to whether the Libyan campaign will have the effect of relieving pressure on the Russians by diverting some of Germany's air-strength.

The great admiration felt by the public for Russia's courage and endurance continues to grow with every week of her resistance. The present attitude may be summed up by the phrase: 'People realise that every Russian killed is one Englishman less to die, and they are not only thankful, they are deeply grateful.' For this reason, matters of apparently small importance tend to be somewhat magnified in the public estimation, if they suggest that we are lukewarm in our co-operation with Russia.

The recent 'discourtesy' shown to M. Litvinov in excluding him from one of our planes, although accepted as accidental, has aroused 'some perturbation lest such stupidity by our officials should jeopardise our good relations with Russia'. There are still suspicions that there is 'less enthusiasm in Government circles' for helping Russia to the utmost of our ability than there is among the workers and the people in general.

(c) ARMY CHANGES

On the whole, little interest has been aroused by the recent changes in the High Command. Such comments as have been reported are, on the whole, favourable, 'the principle of having younger men in command being generally accepted as good'. A minority view is that the sending of Sir John Dill to India indicates some kind of unspecified action in that quarter in the near future.

2. VICHY

There are reports of 'more and more impatience with the Government's alleged tenderness towards Vichy'. The dismissal of General Weygand is widely accepted as heralding much closer co-operation in North Africa between the French and the Nazis. 'There is no indication that much trust has been placed in Weygand, but his presence there was regarded as at least a hindrance to Hitler', and fears have been revived of the French fleet being handed over to Germany.

Concern is also reported over a common belief that 'German and Italian submarines are already operating freely from Dakar'.

3. AMERICA

Considerable impatience and even depression is reported over 'the latest evidence of United States disunity' – the coal strike, and the threat of other strikes seriously affecting war production. 'The most generally expressed opinion is one of surprise and doubt as to whether this country can ever rely upon consistent aid from the USA.' (No comments have been received since the announcement that work had been resumed in the American mines.) President Roosevelt, however, is thought to have demonstrated that his control is 'pretty strong at home'; while in foreign affairs his firm policy in relation to Japan has led to his description as 'our best friend after Churchill'.

4. JAPAN

Opinion on the likelihood of Japan's entry into the war has changed little since last week, when there was a strong expectation of hostilities at any moment. There is now felt to be slightly less probability that Japan will commit herself to a fight from which she has, it seems, apparently so little to gain. Belief that she may be bluffing seems to be gaining ground, and apparently rests on the idea that if she really intended action, she would have taken it by now. A typical comment, however, is still that 'America will look after her'.

5. RUMANIA, HUNGARY AND FINLAND

'Whether we declare war on Rumania and Hungary' is said to be a matter of indifference to some sections of the public, though others are urging that it should be done at once, as a sign of our whole-hearted support for Russia; there appears, however, to be no public feeling *against* such a declaration. Over Finland, there seems to be a rather wider division of opinion. Although in some quarters there is a demand that we should be openly at war with her, 'some of the goodwill towards her, which reached a climax during the winter war, undoubtedly remains, and it is with regret that many people noted her failure to respond to the message from the United States'. In general, however, 'opinion is stiffening against Finland, on the ground that those who are not with us are against us, and that Finland has chosen her part and is now subject to German dictation. People who feel most warmly about Russia are impatient with the apparent reluctance of our Government to break with Finland, and regard it as further evidence that some members of the Government are not all-out in their support of Russia.'

6. BROADCASTING AND PRESENTATION OF NEWS

There is renewed criticism of the importance given to trivial items in the BBC news bulletins: 'too many minor speeches' are said to be included. Again, it is alleged that 'every Russian retreat or withdrawal is presented in such a way as to suggest that little or nothing has been lost'.

In marked contrast to the reception given to the ATS broadcast, *Four Smart Girls*, Chief Controller Knox's *Postscript* was said to show 'sincerity and ideals'. Raymond Gram Swing's elucidation of the vote on the Neutrality Act 'has been received with gratitude by many people. It is suggested that this broadcast should be made available in pamphlet form.'

7. RUMOURS

The rumour that raids are being made by us on the Continental coasts has again been met. It is said that there are many flat-bottomed barges on the east coast which are used in these raids.

A story is reported that two military convoys were sent (from the south-west, via Trowbridge) to the east coast to repel imminent invasion expected by the Government 'because the army fighting in Russia were just Czechs, Hungarians, Italians and Rumanians. The German army, intact, was waiting on the west coast of France, ready to invade us.'

Rumours of enemy bombing of Aldershot, Basingstoke, and Newbury circulated in Reading during the week.

The rumour of the sinking of HMS *Malaya* has been reported in the Southern Region.

It is reported that roundsmen are suggesting that their customers should take homogenised milk – at 9½d per quart as compared with 9d per quart for ordinary milk – 'as this is classed as priority, and not subject to any cut'.

II. SPECIAL COMMENTS

8. INDUSTRY

Complaints of slackness and muddle in munition factories are less numerous this week. There is still criticism, however, of the cost plus 10% system, founded on the belief that it is the basis of all Government contracts, and that it inevitably leads to waste.

STRIKES: Though last week's 'token' strike on Clydeside is said to have been regarded 'as a bit of a farce', it is reported to have caused much public indignation and a feeling that Glasgow shipyard workers will 'sacrifice national needs for personal cupidity'. There has been strong approval for the policy of using the Military to break the Glasgow bus strike.

COAL MINERS: There is still much comment on the amount of absenteeism among miners. But, in the opinion of a speaker who has been addressing them during the Coal Production Campaign in the Northern Region, even if absenteeism were eliminated, the short supply would not be remedied. At most places, he says, 'there is no understanding between the miners and the managements. The men feel that the appeal for increased output is only a stunt, because they see obstructions to it over which they have no control.' The managements 'evidently do not believe output to be urgent if it involves expenditure' to provide new facilities for the men. The same speaker reports that 'managements appear to expect speakers to lecture the men, as though the fault were only due to absenteeism'.

GOVERNMENT INSPECTORS: There are complaints of the workers' time being wasted in waiting for Inspectors to 'pass' jobs, with the result that in some cases skilled men are held up at their work for two or three days. Apparently when the Inspector finally comes to a job, it is sometimes 'passed' in five minutes; it is therefore felt that in such cases skilled men should be allowed to use their own initiative.

9. REGISTRATION OF WOMEN

Public feeling on this subject continues on the same lines as those referred to in our previous reports. The desire for compulsion is still widely reported, and there is now a feeling that sooner or later the Government will use compulsory powers. This, it is said, would make it easier for women who are willing to do war work but who are reluctant or unable to volunteer. The following examples are given:

(a) Married women whose husbands prevent them from volunteering because they feel their wives ought to stay and look after them.
(b) Girls whose parents are preventing them from doing war work.
(c) Women who, having been in good jobs for a long time, feel they owe something to their employers, and that by staying with them now they will be more likely to get their jobs back after the war, if they are compelled to leave.

MR. BEVIN'S APPEAL: Reactions to the Minister of Labour's appeal to married women have, on the whole, been unfavourable, and it is described as having raised a 'storm of disapproval and resentment'. It is felt that he should (a) first apply his compulsory powers to the 'many women without household responsibilities who are felt to be still avoiding service'; (b) 'get on with the job of calling up and placing those already registered'. The suggestion is made that he should first ensure that 'no privileged unmarried women are sheltering in inessential jobs at Government offices'. It is also stressed that any appeal to married women will fail unless there is adequate provision for day nurseries and communal feeding, and some arrangement to facilitate shopping.

PART-TIME WORK: Would-be workers with home responsibilities are said to be held back by lack of part-time work, and also by the fact that the requirements of factories for part-time workers do not always coincide with the time of day when these women could work. In one factory an experiment has been successfully introduced whereby older women begin at 10 a.m. so that they can first do their shopping and housework.

CAUSES OF RELUCTANCE: Several factors, though apparently not strong enough to operate in the case of women who are willing to take up war work, are quoted as having a disturbing effect on the more hesitant:

(a) A strong belief that many men in Ministries and Government offices could be replaced by women. This feeling is reported especially in places to which Government offices have been evacuated.

(b) 'Alleged class-distinction in the application of conscription.' There are persistent grumbles about 'wives of army officers who dodge the registration by following their husbands round the country'. There is also some feeling about the young wives of men in the Services who have no responsibilities, and, in many cases, no homes. It is thought that these women would be more eligible for war work than the wives of doctors and professional men whose homes have to be kept going.

(c) Though stories of alleged slackness in war factories have lately been fewer, these too provide a reason for women not volunteering.

(d) The 'burden of income tax on married women, imposed on top of the extra costs of travelling, etc.', is still quoted as a reason for their not working, particularly as many think they would be losing half their earnings in tax.

(e) The fact that women's jobs are not guaranteed after the war is said to be a deterrent; so, too, is the fact that the difference between their Service pay and civilian salary is not made up by their firms, as is often the case with men.

(f) Complaints have sometimes been made about the interviewers of the Ministry of Labour. It is said that 'instead of being interviewed by competent and experienced people, many women are interrogated by persons so young that they themselves might be considered suitable material'. The 'alleged bullying manner of the interviewers' has also been the subject of comment.

MINISTRY OF LABOUR BROADCAST: The recent broadcast, with Miss Rathbone taking part, seems to have been much appreciated. It is considered to have been far more successful than the previous one, and the policy of giving such discussions is commended.

10. FOOD

Except for milk rationing, satisfaction with the food situation continues. Postal Censorship quotes one writer as saying: 'Sometimes it seems impossible to imagine how we can have so much, when we have been at war so long – it's really a triumph of organisation', and this reaction appears to be typical of many. Complaints about food come from people whose main grumble is lack of variety.

MILK: A feeling of resentment about milk rationing is reported in many parts of the country, dissatisfaction being mentioned by eight RIOs. In one Region, for example, the public is described as being 'up in arms', while in Scotland there is said to have been a 'greater storm over the milk cuts than over any other food restriction since the war broke out'. It is thought that in Scotland the milk shortage is felt more acutely than elsewhere, as porridge is so extensively eaten by all classes. It is suggested that a clear and direct statement is called for on the whole milk situation: 'it is felt that if this subject is not handled carefully it might conceivably affect morale'. The following points are particularly mentioned:

(a) The suddenness of the reduction is not understood. It is pointed out that the seasonal decrease in supplies is gradual, and it is therefore claimed that the available supplies per person should decline proportionately: 'if we received a pint yesterday, and half-a-pint today, what has become of the surplus?'
(b) 'The inability of the Ministry of Food to make a clear statement.' People complain that they were not given 'a straightforward announcement that non-priority classes would have to face a cut far greater than 15%'.
(c) There are numerous complaints of inequality of distribution, both between areas and between families.
(d) It is thought unfair that the rationing should have been left to the retailers, 'some of whom can get better supplies than others and can treat their customers more generously'. Retailers, on the other hand, complain that they are 'left, as usual, to shoulder the blame, and have to try to pacify the public'.
(e) There is said to be much uncertainty about dried and tinned milk; people want to know when it will be available and how much each person will get.

TINNED FOOD ORDER: Favourable comment on the points rationing scheme, though still freely expressed, now tends to be swamped by disappointment at the delay in starting it. There is some criticism of Lord Woolton for announcing the plan before 'he was assured that it could be carried out at the appointed time'; but his reputation is said to stand so high at present that it is unlikely to be damaged by the postponement of the scheme.

SMALL SHOPS V. CHAIN STORES: There is a persistent belief that chain stores are 'favoured with supplies', and that they are selling foods which they did not sell before the war.

11. AGRICULTURAL WORKERS

The general reactions to the £3 minimum wage appear to be that agricultural workers have at last had a square deal, and that there will now be some encouragement for men to stay on the land after the war. The general pleasure is, however, slightly tempered by a fear that food prices will inevitably rise.

12. CLOTHES RATIONING

A Welfare Supervisor reports 'considerable ill-feeling' because coupons must be surrendered for overalls, particularly among workers doing dirty jobs. 'It is suggested that an arrangement should be made to enable firms to give certificates for coupon-free overalls.'

Women's Societies are said to be complaining that the WVS, from whom coupon-free wool must be obtained, 'do not allow any of the credit to local knitting bodies'.

The 'comparative ease with which it is possible to obtain coupons for clothes when the normal ration book is alleged to be lost' is reported to be causing 'grave concern'. There is, also, 'much derision at the loose coupon system through the post, and it is not understood what checks there are on fraud by this method'.

NO. 62: MONDAY 1 DECEMBER TO MONDAY 8 DECEMBER 1941

I. GENERAL COMMENTS

1. GENERAL STATE OF CONFIDENCE AND REACTION TO NEWS

THE FAR EAST

The general reaction to Japan's aggression in the Far East seems to be 'relief that things have come to a head, and that at last we know where we are'. Although great interest is reported everywhere, the latest developments seem to be 'generally accepted without excitement and as a foregone conclusion'. To a section of the public, however, which thought Japan was bluffing, the declaration of war has come as a shock. There is some despondency on the part of a few, but no alarm is reported, nor any feeling of immediate danger. Although preliminary reports speak of 'exhilaration' and of an 'undercurrent of excitement with a general tonic effect', no signs have yet been reported of any stimulus to our war effort.

JAPAN: There is a good deal of speculation on Japan's strength. The general opinion appears to be that 'her army is already fairly fully employed, that her air force is not a serious factor, but that her navy is dangerous'. That she should 'feel herself strong enough, while still engaged in China, to take on the USA and this country too' is interpreted as meaning either that she dare not wait any longer because of the growing strength of America, or that she is acting in obedience to Hitler's instructions.

USA: There is great satisfaction and relief that America is 'at last in with us'. This satisfaction appears to result largely from:

(a) A widespread feeling that America's war potentialities are by no means fully developed, and that she will now realise the necessity for a much greater production effort and will have to exert herself fully to get on a real war footing.

(b) 'Underlying irritation with America', which is reported by several RIOs. There appears to be a feeling in some quarters that she will now do, 'for selfish reasons, what she would not do to co-operate in fighting for democracy'; and there is a certain 'malicious delight' in comments such as – 'Americans will now have a taste of war – and about time too', and 'Bombing will wake them out of their complacency and end labour troubles'. On the other hand, a strong hope is reported from several Regions that America will bomb Tokyo, and surprise has been expressed that she should not have already done so. It is urged that she should 'give the Japs a taste of what they gave the Chinese women and children'.

SUPPLIES

(a) ARMS: There is a good deal of speculation about the question of supplies from America. Although some people anticipate that Lease-Lend material will increase in volume, owing to US production being henceforth on a war footing, the majority fear that it must now inevitably decrease, as she will need it for her own use.

(b) SUPPLY LINES: There is some fear that our supply lines (especially across the Atlantic) will be jeopardised by America being forced to withdraw some of her protection for our convoys. Germany, it is felt, has 'got away with a magnificent piece of timing; at a crucial stage of the Battle of Libya, Japan enters the war and complicates our supply position'.

(c) FOOD: Many people, women especially, are concerned at the possible effect on the food position. In some cases, the idea 'that American supplies of food for this country will be cut apparently impresses the public, especially the working class, more than the possibility of a reduction in our imports of armaments'.

THE LENGTH OF THE WAR

There is said to be much speculation as to whether the war will now be shorter or longer. Some expect a 'shorter but intensified war, with heavier casualties'; others fear that it will be lengthened by twelve months.

2. RUSSIA

'The strength and vigour of Timoshenko's thrust from Rostov, which has supplied a much-needed corrective to public disquiet over Libya', has been enthusiastically praised, and has created a 'fresh thrill of hope'. The recapture of Rostov, and the subsequent Russian advance, constitute a victory which can easily be understood; it is described as 'the only major victory of the war for the allies so far', and as 'Hitler's first real defeat on land'. Although the position round Moscow is still regarded with anxiety, it is thought to be increasingly unlikely that the Germans will penetrate to the Caucasus this winter.

Admiration for the Russians is said to have risen even further as a result of their latest successes. 'There was never greater evidence of complete solidarity with Russia' and there is an 'increased desire to give her every possible aid'. The news that British-built tanks took part in the fighting has been received with satisfaction and has in some measure increased public confidence in the extent of our aid to Russia.

In more than one Region, however, there is still said to be talk of 'persons in high positions who are not one hundred per cent in favour of assisting the Russians', and of others who refuse to sit on the same platform with Communists.

3. LIBYA

Even before the outbreak of hostilities in the Far East, the campaign in Libya was said to be arousing less comment and no longer to be the centre of public interest. There appears to be considerable difficulty in understanding the progress of the fighting, with the result that some people express anxiety and concern, while others feel 'satisfaction over our successes'. The feeling of the great majority, however, seems to be disappointment at the slowing down of our progress. Reports mention criticism of our Intelligence and also of our equipment; and disappointment is expressed at the 'performance and capabilities' of the British and American tanks, as compared with the German tanks, 'whose firepower is said to be superior'. There is said to be more 'confidence, however, in our Eighth Army' than is felt for the British army as a whole. 'It is regarded as young, vigorous and well commanded, and strengthened with the finest overseas troops.' Anxiety is felt about the heavy casualties, particularly among New Zealand and South African troops, and some concern is expressed as to how this news will be received in the Dominions.

CAIRO MILITARY SPOKESMAN: The optimistic and apparently unwarranted statements of this gentleman have again caused a howl of annoyance. He is mentioned by eight RIOs as the target for bitter criticism, on account of complacency, and particularly for representing serious reverses like the Axis breakthrough in the Tobruk corridor as a minor incident. 'This spokesman, by his pronouncements, is said to have performed the greatest single harmful act against this country of the whole war.'

4. FINLAND, HUNGARY AND RUMANIA

'British warnings to Finland, Hungary and Rumania, followed by declarations of war, have been accepted as inevitable, and as part of the welcome clearing-up process', though some people are asking how we intend to wage war on these countries. Even those who admired the Finns' 'resistance to Russian aggression are said to have seen no reason for our remarkable tenderness towards them after their line-up with the Axis'.

5. ATTITUDE TO THE GOVERNMENT AND THE WAR EFFORT

Increased confidence in the Government is reported to have been the public's first reaction to the latest conscription proposals, which are welcomed as 'a new sign of vigour and determination'. According to two RIOs, however, 'the Labour Amendment, calling for the nationalisation of the central industries, appears to find much more general support than the final vote would indicate, and this is by no means only among members of the Labour Party or the working class'. There is said to be a feeling that 'far too much concealed profiteering is going on, particularly among contractors on Government work'.

6. RUMOURS

The alleged use of certain ports on the south-west coast for the embarkation of reinforcements for Libya is said to account for Nazi raids on South-Western districts.

HMS *Sydney* is said in one report to have been sunk 'by the Japanese', and in another by the *Tirpitz*.

During the recent exercises near Bletchley 'the greatest help secured by the Home Guard, who represented a hostile force, came from questioning children'.

In the South-Western Region there is a rumour that 'it is unwise to put money into National Savings because the Government is unlikely to be able to repay in full'.

II. SPECIAL COMMENTS

7. EXTENSION OF CONSCRIPTION

Two RIOs state that until the weekend, the new plans for mobilising man- and woman-power were causing 'more interest and discussion than the actual war news'; all speak of it as a measure which, on the whole, has been welcomed as fundamentally sound and equitable. Two typical comments are: 'It was felt that firmer direction was long overdue', and 'at last we are getting down to it, with equal sacrifice all round'.

The main point of discussion appears to be, not the necessity for the changes, but their individual application. 'Much confusion and anxiety' is reported on all sides by people 'uncertain where they stand – what will, and what will not be considered essential work?' This is said to be especially the case with young women. 'Girls with home responsibilities are reported to be worrying considerably about the possibilities of being sent away; this is apparently because many of them have little or no idea of what constitutes a mobile worker, nor of their rights of appeal.'

THE ATS: There is evidence of widespread anxiety at the idea of being forced into the ATS, and 'tales of the low type of girl in this Service are frequently told'. Marriages are said to be taking place hurriedly in order that girls may be 'saved' from this fate and directed into industry instead. It is again stressed that though the idea of conscription for the ATS is unpopular with the young women themselves, it is the parents, particularly of the upper class, who are the more vocal objectors, mainly on account of the alleged reputation for immorality in this Service.

SERVICEMEN'S WIVES: The new call-up is chiefly criticised because of the exemption of servicemen's wives, concerning whom the public is said to feel 'a considerable sense of grievance'. Though it is appreciated that many of them have volunteered, 'those who have not done so, and who are without children, tend to be regarded as the most noticeable parasite group of the present day'. Other women, who will now be forced to give up their homes and their jobs under the new regulations, are expected 'bitterly to resent the freedom of the camp-follower wives'. There is a feeling that even those servicemen's wives who have homes to look after could more easily go into industry, with their husbands away in the Forces, than many of the civilian wives who will now have to do so. Adherents to the view that it might be inexpedient 'to conscript servicemen's wives at present' appear to include more men than women.

SMALL TRADERS: The extension of the service age for men is thought to fall heaviest on the small trader, particularly the owner of the one-man business, who must shut up shop if he is called up and is likely to be too old to start again when the war is over.

8. INDUSTRY

Reports of slackness in munition factories are said to have reached 'alarming proportions in some Regions, since the stimulus of the debate on manpower in the House of Commons'. Workers are alleged to be asking: 'What is the use of bringing in more people to join us in standing easy?' and also to be saying that better organisation is required more urgently than any increase in industrial personnel. For this reason, 'appeals for increased production are becoming outstandingly unpopular among the workers; their response tends to be bitter talk of the wastefulness, inefficiency, muddle, etc. of the managements'. It is also said that in some war factories, 'work is speeded up for the benefit of inspectors', and that 'such incidents are increasing the workers' distrust of their executives'. In two of the main centres of recent unrest, however – Scotland and Northern Ireland – the situation is thought to have improved, and the workers to be less discontented.

WAGES: 'Bad feeling about the discrepancy in wages increases' especially in cases where 'unskilled boys now earn more than their fathers, who are skilled operatives'. The inequalities of Service and industrial pay are mentioned again as a source of much dissatisfaction. Alleged attempts 'to profit by the employment of women at cheaper rates has led to a renewed call for "equal pay for equal work"'.

TARGET SYSTEM OF CONTRACT: 'The target system of contract, now used extensively in the building trade, is thought to be little better than the cost plus 10%, as, although no profit is made beyond the target figure, the total costs are still met. Even though some attempt appears to have been made to encourage contractors to spend less than the target figure, by offering them a generous percentage of what they save between cost and target, the whole system is condemned by many people as uneconomic.'

INTERVIEWERS: Mr. Bevin's defence of his interviewers 'has encouraged rather than decreased criticism, which continues to be very bitter'. Older women are said to be exceedingly angry when their difficulties in leaving home, husband or children 'are brusquely waved aside by young girls', obviously much more mobile than themselves. There are still fears that women are being told at the Labour Exchanges of industrial amenities such as crèches for their children, and arrangements by which they can surmount their shopping difficulties, when, in fact, such amenities remain 'all too rare' in connection with war factories.

WOMEN WORKERS' DIFFICULTIES: These are still -

(a) the urgent need of part-time work,
(b) day nurseries, and
(c) shopping facilities, all of which are the source of much impatient comment this week.

9. SERVICE DEPENDANTS' ALLOWANCES

The increased intake into the Services which will result from the new call-up has brought dependants' allowances into prominence again. Older men in good jobs are reported to be wondering 'how they can possibly meet their civilian commitments', and many women are said to be in the same position. It is asked once more why there can be no general increase in family allowances; 'the argument that the country could not afford it is not accepted, in view of our other immense commitments, which we somehow meet'.

There are still complaints of 'interminable form-filling', delays entailing hardship, and of difficulty in understanding the new legislation.

10. TRANSPORT

The desire for war-workers' priority passes appears to be growing. As bus services are curtailed the situation deteriorates, especially for the long-distance traveller, and some scheme is demanded by which short-distance travellers could be prevented from 'wasting' the available space.

LIFTS FOR PEDESTRIANS: Special reports from RIOs on this subject suggest that, although members of the Forces seem to have no difficulty in getting lifts, the average motorist does not usually offer them to civilians. Among reasons given for refusing to offer lifts are:

(a) Waste of petrol in stopping and starting.
(b) Fear of offers being refused.
(c) Mistrust of strangers.
(d) Uncertainty about questions of insurance.

(c) and (d) are also quoted as reasons for pedestrians refusing to accept lifts.

Some men are diffident about giving lifts to women in case their intentions should be misunderstood; and some women drivers are apprehensive of 'amorous advances', or assault (particularly after dark) from men passengers.

Among civilians, lifts appear to be generally welcome, although seldom asked for, and there is some resentment against motorists who do not offer them. In general, it appears that fewer lifts are offered than was the case a year ago. RIOs differ on the need for a general appeal to motorists; five feel this to be necessary, and two do not; the remainder appear to have no opinions either way.

11. FOOD

The food situation continues to be generally regarded as satisfactory except for the shortage of milk, the 'severe rationing' of which appears to cause 'more bitterness than any other regulation up to date'. Inequalities of distribution still seem to provide the main grounds for complaint, but there appears to be little understanding – and growing criticism – of the system by which surplus milk in one district is sometimes distributed in another where supplies are short.

Factory welfare workers and doctors are said to be inundated with applications for milk on the grounds of health. Many doctors consider that priority should be extended to include certain illnesses not already covered by the scheme.

TINNED FOODS: The points rationing scheme appears to be 'most acceptable' and the first week to have 'gone off well' with customers. Small traders, however, still seem to dislike the scheme. Salmon, sardines and tongues are said to have been 'quickly snapped up' in preference to American canned meats but 'those who have overcome their reluctance to try "new-fangled foods"' seem to find Spam, etc. 'highly palatable'. It has been suggested that other foodstuffs, such as chicken and game, should be rationed in a similar manner and that the price should be controlled in order to share out stocks available.

DRIED FRUITS: Complaints of shortages for Christmas.

COST OF LIVING: There have been some complaints of the high cost of living, and maximum controlled prices of vegetables 'are thought to be much too high'.

RURAL AREAS: One RIO reports continued complaints from workers in isolated places, such as those working on aerodromes, who are unable to supplement their rations like town workers. It is said that 'housewives are reluctant to billet men who need packed lunches, because of the strain on the rations'.

Much bad feeling is said to be caused by the present rules permitting only servicemen to be fed from Service canteens. There is frequently no other provision for scattered Civil Defence workers.

12. CLOTHES RATIONING

There has been very little comment on this subject this week.

NAVY AND COUPONS: It is reported from the London Region that difficulties have been caused by the Board of Trade's withdrawal of the arrangement permitting men on leave to buy clothes on a note from their commanding officers. It is felt that this arrangement should not have ceased before the new scheme, now under consideration, had come into force.

ISSUING OF CLOTHES COUPONS: Allegations of delay in issuing clothes coupons to people coming from institutions, hospitals and prisons, has caused some dissatisfaction.

NO. 63: MONDAY 8 DECEMBER TO MONDAY 15 DECEMBER 1941

I. GENERAL COMMENTS

1. GENERAL STATE OF CONFIDENCE AND REACTION TO NEWS

The situation in the Pacific has taken first place in the public's mind during the past week. The immense range of events seems to have left most people 'rather breathless with confused reactions'; feeling as a whole is described as 'divided between satisfaction that the United States is now actively in the war on our side, and dismay at the strength of Japan', which was accentuated by the apparent unpreparedness of our new ally. Since Thursday, when, following the news of our serious naval losses, public feeling seemed to have been at its lowest ebb, there has been a steady recovery of spirits; this appears to be mainly due to:

(a) Relief at the number of men rescued from the *Prince of Wales* and *Repulse*.
(b) The fact that the United States is now wholly committed to the war. Satisfaction has been considerably strengthened by the US declaration of war on Germany and Italy; by the unanimity of Congress; and by President Roosevelt's speech to Congress on December 9th.
(c) The continuance of Russian successes.
(d) Our improved position in Libya.

(Nevertheless, there has been much disappointment at our delay in catching up with official forecasts of the campaign's progress.)

Most reports agree in saying that lately the public has 'stood up staunchly to a series of shocks', and that, on the whole, they have had a bracing effect. It is now thought to be generally realised that 'the war has entered a new and more serious phase', and is likely to be considerably prolonged, though confidence in our victory remains unshaken. 'Further hardships are anticipated', and there are 'signs of readiness for greater sacrifices of personal liberty and comfort'.

The hope is expressed, therefore, 'that the Government will take all necessary action swiftly to harness the public effort at this psychological moment'.

JAPAN

'Initial contempt for the Japanese has given way', according to most reports, 'to lively apprehensions', though the Japanese are not apparently regarded as being as formidable as the Germans. All the same, 'the range and power of their attacks have been an unpleasant surprise to the public, which has been fed by certain newspaper "experts" on stories of Japan's crippled economic position, and of the alleged poor quality of her airmen and aircraft'. This surprise has been all the greater because of her 'relative ineffectiveness in China'.

Although the importance of Singapore seems to be 'only very imperfectly appreciated', some apprehension is reported on the strength of our defences there, and on the difficulties of imposing 'Anglo-American superiority in the Pacific and the Far East'. It seems that the public as a whole has not yet grasped the diverse implications of the situation in the Pacific, partly owing to a poor understanding of the geography.

NAVAL LOSSES

Last Wednesday, when the public heard of the loss of the *Prince of Wales* and *Repulse*, was described by many people as 'the blackest day since Dunkirk'; but relief at the high proportion of men rescued has done much to mitigate the public's depression. 'The consternation and distress with which the news was received' gave place, after the first shock, to critical speculation about the amount of air support given to the ships. 'The regard in which the British Navy is held, however, has silenced any criticism of the strategy which resulted in their loss.' Yet many people are said to be making unfavourable comparisons between 'the apparent ease with which the *Prince of Wales* was sunk and the outstanding manner in which the *Bismarck* remained afloat'.

USA

Public feeling about the United States seems to fall under four main headings:

   (a) PRO-AMERICAN FEELINGS: President Roosevelt's speech to Congress on December 9th made a deep impression; it was received with unanimous praise and has been compared with some of Lincoln's speeches. Great satisfaction is expressed at his announcement of 'plans for 100% war effort'.
   (b) ALLEGED AMERICAN UNPREPARADNESS: At the same time, there has been much comment, some of it angry, some contemptuous, on the United States' apparent unpreparedness. There is particularly strong criticism of 'the lack of foresight indicated by the grouping of ships at Pearl Harbour, and the poor defences of her island bases'.

(c) UNFRIENDLY FEELING TOWARDS THE UNITED STATES: Some contempt is also expressed for 'the remarkable unanimity of the Americans in going to war when they are directly threatened, after the years in which they appeared content to let other people do their fighting for democracy'. There is, in short, a feeling reflected in many reports that she has been pushed into the war rather against her will.

This antipathy is reported to be 'strongest among working people, who most admire the Russian resistance'. The difference between the public's attitudes towards Russia and towards America is noted by more than one RIO. It is pointed out that 'people are willing to make immense sacrifices to assist the Russians, even giving up food and materials that are badly wanted here', but America's entry into the war has produced aggrieved remarks about 'the possibility of diminished supplies of food and tobacco'. There are now thought to be signs, however, that 'this mood of slight anger and frigidity is passing, and that there is greater realisation that America and ourselves are side by side and sharing the same dangers'.

(d) SUPPLIES FROM AMERICA: Considerable speculation is heard about our future supplies from America. The general opinion seems to be that they will be 'lessened in the immediate future, but that before long they will assume greater proportions than ever'. Much is expected of 'America's well-nigh inexhaustible material resources, and her vast manpower', though some apprehension has been caused by our offer of Canadian shells, as 'this is considered to reveal a state of unpreparedness even worse than had been anticipated'.

2. RUSSIA

The news of the Russian advances has been enthusiastically received as 'the most encouraging corrective to bad news elsewhere'. 'The Russian capacity for offensive action after all they have been through evokes the greatest admiration'; so does their 'almost legendary bravery', and their 'breaking of the idea of Germany's invincibility'. Satisfaction at these successes is slightly tempered by a feeling that if they are unable to advance in Russia, the Germans will 'break out in some new direction', probably in heavy air attacks here (see 'Air Raids').

Disappointment has been expressed in some quarters that Russia is not at war with Japan, particularly as Russia alone is considered to be favourably placed for air attack on Japanese cities. Apprehension has been expressed lest her inactivity towards Japan may mean that she proposes to make peace now that she has stopped the German offensive. There seems, however, to be a fairly widespread understanding of Russia's reluctance to open up another front, particularly in view of our delay in declaring war on Finland.

3. LIBYA

Disappointment, which marked the earlier stages of the Libyan campaign, has now given way to 'sober satisfaction' that the Germans are in retreat. Criticism of our tanks, on grounds of inferiority in size and armament, continues to be heard.

The change of command is taken by a large section of the public as meaning that 'General Cunningham had blundered in the early stages of the campaign'. The statement that he was suffering from a 'breakdown in health' has been sceptically received, and with some regret, as the Cunningham brothers had apparently caught the public imagination more than General Auchinleck has done up to the present. The appointment of General Ritchie has been very well received, largely, it seems, because he is not yet forty-five.

4. AIR RAIDS

Several regions report that the public is once again expecting heavy air raids. There is apparently a widespread feeling that 'now that the Nazis find they cannot proceed in Russia they will be able to turn their attention to us again'.

5. THE PRIME MINISTER'S SPEECHES

Mr. Churchill's two statements (the broadcast on Monday December 8th, and his speech in the House of Commons on December 11th) appear to have made very different impressions on the public.

(a) THE BROADCAST SPEECH, DECEMBER 8TH: This caused considerable disappointment. Many people found it depressing and 'in strong contrast to the confidence with which he had challenged Japan some weeks before'. The general impression seemed to be that it was 'the speech of a very tired man, and people are worried lest he should strain himself'. It is pointed out that 'the public hangs so much upon his utterances that the least hint of uncertainty gives rise to speculation'.

(b) THE SPEECH IN THE COMMONS, DECEMBER 11TH: His review of the war situation, on the other hand, has been described as 'a masterly exposition', and has done much to 'restore not only confidence but a sense of proportion among the public'. His statement on our losses in the Pacific was much appreciated for its 'candid admission that the loss of these vessels was the severest naval blow ever suffered by Britain. The public prefers such frankness to attempts to gloss over unpleasant facts.'

6. BROADCASTING AND PRESENTATION OF NEWS

Some satisfaction has been expressed this week with the presentation of news. As a result of the swift announcing of the loss of our two battleships, the feeling is gaining ground that bad news is not being withhold. There has, however, been considerable criticism of the 'idiotic Press' for misleading the public as to the strength of the Japanese fleet and air arm. In this connection Dr. Dalton's 'blunt warning' concerning Japan's power and resources, 'which forbids us to underestimate our enemy in the Far East', has been favourably commented on. It is pointed out that such statements, giving a true picture of the situation, 'are much more likely to stimulate morale than to depress it'.

MR. PRIESTLEY: There has been appreciation for his series of *Listen to my Notebook* broadcasts; it is noted that the propaganda is 'wrapped up' and 'does not suffer from the over-emphasis of some of his earlier *Postscripts*'.

MR. BARTLETT: One RIO reports considerable appreciation for his *Postscript* to the 9 o'clock news on December 7th.

7. MOSLEY

At a time when many husbands and wives are threatened with separation, through the extension of conscription for the Services and industry, 'indignant comment' has been caused by the report that Sir Oswald Mosley is to be transferred to the same prison as his wife, in order that they may be together. It is said to be 'time the Home Secretary realised that this man is not only as much an enemy as Hess, but a traitor – and in Germany he would have been shot'.

8. RUMOURS

There has been an increase in the number of rumours reported this week. Singapore is said to have fallen, and from various sources come stories of the sinking of HM ships *Malaya*, *Barham*, *Ramillies*, *King George V*, and *Warspite*. 'Half the US Pacific Fleet' is also said to have been sunk.

The Japanese are said to have found a new steel 'capable of piercing any armour'.

The air raid on Whitley Bay on December 8th led to a crop of rumours that the attack was due to the imperfect blackout of billets occupied by RAF men, a large number of whom were said to have been killed – and that in one billet a chimney was on fire at the time of the raid.

It is now believed that 'any money due under the post-war credit scheme reverts to the state if the creditor dies before it is repaid'.

In Liverpool it is rumoured that a man dressed as a woman is cutting electric cables in air-raid shelters.

From Glasgow comes a story that many women are receiving extra clothing cards 'through their husbands' employment in the Board of Trade'.

II. SPECIAL COMMENTS

9. NATIONAL SERVICE ACT

The new regulations continue to be generally approved, but there is some dissatisfaction on these points:

(a) Fear that newly conscripted and directed labour may not be used to the best effect (this fear being largely due to alleged wastage of manpower in some war factories).

(b) Resentment of certain exemptions, notably the total exemption of servicemen's wives, and the exemption of childless married women from the Services. There is 'a strong feeling that the criterion for calling up a woman should not be merely whether she is married, but whether she has children to look after'. Only one RIO has this week reported approval of the exemption of serving men's wives, who are described by others as 'the most glaring example of drones'.

ALLOWANCES AND PENSIONS: The prospect of a much greater intake of both men and women into the Services has stimulated criticism of dependants' allowances, pensions, and compensation in general. 'The present conditions are regarded as most unsatisfactory.' In particular, it is felt that women who enter the Services, and who have dependants, should be given the same allowances as those of men.

10. INDUSTRY

As reported last week, the increased scope of conscription for industry has focused public attention on the shortcoming of workers and particularly of managements. On the whole, workers are apparently thought to be doing their best; it is felt that any drive for greater production must aim at a serious overhaul of managerial arrangements. Many cases of slackness in munitions factories, through no fault of the employees, continue to be recorded from various parts of the country, and 'the feeling persists that we are still not all out for victory. Aircraft workers have complained of not being given enough to do for weeks on end, and Irish war workers state that they are encouraged to go slow.' A sense of 'disappointment and frustration' is reported among the workers who are stood-off or subjected to delays at a time when, it is felt, the need of the country must be urgent if such drastic measures have had to be taken to secure manpower.

WAGES: Discrepancies in wages are again much discussed, particularly where there are local instances of unskilled labourers receiving more than skilled workers: the high pay of juveniles causes great concern to certain welfare officers and social workers, and it also seems to be a fruitful source of grievance when it is contrasted with Service pay. Opinion is again recorded that the regularisation of pay is something which the Government must tackle sooner or later if industry is to be on a satisfactory war footing, and therefore the sooner the better.

DIFFICULTIES OF WOMEN WORKERS: The introduction of the 'pairing-off' system for women workers is thought by many to be the only means of tapping a very large reserve of woman-power which will otherwise be lost to the country. More and more women with children, or other household ties, are said to be discussing the need for some arrangement by which two neighbours can interchange duties, both at home and in the factory, to make up a full-time shift between them. Few factories, so far, have provided part-time work, even in districts where labour is scarcest; for this, too, managements are generally considered to blame, though there is also apparently some unwillingness on the part of 'reserved' men to see women employed in this way, as it is supposed that the men themselves will be released for the army as soon as the women have mastered their jobs. It is also said to be feared by the men that the women will be able to stick to these jobs in peacetime, once the convenience of the 'pairing-off' system is recognised.

Lack of day nurseries (and the expense and inadequacy of child-minders, where these are available) remains one of the chief problems for women workers, as does also the shopping question. Sunday morning opening of certain shops, for the exclusive use of factory workers with special cards, has been suggested by two RIOs; it is pointed out that for the sake of their own employees, these shops might close instead on Monday, which is often a slack day.

The RIO, Southern Region, writes: 'One difficulty preventing a number of married women from volunteering for industry is said to be that their husbands are paying contributions on their behalf to local medical benefit societies. If the women take up paid work they are no longer eligible for benefit, lose all the money they have paid in contributions, and will have to wait six months after taking up insurable employment before they can draw any medical benefit under National Health Insurance. It is asked whether some arrangement could not be made as a wartime measure to permit benefits under local medical aid societies for married women on war work.' The question of double insurance, to be paid by the employer, is also said to complicate the introduction of part-time work.

11. BILLETING

The problem of finding accommodation near factories, which is already serious in some areas, is expected to become still more acute in the near future, when thousands of new workers will be drafted into industry. 'From Banbury, for instance, it is reported that saturation point has been reached. Transport drivers requiring a night's lodging often have to be accommodated in police cells for want of a billet.'

The opinion is still general that in the reception of evacuee children, the lower-middle and working classes are doing more than their share, while the big houses somehow manage to escape. From the South-Western Region it is reported that 'small houses near a Bristol aerodrome resent receiving billeting notices, on the grounds that there are scores of empty houses near the works'.

The inequalities of billeting allowances, and their disparity with the costs incurred, particularly for young children, is another cause of complaint. There seems to be no justification, for instance, for paying a lower rate when two or more children under ten are billeted in the same house.

Yet another grievance is that those caring for evacuees receive no payment and are yet prevented from doing paid war work. Although willing to undertake the care of the children in a first emergency, many are not prepared to continue without pay for the duration. Failure of the children's parents to provide the necessary clothing often causes additional expenses to kindly foster-parents who do not like to see the children inadequately clad and so provide boots or garments themselves.

12. FOOD

In general, the food situation continues to give considerable satisfaction, though there is some anticipation of a decrease in supplies from the USA.

MILK: Although complaints about distribution continue, far fewer are reported this week. Confusion about tinned and dried milk is attributed to the fact that 'broadcasts and press statements have been so often amended'.

EGGS: The shortage of eggs 'has come to the fore' this week. There is again some confusion as to 'where all the eggs have gone', and the feeling is expressed once more that 'the egg rationing scheme is a lamentable failure'.

TINNED FOODS: Approval of the points rationing scheme seems to be almost unanimous, and it is hoped that this system may be more widely used. American canned foods are gradually growing more popular and the variation they afford to the diet is appreciated.

13. CLOTHES RATIONING

There has again been very little comment on this subject; two RIOs report a feeling that the present system works out to the advantage of the wealthy, as poor people buy cheaper clothing which does not last long.

SHEFFIELD STEEL WORKERS complain that they have not yet received the supplementary clothing coupons promised by the Board of Trade.

YOUNG CHILDREN: One RIO reports enquiries from parents who have run out of coupons and cannot send their young children to school without shoes.

APPENDIX TO WEEKLY REPORT NO. 64

PUBLIC ATTITUDES TOWARDS THE USA

24 DECEMBER 1941

This week special reports on the above subject have been asked for and received from all Regions. The following is a summary of the main points made.

I. ATTITUDE TO THE USA BEFORE THE JAPANESE ATTACK

Over the past 6 months there has been a steady growth in admiration for President Roosevelt, a firm conviction that he was 'all out' to help us, and an increasing realisation of the gap between him and his administration, and American public opinion as a whole. The strength of isolationist feeling was brought home particularly by:

1. The news of strikes and industrial unrest.
2. The narrowness of the margin by which the Neutrality Act was repealed.

While American help both in supplies and in the Battle of the Atlantic was increasingly appreciated, criticism was frequently made of:

1. The volume of talk which was thought to be a characteristic feature of American politics.
2. The use of 'high-falutin'' phrases describing America's part in the war and in the defence of democracy, when we and the Russians were doing the actual fighting and bearing the blows. There was, and still is, a certain 'hang-over' from the supposedly excessive claims of the Americans after the last war.

It is pointed out that the frankness with which British people treat America is very similar to their attitude towards the Dominions, and even to the attitude adopted by England to Scotland, Wales and Ireland (and vice versa). The 'malicious glee' reported after the Japanese attack on Pearl Harbour is not dissimilar to the 'satisfaction' with which certain English blitzed towns received the news of heavy raids on other cities (there was, of course, also a very large volume of human sympathy for the blitzed populations, particularly in the smaller cities attacked). It appears that America is not really regarded as a foreign country, to be wooed with praise, but as a close relative to be chided freely for her shortcomings.

II. ATTITUDE IMMEDIATELY FOLLOWING THE OUTBREAK OF HOSTILITIES

Public feeling during the first few days of hostilities was along the following lines:

1. Great satisfaction that America was 'at last in with us'.
2. The immediate American disasters produced:

    a. Dismay at the evidence of unpreparedness. This was added to by our offer of Canadian shells.

    b. A widespread but apparently superficial 'malicious glee' that she was 'caught napping even worse than us'.

    c. A fear that Lease-Lend supplies – particularly of armaments to Russia and food to us – would 'dry up'.
3. It was felt that 'at last America would really get down to industrial production'.
4. It was hoped that the initial setbacks would prevent the USA suffering from an initial period of complacency such as we experienced.
5. It was believed that the whole of America would at last be united behind the President, and that he would no longer have to 'nurse' public opinion.
6. It was regretted that America had had to be forced into the war by the Japanese attack, and the declarations of Germany and Italy, and that she had not taken the initiative against the Axis.
7. There was much jocular comment on American morale, and a widespread belief, and even hope, that her citizens would stand up to air raids less

satisfactorily than ours. Mayor La Guardia's advice to New Yorkers not to scream was particularly appreciated.

8. The absence of aerial attack on Japanese cities was unfavourably commented on, and there appeared to be little appreciation of the size of the Pacific theatre of war.

9. It was, and is, generally thought that, while the American navy and air force can be relied on, the American army is most inefficient. This belief is attributed to publicity given to 'unwilling conscripts' and to efforts to 'contract out of the army'. The ubiquity of girls in films of American army life is also commented on.

10. It was feared that extreme isolationists of the Lindbergh class constituted a potentially dangerous fifth column.

11. Those who had not sent their children to America 'patted themselves on the back'.

III. SUBSEQUENT REACTIONS

There is evidence of a steady improvement in feeling towards America, and of an increasing readiness to 'work in harness with the USA in spite of minor irritations'. The following points in particular are noted:

1. While it was not for a moment doubted that we should win the war, there had for some time been speculation as to 'how this could be done on land'. (Such speculation had, however, vanished following the Russian victories.) It is now felt that American man- and machine-power supply the 'necessary means to certain victory'. The news that the American army will serve overseas if necessary caused great satisfaction.

2. The sinking of the British battleships, and the vigorous Japanese attacks on Hong Kong and Malaya, convinced the public that the Japanese were 'our business as well as the Americans'', and that we were 'really on the job together'.

3. The President's prompt sacking of the American army chiefs at Hawaii was favourably contrasted with our failure to sack anyone at Singapore.

4. It was hoped that, at the earliest possible moment, a joint strategy would be worked out by a council including Britain, USA, the Dominions and Russia (this was before the news of Mr. Churchill's trans-Atlantic visit).

5. The news that Lease-Lend commitments would be fulfilled was greatly welcomed.

6. The sight of so much American tinned food in the shops was hailed, particularly by women, as evidence that American supplies were still arriving. Spam and Mor were described as 'America's best ambassadors'.

7. That America and Britain are at last full partners is thought to increase the chances of a stable and peaceful world after the war.

IV. SOME GENERAL POINTS

1. While the public are prepared to make any sacrifices necessary to help Russia, it is pointed out that they have no such disposition towards America. There appears to be a widespread feeling that America is 'too damned wealthy', that Americans are too mercenary-minded, and that the hardship and suffering of war will 'do them a lot of good'. Thus, the offer of Canadian shells, in addition to causing comments about unpreparedness, also provoked a temporary wave of bad feeling that we should have to give help to America.

2. It appears that the main picture of America which British people have is that which she has painted of herself in her commercial films – a land of material plenty – with little or nothing of the home and family life as British people understand it.

3. Apart from President Roosevelt, no American public figures have 'caught on' permanently, and there is little interest in their doings or sayings.

4. Very little is known about the traditions, uniforms, and so on, of the American forces.

HOME INTELLIGENCE

II

January to December 1942

22 DECEMBER 1941–14 JANUARY 1942 Washington conference. Churchill, Roosevelt and their advisors set the direction of Anglo-American strategy and devise the mechanisms to coordinate their war effort. It is confirmed that the defeat of Germany is the prime Allied objective.

15 JANUARY Japanese forces invade southern Burma.

21 JANUARY Rommel launches a counterattack in Libya. The Eighth Army falls back towards eastern Cyrenaica.

26 JANUARY The first US troops arrive in the UK and disembark in Northern Ireland.

11–13 FEBRUARY Under the noses of the Royal Navy and RAF, the German warships *Scharnhorst*, *Gneisenau* and *Prinz Eugen* make a successful dash through the English Channel from Brest to German home waters (although the *Scharnhorst* and *Gneisenau* are damaged in the operation).

15 FEBRUARY The seemingly impregnable British naval base at Singapore surrenders to Japanese forces. Some 120,000 British, Commonwealth and imperial troops are taken prisoner during the Malayan campaign and battle for Singapore.

27–28 FEBRUARY British airborne forces raid a German coastal radar station at Bruneval in northern France. Parts of the German Würzburg radar system are brought back to the UK for examination.

3–4 MARCH The RAF bomb the Renault factory in the Parisian suburb of Boulogne-Billancourt. Some 400 French civilians are killed in the raid.

8 MARCH Japanese forces take Rangoon, the capital of Burma.

23–24 APRIL Start of the so-called Baedeker raids: a series of German bombing raids on British cities of special historical or cultural significance.

5 MAY British forces land in Vichy-controlled Madagascar to forestall a Japanese occupation of the island. Control of the island subsequently passes to the Free French.

12 MAY Soviet forces launch an attack to retake Kharkov in Ukraine. The attack soon collapses and some 250,000 Soviet troops are taken prisoner.

20 MAY British, Indian and Burmese troops complete a fighting withdrawal from Burma to India.

30–31 MAY In the first 'thousand-bomber raid' on Germany, 1,047 RAF bombers are despatched to attack Cologne.

4–7 JUNE US carrier forces inflict serious damage on the Japanese fleet off the Midway Islands in the central Pacific.

19–25 JUNE Washington conference. Churchill and Roosevelt agree that plans should be drawn up for an Allied invasion of French North Africa.

21 JUNE The garrison of the port of Tobruk, Libya, surrenders to Rommel. Some 33,000 British, Commonwealth and imperial troops are taken prisoner.

28 JUNE Hitler mounts an offensive in southern Russia with the objective of taking the Caucasus. German forces make rapid advances.

1–2 JULY A vote of censure on the government's direction of the war takes place in the House of Commons. The government comfortably survives the vote by a majority of 451.

1–4 JULY Rommel's advance into Egypt is held by the Eighth Army at El Alamein.

7 AUGUST US Marines launch an amphibious assault on Guadalcanal in the Solomon Islands. Japanese forces tenaciously resist for six months.

8 AUGUST In Bombay, the All-India Committee of the Congress party adopts the 'Quit India' resolution to end British rule. Gandhi and Congress leaders are subsequently arrested. Protests and demonstrations in India are followed by mass detentions.

19 AUGUST A mainly Canadian force mounts a major raid on the port of Dieppe in northern France to test enemy defences and the ability of an amphibious force to establish a foothold in occupied Europe. Of the 4,963 Canadian troops who take part, 3,367 are killed, wounded or captured.

23 AUGUST German forces reach the outskirts of Stalingrad on the Volga River.

13 SEPTEMBER German units unleash an assault on Stalingrad. The Soviet defenders put up fierce resistance.

13–14 SEPTEMBER British forces carry out an abortive raid on Tobruk. Three Royal Navy warships are lost in the operation. Some 750 men are killed, wounded or captured.

3–4 OCTOBER British commandos raid German-occupied Sark in the Channel Islands in order to carry out reconnaissance and capture members of the German garrison.

14 OCTOBER German units make a renewed assault on Stalingrad. Again, Soviet troops fiercely resist.

23 OCTOBER–4 NOVEMBER The Eighth Army under Montgomery attacks Rommel's forces at El Alamein. After a twelve-day battle, Rommel's army is defeated and retreats across Libya.

8 NOVEMBER US and British forces land in Vichy-controlled Morocco and Algeria. An armistice with the Vichy French in North Africa shortly follows.

11 NOVEMBER German units mount a final push to take Stalingrad. The attack soon grinds to a halt.

15 NOVEMBER Britain's First Army advances from Algeria into Tunisia. Over the following weeks, the advance falters in the face of German resistance and worsening weather.

19 NOVEMBER Soviet forces launch a major counter-offensive in the Stalingrad area. Within days, the German Sixth Army at Stalingrad is encircled.

1 DECEMBER Publication of the report of an inter-departmental inquiry, under the chairmanship of Sir William Beveridge, into social insurance and allied services. Beveridge proposes a comprehensive system of social security 'from the cradle to the grave'. This is linked to assumptions about the provision of children's allowances, a national health service and the maintenance of employment. It is reported that the first print run of 70,000 copies is sold within hours.

15 DECEMBER The Eighth Army enters the Libyan coastal town of El Agheila. Rommel withdraws towards Tripoli.

17 DECEMBER British and Indian troops mount a campaign from the India–Burma border into the Arakan region of western Burma.

NO. 68: MONDAY 12 JANUARY 1942 TO
MONDAY 19 JANUARY 1942

I. GENERAL COMMENTS

1. GENERAL STATE OF CONFIDENCE AND REACTION TO NEWS

There appears to be a slight decrease in public confidence this week. Satisfaction over Russia's continued progress is overshadowed by anxiety and disappointment at developments in the Far East – particularly by the increased threat to Singapore.
Other factors influencing public confidence are:

(a) Mr. Churchill's safe return, which has allayed considerable public fear.
(b) What is regarded as 'almost a stalemate in Libya'; this has led to some disappointment.

2. THE FAR EAST

Our withdrawals in Malaya are now causing wider concern, and what is now realised as 'the extreme gravity of our whole position in the Far East' seems to be giving anxiety to a far larger section of the public than were previously affected – 'even to those people whose knowledge of geography is vague'. The outlook about Singapore is not regarded as hopeful and, indeed, its fall is now regarded by many to be 'a foregone conclusion', despite Mr. Churchill's expressed belief that we should be able to hold it. The storm of criticism of what is believed to be our lack of foresight is even stronger this week: 'It looks as if our people in the Far East, Services and civilians alike, have been living in a fool's paradise, and anyone attempting to rouse them has been silenced.' Previous official statements showing over-confidence in the situation are again quoted with much irritation.

3. RUSSIA

There is, if anything, an increase of enthusiasm and admiration for the Russian successes. The dangerous position of large masses of German troops gives rise to continued optimism, and there appears to be every confidence in the ability of the Russian Command to maintain pressure on the retreating Germans. Only one RIO says that 'people would prefer to wait for the better weather before throwing their caps in the air'.
The suspicious circumstances of von Reichenau's death have encouraged people to hope that the German forces are in serious difficulties, although the RIO Scotland mentioned a growing belief in his Region that 'the best German units have been withdrawn and are safely wintering at home'.
Some uneasiness is reported among sections of the middle classes about the possible extent of Russian influence upon the post-war social and economic structure of this country.

SOVIET TRADES' UNION DELEGATION: Several Regions report that the visits of the Soviet Trades' Union delegates have given opportunities for the spontaneous expression of the general enthusiasm felt for Russia as an ally, and the affection in which her people are held. Their outspoken criticisms of our production have not, however, been received entirely without resentment.

4. LIBYA

'The news of the recapture of Sollum and Halfaya has been received with pleasure, but there is a growing belief that our aim in Libya, namely, the destruction of the German forces, is proving increasingly hard to achieve.' There is some fear that Rommel 'may have out-manoeuvred us, and that strong reinforcements may reach him and prolong the battle indefinitely'.

'The out-ranging and out-weighing of our 2-pounder tank guns by the German heavies' has been noted with regret and some foreboding.

5. AMERICA

Colonel Knox's statement that the task of the US Navy was chiefly in the Atlantic has received a good reception. Many feel that his statement is true, but a minority think it was made to cover up Pacific failures; and the question, 'Where is the American fleet?' is widely reported once more. There is some revival of the 'all talk and no do' type of criticism, but General MacArthur's stout defence in the Philippines has won 'widespread respect' and is considered a welcome reassurance that Americans can fight. On the whole, the feeling prevails that 'when America really gets going, she will pull the chestnuts out of the fire'.

Very little interest has been shown in the Pan-American Conference.

6. HOPES OF CABINET CHANGES

Anxiety about Malaya appears to be the principal cause for a demand for wide revision of the Allies' conduct of the war. People 'have a feeling that things are not right', and eight RIOs report hopes or expectations of Cabinet changes. 'It is desired that this shall not merely be a reshuffle but a replacement of those Ministers who are thought to lack the necessary drive, and who, it is felt, are still talking about being prepared, rather than seeing that it is an actual fact. It is felt that the war will not be brought to a successful conclusion unless radical changes are made.' There is a good deal of sympathy with Australia's demand for an Empire Cabinet.

MR. DUFF COOPER: Even though some people are saying that Mr. Duff Cooper 'had not been out East long enough to be responsible for any of the present muddle', the published reasons for his recall are still considered 'unconvincing'.

7. THE PRIME MINISTER'S RETURN

The news of the Prime Minister's safe return was greeted with immense relief; there had been anxiety about his safety earlier in the week. Some criticism has been heard of 'the risks taken in sending several of our leaders together in this long flight over the Atlantic'.

8. EIRE

There appears to be growing impatience with the Irish Free State on the subject of the ports, and the hope is expressed that the Americans may do what we hesitate to undertake – and 'enforce some kind of agreement with Mr. de Valera'.

9. RAF

There is some criticism of Bomber Command for the apparent failure of the 'non-stop offensive against Germany'.

People are said to be 'fed-up' with the repeated bombing of Brest, which they consider as 'singularly ineffective by comparison with the effect of one or two German raids on ports in this country'.

10. BROADCASTING AND PRESENTATION OF NEWS

Strong protests continue to be made against the minimising of defeats in the Far East, together with the repeated mention of our minor successes; it is said that 'ground lost is made to appear valueless until it is regained, when emphasis is laid on its importance'.

'A fresh wave of irritation' is reported at the realisation that 'the information we have been given about Malaya, by all the news services, has been full of lies'. In one Region the decline in volume in important news has produced some feeling of 'a lull before a storm', and there is comment on the undue publicity given to Axis news. The naming of the regiments engaged in Libya was received with approval.

NEWSREELS AND MOI FILMS: The Commando raid film is said to be still drawing large crowds in Scotland. Gaumont-British is criticised for their advertisement, said to give the impression that the pictures were a 'Gaumont-British exclusive'. *Rush Hour* and *Royal Observer Corps* are commented on with approval.

BBC: There is still a demand for more 'facts' in the news bulletins and less 'frills or padding'. In one Region the remark was made 'The BBC treat us like children; the commentary on the Malta bombings was an insult to the public intelligence', while regarding the Far East it was remarked: 'the news service is as inefficient as the military authorities'.

People are now enjoying listening to the German broadcasts about conditions on the Russian front 'which a few months ago made our stomachs turn over'; otherwise, they appear to be paying scant attention to Lord Haw-Haw. Wilfred Pickles' return is welcomed, and the item *Irish Half Hour* has been warmly praised.

PROGRAMME PREFERENCES: During 1941 the Listening Barometer showed a steady increase in listening to the Forces Programme at the expense of the Home Service. In order to ascertain how far this tendency was general, Listener Research correspondents were asked, in December 1941, to differentiate in this matter between the following categories of listeners: men and women; middle and working class; four age groups.

296 questionnaires were returned by the correspondents, from which the following trends are deduced:

1. The Forces Programme is the young people's programme. 'With each step-up in age it loses ground to the Home Service.'
2. There is no evidence that the tastes of men and women differ materially in their preferences for Home or Forces programme.
3. The Forces Programme is above all the working-class programme, and it is overwhelmingly preferred to the Home Service by working-class listeners of all ages; it is also favoured by the majority of young middle-class listeners.

    Nevertheless, of the correspondents themselves, whether working or middle class, 30% prefer the Home Service, 18% the Forces, and 52% have no preference.

SUNDAY NIGHT POSTSCRIPT: Listener Research have summarised thirty of their reports on Sunday night *Postscripts*, broadcast between May and December 1941. These *Postscripts* have had an audience of between 24.4% and 50.1% of the adult population. It is seldom that less than 60% of those who hear the News listen to the *Postscript*; occasionally, as in the case of Quentin Reynold's second *Postscript*, as many as 87% of the News listeners have kept their sets on for the *Postscript*. The index of popularity ranges between 92% for Frank Laskier and 36% for Duff Cooper. Generally speaking, overseas speakers, particularly Americans, have been more popular than speakers from this country: 'They seem better able to establish easy contact with listeners and to put over the impression of a live personality.' Speakers are usually judged on their reputation, experience, technique and particularly on their personality. Subjects are judged on interest, illumination and particularly on their stimulating qualities; Reynolds' pugnacity, for instance, evoked much greater enthusiasm than the more balanced and informed talks by Lord Cecil and Tom Jones.

11. RUMOURS

During the visit of the Soviet Trades' Union delegates there was the usual tendency to attribute an air-raid warning to German knowledge of the presence of distinguished visitors. Workers on the Tyne declare that whenever an advertisement beginning 'Nash' has appeared in the personal column of the *Newcastle Evening Chronicle* there is an air raid seven days afterwards.

It is rumoured that troops and equipment are being moved from the east coast to the south, thus leaving the east coast unprotected.

A story is going about that girls leaving a Borstal Institute are directed into the ATS.

Before Mr. Churchill's return there were rumours that he had been lost in an aeroplane accident, and alternatively, that he was enjoying a holiday in the Bahamas.

Japanese troops were said to have already invaded northern Australia.

Income tax authorities were reported to have lost their books and to be making assessments by guesswork.

In Northern Ireland a report was circulated that American troops were to be landed there immediately, and that pressmen hurried to the scene to describe the landing.

The rumour that Germany has bought the whole of Portugal's sardine-catch for the year is again reported.

II. SPECIAL COMMENTS

12. INDUSTRY

Again this week, criticisms of the industrial front are not numerous, but the feeling is still strongly expressed that 'industry is not yet mobilised for total war', and there is a 'wish for a further tightening up of control, both of managements and of labour'. There is criticism of 'the hesitancy with which Government departments are thought to tackle the problems that arise'. People feel that 'too much is left to the managements to rectify, and that the will to rectify is not always present'.

Concern at periods of enforced idleness is still expressed by workers in war industry and tales continue to circulate of workers being told to go slow; it is felt that the reasons for hold-ups are not yet understood. 'Suspicion is still cast on the financial systems under which some of the factories operate', and the 'cost plus 10% system of contracting is thought to be widely used', according to one RIO, in spite of official statements to the contrary.

RESERVED OCCUPATIONS: There is some ill-feeling because of what is considered to be the 'large number of men between 20 and 30 who are exempt', and who are retained in civilian employment where it is thought that they could easily be replaced by older men. Some depression is reported among men in the 40 to 51 age groups at the extension of conscription, owing to their 'heavy responsibilities, both in home life and in business'.

WOMEN'S CALL-UP: The following points are mentioned this week:

(a) SERVICEMEN'S WIVES: The dissatisfaction of a section of the public (noted previously in these reports) at the exemption of the childless wives of servicemen does not appear to have been silenced by the explanation that they can be directed into industry near their homes. It is felt that the real 'culprits' are the 'camp-follower wives' who have no homes and can travel round the country, thereby evading direction. The feeling among the men is said to be that if their women were compelled to join the Services, 'it would be as bad as Nazism, against which we are fighting, because the only thing worth while is to have a home'.

(b) EMPLOYERS' DIFFICULTIES: Strong feeling is reported on the part of employers that 'their new female staff engaged to replace male labour should not be called up, after time and skill have been spent in training them'. They are anxious to 'have some assurance as to how many of the staff will be permitted to stay, so that they can plan for the future'.

(c) OLDER WOMEN: Older women again complain of the difficulty of getting suitable jobs near home, and, in some cases, of the discouraging attitude of Labour Exchanges to their enquiries.

(d) LABOUR EXCHANGES: The RIO Wales reports a great improvement in the attitude of interviewers, who are now said to be treating the girls 'very sympathetically' in that area.

(e) TRANSFER OF LABOUR: 'Alleged cases of workers being sent from their homes to work in a distant town, while workers from that town are being sent to the other', are reported to be causing 'a good deal of bitterness'.

(f) MARRIAGES TO AVOID CONSCRIPTION: These continue to be alleged, and some clergymen report an increase of marriages of young women since conscription was announced.

(g) DAY NURSERIES: The shortage of day nurseries continues to be reported, and it is not always understood why a stronger line is not taken in the requisitioning of buildings for this purpose. In one case, however, when a Parish Hall was requisitioned, there were protests on the grounds that it was the only building in the village where social events could be arranged for war workers.

13. YOUTH REGISTRATION

Although varied reactions are reported, the public appears on the whole to be favourably disposed to the idea of the registration of young people. There appears, however, to be some disquiet about the lack of information on the Government's proposals, and people are asking 'whether the interview will be compulsory, in view of the stressing of the voluntary character of the scheme'.

There is satisfaction that the 'children should have something to do with their evenings', and it is hoped that the scheme will 'draw in the youngsters who are just wasting their time and drifting'. It is even thought that it may help towards 'lessening juvenile delinquency, chiefly because of the discipline involved'.

Boys are said to be very keen on the ATC, and some are switching to it from the Home Guard, 'in which they feel they do not learn anything interesting'. In some quarters the 'undesirability of drafting children into the Home Guard is stressed, as they would be in close contact with much older men'.

14. INCOME TAX

Dismay and bad feeling about the payment of income tax are reported from three Regions, particularly among first payers. According to another report, the workers accept the requirement to pay income tax quite calmly, but 'are scared as to where it will end'. In Scotland, where the workers, though puzzled, are said not to be grumbling unduly, this is thought to be accounted for by a 'delay in the issue of assessment notices, so that the workers in many important establishments have not yet begun paying'. Postal Censorship, however, quotes a writer as being 'representative of 50% of the comments', who says, 'income tax is somewhat strangling at the moment, but that is nothing compared with the prospects of Hitler's New Order, so we pay up cheerfully'.

In some cases, bad feeling about the payment of income tax is apparently affecting willingness to work. It is reported that 'the workers just clock-off if things don't happen to be going very well with their work, the view being taken that most of what they would have earned would be lost to them in income tax anyway'. Postal Censorship also quotes a writer who says, 'the income tax is awful. Everyone is on about it. I'm going to do less hours, it's not worth it, having to pay it all away.' An employer writes: 'We are very short of staff, owing to the fact that as many as 20 girls stay out a day, so that they won't have to pay the income tax'. The case is mentioned of a workman asking for a rise on receipt of his assessment: 'every time I get an increase on income tax, I look for a rise, so that the firm pays it'.

Doubts continue to be expressed as to whether post-war credit will actually materialise.

15. SERVICE PAY AND ALLOWANCES

Strong feeling continues to be reported at the disparity in pay between soldiers and civilians, even taking into account the soldiers' keep and allowances. 'Fantastic tales' are reported of the high wages paid to munition workers, builder's labourers and dockers (instances are quoted where dockers are said to earn £80 per week for special jobs), and bitter comparisons are made between these amounts, and what a soldier receives. Comparison is also made between the higher pay of Dominion and Colonial troops, and that of our own soldiers. There is dissatisfaction at the 'long time that elapses between the application for a supplementary grant and its payment' – this is sometimes said to be months. In this connection, 'mothers with sons in the Forces are felt to have a very raw deal'.

The rates for pensions of Service casualties are said to be causing disquiet among dependants.

16. FOOD

The general situation remains satisfactory, and Postal Censorship reports many letters to the effect that 'if you can't get one thing there is always something else'. Only a small minority has been upset by the ration cuts; for the most part gratitude has been expressed that the extra had been given while possible.

POINTS RATIONING: There is continued praise and desire for further extension. It is suggested that the large packs and the large choice of foods tend to cause waste.

MILK: Criticism and mild complaints are again more apparent, but it is hoped that the shortage is only seasonal. The wish is expressed that the children's 'school' milk could be added to the family's ration in the holidays. Elderly people living alone are said to suffer under the 2-pint-a-week ration. Too much milk is thought to be consumed at office teas, canteens and clubs at the expense of the children's ration. In Aldershot, 268 gallons a week were said to be used by office tea clubs.

FRUIT AND VEGETABLES: It is suggested that the 'under-fives' are benefiting unduly in the matter of oranges, fruit juices etc., at the expense of the school children, and that oranges might be distributed in schools.

Farmers and smallholders are worried over the Government's failure to buy their potato crops, which are going bad. The quota of cattle food is said to be augmented by potatoes, for which the farmers must pay a higher price than they get when they sell them. Onions are also said to be rotting before they can be distributed.

BRITISH RESTAURANTS AND FEEDING CENTRES: Postal Censorship shows continued praise. Overcrowding is said to make it hard for workmen who can only afford 1/- to get a mid-day meal, and it is alleged that many people use the centres who could well afford to go elsewhere. Certain local authorities are said to be unwilling to open more British Restaurants because of the opposition of local caterers.

It is suggested that the School Feeding Scheme should be extended to release mothers for war work. In one borough, for example, ten elementary schools with 3,500 children are unprovided for.

SALE OF CONDEMNED MEAT: It is suggested at Aldershot that meat condemned by the Ministry of Food is bought by contractors, so that the fat, rendered down, may be used for fish frying.

PREFERENTIAL TREATMENT: Bournemouth grocers complain of certain chain stores securing early deliveries of 'Points' goods, and thus getting an unfair advantage. The official statement that chain stores are not selling food they did not stock before is disbelieved in some quarters, and the allegation has been made that Woolworth now sell branded goods for 6d which were previously unobtainable.

STOLEN LORRIES: Concern is expressed at the amount of food stolen, together with lorries and equipment. It is felt that while the drivers eat and sleep, armed guards should be provided for these vehicles.

17. SALVAGE

METAL: 'The Government's failure to salvage material from bombed buildings' and the 'continued presence of scrap iron dumps' are reported to be irritating the public. The taking of private railings, while public railings are allowed to remain, is also the subject of much criticism. The requisitioning of railings protecting vegetable gardens is causing apprehension in semi-rural areas.

WASTE OF PAPER: Many people are of the opinion that 'despite the frequent Government appeals for the salvage of paper very little enthusiasm will be forthcoming until the Government departments set a better example'. In Tottenham, where there is a large salvage centre, and collections of waste paper were made even before the war, there has been considerable study of the problem of utilising waste. It has been found that though every facility is given to keep the salvageable goods apart from the refuse, there is little co-operation from the public. Despite many 'drives', one of which was in progress at the time when the observations were made, nine out of ten people fail to keep their clean waste paper separate from their refuse. In the case of kitchen waste for pig food, co-operation is much higher, and little or none is put in with the other rubbish. It is felt that 'people still do not realise the necessity and urgency for salvage and they will not realise it until it is made an offence at law to put clean paper in with the refuse. Ordinary publicity methods have ceased to have an appreciable effect.'

APPENDIX TO WEEKLY REPORT NO. 70

IMPRESSIONS OF THE VISIT OF THE SOVIET TRADES' UNIONS DELEGATION

4 FEBRUARY 1942

The following report is by the MOI Intelligence Officer in the North Midland Region who recently accompanied the Delegation, consisting of Mdme. Nikolayeva, M. Solovyev, M. Yakoubov, and M. Rotov, on visits to factories in Nottingham, Derby and Lincoln.

Mdme. Nikolayeva was the moving spirit of the party. Rumoured to be seventy years old, but full of vigour, she has a rugged peasant appearance and a strong sense of fun, though little apparent sense of humour, as we understand it. She appeared to be strong willed to the point of obstinacy, impatient and irritable at times, and at others, spontaneously gay and cheerful, but never easy-going.

M. Solovyev is an unassuming young man, very little different from our own craftsmen in appearance or manner. M. Yakoubov was rather a puzzle to most people as he is very swarthy and looks more like a Persian than like our idea of a Russian. M. Rotov is much the same type as M. Solovyev but, as Secretary to the Delegation, took little part in the proceedings.

RECEPTION OF THE DELEGATES: The various managements differed widely in their understanding of the needs of the situation. Some realised that the Delegation would want to meet the shop stewards and spend most of their time in the factories, and the programme was arranged to that end. One management, to the intense suspicion of the Russians, as good as refused to summon the shop stewards and it appeared that no announcement of the visit had been made to the workers. As there was also no opportunity for speeches, the visit to this factory was counted as a dead loss. Another management, though extremely co-operative, made a bad mistake by arranging for the shop stewards to lunch in an adjoining room instead of with the party, though this was rectified at the last moment. The Delegation preferred to eat in the workers' canteens and some well-intentioned arrangements for them to eat in superior staff rooms were not appreciated.

The Delegation appeared particularly pleased with their reception by the management at the Nottingham Royal Ordnance gun factory and made a special note of the manager's name (Mr. Holyoak). They also remarked on the excellent spirit of co-operation between the management and workers at this factory.

At another factory they were delighted to find that many members of the management spoke Russian, having traded extensively with that country for a number of years, a fact which materially increased their enjoyment of the tour.

They were not at all keen on going to Boots, as this is not a munition factory, and might have refused to do so if it had not been arranged for Lord Trent to receive them there. On arrival, however, they were so impressed with the factory and so interested in the 'School' for young workers, that they were loath to leave to catch their train to London.

The reception given to the Delegates by workers in the munition factories left no doubt as to their enthusiasm. They were proud to be watched at their work, and very proud when given the opportunity to shake hands, and there was much surreptitious wiping of palms in hopeful anticipation. A number of shops organised a cheer of welcome as the Delegation appeared, or broke into the 'Internationale' or rattled their tools. It appears that the Russians heard 'Hip Hip, Hooray!' for the first time, an expression which intrigued them.

The workers in most factories had chalked up slogans and messages of welcome, some of them very ingenious. The 'V' sign and the hammer and sickle abounded, and some shops were decked with flags. The interpreters were busy explaining the various chalkings, especially in one factory, where the cleaners had been busy overnight putting slogans on the floor of every gangway. The Russians were particularly pleased with one which read: 'We want more guns, planes, tanks for Britain, Russia, USA and Ve Vill Vin'. They were also amused by slogans such as 'Berlin via Moscow' which appeared on guns and tanks.

Mdme. Nikolayeva appeared to be in her element. She smiled, waved, shouted greetings, shook innumerable hands, embraced some of the women, and made speeches whenever she got the chance. The men were not so spontaneous but made an effort to emulate their vivacious and quite untiring leader.

It was noticed that the women workers were more tentative in their response than the men, but some individual women came forward to express their personal admiration and gratitude.

REACTION TO SPEECHES: Mdme. Nikolayeva was again the star turn, the only criticism being that she spoke rather too long and there were some signs of restlessness towards the end of all her speeches. It was frequently remarked, however, that she made her meaning clear by the power of her oratory and actions, even though her words were not understood. The translation was, in each case, excellent and the volume of applause at the end was doubly as great as for the speech in Russian.

The speeches of all three Delegates followed very much the same lines and it was noticed that their speeches were interrupted by applause at the same points on each occasion. These were:

(a) 'We must all produce more to beat Hitler.'
(b) 'Hitler made a mistake when he thought Russia was beaten.'
(c) 'There *was* a parade in the Red Square in Moscow on Nov. 7th, but the salute was taken by Stalin – not Hitler.'
(d) 'Long live the friendship between Great Britain and the USSR.'

PRESS PUBLICITY: The Delegates did not appear too pleased with the press reports on the whole. It seems that they were anxious to put over their message and felt that 'personal stories', mixed up with what they considered a distortion of their words, were superfluous and sometimes in bad taste. They were particularly angered by a report of a woman worker, who was said to have addressed them 'with tears in her eyes' which, they said, was untrue.

The reaction of many readers to the Delegates' appeal for more production was not at all favourable. It was said either that 'the Russians have a cheek to come over here and tell us what to do, knowing nothing of our difficulties' or 'It's a bit thick, telling us we are not doing enough, considering we've slaved to help them and have dangerously depleted our stocks to keep them supplied.'

DELEGATES' CRITICISM: The lack of day nurseries and the unequal pay of men and women were two subjects which caused much comment among the Delegates. They could see no possible argument against the principle of equal pay for equal work. The loss of actual and potential production through lack of day nurseries and other facilities to enable married women to work added to their impression that we had a long way to go before we could say we were 100% engaged in fighting Hitler.

HOME INTELLIGENCE

NO. 71: MONDAY 2 FEBRUARY 1942 TO MONDAY 9 FEBRUARY 1942

I. GENERAL COMMENTS

1. GENERAL STATE OF CONFIDENCE AND REACTION TO NEWS

Reports indicate that there has been a further slight decline in public spirits this week. The main causes seem to be:

(a) Our continued reverses in the Middle and Far East, which are giving rise to a feeling that 'we do not seem able to achieve anything anywhere'.
(b) The 'disappointing' changes in the Government, which are generally regarded as 'merely another reshuffle'.

The continued success of the Russian offensive is considered 'the only bright spot in the news', though it no longer counteracts the depression caused by 'the realisation of the gravity of the situation in the other theatres of war'.

2. THE MIDDLE EAST

LIBYA: Profound disappointment and anger continue to be reported over Rommel's 'triumphal progress through Cyrenaica'. It is said that 'people would be much more philosophical and would give full credit to the difficulties if the Prime Minister and other Government spokesmen had not been so confident at the outset'. The public also appears to be extremely bewildered by the reversal of conditions in Libya and fails to understand 'how Rommel, with less men, less material and with serious transport difficulties, can put up a show like that.'

The following theories are advanced to account for it:

(a) That he has received considerable reinforcements through the complaisance of Vichy. (This was before Mr. Dalton's statement in the Commons on 10th February.)

(b) That our successes in attacking enemy convoys must have been less than was supposed.

(c) That some of our troops, aircraft and war material have been withdrawn from Libya to the Far East.

(d) That our army command, by its handling of the military situation and by repeatedly under-estimating the enemy's strength, is responsible for our reverses. There is again mention of our 'inferior armament' and of 'Libya tanks'.

EGYPT: The Egyptian crisis appears to have aroused very little interest but has caused some vague fears of the stability of our position in the Middle East.

3. THE FAR EAST

There now seems to be an almost fatalistic acceptance of Japan's continuous successes in the Far East, though this is to some extent offset by the belief that 'we'll win in the end, once the Americans and ourselves really get going'.

SINGAPORE: The disappointment and criticism with which the general public watched the Malayan withdrawals has now given place to 'a sense of keen drama as the onslaught upon Singapore begins'. Surmise as to whether adequate help will reach the besieged island in time, and whether the reinforcements will go to the island itself, has been stimulated by General Wavell's special order of the day. Nevertheless, there appears to be little real hope that we shall be able to hold the place. There is renewed impatience with over-confident official statements, made both in the past and present, a typical comment on them being: 'As soon as we heard "Singapore will be defended to the last man" we knew the game was up.'

THE AMERICANS AND THE DUTCH: There is continued admiration for General MacArthur's stand in the Philippines, and also for the Dutch resistance in the East Indies. Some comparisons are made between their activities and our own 'lack of achievement in Malaya'. Criticisms of British methods in comparison with those of America have also been made recently, chiefly with regard to the swift and thorough investigations into the Pearl Harbour disaster, followed by a frank report and immediate charges; this is compared unfavourably with our investigations into the loss of the *Prince of Wales* and the *Repulse* and what is regarded as attempts to keep the truth from the public.

THE BURMA ROAD: Interest in the Burma Road is considerable, and feeling for the Chinese tends to become 'not dissimilar from the warmth of feeling shown towards Russia'. There is also some belief that the best hope of 'finally smashing Japan will be from a fully equipped China'.

4. MINISTERIAL CHANGES

As mentioned in the first section of this report, considerable disappointment has been caused by the Ministerial changes which are dismissed as 'just another game of general post'. It is believed in some quarters that 'the Premier has not made the changes as a matter of conviction but as a matter of political expediency'. Eleven RIOs report continued criticism of the Government and from some quarters this criticism is said to have increased in intensity since the debate on the war situation. Although there is unabated confidence in the Prime Minister, and 'everybody desires that he shall be upheld in every way', fears are discernible as to 'whether in his management of his Government he may not weaken his own position'. It is noteworthy, however, that few people have any constructive suggestion to make; Sir Stafford Cripps is the only name which reports mention as a possible addition to the Government.

MINISTER OF PRODUCTION: There has been in general a favourable reaction to the appointment of a Minister of Production. This has given rise to a feeling of hopefulness that 'this move will help to get things done', though some anxiety is expressed as to what the relations of this new Minister will be with the other supply departments. (This was before the issue of the White Paper defining the new Minister's powers.)

Three RIOs mention that Lord Beaverbrook's appointment has met with unconditional approval, but a considerable section of the public appears to view it with reserve. While it is recognised that Lord Beaverbrook has 'great drive and initiative' it is suggested that 'his methods have their own dangers: if tanks are needed then he will bust himself to get tanks, but he may forget Spitfires in the meantime'.

SIR STAFFORD CRIPPS: There is widespread popular enthusiasm for Sir Stafford Cripps, and considerable regret that he has not been absorbed in the Government and 'harnessed to the war effort'. There is some speculation as to why he has not been included, but it is hoped that he will be given an 'outstanding job before long'. His BBC *Postscript* met with lavish and almost unanimous approval and was considered 'one of the best speeches we've had'. People were impressed with both the manner and substance of his address.

5. RUSSIA

The continued Russian advance continues to cause admiration and is welcomed as a relief from 'depressing news from other fronts'. It is beginning to be asked, however, whether their great achievement will be enough to prevent an even more powerful German counter-offensive in the spring.

There is a growing tendency to compare Russian successes with British and American failures and 'the brilliant conduct of the Red Army's offensive is contrasted with our own generalship'.

6. RELATIONS BETWEEN AMERICAN TROOPS
AND BRITISH TROOPS IN IRELAND

The RIO Northern Ireland reports that the rumour is prevalent that relations between British and American soldiers are rather strained. Two reports have been received of fights between these men in the streets of Belfast, and some contacts repeat a phrase often heard in the last war: that the Americans are saying 'We have come to win the war.' But according to the RIO 'there is a total absence of hostility towards the Americans among the civil population, and these troops have, in fact, expressed their appreciation of the hospitable welcome they have received. Many people are asking if, as this contingent is obviously only the first, American troops will eventually replace British troops in Northern Ireland. Uneasiness is noted among many people that the defence of Belfast might be left to these men and there is a general desire that British troops should remain.'

7. BROADCASTING AND REPRESENTATION OF NEWS

MINIMISING OF NEWS: Dissatisfaction with the news bulletins is reported this week by eight RIOs, and it is said to have increased slightly in one Region. The 'completeness and veracity' of these bulletins are questioned: 'lack of real news' is said to arouse suspicion that bad news is being withheld, and to induce listeners 'to give greater credence to the exaggerated claims' made on the German radio. Objection is made to official statements still being 'too often tinged with that sort of hearty, almost perfunctory, optimism, which, in the past, events have often failed to justify'. Criticism is again made of the practice of boosting the importance of territorial gains, and if they are afterwards lost, of making them out to be of trifling value. The news from Libya especially is thought scanty, compared with the 'fulsome accounts of our advance'.

PREMATURE ANNOUNCEMENTS: Again, there are complaints that 'innovations or reforms' are announced before the department or authority concerned has received its instructions. Though the particular matters may be regarded by the public as 'faits accomplis', the local office involved may not receive further details for several weeks. 'Nurseries, school meals, milk scheme etc., are all said to have been introduced in this way.'

AEF IN EIRE: There has been a good deal of criticism in Northern Ireland of the publicity given to this event, and particularly to the mention of the troops being billeted in houses. This kind of information is looked on as 'a direct invitation to the enemy to bomb civilians'.

EUROPEAN NEWS SERVICE: The popularity of this is mentioned by three RIOs. One report comparing it with the Home Service News says it is 'repeatedly mentioned as giving a wider and more comprehensive grasp of the war situation'.

II. SPECIAL COMMENTS

8. INDUSTRY

'This week there seems to have been a new wave of talk about slackness in factories'; this is mentioned by six RIOs – as against three who referred to it last week - in spite of the suggestion that 'the promise of a Minister of Production appears to have had the effect of temporarily decreasing criticism'. The complaints follow the familiar pattern: the workers blame the managements (for profiting out of the war and encouraging slacking); the managements blame the Government (for the necessity of 'form-filling' and 'official indecision') and the workers (for not pulling their weight and for absenteeism). Government inspection is said to be 'nullified by unholy co-operation' between management and workers. 'When an inspector comes round everyone goes raving mad. The workers are told to look busy; then, when the inspector leaves, the "All Clear" is given.' Resentment at the criticisms by the Russian Delegation appears to have given way to 'overwhelming approval of the points made in their reports, and a general conviction that their criticisms were an understatement of the facts'.

WAR PROFITS: Workers' criticism of the cost plus 10% system, though much less than it was three months ago, still continues, together with the feeling that 'there are lots of people making tremendous profits out of this war'. It is suggested that 'some explanation of Excess Profits Tax still seems to be needed'. This grumbling appears to be directed chiefly against 'those owning big firms which do Government work', and 'elements in the Government who are in with the big industrialists and do not want the war to finish too soon because war is a paying business'; but there is also some feeling about sections of the working population 'who do not worry if the war goes on for years – as long as they have their jobs'.

INDUSTRIAL PUBLICITY: The need for talks and films in war factories is again stressed this week. According to one report: 'Many of the workers stand by their machines, day in, day out, week in, week out, making nothing but nuts and bolts or sprocket holes, but often they ask in a tired sort of way "What good is this towards the war effort?" They have not grasped the idea that their job, however small, is but one part of a great whole.'

'Any proof that war material manufactured here has actually arrived in Russia is said definitely to raise production.' An instance is mentioned by the Works Manager of a Wolverhampton factory, where the receipt of a couple of telegrams about British tanks in Russia, containing parts made by this particular factory, 'made the machines fairly hum'.

CALL-UP: The public is said to be puzzled at the 'slowness of the intake of young men and women into the Forces', which is thought to be at variance with the 'plea of urgency'. In the case of women, complaints come both from the girls themselves, who are 'unsettled because they do not know whether they will be left in their jobs or not', and from employers, who 'complain that their work is suffering as a consequence'.

WOMEN VOLUNTEERS: A three-week campaign which has just taken place in Northamptonshire to get volunteers for munition factories has resulted in about 200 volunteers actually signing up, according to the RIO North Midland Region. Over 1,000 were hoped for, 'but local conditions, and actual opposition, weighed heavily against success'. Some of the causes of the failure are summarised briefly as follows:

(a) Feeling that if the Government *really* wanted them, they would be taken.
(b) Good wages and short hours in the boot and shoe trade, and pride in their craft.
(c) Feeling that they are doing a war job already (in comfort), linked with local evidence of slack time in munition factories.
(d) Opposition of employers, all of whom probably use at least indirect pressure. It is alleged that all boot and shoe firms displayed a notice stating that workers were 'regarded as engaged on work of national importance and essential to the nation's war effort'.
(e) Wish to retain the goodwill of employers, 'because of after the war'.

WAR WORKERS' SHOPPING DIFFICULTIES: These are again reported from several Regions, as the cause of both resentment and absenteeism. One engineering firm reports over 50% absenteeism due to early closing of grocers' shops on Saturdays. The need for special shopping facilities for war workers is again emphasised. In many cases, however, the attitude of shop managements and assistants appears to be uncooperative. In spite of the fact that large shops and multiple stores are thought to be better supplied than the smaller shops, there is now said to be an increasing tendency for workers to prefer the latter as they are more sympathetic to shoppers' difficulties.

Various remedies have been tried or are under consideration. In one factory, the women voted 100% for two late shopping nights a week; in another a rota system has been successfully introduced, whereby the workers have every sixth day off. In Luton, under a scheme awaiting Home Office sanction, shops will remain open on Friday evening to serve women with factory passes. 'Considerable exasperation is reported that a straightforward experiment of this kind should be held up, and perhaps frustrated, by red tape.'

9. INCOME TAX

This is mentioned by eight RIOs as a subject of much discussion, and, in many cases, of misapprehension. It is even suggested that 'the belief that the firm gets the income tax is not dead'. 'Continued resentment amongst first payers is reported, and it is thought that, in spite of the publicity, there is little appreciation of the fact that paying income tax is helping with the war.' The following points are emphasised:

(a) Income tax is still reported to be causing absenteeism. This is said to be particularly serious in the mining industry.

(b) The aspect which is now most discussed among the workers themselves is 'the lag whereby a manual worker, in what may be a lean period, pays tax on his earnings during the half year ending some three months before, when his earnings may have been very much higher'. There is 'a widespread demand' that tax should be deducted from the current week's earnings, 'even if this does cause some bother to the bureaucrats'; in view of which it is suggested that some explanation is needed to show that such an arrangement might cause even more bother to the worker, as well as unfairness.

(c) Scepticism about post-war credits continues, together with the wish for some form of non-negotiable certificate to show how much is accumulating. It is also feared that 'compulsory savings will be retained to meet arrears of tax due when, after the war, a man may become unemployed'.

(d) There is some feeling that special exemptions should be made on: (i) Overtime pay; (ii) 'Proficiency pay of young volunteers in the Services'; (iii) Dependants' allowances received by married women at work.

10. TRANSPORT

'Reports of inadequate services, overcrowding and disorders at stopping places continue.'

It is reported that where skeleton late tram services are run (as in Southampton) this has proved a 'boon to war workers'.

11. SERVICE DEPENDANTS' ALLOWANCES

Very little reaction is reported to the recent changes in Service pay and allowances, though some approval is mentioned by one RIO at the increase in the children's allowances. There is said to be continued dissatisfaction over the long time that elapses between the application for a supplementary grant and its payment. It is pointed out that 'the machinery can work quickly enough if it is a question of stopping a grant; if a woman takes up work the grant is stopped immediately, but if later on she has to give up work for health reasons, it takes about five weeks to get the grant again'.

Two RIOs report a belief that 'Service dependants and widows are not even as well treated as refugees in this country'.

Some ill-feeling is reported about 'the hardship caused if a wife moves out of London for a few weeks (as she is encouraged to do) for the arrival of her baby, as she thereby forfeits the right to the 3/6d a week London allowance; this is considered to be very hard, as almost always her London rent continues during her enforced absence'.

12. WOMEN'S SERVICES COMMITTEE

Four RIOs report strong public feelings, ranging from indignation to ridicule, because (a) there are no women on the Committee, and (b) 'the men on it are too closely connected with the different Service departments to be unbiased'. This is cited as 'another example of actions by the Government which are so surprising because they seem to offend against ordinary common sense'.

13. DRUNKENNESS AMONG YOUNG PEOPLE

The high wages paid to young people are held to account for 'the many reports of rowdyism and drinking on the part of young men and girls'. 'Disquiet is being caused by the amount of drunkenness among young people which is visible not only in public vehicles but also in factories'. Though various causes are suggested, the main one is thought to be 'the difficulty, owing to rationing, of finding other outlets for greatly increased incomes'.

14. SOAP RATIONING

Reports on the public's reaction to soap rationing have been received from five Regions. This appears to have caused very little resentment or surprise. A rumour that it was to be rationed was reported from the North-Western Region at the end of last week, but it has been reported several times from different parts of the country during the last six months, and there is no suggestion that the secret had leaked out. It is not thought that the ration is likely to be inadequate except, possibly, in the case of:

(a) Those whose work makes them especially dirty,
(b) Mothers with small children and babies,
(c) People who cannot afford to send washing to a laundry,
(d) Areas where the water is exceptionally hard and where, it is alleged, twice as much soap may be necessary as in places where it is soft.

15. FOOD

POINTS RATIONING: General approval of the extension continues, with the following reservations: (a) that the extra points are disproportionate to the greater variety of goods now covered, (b) that single people and small households are now at a greater disadvantage than ever, (c) complaints from retailers that they are unable to get renewal of stocks on presentation of coupons. In spite of the inclusion of fruits, tinned meats, especially the American brands, still seem to be considered the best 'points value'.

MILK: Some sense of grievance over the milk rationing is reported by three RIOs, and in Wales it is said that the need for such rationing had not been given enough publicity; also that 'a general ignorance exists over the uses of tinned milk'.

FISH: Five Regions report complaints of the shortage and high prices of fresh fish.

ORANGES: It is thought that if there are going to be new consignments of oranges a more orderly method of distribution will be needed, and that 'specific registration would be justified'.

BRITISH RESTAURANTS: Approval of British Restaurants and the wish for more of them continues. But one RIO reports, apropos of this, that there is annoyance with Lord Woolton for 'kowtowing to the caterers' who are thought to have vested interests in the restriction of such restaurants. A considerable minority, however, is still reported to misunderstand and criticise the scheme, their chief objections being that meals without coupons undermine the rationing scheme and that wealthier people have an unfair advantage.

16. CLOTHES RATIONING

The demand continues for special price and coupon concessions to those working in 'dirty trades'.

Farm labourers and working women are reported to be 'hard hit' by the high prices, inferior quality and coupon value of woollen socks and stockings.

There are some complaints from miners that the extra coupons for their use are not easily negotiable, as they are in units of 5 and no change in coupons can be given.

The additional allowance of forty coupons to boys of 14–18, together with an extra thirty if they are colliery workers, is thought to be excessive.

APPENDIX TO WEEKLY REPORT NO. 71

HOME MORALE AND PUBLIC OPINION

11 FEBRUARY 1942

A review of three months' findings, November 1941–January 1942.

NOTE: This paper should be read as a sequel to a longer review on this subject, issued as an appendix to the Home Intelligence Weekly Report on October 1, 1941.

1. INTRODUCTION

In interpreting the present state of public feeling, certain general points mentioned in the previous review should be borne in mind:

a. For the majority of the public, personal experience is the most important factor in forming opinion. It is the immediate impact of the war on their own lives which affects them most strongly. Events happening at a distance have for them a certain unreality. And the greater the distance, the greater the unreality.

    This is illustrated by their much stronger reaction to the killing of the French and Belgian hostages than to reports of mass executions of prisoners and civilians in Poland, Russia, and Yugo-Slavia.

b. When things go wrong, the public tends rather not to blame the enemy, but rather some section of those in authority. In this process, it is not unusual for the wrong scapegoat to be picked on. When no particular scapegoat can be found, the Government and all those in authority are, always excepting the Prime Minister, blamed indiscriminately.

c. The volume of grumbles varies inversely with the immediate difficulties and dangers which the public has to face. This statement requires qualification. If any section of the community feels that its sacrifices are greater than those of another section (e.g. servicemen's dependants, who compare themselves with the wives of munition workers), then a loud wail goes up. Further, if the reasons for a sacrifice are not understood, or if its method of application appears unfair (e.g. income tax), a large volume of complaint also arises.

2. PRESENT STATE OF PUBLIC FEELING

If those points are borne in mind, the present state of public feeling is not difficult to understand.

At home, rationing of food, clothing and petrol are accepted as a matter of course. The schemes are thought to be just, and to be functioning, on the whole, surprisingly well. There is a real sense of gratitude for the abundance of food supplies so far. The absence of air raids and of any apparent threat of invasion have added to the remoteness of the bloody side of war. In the absence of immediate dangers to be faced and overcome, the volume of grumbling has increased.

The news of our retreats in the Near East and the Far East has failed to awaken the British public to a sense of urgency. They feel vaguely that 'something is wrong somewhere' and seek without great success to pin the blame onto some individual or section of those in authority. That there may be connections between events in the Near East and those in the Far East, or between the more distant past and the present, is seldom considered. The desire of the public to see mismanagement publicly condemned is well illustrated by the rise in the popularity of America when those responsible for the Pearl Harbour disaster were dealt with.

One facet of the war overseas is clearly connected with events in these islands. The public is under no delusions about its freedom from air raids being directly connected with Russia's successes. The gratitude and the admiration for the great fight of the Russians far exceeds the feeling for any other foreign country. At the same time, to be told by the Russians that we ought to be working harder was first accepted with ill-grace by the workers, and that we ought to be better organised for production with ill-grace by the managements. British people are ready enough to condemn themselves, but they do not take kindly to hearing home truths from others; nevertheless this irritation died down when the Soviet delegation's report was published and found to be in accordance with the workers' own criticisms.

To return to events on the home front, it is generally felt that the two outstanding problems now to be tackled are:

1. The organisation of production.
2. The organisation of manpower and woman-power. On how this is to be done, the public is inclined to be less specific. The main remedy suggested is 'telling someone else how he ought to be doing his job, and naming some other body who would do it better'.

Yet, if the public appears to be in a capricious mood, its judgement on certain fundamentals seems sound. The entry of Japan into the conflict is generally thought to have greatly lengthened our task. A year ago, a majority of the public anticipated 1–2 more years of war. Now they anticipate 1½–3 more years. And America's active participation is thought to have made our final victory an emphatic certainty. (Before her entry, our final victory was regarded as certain, but how this would be brought about was not clear.)

3. THE LACK OF 'URGENCY'

The main characteristic, then, of public feeling at the moment is a lack of urgency. The problem which presents itself is first, whether it is possible by anything other than the direct impact of immediate events to remove this, and secondly, whether it is desirable so to do. To supply answers is outside the scope of this review, but to marshal such evidence as has been accumulated on these points is justified.

a. In the past, propaganda attempts to create an atmosphere of urgency (e.g. gas-mask carrying campaigns) have been unsuccessful. When propaganda has been used as an adjunct to the impact of events (e.g. 'Going to it', after Dunkirk), results have been achieved. But it was then impossible to tell how much was due to the events and how much to the propaganda.

b. In the second Emergency Report of the Industrial Health Research Council (published last week), it is shown that the increase in production which followed the fall of France was followed in due course by a decline in production as a result of long hours, 7-day weeks and fatigue. When steps were taken to deal with the fatigue (shorter hours, holidays, and a reduction in the length of the working week), production rose again, not always to peak level, but to a level substantially above the 'pre-emergency' level. A genuine emergency had not only increased immediate production, but, when coupled with reduction in working hours, had increased production over a much longer period. Since no figures are available to us, we are unable to say whether more remote emergencies, when coupled with propaganda (e.g. 'Tanks for Russia' week), are of value in raising long-term as well as immediate production.

c. It is, in theory, arguable that it is undesirable to stimulate a sense of urgency except by reinforcing the impact of events. If, as the public anticipate, the war is to last for a considerable period of time, it may be valuable to have in hand a certain reserve of national effort – a bottom gear, as it were, available for changing into when the hill reaches its steepest part.

It is with considerations such as these in mind that the strategy of home front propaganda has to be worked out.

4. ATROCITIES

The findings of Home Intelligence in the past on the subject of atrocities as propaganda may be summarised as follows:

1. The public is ready to believe stories, photographs or films showing Nazi atrocities on German citizens, the people of the occupied territories or on Russians. The pre-war record of the Nazis is such that these cause no surprise, and relatively little shock.
2. A section of the public is acutely concerned that photographs and films of atrocities should not be seen by children. There is no evidence to suggest that children are in fact upset by them.
3. The shooting of the French and Belgian hostages was considered more shocking than the butchering of much larger numbers of Poles, Russians, and Yugo-Slavs.
4. The possibility that such happenings might take place in Britain is only just beginning to be considered. Thus, women are beginning to discuss whether a stay-put policy will not lead to 'worse than death' and are speculating as to whether they and their daughters would not be better dead than in the hands of the German soldiery.
5. The main recorded effect of such atrocity propaganda as has been put out so far has been to increase the desire for a retributive peace and the demand that 'we should drop the kid-glove methods and stop playing cricket'. In this connection, it may be mentioned that the desire for a retributive peace appears to have grown in the last three months, and there is considerable sympathy with what are believed to be Russia's intentions.
6. We have no evidence of the effect of atrocity propaganda on production.
7. We have no evidence of the effect on the public of atrocities on British subjects.

5. NEWS PRESENTATION

In the period under review, there has been considerably less blame of the Ministry of Information for faulty news presentation, or for bad news. (In the past, it was often the public's habit to blame the news services for our reverses.) There has been favourable comment whenever bad news has been released promptly (e.g. the sinking of the *Prince of Wales* and the *Repulse*), and vigorous criticism of military spokesmen in the Near and Far East, whenever bad news has been 'dressed up'. This is regarded by the public as an insult to its ability to take the truth.

SOME SPECIAL COMMENTS

6. THE SERVICES

The popularity of the Air Force with the public has slightly declined. The public appears to be tired of tales of individual exploits. It has been unwilling to accept the weather as a reason for the absence of heavy raids on Germany (though comments on this have declined of late). And the repeated raids on the *Scharnhorst* and *Gneisenau* at Brest are compared unfavourably with the single Japanese attack on the *Prince of Wales* and the *Repulse*.

On the other hand, complaints of army inefficiency, of food wasted at camps, of soldiers doing nothing, and of dangerous driving, have markedly declined. There has been a growth in sympathy for the position of soldiers' dependants.

The silence of the Navy is accepted without question.

7. THE USA

The personal popularity of the President continues unabated.

The popularity of the US as a partner in the war has recently been increased by three factors:

a.   The stout fight put up by General MacArthur and his men.
b.   The prompt publication of the findings of the Pearl Harbour Commission.
c.   The arrival of American troops in Northern Ireland.

The public are still prone to treat the United States as a member of the British family who can therefore be criticised with freedom and vigour.

8. THE DOMINIONS AND INDIA

Interest in the Dominions is at present very limited. Interest in India, negligible six months ago, has slightly increased.

9. WOMEN'S CALL-UP

This is accepted as desirable and essential. The practical problems which arise from it are engaging much attention:

a.   The problems of dependants and young children; the need for day nurseries.
b.   The problems of the immobile woman, the older woman, and the woman who is anxious to work part-time.
c.   The problems of billets and hostels for mobile women.
d.   Transport difficulties.
e.   Shopping difficulties.
f.   Married women's income tax.

The ATS appears to have turned the corner, and its unpopularity is declining.

10. INCOME TAX

The new income-tax-paying classes are finding it an unpleasant novelty. There are many allegations of deliberate absenteeism and reduction in overtime, in order to avoid paying tax. No figures are available to us.

Specific complaints are that a tax based on past earnings but levied on present reduced incomes leads to genuine hardship among certain groups of workers; and that the present rate of taxation on married women means that when they have paid for travel and for the care of their children, they have nothing left at all.

Post-war credit is still generally regarded as a myth.

HOME INTELLIGENCE DIVISION

NO. 72: MONDAY 9 FEBRUARY 1942 TO MONDAY 16 FEBRUARY 1942

I. GENERAL COMMENTS

1. GENERAL STATE OF CONFIDENCE AND REACTION TO NEWS

There is a very marked decline in public confidence this week. Public spirits have not been high for some time past, and last week most RIOs referred to a sense of disappointment and a lack of enthusiasm. Now the public is said to be profoundly disturbed and angry. Depression is reported from several Regions, and in a few areas there are said to be 'some signs of defeatism'. The passage of the German warships through the Channel appears to have shocked the public far more than the fall of Singapore, which was expected by the majority. This is described as having been 'the blackest week since Dunkirk'; eight RIOs refer to Dunkirk – or even in one case to the 'Norwegian campaign' – in seeking a term of comparison for the present state of public feeling. The situation in Libya is felt to be disappointing, and even the Russian advances, though still regarded as the one bright spot, are thought to have been slowed down. The desire to criticise is very widespread, and, although the Service chiefs are greatly blamed, the main weight of public criticism seems to be directed against the Government, and no longer excludes the Prime Minister.

2. THE ESCAPE OF THE GERMAN BATTLESHIPS

This event, which has been described as 'the most bitter failure of the whole war', appears to have caused not only shock, bewilderment and anger, but also a feeling of humiliation and disgrace. One RIO describes public reaction, after the 'first stupendous astonishment', as being 'one big "Why?"', and in the majority of public reactions, query and criticism seem to be inseparable. The chief points disturbing the public – in order of frequency – are as follows:

(a) 'HOW WERE THE SHIPS ABLE TO LEAVE BREST AT ALL, AFTER OUR RAIDS ON THEM?' Our weekly report (No. 68) on January 21st stated that 'people are said to be "fed-up" with the repeated bombing of Brest, which they consider as "singularly ineffective by comparison with the effect of one of two German raids on ports in this country"'. This feeling now comes out strongly. In Wales, for example, comparisons are being made between the destruction in Swansea after three German raids, and what might have been expected to have been the state of the German warships and of Brest itself after over 100 RAF raids. Our whole bombing policy is now called in question, and people are beginning to ask 'how effective has the bombing of German industries been?' A substantial minority express the opinion that they were 'dummy ships at Brest all the time'; and a small minority, in the first outburst of anger, even suggested that 'the RAF never went near Brest at all, because of the flak'. Criticism, however, 'does not seem to be directed towards the rank and file, who, it is felt, did their best', but the whole operation in the Channel is regarded as a 'defeat for the RAF'.

(b) 'WHERE WAS THE FLEET?' Nine RIOs mention this question as being extensively asked, but three RIOs refer to criticism of the Air Force being greater than that of the Navy. Indignation is reported at 'our failure to bring big battleships into action', or at least submarines. Our naval superiority in home waters is now being queried. 'Lack of co-operation between the Services' is repeatedly criticised.

(c) INVASION: Signs of apprehension about invasion are reported by eight RIOs, 'now that it appears that Britannia no longer rules the waves'; and there appears to be some anxiety as to the future activities of these ships, and a fear that they will attack our coastline and shipping, or be used against convoys for Russia.

(d) COMPARISONS WITH THE LOSS OF OUR BATTLESHIPS: Comparisons are made with 'the loss of the *Prince of Wales* and the *Repulse*, sunk at so little expense to the Japanese, while, with a loss of 42 aircraft, we have failed – so far as the public knows – to cripple any of these three ships'. This reaction is reported from seven Regions. Comparisons are also made between 'the fighter aircraft, smoke screens, E-boats, torpedo boats and minesweepers with which the enemy's ships were protected', and the fact that 'we relied on the weather to give ours cover' in the Far East.

(e) OUR INTELLIGENCE SERVICE: Criticism of our Intelligence Service is reported from seven Regions. People are said to be 'staggered that, in the midst of a country presumably seething with Allied sympathisers, no warning appears to have reached us that these ships were preparing for sea. The apparent absence of submarines and big surface craft is taken as evidence of this.'

(f) MISLEADING THE PUBLIC: The suspicion that 'the public have been grossly misled about the damage inflicted on these ships' is being taken as confirmation of 'previous suspicions that official news is unreliable and "dressed-up"'. This is reported from four Regions, and for the same reasons, 'the admitted losses in aircraft are thought to be an understatement'. Blame of the weather appears only to have increased irritation, and 'impatience with official accounts of the action, which are regarded as "the usual excuses"'.

3. THE FAR EAST

THE FALL OF SINGAPORE: The great majority of the public appear to have been 'resigned, rather than reconciled' to the fall of Singapore, which has been received, according to some accounts, 'with a silence too deep for words'. There even appears to be 'some relief that the tragedy is at last over, and the personal suffering in the city finished'. People are said to be dismayed that a 'fortress reputed to be so strong has proved to be so vulnerable'. There are bitter comments on all the money that has been spent on Singapore in the past, on the 'reinforcements that are thought to have been poured in and sacrificed all for no purpose'. The 'excuse that our resources were sent to Russia and Libya is thought not to be good enough, especially after Rommel's advance'; and it is felt that 'such a key point should have received plenty of guns, ammunition and aircraft long ago'. There is criticism of the lack of air support.

BURMA: There appears to be considerable anxiety over Burma; and there are fears for Rangoon, and particularly for the Burma Road. The importance of our supplying the Chinese with arms seems to be increasingly realised, and 'it is felt that if we can equip the Chinese, they will fight the Japanese as the Russians have fought the Germans'. Admiration for China continues.

Our efforts in general in the Far East are compared unfavourably with those of General MacArthur.

GENERAL CHIANG KAI-SHEK'S VISIT TO INDIA: 'Doubts of the adequacy of preparations in India, and of the attitude of the Indians, have been somewhat relieved by the news that General Chiang Kai-Shek is acting as ambassador to unfriendly elements in India, and great hopes are placed in his good offices and organising ability.' This feeling is reported by six RIOs. It is also felt to be 'imperative that we should bring about a measure of agreement in India', and doubts are expressed as to 'whether Mr. Amery is doing much to help'.

4. THE GOVERNMENT

Criticism of the Government appears to be intense and widespread this week, together with a 'growing feeling that the direction of the war is very much at fault'. The general feeling may be summed up in the words of one RIO, who says that 'not since the Norwegian fiasco has there been such grave and widespread doubt regarding the adequacy of the high direction of the war in general and of our staff work in particular. The dominant sentiment appears to be one of frustration that after two-and-a-half years of war, and nearly two of the Prime Minister's leadership, we should, except for the Battle of the Atlantic, be still apparently incapable of conclusive victory over anybody except Italians.' It is also felt that 'the common habit of tracing our failures to the policy of previous Governments is now wearing thin and that, for many previous circumstances and almost all future ones, the present Government must accept responsibility'. There is also a feeling that 'we have got to the stage when it is time to stop accepting excuses and try a change of Government'.

THE PRIME MINISTER: Although 'Mr. Churchill's general popularity remains very great', criticism of him, in one form or another, is reported from every Region. This criticism is primarily of Mr. Churchill in his capacity as Minister of Defence rather than as Prime Minister. A number of people are said to feel that 'he never was a military strategist; naval and military tactics are for the expert'. It is thought, too, that 'he has taken on far too much responsibility and that he will not delegate authority'. His 'protection of his Ministers is still the subject of much criticism'.

THE PRIME MINISTER'S BROADCAST: This appears to have had rather a mixed reception. Some people feel that it has had a steadying influence, but a greater number seem to be of the opinion that it did not succeed in allaying criticism. There is a general feeling that it was a difficult speech to make and that it was 'the best he could do in the circumstances'. Particular note seems to have been taken of his 'call for unity', to which the reaction is reported that 'unity depends on having the right men in the right places'. The appeal to the people not to criticise the Government was regarded by many as 'ineffective, as feeling is too disturbed at present for any such appeal to take effect'. It is considered that comparisons with Russia cut both ways, as people appear to be making their own comparisons between 'the organisation and efficiency of the Russian war machine and our own half-hearted methods'. There has been a good deal of comment, and some dissatisfaction, on the omission of any reference to the German battleships.

SIR STAFFORD CRIPPS: Rumours are said to be current in two Regions that 'a major political crisis is developing and that Sir Stafford Cripps will be the Prime Minister within a few months'. There is also some indication that 'people are beginning to think of alternatives to Mr. Churchill, and that in this connection Sir Stafford Cripps is most often mentioned'. There is reported to be widespread disappointment that he is not in the Government.

5. RUSSIA

'Continued Russian successes still give rise to thankfulness that "someone on our side is doing something, at any rate".' They are, however, less discussed than formerly, and there is some feeling that 'they have ceased to have any directly stimulating effect'. Some fear is now expressed that the Russians are 'slowing up', and there is anxiety as to the German spring offensive. German resistance is thought to have become 'considerably more effective of late'. There is more comment on 'the relative success in the military field of "working" Russia and capitalistic Britain and USA'.

6. LIBYA

'Disappointment' is the most generally reported reaction to the situation in Libya but, in view of more sensational events elsewhere, there is said to have been little comment this week. There seems to be a feeling that 'we are up against a better equipped enemy'. The fact that troops refer to it as the 'Muddle East' is said not to inspire public confidence.

Strong feeling against Vichy is reported from four Regions, and there is some demand that Vichy France should be treated as an active enemy, in view of the assistance she is believed to have given to the Axis forces in Libya. It is felt that our treatment of Vichy 'looks like appeasement'.

7. LONG-TERM TRENDS IN PUBLIC OPINION

As a footnote to the appendix to last week's Home Intelligence Report, the RIO, Midland Region, records certain tendencies observed in that Region.

There seems to be a freely expressed feeling that the Government may be forced, before many months, into a general election, in which event few of the present MPs are thought likely to be returned. More and more people of all classes are said to be taking to 'a kind of home-made socialism, which does not owe allegiance to any particular political party, but which expresses a resentment of the system which has given so much power to so few people'. This feeling is said to be by no means confined to factory workers and the industrial middle-class, though it finds its strongest expression in this section of the community.

Another factor which is thought to be coming to the fore is 'the religious or spiritual aspect of our lives'. Compared with eighteen months ago, an increasing number of people are said to be talking of Christian principles, and 'regretting that this country has so far departed from them as to make this war possible'.

Somewhat similar tendencies are reported by the RIO, Eastern Region. There is stated to be a 'desire among the working classes for some sort of post-war New Order, aimed at contracting the gulf between the "haves" and the "have-nots"'.

There are references to the need for 'Socialism in its purest form in this country after the war', and to this end they mean 'to make their voices heard when the opportunity presents itself'.

8. BROADCASTING AND PRESENTATION OF NEWS

SIR STAFFORD CRIPPS' SPEECHES: Favourable comment is reported from twelve Regions on both his Bristol speeches and broadcast, which have caused widespread discussion. 'His human voice and absence of rhetoric' were appreciated, as was also his 'non-political and helpful factual approach'. The broadcast is thought to have provoked 'self-examination' and a desire to know '*why* we are all so sure we are going to win'. In the London and Scottish Regions, in spite of general approval, several workers are said to have disliked the suggestion that they were not doing enough, and to have taken up a 'What can we do?' attitude, but the vast majority of reports register 'enthusiastic approval'.

MINIMISING OF NEWS: This complaint has now been evident for eight consecutive weeks, in ever-growing intensity. This week nine RIOs, four Police Duty Room reports, in addition to Postal Censorship, continue to report dissatisfaction with the BBC news bulletins, and there is further evidence that 'padding' or excuses are immediately resented by the public. 'A feeling that the leaders do not trust the public with bad news persists, and in some quarters is thought likely to cause serious trouble.'

In two Regions this refers particularly to Singapore, and resentment is felt that the Government allowed hopes to be raised that the place might be held 'long after they must have known it was doomed'. The complaint is said to be less with the events themselves than with the falsity of the outlined position. 'Continued belying of predictions makes people believe that the men in control are, to say the least of it, ill-prepared.' The BBC interpolation that the Singapore announcer 'sounded as cheerful as usual', and the tactlessness of featuring 'The Road to Mandalay' at such a time, are two among other incidents that aroused caustic comments. Playing up minor successes, such as the destruction of *one* tank or some Italian planes in Libya, and the 'balancing of Admiralty losses with successes' are criticised severely. The early official reports on the Channel 'defeat' tend to be regarded as 'too volubly excuse-finding' and to lend confirmation to previous suspicions that official news is 'unreliable and "dressed up"'.

The Eastern Region alone states that, after increasing adverse comment throughout the week on withholding bad news, full praise was given to the Sunday night and early Monday announcements as being 'brief, subdued and exactly as news bulletins should be'.

9. RUMOURS

From Scotland it is reported that 'rumours are more prevalent this week than for many months'.

From various sources come reports that the following ships have been sunk:

The *Queen Mary* (with American – or Australian – troops on board), the *Queen Elizabeth*, the *Duke of York*, the *Warspite*, the *Nelson*, the *Devonshire*, and the *Mauretania*. (Some reports suggest that delay in announcing the sinking of the *Barham* may have stimulated these rumours.) On Clydeside the story is current that a German U-boat entered the Clyde on February 12th and landed saboteurs at several points. One version says that the U-boat was destroyed.

It is rumoured that salt and cigarettes are to be rationed.

II. SPECIAL COMMENTS

10. INDUSTRY

According to six RIOs, the White Paper on the duties of the Minister of Production has caused considerable disappointment. The powers conferred on the Minister are said to be considered insufficient and are taken to be 'only a window-dressing arrangement and just another instance of half-measures and lack of decision'.

Eleven RIOs report dissatisfaction with production in war factories, and it is suggested that 'the far greater realisation of the extreme seriousness of the war situation this week' has increased the desire for the Government to 'exercise its great powers and to take a firm line as regards the organisation of industry and the use of manpower'.

The following specific complaints continue to be made:

(a) There are further reports of dissatisfaction at 'enforced idleness'. Stories on this topic continue to gain currency and workers are said to 'resent being kept idle when they want to work to help the country'. This idleness is in some quarters blamed on the 'cost plus' system of Government contract, which is supposed to lead to overstaffing by the managements. A similar effect is stated to result from Excess Profits Tax, which is also accused of having caused 'swollen expense accounts'.

(b) There is some reference to the 'misuse of manpower', and the demand for greater efficiency in the use of labour continues.

(c) Dissatisfaction is expressed over the distribution of skilled labour. Cases are quoted of skilled men being wasted on unskilled work.

WOMEN'S CALL-UP: The feeling that 'moneyed women are still not pulling their weight' is reported by three RIOs. There is also 'talk of young girls to be seen in hotels and dances who are believed to be evading the call-up', and of 'women with no responsibilities doing no war work at all', or 'just playing at it'.

On the other hand, women with family commitments who are doing national service are encountering an additional difficulty. The problem of domestic help is stated to be accentuated by the position of able-bodied old age pensioners, who fear that if they take employment they will jeopardise their pensions.

LABOUR EXCHANGE INTERVIEWS: 'The unsympathetic attitude of many of these interviewers' has been reported from the South-Eastern Region. They are said to be too young to handle the married women, while the young recruit cannot understand why her contemporary should hold such a post as interviewer and she herself be told to volunteer for factory work.

It has also been alleged that 'older women who are willing and anxious to do work of national importance are not encouraged at the Labour Exchanges' and that 'servicemen's wives, who have asked for part-time work, have been told to "run away and play"'.

UNEMPLOYMENT: Some concern has been caused by the last unemployment returns which showed a 4% increase on previous figures: 'People do not see why there should be any unemployment, let alone an increase in it.'

11. INCOME TAX

There is less general discussion on this subject this week.

SEASONAL TRADES: In the building and other seasonal trades, it is believed that hardship is being caused by high deductions on low wages. Some interest has been aroused by the scheme whereby a Bootle firm has advanced £5,000 to finance their workers' total liability so that the workers' income tax deductions can be spread over 52 weeks.

POST-WAR CREDIT: Scepticism continues to be expressed as to whether these credits will be placed to people's saving accounts at the end of hostilities.

12. CIVIL DEFENCE AND HOME DEFENCE

FIRE PRECAUTIONS: The new Residential Buildings Order by which every house, flat, etc., is obliged to have, immediately outside the door, a supply of water – not less than four gallons – in containers, has led to some criticism because people believe that buckets or other suitable receptacles are not available.

PIKES FOR THE HOME GUARD: Lord Croft's reference to pikes and their use by Home Guards has been greeted with derision and has caused comment on our unpreparedness.

13. FOOD

Satisfaction with the rationing situation appears in most Regions to predominate, but there are a few local complaints.

FISH: Four Regions complain of the scarcity and high cost of fish, mention being made of fresh-water fish and whiting at 4/- and 3/- per lb. respectively.

VEGETABLES: The shortage and high price of green vegetables are reported from three Regions to be causing concern.

POINTS RATIONING: In one district an almost unanimous protest is reported against the inclusion of tinned peas and beans in this scheme; these being regarded as staple foods and as an essential alternative to fresh greens rather than as semi-luxury diets. In London disappointment was expressed over delay in the issue of tinned fruit to the public under points rationing.

MILK: There is less complaint of the milk ration, but ignorance of the scheme still appears to persist. There are complaints that powdered milk supplies are unevenly distributed.

14. SOAP RATIONING

In general, there seems to be no change in the public's attitude to this restriction from that noted in our Report last week. From several areas, however, and especially from Manchester, reports have been received of heavy buying on the Saturday before rationing was introduced.

In themselves the cuts are not considered excessive, although opinion is unanimous in almost every Region that the ration will be found inadequate in the case of:

(a) persons in 'dirty' occupations, and those needing frequent laundering of overalls;

(b) households in which there are babies;

(c) persons living alone.

One RIO reports the following impressions:

'With regard to the soap ration there appears to be a strong feeling of the desirability of purchasing this particular commodity as soon as possible', (a) lest favourite makes should quickly disappear from the market, and (b) from conviction that stocks of soap are severely limited.

It is felt that some priority classes for soap may have to be formed.

15. CLOTHES RATIONING

There are still complaints from men in the chemical industries that they cannot eke out their clothing coupons; and from people engaged in dirty work which damages clothes, even through overalls.

NO. 75: MONDAY 2 MARCH 1942 TO MONDAY 9 MARCH 1942

I. GENERAL COMMENTS

1. GENERAL STATE OF CONFIDENCE AND REACTION TO NEWS

Public feeling, which was reported last week to be in a confused and unsettled condition, now appears to be calmer and less agitated, and even, in some respects, less critical. The greater uniformity of mood reflected in RIOs' reports, however, is coupled with the suggestion that the majority have settled down into a state of frustration, apathy, and war-weariness. It is stated that 'with the exception of the usual happy optimists, the mood of the people at the moment is more depressed than it has been since the war began'. There is a strong 'feeling of futility', and a belief that 'something is altogether wrong'. The outstanding general trends are as follows:

1. THERE IS A DEMAND FOR STRONG LEADERSHIP: Nine RIOs report a 'demand for strong leadership of the kind that orders rather than appeals'. There is an impression that 'the Government is "footling" when the situation is desperate'. People feel that 'the time has come for a drastic effort to be made by mobilising the entire national effort'.
2. HEAVIER BURDENS WOULD BE ACCEPTED: It seems clear that 'people are willing to bear any sacrifice, if a 100% effort can be reached, and the burden fairly borne by all'.
3. MORE DRASTIC PUNISHMENTS ARE WANTED: There is greater impatience with those who are not pulling their weight, and a demand that 'more drastic action should be taken against moral saboteurs on the home front', not only slackers or those who take part in black markets, but 'all those who are not pulling their weight'.

2. THE RAF

THE RAID ON THE RENAULT WORKS: This is described as the 'high spot of the week' and has been greeted with great satisfaction. It is mentioned by three RIOs as having done more than anything else to relieve the growing 'feeling of frustration'. Even this news, however, 'welcome as it was, people received with restraint. The time seems to have passed when people "threw their caps in the air" when something good was done – instead, the general feeling is, 'It's about time, too', and they are eager for more tangible results.' The raid is also said to have done much to restore faith in the RAF, which had been somewhat shaken by the escape of the German battleships. People are particularly pleased with the raid as

(a) an 'indication that we are dropping our kid-glove policy', and at last taking strong offensive action;
(b) a blow at Germany's war production;
(c) likely to 'bring home to Vichy the dangers of collaboration with Germany'. Little regret is expressed at 'the necessity for hurting the French'.

THE AIR MINISTER'S SPEECH IN THE HOUSE OF COMMONS (MARCH 5TH): Sir Archibald Sinclair's speech has aroused considerable interest. The promise of renewed and heavier air attacks on Germany has been generally welcomed and is reported to have done something towards cheering people; it is hoped that the promised offensive will really materialise.

There is reported to have been some critical comment on Mr. W. W. Wakefield's recent description of dive-bombers as 'obsolete', in view of the use made of them by the enemy, and also of Sir Archibald's statement that large quantities of new American dive-bombers were coming along. There is also some desire to know 'which of them is right'.

3. THE PARATROOP RAID ON FRANCE

Further reports confirm the first reaction mentioned in our Report last week. The following additional points have since been reported:

1. The raid was welcomed as a 'minor proof that our offensive spirit is not quite dead'.
2. 'Too much was made of what was only a minor affair.'
3. It was 'unreasonable to risk paratroops', as the 'results achieved, and achievable, are not in proportion to the inevitable loss in men'.
4. A small minority 'linked it up with the subsequent raid on the Renault works, and regarded the destruction of the radiolocation station as only a part of the larger plan'.

4. THE PROPOSED 'COMB-OUT' OF ARMY OFFICERS

A warm welcome is reported for what is variously described as Sir James Grigg's 'purge', 'spring clean', and 'clearing out of the dead wood' in the army. This is said to have raised him in public estimation, and 'it is now taken as clear that it was Captain Margesson who was acting as a brake on his efficiency'. The only disappointment recorded is at the 'limitation of grades to be overhauled', and people are asking, 'Why stop at Lt. Colonels?' and 'Why not start with the higher ranks, among those who have gravitated to the top by virtue of their seniority or blue blood?'

5. SIR STAFFORD CRIPPS

Although admiration for Sir Stafford Cripps continues, together with the 'hope that he will bring realism to the Government', three RIOs report some decline in the first enthusiasm that greeted his inclusion in the Cabinet. His appointment was 'connected in peoples' minds with radical reforms, particularly in industry'; and although there is some realisation that there has hardly been time yet for changes, the fact that 'the public desire for action has not been satisfied leaves a taste of disappointment'. Some people, too, fear that he has 'been put in as a smoke screen'. It is suggested that 'Churchill's greatest stroke of genius was putting Cripps in a position where he *must* defend the Government, right or wrong, good or bad.'

6. THE FAR EAST

'General depression, but little comment' appears to be the feeling of the majority about the situation in the Far East this week. No new aspects of public feeling have been reported, except that resignation about Java and anxiety about Burma seem to be giving way to resignation about Burma and even greater anxiety about India.

A feeling is reported which, though not applying in the case of those who have relatives among the Forces or the residents in the East, appears to be characteristic of the attitude of many people to the situation in the Far East as a whole. They are said to 'dissociate themselves entirely from it and take the line that "it serves them right", meaning by this the white men, and our administration out there'. With the fall of Singapore, the 'more thoughtful' are said to realise that 'the unchallenged prestige of the white man in the East has gone for ever'.

Admiration and sympathy for the Dutch continue, and there is some feeling that 'it is a pity that they did not have more control of the situation before they were actually cut off, as it is thought that their leaders have more guts than ours. The same feeling exists for General MacArthur and the Filipinos.'

AUSTRALIA: The 'possibility of Australia leaving the Empire after the war' is reported as being freely discussed in two Regions. It is felt that 'she has no confidence in us, and is leaning more and more to the USA'.

INDIA: Widespread anxiety about India continues to be reported from most Regions. Our relations are thought by many people to be critical, and they urge the immediate granting of Dominion status. There is said to be 'growing impatience at the Government's attitude'. Apart from 'not attempting to fulfil the clauses of the Atlantic Charter', it is thought that 'we lost Malaya through the lack of the sympathetic help of the natives, and that we are making little attempt to enlist the wholehearted co-operation of the Indians'. Comparisons are made between ourselves and the Dutch, as colonisers.

Opinions differ as to how well India is protected against the Japanese attack, which is felt to be only a matter of time. Some people believe that 'our forces and equipment in India are very strong, and that the Japanese will not find things as easy there as elsewhere', but others feel that she is 'not protected against attack from the South'.

7. LIBYA

People are said to 'have lost all interest in this campaign, beyond wondering when Rommel is going to spring, and if we are prepared for him'. There is also some speculation as to 'why we can't "get one in first"'.

8. RUSSIA

There is little new to report this week on public feeling about Russia. There are the same 'humiliating comparisons', and the same admiration and gratitude for their continued successes. While there is a slight fear that their advance may be slowing down and that their successes may have been exaggerated in the press, many people hope that the Russians may already have succeeded in 'drawing the sting from the German spring offensive'.

Reports from several Regions indicate that 'Stalin is still the most applauded figure on cinema screens'.

9. CURTAILMENT OF SPORTING EVENTS

Continued interest and discussion are reported on the suggestion that sporting events should be curtailed. Although considerable diversity of opinion is expressed, approval appears to be the predominating reaction, 'so long as any interference is on a basis of equality'. Two RIOs report a belief that football matches and greyhound racing during the week are a definite cause of absenteeism, but at the same time it is pointed out that 'some opportunities of relaxation must be left for war workers if morale is not to suffer'.

10. SOCIAL ACTIVITIES

It is suggested that at times like the present, when there is a call for greater austerity, a bad impression is created by:

(a) 'The giving of public luncheons to distinguished visitors at the opening of a campaign.'
(b) The launching of ships 'by ladies in fur coats'.
(c) The publication of 'frivolous' photographs, such as the one which showed Sir Dudley Pound arm in arm with Miss Vivien Leigh, 'when he could have been better employed at the Admiralty'.

11. RECENT DEVELOPMENTS IN PUBLIC FEELING

A special report from the RIO Eastern Region describes certain 'disquieting trends which have recently become apparent in various sections of the public'. As these trends have been reported in one form or another during the last two weeks by most RIOs as well as by MOI speakers, they are summarised briefly below.

It is pointed out that 'undoubtedly a large proportion of the civilian population are still wholeheartedly and actively forwarding the war effort', just as another section continues either to 'profit from the war', or to 'play no part in the war effort'. Since mid-January, however, 'a number of people have been encountered whose mood suggests a slackening of effort and a feeling of lack of purpose. This mood does not appear to be confined to any definite social classes or occupational groups, and has been encountered in members of the professional, small business, industrial and agricultural classes.'

Though varying considerably in its nature and intensity among different classes, it finds expression in the following points of view:

1. WHAT ARE WE FIGHTING FOR? 'The public has no clearly worked out conception of the purpose of the war. The Russians have a clear-cut purpose; they have a way of living that they think worth fighting for and which enables them to fight well. The Germans are believed to have a purpose. We have only vague conceptions, fluctuating between ideas of holding what we have got and ideas of right and wrong.' (A remark is reported by another RIO as expressing the state of mind of many people: 'We've no cause, no banner, no slogan.') People are not convinced that 'the Britain of the future is worth fighting for'; this lack of conviction applies to the Empire also, 'particularly in view of the questioning now arising over the attitudes of the Indian and Malayan peoples'. 'There is at present considerable and widespread discussion of future plans. Policies dealing with social and economic reforms after the war, are looked for even by the non-politically minded.'

2. HOW CAN WE WIN THE WAR? There appears to be a 'lessening of conviction in our ability to win', and a 'growing tendency to believe that we shall not win unless we deserve to win'. Remarks are heard, 'Why not call it a day?' 'What a futile business this all is, but I suppose we must carry on.' (From London Region this week come reports of people 'unable to see how we can recover the ground we have lost'.)

3. LET HITLER COME! From 'the more submerged social groups are reported variations of the remark: "Let Hitler come; he can't do anything so very bad when he does get here." It appears that those classes, believing themselves to have little to lose, are not prepared to exert themselves for anyone else's gain. It is added that these have no conception of what life would be like if Hitler came.'

4. ADMIRATION FOR RUSSIA: A strong underlying tendency is 'admiration for Russia, giving rise to interest and sympathy in her ideals and institutions'. This appears to arise less from any liking for communism

than from a 'conviction of our own inefficiency, resulting in an increasing degree of admiration for efficiency wherever it is found. This applies not only to Russia but to Germany; there is admiration for a system which creates such efficiency.'

12. BROADCASTING AND NEWS PRESENTATION

Public reactions to the presentation of news are reported this week to range from 'apathy to disgust'. The BBC is still criticised for 'glossing over bad news', and for padding its news bulletins unnecessarily. People are said to be sick of talk, and to be asking for the 'barest facts'. The Government, it is felt, is not making enough use of the BBC to further the progress of the war effort and has 'missed an opportunity of instilling a sense of urgency by making the gravity of the position clear'. It is also reported that 'the war news in newspapers is less read now than at any other time during the war'.

References to the switching-off of wireless sets after the News Summary continue, but there are fewer allusions this week to listening-in to German broadcasts.

Details on the subject of switching off have been obtained by the BBC Listener Research Department by a questionnaire put to General Listening Panels in January. They were asked to say whether, when they listened to any bulletin, they usually listened right through or switched off after the most important items. These panels are not a random sample of the listening public, but a sample of keener listeners.

	7.00 a.m.	8.00 a.m.	1.00 p.m.	6.00 p.m.	9.00 p.m.	midnight
Usually –	%	%	%	%	%	%
Listen right through	82	71	60	73	79	48
Switch off after important items	18	29	40	27	21	52
(Average length of bulletin in mins)	12	12	15	22	23	17

CAPT. GAMMANS' BROADCAST: Four RIOs refer to this *Postscript* as being 'widely praised for its straightforward and outspoken tone'.

BRUNEVAL RAID: Comments vary; 'in some quarters it is felt that too much publicity has been given to the raid', and that by the publication of details useful information may have been divulged. The broadcasts about the raid are thought to have been 'deliberately spun out'.

BBC POPULARITY: The latest Listener Research investigation of the views of listeners on current BBC programmes showed that 77% of listeners are satisfied with the programmes, 11% are dissatisfied, and 12% have no opinion. The investigation was carried out on a sample of the listening public of the usual size, about 6,000 persons.

The following figures show the percentage of satisfaction for the first six weeks of 1942:

Week ending	Percentage of listeners expressing satisfaction
	%
Jan. 10th	81
Jan. 17th	80
Jan. 24th	79
Jan. 31st	78
Feb. 7th	79
Feb. 14th	77

It will be seen that the percentage of listeners expressing satisfaction with programmes has steadily decreased in recent weeks. The decrease is not large, but it is slightly greater than the normal degree of variation.

II. SPECIAL COMMENTS

13. INDUSTRY

Dissatisfaction with production and 'disillusionment at the lack of the sense of urgency in war factories' are reported by twelve RIOs this week. This is apparently connected with 'a still greater call for leadership and for the Government to use all the power it has got to make everyone take part in the war effort to the full – instead of acting as if there were plenty of time'.

This widespread dissatisfaction is attributed to:

1. ENFORCED IDLENESS: Tales of idle time in essential industries appear to be increasing in volume and are reported by ten RIOs. Although there are instances of workers attributing such hold-ups to shortages of material or 'red tape' in Government departments, they tend rather to put most of the blame on the managements, for the following alleged reasons:

    (a) Bad organisation, leading to hold-ups.
    (b) Overstaffing on account of the 'cost plus' system of contract. An instance is quoted from the North-Eastern Region of one munition factory where the staff is said to have increased out of all proportion to output – 'in fact, in one department 75 men are said to be doing work previously done by 16 and completing it in less than two days' working time, thus standing idle for the biggest part of the week'.
    (c) 'Window dressing' when Government inspectors or important visitors are expected. 'In order to give such people the impression that the place is busy, the workers are told to "put speed on".'

2. MANAGEMENTS: In addition to being considered chiefly responsible for enforced idleness, managements are also blamed for:

    (a) Looking after their own interests, 'profiting from the war', and thinking about 'their own position after the war'.

    (b) Not taking the workers into their confidence when there is a genuine hold-up of materials or some good other reason for slack time. It appears that this factor is creating 'a very bad spirit among the workers which is detrimental to production'. They are discouraged, and, according to the RIO Midland Region, 'they do not feel called upon to "take off their shirts" when work is urgent, as it means, in their eyes, that the next hold-up will come all the quicker'.

    (c) Running up costs on Sunday work and overtime – again allegedly on account of the 'cost plus' system – which continues to be much criticised by the public.

3. THE WORKERS: A proportion of industrial workers appear not to be pulling their weight in the war effort; reasons advanced for their slackness are:

    (a) The conviction of some that 'in this war it is a case of doing as little as you can for as much as you can get'.

    (b) Grievances against managements, outlined above.

    (c) The 'sense of frustration' mentioned in the first section of this report.

    (d) Income tax.

4. THE GOVERNMENT: As far as industry is concerned, most individuals seem able to quote instances of 'waste and muddle in factories, on aerodrome sites, etc.; drawing conclusions from such instances in their own locality, they are prepared to condemn the Government as a whole and decide that their own individual effort is not worthwhile'.

PRODUCTION COMMITTEES: From the Northern and Midland Regions come reports that there is some suspicion of managements, where such committees are functioning. Fear is expressed that 'they may sometimes oppose changes that might affect post-war working or side-track issues'. It is felt there should be some means whereby suggestions made by the workers should be considered by the appropriate Government department as well as by the management.

WOMEN'S CALL-UP: The demand continues for:

(a) DAY NURSERIES: Some factories are reported 'to be getting desperate and are asking if they may start their own'. Others, which have done so, report great success.

(b) SHOPPING FACILITIES: The RIO North Midland Region mentions 'a scheme which is said to have been a great success in the few factories which have tried it. By the 'C' plan, as it is called, married women work three days and then have one day off'. It is stressed that 'any scheme which deprives women of the opportunity to do their own shopping is bound to fail'.

(c) MORE PART-TIME WORK.

14. INCOME TAX

Seven RIOs refer this week to discontent amongst workers over the payment of income tax. The main causes of complaint are:

(a) Income tax on overtime earnings. This is said to be discouraging overtime, particularly in shipyards and collieries.
(b) Married women's income tax.
(c) The long-term 'debit and credit system', instead of a weekly reckoning.

15. BLACK MARKETS

Feeling on this question is reported from most Regions to be still rising; it is linked with a 'desire for more drastic penalties for these "anti-social" practices'. One RIO states that, in itself, a term of imprisonment is not thought to constitute a deterrent, and that as 'it appears that many local magistrates are still giving paltry sentences, it is felt that it would be better if all such cases were sent for trial'. 'Evidence that the promises of harsher punishment are being put into effect is widely demanded.' Anti-Semitic feeling is, it is said, again connected with black market dealings.

16. FOOD

GENERAL: Although the majority of RIOs report an attitude of philosophical resignation to the prospect of further sacrifices, and it is said that confidence in Lord Woolton prevails, there are also indications that 'the rationing of most commodities is found to be barely adequate, and a cut would not be accepted without complaint'. It is moreover suggested that greater equality in distribution would be welcomed in view of the 'advantages' obtainable by the 'rich' over the 'poor'.

HIGH PRICES: The high cost of living, and the scarcity and high price of fish, fresh fruit and green vegetables, are reiterated.

POINTS: While the equity of this scheme appears to be recognised, it is felt by many housewives that 'with every extension of the scheme, the wise spending of points becomes more difficult'.

INSPECTION OF FOOD STORES IN THE HOME: The news that Ministry of Food Survey workers are entering housewives' homes and weighing food has been misinterpreted by many people – particularly middle-class women – as 'meaning a kind of Gestapo' on household stores. 'I thought this was what we were fighting against' is a typical comment.

17. CLOTHES RATIONING

GENERAL: Workers whose clothing is apt to deteriorate owing to the nature of their employment continue to complain. Overalls, it is suggested, are particularly apt to suffer in chemical factories among newcomers, who are expected to replace them with their own coupons. Replacement of clothing for growing children is still a cause of concern.

UTILITY CLOTHING: Popular reaction to standardisation appears to have been slow. Such reactions as there have been are favourable. It is suggested that the extension of this principle might be welcome.

18. TRANSPORT

RETAIL DELIVERIES: The policy of a number of tradesmen who have refused to co-operate in local delivery schemes is said by one RIO to be regarded as a serious blow to invalids, old people and workers, and it is hoped will be discouraged.

19. SALVAGE

Considerable criticism is being reported in a number of areas over slackness and inefficiency in the collection of milk bottles, railings, and salvage in general. It is thought that 'the fault is more with the authorities than with the public'.

20. RUMOURS

There has been no apparent increase in the number of rumours this week.

It is said that in one Region relatives of men serving in the Far East have been greatly disturbed by tales of Japanese atrocities on our troops. (This was before the official announcement of the Hong Kong atrocities.)

It is believed that impending rationing is to include salt, coffee, cocoa, flour and shaving soap; the allowances of tea and butter are, it is said, to be halved.

The *Queen Mary* is again reported missing.

APPENDIX TO WEEKLY REPORT NO. 77

'HOME-MADE SOCIALISM'

24 MARCH 1942

In view of a reference in our Weekly Report No. 72 to the spread of 'a kind of home-made socialism' among certain sections of the public, Regional Information Officers were asked whether any similar trends of opinion had been noticed in their Regions. They were particularly requested not to make special enquiries into this subject, but merely to report any spontaneous evidence of these trends. The RIOs' replies, while confirming that some such tendencies are apparently widespread, describe them as 'vague' and 'rather inarticulate'. The outstanding characteristics of this amorphous doctrine seem to be:

(a) Its non-political character.
(b) The impetus it has received from Russian successes.

(c) A general agreement that 'things are going to be different after the war'.
(d) A revulsion against 'vested interests', 'privilege' and what is referred to as 'the old gang'.

(a), (b) and (c) were mentioned in seven out of a total of eleven reports; (d) was referred to in six of these.

The material which follows summarises the main points from the RIOs' reports.

NORTHERN REGION: 'The bias in popular political thought seems to be turning from liberty to equality.' Though many people feel that they are working for the community rather than for their own gain, they are, at the same time, doubtful of an equally altruistic spirit among their employers, who are suspected of resisting changes which might affect their post-war profits.

There seems to be 'a desire, largely unexpressed, for greater social security after the war', and it is stated that 'the success of Russia' has tended to prepare the public mind 'for alterations in the present order of society'.

NORTH-EASTERN REGION: Here it seems that 'there is a more apparent leaning towards socialism since Russia became an ally'. Successful Soviet resistance and 'the ruthless speed of Russia's dictatorship' are contrasted with our own constant failures and 'bureaucratic procrastination'. 'Inequalities of sacrifice and reward apparent in our own system' are also said to increase this leaning towards socialism.

This, it is pointed out, does not represent an 'organised political feeling', but rather an outlet for the urge to get on with the war effort.

NORTH MIDLAND REGION: 'It is agreed', says the RIO, 'that there is a strong tendency towards the ideal of socialism in all classes'. Once again this is said to be mainly non-political.

The following factors are suggested as causes of this tendency:

(a) A levelling-up of classes, resulting from bombing and rationing.
(b) The Russian successes.
(c) The blaming of vested interests for 'ills of production'.
(d) The fear that conditions of the last post-war period may be repeated.

It is stressed that, for the most part, these ideas are indistinct and only formulated by such vague expressions as: 'Things will never be the same again – We'll see to that.' Emotional response to Russian achievements is reported to be widespread in this highly industrialised Region which is 'still suffering from the aftermath of the industrial revolution' and where feeling against the employer class is said to be 'very strong'. It is noted that 'comparatively few people link the Russian form of government with British communism but that increasing numbers may do so if there is no satisfactory alternative'.

Fear that post-war conditions may be a repetition of those which followed the last war is said to cause some scepticism about reconstruction plans.

Finally, 'the relation of socialistic ideals to the Christian ethic is becoming more apparent and, though there is little sign of a rebirth of true religious feeling or of interest in the Church, the basic Christian principles, with the possible exception of turning the other cheek, appear to have greater appeal now than in recent years'.

EASTERN REGION: Admiration for the efficiency not only of Russia but also of Germany is said to be resulting from 'our own inefficiency'. These countries are said to have a sense of purpose, with which are contrasted 'our own vague conceptions, fluctuating between ideas of holding what we have got, and ideas of right and wrong'. It is suggested that among part of the lower social groups the advent of Hitler to this country would not be particularly feared.

Discussion of future social and economic plans is apparently widespread among various classes of people. This tendency does not seem to be confined to those who are politically minded, 'though it might be said to show a bias towards the Left'. This view is thought to be stimulated by a desire for:

(a) The removal of existing abuses (e.g. black markets).
(b) Admiration of Russia.
(c) Greater 'security' for workers.
(d) An extension of reforms in certain hitherto 'immutable' spheres (e.g. Excess Profit Tax).

In this way, it is thought, 'drastic changes' are being thought of which 'might permanently improve post-war Britain'.

LONDON REGION: During the last six months it is believed that 'a new trend of opinion' has gained impetus and is now said to be 'growing like a jungle plant'. 'During the earlier part of the war, socialism developed among people who, thrown out of their normal circumstances, were more in contact with the poorer classes.' But more recently it appears to have increased considerably 'among black-coated workers who are said to be reading and discussing a good deal'. The 'employer class', as well as those who formerly always voted Conservative, are also 'turning to this idea'. Many of them appear to feel that socialism is inevitable, and are resigned to the prospect, as it is agreed that 'better social opportunities for everyone, and improved conditions, must come'.

Stories of muddle, inefficiency and complacency at home are unfavourably compared with Russia's successful methods. Of the USSR – and China – it is felt that 'these seem willing to sacrifice everything, because they have something worth fighting for'. Communists are reported to be drawing the public's attention, particularly in working-class districts, to various 'sore points'; but it is thought that they do not succeed in gaining many converts to their doctrine, though some young people, through ignorance, 'tend to swallow it whole'.

SOUTHERN REGION: No similar trends of opinion have been noticed in this area, but the RIO mentions a growing tendency 'to speculate as to whether our Parliamentary system will be able to function much longer'. He alludes to 'a lot of talk about its being out of date' and suggests the possibility that 'the cult for Cripps may be due to a sort of sub-conscious reversion to the Cromwell idea – an austere but democratic dictator'.

SOUTH-WESTERN REGION: 'A distinct swing to what is vaguely called "the Left"' is reported from this Region. It does not appear to be on Labour Party or socialist lines, but it does seem to be directed against the Conservative Party in so far as this represents the so-called 'Men of Munich', the 'old gang', 'Colonel Blimp' and similar die-hard types. For this feeling it is believed that the continued opprobrium of press and Parliament are partly responsible.

'The effect of the Russian war has also been very great. A large population who until recently regarded the Russians as blood-thirsty Bolsheviks, are saying that it would be a good thing if something along the same lines were introduced in this country.' It is very strongly emphasised that in this Region any party manoeuvring is regarded with extreme abhorrence.

WELSH REGION: Throughout Wales it appears 'Labour is predominant in Parliamentary representation' and the industrial areas especially are already accustomed to local government by Labour. As in most other Regions, admiration for Russian resistance is said to be universal, and to have 'awakened interest in the people and the system of government which have made it possible'.

A general feeling is reported that 'things must be different after the war', and it is said that 'a demand is coming for a new order of things, with socialist leanings, though not necessarily in all cases evidenced by socialist Parliamentary representation'.

NORTH-WESTERN REGION: A belief among ordinary people 'that there should be no restoration of the old order' is reported by the RIO. This view is amplified by the remarks of a contact who writes: 'We are on the threshold of an entirely new conception of economic and human relationships ... in which very large incomes will no longer be tolerated, and the motto "Service before Self" must come into its own.' Some are said to regard Cripps as the 'prophet of a new order which will be international'.

'The Russian alliance and the success of Russian aims' are again reported to have had a 'powerful influence' on opinion, and derogatory comparisons are said to be made between 'the apparent unity, strength and purposefulness of the Soviets' and 'corruption and selfishness in the United States'. Nevertheless, though the working classes appear to be 'keenly aware of the differences', it is not thought that they wish to embrace communism.

Very many people are said to regard the war as a religious one, and 'the essential brotherhood of man' is reported to be a popular sentiment. Those who believe it to be a war between the 'haves' and 'have nots' believe also 'that sacrifices must be made by all "haves", whether as individuals or nations'.

In this Region there appears to exist some belief in the recovery of liberalism, which it is felt may be possibly due to 'a traditional free trade outlook'. In wartime, however, 'political manoeuvring' is regarded by the majority with disgust.

SCOTTISH REGION: While it is stated that 'nothing so definite as "a group" is growing up', political consciousness in this Region seems to be increasing. The three orthodox parties have either 'fallen from grace' or are making no headway, and attention is drawn to the 'awakening' of the Communist Party since Russia's entry into the war; it is reported that 'over 1,200 new members enrolled during the first six weeks of this year'. This RIO stresses the general impatience with or indifference to political party machinery. This contempt for politics, and its accompanying symptoms, is considered by one contact to be 'exceedingly dangerous, for it is almost fascist in tendency'. The opinions reported from this Region indicate a general determination that 'after the war things will be different, and there must be better opportunities for all'.

SOUTH-EASTERN REGION: In the urban and industrial areas of this Region an 'inclination to think socially' is said to exist among people who have hitherto never 'embraced political socialism'. Vested interests, and 'string-pulling behind the scenes', are said to have aroused fairly widespread complaint, and 'there is a belief that our failure to reach a 100 per cent war effort is attributable to them'. There appears to be as well 'quite a strong feeling that there must be something seriously wrong with the existing regime which is held responsible for the country's present difficulties'.

It is, however, questioned whether, in the many rural areas of this Region, any real desire exists for a complete change in the social order. In these areas, respect for 'the parson, the doctor and the old families who are all part and parcel of the locality' is still apparent.

CONCLUSIONS: It will be seen that nothing so definite as an organised political movement can be said to underlie these reported tendencies. They seem mainly to spring from dissatisfaction with 'the lack of Government leadership; hence there arises a groping towards an unofficial and non-party type of social policy'. Five RIOs indicate some desire in their Regions for methods approximating to a dictatorship. It is not, however, stated whether there is any connection between this idea and socialism as an instrument of national policy. One thing is apparently agreed by all: that there must and will be 'alterations in the present order of society'.

HOME INTELLIGENCE DIVISION

NO. 83: MONDAY 27 APRIL 1942 TO MONDAY 4 MAY 1942

I. GENERAL COMMENTS

1. GENERAL STATE OF CONFIDENCE AND REACTION TO NEWS

The level of confidence has been maintained this week, and indeed a further rise in public spirits is reported from five Regions. Our sustained air offensive on Germany and the occupied countries is held to be largely responsible. Other features making for confidence are:

(a) Hitler's speech in the Reichstag, which is regarded as some indication of 'internal weakness in Germany'.

(b) 'The comparative ineffectiveness of the Luftwaffe's blow for blow reprisal policy' on this country.

(c) An unexplained feeling of optimistic 'cheerfulness divorced from the war', due perhaps in part to the weather, and in part to a reaction from the long period of depression coinciding with the last months of the winter.

A feeling of 'almost pleasurable expectancy' is still reported, though it appears to be rather less marked than in previous weeks.

Interest appears to be chiefly centred on Europe, and anxiety about the situation in Burma is overshadowed by events nearer home. Lack of interest in all war news, however, continues to be reported from some areas.

2. THE RAF OFFENSIVE AND 'REPRISAL RAIDS' ON THIS COUNTRY

THE RAF OFFENSIVE: The 'magnificent' RAF non-stop offensive against German key towns and war industry in occupied France is having 'a great tonic effect on people'; profound satisfaction is expressed that 'the Germans are getting a taste of their own medicine in increasingly bigger doses', and that 'we seem able to give them more than we get'. Raids on Paris are still rather less popular than those on Germany.

All evidence going to prove the weight of our blows is eagerly studied, particularly the photographs of damage inflicted at Lubeck, Augsburg and Rostock, and the comparative figures of bomb loads dropped by the enemy and ourselves. The damage to German workers' homes is regretted, but is regarded as inevitable, even with the best bomb aimers.

REPRISAL RAIDS ON THIS COUNTRY: Reprisal raids are expected as a result of our offensive, and satisfaction is expressed that 'the weight and scope of our bombing outweighs the damage here'. They are regarded as the work of 'a foe on the run'. To quote a report from the South-Western Region, where Bath and Exeter suffered heavy raids: 'Our Government's bombing policy is considered right and must be continued.'

The choice of cathedral towns as targets is considered 'typical' and as 'a proof of German weakness in that they dare not come where they know they will get a hot reception'. A minority view expressed is that 'anyway historic buildings won't help us to win the war'.

'Some uneasiness', and in some cases 'considerable apprehension', is reported from Cambridge, Edinburgh, Durham, Lincoln, Oxford, Stratford-on-Avon, Winchester, and Chichester, all of which fear that 'they may be next on the list'. In Reading, too, some talk has been heard of possible raids on that town not as a 'three-star Baedeker' but as a railway junction. The fact that it houses Government staffs – and that Bath may have been raided 'because of the Admiralty' – is another reason advanced.

Sympathy is expressed for the towns which have suffered, particularly for Bath as it is believed to be full of old people and invalids; though in a few working-class areas, the belief that rich evacuees are now 'getting their fair share' is expressed.

In the bombed towns themselves, morale appears to have been good during, and after, all the raids: there was 'no weakening nor wanting to call things off'. From the South-Western Region comes the report, however, that 'perhaps one per cent of uninformed lower-middle-class workers reacted to the first news of raid damage in this Region with talk against continuing the war and against the Government'.

The raids led to widespread rumours along the same lines as after previous blitzes. These were:

(a) Rumours exaggerating casualties and damage. Casualties at Bath were said to be about 17,000 killed, and in Exeter, 6,000 killed. Similar rumours circulated about Norwich.

(b) Rumours of further towns to be bombed. In many cases, 'Haw-Haw' is quoted as having broadcast the names of such places, the dates on which the attack is to take place, and local circumstantial details.

(c) A rumour alleging the breakdown of emergency services in Bath.

Other reactions reported are:

(a) Trekking from the bombed towns in the evenings. A new development is that at Norwich such trekkers, if unessential to Civil Defence, are regarded by the public as behaving in a sensible rather than a cowardly way.

(b) Widespread protests about official announcements that York Minster and 'historic buildings' in Norwich escaped. Such announcements are looked on – particularly by the blitzed population – as 'an invitation to the enemy to return'.

(c) 'The keenest satisfaction' in the Northern Region, 'that on the night of the raid on this Region (30th April) eleven enemy bombers were destroyed'.

(d) The heartening effect of the barrage.

3. HITLER'S SPEECH

Reports from eleven Regions mention that this speech was taken to indicate internal trouble in Germany; this feeling ranges from 'hope that this is the beginning of the end of Hitler's power' to 'realisation that there must be a good deal of strain within the Reich but not serious internal dissension; the Gestapo is still thought to have a tight grip on the German people'.

There is some speculation as to whether this speech foreshadows 'greater ruthlessness in the waging of the war such as gas or bacteriological warfare' or is 'primarily intended to mislead us and lull us into a false sense of security'.

The Hitler-Mussolini meeting has led to little comment. The belief that Italian morale is near breaking point is fairly widespread; rumours that Italy was making a separate peace were reported from Scotland. But the general view is that Germany has Italy completely in her control.

4. THE FAR EAST

There continues to be relatively little discussion of the Far Eastern situation, apart from continued 'uneasiness at our inability to stem the tide of Japanese advance'. The situation in Burma is, however, regarded as 'very grave' by those 'who follow the progress of the war in remoter fields'.

5. A SECOND FRONT

A more cautious attitude appears to be shown by the public this week on the question of the opening of a second front in Europe. While continued and increased demands for action in the West come from some sections of the public, others are more concerned about its feasibility. There is discussion as to whether 'a diversion, not a full-scale attack, would perhaps be sufficient'; and some 'fear that the Government may be led into taking this action against its better judgment, thereby risking a knockout blow to us when our forces are weakened'.

6. THE BRITISH LANDING IN MADAGASCAR

Only preliminary reports of the public's reactions to the British landing in Madagascar have so far been received; these mainly show extreme satisfaction that 'we have at last taken the bull by the horns and done something first'. Other reactions are:

(a) 'It should have been done long ago.'
(b) 'We'll come to blows with France before long – and a good thing too.' Laval is regarded as 'no better than a Jap – i.e. subhuman'.
(c) 'Where is Madagascar?' The 'man in the street' is said to be hazy about Madagascar's position, size and strategic importance.
(d) 'We don't want another Crete'. Satisfaction is mixed with anxiety 'lest we have not enough strength to hold Madagascar'.
(e) 'What about America's attitude to Vichy now?' The official American statement is welcomed, but 'one American warship helping us as a token would have been even better'.

7. BY-ELECTIONS

The return of Independent candidates to Parliament appears to have given satisfaction, particularly to 'the people who have become distrustful of the various party machines, or are tired of party politics'. The results are, in some cases, attributed to dissatisfaction at Government measures, such as fuel rationing; but they are more frequently considered as 'a pointer from the people to the Government to get on with a more progressive policy and intensify offensive effort'.

8. BROADCASTING AND PRESENTATION OF NEWS

SIR STAFFORD CRIPPS' POSTSCRIPT (SUNDAY 3RD MAY): Only preliminary reports have so far been received of public reactions to this; they may be summed up as 'mixed, though generally favourable'. Praise of Sir Stafford's manner, and particularly of his 'restraint and sincerity', come from three Regions. Where disappointment was reported, there seems to have been some uncertainty as to 'what was his real point. He began with the Poles, went on to the Indians, and ended with reconstruction.' Although his clear statement on India was appreciated, some people are said to be 'rather sick of India'. The chief interest appears to have centred in 'his picture of the post-war world'. His 'statement to the effect that the new order would be achieved without reference to class or creed' was particularly liked, and it is said that 'coming from Cripps, people believe that this will be achieved'.

MR. OLIVER LYTTELTON'S POSTSCRIPT (SUNDAY 26TH APRIL): Only four Reports mention this. While some people liked its 'sober realism', others criticised its joint blessing of socialism and capitalism, on the ground that 'unrestricted private enterprise has encouraged the selfish adventurer too much in the past, and that there should be Government control of large-scale private enterprise, to avoid the dangers of monopolies'.

Again this week there has been little dissatisfaction with news presentation in general; there is some criticism of the BBC for 'making too much of minor activities of the RAF', whereby 'incidents given only a small paragraph in the newspapers are sometimes magnified out of all proportion in the broadcast news'. Some criticism is reported from Wales of the broadcast and press announcements of the Commando raid on Boulogne, particularly 'the splashing of nonsensical details such as the ex-policeman's adventure in carpet slippers', when 'we want to know the result of the raids'.

Favourable comments are reported on 'the descriptive talk on what Nazi Germany is doing to the children' (in *Marching On*, Home Service, 30th April); it is felt that 'this is the kind of talk likely to stiffen the morale of our people'.

James Urquhart is not popular, and his pronunciation is thought to be too close to 'Haw-Haw's', particularly over the word 'Jairmany'.

II. SPECIAL COMMENTS

9. INDUSTRY

Public criticism of, and interest in, industry are reported to be dying down: people are 'more satisfied that things are being got on with better'. Tales of absenteeism, slackness and idle time still occur, as also do complaints of 'bottlenecks created through bad organisation', and the 'plethora of Government forms in industry'. The 'profit-motive' and 'cost plus' continue to be criticised. In one Region munition workers are described as 'not anxious that the war should end as they have never been so well off'.

It is said that young workers in particular are only interested in production as a source of income, for which they are prepared to risk both their health and their efficiency.

JOINT PRODUCTION COMMITTEES AND ABSENTEEISM: Two Regional reports refer to Joint Production Committees, 'high hopes' of which are entertained. But it is said that 'miners who attended a Production Council in the afternoon themselves cut the night shift'; and 'when absentees were brought before them, the men's representatives on the Production Council were frequently strongly biased in the miners' favour'. Allegations are made of young miners in court on drink charges 'that if they had money after the weekend's spree they continued to enjoy themselves on Monday'.

10. WOMAN-POWER

While 'continued enthusiasm' is reported in factories adopting the part-time system for women workers, many managements are described as being 'still reluctant' to embark on their training. The idea that part-timers should be used to free women in the distributive trades for full-time factory work is regarded with favour. There is, however, some criticism of 'appeals for housewives to provide billets for war workers and also do part-time work'. These appeals are, it is felt, 'mutually destructive'.

SHOPPING DIFFICULTIES: Two Regional reports, supported by Postal Censorship, confirm the 'very considerable shopping difficulties' experienced by married women in industry; the shops, it is suggested, are not being as helpful as they could. According to Postal Censorship, 'they seem to think they are hard done by, opening at 9, closing at 4.30 or 5, with 1¼ hours for lunch and a regular half day each week'.

In the Manchester area the Lord Mayor's Committee is reported to have 'voted for the late opening of shops on two nights a week'. This proposal is thought to be unlikely to gain the co-operation of shops; one of them taking the view that absenteeism means 'the desire to replace the funeral with some other excuse for taking a rest when income allows it'.

DAY NURSERIES: The care of children continues to be 'a burning problem'; two Regions report the view that 'if married women are to be brought into industry the schools and nurseries must be available in advance'; if women must wait 'for months after they volunteer their enthusiasm tends to disappear'.

11. HIGH WAGES OF JUVENILES

Social workers are greatly concerned 'at the harm done to youngsters' by high wages; these they spend 'wildly in cafés, pubs, and amusement arcades, and in buying cheap jewellery for girls'. They are alleged to 'drink more than is good for them, and then get girls into trouble'.

Girls of 16 and 17 are said to be earning £2 a week for peeling potatoes at camps. It is said that 'they beg clothes coupons so as to "deck themselves with fine feathers", and the rest they put on their faces'.

12. THE BUDGET

The tax on tobacco continues to be lamented in seven Regions; it being generally agreed that old age pensioners are the hardest hit. Two references are made to the decline in the trade of tobacconists; of one of them it is reported that 'his average number of pensioner customers is thirty-one, but the last time they drew their pension he had only one'. This hardship is stated to have resulted in 'a fairly widespread demand for the raising of old age pensions, which have long been considered inadequate'.

13. TRANSPORT

Dissatisfaction is reported in six Regions over the transport problems of industrial workers and country people. From three Regions come complaints of 'short-distance travellers crowding out long-distance travellers'; there are requests for some form of priority system. In many country villages, it is said to be 'impossible for villagers to get on buses passing through, and it will be still worse when it is no longer possible to get a lift in a local car'.

14. THE HOME GUARD

There are requests for a clarification of the position. Civil Defence workers who have joined the Home Guard are said to have 'no clear idea of their obligations to the two services'.

15. THE PROPOSED RATIONING OF FUEL

Further reports confirm the first reactions of the public, mentioned in our Report last week. The attitude of the great majority seems to be one of 'apprehension and annoyance'. The only recorded satisfaction comes from rural areas, where it is felt that 'rationing might give the villages a better deal, as then the Government would have to deliver the allotted amount somehow'; those who suffered from the caprices of coal merchants last winter think that it might be 'better to be in the hands of the Government'.

It is pointed out that 'comment has tended to follow the lines laid down in Parliament and press', and criticism is still chiefly of the Government for having allowed the present situation to arise, and in particular for having drafted so many miners into the army. Particular annoyance has been caused by the great number of civil servants needed to work the scheme; it is thought that it would be better to send them into the army and release the miners. That these requirements are temporary is not appreciated.

Several reports speak of the hardships and discomfort which are anticipated as a result of rationing fuel, and two reports stress the danger to morale. 'Lack of heat would be the last straw.' It is taken for granted that the ration would be smaller than last winter, and indignant housewives ask if the Government thinks they are wasting fuel at the price it is.

Criticism – last week, confined to the Government – now includes the miners 'who are alleged to have made this scheme necessary by absenteeism', and the mine owners 'who are accused of opening up the bad seams and keeping the good ones till after the war'. There is some demand for the nationalisation of the mines.

The terrors of meter-reading and being without gas for cooking husbands' dinners continue to be stressed. Many practical difficulties are mentioned; for example, the position of women with troops billeted on them 'for whom they are *bound* to provide heat'.

16. FOOD

Satisfaction with the general food situation continues; praise of Lord Woolton comes from two Regions, one of which is Scotland.

MEAT: Some disappointment has been expressed that the meat ration is to be reduced, although it seems to be accepted as inevitable. Concern at the withdrawal of corned beef from the market is reported from three Regions; this is said to cause special difficulty in some rural areas, 'where no alternatives are available'. The absence of corned beef and the 'difficulty in finding offal' are said to make meals very difficult towards the end of the week.

EXTENSION OF RATIONING WANTED: The demand continues for goods in short supply to be rationed, or included in points, so as to 'put an end to the unfair disadvantages' to:

(a) Women who are working,
(b) People who have left their own districts, and removed to another town,
(c) People in rural areas who cannot get to the shops before goods in short supply are sold out.

SHORTAGE AND HIGH PRICE: Complaints have been reported on the shortage or high price of the following:

Green vegetables (six Regions)
Fruit (three Regions)
Fresh fish (three Regions)
Sweets (two Regions)

NEW POINTS VALUES: Only one report has been received so far on the increase in points value of certain foods, and this indicates that 'it was taken quietly, but with some dismay'. Some comments are, however, reported on the 'subtle way in which more and more things are being put on points without any rise in the value of the coupons'. People are said to be finding that considerable mental effort is needed in spending their points wisely; more publicity, in the form of a list of goods with their points values, displayed in the shops and the press, is suggested.

NO. 87: TUESDAY 26 MAY 1942 TO TUESDAY 2 JUNE 1942

I. GENERAL COMMENTS

1. GENERAL STATE OF CONFIDENCE AND REACTION TO NEWS

To assess public feeling during the past week, the period must be divided into two parts – before and after mid-day, Sunday 31st May, when the news of the RAF raid on

Cologne was announced. Until then there had been little change since the preceding week, confidence and optimism being widespread, together with some apparent lack of interest in war news. The news of this raid, however, had a 'tremendous effect, and was undoubtedly the most stimulating event for many months'; 'since mid-day on Sunday it has been the subject of universal comment'. As a result of this raid, the high level of confidence of recent weeks – which appeared to many people to be based on over-optimism – is now considered to have a real backing of fact.

Other factors making for increased confidence – though to a lesser extent – include:

1. The power of Russian resistance,
2. Our successes in Libya,
3. 'Increased confidence in the power of the Allies to strike and a conviction that they intend to strike soon', supported by the confident tone of our leaders,
4. News of unrest in occupied countries, and particularly the attack on Heydrich,
5. A belief in the unsteadiness of German morale, confirmed by Himmler's taking over control of the German ARP organisation.

The only discordant note (for the Far East 'still tends to be disregarded') is the coal situation, and in particular the number of strikes; in spite of dislike of the tactics adopted, most people are reported to sympathise with the miners.

EXPECTATION OF THE END OF WAR: The feeling that the war may be over this year continues to be mentioned frequently both in Regional and Postal Censorship reports. It is suggested that this may largely account for the fact that 'interest in post-war reconstruction seems to be becoming more prevalent'.

2. THE RAF RAID ON COLOGNE

Reports are almost unanimous in suggesting that 'nothing has given such a lift to public confidence for many months' as the raid on Cologne. The public's astonishment and awe appear to have been almost as marked as their elation and satisfaction. The scale of the raid, and 'the threat of continued raids on German towns on the same scale has rather taken people's breath away'. Five reports mention surprise that 'our air strength is now sufficient to carry out a raid of such magnitude'. Misgivings that the 'RAF did not appear capable of repeated and sustained attack' were reported to have been quietened when the Cologne raid followed immediately upon the Paris raid, and it may be assumed that any such doubts have been completely allayed by the Essen raids.

Further reactions may be summarised as follows:

OUR LOSSES: These are 'not felt to be disproportionately heavy'. One report even refers to them as being considered 'staggeringly small' and some people point out 'how much greater they would have been if similar damage had been achieved by land attack'.

GERMAN REPRISALS: 'Reprisal raids are expected', but 'Germany is thought to have too many planes locked up on the Russian front to do any large-scale damage here'.

'CITY BY CITY': The message of congratulation from the Prime Minister has been commended, particular satisfaction being expressed at his promise that city after city will suffer in the same way. The demand for a 'special effort against Berlin' comes from three Regions; the wish that Italy may also be heavily bombed comes from two.

THE ORGANISATION: 'The splendid organisation required to make such a raid possible' has caused general admiration.

SYMPATHY FOR THE 'ORDINARY CITIZENS' OF COLOGNE: Some regret has been expressed, 'particularly by older people, that women and children should have to suffer from our bombing; but no one has been heard to suggest that we should limit our attacks on this account', and 'even the most soft-hearted' feel that it is 'the only way, however distasteful, to drive home to the German people what their airmen have been doing in other countries'.

'A REAL SECOND FRONT': A raid of this size is 'accepted as unquestionably of major assistance to Russia'. Many people are said to consider it 'as good as a second offensive'.

THE VALUE OF LARGE-SCALE ATTACKS: While in general the value of large-scale attacks does not seem to be questioned, two reports mention some uncertainty on the part of a very small minority. These people feel that 'raids on ten towns with a hundred planes would be better than a raid on one city with a thousand planes'. A few of the 'more thoughtful', believing that Coventry was in some sort of working order one month after its heavy raid, ask: 'Might it not have been better to send 2,000 fighters to Burma than 1,000 bombers to Cologne?'

EXACT FIGURES GIVEN: Great satisfaction is reported at the 'exact details given of the number of planes used', and the 'very high belief accorded our own Air Ministry's figures' are contrasted with the general disbelief in Russian figures.

THE BOMBING OF ESSEN: Only two short references have been made to this so far. 'Immense satisfaction' is reported in both, 'the more the better' being a typical comment.

'HAW-HAW': According to the Scottish report, 'many people tuned into "Haw-Haw" on Sunday evening, gleefully hoping that for once he would be at a loss, but his statement that the raid on Cologne was a reprisal for the big Russian defeat at Kharkov puzzled some listeners and, though not widely believed, disturbed many. It was considered "a clever twist".'

3. AIR RAIDS ON THIS COUNTRY

CANTERBURY (1ST JUNE): Excellent morale is reported from Canterbury, following the recent 'Baedeker raid'. It is stated that co-operation was very satisfactory between all departments. In London the raid was looked upon as 'sacrilege'; as the cathedral was not mentioned, a number of people are said to have assumed that it is 'down'.

HULL: After the great Cologne raid, 'signs of uneasiness at possible German counter-measures' have been reported from Hull. This followed a wave of discontent resulting from the raid of 19th May, when strong criticism had been made of the alleged weak defences. The scant publicity accorded to Hull compared with that to York was an additional cause of complaint.

According to a report from the Eastern Region, 'the bringing of guns to "Baedeker towns" has had different effects with people of varying temperaments'. Some are said to anticipate attacks; others to feel less concern because 'we know we can hit back'. The raids are regarded as 'more than ever the work of a mad nation'.

4. RUSSIA

The most widespread reaction to the campaign in Russia appears to be a disbelief in the claims of both sides, which is reported in one form or another from eight Regions. Particular points causing scepticism are the Russian figures of air losses, their claim that 5,000,000 Germans have been killed on the Russian front, and their habit of suppressing all place-names in their communiqués. German claims 'are regarded as even less reliable'. Possibly as a result of this scepticism, some confusion is reported as to which side has won at Kharkov. The report from the London Region seems to sum up the general feeling: 'Thinking people of all types feel that it is a crucial period, but the majority display a calm confidence. Over-optimism, although still evident among some people, is less than it was.'

5. LIBYA

Reactions to the battle in Libya are said to be 'rather confused' at present. There appears to be considerable interest but little talk. A 'wait-and-see' attitude is reported to be fairly general, as 'the public feel that they have too often before been misled'. Although there is 'considerable respect for Rommel as a general', he appears, however, to be 'no longer the legendary figure he was in the past' and there is 'confidence that we have now taken the measure of his abilities'.

Some satisfaction is expressed at:

1) The firm opposition with which Rommel's main thrust has been met.
2) Reports of our air strength and the quality of our equipment.
3) The capture of the Afrika Corps Commander.
4) The manner in which the news of the battle has been given, and particularly 'the absence of the Cairo spokesman'.
5) General Auchinleck's remarks about unnecessary form-filling, paper work, and red tape.

There was some disappointment that 'once more the enemy have been allowed to make the first move'.

6. A SECOND FRONT

Interest and discussion appear to be on almost exactly similar lines to those reported last week, and may be summarised thus:

1) Desire for a second front, 'but not until we are absolutely ready'. 'Another Dunkirk would be too awful.'
2) It is already planned and is 'coming reasonably soon'.
3) The Government knows best.
4) Impatience with the Communists and the 'open-at-any-price' brigade.
5) Until the Cologne raid 'RAF raids were not regarded as a second front', but – as mentioned in the first section of this report – there is now a minority feeling that attacks on such a scale are 'a real second front'.

7. THE ATTACK ON HEYDRICH

The shooting of Heydrich is reported to have caused a good deal of interest and to have had 'an effect perhaps out of proportion to its real importance'. It is said to have shown 'the extent of the unrest in occupied countries, news of which was previously apt to be dismissed as propaganda', and the shooting of hostages and the disturbances in Paris are taken as confirming this. 'The persistence of risings in spite of cruel reprisals has excited great admiration and a wish to aid the repressed peoples and punish the offenders.'

One report refers to a feeling that 'the assumption of command by Himmler of the German security services indicates not only the great effect of the Cologne raid but also, probably, serious collapse of morale among the older Germans, from whom opposition to the Nazis is most likely'.

8. VICHY AND ITALY

Friction between Laval and Mussolini over Nice, Corsica and Tunis is reported to be the cause of slight bewilderment and speculation as to the 'possibility of a split in the Axis camp and the downfall of Laval'. Impatience and irritation against France continue.

9. MEXICO

The slight interest expressed at Mexico's entry into the war may be summed up in the words of the report from the South-Western Region: 'Few comprehend what effect her entry into the war may have, but a new ally is always welcome.'

10. FAR EAST

Except for an anxious minority, interest in the Far East seems to be practically non-existent. Belief in the ultimate defeat of Japan appears to be fairly strong, but it ranges from a feeling that she will 'take a lot of beating' to confidence that 'we shall soon settle the Japs when the Germans are fixed'. Dr. Evatt's plea has made people appreciate Australia's needs, but the general view is still that 'we *must* finish off Germany first'.

Such interest in the Far East as is reported relates to China. There is fear for China's supply line, and considerable anxiety and regret that we cannot do more to help.

General Stilwell's comments on the Burma campaign were much appreciated for their frankness and honesty.

11. POST-WAR CONDITIONS

There appears to be a considerable awakening of interest in post-war conditions, both immediate and long-term. The greatest concern is reported to be on the question of unemployment, and there seems to be some fear that 'men returning from active service will be denied a square deal and that people who have taken over servicemen's posts will receive preferential treatment and promotion over those who have made a greater sacrifice'. It is suggested that 'Conchies and munition workers should have to wait till servicemen have picked their jobs', and that 'any army of occupation after the war should be formed of eligibles who stayed at home, and that their jobs should be taken over by men returning from the colours'. Some people think that 'compulsory emigration should be introduced to counteract unemployment'.

Other points mentioned during the last fortnight include:

1) EDUCATION: State schools with equal opportunity for all. The raising of the school-leaving age is favoured by 'many of all classes'.
2) CARE OF THE DEPENDENT: The raising of old age pensions and the removal of economic hardship – in the case of the wage earner and of sickness – are advocated.
3) STATE MEDICAL SERVICES: Many people want to see the state take over all medical services, including hospitals.

12. THE LABOUR PARTY CONFERENCE

This does not appear to have aroused widespread interest, but there has been some comment on the following points:

1) THE ELECTORAL TRUCE: The resolution to support this was the more admired as the truce is felt to 'operate to the advantage of the Conservatives'. There is some suspicion of their 'domination over Labour members', and further criticism of Mr. Churchill's position as leader of the Conservative party.
2) THE SUBJECTS DISCUSSED: Some surprise is expressed at the lack of interest in the conference, in view of the fact that many of the subjects discussed were topics of some interest to the public at the moment, such as post-war conditions. This is attributed to 'lack of faith in party politics, party politicians, and the old pre-war way of running the political machines'.

3) THE BBC: Some criticism has been expressed that the BBC should have given so much time to the conference. Some considered it 'was trying to sell the Labour Party'; others thought it 'killed the conference with too much publicity'. A few people, however, were interested in 'the BBC's new departure'.

13. BROADCASTING AND PRESENTATION OF NEWS

Some satisfaction is expressed at the 'recent improvement in the news bulletins'.

MR. DUFF COOPER'S EMPIRE DAY POSTSCRIPT: Four more reports refer to this. The only reaction not mentioned is indifference, and its mixed reception is once more stressed. While many are said to have liked it, others condemn it as 'arrogant and boastful', as 'jingoism', and as a 'weak imitation of Churchill'. Some people are reported to have disliked it so intensely as to suggest that Mr. Duff Cooper should never be allowed to broadcast again. It appears that those who have 'some personal interest in the tragedy of Singapore' are the most critical and consider him 'the worst possible man to talk to or about the Empire'.

FAVOURABLE COMMENT is reported on the following: Admiral Cunningham's broadcast; the talk by Group Captain Helmore (May 28th); the *Postscript* by a Squadron Leader (May 31st); and the series *Marching On.*

SUBJECTS ON WHICH MORE INFORMATION IS SAID TO BE WANTED include the following: 'The ordinary life of our brothers and sisters in the Dominions and Colonies', Dominion troops being 'appalled at our ignorance' on this subject; the 'root causes of the traditional hostility between the Chinese and the Japanese'; and 'the internal structure of Russia'.

BBC ANNOUNCEMENTS: 'The preliminary announcements of goods shortly to come off the market' continues to be reported as causing grumbling on the part of poorer people, on the lines of 'Mrs. X has bought enough floor polish to last for two years, but we can't afford to do that'. There are again complaints of the inconvenience of announcements being given after the 6 o'clock news, on the grounds that many workers are not home then, or are only just home and are preparing a meal.

II. SPECIAL COMMENTS

14. INDUSTRY

On the industrial front little criticism is reported except where 'the miners provide a jarring note in a happier world'. Some complaints, however, concern the following subjects:

(a) PART-TIME WORK FOR WOMEN: Allegations are made of 'deliberate obstruction' by some employers to part-timers, and the refusal 'to up-grade suitable women so that men may be released'. Part-time women appointed to jobs outside their home towns 'find themselves virtually on full-time work because of transport delays'. Transport and shopping difficulties are stated to be causing women 'to drift back into their homes'.

(b) COST PLUS SYSTEM: 'Among those in the know' there is some renewal of complaints of the cost plus system. It is described as 'the root of the trouble' in the shipyard strike at Leith.

(c) WAGE ANOMALIES: New employees in one group of factories in the Southern Region are said to be experiencing difficulties, as they have to work two weeks before receiving one week's pay. They are alleged to get into debt while 'struggling to make both ends meet'.

(d) JUVENILES: The 'demoralising effect' of the high wages earned by juveniles continues to be reported. Some fathers are 'complaining that their sons are earning more than themselves'.

(e) PROPOSED INCREASES IN HOURS OF WORK: These are criticised among progressive employers and many workers. Mr. Bevin himself is quoted by workers as having said: 'It isn't the hours you work, but the work you put into the hours you work that counts.'

15. THE COAL SITUATION

(No reports have been received since the issue of the new White Paper.)

Widespread anxiety over the coal situation, which in some Regions is reported to be causing 'grave discontent', continues to keep the prospects of rationing and eventual nationalisation in the public mind. While strikes are regretted, considerable sympathy is reported for the miners over their demands for increased pay; the rigours of their ordinary work are contrasted with those of the men in the new munition factories, to the detriment of the latter. The miners are alleged 'to have stood all they are going to stand', and 'unless some drastic steps are taken there will be less coal, not more'.

From three Regions 'a general opinion is that it is up to the Government to settle the dispute by nationalisation'. Minority fears are expressed that something so bitterly controversial may divert attention from the main issue of the war.

In the North Midland Region, Communists are said to be capitalising on existing discontent; a tour of the coalfields by the King or the Prime Minister is suggested.

FUEL RATIONING: People are said to be resigned to some sort of coal rationing; but they are hoping it will be made up in gas and electricity. 'Strong opposition by the masses' would, it is believed, greet any re-introduction of 'a Beveridge-like scheme'.

There is satisfaction at the permission to purchase for storage reasonable amounts of coal, particularly among 'those who have been accustomed to this provident practice'.

16. FOOD

In general, satisfaction continues unabated with the food situation. The following points, however, continue to cause special dissatisfaction and comment:

THE HIGH PRICE AND SCARCITY OF GREEN VEGETABLES: The price disparity of vegetables as between growers and retailers, and retailers and the public, is the cause of very strong feeling: 'lettuces at Poole purchased from a grower at

1½d each were sold at 8d and 10d each'. This is confirmed by Postal Censorship as the following extract shows: 'Veg is not to be got up here, and what there is is beyond our purse in some places ... it's all rotting.'

JAM: A sense of grievance is reported among country people that, having sent their fruit to the Women's Institutes for jam-making, 'they had to buy it back from the shops'. It is also felt that owing to insufficient demand the jam may again not be used. In Wales, a surplus in the shops is reported.

RESTAURANT MEALS: The new maximum price is said to arouse 'sarcastic comment'; some demand is reported for coupons for all food, no matter where consumed.

RURAL MEAT PIES: The rural distribution of meat pies is causing great satisfaction in the receiving areas.

MINISTRY OF FOOD INVESTIGATORS: The 'very zealous' enquiries of Ministry of Food Investigators have been causing resentment in Scottish shops. In one district they are alleged to have 'worked on the sympathy of grocers by hard luck tales'. It is suggested that 'the Ministry should differentiate between accidental or inexperienced mistakes, and deliberate exploitation of the public'.

17. RATION BOOKS AND IDENTITY CARDS

'Continued irritation' arising from the recent issue of ration books is still reported from many Regions: 'the national loss of millions of man and woman hours' wasted in queues is deplored. The Government is accused of 'making people think they would only have two days, or at the most a week' in which to get their new books. On the authorities' side the complaint is, however, made of the public's laxity over identity cards; people are said to have changed their addresses three or four times, and to have 'scribbled all over their cards', causing 'a terrific amount of unnecessary work'.

18. FURNITURE AND CROCKERY

The difficulty and expense of replacing furniture and crockery in bombed areas is reported. The suggestion is made that 'special stocks of crockery should be held for release to towns that have suffered a heavy raid'. The need for utility furniture is stressed.

19. ANTI-SEMITISM

A 'flare-up of the always underlying feeling against the Jews' is again reported from four Regions. In black market operations they are considered the worst offenders; and it is said: 'They rob us while we fight for them.'

20. WAR CASUALTY BUREAU

Concern is reported from two Regions among the recipients of official letters marked on the outside 'War Casualty Bureau'. Relatives at once think that their boy has been injured. The letter begins with the name of a serving relative and only enquires for routine details about his next of kin. 'A little thought' would, it is felt, have avoided 'much unnecessary distress'.

21. NATIONAL SAVINGS

From the South-Western Region the following 'subtle form of blackmail' is reported over the possession of National Savings Certificates by workers disputing for higher wages: 'If you are able to buy Certificates you can't need more money.' Workers are also being told that the Government will not pay up on these Certificates until after the war. 'A noticeable liquidating' is reported from Bristol, where the proceeds are being apparently spent.

22. RUMOURS

It is rumoured in Oxford that our Commando raids are starting from the Isle of Wight. From Luton come rumours that there is a strict postal censorship on letters to and from the Isle of Wight.

Rumours in Northern Ireland of friction between the American troops and the Ulster people are thought to be deliberately spread by the IRA.

A 'whispering campaign' is reported from Scotland about the behaviour of the Australians at Singapore; it is said that they threw away their rifles and refused to fight because of lack of promised air support.

Lyndoe's astrological predictions in *The People* (which has a particularly large circulation in the North) that there will be no invasion of Britain are widely commented on.

There are rumours that 'there is more behind our lack of dive-bombers than meets the eye'. To be without them at this stage of the war is regarded as 'far from satisfactory'.

NO. 90: TUESDAY 16 JUNE 1942 TO
TUESDAY 23 JUNE 1942

I. GENERAL COMMENTS

1. GENERAL STATE OF CONFIDENCE AND REACTION TO NEWS

Events in Libya appear so completely to have dominated public interest this week that 'most other subjects have been completely eclipsed'. People are stated to have been shocked out of the optimism of recent weeks. Disappointment, exasperation, shame and rage are only a few of the very widespread reactions which have been reported. Although confidence in ultimate victory is still said to be strong, it is thought, as regards our immediate prospects, to have been considerably shaken – an effect which is augmented by fears of the 'ominous threat' to Allied shipping, and doubt of our ability to maintain a heavy bombing offensive. A slight increase in war-weariness, not unmixed with defeatism, is reported, and there is a recurrence of the belief that 'we are in for a long war'.

2. LIBYA

While people seem to have been fairly well prepared for unfavourable developments, the sudden capitulation of Tobruk appears to have constituted what, in four Regions, is described as 'the greatest single blow to public confidence since Singapore'. Comparison is made between 'the shining example of the Russians at Sevastopol and our inexplicable caving-in at Tobruk'; although the fighting quality of our men escapes adverse comment, people are anxious to know how this can have happened so suddenly with what is believed to have been a substantial garrison of troops. Blame for the 'Libyan disaster' is being ascribed to the following causes:

(a) THE GOVERNMENT: The Government as a whole, and the Prime Minister in particular, are being criticised for 'the present turn of events'. The fact that Mr. Churchill and General Ritchie 'both gave the impression that all was well seems to have upset people more than anything else'. The Government is strongly criticised for its handling of news, both in the press and on the BBC. 'People are stated to be absolutely fed up with misleading news, saying: "we were led to expect differently".'

The Government is also criticised for 'not learning from the Russian successes in generalship or revising the system of promotion to give modern-minded officers a chance'.

(b) THE GENERALS: The belief that we have been 'out-generalled' is reported to be widespread; our generals are, in a number of Regions, contrasted with Rommel, for whom the public is said to be feeling an increasing respect and 'unwilling admiration'. It is felt that 'our whole Army High Command is out of date in its strategy and is impervious to new ideas'. In this the enemy is felt to be superior, and anger is expressed that our ranks should have been so badly led. In this connection the following comment has been reported from the London Region: 'The best thing that happened in Libya was the capture of five British generals.'

The practice of 'writing up' and of prematurely congratulating generals is deplored.

(c) OUR EQUIPMENT: It is being asked why, 'after three years of war, the Germans should have better weapons than ourselves'. We are criticised for being 'always one step behind the enemy in the question of arms'; many are said to wonder 'whether the men in charge of our supplies are "on top of their job"'. The General Grant tank comes in for strong criticism. It is thought 'good enough for 1940 battles'.

(d) AIR SUPERIORITY: The ineffectiveness of our air superiority is the subject of bitter criticism; it is recalled that 'we were led to believe we had air superiority, yet Rommel was able to inflict a terrific bombardment by dive-bombers'.

In two Regions the need is stressed for 'a resounding victory to make people put out their greatest effort'; it is felt that 'the kind of criticism that is going the rounds today is inevitable after a major military defeat, and that much of it could be immediately stopped by an intelligent broadcast from a senior member of the Government, but by no one less respected than the Prime Minister or Sir Stafford Cripps'.

3. RUSSIA

From eight Regions there are indications that the fall of Sevastopol is not unexpected; praise for and admiration of Russia's tenacious resistance is stressed. At the same time, people are reported to be confident that the Germans will not be ultimately successful; the failure, so far, of their efforts is considered a good omen, and there is some belief that a major engagement is still to come. References to 'the time when the Russians have won the war for us' occur in two Regional reports. There is still said to be a considerable demand for information about Russia, and interest in Anglo-Soviet post-war relations is said to be keen. There are few comments on the Anglo-Soviet Treaty this week, other than satisfaction, which is reported from a number of Regions.

4. THE SHIPPING SITUATION

A rapid increase in anxiety over Allied shipping losses is reported from nine Regions, in seven of which it is said to be believed that bad news is being withheld and the public asking for definite information. It is thought that hints by MPs and other speakers are increasing this anxiety, even, it is also pointed out in inland districts, 'where the dangers of the sea are not fully appreciated', and where complacency has existed: 'The speeches of Mr. Curtin and Mr. Shinwell have brought people up with a jolt and made them aware of the U-boat danger.' Some feeling exists that the food situation is likely to be worse next winter, having regard to the increased strain on shipping; 'It is generally believed that publication of present figures would dissipate complacency and stop waste.'

MEDITERRANEAN CONVOY LOSSES: Concern for our ships in the recent Mediterranean convoy attack is reported from three Regions. Our losses are suspected to have been 'very much greater than has been reported'.

5. THE PRIME MINISTER'S VISIT TO THE US

The Prime Minister's present visit to the United States was at first reported to have aroused considerable interest. Since the news of our Libyan reverses, however, this interest seems to have declined. In five Regions some cynical comments have been reported on Mr. Churchill for having 'skipped off to the States at such a time'.

The purpose of the visit does not appear to have been widely discussed; some speculations are said to connect it with a second front; others with the urgent shipping position. In one Region the loss of Tobruk is reported to have caused a demand that the Prime Minister 'should come home and clear up the mess'.

Renewed talk of Sir Stafford Cripps as Mr. Churchill's successor is reported.

6. RAF OFFENSIVE

A decline of interest in the RAF's most recent raids is reported, as well as criticism of the 'spasmodic' nature of the heavier attacks. Some doubt appears to exist 'as to whether we can keep up the pace set by the 1,000-a-night raids', and a feeling is reported that 'something has gone wrong with our bombing offensive against Germany'. Some disbelief in the 'bad weather excuse' is indicated, and the inclement period is thought to be lasting too long.

There are renewed demands for the heavier bombing of Italy, including Rome; the belief is reported from two Regions that the weight of our bombers would have been of greater advantage if used on the Libyan or Russian fronts, or, alternatively, on the U-boat ports in order to implement an anti-U-boat campaign.

7. THE SECOND FRONT

Doubts and misgivings, caused by our Libyan reverses, are reported in five Regions to have arisen over the establishment of a second front; comments are said to be on the following lines: 'Well, if we can't do better than this, why talk about having a second front?' At the same time the necessity of helping Russia is recognised to be greater than ever; in two Regions the belief persists that 'it is coming soon'.

8. THE FAR EAST

Little concern is again reported over the Far Eastern situation; on the whole the attitude appears to be that 'it can wait until we have given Hitler the KO'.

9. THE MEDITERRANEAN

MALTA: Anxiety for Malta, and fears that our Mediterranean fleet may be now unable to help her, are reported from four Regions. It is thought that the constant air attacks on the island were intended to divert attention from the enemy's preparations in Libya.

EGYPT: Fears are reported that 'Egypt is at the Germans' mercy, and that the long anticipated "pincer" threat to the oil fields of the Middle East is at last materialising'. From contacts with relatives serving in the Middle East come stories suggesting that 'all is far from well in Cairo, where it is suggested that the whole atmosphere is one of luxury and ease, such as was thought to be partly responsible for our failure in Malaya'.

10. POST-WAR PLANNING

Interest in post-war planning appears to have declined sharply during the past week, according to reports from three Regions. 'Adverse events' are held responsible for an increase in comments such as: 'We must think of winning the war first, or we shall be reconstructing ourselves into defeat. We should use all our best brains now for winning, not for reconstruction plans.' Many comments are reported from Scotland on what is described as the Archbishop of Canterbury's 'dynamic peace sermon'; one remark, quoted as typical, is: 'Let's have some dynamic war and less prating about peace!'

There is, however, said to be 'a demand that the fundamental aim, after we have beaten Hitlerism, should be to provide social security'.

11. BROADCASTING AND PRESENTATION OF NEWS

Dissatisfaction – varying from 'strong criticism' to 'exasperation' – with the presentation of the Libyan news is reported from eleven Regions this week.

The following familiar criticisms are made:

(a) 'The raising of false hopes and crowing before victory is won.'
(b) 'The irritating habit' of breaking news gently, by the use of 'stock phrases' such as 'our troops re-forming', 'our forces have withdrawn to new positions'; these are said to imply that 'we were doing things to please ourselves rather than things we were forced to do'.
(c) That the Axis news seems frequently to forestall ours. Examples quoted are the attack on the Mediterranean convoy and the fall of Tobruk.

LISTENING-IN TO ENEMY BROADCASTS: This is said to be increasing as a result of the tendencies (b) and (c).

OFFICIAL COMMUNIQUÉS AND THE PRESS: Although some sections of the public tend to blame the press rather than official communiqués for over-optimism about the present Libyan campaign, others 'fail to differentiate between official news (communiqués), semi-official news (Richard Dimbleby's BBC dispatches) and the messages sent by war correspondents to their newspapers. People have the impression that all news is censored and therefore what gets through can be regarded as "official".'

MR. BEVIN'S POSTSCRIPT (JUNE 21ST): 'The shock of Tobruk' is said to have made this *Postscript* seem irrelevant, and it is asked 'why a Government spokesman could not have given a last-minute "steadying talk" on Libya in its place'. Although many people thought the speech too long, admiration for Mr. Bevin's 'obvious sincerity' is reported from the North-Eastern Region.

II. SPECIAL COMMENTS

12. INDUSTRY

For the fourth week in succession no general criticisms of production are reported. Very little discussion is quoted, and 'the general picture appears to be satisfactory'.

THE LIBYAN SITUATION: Two industrial reactions are mentioned in connection with our setbacks in Libya:

(a) Criticism of our production system, and especially of the Ministries of Labour and Supply, are said to have resulted from reports of enemy superiority in tanks and guns. There is some feeling that 'the Ministry of Labour deals too sympathetically with the worker in cases of slackness and absenteeism'. There are also complaints that 'those responsible for designing our military equipment are continually preparing a reply to a German arm which has already been superseded by a more efficient model'.

(b) 'A general spirit among the workpeople of resentment that the things which they manufacture are so speedily lost by the army', and a falling off in production, are reported from a factory making component parts for tanks and aeroplanes.

WHAT IS ESSENTIAL WAR WORK? A report from an industrial Region (Midland) says: 'Among some war workers there is still a fair amount of non-realisation that they are directly connected with the war, if the particular job they do is not obviously an armament, or if explanations in the factory have not been sufficient.' It is also pointed out that 'the public are prone to say that we must have such enormous stocks of unused ammunition now stored in this country that perhaps we can "sit back a bit"'.

PART-TIME WORK: From three Regions a demand is reported for part-time work, primarily for 'older women, untrained but of the intelligent type', and also for 'persons already fully employed, though engaged on tasks not apparently directly connected with the war effort'.

ESSENTIAL WORK ORDER: Complaints about the working of this order come from two Regions, but with little supporting detail. There is a repetition of the feeling that 'the wage earners are the only victims', though 'employers are also reported to believe that their authority is being undermined'.

The 'resignation of a key ARP official in Workington (North-Western Region) to go to private employment is compared with the position of a miner who can be diverted back to less lucrative work'.

WORKMEN'S TOOLS: 'The almost impossible position of the ordinary workman requiring tools for non-Government – yet highly necessary – work' is mentioned in a report from one Region. It is suggested that 'while the serious shortage is understood … supplies of certain essential tools, such as drills, required as replacements of those worn out should be available, in view of the importance of repairing such necessary equipment as newspaper machinery and refrigerators'.

WAR PRODUCTION IN ULSTER: 'Criticism of Ulster's contribution to the war effort, which was rather marked at one stage, is lessening considerably at the present time', according to the report from Northern Ireland. The chief reason for this is said to be the statement in the Northern Ireland House of Commons by Sir Basil Brooke, Minister of Commerce and Production, which gave a 'most satisfactory picture of Ulster industry in war'. It is considered that 'much of the criticism of the war effort has been due to ignorance of the war work being carried on in the Province'.

13. THE COAL MINERS

'The recommendations of the Greene Committee regarding minimum wages for miners is approved by the general public', according to reports from six Regions. There appears to be a fairly general acceptance of their claim to have their wages brought more into line with those of munition workers. Though the public's sympathy continues to lie mainly with the miners – as opposed to the mine owners – there is some criticism of them for having gone on strike, and cynical comment on the fact that they 'pick good weather to strike in'. Some people ask 'why nothing was done with Mr. Bevin's great powers to control labour'.

Strong criticism, particularly among working people, is reported from one Region over the intention to pass on the cost of the extra wages to the consumer. 'It is felt that this will unfairly reduce coal consumption among poorer people, who can only with difficulty meet the present high price, and it is hoped that the Government will reconsider their decision not to give a subsidy.'

BAD SEAMS BEING WORKED: In Scotland, where 'bitterness and dislike of coal owners' is reported, there is said to be 'a common belief that coal owners are working poor seams now to save the good seams for after the war'.

14. FUEL

Although the fuel situation is still arousing a good deal of interest in several Regions, it is said to be less discussed at present because of the news from Libya and the warmer weather. Points which continue to be stressed are:

(a) Voluntary coal economy is not much favoured.
(b) It might be 'better to introduce restrictions now than risk a crisis later'.
(c) Poor people, 'who had a very bad time last winter over coal supplies', are said to feel that a rationing scheme might ensure their getting a fair share.

WARTIME SOCIAL SURVEY'S REPORT ON THE PROPOSED FUEL RATIONING SCHEME: At the request of the War Cabinet Offices, a survey was made of the public's attitude to the proposed fuel rationing scheme. The sample was designed to give national representation, all the main segments of the population being represented proportionately. Interviewing was carried out during the week of May 26th–30th.

The main questions which this survey sought to answer were:

(i) WHAT IS THE PUBLIC'S ATTITUDE TOWARDS RATIONING AS A DEVICE FOR MEETING THE FUEL SHORTAGE?

The survey showed that 53.5% approved and 35.3% disapproved of rationing. Disapproval was more marked among men than among women. 60% of miners who were interviewed disapproved of the idea.

(ii) WHAT IS THE PUBLIC'S ATTITUDE TOWARDS POINTS RATIONING AS A SUITABLE RATIONING SYSTEM FOR FUEL?

The survey showed that 48.6% approved of points rationing, and 26.8% disapproved. Approval was more marked among people in the lower income groups.

(iii) WHAT IS THE PUBLIC'S ATTUTUDE TOWARDS THE NEED FOR INDIVIDUAL READING OF METERS?

The survey showed that 29.5% had read their meters and 70.5% had not done so. Some 85.3% of women had never read meters; of those who had never done so, 83.4% expressed the belief that they could learn to read them.

15. FOOD

'Spontaneous satisfaction' with the food situation and the Ministry of Food continues to be reported from several Regions. Postal Censorship reports that 74% of 4,000 writers commenting on food do so on the lines of 'we are OK over here so far and have bags of food'. The main reasons given by Postal Censorship for this satisfaction are:

(a) That rationing is 'the fairest way as everyone gets their share; the people with money can't buy it all'.
(b) 'The children of this country get the best.'
(c) 'Our rationing seems to be arranged very cleverly to give us just enough things, so that by careful management we can get as much as is good for us of all the foodstuffs that matter.'
(d) 'The health of England is remarkable after two-and-a-half years of war.'

LORD WOOLTON: Not only is he thought to be 'a wonderful man to do such a tremendous job so efficiently' but is being 'thought of with affection by women'. To quote a rural widow in the South-Western Region:

'There's times when that Lord 'Oolton do do right and times when he do do wrong; but do 'ee tell 'en from me as all us poorer folks be beholden to 'en for all what he do do for we.'

THE NATIONAL LOAF: Some approval of this bread is reported this week, but nevertheless it continues to be held responsible for 'the unusual amount of skin rashes, boils, joint inflammation, lumbago, sciatica, and the vast range of disorders at present experienced'; not to speak of being 'at war with my inside'.

There is also a general impression among the public that wastage of bread has increased since the introduction of the National Loaf.

EXTENSION OF RATIONING: The demand continues for the rationing of goods in short supply, as 'there is no equity at all in the amounts received by different families'. The following cases of discrimination are reported:

(a) Greengrocers are refusing to supply customers who have allotments with fruit and tomatoes 'as they do not buy enough general produce'. (Complaints on these lines were reported in Home Intelligence Reports in July 1941.)
(b) Shopkeepers are only selling tomatoes and luxury fruits to customers registered with them for other commodities.

SOFT FRUIT: 'Real anxiety continues at the possibility of muddle and wastage over the disposal of soft fruit crops. Last year's unsatisfactory arrangements are well remembered and there is irritation at the likelihood of such mistakes being repeated.'

RESTRICTION OF RESTAURANT MEAL PRICES: This is considered 'a farce' on account of the house charge system. From Scotland comes the report that in some restaurants it is now impossible to obtain a meal costing less than 5/-.

British Restaurants, however, are said to be 'particularly appreciated as they give the poorer folks a chance to do what the rich have always been able to do – have meals without giving up coupons'.

16. CLOTHES RATIONING

UTILITY CLOTH AND CLOTHING: From three Regions and by Postal Censorship, women's utility garments are reported to be 'very much liked' and to be 'a pleasant surprise'.

'INSUFFICIENT COUPONS': There are further complaints this week about insufficient coupons for the following:

(a) Certain workers who are not eligible for supplementary coupons. To quote a typical letter on the subject: 'I am worried to death with your Dad's working clothes as you cannot get them without coupons. It takes all his coupons for overalls … I do not think any trade is as bad as the building trade for wearing their clothes out; the shipyard men get more coupons for clothes but building trade does not; it is a very unfair world.'

(b) Growing children. 'It is some job trying to keep children in clothes; neither Agnes or myself have had a new stitch since the clothing ration came out and yet we can't keep them going.' The increase in the number of coupons required for children's shoes is also criticised.

(c) Air-raid victims. 'The meagre supply allotted to blitz victims' is the subject of bitter comment, particularly from Bath after the recent blitz.

CLOTHING SHORTAGES: Children's underwear and particularly children's shoes are said to be in very short supply. From three Regions come reports of a shortage of outsize garments.

NEW CLOTHING COUPONS: There is a general impression among the public that people rushed to buy clothes as soon as the new coupons were available.

CURTAIN MATERIAL: The announcement that coupons now have to be surrendered for curtain material has been welcomed as putting an end to a well-known evasion but has 'aroused regrets about the curtains which must now be foregone'.

17. PETROL

The announcement that petrol saved from the basic ration can be used until the end of July appears to have produced two reactions:

(a) Criticism – chiefly, it seems, from non-motorists – that 'this unnecessary concession postpones for a month the control of the unscrupulous'. It is cited as an example of 'the Government's pandering to the rich'. Some people are even reported to feel that 'the non-issue of petrol to unessential motorists came two years too late'.

(b) Confusion and regret on the part of those who 'de-licensed and de-insured their cars before they knew of the concession'.

Criticism – in each case from one Region only – is reported of 'inequalities in the grants of supplementary rations'; of the 'use on official business of big cars which must be extremely heavy on tyres and petrol'; of the 'waste of petrol by the Services'; and of the petrol concession to churchgoers.

Adverse comment is reported from Scotland on 'the King's attendance at two race meetings in one week with an entourage of six large cars'. The difficulty of securing taxis 'for legitimate purposes' has aroused 'anger that racegoers attending Newmarket should park their cars in Newmarket or neighbouring towns and take taxis to the course'.

18. HOLIDAYS AT HOME

There appears to be a persistent feeling in some quarters that 'the Government should have done more than request people to take holidays at home', and that 'the rich, the idle, the selfish' and 'the professional classes' will not comply. Reports from two Regions mention appreciation for the efforts that some local authorities are making 'to brighten up towns' so as to 'enable workers to have enjoyable holidays', and open-air dancing in Princes Street Gardens is said to be 'a huge success'. In spite of this, however, the Scottish report says that 'a special enquiry shows that workers are arranging to holiday away from home as far as possible'. A movement to withdraw savings, which is reported from one of the largest factories in the South-Western Region, is believed to be accounted for by the arrival of the holiday season.

19. CIVIL DEFENCE

There is some doubt about the relative claims of (a) Home Guard duties, (b) fire-watching at home and (c) fire-watching at business premises. Doubt is expressed as to whether Home Guard service takes precedence over fire-watching duties. People who are required to fire-watch at work, in addition to doing so at home, feel that the duties are unevenly distributed, especially where there is considerable variation in the hours of duty. There are also complaints that fire-watchers are drawn from insufficiently manned parties in residential districts (which may be near danger zones) to fire-watch on business premises.

20. VADS AND ATS

Serious apprehension is reported from three Regions at the Army Council's proposal to merge mobile VAD detachments with the ATS. This objection is said to be 'not *entirely* snobbish', but to be due mainly to 'the desire to remain under feminine direction and to preserve their special nursing status, as well as to a feeling that VADs with several years' service ought not to be demoted below conscripted ATS'. The VADs, it is pointed out, 'have their own uniform and traditions which they do not wish to surrender'.

21. BOOKS

Reports from two Regions mention recent comments on the fact that while 'trash is still published, serious books are hard to obtain'. The report from the Eastern Region, based on 'comment received from public libraries and library users, bookshops and purchasers of books', points out that 'a trend towards more serious reading has coincided with a reduction in the supplies available of the former 6d. and 1s. books on serious subjects. Stocks of cheap fiction are comparatively more plentiful, and purchases of these are being reported "simply because nothing else can be had".'

NO. 92: TUESDAY 30 JUNE 1942 TO
TUESDAY 7 JULY 1942

I. GENERAL COMMENTS

1. GENERAL STATE OF CONFIDENCE AND REACTION TO NEWS

The depression following our defeat in Libya and Egypt shows some signs of lifting as a result of the check to Rommel's forces at El Alamein. This improvement in public spirits – reported from eleven Regions – ranges from 'being afraid to hope' to 'a considerable measure of confidence', but it is coupled with uneasiness or anxiety which is attributed to:

(a) A feeling that 'there is something wrong somewhere in the direction of the war', and that 'all is not well with our supply arrangements'.
(b) The news from Russia. Confidence in Russia's powers of resistance, however, appears to be unshaken.
(c) The continued threat to Egypt, and particularly to Alexandria.
(d) The belief that 'the war will now drag on for a long time'.

Some 'pessimistic and even defeatist talk' is reported from the South-Western Region.

Although the debate on the motion of 'no confidence' aroused a good deal of interest, there was little strong feeling expressed about it. Reports from two Regions suggest, however, that it may have 'cleared the air'.

2. NORTH AFRICA

This front continues to be the main subject of interest.

EGYPT: At the beginning of the week our retreat was followed with anxiety and deep concern and 'many people were prepared for the fall of Alexandria and the early loss of Egypt'. Since then, news of the check to Rommel's forces at El Alamein has been received with cautious relief and 'it is felt that there are now real grounds for hope that further disasters may be avoided, and Rommel held'. The public are, however, 'afraid to be optimistic and are waiting with "their fingers crossed" for the results of the present battle'.

Satisfaction is expressed with 'the increased co-operation between the RAF and the army', and with the 'heroic efforts' of the RAF as well as with the fighting qualities of our men.

Some suspicion is reported from two Regions of Egypt's passive attitude. 'The blighters will let us down if they dare' says one report.

LIBYA AND TOBRUK: The bewilderment felt over our Libyan defeat is said to have been increased by Mr. Churchill's statement that both he and the High Command were surprised at the loss of Tobruk. There is some talk of treachery and a story is circulating in the London Region that 'Tobruk was prematurely surrendered by General Klopper because of anti-British sympathies'. Comparison is also made between 'the holding of Tobruk by Australians and New Zealanders and its fall when South Africans were there'. But blame for our Libyan disasters is not so much attached to individuals, as to the following factors:

(a) Our equipment.
(b) General Wavell's transfer to India.
(c) The 'die-hard attitude' of Service chiefs and the War Office.
(d) 'High and low having too good a time in Cairo and Alexandria.'
(e) 'Politicians overrule soldiers, and the General in Command is denied local freedom of action.'
(f) Lack of sufficiently ruthless Commanders.

3. THE MOTION OF 'NO CONFIDENCE'

The result of the debate on the conduct of the war seems to have been regarded as 'a foregone conclusion'. It appears, however, that the overwhelming vote for the Government is not considered to reflect the amount of criticism which exists. 'The failure of our production organisation to match the German arms, and the story of the shortcomings of the equipment of the Eighth Army', have caused disquiet and 'have increased frustration and bewilderment'.

On the other hand, 'there are signs of developing intolerance at this washing of a lot of dirty linen which serves no useful purpose, but only depresses the spirits of the British public and encourages the enemy'. It seems also to be fairly widely felt that the debate was 'a waste of valuable time which could be used more profitably in considering constructive measures for the more effective prosecution of the war'. It is suggested that such debates tend to lower the prestige of Parliament.

While little sympathy is reported for the 'enemies of the Prime Minister', praise of Mr. Aneurin Bevan is reported from the Northern Region. 'Approval for the frankness of other speakers and some praise for Sir John Wardlaw Milne' are reported from the North-Western Region, though his proposal for the Duke of Gloucester's promotion is said to have caused in various Regions 'blank astonishment', 'derision' and 'uncomfortable speculation' as to what was in his mind.

4. THE PRIME MINISTER

Mr. Churchill's position as 'the obvious leader of the people' appears to have been unaffected by the debate, and he 'still inspires widespread loyalty'. Some criticism is still, however, reported on familiar lines:

(a) That the post of Minister of Defence places too great a strain on him.
(b) That he continues to take responsibility for 'the errors of his second-rate colleagues'.

5. RUSSIA

Signs that the long-awaited German offensive may have begun have turned public attention once more to the Russian front. The fall of Sevastopol was expected and has been attended by 'glowing admiration for the defenders', whose prolonged resistance is contrasted with the sudden capitulation of Tobruk.

It is realised that the struggle on the Russian fronts is serious and intense, but there appears to be little doubt 'in the minds of most people that the Russians will not be beaten and will always be able to stage a come-back'.

6. RAF OFFENSIVE

The public is still reported to be mystified at the need for the RAF to pay return visits to Bremen after our thousand-bomber raid: it is asked why, 'when so few planes can do so much damage here, isn't one visit from us as effective?'

Some disappointment is also expressed that 'the thousand-bomber raids on Germany haven't been kept up'.

7. SHIPPING LOSSES

Concern continues to be reported about our shipping losses and 'the hope is expressed that it may be possible to make some official statement on the matter'.

8. ANGLO-AMERICAN RELATIONS

A report from Scotland attributes growing confidence in the US war effort to the following factors:

(a) The Londonderry naval base; two Regions, however, criticise publication of this news as 'an open invitation to Hitler to bomb Londonderry'.

(b) The increased number of US troops in Great Britain.

(c) The *Wasp*'s Malta exploit.

(d) The presence of US troops in the Middle East.

(e) A feeling that US help 'may come in time'.

In contradiction of the last factor there appears to be in other Regions some scepticism of official promises about forthcoming US aid; it is being said that 'they talk too much and do too little', and that 'a tank in Libya is worth two in Chicago'. The fear is mentioned that the US press may cause strained relations between the two countries unless they restrain their denunciations and carping 'criticism of England'.

US TROOPS: From the North Midland Region there are indications of some difficulties over the treatment of US coloured soldiers: 'The kindness meted out to coloured Americans by their British hosts is said to be resented and misunderstood by the white Americans who do not mix with them.' Guidance is asked for in Northampton on this subject, and it is suggested that it would be useful to local authorities, hotels, canteens, etc.

9. THE SECOND FRONT

There appears to be less talk this week about a second front and some feeling is reported, since the loss of Libya, that it would be useless to start one 'when we can't hold what we've got'.

Some sections of the public, however, continue to desire a second front, 'as the only way of really getting at Germany and ensuring Russia's continued resistance'.

10. POST-RAID FEELING IN NORWICH

At the request of the Regional Commissioner, the Senior Assistant Officer, Eastern Region, visited Norwich on 2nd July to discover whether recent raids had produced any demand for the town to be made an evacuation area. The raids occurred on April 27th and 29th, May 8th and June 26th/7th. On the night of June 29th, however – although there were apparently no raiders – the alert was sounded, and as during a heavy thunderstorm a number of balloons caught fire or were struck down, some people thought a raid had occurred.

It appears that although 'morale was reported by everyone to be higher than ever', the raid on June 26th/7th and the thunderstorm on the 29th made people 'aware of the limit of their endurance'. Those spoken to 'were noticeably more fatigued and shaken' by the recent raids than after the earlier and more severe ones, and it is thought that 'a considerable deterioration of the situation might ensue if there should be further raids'.

The main conclusions of the report may be summarised as follows:

EVACUATION: The people interviewed, with one exception, all have children of their own or had children in their charge during the raids. None of these people indicated a wish to send their children away from Norwich, and no one referred to anyone else having expressed this desire. Some had, however, sent children for a brief rest into the neighbouring country, but in each case the child had already returned home. People's attitude to the question of evacuation is said to be influenced by the following points:

(a) RAIDS ON NEIGHBOURING RECEPTION AREAS in remote parts of East Anglia have been so frequent that people in Norwich are not convinced that evacuation gives immunity from bombing. It is suggested that the 'evacuation of houses in the immediate vicinity of a likely industrial target' is the most desirable type of evacuation.
(b) THE TENSIONS ARISING FROM THE BREAK-UP OF THE FAMILY are recognised, special stress being laid on the desirability of keeping the family unit together.
(c) THE POSSIBLE FRICTIONS CONNECTED WITH BILLETING.

UNEMPLOYMENT: As a result of 'considerable industrial damage' some sections of the population are said to fear being either unemployed or compulsorily moved to other work.

INCENDIARIES V. HIGH EXPLOSIVES: Considerable divergence of views is reported on the 'comparative horror' of incendiary and high explosive raids. 'The more educated' claimed that the fire-bombs on June 26th/7th had a far less shattering effect on the community than had the earlier raids in which HEs predominated, while 'the more ignorant' said they found the fire raid much more difficult to stand. 'Watching a row of their own homes burning' seems to have a far worse effect on the poorer families 'than to emerge from shelter ... and find one house has been erased'. Considerable criticism of the NFS was expressed, from a belief that 'they concerned themselves with industrial fires at the expense of fires in private houses'.

Much controversy centred round the question whether fire-watchers should, or should not, take shelter during the zenith of a raid; in practice the deciding factor in keeping a party at its post seems to have been the 'presence of a strong personality as leader'.

REASSURING FACTORS: The following factors are mentioned as having a reassuring influence:

(a) SHELTERS: The public appear to place considerable confidence in the 'ample shelters provided for all in close proximity to their homes', and praise for street shelters and Anderson shelters was high. In view of the great damage done by fire, the Morrison shelters were regarded by many people as 'worse than a trap'. One advantage of an Anderson shelter is that it combines 'effective shelter with an active watch against fire in the shelterer's house'.
(b) THE BALLOON BARRAGE: This is said to have given 'very considerable reassurance' to all classes, and there was comment that 'nothing could be more damaging to morale than its removal'.

11. BROADCASTING AND PRESENTATION OF NEWS

Criticism of news presentation – chiefly with reference to Libya – continues, though it appears that 'the earlier intense irritation' has subsided to some extent, and that 'criticism is perhaps less violent than last week'. 'Disbelief in the news as given over the wireless or through the press' is widely reported, either directly or by implication. The demand is for 'plain facts' and for 'dispassionate and factual statements', a desire which is summed up in a Postal Censorship quotation: 'Tell us the truth – tell us we're in a damned tough spot and we'll get out of it. But tell us we might be worse off, and we'll sit back and wait until it happens.'

Though 'reports still stress that rosy presentation of the Libyan battle news contributed largely to the severity of the fall in the level of public spirits', dissatisfaction with news presentation for being too optimistic seems to have died down almost completely, and one Regional report now refers to 'appreciation of the more soberly worded communiqués from Egypt'.

Criticism appears to be made chiefly on the following grounds:

(a) MINIMISING OF BAD NEWS: There are complaints of 'the flattering platitudes of the news and papers, minimising everything' and 'making one believe nothing they say'. There is said to be a constant demand for news 'to inspire rather than to produce complacency, and for no spoon-feeding of syrup in preparation for the release of bad news' ... As another writer quoted by Postal Censorship says: 'We writhe under sweet words of consolation.' According to the Scottish report, at a time when the early loss of Egypt was expected, people were speculating bitterly 'on the way this would be put over' anticipating that 'the BBC and MOI have their communiqués already prepared telling us that Egypt, after all, is of very little importance'. People are reported to ask why the news bulletins on the Home Service 'quietly alter miles to kilometres as the Germans approach Alexandria', which seems like 'an attempt to make the bad look better'.

(b) INDISCRETION: It is felt that 'we give away too much information' (some people are said to believe that 'MPs are particularly prone to this error'). The BBC is criticised for 'allowing the world to know on Wednesday night, July 1st, in the midnight news, that the House was still sitting'. It is complained also that the BBC 'gives information to the enemy by stating that troops are in certain areas, and by disclosing too much information about war industries'. There are complaints, too, that 'to announce the successful arrival of a convoy at Malta is nothing less than an invitation to the enemy to bomb the ships in port'; 'those with friends or relatives in the Navy and Merchant Service' are said to 'lay particular stress on this point and urge that nothing should be disclosed concerning the arrival of convoys until the ships have been unloaded and have dispersed again'.

(c) PADDING AND REPETITION: There are demands for 'terser bulletins' and the 'cutting out of irrelevant detail'. Owing to 'the repetitive quality' of the BBC news, the morning bulletins are said to be preferred to the evening.

BBC AND PRESS COMPARED: There is some tendency since the loss of Tobruk to think that the BBC smacks too much of propaganda and 'gives only half the truth', and is 'no more reliable than the news we get in the papers'. (It may be of interest to compare this with the findings of BBC Listener Research, on the public's estimate of the relative standings of BBC news bulletins and the press, mentioned in our report No. 88, 11th June; in this it was stated that 'the great majority consider the BBC news bulletins more reliable than the press'.) 'The press, on the other hand, is criticised for being "exaggerated" and "extravagant in reporting either advances or reverses".' The public is said to be 'bewildered by the diverse accounts of the fighting given by the military correspondents on the war fronts', and 'completely contradictory versions of the same incident are said to have been given in different papers'.

LISTENING-IN TO ENEMY BROADCASTS: This continues to be reported on the grounds that (a) 'You get the news earlier and undisguised', and (b) the names of men reported missing may be included in the lists of prisoners of war.

BBC ANNOUNCERS: Some criticism is reported of the 'Everything-in-the-garden-is-lovely voices' of the BBC announcers, which are unfavourably compared with the 'deep, powerful and convincing tones of American news announcers'. Two Regional reports, however, refer to favourable comment on 'the wonderful diction' and 'good speaking personality' of the new announcer, Mr. Robert Robinson.

II. SPECIAL COMMENTS

12. INDUSTRY

On the whole, little criticism of production is reported this week, but from three Regions disappointment and discouragement are reported among war workers because 'we are apparently turning out duds'. It is thought that this refers not to specific examples of faulty work but implies that organisation throughout the whole arms industry is being widely questioned. Only one case is reported of a drop in production; this comes from the Midland Region, where the news from Libya is alleged to have caused in one factory a 37% drop in output of shells; in spite of some improvement, a 20% drop is still reported.

SHIPYARDS: Some criticism is reported of idleness in shipyards. In the Falmouth area reserves of labour are said to be 'kept in idleness between repairing spells'. In one yard, where 3,000 men are said to have such periods of idleness, the effect on the population is described as very bad.

According to the Scottish report, 'people living near shipyards are wondering why these are idle at weekends'. Workmen at Rosyth Dockyard are thought to believe that 'as quotas frequently under-estimate what the men can do, the "quota" system leads to slackness'.

WAGE RATES: From two Regions dissatisfaction among wage earners is reported. The increased miners' wage is said to have been very well received, and the public 'now definitely expect increased production and peace in the industry'. The miners are, however, said to be not completely satisfied, and in the North-Eastern Region an ever-increasing demand is reported 'that the grades of all workers should be classified, and that basic rates of pay should be standardised'.

From London and Wales, there is some recurrence of stories that 'scores of people get paid high wages for doing next to nothing'.

13. WOMAN-POWER

Following the call by the Minister of Labour for increased use of women in war industries, and the recent campaigns for the recruitment of women, public interest in the subject has been revived. While it is felt that, on the whole, the situation is fairly satisfactory, criticism is still voiced along familiar lines:

(a) THE EVASION OF RESPONSIBILITIES BY YOUNG MARRIED WOMEN, whom, it is said, 'nothing short of compulsion is likely to recruit'. Against this it is pointed out in the London Region that some married women have found increased working hours 'the last straw', as previously 'they had just been able to cope with home affairs as well'.

(b) INSUFFICIENT 'DEMANDING' BY THE GOVERNMENT: Volunteers and others are still of the opinion 'that a far greater measure of compulsion is needed'.

(c) UNSUITABILITY OF WOMEN INTERVIEWERS: This complaint is again renewed. During the Sheffield campaign 'girls with painted faces and fingernails, sipping cups of tea', were considered 'not the type of interviewer to appeal to local working women'.

(d) INSUFFICIENT EXPLANATION TO WORKERS OF THEIR JOBS' RELATION TO THE WAR EFFORT.

(e) THE DELAY IN CALLING UP GROUPS OF WOMEN WHO HAVE ALREADY REGISTERED.

(f) FULL-TIME V. PART-TIME WORKERS: Certain types of full-time workers tend to ask why they should be kept on full-time where part-timers are now employed. Some signs are reported of victimisation of part-timers by full-time colleagues on this account.

14. FOOD

General satisfaction with the food situation continues to be reported from several Regions and is confirmed by Postal Censorship.

POULTRY RESTRICTIONS appear to have provoked resentment and criticism in five Regions among 'backyard poultry keepers' who feel they should have been given notice before the spring breeding season and before winter preparations had been made. In accordance with the Government's policy to encourage the keeping of backyard poultry, many poor families are reported to have 'spent much money on buying birds and equipment at high prices', and now 'money, time and trouble' are said to have been 'thrown away'. There appears to be some confusion about the meaning of the order itself, which 'does not apply to those able to feed their chickens without buying food'; among those who cannot do so, 'an enormous killing of birds' is predicted from one Region. The suggestion that neighbours should surrender their shell egg coupons is considered unpractical 'because of the likelihood of disagreement when supplies are short'.

In the South-Western Region it is suggested that the new restrictions will bring special hardship to families in rural areas where fish and unrationed cooked meats are 'scarce and almost unobtainable', and where housewives rely on eggs, especially for children. From two Regions it is reported that the public favour the restrictions.

FRESH FRUIT AND TOMATOES: Complaints about the scarcity and unequal distribution of fresh fruit and tomatoes continue to be reported from five Regions and by Postal Censorship. Exception is taken to the fact 'that so much fresh fruit should be allocated to jam and canned fruit manufacturers' when it would be 'more desirable to eat fruit in its fresh condition'. There are continued complaints of unfair discrimination by some shopkeepers against 'newcomers', of favoured customers being allowed 'to place orders every day for strawberries', and of retailers refusing to 'sell tomatoes to any but registered customers'.

NATIONAL BREAD AND WHEATMEAL FLOUR: There are continued complaints of digestive and stomach trouble attributed to the national bread, and from two Regions come reports of housewives sifting wheatmeal flour to obtain 'something approximating to white flour'. According to reports from one Region the rougher unsifted part is fed to poultry.

MEAT PIES AND RATIONS FOR AGRICULTURAL WORKERS: Difficulties in the distribution of meat pies are reported from three Regions, but it is said that where distribution is done locally by the WVS and Women's Institutes it is more successful and popular than when it is carried out by local authorities. In Oxfordshire the scheme is said to be working well. There is some suggestion that extra meat and cheese rations for farm workers would be a better solution, and in Dorset the Agricultural Workers' Union have put this forward as a definite demand, but it is said that some wives support the meat pie scheme because it adds to their husbands' rations and saves their doing 'extra cooking'.

From the South-Eastern Region come complaints that tea and fat rations for farm workers are inadequate, the latter being so because of the workers' sandwich meals.

CHILDREN'S RATIONS: Some feeling among women is reported from two Regions that the under-fives' rations are too generous, and that older children do not get enough. It is suggested, for instance, that babies do not need 'orange juice, oranges and four eggs a week', and that an allowance of oranges for the 5-to-14-year-olds would be welcome.

15. TRANSPORT

Allegations of 'intolerable conditions' on trains 'packed with holiday-makers', petrol waste and evasion of restrictions, and of the inadequacy of bus services, particularly in rural areas, once again form the subject of much criticism and complaint. In the North-Eastern and North-Western Regions, as well as in Wales, liberal abuse of petrol is alleged; in Sheffield it is said that 'the first week in July has brought no vast difference in the number of private cars on the road', and much indignation has been caused by the misuse of petrol by hirer-drivers of cars and taxis.

HOLIDAY TRAVEL: What is described as 'the complete failure of the Ministry of War Transport to plan ahead for the holiday period and ration travel' is the subject of widespread comment, causing serious apprehensions of 'a breakdown in passenger-train traffic when the peak period, August, is reached'.

In certain parts of the country the running of special trains is reported to be having a disturbing effect among workers: 'Local authorities are furious.' Many people had apparently planned to stay at home in response to the Government's request, and although there are signs that they are doing so, there is anger 'that the Government should not know its own mind on a point of this sort, and fury at tales of black markets in holiday railway tickets'.

Serious inconvenience to official or essential travellers by the movements of holiday-makers is again reported; from three Regions the desirability of priority passes or vouchers is stressed.

16. FUEL

WASTE OF FUEL ORDER: The reception of this order is reported on the whole to have been favourable. The public is stated to be willing to assist the Government, though in one Region there are reported 'tendencies to treat voluntary economies lightly'. Concern is also reported 'at the possibility of a repetition of a shortage of coal during the winter (particularly for occupants of upstairs flats)'.

In three Regions there is criticism of 'the great waste of light' in works, stores and public places; the following instances are given:

1. The Conference Hall, County Hall, for the lunch-time War Commentary.
2. Harrods.
3. Barkers' bargain basement.
4. Lighting of display boards and public buildings.

From three Regions there is approval of Major Lloyd George's fuel broadcast: 'a fair and reasonable approach to a difficult subject'.

17. PUBLIC HEALTH

While there appears to be no widespread apprehension on the subject, there seems to be some evidence for the belief, reported in three Regions, of a deterioration of the nation's health. A doctor is reported as saying that 'medical men all over the country will confirm that, while there is an absence of serious illness at the moment, the majority of the population are distinctly below par. The majority of practitioners are frequently refusing to issue certificates of unfitness although on pre-war standards they would have done so.'

SMALL-POX IN GLASGOW AND SWINDON: Outbreaks of small-pox in Glasgow and Swindon are reported to be causing agitation and alarm in the former, and anxiety in the latter locality. In Glasgow 'huge queues are to be seen outside doctors' surgeries for vaccination and, in spite of public announcements about the number of cases, rumours are current that the number is greater than that published'. In the suburbs, news of almost any illness in a street sends all the neighbours to clinics to be vaccinated.

18. THE PROPOSED CONCENTRATION OF RETAIL SHOPS

Three Regional reports refer to feeling about the proposals of the Craig Henderson Committee for the wartime 'concentration of the retail non-food trades'. On the whole, opinion appears to be divided, with 'a larger proportion against than in favour' of the proposals, but there is no evidence to suggest that the public – as opposed to the retail trade – is showing much interest in them. From the London Region, however, some apprehension is reported on the part of those who look to the private shopkeeper 'for that personal service which is peculiar to the small trader'. Some traders are said to feel sceptical of 'official assurances about post-war opening', as it is felt that 'conditions may make it impossible to implement them'.

19. RUMOURS

Rumour-mongers have again been active in retailing alleged incidents between US and British troops. For example, American soldiers are reported to be saying that 'yellow' is a fourth colour of the Union Jack. Another example – reported from Reading, Winchester and London – is of an American asking to be served with a drink 'as quickly as you left Dunkirk'. Other rumours relate to the large sums of money which American troops are thought to possess. It is suggested in one Region that these rumours are being 'deliberately put about'. In Oxford many stories are reported to be circulating about the large number of American troops said shortly to be coming to the South of England, and a house in Banbury Road is being pointed out as an American headquarters.

Miscellaneous rumours include the following:

'The British Fleet left Alexandria and went through the Suez Canal on June 30th.'

NO. 96: TUESDAY 28 JULY 1942 TO TUESDAY 4 AUGUST 1942

I. GENERAL COMMENTS

1. GENERAL STATE OF CONFIDENCE AND REACTION TO NEWS

The general level of public feeling appears to have changed very little since last week. Anxiety about Russia, which still takes first place in the minds of most people, is said to have increased in eight Regions, in three of which some lowering of public spirits is reported.

As before, concern for Russia has resulted in 'a call for greater action on our part, whether it takes the form of a second front – most frequently mentioned – more and heavier air attacks on Germany, or an increase of supplies to the Soviets'. In six Regional reports 'a feeling of helplessness and frustration' is referred to: people are said to be 'aching to hit hard, and yet are forced to be the unwilling spectators of a fight which is really their own'. Opinion seems to be growing that 'there remain sections in the Government who are still not willing to give the utmost aid to our ally', and that they 'are holding back in the hope that Russia and Germany will exhaust one another'. These suspicions, which appear in reports from eight Regions, are directed not only to certain sections of the Government but also to those of whom it is believed that their 'old die-hard prejudice against Russia is still influencing or retarding a 100 per cent policy of co-operation'.

A further decline of interest in the Egyptian campaign is reported, and there has been little comment on India or the Far East.

The recent heavy raids on Germany have given some satisfaction, but the conviction persists that 'we have not kept up the sustained raids on Germany as they did on London – despite the many speeches saying we would'.

A considerable section of the population is still said to be complacent and apathetic and to take little interest in the war. Even in their concern for Russia many people appear to be detached, and to have only 'a slight appreciation of what the Russians are actually suffering'. Such people, it is said, appear to be satisfied with wartime conditions, as they have plenty of food and are earning more money than they were.

2. RUSSIA

Anxiety about Russia appears to be still greater this week: apprehension over the Germans' advance into the Caucasus 'is only partially offset by the spirited Russian defence against the thrust aimed at Stalingrad and by the progress made by our Allies near Voronezh'. The 'deep-rooted confidence which makes people hope for, and half expect, a sudden recovery by the Russians', seems to have been shaken, and people 'now find it difficult to believe that Timoshenko has an ace up his sleeve or that, by some dramatic stroke, he can stop the enemy's progress into the heart of the oilfields'. A minority, however, are described as 'still hopeful, as usual'.

The following reactions, arising from the public's concern over the Russian situation, are widely reported:

(a) FEAR OF A RUSSIAN COLLAPSE: Reports from nine Regions mention a fear – mostly on the part of a minority – that Russia may be unable to withstand the German onslaught, and will collapse, either entirely or at any rate on the Caucasus front. In Northern Ireland people are said to be 'steeling themselves for the bad news they fear is coming'; while, according to the Scottish report, 'rumours that Russia is about to collapse were rife in Falkirk last week'. Some fear is reported from two Regions that 'Russia may jump at a German offer of a separate peace'.

(b) FEAR OF THE CONSEQUENCE TO THIS COUNTRY IF RUSSIA COLLAPSES: 'What will happen to us if Russia is defeated?' is said to be a constant supposition, and anxiety and speculation on this score are reported from six Regions. 'Germany is finishing off countries one at a time', it is said, and will 'turn the full brunt of her forces against Britain when she has finished Russia'.

(c) SUSPICION OF ANTI-RUSSIAN FEELING 'IN HIGH PLACES': The idea that 'Britain is leaving Russia and Germany to fight it out because the Government doesn't want Russia to come out of the war too strong' is reported in one form or another from eight Regions; in one instance the US and British Governments are jointly accused. (There is nothing in any of the reports to indicate that Lady Astor's speech has helped to stimulate these suspicions.)

(d) FEAR THAT JAPAN MAY SOON ATTACK RUSSIA: Some apprehension and, in one case, 'a fairly general conviction' are reported from four Regions that 'Japan will attack Russia at the favourable moment'.

3. THE SECOND FRONT

The public's feelings on this subject – though in many cases more intense than last week – do not seem to have undergone any radical change, and may be summarised as follows:

(a) DESIRE FOR A SECOND FRONT: Although one report speaks of 'the clamour for it coming from sections not previously in favour', it would appear on the whole that 'the agitation for the second front has not spread to any more people, but that those who were agitating before are now more desperately alarmed'. Some reports make it clear that the demand – however intense – comes only from a minority, and there is some indication that where the demand is particularly strong, it is the result of pro-Russian or Communist Party propaganda.

(b) DESIRE FOR GREATER ACTION AND A MORE OFFENSIVE SPIRIT ON OUR PART: Although this feeling is not reported from as many Regions as is the demand for a second front, it seems to come from a far greater number of people, including – as it appears – all those who wish we were in a position to invade the Continent but who feel that 'to do so prematurely would be suicidal', and who 'dread another Dunkirk'. Suggested alternatives include heavier bombing of Germany, more Commando raids, and increased supplies to Russia, but there appears to be an uneasy feeling that these would only be 'a second best'.

(c) FEAR THAT WE SHALL BE TOO LATE: Many people fear that by the time we are ready to open a second front, we will be 'too late again – as we were in Norway, Greece and Crete', and that Hitler will have been allowed to carry out his usual method of destroying his enemies one by one.

(d) CONVICTION THAT THE GOVERNMENT KNOWS BEST: The more thoughtful feel that 'the Government is as keen as anyone', and the decision must be left to them. There is said, however, to be a feeling that 'the Prime Minister or another responsible minister' should give some assurance that 'a new front will be opened at the earliest possible moment'.

(e) 'OUR SHIPPING POSITION DOES NOT ALLOW OF A CONTINENTAL LANDING.'

(f) 'THERE MUST BE SOMETHING WRONG, IF WE AREN'T READY TO TAKE ACTION YET.'

(g) IRRITATION AT RUSSIAN PROPAGANDA: Irritation is reported in Northern Ireland at 'Russian propaganda designed to force Britain's hand in regard to the opening of a second front'. This is said to have been increased by 'the publication of a Reuter message quoting passages from a *Pravda* article broadcast by Moscow Radio'. (This was quoted in the *News Chronicle* of 1st August, and possibly elsewhere.) Particular objection is said to have been taken to the statement that the Red Army is resisting alone. This is considered 'an unwarrantable slight on Britain', and as 'the surest way to create friction between the two countries'. (In the North-Western Region there is a rumour that the Russians broadcast a demand for 'a second front now, or we pack up'; presumably this is a reference to the same broadcast.)

4. THE WAR IN THE AIR

RAF RAIDS: Increased interest and satisfaction is reported at our recent raids on Germany, the attack on Dusseldorf in particular being said to have 'caught the popular imagination more than any since the 1,000-bomber attacks'. 'Frequent hopes are expressed that Bomber Command is now beginning to fulfil the Prime Minister's promise that German cities would be razed one by one'; considerable impatience is reported at the slowness with which our promised air offensive is thought to be getting under way.

Some criticism is reported of the policy of returning a second night to the same objective, as it is thought that the defences there will be considerably strengthened in expectation of this. The 'extraordinary number of raids on Hamburg' has also evoked some 'criticisms about our effectiveness'.

RAF LOSSES: A good deal of comment is reported on the number of our bombers lost in recent raids, and opinion seems to be divided as to whether the number is excessive or not. Some people 'hear only that thirty-six planes are missing, and do not take into consideration the total number used', while others appear to regard the number of our casualties as an indication of the size of the raid. There is some feeling that 'the total number of planes taking part is not revealed so that the percentage of loss cannot be gauged', and it is asked whether we can afford this rate of losses in machines and crews, and if the results are worth the sacrifices made.

EXPECTATION OF REPRISAL RAIDS: Fear of reprisals – though it exists – is said to be small. Although there appears to be some feeling that a new series of

German raids on this country is just beginning, 'most people believe that we have suffered the worst that Germany is able to give. If necessary, they are ready to stand more, but they do not think the Luftwaffe capable of hitting so hard now; it is felt that our new raids are paying off an old score'.

GERMAN RAIDS ON THIS COUNTRY: Recent enemy raids on the South-Western Region are said to have been 'taken well and calmly, very much as part of the day's work'; while those in the Eastern Region are 'regarded by many people as a useful corrective for slackness, and have awakened people from their feeling of comfortable security'. They are described as 'having done us a hell of a lot of good'.

The recent raids in the Midlands are also regarded as having had 'a jolting effect on many people who had become complacent'.

THE NEW GERMAN INCENDIARY BOMBS: Concern about these is reported from two Regions, and there are rumours of 'the dreadful casualties caused by these bombs'. From both these Regions comes the demand for 'definite information about them, and how they should be dealt with'.

OUR 'OTHER DEVICES': A good deal of interest is reported in these, and some talk about 'the damage they do'. It is felt that the lot of the Civil Defence Service in air raids will be 'even less enviable', and it is asked, 'What will be the position of fire-watchers under the recent request that people shall not stand out of doors to watch the new anti-aircraft defences going into action?'

AIR MARSHAL SIR ARTHUR HARRIS'S BROADCAST TO GERMANY: Reactions to this appear to have been mixed. The majority view is reported to have been that we have told Germany often enough what we intend, and that we should do the job first and tell them about it afterwards. It is felt not to be 'like us to brag', and that 'if the speech was intended for Germany, it should have been broadcast to Germany alone'. A minority feel that 'at last we are getting down to real propaganda'. The question of allowing Government policy to be announced by someone who is not responsible to Parliament seems to have interested only 'an intelligent few'.

5. US TROOPS IN GREAT BRITAIN

Regional comment on American troops appears to be on a reduced scale this week. Interest in our visitors continues to be reported from Regions in which they are stationed, and where the organisation of hospitality is being attempted; in short, 'the opportunity and necessity for cementing cordial feelings' between the two nations seems to be realised.

A Special report by Postal Censorship (OPINION ON AMERICAN TROOPS IN GREAT BRITAIN) analyses the results of an examination of all civilian mail from 24th June dealing with this subject. This analysis shows that out of a total of 171 comments, opinions appear to have been almost equally divided between appreciation and criticism, the latter slightly preponderating.

Although in the main adverse talk seems to be decreasing, various Regions (strongly supported by Postal Censorship) criticise the following aspects of the Americans' behaviour:

THEIR LAVISH SPENDING OF MONEY is reported to be having an unsettling effect on our men causing jealousy, as 'all the girls are going mad about them and giving their own fellows up'.

THEIR ATTITUDE TO COLOURED TROOPS: From the Midland Region 'local experience' is reported to show that 'it is inadvisable to station black and white troops in the same area'.

THEIR TACTLESS REMARKS: Variants of the already familiar taunts are still reported; the most frequent refer to the 'Dunkirk Harriers', and the addition of 'yellow' to the British colours. In this connection evidence that these tales are largely circumstantial seems to find support in the Postal Censorship analysis, in which the incidents are alleged to have occurred in such widely separated areas as 'a Bristol Hotel', the 'John Cockle' Inn at Warsop, the 'Crown' at Shrewsbury, and the 'Bull's Head', Amersham.

6. EGYPT

Interest in this front continues to wane, and, according to reports from eight Regions, there is little comment on the subject. There appears to be a slight increase in optimism, and in the feeling that 'we shall be able to hold out'. Such interest as is reported is said to take the form of 'settling down to await developments'. People seem to be uncertain as to how to interpret the news that the enemy is digging in: some are cheered, while others regard it as a bad sign, a minority being anxious over the deadlock and feeling that the Germans are 'too near Suez'.

7. SHIPPING LOSSES

Concern over our shipping losses, particularly in the Northern Region, 'where large districts are engaged in the shipping industry', continues to be reported. At the same time, the publication of figures seems to be thought inadvisable; and 'it is often stated that Parliamentary demands for disclosures of facts and figures are considered childish and irresponsible'. It is being asked, however, why, though the United States' losses are published, ours must remain secret. It is also asked why the United States do not provide better protection for coastal shipping, though some belief is reported that the Caribbean Sea is now somewhat safer.

From the South-Eastern Region the feeling is reported that 'the seriousness of the situation is holding up a second front'.

8. THE GOVERNMENT

Criticism of the Government – in addition to that referred to in Section 2 (c) above – is reported on the grounds that:

(a) The Government should order and act more and should not resort to requests and appeals. The Government's 'weak handling of the holidays at home' in particular is criticised.

(b) Parliament should not be allowed 'to disperse for the summer recess at so critical a time', and without making any statement on the war situation.

'Growing disapproval of party politics is reported' from one Region. 'The feeling that members are often compelled by the Party machine to vote against their personal convictions and the wishes of the people they represent is frequently expressed.'

MR. BEVIN'S SPEECH at the Conference of the National Chamber of Trade on 16th July is said to have caused considerable dissatisfaction, chiefly on account of his prophecy that the 'rentier class' would be entirely gone by the end of the war. What is taken as his criticism of this section of the population is considered as 'contrary to all ideas of thrift and self-denial'.

9. BROADCASTING AND PRESENTATION OF NEWS

PRESENTATION OF NEWS: Criticism of the 'treatment of news which is not calculated to bring home the seriousness of the situation to the public' continues on familiar lines and is reported from eight Regions:

(1) Criticism is made of the 'bad handling of news' as regards both 'the material used and the style of delivery', and also of the 'glossing over of bad news'. An example quoted is 'the sharp practice' of announcing our air losses 'by averaging over three nights'.

(2) Complaints are made that the Germans 'get their news out first, especially when it's bad for us', and a desire is expressed for 'earlier confirmation of news given out by the enemy'.

Preference for the 'liveliness' of the European News service, and the 'snap' of the Empire News, is again reported from two Regions. Reports from one Region express appreciation 'for what is said to be the more guarded tones of the news bulletins'. A continued decline in listening to the wireless is reported from five Regions; the following reasons are given:

(1) 'People do not want to listen to talk; they want – and wait for – events.'

(2) The monotony and repetitiveness of news bulletins: 'people who formerly listened now switch off after the news summary'.

(3) 'The news is so depressing that it makes people too miserable to listen to it.'

'INDISCRETIONS': 'Strong feeling' against so-called 'indiscretions' of MPs and of statements in the press and on the radio are reported again this week from five Regions. During the last three months complaints on the following lines have been received:

(1) Information given out during the 'Baedeker raids' as to whether or not historic buildings had been hit were said to 'invite the Germans back again'; announcements about movements of population, either for industrial purposes or to holiday resorts, are also said to invite bombing.

(2) 'Too much information is given over the radio' and in the press on the arrival of convoys or troops; about invasion exercises and the training of

troops; and of war materials going to Russia, and other industrial particulars which are regarded as 'giving valuable information to the enemy'.

(3) Complaints about MPs who ask questions in the House 'without considering the effect it has on the country or on the enemy', and who are accused of 'abuse of privilege regarding secrets and the quoting of production figures'.

BBC PROGRAMMES: Satisfaction continues to be reported from four Regions at the BBC's decision 'to drop "slush"'.

LORD WOOLTON'S POSTSCRIPT is reported to have been well received; 'his reference to the family and the need to consider the individual are particularly welcomed', and he is praised for 'his strong human sympathy'.

'I AM JOHN CITIZEN' BROADCASTS are also reported to have been 'well received', but a suggestion is made that 'the choice of a young man not in the armed forces is not particularly representative, and his ardent patriotism is rather suspect among Service listeners'.

GOVERNMENT INSTRUCTIONS: 'The changes in Government policy in connection with the carrying of gas masks' is reported to have been greeted with 'amusement and mystification'. It is asked 'what about the poster "Hitler will send no warning"?'

II. SPECIAL COMMENTS

10. INDUSTRY

(No reports have so far been received on public reactions to the Minister of Supply's review of Royal Ordnance Factories in the House on July 5th.)

Criticism continues along familiar lines, which may be summarised as follows:

(a) ENFORCED IDLENESS IN FACTORIES: Specific mention is made of the Bristol Aeroplane Co. at Winterstoke Road, and Westinghouse Ltd. at Chippenham; also mentioned in this connection is a maintenance depot near Carlisle where 'young women are alleged to do two hours of work a day'.

(b) MANAGEMENTS are blamed for:

    (i) Being 'more concerned with profit and preparations for after the war than with putting a 100% effort into a drive for victory'. Fifty per cent of the machines at the Bristol Engineering Co. are said to stay idle at night while the small staff on duty are put on commercial work – not on war work'.

    (ii) Laziness, and 'for refusing to adopt schemes calculated to increase production'.

(c) WORKERS are criticised for being 'more concerned with their pay packets and conditions of employment than with the war effort'.

WOMEN WORKERS: From ten Regions and from Postal Censorship comes 'wholehearted praise of the work being done by women in factories'. It has been suggested, however, that 'their enthusiasm, in particular, is damped by instances of slackness'.

IRISH LABOURERS: Those working on construction sites are again said to be a source of trouble in some districts: 'They will go miles for a drink and then become fighting drunk.'

ESSENTIAL WORK: The question is again revived of the effect upon workers of knowing the ultimate use of what they are making. They are said to be encouraged by knowing the destination of their products. As a writer quoted by Postal Censorship says: 'This work makes me feel very important; when I read of a thousand bombers over Germany – to think I have had parts of them in my hand!' Service speakers, who tell workers of the uses made of their products, are also quoted as a source of encouragement.

It is felt in the Eastern Region 'that if workers were to *see* where their particular share of the work goes (for instance, if makers of aeroplane parts were to see bombers when assembled) they would be very encouraged'.

11. WAGES

The following complaints continue to be reported about disparities in pay:

(i) between industrial workers (including labourers on aerodrome sites) and servicemen. It is felt that servicemen's dependants, particularly, should be better provided for. 'Everyone here, except the soldier's wife, has money' says one letter; while a report from London Region states that: 'The cut in the hardship grant corresponding to any rise in the soldier's pay through promotion or proficiency, is said to cause distress in cases where the man does not make up the amount to his wife.'

(ii) between US and British soldiers.

(iii) between industrial workers and miners.

There are also complaints about wives earning more than their husbands who are in the same factory, and of the high wages of juveniles and the demoralising effect of their 'earning sums out of all proportion to their usefulness'. It is felt to be 'a great pity that youngsters should go into dead-end jobs with good pay instead of into less well-paid work where they could learn a trade'.

12. WOMEN'S CALL-UP

Reports continue of 'people asking why some women are compelled to go into war work, while others "get off"'. The 'too many idle women' who are believed to be making virtually no contribution to the war effort include the following:

(a) Young married women with no family ties. Dissatisfaction with them is particularly expressed by workers with young families, and also by women of forty to forty-five.

(b) Middle-aged women with husbands and grown-up families away from home.

(c) Healthy women who obtain medical exemption certificates – granted too easily, it is thought, by certain doctors. Some young married women are said 'to claim exemption on the grounds of non-existent pregnancy'.

DOMESTIC LABOUR: Mention is made of the shortage of domestic labour for women who are themselves in war work; as regards voluntary work, it is felt 'among wealthier circles' that this will have to be reduced on account of the servant situation.

On the other hand, the servant question is not worrying everybody. To quote from Postal Censorship: 'I am still in the same old place. The new people, one gentleman and one lady, have brought their own cook and lady's maid and chauffeur, so that we are now, with the gardener, six employees for two people ... and at that they are in London for half the week.'

13. MANPOWER

Dissatisfaction is again expressed at 'the dozens of young men eligible for service who have still not been called up'. Many are said to be 'hiding in munition factories', having entered them for that purpose. They cannot be regarded as skilled in their new calling and their deferment is considered 'unaccountable'.

It is also felt that clerical staffs in factories, young men in the shoe trade, and others 'who could be replaced by women and older men, should be de-reserved'.

14. FUEL

The fuel economy campaign is said to be causing interest, and there appear to be signs of 'economy consciousness' among the public.

Other comments, each reported from only one or two Regions, refer to (a) queries about filling in the fuel consumption forms, particularly where more than one family lives in the same house; (b) anxiety at the possible prospect of fuel rationing; belief that this is inevitable, and from one Region a preference for it, since 'it would be fairer all round'; (c) anticipated difficulties in rural areas of transporting fuel in the winter; (d) dissatisfaction in an area where 'supplies of coal were so short that in June and July people were unable to obtain more than half the 10 cwt. "allowance"'; (e) discontent at flat rates of electricity which mean 'paying for fuel economised'.

15. HOLIDAYS

Criticism of Government 'shilly-shallying' over holidays continues to be reported in five Regions, and the 'running of excursion trains' is thought to be 'contrary to the holidays-at-home policy'.

Difficulties of travelling, feeding and accommodation are said to have been experienced by many of those who have gone away. 'It was hardly worth while' is reported to be a frequent comment from Scotland, and there are reports of visitors having had to return from Bournemouth 'for lack of accommodation'.

Reports from three Regions express appreciation of facilities for holidays at home, and in Gloucestershire people are reported to have 'responded well to the stay-put arrangements'.

HOLIDAY OPENING OF SCHOOLS: The response to the opening of schools is said to have been poor in Scotland and in some districts of the North-Western Region. A child quoted by Postal Censorship writes: 'Nobody is coming (to school) from our form, and nobody from two other forms, so I bet it's a farce. The staff will be mad.' Many teachers criticise the scheme and are reported to feel 'that their energies could be better employed than in supervising the few children that do turn up'.

16. FOOD

Satisfaction with the food situation, and with Lord Woolton and his Ministry in particular, continues to be widely reported in all Regions. Of the Minister himself, a writer quoted in Postal Censorship says: 'Wish we had others like him, then the war would end this year.'

SWEETS RATIONING: Sweets rationing is reported to be approved, although in a number of Regions the feeling is expressed that children should receive a larger allocation, even if this should entail some sacrifice from adults. Considerable surprise and some amusement seem to have been shown at 'the large amount and wide selection of sweets and chocolates now on view'. A certain amount of cynical curiosity is expressed as to why these stocks were not available before. 'The recently unfamiliar courtesy of sweet shopkeepers is also attracting comment.'

TOMATOES AND SOFT FRUIT: The scarcity of tomatoes and soft fruit is criticised, and 'the belief that retailers have given preferential distribution to monied customers' is reported to have caused some discontent.

DRIED EGGS: These still win approval, but growing ill-feeling is reported 'because of their unequal allotment by different grocers, some allowing one tin per ration book per month, others only one tin per family per month'.

AUSTERITY MEALS: In two Regions, comment is aroused at the 'fatuous' order regulating meals in restaurants; the measure is felt to be 'a farce'. Increasing difficulty is reported in purchasing a light meal; some hotels and restaurants are said to be 'demanding the price of a full dinner when only a plate of soup or some similar item has been ordered'.

FOOD OFFICES AND HOLIDAY-MAKERS: Congestion at Food Offices by people requiring emergency cards is reported from two Regions; it is felt that large towns, such as Manchester, require more than one Food Office.

17. AGRICULTURE

From six Regions come reports of farmers' difficulties over 'shortage of labour, filling up of forms, and keeping books for tax purposes'; these problems are said to be keeping farmers so busy 'that they have little time to think about the war'.

POST-WAR SUBSIDIES: It is felt that farmers should be given 'some reassurance about post-war subsidies if the increased "ploughing out" is to be a success', as they feel that they will be left after the war 'with crops they can't sell with profit, and will not be able to regain their markets for milk and beasts'.

INCOME TAX: In the Eastern Region the dislike of income tax among farm labourers is reported to be arousing criticism. 'It is felt that they are getting a "good deal". They have new bicycles and their wives new rig-outs.'

18. POST-WAR PLANNING

While the subject of post-war planning appears to have lost favour in most parts of the country, there seems to be some support for the feeling reported from the North-Western Region: 'Plan by all means, but do not talk "until victory is won".'

19. PETROL RESTRICTIONS

There appears to be 'a good deal of comment on the number of private cars still seen, particularly parked outside shops and restaurants – and pubs at night'.

There are some complaints of petrol wastage by the military and by 'officials' and also of 'the issue of petrol to young boys for motorcycles for pleasure alone'.

The more vigorous rationing is said to have been accepted 'with no more than healthy complaining, and more and more unexpected people are to be seen on bicycles'.

20. SMALL FIRMS

Considerable concern is reported for the position of the small business and small shopkeeper, who are thought to be getting 'a raw deal'. It is felt that 'the trend of the Government is in favour of large concerns', which, if it entails the elimination of the small and medium trader from the life of the nation, 'would be generally considered disastrous'.

There is strong feeling in the South-Western Region about the call-up of heads of small businesses, which are thus compelled to close down, 'while, at the same time, younger men are allowed to go free'.

21. RUMOURS

This week again the principal rumours are concerned with the imminence of a second front. Evacuation rumours are reported to persist in Southampton, Bournemouth, Portsmouth and Middleton. From the Southern and South-Western Regions, the second front is said to be due either this week or next.

NO. 99: MONDAY 17 AUGUST 1942 TO
TUESDAY 25 AUGUST 1942

I. GENERAL COMMENTS

1. GENERAL STATE OF CONFIDENCE AND REACTION TO NEWS

The Dieppe raid and the Prime Minister's visit to Moscow were responsible for a sharp rise in public spirits which appears to have been at its highest after the one o'clock news on Wednesday, August 19th, while the raid was still in progress and people were thinking that our invasion of the Continent might possibly have begun – in spite of the warning to the French that this was not the case. When, however, it became known that our troops had re-embarked, there began to be a feeling of disappointment that the raid had not developed into something bigger. There is reported to be a widespread tendency to believe that 'if it had been successful, it would have been invasion', but that it resolved itself into 'just another Commando raid'. The news of our losses in relation to the apparent results of the raid seems also to have helped to reduce elation.

While most reports agree that the general level of public feeling is higher than it has been for some weeks, the rise in spirits is reported as 'not very substantial in some cases'; and three Regional reports indicate that there has been, to some extent, 'a drift back towards the earlier mood'. Delight at this sign of offensive action on our part has not distracted people's attention more than temporarily from anxiety about Russia, where the situation remains, 'for many people, the crux of the war'. The sense of frustration at our apparent inability to bring much relief to our ally is still reported.

The announcement of the Prime Minister's visit to Moscow seems to have come as no surprise, in view of the widespread rumours which have been current for the past three weeks. It is reported, however, to have caused the greatest satisfaction, and a good deal of hopeful speculation, though little excitement. As a topic of discussion, it seems definitely to have taken second place to the Dieppe raid.

The American action in the Pacific is said to be causing increasing interest and satisfaction to a large minority, though there seems to be no tendency to be prematurely optimistic about it.

Brazil's entry into the war appears to have aroused only slight interest.

Apart from anxiety about Russia, other factors reported to be keeping spirits low include:

(a) The depressing effect of the return of the blackout and dread of another long winter with the prospect of 'limited light and warmth'.

(b) The 'probability of a long-drawn-out war'.

(c) A feeling that 'the post-war world will be a worse mess than it was before', the return of unemployment being particularly dreaded.

Though less widely reported than last week, apathy and lack of urgency continue to be mentioned, in one form or another, in four Regional reports, special reference being made to those earning high wages and to people living in small un-bombed towns.

2. THE DIEPPE RAID

Reference has already been made to the stimulating effect of this raid, which was welcomed primarily as 'a sign of a more aggressive spirit'. People's secondary reactions are, however, reported to have been conflicting, with considerable uncertainty both as to the purpose and the success of the operation; the main trends of feeling may be summarised as follows:

(a) 'IF THE OPPOSITION HAD NOT BEEN SO STRONG, WE SHOULD HAVE DEVELOPED A FULL-SCALE OFFENSIVE.' This reaction is reported in one form or another from ten Regions – in some cases, as being the belief of the majority. The landing of tanks is particularly mentioned as giving rise to the idea that this was intended to have been more than just a Commando raid. A few are said to have regarded it simply as an attempt at invasion which failed. The warning to the French that this was not the real thing was apparently thought by many to be 'a bluff to deceive the Germans', and by a few as 'a blind to enable our High Command to cover itself in case the landing was not a success'.

(b) 'WERE THE GAINS WORTH THE LOSS OF LIFE AND EQUIPMENT?' 'The actual objectives gained, a radiolocation station and two batteries of naval guns ... are considered as very little to show for such a great sacrifice of men and equipment', and it is asked: 'Could not heavy air raids have achieved more without such loss of life?' On the other hand, it is thought that if it was done for practice, 'it could have been done just as easily on our own shore at less expense'. 'If we have gained invaluable experience', it is asked, 'may not the Germans have done the same?' Others say: 'Did the Germans need a practice invasion of Norway or Crete?' There is some feeling that the raid was intended as 'a spectacular token action to give the Russians some hope of further help soon'. Many people connect it with Mr. Churchill's visit to Moscow.

(c) 'DID CARELESS TALK BEFOREHAND WARN THE ENEMY OF THE RAID?' The claim that our plans were upset by the encounter with an enemy naval patrol is thought by some to be 'very weak, since the Germans might be expected to patrol this coast'.

(d) 'THE SUCCESSFUL CO-OPERATION OF THE THREE SERVICES', and 'the skilled planning' involved, have received appreciative comment from four Regions.

(e) 'WAS THE GREAT AIR BATTLE A VICTORY?' Although a few people are reported to ask whether 'command of the air can be reconciled with the loss of nearly a hundred planes', the number of our losses 'does not seem to have created anxiety', particularly if the action 'results in the diversion of German fighters from the Russian front'.

(f) THE CANADIANS: There appears to be a minority who ask why the lion's share of the action was left to the Canadians and why they were given so much publicity. A few are even said to believe that the raid was 'staged to please the Canadians, to keep them from quarrelling with themselves and us'.

3. THE PRIME MINISTER'S VISIT TO MOSCOW

'Satisfaction' is the word most often used to describe people's reaction to the news of Mr. Churchill's travels. The general feeling is that the trip to Moscow 'is bound to have done good', and that 'whatever the nature of the discussions, movements will have been set on foot which will ease the burden on Russia'. Many people think that the visit 'presages the opening of the second front'. It is widely hoped that a better understanding between the two countries will result and that 'the Prime Minister's personality will have overcome Stalin's previous suspicions on account of his well-known anti-communist attitude'. Some people, however, were worried by Mr. Churchill's reference to the need for him 'to express himself', and hoped this did not indicate any serious divergence of view. The Prime Minister's statement on his travels is 'eagerly anticipated'.

The following points of view are reported to come from a minority:

(a) The visit was necessary (i) 'to keep Russia in the war' ('It was horribly reminiscent of his journey to France before her capitulation'); (ii) to 'hear the facts regarding the critical situation of the Russian armies'; (iii) to 'smooth over disagreement among the Allies'.

(b) 'Why must Churchill do all the travelling? Why can't Stalin or Roosevelt come here?'

THE PRIME MINISTER IN EGYPT: Particular pleasure was caused by Mr. Churchill's visit to the Egyptian front, and the fact that he looked so cheerful has heartened many people. It is thought that he 'must have done a lot of good in Egypt, especially as he talked with the men as well as the officers'.

Rumour has it that Mr. Churchill has also been to India, and/or China.

THE PRIME MINISTER'S POPULARITY: Mr. Churchill's position is said to have been considerably strengthened as a result of his travels. His energy and courage are much admired, and great relief is expressed at his safe return. People are impressed at the way he goes and sees things for himself rather than relying solely on other people's reports.

Though a few are said to regret his 'playing to the gallery' and his frequent use of the 'V' sign, others are reported to 'love to hear of his boyish tricks'.

4. RUSSIA

Anxiety for Russia continues to be reported, but although attention has been to a great extent diverted from the Caucasus to Stalingrad ('a name that means more than most Russian towns'), apprehension does not appear to be greater than it was last week. In the case of four Regions, in fact, 'the fears that were expressed about the possible collapse of Russia were more than countered by the impression created by the Moscow talks': in the words of the Scottish report, 'people were getting very despondent about Russia until Churchill's visit to Stalin which seems, in the minds of the public, in some extraordinary way to have immediately improved the position in the Don Basin'. Nevertheless, so far as the majority are concerned, anxiety as well as admiration appear to be deep, and fears that Russia will be forced to make a separate peace or that she will at any rate be immobilised continue to be expressed.

Some belief is reported that we may be able to help Russia with 'our forces in Persia' and that General Wavell's presence in Moscow may have had something to do with such a plan. A few are said to believe that 'Stalin is jettisoning the Caucasus area and shepherding the Nazi armies into the Middle East where we shall be compelled to contend with them'.

Less comment is reported this week about 'anti-Russian feeling in high places', and this is thought to be largely due to Mr. Churchill's visit to Moscow. Lady Astor's Southport speech continues, however, to be quoted as 'an example of such feeling'.

5. THE SECOND FRONT

There is little change to report about the public's feelings on this question. Although the desire for a second front continues, demands for its immediate opening are said to be less numerous and less insistent since the raid on Dieppe, and increased confidence in the Government is reported in this connection. There seems to be a fairly general belief that 'the second front is very near', and that it will be established this autumn.

There appears to be increasing realisation – and resentment – of the part played by the Communist Party in propaganda for a second front.

6. INDIA

There is little that is new to report about people's reactions to the situation in India, discussion having to a great extent died down. The views most freely expressed are:

(a) Approval for the strong measures of the Indian Government.
(b) Sympathy for Indian aspirations, and the hope that negotiations will be reopened as soon as the campaign of civil disobedience ends.
(c) Fear that we may be 'creating another Irish problem'.

7. CHANGES IN MIDDLE EAST COMMANDS

Little comment is reported on the situation in Egypt, though there is 'still a background of apprehension', and at the same time 'a corresponding impatience as to what may happen when Rommel is reinforced'.

A good deal of interest is, however, reported as a result of the changes in Command. While the public as a whole appears to be mystified, a good many people are reported to have greeted the changes with 'cynical comment', and others with 'disfavour' or 'regret'. It is thought that:

(a) It is not a good thing to move generals from one front to another so often, as 'it deprives them of the valuable asset of familiarity with the ground on which they have to fight'.

(b) General Auchinleck 'is needed for a more important job – the second front'.

(c) He was removed 'because of failure'.

(d) He has been 'removed for the same reason as General Cunningham – because he is not prepared to undertake an offensive with the material and personnel available'.

(e) 'As the intensive build-up of "the Auk's" reputation was considered to be officially inspired, his apparent dismissal shows that not much credence can be given to eulogies of generals'; as a result of which there is a tendency to 'accept the present tributes to the new commanders as so much dope', though General Maitland Wilson, as Wavell's former henchman, 'has some of the popularity that has always been given to Wavell more than any other general'.

8. THE US OPERATIONS IN THE SOLOMON AND GILBERT ISLANDS

Increasing – though still cautious – satisfaction is reported at the US Pacific offensive, and there is some belief that this is intended 'to divert Japan from Siberia'. There is, however, a feeling that the Pacific is 'a long way from Berlin and Tokyo'.

9. US TROOPS IN GREAT BRITAIN

Praise for the good behaviour of US troops continues to be reported, and though there is said to be 'some hostility' at the news of their arrival, there also appears to be a 'subsequent thawing'. In the Southern Region a desire is expressed 'that particulars of the American uniforms and badges of rank should be published in the press and elsewhere, because people offering hospitality are said to be embarrassed by their lack of knowledge of the unfamiliar uniforms'.

HIGH PAY: The high pay of US soldiers compared with that of British troops continues to be a source of critical comment from three Regions. In the Southern Region the lavish display of dollar bills is commented on: 'wads enough to choke a cow' is the local description of such riches. Reports from Northern Ireland indicate that US soldiers 'resent the inference that they are well paid compared with their British comrades'. They are said to feel entitled to their pay, and even to feel underpaid, compared to their comrades in war industries at home.

COLOURED TROOPS: Criticism of white girls' behaviour with coloured troops is again reported from three Regions. In the South-Western Region it is said that there appears to be an increasing tendency for coloured men to accost girls in passing, but 'the white girls are held to blame' and there is a demand for action by the police.

Dislike of American soldiers' discrimination against their coloured brethren is reported from three Regions, and it is pointed out that Canadians differ from Americans in their attitude to Negroes, 'showing far less discrimination and fear'.

DRUNKENESS: Complaints of the rowdiness and drunkenness of US soldiers are reported from two Regions, and in the Southern Region they are criticised for 'treating' English girls 'who are not accustomed to drinking on this scale'.

10. THE MEDITERRANEAN CONVOY BATTLE

There still appears to be some discussion on this subject, opinion being divided between (a) considering the enterprise 'abundantly worthwhile, in spite of our great losses'; and (b) 'doubt as to whether the fleet should have been hazarded in this way – or could be again'. Admiration for the heroism of those taking part is again reported, the general feeling seeming to be that 'it was a damned good show'.

11. RAF BOMBING OFFENSIVE

Comment continues on the same lines as that reported during the last two weeks, and may be summarised as follows:

(a) Disappointment at 'our failure to carry out our threats of uninterrupted and heavy raids on Germany'. It is felt that 'failing a second front, raids are the most effective way of helping Russia'. A minority opinion, however, reported from one Region, is that 'the raids have not delayed the German advance in Russia, and have only served to bring the German raiders back over Britain'.

(b) Criticism of any promises of heavy bombing in the future: 'We do not want to hear what is going to happen – let us hear the results.' According to the report from the Southern Region, 'the definite information of the effect of our bombing' given in Sir Archibald Sinclair's speech at Swansea on 22nd August 'has been received with considerable satisfaction'. (No other references to this speech have been reported.)

(c) Little interest in raids 'which have not assumed the proportions hoped for'. (It is reported from London Region, however, that recent raids are cheering the working people considerably: 'Somebody has scrapped the talk and got on with the job.')

(d) A demand for the bombing of Italy: 'Just fancy, not a single bomb on Rome, and poor Malta bashed.' From the Southern Region comes a reference to renewed feeling that 'the lenient treatment of Italy is due to pro-Italian sentiments in high quarters'.

12. BRAZIL

The entry of Brazil into the war on the side of the Allies does not appear to have excited much comment, beyond a feeling of mild satisfaction on the lines of 'it all helps' and 'it's one less for Hitler'. Some pleased surprise is, however, reported at

Brazil's size and potentialities, and it is hoped that the shipping situation off the American coast may now be improved.

13. BROADCASTING AND PRESENTATION OF NEWS

THE DIEPPE RAID: From seven Regions comes praise of the way in which the news of the raid was presented: 'Accounts have been eagerly read and found satisfying.' Reports from three of these Regions show appreciation for the promptness of the announcement – 'for once we have left Goebbels standing at the post!' On the other hand, reports from four Regions complain that 'the policy of non-contradiction of German claims was unwise' and that 'German casualty figures were generally accepted' as none were given by us. Reports from two Regions suggest that 'too much prominence has been given to the raid', and by Friday people were reported to be saying, 'I hope they will stop plugging it soon, we are tired of it already.'

FRANK GILLARD'S BROADCAST: This description of the raid was considered 'most effective publicity' in one Region, though in reports from two others, he was criticised for his 'exaggerated claims that we had destroyed 270 German aircraft', and for his 'gory details' and alleged inaccuracy about 6 ins. howitzers.

PRESENTATION OF NEWS: There is less criticism of news presentation this week, though from three Regions come the familiar allegations that:

(a) 'Successes are magnified, and reverses played down.'
(b) That 'we are not told the whole truth'; the usual criticisms are heard 'whenever an enemy claim is subsequently admitted'.

ENEMY BROADCASTS: From three Regions and Postal Censorship come reports of listening-in to enemy broadcasts in the hope of picking up 'items of news in advance of the BBC', and information about prisoners of war. One writer says: 'What do you think of Richard's name coming over the wireless from a German station last Monday? So he's a prisoner! Haw-Haw gives six names every night, quite a few heard it.'

BBC NEWS BULLETINS: Two Regions still report a tendency to 'switch off after the summary' and a woman quoted by Postal Censorship writes: 'As I have said, dear, I do not listen to the news any more. If I feel low, it only makes me lower.'

The suggestion that official announcements should be given in the press is reported again from one Region, as 'many people are said to miss them after the news bulletins'.

EUROPEAN NEWS: Praise for the European News Service comes from two Regions and, in another, listening to this service is said to be on the increase.

COMMANDER KIMMINS' BROADCAST: This 'superb description' of the convoy to Malta has been praised in reports from seven Regions: 'It was sincere and real, and there was nothing mannered about it. It captured the imagination.'

MR. BROCKINGTON'S POSTSCRIPT, Sunday 16th August: Favourable comment has been received from three Regions on this *Postscript*.

II. SPECIAL COMMENTS

14. INDUSTRY

Little criticism is again reported of industry as a whole. In fact, from two Regions 'a definite spurt amongst the workers' was reported as 'a result of the Dieppe raid: they again felt that their work was for a definite purpose'.

MANPOWER: A continued demand is reported for 'the combing-out of young men in sheltered jobs', specific mention being made of those in Government departments, on the staff of contractors engaged on Government work, and in industry – where 'inspectors and clerks are looked upon by manual workers as no good because they are non-productive'.

PART-TIME WORK: According to reports from three Regions, it is believed that more accommodation for young children would 'give a valuable impetus to the recruiting of part-time workers'. In the Southern Region, however, such hopes, raised by the anticipated opening of a day nursery at Hungerford, are said to have been dashed by the alleged 'refusal of Vickers to consider any shift of less than twelve hours'.

WOMEN'S HEALTH: 'The tiredness of women workers' is reported from the Eastern Region to be 'beginning to affect their interest in their work and the war effort'. The following factors are held to be chiefly responsible: (a) long hours of work; (b) transport difficulties; (c) shopping difficulties; (d) the blackout – sometimes they scarcely see daylight at all.

ACCOMMODATION FOR WAR WORKERS: The difficulties connected with the billeting and feeding of war workers are again reported this week from the Eastern Region. The report from the Southern Region refers to 'an already impossible position in Newbury Rural District', and to 'constant new demands for accommodation there'; 'the latest being for anything up to a thousand workmen employed in laying a double track on the Winchester–Didcot railway line'.

CRITICISM OF MANAGEMENTS: The suspicion that 'this war will go on just as long as large profits can be made by war contractors' is reported from two Regions. Talk of the 'cost plus 10% basis of contracts' is said to have revived in Wales.

15. FOOD

Though praise for the general food situation continues to be reported from five Regions and Postal Censorship, there is said to be some apprehension because the number of points has not been raised; the reasons being the inclusion of biscuits on points, though this is welcomed by housewives and especially war workers, and 'the doubling of syrup and treacle pointage'.

SWEET RATIONS: Pleasure at the increased sweet ration is reported from four Regions and Postal Censorship, but there are 'caustic comments on the fact that the shops are overflowing with sweets'. The alleged admission by Lord Woolton that he has had to increase the sweets ration to reduce surplus stocks is criticised in one

Region by people who feel that, since hoarding by consumers is punishable, Lord Woolton has 'one law for his fellow traders and another for the general public'. In the London Region, instances have been reported of customers being offered sweets off the ration 'because they will go bad if they are not sold'.

EGGS: Confusion over the allocation of dried eggs is reported again from three Regions. Shortage of fresh eggs is reported from two Regions.

FOOD WASTAGE: Complaints of food being wasted by the Services come from two Regions and Postal Censorship. Two RAF camps in the North and army camps in East Anglia are specially mentioned. In the North-Eastern Region complaints are made that market stall holders 'throw away fruit and vegetables, rather than sell them at lower prices'; and in the Eastern Region it is asked why potato clamps cannot be sold faster as some are said to be rotting.

16. FUEL ECONOMY

People continue to be 'full of resentment over any instances of wastefulness in others'. Complaints are made chiefly about Government buildings, local authorities, business premises, factories and shops. It is also suggested in one report that 'quantities of fuel are used in heating churches and cathedrals, the doors of which are continually being opened, allowing the heat to escape'.

This resentment appears, however, to be coupled with 'a very conscientious effort on the part of most of the public to economise in the domestic consumption of fuel'.

Complaints are still reported over (a) the electricity two-part tariff 'where people pay more for the privilege of saving fuel than if they did not have it' and (b) 'requests to replace high-wattage bulbs by low-wattage ones when the latter are difficult to get'.

'YOUR FUEL TARGET': Few reports have as yet been received on this advertisement. In one Region there is said to be a good deal of talk about it, 'the facts of saving having been seized on' in preference to 'the rhetoric of the Sunday broadcast appeal'. 'The more generous treatment of the North' is reported from the North-Western Region as 'likely to meet with favour', though in the Southern Region, annoyance is said to be caused by 'the differentiation between the North, the Midlands and the South'.

17. WOMEN'S FIRE-GUARD ORDER

A feeling of resentment and objection to the Fire-Watching Order for women is reported this week from four Regions, and is borne out by Postal Censorship; the chief reasons for complaint are that:

(a) There are thought to be still a lot of men who are avoiding fire-watching duty; women feel that all men should be called upon first. It is suggested that the ARP Service and Home Guard, 'who spend long hours of duty doing nothing', and older men up to 65 or 70, should be brought in to fire-watch.

(b) Fire-watching is not a fit job for women; this opinion appears to be held chiefly by men, who are said to be doubtful of women's ability to tackle difficult fires, and dubious 'about the propriety of girls being on duty with men employees at night'.

(c) Fire-watching in target areas should be left to men; women should only fire-watch in residential areas.

(d) Women with elderly relatives in their care should be exempted in the same way as women with children.

It appears that women are still not clear about the provisions of the order, and particularly how the hours of duty are to apply.

18. TRANSPORT

'Inadequate transport facilities' for workers and in rural areas have been referred to in reports from ten Regions this week; from the South-Western in the following terms: 'The growing difficulties, the inordinate waste of time and the downright impossibilities in journeying by public service vehicles, are becoming a major issue.'

Specific complaints follow familiar lines: (a) workers are crowded out by holiday-makers; a case is also quoted of business men crowded out of their train to Cambridge for a vital appointment by racegoers; (b) short-distance passengers with alternative transport using long-distance buses; (c) non-observance of the queuing regulations; (d) the discomfort of war workers who have 'to make long journeys in overcrowded buses at the start and end of their day'; (e) lack of compulsory control over travellers, and failure to eliminate non-essential travelling.

PETROL: Petrol wastage appears to 'be fused in the public mind with transport difficulties', and critical comment is reported about:

(a) The number of motor cars – often high HP – taking 'well-dressed people to dinners or dances' or used for shopping. It is asked 'how are they managing to wangle petrol'?

(b) Wastage of petrol by the NFS, the army, the police and Government officials.

19. RUMOURS

Among rumours reported this week are stories that:

(a) Matches are to be rationed and the tea and sugar rations are to be cut.

(b) The WVS have been told that on no account should American coloured troops be entertained in private homes owing to the prevalence among them of venereal disease.

(c) US Forces are going 'to take over the Southern Command'.

(d) United States forces 'are to seize the vital ports of Eire when the time for definite action arrives'.

NO. 103: TUESDAY 15 SEPTEMBER 1942 TO TUESDAY 22 SEPTEMBER 1942

I. GENERAL COMMENTS

1. GENERAL STATE OF CONFIDENCE AND REACTION TO NEWS

Interest, apart from that taken in home affairs, seems to have been focused almost entirely on the defence of Stalingrad this week. Admiration for its 'heroic defenders' and a feeling epitomised by the question, 'Is there nothing we can do to help Russia?' appear to be almost universal. Opinions conflict as to whether the city will be able to hold out, but there is considerable anxiety about its fate.

Although not much discussion is reported about other war zones, satisfaction is mentioned at 'our large-scale bombing of Germany' and, to a lesser extent, with our action in Madagascar. The announcement of Canadian casualties at Dieppe has in some areas revived discussion about 'the worthwhileness' of the raid.

According to reports from eight Regions and Postal Censorship, people continue 'to be much preoccupied' with the following apprehensions about the winter: (i) the blackout – 'It's the blackout that's worst'; (ii) the fuel shortage; (iii) air raids: 'When winter comes on the Russian front, the Germans will send their planes to bomb us'; (iv) transport difficulties 'of all kinds'.

From the North-Eastern Region and, for the third week in succession, from the South-Western Region 'the unequal distribution and misuse of petrol' are referred to as the main or one of the main topics on the home front.

2. RUSSIA

Admiration for the defenders of Stalingrad, the desire for us to give help to the Russians, and the feeling that we are not doing enough to relieve pressure on them, are again reported this week, with increased intensity.

Although a growing number of people seem to feel that Stalingrad is sooner or later bound to fall, a minority still believe that 'the astounding tenacity of the Russians will save it'. The majority seem, however, to be confident that 'whatever happens to the city, Russian resistance will continue'.

'People in high places who are wanting the Germans and Russians to exterminate each other' are again referred to, being mentioned this week in reports from six Regions.

Feeling about a second front continues on the lines reported last week.

3. EGYPT

Although little comment on the Tobruk raid is reported from some Regions, 'a sudden flare of interest' is reported from others. There is some belief that the raid was a failure and that, 'as at Dieppe, we paid a high price for the results achieved'.

The loss of the two destroyers is specifically mentioned, and in addition 'it is feared that casualties may have been heavy'.

It appears to be fairly generally felt that 'the position in Egypt is now in hand'. There continues, however, to be some impatience at our lack of action, and also 'disappointment that our victory was not followed up, and that we have given the enemy a chance to recover'.

4. MADAGASCAR

Satisfaction is reported that 'we are gaining a firm control over the island', though there is some comment on what is thought to be our slow progress. (This was before the capture of Antananarivo.)

The rejection of our armistice terms appears to have increased feeling against the Vichy Government and impatience at 'any soft handling of Laval and his gang'. In the Southern Region this anti-Vichy feeling is said to be extended in some cases to the Free French on whom 'not much reliance is placed and who are unpopular in some parts of the Region where they've been stationed'.

5. THE ALLIED AIR OFFENSIVE

From seven Regions there are reports that the Allies' large-scale raids on Germany are being followed with the greatest interest. Although there is still some demand for more thousand-bomber raids, it is now felt that 'the oft-repeated threat to make Germany suffer is really being executed'. Astonishment is expressed at the use of our 8,000 lb. bombs, and it is hoped that the enemy is not similarly equipped. Anxiety about our losses increases a desire to know their proportion to the number of planes employed. Lack of such information is said to 'make people feel that the percentage of losses must be high'.

Four Regions report a hankering for the bombing of 'Italy, preferably Rome', and the Italian industrial towns generally; it is not understood 'why Italy remains immune'. It is also felt that 'the bombing of Berlin is our job and should not be left to the Russians'.

6. ENEMY RAIDS ON THIS COUNTRY

Expectation of German raids on this country during the coming winter is said to be fairly strong; it is believed that the Luftwaffe in Russia will 'turn westwards if Hitler's armies can dig themselves in'.

Great concern is still reported from three Regions at the late sounding of sirens, the lack of fighter protection and the failure of the AA defences in coastal areas. On the other hand, great satisfaction is expressed in one south-coast town at the defences which have now been allotted to them. These, it is claimed, have had a noticeably heartening effect on the population.

INCENDIARY BOMBS: These are reported in one Region to be 'better left alone, as so much confusion still persists as to methods of treatment'.

7. THE DIEPPE RAID

The announcement of the Canadian casualties at Dieppe is reported to have caused some concern and has 'increased doubts as to whether the raid was worthwhile'.

In two Regions, there is said to be 'an unhappy feeling that the 3,367 Canadians are only part of the total casualties' – which are variously estimated in the Eastern Region at ten or fifteen thousand.

The belief that the raid was 'an invasion attempt that failed' has not entirely died out.

8. THE WAR SITUATION DEBATE (8TH SEPTEMBER)

Feeling ranging from severe criticism to all-round disgust at the action of Members of Parliament in 'walking out for lunch after the Prime Minister's statement' is reported from five Regions this week; two reports refer to 'the bad effect of such behaviour on workers in industry'.

The following letter, quoted by Postal Censorship, typifies reactions to this incident: 'At a time when England is fighting for her life ... less than twenty members of Parliament are sufficiently interested to be there on the job. These are the people who get on their hind legs and shout about absenteeism if a miner or a docker or a factory worker loses an hour. It makes me mad; they should get the same penalty as the workers, or better still, as the deserters.'

The rebuke administered by Sir Stafford Cripps is thought to have been 'richly deserved'.

9. THE FAR EAST AND THE SOUTH-WEST PACIFIC

Interest in 'this distant front' is still confined to a small minority. There appears, however, to be increasing confidence in the Americans' ability 'to handle the Japs on land and sea', in spite of some concern over the Solomons and Port Moresby. A demand for the bombing of Tokyo and other Japanese cities and for greater aid to China is reported from the Northern Region.

10. INDIA

'The great extent' of the sabotage in India, as lately revealed in the press, is said to have caused some uneasiness; at the same time approval of 'our firm handling' continues, as does lack of sympathy for Congress.

11. BROADCASTING AND PRESENTATION OF NEWS

There is again little criticism of news presentation this week; there is, in fact, some indication that it is regarded by a considerable number of people as 'not unsatisfactory'. Three aspects are, however, unfavourably commented upon in several reports:

(a) GIVING THE ENEMY VERSION FIRST AND CONFIRMING IT
    LATER: This criticism is applied to the BBC and press alike, and the

practice is said to lead to confusion on the part of the public, who 'often
accept German communiqués as official British communiqués'.

(b) GIVING TOO MUCH AWAY TO THE ENEMY: This familiar complaint
is still heard. References to the American naval base in Northern Ireland
are cited again, and another example is said to be the announcement
(presumably by the BBC): 'I am about to take you over to Wallsend, where
they are laying the keel of a new vessel ...' The MP for Derby is also
criticised for referring to the fact that 'he represented a town where railway
engines and aero engines are made', and it is felt that 'the BBC need not
have repeated it in two or three bulletins'.

(c) TOO MUCH WRITING UP OF SMALL SUCCESSES.

Talks and programmes particularly commended include:

(a) WALTER LIPPMANN'S POSTSCRIPT (13TH SEPTEMBER), which is
praised in four Regional reports and described as 'the best help we have
had towards good Anglo-American understanding'.

(b) W. A. SINCLAIR'S TALK (8TH SEPTEMBER) on German propaganda.
'He is excellent; why don't they use him more?'

(c) THE 'BATTLE OF BRITAIN' BROADCAST (14TH SEPTEMBER).

MR. LYTTELTON'S '80 DAY SPEECH': Some interest is reported from four
Regions in Mr. Lyttelton's further references to this in Sheffield on the 16th
September, and it is thought that: (a) 'He expects some considerable improvement
in our position before long'; (b) 'It will increase wishful thinking', and that 'if we
survive the next three weeks without a major disaster people will then think they
can sit back and wait for victory'; (c) 'We shall be opening a second front within
this period.'

'DISTRESSING ARTICLES' IN THE PRESS: Two features in the press are
criticised as causing 'distress and misery' to soldiers' next of kin. One is an account,
said to have appeared in the *Star* (7th September) and in the *Daily Telegraph* (8th
September), of how our men in Libya were made to dig trenches in front of the
German guns and were then mown down, the Germans remarking: 'Less to feed, if
we don't take them prisoner.'

The other is an article in the *Sunday Express* of 13th September, by O. D. Gallagher,
describing how 'the last troops to enter Singapore were tortured and killed by the
blood-lusty Japanese'; this is being 'widely discussed in the Peterborough area', as it
is believed that these troops were mainly Lincolnshire men.

THE PUBLIC'S ATTITUDE TO BROADCAST MUSIC

Recent enquiries by BBC Listener Research indicate a growing appreciation for
symphony concerts and a decline in enthusiasm for the theatre and cinema organ.
Two enquiries based on random samples, each of 5,000 listeners, show the following
changes in the public's attitude to symphony concerts:

	Sept. 1941	Aug. 1942
Very enthusiastic	10%	11%
Quite enjoys them, when in the mood	13%	14%
Doesn't feel strongly, either way	17%	23%
Doesn't much like them	20%	23%
Strongly dislikes, avoids if possible	40%	29%

If the second group, who are predisposed to favour concerts without being enthusiasts, are regarded as part of the symphony concert public, it appears that this kind of music interests about one listener in four. A comparison of the two enquiries shows that, whereas a year ago 40% of the listening public were strongly antipathetic to concerts, this figure has since decreased by more than a quarter. In the majority of cases this change is merely from active hostility to a more passive dislike, but the fact that this movement of opinion has already increased, however slightly, suggests that if it continues, more positive changes may be expected in the future.

Similar enquiries about the public's attitude to cinema organ music show the following results:

	Aug. 1941	Aug. 1942
Very enthusiastic	34%	27%
Quite enjoys it, when in the mood	26%	23%
Doesn't feel strongly, either way	23%	27%
Doesn't much like it	10%	13%
Strongly dislikes, avoids if possible	7%	10%

Last year the keenest enthusiasts exceeded one-third of the whole listening public; they now number little more than a quarter. At the same time antipathy towards cinema organs has increased from 17% to 23%. In a word, the marked decrease in hostility towards symphony concerts runs parallel with the decrease in the popularity of the theatre and cinema organ.

II. SPECIAL COMMENTS

12. FUEL ECONOMY

Discussion of this subject appears to be increasing, although few new points have arisen. There is a marked desire to do everything possible to economise, but indignation is expressed at the necessity for the campaign: 'People are willing to go short of imported goods, but when it comes to coal they want to know the reason why.' It is felt that the gap between production and consumption could be bridged by improved methods in mine management and a greater effort on the part of the miners, and there is again suspicion that workings are being prepared for post-war coal production at the expense of the present output. There is renewed comment on waste in public buildings, Government offices, cinemas and shops, and it is suggested that the campaign might profitably be directed to these culprits rather than to the domestic consumer.

Points particularly affecting the housewife are:

(a) The shortage of matches, which is reported from seven Regions, and which results in waste through small lights or fires continually burning, and the switching on of electric fires to light cigarettes, etc.

(b) People on the 'all-in' rate for electricity resent not being able to get a reduction in their bills if their consumption is below the minimum amount.

(c) Special consideration is again asked for those who do baking and washing at home.

(d) The proportionate rations of paraffin and coal are considered unfair and there are fears of a paraffin shortage in some country districts.

FUEL ECONOMY ADVERTISEMENTS: One Region reports that people are taking the campaign more to heart and suggests that a 'repeat advertisement' of the Target Tables in the press would now receive greater attention than the first issue. Another Region calls for 'more and continued publicity'. It is said that the advertisement, 'Do not use fuel for space heating' is not understood, and criticism is again made of economy posters being shown in districts where gas and electricity are not available.

There is also criticism from one Region of the 'lavish brochure' issued by Commander King-Hall giving information on the fuel campaign weeks. Further comment this week on his broadcast talk is that 'to be lectured for a state of affairs for which the Government is to blame is a natural cause of resentment'.

FUEL FLASHES: Reports on these are equally divided between approval and sarcasm: 'I am fed up with being talked at, lectured at and given advice.'

FUEL ECONOMIES IN THE ROYAL HOUSEHOLD: These have been received in Scotland with interest, but objections have been taken to mention of the King's bath having a 5-inch water line painted on it. This is considered 'going too far' and an intrusion on the King's privacy.

13. TRANSPORT

Transport – described in one report as 'a major evil and a subject of constant discussion throughout the Region' – continues to be widely reported as a matter for complaint. This week nine Regional reports (as against seven last week) refer to transport difficulties of some kind, particularly in country districts.

While complaints for the most part follow familiar lines, the difficulties and hardships of elderly people are mentioned in two reports this week: 'From various parts of the Southern Region there are complaints from elderly people, compelled to undertake train journeys on business, of the strain of spending hours standing in crowded corridors. Some of them are saying that they do not think that they can survive a winter of such travel with the added trial of the blackout.'

People are said to be asking 'why the number of trains is to be reduced, as this will throw increased traffic on to the buses. It is pointed out that the trains are powered from coal which we produce, while buses run on petrol which we have to import.'

PETROL: Unfavourable comments are reported from five Regions on 'the number of private cars being used for journeys obviously not of national importance', and of 'the various loopholes which apparently exist, and are taken full advantage of by many business people and owners of private cars, to obtain petrol'. 'Cases are quoted', according to the report from the North-Eastern Region, 'of thirty cars being drawn up outside a building while a lecture was being held, twelve or sixteen outside a house where a sale was in progress, and twelve outside a hotel and dance hall'.

It is thought that the police are lax in checking up on petrol usage, and the suggestion has been made that 'motorists should have a card or endorsement in their registration books indicating the purpose for which they are allowed to use petrol'.

Suspicion of abuses on the part of farmers – who 'seem to have unlimited petrol' – is again mentioned; it is believed that 'empty sacks, bulb trays and similar articles used in connection with agriculture are carried with the sole object of providing an excuse for the drivers if they are called upon to explain the use of petrol'.

There are also 'complaints that discrimination is shown in the allocation of petrol, one businessman having to lay up his car while another, in apparently similar circumstances, is allowed petrol'.

SHORTAGE OF SPARE PARTS FOR BICYCLES: The difficulty of replacing spare parts of bicycles, and particularly ball bearings, is said to be the cause of considerable hardship to munition workers, who 'depend on their machines for getting to work'.

GREEN LINE COACHES: Some grumbling is reported from the Eastern and the London Regions about the 'imminent suspension' of these buses. It is feared that the parents of evacuated children who have been in the habit of taking a cheap day return to see their children on Sundays, will not be able to afford the more expensive train fare, and will bring their children home.

14. INDUSTRY

Again this week little comment is reported on production as a whole, and the general feeling seems to be that it is 'fairly satisfactory'.

THE CALL-UP: Two subjects are, however, arousing a great deal of discussion in connection with the call-up:

(a) 'WOMEN OF FORTY CALLED UP, WHILE GIRLS REMAIN': Comment is reported from four Regions about 'the call-up of older women for the Services' and 'the number of women of about forty who are being directed into industry', while apparently young girls are left in Government offices and departments. Feeling on this subject may be summed up in the words of a writer quoted by Postal Censorship: 'I have to go for an interview ... they must think I haven't enough to do when John comes home for his tea at five o'clock, Daddy at six o'clock, Beryl at 6.30 and Fred at 7.45 p.m. and besides me giving a day a week at the hospital. There are a lot of single girls of nineteen round about who are doing nothing to help the war effort ... I don't know why a woman of forty with a grown-up family has to be interviewed.'

(b) 'YOUNG MEN WHO APPEAR TO HAVE EVADED SERVICE IN THE FORCES': Criticism about this is reported from four Regions. It is asked: 'How are so many apparently strong, healthy young men in the thirties still in non-essential work and filling in their time in the NFS or Special Police, while the forties to fifties are being called up and sent away?'

15. MINERS AND THE ESSENTIAL WORK ORDER

Preliminary reactions to the Essential Work (Coalmining Industry) (Amendment) Order, 1942, are referred to in reports from nine Regions. The general public are said, in the main, to be unaware as yet of the existence of the new amendment, but the few who know about it think that 'it's about time'. In some Regions (particularly in the Northern Region, where the amended order was only circulated towards the end of last week) the miners themselves seem not yet to have 'appreciated the object of the amendment' or, at any rate, 'how it would operate in particular cases'.

THE MINERS' REACTIONS: Most reports indicate that, on the whole, the miners are accepting the amendment 'very calmly ... as a matter of course, and are not at all perturbed'. Many are said to welcome it and 'to be beginning to realise that voluntary absenteeism must be eliminated'. Exceptions are, however, mentioned, notably in the Midland Region where at first the miners were said to be 'very disturbed' and to feel that they were 'having the whip applied'. In Scotland, too, the miners are said in some cases 'not to be taking it very well'.

The following points of view have been expressed by the miners:

(a) It will be a good thing for all of them because –
   (i)   only the bad miners will be affected,
   (ii)   the good will no longer be 'vilified on account of the bad',
   (iii) production and qualification for bonus will be improved,
   (iv)   responsibility for drastic action becomes less personal for the workmates of the offenders.

(b) Miners feel that they will now be 'tied to one pit', though one report indicates that 'the fact that free movement from pit to pit is now forbidden does not appear to be understood by miners as yet'.

(c) Two reports indicate a strong feeling that due allowance should be made for the exhausting nature of the miner's work, and for the fact that 'tiredness often compels a miner to take a day off'. (55% of the Warwickshire miners, it is said, are over 40.)

(d) 'The managements should be liable to investigation too, in the same way as the men.' The miners' distrust of the managements is stressed in two reports, and implied in others.

(e) Miners resent the comparison between themselves and factory workers.

THE MANAGEMENTS' REACTIONS: The managements and owners appear to have welcomed the amendment to a man: mine owners, according to two reports, 'welcome anything that puts pressure on the men'. The new procedure, it is thought, will be an improvement on the 'ineffectiveness of Pit Production Committees in dealing with the absentee problem, which is said to have been due to the policy of the men's representatives'. It is pointed out that 'the Committee members were the elected officers of Union Branches, and their re-election to these offices was often more important to them than the prosecuting of a miner for an offence, the miner's vote being lost if he received a fine for absenteeism'. It is, however, felt that any action under the new amendment should be 'taken immediately after an offence, as this would impress on the offender that he was getting his deserts and would cut down the resentment which grows as a result of discussion, consideration and other delays'. But even under the amendment it is thought that prosecution will still be 'indirect and lengthy. The Fuel Investigation Officer has to report to the National Service Officer who, in turn, investigates the case, after which it *may* be passed on to the courts. All these investigations mean further loss of working hours for the miner, who begins to feel that his avoidable holiday is being lengthened by the Government.' The suggestion is made that 'the Fuel Investigation Officer himself should have power of prosecution, and that after a miner has received one warning he should, immediately upon committing a second offence, be prosecuted'.

THE FUEL INVESTIGATION OFFICER: Two reports stress – and others imply – that the Fuel Investigation Officers should be 'independent of both sides' and that they 'will have to be very careful in implementing the order, as mistakes on their part will have dire results'. It is, however, felt that 'if he shows that he means business, he will have the public's backing, the respect of the majority of the men and the welcome of the managements'.

'A LOOP-HOLE FOR SLACKERS': It is suggested in one report that the fact that 'shifts can be lost quite legally if the time is spent in a visit to a doctor' may provide a loop-hole for slackers, and it is said that 'about 10% will take advantage of this as they habitually visit the doctor on the slightest pretext'. According to the report from the Midland Region, 'the Warwickshire Miners' Federation states that "sick notes" have poured in, since the order was announced, from men who were absent before but who never bothered with sick notes'.

POINTS NEEDING CLARIFICATION: In addition to the question already referred to of 'the free movement from pit to pit', which is said not to be understood at present, other points which are thought to need clarifying include the meaning and interpretation of certain phrases in the order, such as 'reasonable excuse', 'persistently late' and 'lawful and reasonable orders'. In connection with this last, the Welsh report states that there are at present 'a large number of young colliery managers, highly qualified in theory but naturally lacking in practical experience', and there is said to be some difficulty in visualising 'a ripened collier with twenty, thirty or even fifty years' experience on the face taking instructions from one of these'.

16. FOOD

Praise for the general food situation is again reported. 'Food Facts' are also commended. 'Their up-to-the-minute hints' and 'reminders of the current four-weekly period' are commended. 'These Ministry Notices are getting to be looked for and relied upon.'

Aspects of the food situation causing unfavourable comment include:

(a) The shortage of shell eggs.
(b) The waste of fruit owing to: (i) the high controlled price, (ii) the insufficient ration of sugar for preserving it or for making jam, (iii) the shortage of jars for preserving.
(c) The proposal to ration milk and the enforcement of rationalisation schemes, particularly when the latter are thought to favour the big distributor at the expense of 'the small man'.
(d) The increased cheese ration, which is considered too large, and which is difficult to prevent from going mouldy.
(e) The points allocation, which is considered inadequate.

It is suggested that more ideas should be given to the public about how to use potatoes instead of bread, and that better and more varied cooking of potatoes in restaurants and canteens would increase their consumption. The 'Potato Pete' advertisements are said to be disliked in Scotland, though the campaign is reported to be having some effect there.

No comment on the rise in the price of bread has been reported.

17. WOMEN'S FIRE-GUARD ORDER

Comments on this order continue on the same lines as were reported last week, and may be summarised as follows:

(a) Equality of compensation is necessary.
(b) Women should not watch in target areas.
(c) They should have proper amenities.
(d) Men should not be allowed 'to dodge'.
(e) 'The new German bombs are too dangerous.'

People are still reported to be uncertain of what they will be required to do, and Miss Wilkinson's talk on 11th September is described as being 'evasive'. The 'incomprehensibility of the official wording of the public notices' about registering for fire-watching is also commented on.

18. US TROOPS IN GREAT BRITAIN

Reports show that relations with the US troops continue to be good, on the whole, and there is an increasing desire for greater knowledge of them and their country. There is a feeling that they are now being welcomed and 'accepted as part of the community', and their reaction to hospitality is considered appreciative. On the other hand, there are still complaints that some of them make a too lavish display of wealth, of too much treating of young girls who are not accustomed to drink, and of a lack of discipline. Reference is also made in one Region to their being guilty of 'careless talk'.

It is of interest that in a special Postal Censorship Report (23rd September) on opinion on US troops in Britain over the last two months, references to them appear to be almost equally divided between appreciation and adverse criticism. (Home Intelligence Reports over this period, though giving these two aspects of public feeling, show a slightly greater volume of appreciation than adverse criticism.)

Renewed complaints, this time from Scotland, are reported of shopkeepers who are alleged to be taking advantage of US troops who are ignorant of our currency.

19. SERVICEMEN'S PAY AND ALLOWANCES

Discussion on this subject seems to be as widespread as ever, and the familiar comparisons are made between the pay of UK troops and that of:

US troops
Munition workers

(Adverse comment is also reported from the relatives of servicemen on the 'numerous uniforms provided for the American troops': it is said that 'American privates have as many dresses as a debutante'.)

The recent increases in servicemen's pay are still described as inadequate, and there is a feeling that 'the Government has had the increase forced upon them by the presence of so many better-paid American and Dominion troops in this country'. The belief is expressed that 'trouble will ensue if more is not done to bridge the gap in actual cash received between the British forces and the US men. This is said to apply equally to junior officers with wives and children to support.'

The hardships and difficulties of servicemen's dependants are mentioned in two reports, particularly in the case of 'widows with young children, who have received no commensurate increase'.

20. SERVICES' COMFORTS

The removal of the Board of Trade's concession to supply coupon-free wool for knitters of Service comforts is said to be causing concern to relatives of servicemen: 'It has taken away the last opportunity women had of making something for their menfolk.' Old ladies 'who wanted to feel they were helping a soldier' now, apparently, consider themselves 'quite useless'.

21. LACK OF DOMESTIC HELP

The lack of domestic workers for the sick and aged is said to be causing much hardship. The bright side of the picture is, however, mentioned in the report from Wales, according to which general practitioners agree that there is 'a progressive decline in the minor neuroses'. This is thought to be 'obvious in the case of the more wealthy who have had to undertake a serious job of work. In particular, the lady of the house, left without maids or car, seems to have gained much in health and, quietly, in self-esteem. The maidless cease to grouse, and boast about it.'

NO. 106: TUESDAY 6 OCTOBER 1942 TO TUESDAY 13 OCTOBER 1942

I. GENERAL COMMENTS

1. GENERAL STATE OF CONFIDENCE AND REACTION TO NEWS

Once again, the general level of public feeling is reported to have undergone little change. Greater hopefulness about Stalingrad, though still tempered by caution, is widespread, but it appears to be counterbalanced by a growing impatience at 'the failure of the United Nations to take offensive action in support of Russia'.

For most people, however, the major issue of the week seems to have been the chaining of prisoners of war, which in nine Regions is said to have superseded Stalingrad as a subject of interest. The action of the Germans in manacling the Dieppe prisoners has aroused anger and consternation, and is reported to have 'increased and hardened feeling against Germany'. It is pointed out that 'had Hitler deliberately wished to stimulate the people of this country he could not have selected a more successful way of doing it'. Opinion on the wisdom of our retaliating is divided, and there are indications that support for the Government's action is losing some of its strength.

Reports nevertheless suggest some increase in complacency, as well as lack of interest in the war. There is an indication that this may partly be the result of 'a feeling of frustration at our own continued inaction', and because 'people are fed up with waiting for something that does not look like coming'. It is said that, 'especially in the lower grades of the social scale, the seriousness of the war situation is little appreciated', and inspiration for the war effort is still lacking for many people.

There is also 'a certain amount of apprehension that this winter is going to be nastier than the last one'. The blackout is disliked, particularly by women. To this are added, in people's minds, the discomforts of fuel shortage and fire-watching duties, as well as the possibility of renewed German air raids if the Russian front becomes stabilised.

2. THE CHAINING OF PRISONERS OF WAR

The whole subject of the chaining of prisoners of war has aroused intense and widespread interest on the part of all but a very few, 'who seem to be left unmoved'; by the end of the week, it appeared to have ousted Stalingrad as the main talking point in nine Regions. The following reactions have been reported, and are arranged in order of the frequency with which they were mentioned:

(a) 'RAGE AND A HARDENING OF SENTIMENT AGAINST THE GERMANS': Their action is said to have 'aroused a greater outburst of anger than any other example of Nazi brutality for a considerable time past'. ('Tales of atrocities in occupied countries', it is said, 'were becoming unreal through too much repetition.') The wave of hatred for the Germans is said to have 'stepped up production in some factories'.

(b) DESIRE FOR STRONG RETALIATORY ACTION ON OUR PART: At first there was some 'impatience against our Government for not taking immediate action', but the statement that we would chain a similar number of Germans met with the support, apparently, of the majority. Feeling ranged from impatience that we were going to wait till Saturday before doing this, to a feeling of 'I don't like the idea, but I expect there is nothing else we can do.' There is now some indication that many people are changing their minds and are no longer convinced that we are adopting the best course in retaliating in kind.

(c) 'WE SHOULD NOT DEGRADE OURSELVES TO THE GERMAN LEVEL' has from the first been the opinion of a large minority, which is said to consist, in the main, of older or more educated people, and of those whose relatives are prisoners in German hands. This minority is now said to be increasing. Objections to our retaliating are said to be for the following reasons:

   (i) 'Where will this competition in brutality end?' It is a vicious circle, and the Germans will always be prepared to go one worse than ourselves.

   (ii) Germany holds the greater number of prisoners and will not care if we make up the numbers with Italians.

   (iii) The Germans don't care what happens to their men. It is suggested that 'the German High Command would prefer us to shoot prisoners attempting to escape, rather than that we should get useful information from them'.

   (iv) Whatever we do, it 'will make no difference to the Nazi attitude' and 'the only thing for us to do is to get on with the war, hit them hard and wait until we are in a position to talk to them'.

(d) THE BEST RETALIATION WOULD BE TO INCREASE OUR BOMBING OF GERMANY, starting with a 'terrific raid on Berlin'.

(e) 'THE GERMANS MUST BE DESPERATE TO DO IT'. There is some bewilderment as to why the Germans should make such a fuss; it is suggested that 'the chaining is a red herring to draw the German public opinion from Hitler's other failures', or that it is 'a desperate attempt on Hitler's part to work up dying enthusiasm for his cause'. (This point of view has found support in Hitler's and Goering's recent speeches, which are thought to have shown their anxiety and discomfort.)

(f) THE STATEMENT BY THE GOVERNMENT ON SATURDAY (10TH OCTOBER) is said to have been well received and to have cleared away people's doubts: 'The fact that we had tied the hands of some of our prisoners in the field is accepted by most people as totally different from the manacling of prisoners under detention under proper guard.' Before the appearance of this statement there had been some uneasiness and suspicion on this score, and it is felt that the admission should have been made immediately the Germans made the claim. According to one report, 'Universal comment has been – "Why didn't they say so before?"'

(g) A RENEWAL OF INTEREST IN HESS is reported from two Regions, much of which is described as mere speculation, but there is a suggestion that 'Hess should be made to suffer'.

(h) There is some questioning as to what 'being put in chains' actually means: 'Is it for an hour or two, or for all the time?' 'Does it cause pain or discomfort?'

3. RUSSIA

Feelings about Russia may be summarised this week as follows:

(a) Less interest and less anxiety. 'For the first time for many weeks, the Russian front has had a real competitor for attention, and the fact that no reports of any great variation in the position have been received has caused interest to decline.'

(b) Continued 'strong and widespread admiration, particularly for the defenders of Stalingrad'.

(c) 'Rising belief that Stalingrad will not fall.' There is a fairly widespread belief that the Germans have been 'baffled and have failed in their storming tactics, and this is regarded as particularly cheering after Hitler himself had promised that Stalingrad should fall'. There is 'delighted amusement at the efforts of the German propagandists to make the best of this situation'.

(d) 'Are we doing all we can to help?' 'Why haven't we sent bombers – a thousand of them – to Russia to operate from there instead of over western Germany?' 'Since Churchill flew to Russia, why can't other bombers be flown there too?'

(e) The 'quality of Russian resistance at Stalingrad has continued to arouse some disparaging comment about our own troops'.

(f) If Stalingrad were to fall, it is feared by some that Russia would ask for a separate peace. One explanation of M. Stalin's recent statement was that 'he may be preparing the way for opening separate negotiations with Hitler'.

4. THE SECOND FRONT

Although an increase in 'second front talk' is reported from three Regions – in one of which it is said to have been greater than at any time in recent weeks – the majority still seem ready to 'leave it to the experts' ... 'but let it be soon rather than late'. Strong though the desire is that we should wait till we are properly prepared, this is offset by a fear that we might leave it until it is too late or by a belief, in the case of a good many, that it is already too late. Expectancy that 'something will happen soon', which appears to be fairly widespread, is said to have found some support in Mr. Churchill's reference to 'this significant time'.

Reference continues to be made to 'anti-Russian feeling in high quarters', to the discouraging effect of the Dieppe casualties, and to the agitation of the Communists for a second front.

5. M. STALIN'S REPLIES TO MR. CASSIDY'S QUESTIONS

Reports differ as to the amount of interest aroused by M. Stalin's remarks, but the general opinion seems to be that his statement was 'a puzzle that uninformed ingenuity cannot solve'. Reactions differ little from those mentioned in our last report and range from indignation at his ingratitude to shame that he should have to ask us to keep our promise. His statement, together with various utterances by Mr. Willkie, is held to account for the increased second front talk.

What seems to have made a particularly strong impression on many people is the indication that 'there is some deep misunderstanding between our country and Russia'; there is disappointment that 'such a statement should have been made so soon after Mr. Churchill's visit'.

6. THE RAID ON SARK

This raid has been overshadowed, for most people, by the chaining of the Dieppe prisoners. The following reactions have, however, been noted:

(a) Anger and bitterness at the enforced deportation of British subjects. This is taken as showing how short of manpower the Germans must be.
(b) 'Why haven't we retaken the Channel Islands before now, when they are on our very doorstep?' It is asked why we leave the Channel Islanders at the mercy of the Germans, when, it is thought, 'a few Commandos could turn them out'.
(c) People have noted with pleasure the fact that this is only one of several such raids. 'I thought this was happening, but I'm glad to know for certain.'

7. THE PRIME MINISTER'S SPEECH AT EDINBURGH
(12TH OCTOBER)

(Reports have not yet been received from all Regions.)

The speech appears to have been well received and people are said to have approved 'his references to our having stood alone for a year, as a necessary reminder for both Russian and American critics of Britain'. In Scotland 'his more hopeful view of the situation was noted, and this has heartened most people as Mr. Churchill is not generally considered over-optimistic'. On the other hand, some Scottish critics 'thought he was too buttery towards Scotland', and some working-class people on Clydeside seem sceptical of his remarks about the improved health of this country. They do not see 'how this squares' with the Dawson Committee's findings on the increase in tuberculosis.

8. MR. LYTTELTON'S '80 DAY' SPEECH

There are some references to slight interest in Mr. Lyttelton's '80 day' speech, and he is accused 'of making us count to no purpose'. People were 'expecting some spectacular development' at the end of 80 days, and his speech is therefore considered to be 'a bad form of ministerial oratory, which can only lead to public cynicism'.

9. ENEMY RAIDS ON THIS COUNTRY

Expectation of reprisals by the Luftwaffe is reported from seven Regions but is 'not causing much concern': 'most people seem resigned rather than acutely worried'. One Region reports a divided opinion as to whether we shall get raids: 'there is much less fear now that the Russians are holding out at Stalingrad'; and there is said to be a feeling of confidence that we would still 'have the Germans' measure even if they withdrew large numbers of planes from the East'.

BLACKOUT: Indignation has been expressed in Norwich that the BBC should have broadcast a statement of the city's defective blackout. There are reports from two Regions expressing uneasiness about blackout arrangements in some places; it is thought the regulations should be more strictly enforced.

10. THE ALLIED AIR OFFENSIVE

There is little comment this week. The raid on Lille by Flying Fortresses has given satisfaction, though people cannot understand why their losses were so slight and their fighting capacity so great as compared with our bombers.

Four Regions refer to our air losses published a few days ago. Although these are deplored, the proportionate losses are thought to be 'not unsatisfactory', and the view is expressed that they 'show the great strength of a force which can stand such losses and still maintain superiority in Egypt and elsewhere'.

The desire for the bombing of Italy is again reported, this week by four Regions, two of which refer to a feeling that the Government is being influenced by the Catholics in this country; it is suggested that a speech by a Government spokesman might clear up the position. Two reports mention some demand for the 'bombing of Berlin as a reprisal for the chaining of our prisoners'; another urges that any chaining of our prisoners by Italians should be 'answered by the bombing of Rome'.

11. INDIA

Some 'slight renewal of interest' in the Indian situation, possibly stimulated by the recent debate in the House of Commons (9th September), is reported this week. A desire 'to see an attempt made to end the present deadlock' is reported from three Regions, and it is felt that the Government should make greater attempts to negotiate with 'those leaders in India who are willing to do so'. Congress and Gandhi are still said to be in 'bad odour'.

12. FAR EAST

Interest is limited, but people are pleased 'with the way things are going in the Solomons and New Guinea'; fear is, however, again expressed by a small minority that 'our troops may be advancing into some ingenious Japanese trap'.

Only one Region reports expressions of 'appreciation' at our readiness to 'relinquish extra-territorial rights in China'; it is described as 'an earnest of our good intentions'.

13. MIDDLE EAST

Interest in this theatre of war continues to be at a low level, though people are reported to be less 'bewildered' by the long lull, and to be 'slightly more hopeful' that 'a big offensive' will start soon.

14. THE DAWSON COMMITTEE ON TUBERCULOSIS

The findings of this Committee have aroused some interest. The public 'do not see how this increase in tuberculosis can be reconciled with other Ministry of Health statements that the health of the population is good'; it is felt that in fact 'our powers of resistance have been considerably lowered'.

High approval is reported from the North-Eastern Region for the suggested provisions 'for the maintenance of sufferers and their families'; in London some factory workers are said to have commented to the effect that 'we are following the Russian lead'.

15. BROADCASTING AND PRESENTATION OF NEWS

Once more there have been few reported comments on news presentation and on the whole people seem to be satisfied. References are made to a preference for the European News Service, and to people reading only press headlines and listening only to the summary at the beginning of the news bulletins.

There has been criticism in two reports of 'the BBC's handling of Goering's speech; there is a preference for verbatim reports of enemy leaders' speeches, or for faithful summaries, rather than so much ironic comment'.

MINISTER OF AGRICULTURE'S POSTSCRIPT (SUNDAY, 10TH OCTOBER): This has earned what is described as 'unusually widespread praise'. Mr. Hudson is 'praised for his sincerity, his modesty in claiming no credit for himself in the achievement, and for his courage in referring to a "Higher Power" having provided for us in our need'.

'CONVOY TO RUSSIA' NEWSREELS: The greatest satisfaction is reported with these for 'showing that help really is getting through to Russia'.

II. SPECIAL COMMENTS

16. WOMEN'S FIRE-GUARD ORDER

Although 'a hardening of opposition' to the order is reported from the North-Eastern Region (where even a women's strike is talked about), 'resignation' and 'less discussion' are reported from five Regions and Postal Censorship. In the 'pockets of resistance' which still remain, the objection is not so much to women fire-watching, as to 'an almost passionate feeling of resentment against men who are considered to be shirking their duties', and an insistence that 'all available men should be roped in first'. Other criticisms follow along familiar lines: opposition of the menfolk, reluctance of women with household responsibilities to fire-watch away from home, and a desire for equal rates of compensation.

There are allegations that many women are claiming exemptions from duty, up to 80% in some places. Feeling persists that some women have not registered at all and the hope is expressed that 'they will check up, to trace the evaders'.

'Adverse criticism' of Miss Ellen Wilkinson's recent speeches on the subject has been received from three Regions, and it is asked: 'On what grounds does she claim to speak for women collectively?' In Liverpool the situation is reported to be 'much quieter', but both Mr. Morrison and Miss Wilkinson are reported to be unpopular.

An article in the *Sunday Dispatch* of 4th October has been 'specially praised' for the 'interesting light' it threw on the question.

17. FUEL ECONOMY

Thanks apparently to the weather, the ban on central heating and the 'moral blackmail' of telling people not to light fires before November 1st is the most discussed aspect of the economy campaign this week. An epidemic of colds is reported from six Regions, thought to be due to the lack of heating during the cold spell, and the Scottish Region states that 'reports of shivering conditions in offices and especially schools come from all over the Region'. It is suggested in one report that the ban on central heating is forcing many people to light fires, thereby causing a greater fuel consumption than would be the case with a central heating boiler; also that much fuel will be used by people who have to stay away from work through illness.

Coupled with a great desire to do all that is possible to economise, there continues to be strong resentment against the Government for its failure 'to take a grip of the question', and for 'playing unfairly by trying to lay the responsibility at the consumers' end'.

FUEL TARGET: The difficulties of reaching the Target are again emphasised by seven Regions; one report suggests that 'now is the time to re-issue the Fuel Target notice when public interest is so awake'.

Renewed complaints are made of waste of light in Government and municipal offices and large shops, and of a market 'where butchers have a blaze of lights'; there is a report of a Law Court in one Region being centrally heated while the schools are cold. It is asked that more gas lighters should be made available, as 'some people have had no matches for three weeks and the gas has had to be kept lit for hours on end'.

FUEL RATIONING: There is some demand for rationing as being the best way of securing equal distribution, although there is some realisation that equitable rationing would be difficult without guaranteed supplies.

'FUEL FLASHES': Fuel Flashes are described in six reports as having 'outworn their welcome'; on the other hand, three Regions report favourable reception: 'People like Freddie Grisewood's persuasive tones.'

It is reported that press publicity given to local pits who 'make their targets' is appreciated and that there is a general improvement in output and an atmosphere of greater effort about the pits.

18. COAL PRODUCTION

Reports from four Regions refer to factors affecting coal production as follows:

(a) Lack of discipline, chiefly among the younger colliers 'who fail to appreciate the national need and are conscious of their indispensability'.

(b) Absenteeism attributed to: (i) increased wages; colliers are now able to spend more on recreations such as dog racing; (ii) fire-guard duty, 'which is often given as an excuse'.

(c) The strain of work among older men: 'six or seven shifts are too much for them'.

19. THE TYNESIDE STRIKE

There appears to have been little interest in the Tyneside strike outside the districts involved. Locally, however, as is shown by a special report from the RIO, Northern Region, an 'overwhelming majority of the public feel considerable bitterness towards the men concerned', though there is some support for them in their own districts. It is also said that some of their complaints about inefficiency in the management of the yards are justifiable.

Among the men who remained at work some are said to believe that Mr. Bevin's concern for his future inhibited him from taking 'necessary action'.

The reasons given by the strikers ranged from the trade unions' agreement to a pay-day change without consulting the men, to complaints about their welfare facilities. When questioned, they have hinted that 'a great deal more' lies behind the strike than has been published, but refuse to say what. As 'many of them appear somewhat shamefaced at the relative unimportance' of their reasons, this attitude is thought by some people to be only a 'face-saver'.

The strike leaders are said to have been known for some time as the instigators of feeling against the trade union leaders, and to have seized this opportunity, by appearing to represent the men, to discredit the leaders for failing to do so. While some of the Central Strike Committee were apparently shop stewards, others were merely vociferous 'spokesmen'; it is said that despite their promises to the men, they took no steps to bring about a settlement, and, indeed, without referring to the men, told the employers 'the men wished the strike to continue'.

20. MAN- AND WOMAN-POWER

Complaints about the alleged waste of man- and woman-power are reported from nine Regions this week.

The main criticisms are that:

(a) People are evading their responsibilities: (i) 'hundreds of young people in soft jobs'; (ii) childless servicemen's wives; (iii) young women 'who have married to avoid conscription'.

(b) Men and women 'put into the wrong jobs', particularly skilled workers into unskilled jobs.

(c) Men kept on where they cannot be fully employed, instead of being transferred to work where they could be. In this connection 'a great amount of feeling and a strong sense of frustration' are reported amongst workers at shipbuilding yards at Hull.

(d) Overstaffing at labour camps. According to an employee quoted by Postal Censorship: 'I for one can't understand the waste of manpower, for every job I have been in since the war, they have three men doing one man's work and it makes my blood boil to see the campaigns for more women for all sorts of things, and thousands of us men kept doing nothing to help in the struggle against Hitler and his gang.'

(e) The increasing difficulties of many types of employers through the call-up of trained personnel.

COMBINED SERVICES' RECRUITING CAMPAIGN: Little interest appears to have been aroused by this campaign, which is only mentioned in reports from three Regions; reactions given are as follows: (i) women are 'left cold' by the campaign as they are mostly busy already with evacuees, Civil Defence, etc. (ii) 'an increasing feeling', to quote from the Northern Region report, 'that women with children should look after them and neither volunteer for, nor be directed into, the Services or industry; this feeling is said to be created by the noticeable increase in juvenile delinquency'.

21. WAGES AND PAY

There is further reference this week to feeling, described in the North-Eastern Region as 'rising discontent', at 'the inequality of sacrifice and reward between servicemen and women and their dependants on the one hand and civilians, particularly munition workers, on the other'. 'The inadequacy of allowances' to servicemen's wives is again particularly mentioned, though it is also suggested that (i) in some cases 'exploitation by landlords charging high rents is the chief cause of financial difficulty'; (ii) 'far too few' know about the availability of war service grants; (iii) delay in dealing with some cases causes hardship: 'every day of waiting deepens personal distress'.

Two Regions also refer to war widows being 'very badly off since prices have increased so greatly; it is asked why their pension was not increased at the same time as the Old Age Pension'.

Unfavourable comparisons continue to be made, in addition to the above, between the pay of:

(a) UK troops and (i) US troops (ii) juveniles.
(b) Skilled and unskilled workers.
(c) Women and men.

22. SHOPPING DIFFICULTIES OF WAR WORKERS

Workers are reported 'to be faced with a serious dilemma as a result of the early closing and lunch-hour closing of shops and the late hours they are expected to work. Either they must take time off for shopping or they cannot obtain their fair share of goods.'

23. CLOTHING COUPONS

Initial reactions to the new coupon values for clothing are not very favourable.
The rationing of towels is described as 'the last word' because:

(a) In places where there are billetees and evacuees, good pre-war-quality towels are quickly worn out, and can only be replaced by poor-quality towels.
(b) The fact that towels have been difficult to obtain for some has meant that in many households 'stocks are very low'.

The increase in coupon value for fully-fashioned stockings is described as 'disappointing', although pleasure is expressed at the possibility of obtaining 'a good pair of fully-fashioned stockings that will wear better than the present ones'. It is felt that 'purely medical necessities such as surgical and abdominal belts which cannot be used for non-medical purposes' should be coupon-free.

The 'counter-balancing concessions' are thought to be 'unsubstantial' and 'the fact that the new issue of coupons will take place in March instead of April is too remote at the moment to make much difference'.

24. INCOME TAX

Three Regions report some worry or irritation over income tax among workers. The specific points raised are as follows:

(a) If deductions could be made at a fixed rate in the pound on each week's earnings, the men would be 'much more satisfied'.

(b) When a man changes his employment 'his new employer does not deduct income tax from his pay until a return of the man's income tax is made for the next period; and then the arrears are brought forward, making the deductions very heavy'.

People are also reported to be saying 'that to pay income tax and to save is now impossible'.

25. SALVAGE

Although criticisms about non-collection of salvage and the collection of railings continue on familiar lines, a few additional points have been reported this week:

(a) 'Why are rubber mats to be seen in shops and public houses not called in?' To quote from the London Region report, 'In many public houses there are said to be mats supplied by the Imperial Tobacco Company, which measure nine-foot-by-six and weigh about five or six pounds.'

(b) Scrap metal dealers are said to be conducting 'a ramp' over salvage.

26. US TROOPS IN GREAT BRITAIN

Comment on this subject has largely died down, but reports continue to show that where personal contact is made the US troops are, on the whole, popular, and 'settling in well'. There is still some criticism of the amount of money they have to spend, of their apparently 'casual behaviour', elaborate uniform, and 'heavy drinking'; and one Region reports a feeling of discouragement among the local people because their offers of hospitality to American troops have not been taken advantage of.

The coloured troops are said to be well behaved and sympathy for them, 'in a strange cold country' ... 'with no lady friends', is expressed. The behaviour of white girls is criticised in two reports.

In some areas, it is wondered if our offers of hospitality to the US troops are being overdone, in comparison with what we did for our other allies.

Two Regions report the belief that in some cases US troops are being overcharged by taxi drivers and bartenders.

27. TRANSPORT

There are fewer references to transport difficulties this week, though some complaints are still reported from rural areas particularly on the difficulty 'of obtaining rations from neighbouring towns owing to inadequate bus services'.

There are also complaints that 'the increase in railway fares has made more people travel on the already overcrowded buses'. It is suggested that this congestion may not only cause ill-health but also be one of the causes of the increase in tuberculosis.

28. PETROL

There appears this week to have been a further decrease in the intensity of complaints about the waste or misuse of petrol. References, however, to the following allegations continue to be reported: (i) car owners use their petrol allowance for purposes other than those for which it was issued; (ii) taxis are used for pleasure purposes; (iii) petrol is wasted by servicemen and by Government officials.

29. FOOD

The 'familiar bouquets for Lord Woolton' continue. Even his threat to tighten our belts is described as popular.

Minor points on which there is comment are as follows:

(a) The new milk distribution arrangements are criticised in some places. They are thought to 'favour the Co-ops'.

(b) It is asked, 'How are we to eat more potatoes and at the same time save fuel'?

(c) There are a number of complaints about the shortage of shell eggs and the disappearance of dried eggs.

(d) Shortage of fish is mentioned, 'though it is realised that distribution is in a transitional stage'. Pink salmon is said to be unpopular; it is doubted if it is even a distant relative of red salmon.

(e) There are some complaints at the shortage of 'Christmas foods' – in particular dried fruits for puddings and cakes.

(f) 'The availability of oranges to persons up to eighteen years of age has been welcomed'.

30. RUMOURS

There are few rumours this week. The *Ark Royal* story continues, and the story about the Jap atrocities recorded on the back of a prisoner's postage stamp has recurred. Commando units are said to be going to Dakar. There are said to be large concentrations of barges on the south coast. It is rumoured that a Commando training film gives instructions in how to tie up prisoners.

An increase in careless talk is reported specially from the South-Eastern Region. RAF men, Canadian soldiers, and civilians working on secret Government contracts are regarded as the worst offenders.

NO. 110: WEDNESDAY 4 NOVEMBER 1942 TO TUESDAY 10 NOVEMBER 1942

I. GENERAL COMMENTS

1. GENERAL STATE OF CONFIDENCE AND REACTION TO NEWS

In what is described as 'the best week of the war', events in North Africa have 'eclipsed' all other news. Public spirits, which had been steadily rising as the week progressed, 'soared with the news of our success in Egypt, and rose to fresh heights' over the Anglo-American landings in French North Africa; they are now described as at a higher level than 'since the war began'. While 'a good many people still try to remain cautious in the midst of general jubilation', reports from ten Regions indicate a growing belief that the war will be over within the coming year – 'the less thoughtful suggest the spring or even Christmas'.

The stimulating effect on workers of the North African news is reported from eight Regions, and the volume of critical comment on almost all subjects has declined.

2. NORTH AFRICA

'The double news' from North Africa has encouraged people to believe that 'a large-scale offensive plan, showing inter-Allied and inter-Service co-operation and perfect timing, has begun'. There is expectation of 'more to follow'; a great studying of maps is reported, and 'armchair strategists are having a field day'. Speculation is on the following lines:

(a) North Africa will be 'cleared up' by the complete destruction of Rommel's forces, 'sandwiched' between the Eighth Army and Allied troops advancing eastward through Tunisia.

(b) When this has been completed, we shall invade (i) Italy, via Sicily or from 'our southern Mediterranean springboard'; (ii) Greece, via Crete, or 'as Turkey will be on our side now, we shall be able to get through Turkey into Greece'; or (iii) southern France, or Spain from Gibraltar.

THE EIGHTH ARMY'S OFFENSIVE: The news of our victory in Egypt has caused almost universal elation. Most people are satisfied that Rommel has been decisively defeated; proof of this, it is felt, has been furnished by 'the thousands of prisoners, enemy admissions and General Montgomery's statements'. But many are still cautious: 'I daren't quite believe it's as good as it sounds.' A few people in this category have found in General Montgomery's statements 'reminders of Cairo military spokesmen'.

Further reactions are:

(i) Praise for, and restored confidence in, our leadership, generals, officers and men.
(ii) Praise for our air support.
(iii) Pride in the 51st Highland Division (reported from Scotland) and in the north country regiments (reported from the Northern Region).
(iv) Admiration for General Montgomery's ability.
(v) Hope and belief that Italy will soon be out of it.
(vi) Continued respect for Rommel.

The picture in the press of General Ritter von Thoma entertained by General Montgomery is said in some Regions to have aroused 'extreme annoyance'. People are saying: 'It will be just like after the last war; our leaders will have their arms round the Germans' necks in no time'; they are also wondering how the Greeks and the Poles will greet this spectacle.

ANGLO-AMERICAN LANDINGS IN FRENCH NORTH AFRICA: News of this action 'which has rounded off an excellent week' came as a 'grand surprise to most people' and has been received with great enthusiasm. It has increased confidence generally and has 'even made those who are cautious about Egypt rather grudgingly cheerful'. Other reported reactions are:

(a) Praise for 'the wonderful organisation necessary for such an undertaking'.
(b) Praise for the part played by the Royal Navy in conveying the troops and equipment.
(c) Desire that no leniency shall be shown to the resisting French. It is hoped that 'the Americans won't be too kid-gloved in dealing with them'.

3. RUSSIA

Although the Russian news has been 'overshadowed' by events in the Middle East and Africa, 'admiration for her fighting efforts continues to be deep and widespread'. The belief that Stalingrad will hold out is increasing and it is hoped that the 'on-coming winter' and the African offensive will help to 'relieve her burden'. Some hopes are also expressed that the 'Red Army may yet be able to take the offensive' during the winter. Less interest is reported in the Caucasian fighting, though it is hoped that the new German drive 'won't be very much after all'.

STALIN'S SPEECH: M. Stalin's speech was, on the whole, well received, and was appreciated for its 'frankness, bluntness and realism'. His pronouncements on the second front caused some discussion as to 'how much help we are giving Russia', and some resentment is reported; but his 'references to complete understanding between himself and Mr. Churchill' were appreciated, and events in North Africa are considered to 'have illuminated his statement on unified strategy'.

His comments on the African campaign are criticised for 'slighting our efforts', in one report, but in Northern Ireland they are thought to 'have helped the ordinary people of Britain to regard the Western Desert offensive in its right perspective'.

4. THE SECOND FRONT

The demand for a second front in Europe has died down considerably since the North African offensive began. Opinion appears to be divided, however, as to whether this constitutes 'the promised second front'. Some people have accepted it as such, others as a step towards it – 'By clearing the Mediterranean we shall be able to release shipping for the attack on Europe'. But a few are unwilling to consider the Allies' action in that light – 'We have let Russia down; if we could open a front at all, then it should have been in Europe.'

5. FAR EAST

A more 'hopeful' attitude towards the fighting in the Far Eastern zones is reported this week from six Regions, but the subject is reported to be 'crowded out by news from the Middle East'.

6. THE ALLIED AIR OFFENSIVE

Our raids on Genoa have given 'great satisfaction', and the hope continues to be expressed that we shall bomb Rome.

7. HITLER'S SPEECH

Only five Regions report any mention of this speech. His 'obvious change of tone' is said to have been noted, and his explanations and taunts were greeted with 'scornful amusement'.

8. MRS. ROOSEVELT'S VISIT

Mrs. Roosevelt's presence in England continues to be a subject of interest. It is thought to be 'yet another link between our two countries', through which 'some of the prejudices and misunderstandings between America and ourselves may be cleared up'.

There is some criticism of the 'intensive overcrowding of her itinerary', and a feeling that 'she is spending too much time with the heads of the Services and the nobility and too little time among the workers'; also that 'there is too much WVS about the whole tour'. Her visits to Canterbury and Cambridge were much appreciated.

POSTSCRIPT ON SUNDAY EVENING (8TH NOVEMBER): This 'was eagerly awaited', and was liked as a 'simple straightforward talk, well-delivered'. Her voice came as a surprise 'because it was less American than expected'. Mrs. Roosevelt's description of the blackout in this country is reported to have attracted attention – 'people had forgotten their own first impression' – and her praise of women's work was much appreciated.

9. ELECTIONS IN THE USA

Comment on the elections in the United States has been received from six Regions. Interest in the results among more thoughtful people has been considerable, but 'attempts to interpret them have ended in puzzled bewilderment'. There is some anxiety about the 'possible post-war effect of the elections': 'Isn't this a move towards post-war isolationism?'

Disappointment is expressed at the size of the anti-Roosevelt vote, but the great majority regard this as 'only important internally', and 'so long as Roosevelt gets continued backing for the war effort the man in the street is quite happy'.

It is also said that Mr. Willkie's statements during the past few weeks are now 'considered by the intelligent to have been put over for election purposes'.

10. THE CHAINING OF PRISONERS

Discussion has now diminished considerably, but the general opinion seems to be that 'we cannot compete with the Germans in inhumanity' and that 'it is a mistake to try'. The friendly treatment accorded to the captured General von Thoma is, however, regarded as going much too far in the opposite direction.

11. ENEMY RAIDS ON THIS COUNTRY

Comment on this subject comes from three Regions only. It is thought that 'the more Germany is thwarted in her plans the more likely she will be to launch desperate and vengeful air attacks upon us', but 'we shall be ready'.

It is said that tip-and-run raids are particularly disliked because 'the feeling of defencelessness seems much stronger than in the case of night raids'.

THE RAID ON CANTERBURY (31ST OCTOBER): According to a special report from the South-Eastern Region: 'No one could fail to be impressed by the almost normal appearance both of the city and the people.' The morale was excellent, and the following overheard comment is said to be typical: 'When I found my home destroyed, I immediately thought of my week's shopping and the cob nuts I had bought and said to my neighbour – "Jerry has cracked the nuts for me."'

Other points which are mentioned are:

(a)   People were cheered by the fact that nine enemy planes were brought down, but there was some criticism of the balloon barrage, which was not thought to be high enough to prevent dive-bombing.

(b)   'Unofficial casualty figures were not exaggerated; on the contrary, they were minimised.'

(c)   The BBC statement, in the nine o'clock news, that 'if it was a reprisal raid it was a very poor one' was criticised and thought to have been the 'reason why the Germans raided later in the night'.

(d)   The only examples of somewhat shaken morale came from the rest centres, which were on this occasion used mainly by 'people of a low mental order and of the helpless variety'. The more virile members of the public had 'made their own arrangements'.

12. RECENT SPEECHES

GENERAL SMUTS: Appreciation of his visit to this country and of his speech continue to be reported.

MR. HERBERT MORRISON'S TWO SPEECHES: Further praise is reported, from four Regions, Civil Defence workers being especially gratified at his having 'done so much to give them status'.

13. BROADCASTING AND PRESENTATION OF NEWS

This week 'the hungry public' is described as 'eagerly snapping up the information from the Near East'. Reports of switching off after the news summary have given place to accounts of 'people scurrying to their radio sets a quarter of an hour before the news bulletins are due'. Complaints of 'repetition' are heard no longer and the public are 'just as keen to listen to good news twice, as the BBC are to give it'.

The presentation of the North African news appears to have given entire satisfaction: as one report says, 'people who are hungry for good news do not quibble about the way it is served up, and there are no complaints'. 'The restraint shown both by the BBC and the press in handling the news' has been especially appreciated, according to ten reports.

Appreciation is reported at the recapitulation of the main items at the end of bulletins, but it is suggested that 'announcers should give the time of communiqués, instead of merely referring to them as the latest'.

SIR WILLIAM JAMESON'S BROADCAST (23RD OCTOBER): Further praise of this is mentioned in three Regional reports, two of which say that people would like even greater frankness about venereal disease.

THE INTENDED TRANSFER OF THE FORD RUBBER TYRE PLANT TO RUSSIA: The announcement of this is referred to as 'an indiscretion' in two reports.

INDIVIDUAL BROADCASTS WHICH HAVE BEEN PRAISED include Captain Gammans' talk (6th November), Peter Masefield's talk (27th October), and the programmes in honour of the Soviet anniversary. 'More of Helmore' is asked for.

II. SPECIAL COMMENTS

14. INDUSTRY

INCREASED PRODUCTION: 'The impetus to war workers given by the good news from the battlefront' is mentioned in eight reports. Workers in the Northern Region 'feel they have contributed to the success of the Eighth Army', and 'express pride at the news of north country regiments employed in the desert, and in the ships that have carried the men and materials for this great effort'.

CRITICISM OF PRODUCTION: There is a revival of 'complaints of slackness in management and of workers standing about idle', though these complaints are described as 'vague and unspecified' and do not make it clear whether the idleness is voluntary or enforced. This criticism of shortcomings is said to have been 'sharpened by the war news'.

SHOPPING DIFFICULTIES OF WORKERS: Shopping difficulties are mentioned in nine reports, six of which refer specifically to those of workers. Now that shops shut earlier, it is urged that they should keep open during lunch, as this is the only time that many factory workers can do their shopping. Two reports, however, refer to women workers having to go without their lunch to do their shopping; it is strongly felt that the best solution would be an arrangement whereby they would be released 'for one hour *during ordinary shopping hours*'.

WOMEN'S LONG HOURS OF WORK: Three reports mention 'the effect of the continued strain on women' – ranging from general irritability to hysteria – due to long hours of work, allied to the difficulties of running a home.

15. MANPOWER AND THE CALL-UP

Manpower is 'felt to be one of our greatest problems at the moment', and 'the difficulties due to the withdrawal of men and women to the Forces continue to be talked about everywhere'. Particular 'matters of complaint' are:

(a) Young men who are in reserved occupations, 'often through influence', should be combed out before the 'eighteens' and the older men are called up.

(b) Many men and women doing skilled and important work are transferred to inferior occupations where they are wasted.

(c) Young and childless married women are exempt, while older unmarried women are called up.

(d) 'Many voluntary workers (e.g., WVS) are not really contributing full service, and should be called up for transfer first.'

MISUNDERSTANDINGS: Many misunderstandings as to the women's position are reported, from the husbands as well as the women themselves: (a) there is uncertainty as to whether or not women can be compelled to do part-time work; (b) 'Women in munitions firms but who are not in reserved occupations think they cannot volunteer without their employer's permission'; (c) it is not understood 'why, in some districts, women are directed into war work, while friends with similar circumstances in other districts are left alone'.

MINISTRY OF LABOUR AND NATIONAL SERVICE:

(a) INTERVIEWERS: Great appreciation is reported from the Southern Region at 'the Ministry's handling of the manpower problem', the Petersfield and Wokingham Exchanges being particularly commended for 'the tactful and sympathetic handling of the women registering' and 'for consideration shown to local business people in allowing them time to train substitutes before call-up'.

(b) APPEALS BOARDS: Complaints are made of 'strict treatment at the hands of the Appeals Board', especially in 'cases of girls, with invalid parents dependent on them, being treated as mobile'.

16. PETROL

There are references from eight Regions this week to the misuse and waste of petrol, as against six last week. There are allegations of (a) people going by car when good alternative transport is available, (b) the numbers of cars with only one occupant, (c) 'wives' still using cars for shopping (in Huddersfield), (d) unreasonable use of taxis, e.g., for shopping, (e) use of petrol by ministers and teachers (in Fifeshire), (f) fleets of cars seen recently at the Brighton dog races.

It is suggested that car owners should have with them a statement showing why they have been granted petrol, and that petrol wasters should be compelled to travel on a tanker as a punishment.

17. TRANSPORT

Transport difficulties, especially for war workers, are arousing the most 'bitter complaints', and in the North-Eastern Region are referred to as 'the main topic of conversation on the home front'. The imposition of the 'transport curfew' is regarded as 'drastic', and war workers and the general public in the North-Eastern and North Midland Regions are reported to be 'unsettled and dissatisfied'. Reactions to its recent introduction in the South-Eastern Region have not yet been received, though Home Guards are already 'worrying' about their Saturday night AA duties.

Other complaints of transport services follow familiar lines:

(a) The restriction of bus services (especially Green Line buses), the long bus queues, and the overcrowding of buses alleged to be due to the cancelling of cheap train fares.

(b) The overcrowding of trains, and the delay in train services which make workers late for work.

(c) The special difficulties of country dwellers who are alleged to 'be becoming marooned'.

(d) Grumbles about the priority ticket system. In Glasgow and Manchester, office workers consider they are entitled to these tickets, and in the Northern Region people complain that office typists should not be allowed to use them.

(e) In Belfast, war workers are demanding the early closing of shops in the city centre 'in order to relieve transport congestion in the early evenings'.

18. THE PRIME MINISTER'S MEETING WITH
THE MINERS (31ST OCTOBER)

Public interest continues to be slight, 'outside the mining fraternity', though curiosity is still reported about what was said. Good results are expected and, according to six reports, have already begun to be apparent in the improved spirit of the miners, though the news from Africa is also said to have done its share. It is felt that more contacts between the workers and those responsible for war strategy would produce good results, but there is still criticism of the time, expense and loss of fuel involved by this means of achieving it, and some think that a meeting-place nearer to the main coalfields should have been chosen.

The following reactions are reported from some of the miners:

(a) Mr. Churchill did not tell them anything they did not already know: it was 'his personal touch that convinced them'. Some would have welcomed an allusion to the industry's future, as well as an opportunity for discussion.

(b) Miners are 'frequently very suspicious of their own selected representatives', and some of them complain that 'it's always the same men who are away at TU or PPC meetings', and who are, in consequence, 'doing little to win coal'.

(c) Criticism, and in some cases indignation, was caused by reports that 'each man attending was to be allowed £7. 10. 0'.

LACK OF CONFIDENCE BETWEEN MINERS AND MANAGEMENTS: This is referred to in four reports. 'Miners state that much absenteeism could be avoided if the men felt that the management were co-operating instead of pulling in the opposite direction.'

19. FUEL ECONOMY CAMPAIGN

There is less comment on this subject this week, but it is reported that in spite of increased cold, efforts to economise are genuine and effective: 'We thought we were as careful as could be before, but we've cut down electricity 20% and gas by nearly 50% on the corresponding period of last year.' Some demand for rationing is reported from four Regions, and many working people think that it was 'abandoned because the rich would suffer most'. It is asked whether, in the event of rationing, economies made now will affect the basis which may be used.

The announcement that householders can purchase up to 15 cwts of coal during the next few months has been well received, but as this amount is not always obtainable it is suggested that in such cases people should be permitted to change to retailers who can supply them. There are complaints from four Regions of the uneven distribution of coal and coke, and it is asked if more authority could be given to local Fuel Overseers 'who know the requirements in their districts'.

The idea of 'sharing fires and ovens with neighbours' is said to be 'disliked by most working-class women'. 'After long working hours they feel entitled to some privacy', and space is often very limited both round the fire and in the oven.

Comment is again made on waste caused through permanent blackout, and it is said that workers 'dislike having no daylight at any time'. A shortage of matches, reported from three Regions, is also said to be causing a substantial waste of fuel.

FUEL FLASHES, COMMUNIQUÉS AND LIMERICKS: Fuel Flashes are adversely criticised: 'Freddie Grisewood's ears would burn if he knew what women said about him.' It is said that housewives are indifferent to the communiqués in the press, and that the reactions to limericks were unfavourable because the 'cockney voice was quite unintelligible'.

PARAFFIN: The scarcity of paraffin is again reported from a rural area and there is complaint of 'townspeople using it when they have other means of lighting and heating'.

20. FOOD

Praise for, and satisfaction with, the food situation continue to be reported. There are, however, some criticisms which may be summarised thus:

(a) THE FISHING ZONE SCHEME: Complaints of shortage of fish come from nine Regions; many hold the zoning scheme responsible, but a few think that things will get better when the scheme is working properly.

(b) THE CUT IN MILK RATION: Four Regions report that the reason for the cut is realised, though it is said not to be understood in the North-Western Region. In the Southern Region it is asked whether Service canteens and American Service clubs are going to have their supplies cut, because it is not considered that fit men should take the milk more necessary for others.

(c) THE TEA RATION: This is thought to be insufficient for people living alone.

(d) BISCUITS ON POINTS: It is asked if they could not be put on the personal ration book for the sake of people living in institutions and boarding houses, etc.

From the North-Western Region, approval is reported of the school meal system and it is suggested that 'if the system was extended there would be fewer children on the public transport at lunch time'.

21. US TROOPS IN GREAT BRITAIN

Comment on this subject appears to have declined in volume, and on the whole it is said that the American troops are liked and 'seem to fit in'. There is still criticism of their high pay as compared with that of our own men, and of their attitude to the colour question; also it is pointed out that 'hospitality on a lavish scale, such as is being shown to the Americans, has not been given to other "visiting" troops in this country'.

Information Bureaux and recreational facilities are said to be 'more and more urgently required', and there is again demand for extensive publicity about the status of British girls who marry US soldiers.

The American nurses are said to be 'much liked'.

22. THE EXECUTION OF THE MERCHANT
SEAMAN FOR TREACHERY

This is said to have 'created wide interest', and to have been regarded 'largely as an example to deter others'. The news 'gave rather a jolt to some seamen, who admitted that they would be quite ready to speak pretty openly to "one of themselves"'.

23. WASTE OF PAPER

Adverse comment is reported on the waste resulting from:

(i) CHRISTMAS CARDS: These are described in two reports as 'a waste of paper and manpower, both in the manufacture and in the Post Office'.

(ii) CATALOGUES: 'Charging for catalogues', it is said, 'will not prevent their being published; only the publishers will gain, who supplied them free before'. Firms are said to send out calendars to customers who did not order them, but who are told that a small charge will be made on their account.

(iii) ADVERTISEMENTS of 'goods which will not be available until after the war'.

24. CLOTHING COUPONS

The following comments on clothing and clothing coupon difficulties are still reported:

(a) There is said to be 'considerable distress' among housewives because of the rationing of towels. Nursing homes, boarding houses, and invalids are now added to the list of special sufferers.

(b) A shortage of children's shoes and Wellingtons, and complaints of the poor quality of children's utility shoes.

NO. 114: TUESDAY 1 DECEMBER 1942 TO
TUESDAY 8 DECEMBER 1942

I. GENERAL COMMENTS

1. GENERAL STATE OF CONFIDENCE AND REACTION TO NEWS

The level of public spirits appears almost everywhere to have 'declined from the peak reached during the last two weeks'. The general state of confidence 'remains at a higher pitch than at any time in the pre-North African days', but 'elation' is now confined to a minority. This is said to be due to:

(a) Uneasiness over the situation in Tunisia.

(b) Misgivings over the position of Darlan and his 'apparent increase in power'.

(c) The Prime Minister's 'salutary warning against over-optimism'. In spite of this, many still believe that the war in Europe will be over by this time next year, if not sooner.

On the other hand, the Russian offensives and the publication of the Beveridge Report have helped to keep spirits up.

The Beveridge Report is everywhere said to have been the main subject of conversation, and 'the war news has tended to take a back seat'. It appears to have been welcomed by the great majority – enthusiastically, by many: 'wage earners' are said to be particularly pleased with it. It is thought that enthusiasm would have been even greater, however, but for the belief that vested interests will succeed in 'killing or mutilating it'.

2. THE BEVERIDGE REPORT

The Beveridge Report has been the most discussed topic of the week – or 'of recent times', according to two Regions. Interest appears to be based chiefly on a preliminary study of the Report, on 'the great amount of information given in the press', and on Sir William's 'easily understood and becomingly modest broadcast'. Only in Scotland are people 'now getting down to details'. The press treatment of the Report is highly praised. A shortage of copies is mentioned in the Midland and North-Western Regions.

THE REPORT AS A WHOLE:

(a) FOR: The Report has been welcomed with almost universal approval by 'people of all shades of political opinion and by all sections of the community'. It is felt that 'this comprehensive and clear-cut scheme' marks a step towards post-war reconstruction – 'it is the first real attempt to put into practice the talk about the new world' – and has done something to allay the widespread fear of post-war unemployment.

(b) RESERVATIONS:

(i) People 'in all walks of life' fear that 'the high rate of benefits may prove an incentive to laziness and thriftlessness'.

(ii) 'To plan social security before planning employment and trade is to put the cart before the horse.'

(iii) Some 'left-wing' people, while in favour of the proposals, feel that the Report 'does not go far enough'.

(c) AGAINST: Only a very small minority fall into this category; but reasons for objecting to the plan vary considerably, the following sections of the public each having their own view:

(i) Some businessmen – those 'in cotton' are specially mentioned – who fear that the tax on industry will be too great, that prices of goods will have to be raised, and that we shall therefore be in no position to compete in post-war export trade. Fear of inflation is also expressed.

(ii) People who think 'the time is not yet ripe for talking reconstruction'; however, even some of these are pleased with the Report.

(iii) 'The more extreme elements' who feel that 'the plan is a palliative and that what is really wanted is the socialisation of industry'.

(iv) Those who think that there is too much 'Soviet flavour' about it. Farmers in Scotland feel that 'this daft socialism will lead to the nationalisation of land next'.

(v) 'The man with shares in the Prudential.'

WILL IT MATERIALISE?

There is, according to reports from eleven Regions, 'very real anxiety' that the plan will not materialise because of the following:

(a) 'VESTED INTERESTS': Particularly mentioned are insurance companies, the BMA and big business. It is felt 'amongst the rank and file that even if these powerful interests do not jointly succeed in completely wrecking it, they will hotly contest every inch of the ground. The final plan will therefore be so mutilated that the benefits ultimately received by working people will be very small.'

(b) THE GOVERNMENT: There is some doubt as to whether the Government is wholeheartedly behind the scheme. A minority of working-class people in Wales and Scotland, 'who remember promises made in the last war', are saying: 'This is merely propaganda to keep us "at it" till the war is over.' On the other hand, the Report is regarded as the first real sign that the Government does in fact mean to tackle post-war problems seriously. There is also a small minority of 'uninformed people who think the plan is already an Act of Parliament'.

(c) PARTY POLITICS: It is felt that 'unless the Beveridge Report is passed before the end of the war, little or nothing will be done to ensure social security because it will become the subject of wrangling between the political parties'.

(d) THE COST WILL BE TOO HIGH.

At the same time, the public are reported to be determined that the plan must go through: 'If not, things will be damned unpleasant for whatever government is in power; if it's mucked up, there will be hell to pay.'

THE REPORT IN DETAIL: The following points have been raised:

(a) CONTRIBUTIONS FOR SOCIAL INSURANCE: Wage earners, particularly farm labourers, feel that 4/3d. a week is too much. In Scotland, however, there are said to be 'few grumbles' about it.

(b) PENSIONS:

 (i) It is felt that the elderly should have the full amount now: 'I will not live long enough to see it.'
 (ii) There is a certain amount of confusion about 'the transitional period of twenty years'. Some people believe that full benefit will be obtained only when the age of eighty is reached.
 (iii) '£2 for a married couple is too little.'

(c) THE POSITION OF PEOPLE WHO HOLD AN INSURANCE POLICY OR CONTRUBUTE TO A SUPERANNUATION SCHEME: 'Will they lose their premiums?'

(d) MEDICAL TREATMENT: The proposals have been warmly welcomed, but, according to the report from the South-Western Region, 'the omission of any mention of state control of hospitals has been noticed'. The Report is said to have brought out 'the existence of very deep resentment, especially amongst workpeople, against the present medical system: e.g. long waiting lists at hospitals and the somewhat cursory examinations and hasty diagnoses given by many panel doctors'.

(e) 'WHY MUST FUNERALS COST £20?'

(f) RENT: If the plan is really to abolish want, rents will have to be controlled. People in towns may pay 20s. a week while those in the country pay only 5s.

3. ADMIRAL DARLAN

Darlan is said to come second only to the Beveridge Report as a subject of discussion. Views differ as to whether comment has increased or declined in volume, but all agree in saying that distrust of Darlan and dissatisfaction with the present position are as strong as ever; three reports say they are even stronger than last week.

The promise of a debate in the House gives 'slight reassurance' to some; a greater number are said to be critical of the fact that it is to be in secret, which is taken by the 'most suspicious' as 'proof that there's something to cover up'.

The setting up of a French Imperial Council has caused some shock, and 'the fact that Darlan did this without so much as a bow to Roosevelt's assurance that the French would be allowed to choose their own leaders, is held to mean that he is telling the American President to mind his own business so far as the administration of the African Empire is concerned'.

Other reactions may be summed up as follows:

(a) There is 'too much mystery about it all', and a clear statement is asked for.
(b) The Americans are responsible. Some think that the American Government, which is suspected of being pro-Vichy, 'has neatly diddled both the British Government and people'. A few say: 'Hence the need for a debate in secret.' Respect for America is said to have declined since the Darlan affair.
(c) Darlan is still 'the tool of Vichy and the Germans' and will betray us. It is thought not to be fair on the First Army 'to have such a man in their rear'.
(d) 'Get as much as possible out of him, and then to hell with him.'

(e) The Government must be trusted for the time being.
(f) We shall lose the support of the occupied countries, and of Russia. 'How can we tell the workers of France to rise when we are hand in glove with a traitor like Darlan whom they loathe?'
(g) 'Are we selling the pass to fascists?' 'What is the difference between Darlan and Laval – or Goering?'

4. GENERAL DE GAULLE AND THE FIGHTING FRENCH

As a result of the Darlan affair, there continue to be reports of increasing sympathy for General de Gaulle and the Fighting French, and a growing feeling that the General has had 'a raw deal'; the Government is again blamed for 'giving the impression of cold-shouldering him'. There is further praise for 'his solidarity with the Allied cause, which has been a lead to all the occupied countries through the darkest days of the war'. Some consider he should have been put in command in North Africa.

General de Gaulle is said to be particularly popular on the Merseyside, but 'even where de Gaulle and the Fighting French are extremely unpopular (e.g. in Portsmouth) the English love of fair play makes people consider they have been very shabbily treated'.

5. NORTH AFRICA

Confidence that the Allies will eventually drive the enemy from the African coast is said to be almost universal, but there appears to be growing disappointment that it is taking so long to do it, and increased realisation that there will be 'some pretty desperate tussles before they are driven out'. The more thoughtful, helped by 'official warnings of the difficulties which lie ahead', are said to realise that 'a slowing-down was inevitable', but initial successes, and press headlines of 'German Dunkirk' and 'Rommel's armies trapped', had given many people the impression that 'the remnants of the Axis forces would soon be out of Africa'.

Other reactions may be summed up as follows:

(a) The news that the enemy are getting reinforcements both in Tunisia and Libya is causing disappointment.
(b) People are concerned at the lack of full air support.
(c) It is feared that the First Army's losses may be high.
(d) The campaigns are said to be difficult to follow, and accounts confused. Distances are not realised.
(e) There is comment on the lack of news; the shortness of the bulletins is taken by some as 'the prelude to some really bad news' – it 'always has been'.
(f) Anxiety is reported in Northern Ireland about the losses of ships in connection with the North African landings: 'the impression was given at the time that the convoys had arrived without loss'.
(g) 'The military setbacks are giving rise to some slight suspicion that friction exists, either among the Commands, between the Americans and ourselves, or among the various French authorities.'

6. RUSSIA

'Admiration' for Russia continues to be expressed, though less comment is reported this week. 'Keen interest' in the Red Army offensives continues, and there appears to be a growing hope that the German retreat may become a disaster.

A desire to help Russia more is again reported, and sympathy is described as 'deep-seated', especially among working-class people. She is alleged to be 'the true country of the ordinary people', and a feeling of 'personal pride and relief' at the lifting of the Stalingrad siege is mentioned in two Regions; in one it is suggested that 'people seemed to identify Stalingrad with their own home town'.

In seven reports this week there are references to a minority who are inclined to 'disbelieve stories of the Red Army's successes'. Others are said to 'fear her potentiality after the war'.

7. ITALY

Widespread approval for the raids on Italian cities is again reported. Some think we have delayed bombing Italy too long, and that 'the hold Hitler has now gained upon the country will be so strong that the Italian people will be unable to ask for a separate peace, even if they wish to'. There is a persistent belief, however, that 'their effective part in the war will cease before long', and that, if we keep the bombing up, she will 'soon crack up'.

A minority persist in wanting Rome bombed, and the rumour that the Pope would move into Rome from the Vatican City if this happens made some people ask 'why he didn't come to Birmingham and the docks in the blitz, to guard his English Roman Catholics?'

Three reports indicate that people do not dislike the Italians as much as the Germans, or in the same way; contempt and pity for them are expressed, the latter 'mostly by middle-aged women'. 'Merseysiders' and people in other blitzed towns feel strongly, however, that 'Italy mustn't be allowed to get out on too easy terms'.

8. THE SCUTTLING OF THE FRENCH FLEET

Comment is now said to have died down for the most part, and the points of view expressed differ little from those reported last week. Admiration still seems to be the predominating emotion and, in spite of some indications to the contrary, the incident is thought on the whole to have 'caused French stock to rise'. Other reactions may be summed up in the words of a writer quoted by Postal Censorship: 'Thank God the French were able to sink their fleet. What asses they were not to have sailed away when they could! They *have* made a mess of this war.'

9. THE PRIME MINISTER'S BROADCAST (29TH NOVEMBER)

Further reports confirm the preliminary reactions mentioned last week. Although 'praise has not been quite so eulogistic as usual', the speech was very favourably received by the great majority, many of whom were enthusiastic. While 'other members of the Government speak too much', Mr. Churchill is considered to speak too little. His popularity is now said to be very high, and 'his modest tone and the realisation that much of the criticism levelled against him has now proved unjustified has greatly increased people's affection for him'.

The two points in his speech most appreciated are still:

(a) His 'mention of the hard years ahead of us', with 'its sobering effect on the optimistic', many of whom are now reported to be disappointed and pessimistic as a result. As a writer quoted by Postal Censorship says: 'I fancy he's put paid to a lot of people thinking the war'll be over in a few months.'

(b) His appeal to the Italians, which was considered 'brilliantly designed to sow alarm and despondency, as well as division among the Italian people'. Those who did not at first think this particularly effective were 'persuaded it was worth while by Mussolini's reply'; this was described as 'a very poor comic opera effort', and has been generally ridiculed. Mr. Churchill's 'pungent references to Musso' were particularly enjoyed by workers.

Regret is again expressed that the Prime Minister 'was not drawn into giving any news regarding Darlan and de Gaulle', that he 'made no mention of post-war planning' and that he 'told us nothing new'.

Little reference is made to Mr. Churchill's Bradford speech (5th December), but it seems to have been regarded as even more 'anti-optimistic' than his broadcast.

10. FAR EAST

Interest in the Pacific war zone is reported to be still at a low level, though the Prime Minister's broadcast is thought to be having the effect of making people pause and think. The 'ordinary man' is said to be satisfied that matters are progressing in the Allies' favour but considers this theatre of war to be primarily American and is willing to leave the job to them.

Opinion is reported to be divided as to whether the Japanese are an 'easy prey' or will take a lot of beating, and the slow process of defeating them in New Guinea and Guadalcanal is noted as an indication of the difficulties to be faced when the time comes to drive them out of the other lands they have occupied.

11. THE CABINET CHANGES

These are said to be still widely discussed. Comment, which is reported to be 'less detailed and critical', follows familiar lines, and regret at Sir Stafford Cripps' 'demotion' appears to be the predominating reaction.

12. AIR RAIDS ON THIS COUNTRY

There are further reports of 'growing complacency about the possibility of air raids on this country' and some people refer to 'the waste of money in keeping up Civil Defence'. Only on the south coast is there said to be some slight renewal of anticipation – but not alarm – 'when the Russian front settles down for the winter'.

13. BROADCASTING AND PRESENTATION OF NEWS

Satisfaction with the handling of the war news is again reported. Praise for the repetition of the headlines after the broadcast news continues.

In the South-Western Region, where wireless reception is said to be bad, people are pleased that 'all emergency matters such as sirens and announcements' will be transmitted by Radio Relay.

BRAINS TRUST: The *Brains Trust* is thought 'not to be so good as it was'. Some listeners miss the 'companionable spirit of the original trio'; others complain of the 'pomposity and dullness' of the 'Eminent Physician', and it is suggested 'that the deference shown to His Eminence cramps the style of the whole party'.

VARIETY PROGRAMMES: *Monday Night at Eight* is 'very much enjoyed', while Tommy Handley is both praised and 'slanged'.

THE EUROPEAN NEWS SERVICE continues to be praised, especially the comments of the 'Man in the Street'.

The following individual speeches and broadcasts are specially praised:

MR. EDEN'S SPEECH ON POST-WAR FOREIGN POLICY (2ND DECEMBER) met with 'warm approval', and his 'further references to the twenty years pact with the Soviet Government is specially praised'.

MAJOR HASTINGS' WAR COMMENTARY (3RD DECEMBER) is again praised. It is considered both 'interesting and comprehensive'.

GENERAL SMUTS' RECORDED BROADCAST (6TH DECEMBER): Preliminary reports suggest that his speech was liked, and his references to the Battle of the Atlantic were specially appreciated on the Merseyside.

II. SPECIAL COMMENTS

14. INDUSTRY AND MANPOWER

PRODUCTION: This week there are again contradictory opinions about the effect of the recent war news on workers' 'zest for work'. On the one hand, 'a falling off of work due to complacency' is reported; on the other, there are still references to 'increased effort'. Certain workers – for example workers in Derbyshire and some miners in the North Midland Region – are still said 'to have little or no realisation of the issues at stake. They cannot forget the past and think that the end of the war will be to their personal disadvantage.'

'Vague stories' of idle time in factories, or in some cases allegations of enforced idleness in particular firms, are reported from four Regions. A specific instance quoted from the Northern Region is as follows: 'Stories that many men were idling for days at a shipyard are believed to be due to the unwillingness of employers to release men when one ship is "got away" and the new ship does not as yet require the same number of men. It is felt that this should be overcome by the transfer of surplus men to another yard immediately a ship is launched, and their re-transfer to the original yard when sufficient work is available.'

MANPOWER: There is less reference to this subject this week. Points raised are: (i) the comb-out of men for the Forces is not as thorough as it might be; (ii) 'The haphazard way men are selected for transfer'; (iii) confusion amongst women about their obligations under the call-up, particularly as regards part-time work; (iv) discrimination against women workers. It is reported that 'foremen are unwilling to use woman labour to its full extent. Even when commanded by the management to put a woman on a certain job, the foreman can get out of doing so; as he has to supervise her training, he is in a particularly good position to say that "she is not much good".'

15. TRANSPORT DIFFICULTIES

There are references from eleven Regions to transport difficulties this week. Public transport is described as 'the greatest difficulty with which the public is contending'. It continues to be a major topic of discussion.

It is felt that many people do not appreciate the necessity for the curtailment of the bus services. Those who do realise that cuts must be made are of the opinion that the best use is not made of the available buses; thus, it is suggested that fewer buses should be run in the afternoons to allow more at night.

Complaints are on familiar lines and may be summarised as follows:

(a) The overcrowding of buses (i) by shoppers and pleasure seekers; (ii) by train travellers because of the abolition of cheap rail facilities; (iii) by short-distance passengers, on long-distance buses.

(b) The lack of a priority scheme for workers and complaints of long waits at bus stops.

(c) Inadequate rural transport services.

(d) Buses and trains not running to time.

CHRISTMAS TRAVEL RESTRICTIONS: Some grumbles that no extra trains are being run are reported from evacuated workers who are very keen on going home for Christmas. From Bournemouth it is reported that, once it was clear that no extra trains would be run for Christmas travel, bookings at local hotels, which had previously been very heavy, were cancelled in large numbers.

16. FUEL ECONOMY

People are reported to be economising and doing their best to save fuel, but there is still some feeling that coal should be rationed to deal with the selfish minority. People without storage space for fuel are said to be anxious about supplies, and complaints are made about the alleged misleading statements as to the amount of supplies which people are allowed.

The Fuel Campaign is arousing less interest. Criticism of Fuel Flashes continues, 'but at least they *do* make people talk about fuel saving'. Fuel and Light Economy film shorts are, however, praised; Fuel Communiqués are said to be read more extensively in Wales.

The quality of coal is again criticised. It is said to be 'poor and does not heat as much water or do as much cooking as it should'.

17. PETROL

There are fewer references this week to the misuse and waste of petrol. Complaints are as follows:

    (a) Men on bus routes using cars to travel to business.
    (b) Misuse of petrol allowances.
    (c) Misuse of taxis.
    (d) Waste of petrol by the army and the Civil Defence Service.

Factory workers in a town in the North Midland Region are reported to be complaining that the mayor is travelling in a Rolls-Royce (8 to 10 m.p.g.) to give canteen talks.

18. FOOD

'General satisfaction' with the food situation is again expressed this week: 'Woolton is a great manager'.

The chief criticisms reported are:

    (a) FISH ZONING SCHEME: This is said to have resulted in shortage, poor quality and the uneven distribution of fish, and to have 'brought back queuing'. It is urged that 'every step should be taken to end any dispute that may exist'. Complaints are made that hotels, restaurants and large stores are favoured and that 'under-the-counter trade takes place'. One report suggests that fish should be put on points.

    (b) MILK: The difficulties of housekeeping due to the cut in milk are again stressed though it is said that 'people are accepting the situation with good grace'. Although many people would prefer more milk in place of the large cheese ration, others are said to find that the 'many recipes available make cheese a popular item on the wartime menu'.

    (c) People are said to be 'out to make Christmas as much like normal times as possible', and some disappointment is expressed in three reports that there will be no extra supplies for Christmas; but this, like the milk shortage, is also 'accepted with good grace'.

    (d) DRIED FRUITS: A shortage of dried fruits – especially currants and raisins – is reported, and it is suggested in one report that these 'should be rationed by coupon and not by points, as at present only favourites with the tradesmen are supplied'.

    (e) FRUIT JUICES AND COD LIVER OIL: One Region reports that 'many mothers are indignant at Government admonitions concerning the failure to take up fruit juices and cod liver oil'. They say the 'machinery is far too cumbersome'.

19. TOYS

Complaints of 'the ridiculously' high price, 'rubbishy' quality, and shortage of children's toys is reported from seven Regions, as compared with four Regions last week. 'Woollen and cuddly toys' and second-hand toys are said to be 'particularly dear'. 'Small firms of mushroom growth' are thought to be 'exploiting the present situation of restricted supplies', and there is a demand for price control.

20. CIVIL DEFENCE

Only preliminary reports have been received so far on the increases in pay for Civil Defence workers. In the South-Western Region they are described as 'helpful'.

Desire for equal war injury compensation for women, and approval of Mrs. Tate's campaign, continue to be reported from three Regions.

'FRONT LINE': A big demand for this book is reported from four Regions and is mentioned in Police Duty Room reports. Both the pictures and the reading-matter are praised, and the only criticism of 'both buyers and sellers is the difficulty of obtaining copies'. Booksellers are reported to have 'sold out' in many places, and for this reason exception was taken to an announcement by the BBC on Sunday night (6th December) to the effect that copies could be obtained at HM Stationery Office, or any bookseller.

21. TORCH BATTERIES

A serious shortage of No. 8 (hand) and No. 800 (cycle) batteries is again reported and the difficulties of cyclists getting to and from work are again stressed. The risk of accident through riding without lights is pointed out in Police Duty Room Reports. One Region reports the comment that the shortage may be due partly to selfish buying by hoarders: '500 batteries were sold in one shop inside an hour'.

22. CLOTHING

COUPONS: The demand for a separate household coupon allowance is again reported. There is 'general dissatisfaction' at the present situation, with regard to towels, of factories, schools, canteens, business houses, hospitals, etc. It is felt there is an 'urgent need for some statement'.

WELLINGTON BOOTS: Two Regions point out the hardships caused to country children through the shortage of Wellington boots. It is 'wondered whether it would be a practical proposition to encourage mothers to buy clogs'. Repairs to rubber boots are also said to be very difficult owing to manufacturers being occupied with Government contracts.

BOOTS AND SHOES: It is thought that footwear may become a 'very serious problem for the poorer sections of the community'. Children's shoes of all types are said to be difficult to obtain, high in price, and of poor quality. An added difficulty is the length of time required for repairs, and their high cost, which results in children having to go about in unmended shoes.

TRAFFIC IN CLOTHING COUPONS: It is reported from two Regions that the traffic in clothing coupons is believed to be increasing.

23. USA TROOPS IN GREAT BRITAIN

Postal Censorship and Police Duty Room reports indicate that the American troops are, on the whole, well liked and well behaved. Only two Regional reports refer to them this week, for the most part in favourable terms.

24. MR. CLAUDE MULLINS

'Resentment' has been expressed at Mr. Mullins' remarks on the subject of housekeepers and it is held that 'too many judges and magistrates are using the Courts as platforms for stating their pet theories'.

25. THE RINGING OF BELLS

Our Weekly Reports of 19th and 26th November indicated that opinion was sharply divided over the ringing of the bells. An independent report (for November), just received, refers to 'the lack of enthusiasm which was displayed when it was announced that the joy bells would be rung', but mentions 'the curious fact that everybody who heard the bells, whether they agreed with them being rung or not, seemed to have appreciated hearing them again'. The information slips from the Liverpool Postal Censorship Unit during the week ending 4th December show overwhelming approval, with 509 appreciations and 78 critical comments. 'Disapproving writers either consider that it is premature to rejoice over victories or that such rejoicing will give sorrow to many.'

26. RUMOURS

There are few rumours this week. The only ones worth noting are as follows:

More transatlantic troops are said to be coming to Swindon shortly, including Mexicans.

In the North-Western Region, six American troops are said to have died through drinking doctored liquor.

Jimmy O'Dea, the comedian in *Irish Half Hour* on the radio, is said to be sending messages in code to the enemy, announcing the names of places about to be bombed by the RAF.

In Scotland, it is rumoured that the Duke of Kent was piloting his plane when it crashed.

NO. 115: TUESDAY 8 DECEMBER 1942 TO TUESDAY 15 DECEMBER 1942

I. GENERAL COMMENTS

1. GENERAL STATE OF CONFIDENCE AND REACTION TO NEWS

Confidence is everywhere said to remain steady, but generally on a slightly lower level than last week. Pleasure at Rommel's retreat from El Agheila is slightly outweighed by a sense of disappointment at 'the slowing down in Tunisia and Russia', and by concern at Darlan's position. Jubilation has almost entirely disappeared, and there are now 'far fewer people who prophesy an early victory'.

Four reports refer to 'a quiet week', and there are many indications that the news is arousing less interest and discussion than of late. 'Lack of exciting war news' and the approach of Christmas are reported to have 'turned most people's thoughts to private affairs'. People are said to be concentrating on such subjects as 'the ramp in Christmas toys' and the shortage of batteries.

The Beveridge Report continues to arouse great interest and discussion, but apparently not to quite the same extent as last week.

2. ADMIRAL DARLAN

Darlan now appears to have ousted the Beveridge Report from its first place as a subject of discussion. Distrust of Darlan and dissatisfaction with the present position are said to be as strong as – and in three Regions, even stronger than – last week, and comment continues on the same lines. The only notable difference is a further increase in the desire for a frank statement from the Government on Darlan's position. It was hoped that such a statement would follow the Commons' secret debate, which some people regarded as 'a sign that the Government has had to bow to Washington'.

A special monthly Postal Censorship report, for November, containing opinions from all parts of the country, has classified 360 writers' comments on Darlan as follows:

(a)   Distrust of Darlan. 'I hope our people do not get taken in by that dirty reptile Darlan; he would sell us tomorrow, if the position became reversed.'   205

(b)   'The policy of befriending Darlan is very harmful to the cause of French liberation.' 'It must look to the Fighting French, inside France and outside, as if we are betraying them.'   66

(c)   'I feel that the Americans are much to blame in the matter.' 'Eisenhower may be using Darlan. Is he certain that Darlan isn't using him?'   52

(d)   'Although the Darlan coup was rather a shock, we must wait and see. There may have been good reasons for choosing him, which cannot be revealed yet.'   18

Nineteen comments defied classification.

3. THE BEVERIDGE REPORT AND POST-WAR RECONSTRUCTION

Although discussion of the Report appears to be slightly less than last week, it continues to be very widespread and on the same lines. Opinions expressed, all of which are confirmed by Postal Censorship, may be summarised thus:

(a) General approval of the scheme, followed – 'almost in the same breath' – by fear that it may be 'too good to go through'. 'Wouldn't the Beveridge Plan be Utopia, if ever it becomes to pass?' is a typical comment.

(b) Vested interests, both financial and political, but particularly the insurance companies, are 'its chief enemies'. They are expected 'to put up a stiff fight and it is feared that they may hold up, cut down or smother the Report'. At the same time, it is suggested that 'if the Government allows itself to be swayed or influenced by them, people are ready to make trouble'; and 'any MP who votes against the Report will certainly lose his seat'. To quote from Postal Censorship: 'The lads in khaki have now got something to fasten on when they come home, and any shilly-shallying by the big guns will cause a riot.'

(c) How will the necessary money be found? On the other hand, reports from three Regions refer to 'people being sceptical of talk about "the country can't afford it" – we can afford fourteen million pounds a day for war'.

(d) 'It's the provision of work that needs guaranteeing.'

(e) The rates of benefit will encourage 'workshyness' and thriftlessness.

(f) The hope that further broadcasts and press summaries will help 'elucidate various points, so that the simplest among the public may understand the Report'.

(g) 'This Report is just bluff: the carrot to keep the donkey going.' To quote a 1914–1918 ex-serviceman (Postal Censorship): 'This new plan for social security makes me laugh, I don't forget the Land Fit for Heroes of the last war.'

(h) Anxiety among people holding insurance policies or contributing to superannuation schemes.

(i) Criticism of certain details: (i) cynicism at the proposal that 'Old Age Pensioners should not reach the full benefit for twenty years'; (ii) 'The 4/3d. per week contribution will weigh heavily on the poorer wage earners'; (iii) the added burden on employers will hamper our export trade, and without that we shall not be able to keep up the necessary standard of living.

POST-WAR RECONSTRUCTION: Interest in post-war reconstruction is said to have been stimulated by the Report. Fear of unemployment continues to be a major preoccupation, but there is slightly more hope of 'a brighter world with poverty and unemployment done away with'.

This week for the first time, there is mention of interest in the rebuilding and replanning of London – this from one Region.

4. NORTH AFRICA

On the whole, confidence is maintained that we shall drive the Axis out of North Africa, but disappointment is again expressed that it should take so long – particularly after the press had 'given the impression that the enemy would be turned out in a few weeks without a major battle'. There does, however, seem to be a growing appreciation of the difficulties involved (particularly in Tunisia), and a greater realisation that 'it will take some time to close the pincers'.

TUNISIA: Comment and speculation are reported on the absence of news from this front, which is taken by many as 'an indication that we have had some sort of a setback'. Surprise and uneasiness are reported 'that the Axis should have been able to reinforce so easily', and there is some speculation as to whether we have 'enough equipment to keep up the pace'. Anxiety is again expressed at our having advanced so far without more air cover and 'with no armoured units except a few American tanks'.

The feeling is said to persist in some quarters that 'the Americans are leaving the difficult spearhead job to us'. It is asked: 'When are the Americans going to fight?'

LIBYA: First reports indicate that people are pleased, but not elated, that Rommel has been dislodged from El Agheila. Pleasure appears to be tempered by disappointment that again we have not had a chance to beat the Afrika corps.

5. RUSSIA

Admiration for, and confidence in, the Russian war effort continue to be expressed, especially among poorer people. The present attitude is said 'to be calmer and less intense', although interest in the campaign is maintained. There is some speculation as to 'how long the Russians will be able to maintain their attack before their tanks and lorries are hampered by the snow', but the general feeling is that 'the Russian army has already denied the enemy his two vital objectives – the Caucasus oil and the Volga communications'. The accuracy of the Russian claims is still said in reports from four Regions to be doubted 'by quite a number of people'.

6. ITALY

The bombing of Italy continues to meet with general approval, though there is now a tendency to take the raids for granted. Our small losses are noted with pleasure. It is hoped we shall keep it up; many people feel that 'Italian morale will break under heavy bombardment' and that 'Italy will soon be out of the war'. There are further demands that Rome should be bombed.

A minority are again said to be sorry for the Italians – regarded by some as 'a harmless people' – but it is felt that 'as long as the Italian people stand behind Mussolini they must take their medicine'. Some people are, however, said to 'deprecate what is described as the lowered moral sensibilities of the public, noticeable in the pleasure taken in reports of air bombardment, even of civilians'.

Some criticism of the present policy of bombing Italian cities is mentioned on the grounds that:

(i) 'Bombs on Italy mean fewer bombs on Germany, which is a pity.' (Some are asking when the 1,000-bomber raid on Berlin is to take place. 'Will this be Churchill's Christmas present to us?')

(ii) 'Bombing only hardens morale.'

7. THE FIGHTING FRENCH

Opinion about General de Gaulle and the Fighting French is reported on the same lines as last week. Any past distrust now seems to have been swallowed up in the greatly increased sympathy expressed for General de Gaulle, and it is hoped that he will not be 'pushed aside for a Vichyite'.

General Catroux's speech (7th December) appears to have aroused a fair amount of interest and to have been generally appreciated. It is said to have contributed to the hardening of feeling against Darlan and to have increased the belief that he 'must be got rid of'.

8. THE SCUTTLING OF THE FRENCH FLEET

The 'authorities' and the press are criticised in connection with 'the release of the news about the scuttling of the French fleet', which gave people the impression that every ship had been scuttled and made useless to the enemy. There is now some disappointment at the news that 'the Germans will have the use of at least a quarter of the Toulon fleet'.

9. GENERAL FRANCO

Distrust of General Franco is referred to in four reports. Some people feel that he would turn against us if things went badly for us in North Africa. It is thought that, if the Germans were to try to get at Gibraltar through Spain, Franco would offer little or no resistance.

His speech (8th December) has passed almost unnoticed except for his praise of Mussolini. Our 'tenderness' to Darlan is thought to have encouraged him to 'talk smoothly' to the Axis.

10. THE UNCHAINING OF THE GERMAN PRISONERS

The British Government's initiative in unchaining the German prisoners appears to have met with general approval, and people's relief is said to be obvious.

'No action by the British since the outbreak of the war' is said to have been so unpopular as our retaliation; it is described as having been 'a mistake from the start' and it is 'generally hoped that we shan't again take retaliatory measures'. The German reply is 'anxiously awaited by those with friends or relatives who are prisoners of war'. Some speculation is, however, reported as to 'what we shall do, if the Germans continue the shackling'.

11. FAR EAST

The fighting in the Pacific war zone has not attracted much attention this week, though appreciation of the allied successes is reported. Interest is said to be taken in the Japanese shipping losses, which are linked up with the home food situation.

The Prime Minister's statement that our energies will be devoted to Hitler's defeat before the Japanese feel the full weight of our arms is thought to be right and sensible. The feeling is again reported that the Japanese will be hard to beat.

Interest in Burma, and the expectation that its reconquest will soon take place, is reported from two Regions.

12. GERMAN ANTI-JEWISH ATRICITIES IN POLAND

The 'wholesale murder of Jews in Poland' is said to have caused 'extreme horror', and the suggestion is put forward that the Prime Minister should make a public statement on this subject 'similar to his broadcast warning Hitler against the use of gas'. It is hoped that something may be done to save the children.

ANTI-SEMITISM: In contrast with this, anti-Semitism, aggravated by reports of 'regulation dodging' and the prosecutions for black-market offences, is once more mentioned in reports from three Regions.

13. VENEREAL DISEASE AND REGULATION 33B

Mention is made in four reports of the recent publicity given to venereal disease and Regulation 33B. There is said to be 'considerable comment on the rise in the number of cases'; and 'appreciation of the *Daily Mirror* for its candour in publicising the facts' is also reported. The details of the regulation are little understood.

14. BROADCASTING AND PRESENTATION OF NEWS

Satisfaction with the handling of the war news continues, though the public appears to be a little more critical this week. Reports from two Regions suggest that 'the comparative quietness on the battlefronts has seen a growth in the tendency to switch off the wireless after the main headings have been read'. There is 'continued appreciation' of the repetition of headlines after the news, though there is some demand from the South-Western Region that they should be more detailed; in two Regions the importance of the 9 p.m. news bulletins to war workers is stressed 'as so much time is taken up travelling in the blackout that they have little opportunity to read the newspapers'.

Critical comment follows familiar lines:

(a) The indiscretion of the BBC in broadcasting information 'which could be useful to the enemy'; the following instances are given: (i) 'The revelation of how the Russians built their under-the-water bridge', (ii) Peter Masefield's description of the new Spitfire engine (10th December).

(b) The news bulletins are 'too full of padding and unnecessary repetition'.

(c) The 'lack of news' from North Africa is commented on, and there is a demand 'for fuller war news to counter popular suspicion that we are holding up something bad'.

The printing in some newspapers of maps of North Africa, with inserted maps of Great Britain drawn to scale, is said 'to help the public to realise the vast distances which the campaign involves', and it is suggested that all war maps should follow this practice.

VARIETY PROGRAMMES: The 'low level' and 'coarseness' of variety programmes is commented on in reports from four Regions this week. There is said 'to be a continuous demand for variety worth listening to', and for more 'good drama and music for the Forces'.

THE EUROPEAN NEWS SERVICE is praised in three reports for its 'more vivid presentation'.

Reports have been received on the following broadcasts and speeches:

GENERAL SMUTS' RECORDED BROADCAST (6TH DECEMBER): While the speech was thought to have been of a 'high standard', and 'plain and practical', little comment is reported, and it is suggested that 'the recording was so poor that many people switched the wireless off after a few minutes'. It is thought that the speech would have made a better impression if it had been read by an announcer.

MR. MORRIS'S BROADCAST ON JAPAN (7TH DECEMBER) met with general approval, according to reports from two Regions, and is thought to have 'stimulated interest in the Far East'.

II. SPECIAL COMMENTS

15. CHRISTMAS

People's minds are said to be turning towards Christmas this week. War workers are looking forward to 'a welcome rest'; others are 'doing what they can to celebrate' but realise that the scale 'must be less lavish' than in former years. Some people, 'of the more patriotic and thinking type', are said to feel that it would have been fairer 'if the Government had taken firmer steps with Christmas shopping and encouraged everyone to treat this as a really war Christmas'. It is thought that this would have avoided 'the quantities of rubbish sold at exorbitant prices', and relieved many housewives of 'hours of shop crawling and enquiring for small supplies of trimmings and mincemeat, etc.'

TOYS: From nine Regions this week 'anger' is reported at the 'ramp in Christmas toys'. Toys, both new and second-hand, are said 'to be at ridiculous prices': 'objects knocked together out of two bits of firewood cost 5/-', 'a rag doll at 25/- worth 9d.', are among examples cited, and it is said that working-class mothers and wives of servicemen 'who want to make Christmas a happy time, cannot afford toys, as the prices are beyond them'.

The order made by the Board of Trade on 12th December, to release more toys, has met with approval, but it is thought 'to have come too late', and people do not feel confident that prices will be brought down to a reasonable level.

16. MANPOWER

NATIONAL SERVICE BILL 1942 (SECOND READING 8TH DECEMBER): Reference is made to this Bill in reports from six Regions, but comment on it is limited. There does, however, appear to be some adverse criticism, particularly in 'educational circles', of the decision that 'no young man will now be permitted to complete an Arts course at a University: where are our leaders, professional men and teachers of the next generation to come from?' It is suggested that 'very special consideration should be given in special cases of outstanding ability'. Boys who have worked for two years for their entrance examination are reported in the North Midland Region to be 'very unhappy'. At the same time, however, resignation to such measures, 'if they are essential to the war effort', is also reported. Among less educated people, Arts students are confused with art students.

The press accounts of the second reading of the Bill seem to have stimulated talk about: (i) the number of 'men of military age in cushy jobs' and of young women in offices and Government departments; (ii) 'The right people not in the right jobs', both in the Services and factories. An example is quoted of 'women trained as bench fitters being put to riveting'.

WOMEN'S CALL-UP: Reports from two Regions again refer to 'the need for a clear statement on women's obligations under the call-up, particularly as regards compulsory work for married women'.

17. INDUSTRY

Less comment about industry is reported this week than in the two previous weeks. It is, however, suggested that production tends to be slowed up by long hours, income tax, shopping and transport difficulties, and women workers' 'worry about their children'.

18. TRANSPORT DIFFICULTIES

There are references from ten Regions this week to transport difficulties. A considerable increase in transport complaints is reported from the Northern Region.
Complaints are on familiar lines:

(a) The curtailment of Sunday morning transport.
(b) The overcrowding of buses by (i) shoppers and pleasure seekers; (ii) train travellers, because of the abolition of cheap train fares; (iii) short-distance passengers on long-distance buses.
(c) Buses running empty in the afternoons.

In the Northern Region, small children are said to be joy-riding on the trolley buses because they have nothing else to do with their pocket money – thus taking seats from people anxious to get home before the workers.

Complaints of the 'revolting conditions' of lavatories on trains and stations come from the Southern Region. The filthiness of lavatories on long-distance trains is said to be partly due to the fact that they are often unlighted at night. Those on the stations are alleged to be due to 'the years of neglect by railway companies before the war' and accentuated now by careless use by troops travelling in large numbers. Lavatories maintained by local authorities have been noted as being invariably cleaner and better equipped than those on stations. It is thought that a serious increase in disease will result unless the railway lavatories are improved without delay and regularly cleaned and disinfected.

19. PETROL

There are references from four Regions only this week to the misuse and waste of petrol:

(a) Cars being used when buses and/or trains are available.
(b) Misuse and waste of petrol by farmers.
(c) Waste of petrol by people who ought not to receive allowances.

20. CLOTHING

COUPONS: The hope is again expressed that the 'Board of Trade will give consideration to the matter of a household ration book'.

UTILITY CLOTHING: There is some complaint that utility clothing wears out quickly 'owing to insufficient turnings having been taken'. 'The seams all burst when you put the garment on.'

STOCKINGS: Fully-fashioned stockings are said to be practically unobtainable and there are complaints from four Regions of the 'shoddy quality' of utility stockings which are said not to be worth two coupons. 'If a shopkeeper sells shoddy goods he can be pulled up for it, but the Government takes our coupons for rubbishy stockings.'

WELLINGTON BOOTS: It is reported from one Region that requests for children's Wellingtons pour into the shops but almost invariably there are no stocks. It is felt to be 'unfortunate that the public should have been given the impression that even a limited supply of Wellingtons would be available'.

21. BATTERIES

There are widespread reports this week of the shortage of both cycle and No. 8 batteries, and some criticism of the lack of foresight on the part of the Board of Trade to meet the needs for 'safety in the blackout'.

CYCLE LAMP BATTERIES: The shortage of these is said to be causing 'widespread anxiety'. Mention is made of the number of police court cases of 'riding without lights' and of the increasing use by cyclists of already overcrowded buses. It is suggested in one report that some form of priority system might be devised which would ensure supplies of batteries, when available, to workers who are dependent on cycle transport.

NO. 8 BATTERIES: The hope is expressed that if no more No. 8 battery cases are to be made the Government will 'issue a standard torch for civilians', as people are said to ask why they should have to buy a more expensive size. There is some feeling that this may be a 'trade racket to force people to buy new torches'.

22. FOOD

A special report from Postal Censorship shows that of the letters mentioning the food situation eighty-one per cent express appreciation. 'Lord Woolton's management of supplies is masterly.' 'A good cook can do wonders with the rations.'

The chief criticisms reported from the Regions are:

MILK: Eight reports refer to the difficulties caused by the smallness of the ration but 'it is regarded as a necessary evil'. There are complaints also of unequal distribution and of quality, the milk being said sometimes to be a day or two old when delivered.

FISH: 'Lord Woolton's firmness in dealing with the fish trade' is approved, and 'it is hoped that the zoning scheme is beginning to work better'. There are still complaints of shortage of supplies and of favoured customers, but the 'limitation of supplies to hotels has been favourably received' and 'it is thought this will make things easier for the housewife'.

CHRISTMAS FARE: Disappointment is again reported at the lack of any 'extras' for the Christmas season, but most people 'accept the necessary restrictions, consoling themselves with the hope that this will be the last Christmas of the war'.

BRITISH RESTAURANTS, AND CANTEENS IN FACTORIES: Approval is expressed of British Restaurants, which are said to compare favourably with canteens in factories. It is stated in one report that there is 'some demand for works canteens to be put under Government control when they would be less likely to be run inefficiently'.

23. FUEL ECONOMY

There is less comment this week on fuel economy. It is thought that the majority are doing their best to economise and that the Economy Campaign has therefore achieved its purpose. Some uneasiness is reported from the Northern Region, where it is felt that people will find their fuel allowance inadequate when the worst of the winter comes.

Two reports criticise the Fuel Flashes. They are said to be 'heartily disliked', and conscientious people are sick of being worried by them.

The quality of coal is again criticised. People in Sheffield are said to wonder where the reason lies for the increase in the cost of coal.

A LISTENER RESEARCH ENQUIRY: During October 1942, the BBC Listener Research department made an enquiry into the prevalent feeling of the public on the Government's Fuel Economy Campaign. Reports were received from 823 correspondents. The results of the enquiry confirm the findings of Home Intelligence, and may be summarised thus:

(i) Bewilderment that such a situation should have arisen in a land where coal is plentiful (this, it is thought, suggests that *labour* shortage as a factor may have been inadequately stressed in the Campaign, or at least inadequately perceived by the public).

(ii) Readiness to put up with the situation and accept any hardship that the Government imposes on them, *provided that such hardships are common to all*, and not the burden of the conscientious few. Here opinion divides fairly evenly between those who favour compulsory rationing as the only fair method of tackling the problem, and those who urge the continuance of the voluntary scheme, with the campaign directed less against the ordinary householder than the large consumer such as offices, stores, hotels, and factories.

24. FIRE-WATCHING

Some renewal of complaints about the Fire-Guard (Compulsory Enrolment) Order is reported this week. Feeling still persists that women should not fire-watch on business premises, especially married women with home responsibilities; and there is a demand for 'a clear statement on what is a danger zone, and what is a woman's duty on business premises'. Grumbles are also reported at 'the delay in issuing the amended order'.

'FRONT LINE': Appreciation of this book continues to be reported, but in the Southern Region there are still complaints of the limited supplies available. In Liverpool, pleasure is noted that 'it has been given its rightful place next to London', while Manchester thinks its quota of bombers has been under-estimated.

III

January to December 1943

14–24 JANUARY Casablanca conference. Churchill and Roosevelt agree an Allied invasion of Sicily and a combined bomber offensive against Germany. The policy of unconditional surrender for the Axis powers is announced.

23 JANUARY The Eighth Army takes Tripoli unopposed. Rommel withdraws into Tunisia.

2 FEBRUARY The remnants of the German Sixth Army at Stalingrad capitulate. Some 100,000 Axis troops are taken prisoner.

14–22 FEBRUARY In their first large-scale encounter with Axis forces, US troops suffer a reverse at Kasserine Pass in west-central Tunisia before Rommel calls off his attack.

16–18 FEBRUARY The House of Commons debates the Beveridge report. The coalition government accepts the report in principle but gives no final commitments. Many Labour backbenchers want 'Beveridge now'. In the division, 121 MPs, mainly from the Labour party, vote against the government.

3 MARCH In one of the largest losses of British civilian life in a single incident during the war, 173 people, including 62 children, are crushed to death at Bethnal Green tube station in London as they hurriedly enter the station to shelter during an air raid alert.

9 MARCH Rommel leaves Africa for Germany.

6–7 APRIL The Eighth Army dislodges Axis forces from Wadi Akarit on the eastern coast of Tunisia. The latter withdraw towards Tunis.

12–25 MAY Washington conference. Churchill and Roosevelt agree to exploit the forthcoming invasion of Sicily to eliminate Italy from the war and to mount a cross-Channel invasion in the spring of 1944.

13 MAY Axis forces in North Africa surrender after Tunis is captured by the First Army and Bizerta by the US Second Corps. Some 250,000 Axis prisoners are in Allied hands. Alexander informs

Churchill that the Tunisian campaign is over: 'We are masters of the North African shores.'

14 MAY The Arakan campaign ends in failure with British and Indian troops pushed back by the Japanese to their original starting positions close to the India–Burma border.

16–17 MAY The RAF's 617 squadron, led by Wing Commander Guy Gibson, attacks the Ruhr dams in Germany using bouncing bombs designed by Barnes Wallis. Gibson is awarded the Victoria Cross for his gallantry.

5 JULY German forces launch a major assault around Kursk on the Russian central front. The assault soon falters in the face of determined Soviet resistance.

10 JULY US, British and Canadian forces land on the southern coast of Sicily. The Allies establish a beachhead and advance inland.

12 JULY Soviet forces counterattack at Kursk. Over the weeks that follow, the Germans are pushed back in western Russia.

16 JULY The government publishes a white paper on educational reconstruction.

19 JULY US aircraft bomb Rome. The San Lorenzo district, the least Fascist quarter of the city, is heavily damaged. Some 1,700 Italians are killed.

25 JULY Mussolini is dismissed from power by King Victor Emmanuel and placed under arrest. A new Italian regime under Badoglio is established.

14–24 AUGUST Quebec conference. Churchill and Roosevelt endorse preparations for operations against mainland Italy as well as the cross-Channel invasion of France: Operation Overlord. As an auxiliary to Overlord, a prospective landing in the south of France is agreed. A South East Asia Command is established to coordinate Allied operations against the Japanese in this theatre.

17 AUGUST US troops capture Messina, ending the campaign in Sicily, but 100,000 Axis troops are evacuated to mainland Italy.

23 AUGUST Kharkov in Ukraine is recaptured by Soviet forces.

3 SEPTEMBER The Eighth Army lands in Calabria in southern Italy. There is little opposition. Six days later, the US Fifth Army lands further north at Salerno. German forces fiercely contest the Salerno beachhead.

8 SEPTEMBER The surrender of Italy is announced.

12 SEPTEMBER In an audacious airborne operation, Mussolini is freed by German forces from his mountain confinement at the Hotel Campo Imperatore in Abruzzo. He is subsequently placed at the head of a puppet fascist regime based at Lake Garda – a rival government to that of Badoglio.

16 SEPTEMBER German forces at Salerno begin to withdraw and the beachhead is secured.

22 SEPTEMBER Two Royal Navy midget submarines attack the German battleship *Tirpitz* at Kåfjord in Norway. The ship is put out of action for several months. For their gallantry during this daring attack, Lieutenant Donald Cameron and Lieutenant Godfrey Place are awarded the Victoria Cross.

22 SEPTEMBER The government announces its intention to introduce a 'pay-as-you-earn' system of income tax.

1 OCTOBER The US Fifth Army enters Naples.

4 OCTOBER German forces capture the Dodecanese island of Cos in the Aegean Sea. The island had recently been occupied by the British after the Italian surrender.

13 OCTOBER Badoglio's government declares war on Germany.

6 NOVEMBER Soviet forces retake Kiev.

16 NOVEMBER German forces capture the Dodecanese island of Leros from the newly installed British garrison. The garrison on the island of Samos is subsequently evacuated.

28 NOVEMBER–1 DECEMBER Tehran conference. The three Allied leaders – Churchill, Roosevelt and Stalin – meet together for the first time. Stalin promises that Soviet forces will mount an offensive on the eastern front to coincide with Operation Overlord in the spring of 1944.

15 DECEMBER The government presents to parliament a bill to reform the education system in England and Wales.

NO. 121: TUESDAY 19 JANUARY 1943 TO
TUESDAY 26 JANUARY 1943

I. GENERAL COMMENTS

1. GENERAL STATE OF CONFIDENCE AND REACTION TO NEWS

A slight rise in spirits is reported and many people are said to be more cheerful than they were last week. For this, continued Russian successes are said to be chiefly responsible. There is also great satisfaction over the taking of Tripoli and the subsequent advances of the Eighth Army, and these have 'in some degree taken people's thoughts away from the political difficulties in Tunisia', where the situation continues to cause considerable anxiety. The shipping situation is said to be another 'sobering influence', and increasing realisation of the U-boat menace is reported from seven Regions.

There seems to have been a slight decrease in talk of early victory, though many are still reported to 'believe that the Germans and Italians will be knocked out by Christmas, 1943'.

Several reports refer to people feeling tired and flat, and to the prevalence of colds, chills and influenza. Long hours of work, the blackout, lack of proper holidays, and of vitamins, are thought to account for this.

On the home front the shortage of batteries is still reported as 'a widespread, major difficulty', though the position is said to have eased a little in some places. Other 'frequently discussed topics' are the fish shortage and transport difficulties.

(1. 2. 3. 4. 5. 7. 8. 9. 10. 11. 12. 13. 14 North-Western Region. 21 six provincial PCs. No report from Region 6 this week)

2. THE PRIME MINISTER'S MEETING WITH PRESIDENT
ROOSEVELT IN CASABLANCA

No reports of public reaction to this news have yet been received, though speculation about Mr. Churchill's whereabouts is reported from eight Regions, opinion being equally divided as to whether he had gone to America or North Africa. The earliest signs of this speculation were reported last week – from the South-Western Region.

(1. 2. 3. 5. 8. 9. 10. 12)

3. RUSSIA

Admiration for the Russians continues, apparently more strongly than ever, and 'Russian prestige has never stood higher'. 'People talk in superlatives of Russia but that doesn't really express how much they admire her achievements.' The relief of Leningrad made a particularly deep impression, without 'giving rise to the almost emotional relief caused by the liquidation of the threat to Stalingrad'. Other reported reactions include (a) admiration for the leadership, organisation and mobility of the armies and supplies; (b) comparisons between Russian activity and our 'quietness'; (c) satisfaction at the amount of material sent to Russia by US and ourselves; (d) scepticism of Russian claims; (e) interest in, and desire to know more of, the Russian social system and conditions of life. Some admiration for 'the tenacity of the encircled German force before Stalingrad' is mentioned in two reports.

SUSPICION OF RUSSIA, in various forms, is mentioned in reports from five Regions, though apparently on the part of a small number of people only, who are 'concerned over the peace, if Russia "pulls it off" by herself'. 'Will Joe stop at the Channel?' is another sentiment expressed. Many people in Scotland are said to be 'irritated, some bewildered, and a few impressed by the outspoken anti-Russia feeling expressed by the Poles stationed there'. Those who are impressed say: 'After all, they have been neighbours of the Russians for so long, they know better than the BBC.'

SECOND-FRONT TALK is mentioned in four reports. People want to 'make sure that the war is definitely carried into German territory', and some feel that 'there never was a more favourable time for attacking the Germans than when they are in difficulties on the Russian front'.

THE SIZE OF RUSSIAN TERRITORY is still not appreciated by many, according to three reports, two of which mention 'increasing criticism of the maps of battlefields appearing in the press'. These are said to 'cause the general public to form a most erroneous impression of the scale of operations and territory involved' – particularly 'the size of the areas recaptured by the Red Army'.

(1. 2. 3. 4. 5. 7. 8. 9. 10. 11. 12. 13. 14 N.W. Region. 21 twelve provincial PCs)

4. THE CAPTURE OF TRIPOLI BY THE EIGHTH ARMY

The capture of Tripoli is described as 'a milestone in the public mind' and has caused great satisfaction. Although it was not unexpected, people are said to have 'liked a silence, succeeded by great news'. This success has 'heightened the already great prestige of the Eighth Army and established the confidence in this command even more strongly'. According to the report from Scotland, 'with working people especially, Montgomery will soon be as popular as Timoshenko'. 'The feat of organisation which enabled the Eighth Army to make so great an advance in strength, and with full supplies, is highly praised' in three reports.

Many people, however, are said to expect that 'great difficulties still lie ahead', and it is pointed out that 'the Eighth Army has not yet got to grips with Rommel's forces'. Though 'Rommel's pursuit into Tunisia is greeted with relish', some now fear that he will be able to join up with the Axis forces in Tunisia and that part of the Allied armies 'may find themselves sandwiched between two German forces'.

At the same time, it is hoped that 'the arrival of the victorious Eighth Army will hasten things'. The comment is reported that 'it will be the Eighth Army that will destroy the Axis in Tunisia, not the First – and certainly not the Fifth'.

(1. 2. 3. 4. 5. 7. 8. 9. 10. 11. 12. 13)

5. TUNISIA

Up to the announcement of the Prime Minister's visit, public feeling about the situation in Tunisia was reported to be substantially the same as it was last week, the only new development being widespread disapproval of M. Peyrouton's appointment. The predominating reactions continued to be (a) bewilderment and dissatisfaction at our lack of progress; (b) criticism of the Americans on the grounds that they were not doing their share of the fighting and were responsible for the political situation; and (c) a belief that the military hold-up was due less to the mud than to political difficulties.

(1. 2. 3. 4. 5. 7. 8. 9. 10. 11. 12. 13. 21 seven provincial PCs)

6. THE WAR IN THE AIR

THE RAIDS ON BERLIN: The RAF offensive, and particularly the raids on Berlin, are said to have given much satisfaction. The great majority seem to 'hope that they'll go on – reprisals or no reprisals'. Further reports mention a belief in 'the psychological value' of raids on the German capital, particularly at a time when they are suffering reverses elsewhere. The raids on Berlin are said to have 'ended a rumour, which very many found unpalatable, that there was a London-Berlin bombing truce'. One report mentions 'some feeling against the bombing of Berlin, on the grounds that there are targets of military importance which do not involve so much bombing of civilians'.

'WHY DON'T WE BOMB ROME?' is a question reported from six Regions, together with the demand that we should do so. Although one report refers to 'a strong feeling that Roman Catholic influences in this country are working to ensure that Mussolini's capital remains immune', the report from Wales says that 'some Roman Catholics would not object to Rome being bombed if Mussolini is increasing the military importance of the city and if it would end hostilities more quickly'.

THE RAIDS ON LONDON were expected and were regarded by many as propaganda raids: 'anything else would have been too open a confession of Luftwaffe weakness'. They were thought to have been 'nothing in comparison with ours'. Satisfaction is again expressed with 'the excellence of the barrage', though there is thought to be some need for renewed warnings of the danger of sky-gazing, while it is in action.

THE BOMBING OF THE SCHOOL (20TH JANUARY) has aroused great indignation and sympathy. Opinion is divided, however, as to whether or not it was deliberate.

CIVIL DEFENCE: The daylight raid on London has given rise to much discussion – not only in London – on the question of locked shelters, of the balloons not being up and, particularly, of bombs being dropped before the alert. There is some feeling that 'the Civil Defence authorities were caught napping'. 'Though not unduly worried about air attack, the public do expect the very extensive and expensive services which absorb considerable man-and woman-power to be capable of handling efficiently a situation such as this.'

EXPECTATION OF FURTHER RAIDS: Speculation is reported as to the possible resumption of heavy raids. There is some expectation of further reprisals, but it is not thought that they will be severe, and most people express great confidence in our anti-aircraft defences and the RAF. In Scotland, however, 'the death roll at the school near London has reawakened in the minds of many parents questions about evacuation'.

POISON GAS: Expectation that Hitler may use gas, 'as a last terrible bid', appears to have been stimulated by Lord Halifax's reference to this possibility in his speech at Rochester, New York (18th January). It is suggested that 'if the British authorities believe this, some arrangements should be made for the overhaul of anti-gas equipment'.

(1. 2. 3. 4. 5. 7. 8. 9. 10. 11. 12. 13. 21 eight provincial PCs)

7. THE WAR AT SEA

Anxiety about 'the U-boat menace' is increasing, particularly among those who live in ports and 'more thinking people', who are said to be uneasy because 'they do not know where we stand'. 'No one wants exact figures', but it is felt that some statement should be made because: (a) 'People don't want to be treated like children: what's bad enough for the Government to know is not too bad for us'; (b) 'Silence blinds the mass of people to the gravity of the situation, whereas more factual news would rouse them from complacency and give an impetus to all war effort.'

Some anxiety is reported at alleged deficiencies of Fleet Air Arm aircraft.

(1. 2. 3. 4. 7. 8. 9. 10. 11. 13. 21 four provincial PCs)

8. IRAQ AND CIIILE

Very little interest has been shown in the declaration of war on the Axis by Iraq (16th January), or in Chile's break with the Axis (20th January). There is some tendency to regard both events as 'a barometer of our degree of success'.

(2. 4. 7)

9. THE BEVERIDGE REPORT

Interest continues at a reduced level, and comment follows familiar lines. There appears, however, to be 'increasing fear that the recommendations may be sabotaged by vested interests', and it is hoped that 'the Government will reassure the public with an authoritative statement'.

'Uneasiness' continues to be reported in six Regions at the ban on the ABCA pamphlet, containing the Beveridge Report summary. According to reports from two of these Regions, 'the defence offered by Sir James Grigg is described as very weak'.

(1. 2. 3. 4. 5. 7. 8. 9. 10. 11. 21 four provincial PCs)

10. ANTI-SEMITISM

Reports from five Regions (as against four last week) refer to 'an increase in feeling against the Jews'. This is again variously ascribed to 'the number of black-market offences committed by people with Jewish names, their indifference and meagre contribution to the war effort', and their success in getting houses in areas where the demand is greatest. It is also suggested in the North Midland Region that 'rumours are going around of the number of Jewish turns – especially in variety shows – being broadcast by the BBC; and any preponderance of Jews in any particular industry or department does get an Englishman's goat'.

Sympathy for Jews in occupied Europe is reported from two Regions.

(2. 3. 4. 9. 10. 21 two provincial PCs)

11. BROADCASTING AND PRESENTATION OF NEWS

There continues to be little comment on the presentation of news, but some criticism is reported this week about the following:

(a) 'The BBC bulletins are overweighted with Russian material' (three Regions). There is some anxiety lest 'people are being led to believe that Russia is bearing the whole burden of the war and that our own efforts are insignificant'.

(b) We are trying to minimise our losses in Tunisia (three Regions).

THE BRAINS TRUST: Comment on the *Brains Trust* is reported in five Regions. Although opinion appears to be sharply divided, unfavourable reactions are said to predominate.

APPRECIATION is reported for Major Hastings' *War Commentary* of 21st January, and for the further instalments of *War and Peace* (four Regions each).

SUNDAY NIGHT POSTCRIPTS: Reports from three Regions again suggest that these are not considered as interesting as they were.

(1. 2. 3. 4. 5. 7. 8. 9. 10. 32)

II. SPECIAL COMMENTS

12. INDUSTRY

Criticism of production continues to be on a small scale, and in two Regions the public are said to be more satisfied with the position. 'Lack of enthusiasm' among the workers is mentioned in two Regions, though in the South-Western Region instances of 'good spirit and readiness for sacrifice' are commented on. Familiar complaints reported are (a) absenteeism, especially among transferred workers and wives of serving men (four Regions), and (b) stories of idle time (four Regions).

In the Northern Region 'the burden of the war' is thought to be 'falling far more heavily on women workers than on the men'. It is pointed out that 'many women workers are housewives with an already full-time job on their hands', and 'strain and fatigue' (reported from three Regions this week) are thought to be aggravated by (a) shopping difficulties (five Regions and Postal Censorship); (b) long hours of work, especially night work (three Regions); and (c) fire-watching duties (two Regions).

STRIKES and the threat of strikes continue to be criticised (five Regions), especially by the relatives of serving men. In Scotland, however, 'considerable sympathy' is said to be shown by industrial workers for the Scottish miners' wage claims, and in the South-Eastern Region a 'minority' are reported to feel sympathy with the locomotive men – 'Give them a fair deal and they will not strike.'

(1. 2. 3. 4. 5. 7. 10. 11. 12. 13. 21 three provincial PCs)

13. MANPOWER

The extension of the National Service Acts (1939–42) has evoked some comment that girls of nineteen should not be called into the Forces until (a) 'women in their twenties' have been called up (four Regions), and (b) married women 'without encumbrances' have been 'forced into war work' (four Regions).

Other criticisms of the manpower situation are (a) the handling of women at Labour Exchanges, and complaints of 'their unfair direction into industry' (four Regions); (b) the number of 'young men in reserved jobs, shirking the call-up' (three Regions); (c) 'the inefficient use of manpower' (three Regions); (d) 'the drain on essential industries and civilian services caused by the call-up of young men and women' (three Regions).

(1. 2. 3. 5. 7. 9. 10. 12)

14. SHORTAGE OF BATTERIES, AND CYCLISTS' DIFFICULTIES

Shortages of torch and cycle lamp batteries are again reported (torch, eight Regions; cycle lamp, seven Regions). 'Although the situation appears to have eased a little', the shortage 'still remains an outstanding topic', and 'workers find that getting to their employment is a hazardous undertaking'. The bad effect on time-keeping and the overcrowding of transport at rush hours are again pointed out, and there is criticism of the whole situation, which 'must have been foreseeable'. A report from the South-Western Region states that 'the more understanding attitude' shown by magistrates to cyclist offenders 'is remarked on and approved'.

(2. 3. 4. 5. 7. 9. 10. 11. 12)

15. TRANSPORT DIFFICULTIES

From ten Regions this week come reports of transport difficulties. These include the familiar ones of the overcrowding of buses, the failure of buses to pick up passengers at intermediate stops, the crowding out of long-distance passengers by short-distance ones, the curtailment of evening and Sunday transport and the departure of buses before their scheduled time.

(1. 2. 3. 5. 7. 8. 9. 10. 11. 12. 21 one provincial PC)

16. PETROL

Complaints about the waste and misuse of petrol are reported along the usual lines this week from seven Regions. They are: the misuse of taxicabs; misuse of special allowances; waste by the army, farmers, Home Guard and NFS; and the number of high-powered private cars still being used.

(3. 4. 5. 8. 10. 12. 13. 21 one provincial PC)

17. HEALTH

From seven Regions this week come reports of 'a good deal of talk about people being away ill'. The prevalence of colds, influenza, 'tummy troubles' and tiredness is specifically mentioned, and it is suggested in three Regions that 'people are not getting the right sort of food to help them shake off these ailments'.

VENEREAL DISEASES: Instructions and publicity are said 'to be doing much good', and approval is reported for the BBC talk on the subject given on 19th January (five Regions). According to the report from the Eastern Region, however, 'there is some feeling that the Government is not tackling the matter in a strong enough manner; many people believe that venereal disease should be notifiable, otherwise local authorities cannot co-operate as they are supposed to do'.

THE CARE OF THE SICK: 'The growing difficulties' in obtaining nurses, doctors, and midwife attendance and hospital or nursing-home accommodation are reported from three Regions.

(1. 2. 3. 4. 5. 7. 9. 10. 14 North-Western Region)

18. FOOD

Satisfaction with the general food situation continues to be reported.

Complaints are, however, reported of (a) the fish shortage and zoning scheme; (b) the high prices at which green vegetables are controlled; (c) the distribution and shortage of shell eggs; (d) the shortage of sweets, apples, biscuits, onions and rabbits; (e) the inadequacy of the points allocation for small families.

BREAD: Six reports refer to the waste of bread this week. It is suggested that much could be saved if (a) it were only served in restaurants and cafés on demand; (b) larger helpings of vegetables were served. People in the Northern Region are said to be disturbed at the idea of potato flour being used in bread.

CHEESE: Little comment is reported on the reduction in the cheese ration (four Regions). It is said that in many cases people did not previously use the full ration.

TINNED FRUIT: The announcement that tinned fruits will be available on the points ration is said to have been welcomed (two Regions). Some fear is expressed in the rural areas of the North Midland Region that 'they will be less well treated than the urban areas'.

(1. 2. 3. 4. 5. 7. 8. 9. 10. 11. 12. 13. 16. 21 fourteen provincial PCs)

19. CLOTHING

COUPONS FOR HOUSEHOLD LINEN AND TOWELS: This week eight Regions report the need for a separate coupon allowance for household linen. It is said that 'the problem is becoming more and more acute', particularly for those households who have people billeted on them and where there are growing children.

CHILDREN'S CLOTHING AND FOOTWEAR: Seven Regions report difficulties arising from the shortage of children's clothing and footwear, particularly the latter, and it is said that 'children have to stay away from school while repairs are being carried out'. The 'present method of patching' is described as 'false economy' as the shoes are not made watertight.

STOCKINGS: The poor quality of stockings is again mentioned (three Regions) as the cause of 'much grumbling'.

WELLINGTON BOOTS: Two Regions report a shortage of Wellington boots, and there is said to be 'much heart burning at the scarcity', particularly among women working on the land and those with children. 'Evacuated children are supplied with Wellingtons by the WVS, and Italian prisoners of war working on the land are also given them, while every difficulty is put in other people's way.'

(2. 3. 4. 5. 7. 8. 9. 10. 12)

20. FUEL

There is less comment on this subject this week. People are said to be 'doing their best', but the difficulties of country people who can use only coal and paraffin – 'the two fuels most strictly rationed' – are again pointed out (two Regions). The Northern Region reports some discontent 'on account of what is believed to be the threat of proceedings against those who exceed last year's fuel consumption', and it is hoped that any rationing system introduced 'will be decided by pre-war figures of consumption' in order not to victimise the patriotic. There are more complaints about the poor quality of coal.

FUEL FLASHES AND ADVERTISEMENTS: While opinion is divided about radio Fuel Flashes, and some people are said to be 'heartily sick of them', there is praise for Government fuel advertisements and for the flashes shown in the cinemas, 'because they have catchy rhymes and amusing sketches'.

(1. 3. 4. 7. 8. 11. 21 two provincial PCs)

21. SHOPPING DIFFICULTIES

There are complaints from four Regions this week of shopping difficulties, the chief of which continue to be the early and lunch-hour closing of shops.

Requests that shopping hours should be adjusted to suit workers are reported from the North-Eastern Region, it being pointed out that the shops are sold out on Saturday afternoons when workers are free.

(2. 4. 5. 7. 10. 21 one provincial PC)

22. BLACKOUT

Pleasure at the promised relaxation of blackout restrictions for travellers is reported from three Regions, although it is suggested that 'what is more needed is insistence that the railway companies maintain lighting to the full extent of the permitted limit' (one Region). It is said also that 'some people are disappointed that the Government did not include some form of 'starlit' street lighting in those towns which are still in darkness (one Region).

(3. 5. 7. 12. 14 North-Western Region)

23. INCOME TAX AND POST-WAR CREDITS

During the past six weeks very few complaints about income tax have been reported, though four references have been made to 'distrust of any repayment of post-war credits' (three Regions). In one Region it is suggested that 'these grave doubts' are due to fears that 'after the war, post-war credits will be subject to the means test'.

(2. 3. 8. 9. 10. 21 two provincial PCs)

REFERENCES

1. Northern Region (Newcastle)
2. North-Eastern Region (Leeds)
3. North Midland Region (Nottingham)
4. Eastern Region (Cambridge)
5. London Region (London)
6. Southern Region (Reading)
7. South-Western Region (Bristol)   } Weekly Reports from RIOs
8. Wales (Cardiff)
9. Midland Region (Birmingham)
10. North-Western Region (Manchester)
11. Scotland (Edinburgh)
12. South-Eastern Region (Tunbridge Wells)
13. Northern Ireland (Belfast)
14. Special reports from RIOs
15. Regions Adviser's Reports
16. MOI Speakers' Reports
17. Local Information Committees' Reports

18. Home Press Summaries
19. Regional Press Summaries $\left.\right\}$ MOI
20. Hansard
21. Postal Censorship
22. Police Duty Room Reports
23. Wartime Social Survey Reports
24. BBC Listener Research Papers
25. BBC Special Papers
26. Citizens' Advice Bureaux Reports
27. WVS Reports
28. Scottish Unionist Whips' Reports
29. Liberal Party's Reports
30. Economic League's Reports
31. War Office Post Bag Summaries
32. Primary Sources

NO. 125: TUESDAY 16 FEBRUARY 1943 TO TUESDAY 23 FEBRUARY 1943

I. GENERAL COMMENTS

1. GENERAL STATE OF CONFIDENCE AND REACTION TO NEWS

Russian successes and, to a lesser extent, anticipation of an early British and American offensive in Europe have helped to maintain public confidence on a high level. But it is slightly lower than last week, as a result of:

(a) The Axis successes in Tunisia. Some uneasiness about the situation is, however, linked with 'malicious pleasure that the Americans are learning that "it's not so easy"'.

(b) Disappointment at what is believed to be the Government's attitude to the Beveridge Report.

(c) Mr. Churchill's illness.

There is less reference than recently to expectation of early victory, and rather more talk of difficulties on the home front and war-weariness. People are said 'to be accepting hardships, and wanting to go all out in order to get on with the war and to get it over'.

2. NORTH AFRICA

Although there is disappointment over the reverses in Tunisia, particularly at 'the loss of three forward airfields', people appear 'to be chiefly anxious lest the Axis successes delay our whole programme for a big offensive'. They are also wondering: 'What is Stalin thinking of the Tunisian show?' Faith in the Eighth Army – *'they* can look Russia in the face' – is responsible for 'every confidence in the ultimate outcome'.

The most marked reaction, however, has been satisfaction, going as far as jubilation in some cases, at 'the American setback'. 'As long as it's not too disastrous for our First Army, and doesn't last too long', it is felt that 'getting a few knocks will have done the Americans good by teaching them some salutary lessons':

(a) 'It will take them down a peg; they shouted so much about the help they would give.'
(b) 'They'll be less inclined to criticise our boys' ... 'Who called us the Tobruk Harriers?'
(c) It will show them the need for discipline and 'will make them into a decent fighting force for the stiff fight ahead'.

At the same time, according to reports from five Regions, while there is some criticism of the fighting quality of the American troops, people are 'ready to make allowances for them because of their lack of battle experience. It is understandable they should not show up well against Rommel's seasoned troops.' It is, however, regretted that 'they have not been able to profit from our own ordeals but should have to start where we started'.

Two reports mention some apprehension as to where this spirit of criticism of the Americans may lead.

GENERAL EISENHOWER: It is suggested that the retreat in Tunisia has increased doubts about the appointment of General Eisenhower as Commander-in-Chief in Africa. Reasons for this feeling are said to be:

(i) Our own generals are tried and successful and have been put under him.
(ii) He is inexperienced.
(iii) He is almost completely unknown. It is suggested that people should be told more about him.

Some hope is, however, expressed in two reports that 'General Eisenhower is a figurehead', and that 'as General Alexander is in actual command of the men nothing serious can go wrong'.

THE POLITICAL SITUATION: There is much less discussion, but still some uneasiness. The release of political prisoners, however, and the passage of French naval vessels to the United States are taken as signs of 'some improvement'.

3. FIRST REACTIONS TO THE HOUSE OF COMMONS DEBATE ON THE BEVERIDGE REPORT

The debate seems to have been eagerly awaited and to have aroused much interest. At present, however, a confused state of public feeling is reflected in most reports. With the exception of one reference to Mr. Quintin Hogg, the speeches of the three Government spokesmen are the only ones referred to, and it seems clear that the whole debate has not been studied in detail. The great majority appear 'more inclined to judge the Government's attitude to the scheme than to take its proposals one by one and to compare them with the recommendations of the report'. (There is, for example, no reference in any report to children's allowances.)

Many feel that 'the presentation of the Government's case was mishandled', and that it was this, rather than their failure to adopt the report as a whole, which caused disappointment. Mr. Morrison's speech has, however, been generally praised.

With reference to what are believed to be the Government's intentions regarding the report, the public seem to fall into two main groups – a large, disappointed majority and an approving minority. This is apart from a considerable number of people who are not interested, or who say: 'Let's get the war over first.'

A. THE DISAPPOINTED MAJORITY: Though reports vary, the majority seems to include 'the working classes', Liberals, Labour and the Left, a proportion of the middle classes and, according to three reports, a number of the rank and file of the Conservative Party. The majority are said to be disappointed, cynical or angry because:

(i)　The Government is thought to be trying to kill or shelve the Report and is thought to have 'whittled down the expected benefits and to have promised little or nothing'.

(ii)　This is 'a forecast of what we may expect when the war is over'. The Government's attitude 'augurs ill for the future of social security' and has 'crystallised people's worst fears of the post-war period'. The opposition to the Catering Bill was another 'straw in the wind'.

(iii)　'Vested interests have won again' and are 'at work to ensure that things will remain as they did after the last war'.

(iv)　The Beveridge Report is 'a symbol, not only to us but to the whole world', and it is feared that the Government does not realise that it 'has become a religion to some people'. By such, the Report seems to be regarded as sacrosanct, 'like the Ark of the Covenant', quite apart from the actual benefits it promises.

(v)　'The Government's failure to set up a Ministry of Social Security' is regretted and is taken by some as 'perhaps the most definite evidence that the Government intends to mark time'.

B. THE APPROVING MINORITY are said to sympathise with the Government's attitude, because:

(i)   Finance ought to be taken into consideration.
(ii) 'Socialist extremists are making capital out of their present opportunities.' 'Why are these controversial subjects allowed to be brought up by the Socialist Party?'
(iii) The Government is right not to be rushed into hasty decisions now, since we cannot know what conditions will be like after the war. 'It is wise not to raise false hopes.'
(iv) Controversial legislation must be avoided now, lest it 'split the country, and make us lose the war'. (Even many of those who are dissatisfied with the Government's attitude are anxious that nothing should threaten national unity.)
(v)   The Government has conceded a good deal and 'can be compelled by public feeling to go even further'.

4. THE PRIME MINISTER'S ILLNESS

'Very real concern' over the Prime Minister's illness is widespread. 'His illness is connected with the strain of his travels', and it is felt that 'he has worn himself out on our behalf'. Reports from six Regions refer to his 'indispensability' ... 'what a calamity if anything happened to him!' 'He is irreplaceable – if he's out of it, we're done.' Fears that he may be more seriously ill than the public realise are mentioned in one report.

5. RUSSIA

Although Russia's 'magnificent achievements' continue to arouse 'boundless' admiration, discussion of them has taken third place to Tunis and the Beveridge debate. Reactions are on familiar lines:

(a) 'How far will they get?' Few people now expect the Germans to be able to stage a comeback in the spring.
(b) Embarrassment that we are still not yet doing enough for Russia, and a continued desire for all possible help to be sent to her. The opening of a second front in Europe this spring by us and the Americans is particularly hoped for, and confidently expected.
(c) Will Russia make a separate peace, or 'go so far and then stop and hold the Germans, and tell us to get on with it?'
(d) Uneasiness that 'if Russia goes on like this, she may want to dictate the peace terms'. On the other hand, 'a leaning towards the ideals of communism' is also reported.

RED ARMY DAY: The celebrations in Great Britain appear to have been 'greatly enjoyed' ... 'a fitting sign of our feelings for the Red Army'. Although some people believe it was 'all done with our tongue in our cheek', the majority appear to feel 'it has done much to dissipate a suspicion that the alliance between Britain and Russia was artificial'. There has been some amused comment at seeing Red flags hanging where not so long ago it would never have been thought possible.

Individual speeches are little mentioned, but many Scots people considered the broadcasts from London 'to be hysterical in tone and reminiscent of Nuremberg'.

6. THE FAR EAST

GANDHI'S FAST: There appears to be little sympathy with Gandhi – 'it's entirely his own choice', and 'let him die and good riddance' are the most widespread sentiments. Although it is again suggested that 'with Gandhi out of the way, there might be some chance of negotiating with other Indian leaders', the opinion of more thoughtful people is that 'Gandhi dead and a martyr' may cause more difficulty in India than Gandhi living. On the other hand, it is thought his release would soon bring trouble. 'Thank goodness, it's not for me to decide' is the final summing up.

MADAME CHIANG KAI-SHEK'S STATEMENTS IN THE UNITED STATES (18TH AND 19TH FEBRUARY) have increased both sympathy and anxiety for China. While 'President Roosevelt's promise of more aid' has been welcomed, it is also asked 'why has there been so little Lease-Lend to China?' It is suspected that 'it'll take years to drive the Japs from the South Pacific'.

7. THE WAR AT SEA

More confidence, and with this some decline in interest, in the shipping situation is reported as a result of the Prime Minister's statement in the House of Commons (11th February). 'People know more where we stand now.' The demand for the publication of shipping losses is much abated.

8. RAF RAIDS

'Steady interest' in the RAF bombings is reported from seven Regions; according to one Report 'a night without bombing, is like a meal missed'. The continued bombing of U-boat bases – particularly the raid on Wilhelmshaven – is specially praised, but the demand that 'Rome shall not escape' is reported again from three Regions.

9. BROADCASTING AND PRESENTATION OF NEWS

Again this week no general criticisms of news presentation are reported.

THE AMERICAN REVERSES are thought to have been 'handled with skill and restraint by both press and radio', though *The Scotsman* of 23rd February is considered to have been 'rather malicious' for using heavy type in stating that 'The Americans were out-manoeuvred and out-fought'. The references to 'straightening our line' led to criticism of the usual type.

THE BBC SUMMARIES OF THE BEVERIDGE DEBATE are praised, in one report, as 'balanced and objective'.

WAR CORRESPONDENTS' REPORTS would, it is again said, be preferred by some if they were read by the announcer, as 'the reception is so poor at times'.

MR. CASEY'S POSTSCRIPT (14th February) was praised for its defence of the British Empire which – like other recent speeches on similar lines – was thought to be intended for American consumption. Some people in Northern Ireland, however, ask: 'What is meant by nations giving up part of their nationalism?' They are 'suspicious of any proposal that appears to cut across national sovereignty'.

PRAISE is reported for the European News Service, *Into Battle*, and the talk about the convoy to Russia (20th February).

REGRET for *ITMA* and Alvar Lidell.

CRITICISM of the 'dull BBC entertainment programmes', of the *Brains Trust* (which is 'going down in popularity'), and of the 'disappointing *Postscripts*'.

DESIRE for 'light entertainment as a change from the war', good light music, and more straight plays.

II. SPECIAL COMMENTS

10. MANPOWER

Comment continues on familiar lines. The manpower situation is still reported to be 'in the forefront of home news'. Complaints reported are: (a) the alleged 'waste of man- and woman-power' when workers are directed into 'less skilled' or 'less useful' work; (b) the number of young people 'lurking in soft jobs'; (c) shortage of labour and fears about the further effects of the call-up on the staffing of civilian services; (d) transfer of labour, which is often considered 'wasteful and unnecessary'; (e) hardships caused to small traders by the call-up.

Comments on the call-up of married women include complaints of: (a) 'unsympathetic treatment' by Labour Exchange officials and by the personnel of Hardship Tribunals; and (b) the number of young women – especially officers' wives – still evading work of any kind. 'Bewilderment by those affected by the regulation' is reported from two Regions, in one of which Citizens' Advice Bureaux are said to be 'inundated with inquiries on this score'.

11. INDUSTRY

Very little comment on production is reported this week. 'People are, for the most part, reported to be working well', though familiar complaints of shopping difficulties, slackness and idle time, and long hours are again mentioned.

12. TRANSPORT AND PETROL

Transport difficulties are reported from eight Regions. Complaints are: long queues; long-distance passengers being crowded out by short-distance fares; inadequate bus services; long distances between stops in rural areas; and increasing overcrowding and delays on railways. One report suggests that 'many difficulties could be removed by schooling the public to understand the problem better and to observe queuing and other regulations'. The same report mentions the hope that women may be 'brought on as part-time workers, as the shift system on buses is thought to be particularly suitable for part-time employment'.

PETROL: Five Regions report complaints of waste of petrol. 'Seventeen WVS cars outside a hall for an ARP show produced extremely strong local comments.' The use of taxis to take spectators to football grounds and greyhound tracks, the waste of petrol by farmers, and the use of cars by local Government officials when buses and trains serve the area are all mentioned; at the same time 'it is felt that Government servants do most of their journeys on foot and are playing their part in petrol economy'. There is criticism of the use of large cars to transport military officers of high rank, and of the 'waste of both time and petrol' by army 'L' drivers driving about for practice in empty lorries. It is felt 'these might be used for the transport of salvage, particularly in rural areas where dumps of various kinds are accumulating'.

13. THE VD CAMPAIGN

Three reports indicate that the campaign is approved, and the advertisements welcomed – though some feel that they could be made even stronger. It is also thought some reference should be made in the advertisement to 'the consumption of alcohol as a contributing factor'. It is thought, too, that attention should be drawn to 'the responsibility of parents for educating their children in matters of this sort'. 'John Hilton's VD broadcast' (19th January) is still the subject of favourable comment.

14. CLOTHING

Difficulties in managing on the coupon allowance now that former clothes are worn out are reported from four Regions this week. Those who can afford to buy expensive and lasting clothing, or who had good stocks, are said to have a great advantage over the poorer people who can only afford 'shoddy' goods which need constant replacement. Men are said to find the issue of coupons insufficient; if any outer garments are bought no coupons remain for necessary underwear.

COUPONS FOR HOUSEHOLD GOODS: The demand for a special allocation of coupons for household goods continues. Two Regions report feeling that newly married people should be allowed extra clothing coupons now that coupons are required for towels. Complaints of the shortage and high price of household linen are reported from four Regions.

UTILITY STOCKINGS: There are again complaints of the poor quality of utility stockings.

SHOE REPAIRS: Difficulties experienced in getting shoe repairs done are reported from four Regions. The inability of shoemakers to secure sufficient leather to carry out repairs, the poor quality of the leather used, and the bad workmanship on patched shoes which are not watertight are commented on.

CHILDREN'S CLOTHING AND FOOTWEAR: The shortage, poor quality, and high price of children's clothing and footwear are reported from three Regions.

Absence (now called 'absenteeism') from school due to the fact that many mothers have no coupons left for shoes is reported from the London Region.

RUBBER BOOTS: The shortage of rubber boots for farm workers and children is reported from three Regions. Agricultural workers complain that although they hold permits they cannot get the boots, and that Italian prisoners have them.

CLOTHING COUPONS: Planning ahead is said to be difficult unless the Government say how long coupons are to last, and some vagueness about the length of availability of the new clothing coupons is reported. A rumour current in the London Region is 'that the green clothing coupons are to expire shortly'.

15. UTILITY FURNITURE

Various references to utility furniture made during the past five weeks may be summarised as follows:

(a) Considerable disappointment at the high prices. 'Utility furniture is said to be too expensive for young people getting married.' One CAB has found that 'a number of people expect a permit for utility furniture to entitle them to furniture free of charge'.

(b) Comment on the limited amount of furniture available. 'Some people have expressed astonishment over having obtained the necessary permits only to find there is no furniture available.'

(c) Adverse criticism of 'complicated procedures necessary' for obtaining a permit.

(d) 'People do not seem to want it'; 'they have the idea it is not going to be very good or of lasting quality, e.g. green and shoddy woods'.

(e) The public would 'welcome greater smartness of design'.

(f) Secretaries of CABs report 'active interest' and add that 'general approval is expressed by people who examine the illustrated catalogue'.

The high price of other furniture, both new and second-hand, is remarked on in four reports. 'Dealers are considered to be taking it out of people who have been bombed and must have furniture', and it is suggested that 'many people are buying to store, hoping for a big demand in the future'.

16. FOOD

Praise for the food situation continues to be reported. 'The food control people are the best of the bunch and have done their job well for the nation.' At the same time, four Regional reports mention difficulties of small families and those living alone who are 'having the worst of it and finding rations sparse'. There is also some complaint of monotony. Two reports refer this week to the difficulty of feeding heavy workers on the allotted ration.

FISH: The shortage of fish is again a major topic. 'Fish is still short and queues for it still long.' One Region reports 'slightly better supplies lately'. Complaints of 'under-the-counter trade', preference given to telephone orders, and 'the favoured customer' are again made.

EGGS: A shortage of shell eggs is mentioned in four reports. 'Uncollected eggs' are said to be causing criticism in some North Midland Region rural areas where it is said that 'farmers' wives have to fill every available box, and it is three or four weeks before the overworked collector is able to call'.

GREEN VEGETABLES: The high price of green vegetables is again criticised, and it is said that 'many shopkeepers include excess leaves, stalks etc.'

MILK: Complaints of uneven distribution are again made: 'Ten pints were delivered at one household of two in three days while a neighbour had none.' The difficulty of getting TT milk is reported, and the 'dirtiness of milk' in one district is said to be 'causing concern'. A black market among recipients of priority milk is mentioned at Burton-on-Trent.

TINNED FRUITS: It is asked why canned rhubarb should remain on points when fresh rhubarb can be bought, and it is thought a 'waste of cans' to preserve rhubarb and prunes which are so easy to obtain. It is said that some 'multiple stores have gained an unfair advantage in obtaining certain canned fruits from their headquarters in London'.

WASTE OF FOOD: Three reports refer to 'waste of food' (especially bread), in restaurants and cafés, by those who feed it to chickens, and on aerodromes sites: 'All the pigs in the neighbourhood are well fed by the "drome".'

17. AGRICULTURE

The ban on sending out flowers by rail or post is commented on in three reports. In the South-Western Region, it is both commended and criticised. The better type of grower is said to have regarded the 'suitcase traffic' with strong disapproval, whereas some farmers feel that the Government has let them down over the flower scheme. Two Regions report indignation and disappointment that flowers can no longer be sent to friends, hospitals etc. because the practice has been abused by the unscrupulous. The high price of flowers is also criticised.

HOUSES FOR FARM WORKERS: Dissatisfaction at the small number of cottages allotted to Derbyshire, Leicestershire, and Lincolnshire is mentioned. The conviction that until there has been more improvement in the housing position, there will never be any prospect of real solid extra labour on the land, is reported from North Wiltshire.

SEEDS AND FERTILISERS: The shortage and price of these are commented on in two reports. Complaints at the difference in retail and wholesale prices are reported, and it is suggested that something should be done to regulate or control these prices.

'DIG FOR VICTORY' CAMPAIGN: Comment on the 'Dig for Victory' campaign comes from the Midland Region: 'It's all very fine for the Government to tell us to grow our own vegetables – we haven't any time to do more.' The Northern Region reports that the agricultural film *Diggers for Victory* is thought to be good, but it is pointed out that nowhere in the film did it state prominently where the Ministry of Agriculture and Fisheries 'Cropping' leaflet could be obtained.

18. FUEL

Again this week there is little comment about fuel economy. People are still thought to be doing their best, though in one Region it is said that the 'pat on the back' which the public received for fuel saving was unwise, as it tended to make people relax their efforts. The longer days are said to be welcomed by housewives as they can now save on artificial light.

Complaints continue about the poor quality of coal, Welsh coal being particularly mentioned in two reports. A shortage of coal is referred to in two Regions.

Coal merchants in the South-Eastern Region are complaining that they are asked to deliver coal weekly to customers on an impossible ration of petrol. The distance of the railway station from the depot and the customers does not, it is said, seem to have been taken into account.

19. YOUTH

During the past five weeks, there have been several references to youth problems. Chief among these are the increase in drunkenness, which is alleged to be due to the high wages being earned by juveniles, and the lack of recreational facilities; the increase in immoral behaviour, also said to be due to lack of recreational facilities; and the ineffectiveness of Youth Movements, which are said not to be running too satisfactorily, as they are insufficiently educational in character and the leaders are not sufficiently good disciplinarians.

Juvenile crime is also said to be causing anxiety. This is thought to be due largely to lack of parental control and discipline, fathers being in the Forces and mothers out at work.

20. SHORTAGE OF BATTERIES AND CYCLISTS' DIFFICULTIES

Complaints of shortages of cycle lamp and torch batteries are reported this week from nine and seven Regions respectively. The efforts of the Government to remedy the shortage are said to be appreciated, though the public is asking when the new supplies of batteries are to be released. It is asked in the Northern Region why a standard size in torch cases and batteries is not introduced.

Complaints are reported in the Southern Region that different magistrates take opposite decisions when people are charged with riding without lights. Some impose fines and others decide they cannot fine people for technical offences for which they are not really responsible. The shortage of bicycle bells is reported from the South-Western Region. It is said 'that as new cycles are not sold with bells and they can't be bought separately people run the risk of "being run in" for cycling without bells as well as without lights'.

21. INCOME TAX AND POST-WAR CREDITS

During the past three weeks, four references have been made to lack of faith in the repayment of post-war credits – especially among workers. Grumbles about paying income tax, and refusal by cotton mill workers to work overtime because of income tax, is reported constantly from the North-Western Region.

22. NATIONAL SAVINGS CAMPAIGN

During the last fortnight further appreciative comment on the 'Squander Bug' advertisements has been reported – 'it makes people think twice before spending'. During this period there have also been references to: (a) people holding back from buying Savings Certificates because of 'lack of faith in the Government's post-war standing', and (b) 'wastage of material' on aerodrome sites, preventing building workers from joining Savings Groups. On the other hand, in one report 'the better news' is said to have been responsible for a great increase in National Savings during January.

NO. 127: TUESDAY 2 MARCH 1943 TO TUESDAY 9 MARCH 1943

I. GENERAL COMMENTS

1. GENERAL STATE OF CONFIDENCE AND REACTION TO NEWS

The general level of spirits remains high – if anything a little higher than last week – but still not quite back to the February level. Cheering factors include:

a) Continued Russian successes, especially the capture of Rzhev.
b) The annihilation of the Japanese convoy in the Bismarck Sea.
c) The non-stop bombing of Germany, especially the Berlin raid.
d) The repulse of the German attacks in Tunisia.
e) The satisfactory position on the home front, the fine weather and the lengthening days.

'The most marked feature of public feeling' this week is a spirit of expectancy, mentioned in ten out of twelve Regional reports. There is said to be a fairly widespread belief that our invasion of the Continent will not be long delayed, and there is much speculation as to when and where it will be.

On the home front, the chief topic of discussion has been the London tube shelter disaster, which is said to have 'horrified the public' and to have 'left many people sceptical of the official statement that there was no panic'. The qualifying words *'before* the accident' have been entirely overlooked by the public.

Six reports speak of people feeling tired, run down, in need of a holiday, or 'war-weary' – especially women; but, though 'many people complain that they are now thoroughly tired of the war', there is said to be 'nobody who is not prepared to fight on'.

2. ANTICIPATION OF THE SECOND FRONT

The general feeling about a second front is now said to be 'expectancy rather than clamour'. There is a general belief that we are pledged to invade the Continent, that we are actively preparing to do so, and that preparations are nearly complete. Many people regard the increasing RAF offensive as 'a prelude to our big attack', but there is 'a notable tendency to interpret all possible signs as clues to the coming offensive'. Thus, a variety of incidents – whether it be 'a large-scale military exercise in the Southern Region', 'military convoys moving down the Great North Road', or 'WVS drivers rushing tons of blankets to the docks' – are regarded as 'straws in the wind, indicating almost immediate action'.

There is now only a small minority of 'noisy second fronters', but the wish is general that we shall not delay too long, because:

a) People are genuinely anxious to help Russia as much as possible;
b) There is some fear that 'Russia will lick Germany all by herself', and will then 'dictate as to how Germany is to be dealt with after the war';
c) 'If we delay, it will be harder.'

Two reports mention 'frequent comment about the exceedingly heavy casualties that must be expected when the attack is launched'. These feelings are specially mentioned among relatives of servicemen.

3. THE LONDON SHELTER TRAGEDY

People everywhere have been shocked and mystified by 'this appalling shelter tragedy'.

PANIC: The main belief appears to be that only panic, or something very like it, could have been responsible for an accident 'involving such a loss of life'. In some cases, the panic is attributed to a special cause, as for instance:

(a) Our barrage: 'People must have run away from this and rushed to get under cover'.
(b) 'Those East End Jews; they were so terrified, they stampeded.' Two significant features in this connection are:
    (i) Two of these Regions, London and the North-Western, have been most consistent in reporting anti-Semitism.
    (ii) The suggestion that 'the trouble was occasioned by the Jews is reported from all parts of London, with the exception of Bethnal Green where there is full knowledge that any such statement is untrue'.
(c) 'It was fifth column or fascist work'. A typical rumour in London was that 'someone frightened the crowd at the entrance to the shelter by calling out that an oil bomb was falling'.
(d) People were jittery about the possibility of a heavy reprisal raid following the attack on Berlin.
(e) 'Crowds often get out of hand.'

Some responsibility for the disaster is also attributed to 'the authorities', because, it is suggested in London, 'people seem to be trying to find a scapegoat on which to focus their feelings'. Reasons are not always given for blaming 'the authorities', but there is specified criticism of: (a) insufficient personnel on duty; (b) bad lighting; (c) lack of handrails; (d) the shelter's construction: 'Had it been passed as conforming to official requirements?'

THE INQUIRY: The immediate promise of an inquiry has been widely welcomed and its findings are awaited with interest. People want to be assured 'that it cannot happen again'; but in Bethnal Green indignation is said to be 'far from allayed by safeguards put into operation for the future'.

Other reactions include:

(a) A feeling of 'what a chance for Jerry's propaganda'. In Wales, on account of this, 'the press and BBC are condemned for revealing the total number of dead and injured'.
(b) 'Will the suggestion of panic bring a renewal of raids on London and other large centres?'
(c) Pleasure that the Ministry of Pensions is being generous.
(d) Criticism of 'the administrative problems that arose in connection with burial certificates and questions of compensation'.

4. THE BEVERIDGE REPORT AND THE POST-WAR WORLD

Discussion continues to be reported from all Regions on the Beveridge Report and the Parliamentary debate. In five Regions, it is still described as 'a lively topic', though in three Regions 'the volume of comment' is said to be reduced.

While it appears to be generally assumed that the Report has been 'shelved', three reports refer to 'uncertainty in the public mind as to what the Government have agreed upon'. The average man in the street is said 'to have no very clear picture of the nature of the report itself or the Government proposals'; and it is suggested that 'definite information is needed in simple language as to what the Report means and which parts the Government has adopted'. Generally, opinion follows the lines reported last week:

A. THE MAJORITY, chiefly working-class people, who deplore the 'shelving of the Plan', and whose feelings are reported to vary from 'anger' to 'despondency' at the 'betrayal of their interests'. They blame:

(i) VESTED INTERESTS for 'over-aweing the Government'. The opposition to the Catering Bill and to the Report are alleged to 'show the strength of the reactionary forces who want to go back to 1939', and it is suggested that 'they will have to be overcome before the Report will see fruition'.
(ii) THE GOVERNMENT for 'their attitude to the Report', which is said to have created a good deal of 'pessimism and cynicism about the post-war world'. 'Why get Beveridge to make a plan at all, if you are going to turn it down?' In three reports it is suggested that this 'valuable social document

has now become a political issue which may at a very inconvenient moment develop into a political battle and detract from the unity of our war effort'.

B. THE MINORITY who approve of the Government's attitude. Though businessmen and tradespeople are mentioned in this category, 'understanding comments from those who are most likely to benefit from the Plan' are also reported. Their points of view can be summarised thus:

(i)   The cost of the scheme will be too heavy, and 'no one would expect the Government to undertake reforms which it will be unable to afford'.
(ii) 'The war must be won first.'
(iii) 'The promised Utopia is far from being just round the corner; the Beveridge Plan cannot bring heaven to earth by a stroke of the pen.'

5. THE WAR IN THE AIR

RAF RAIDS: All Regions (as against eight last week) refer to the Allied bombing offensive on Germany and the occupied countries as giving 'tremendous satisfaction'. Particular pleasure was caused by the attack on Berlin. It is hoped that the raids will long continue and will have a serious effect on the German war effort and morale. Only one report mentions 'regret at the suffering we are inflicting on non-combatants'. Other reactions to the RAF raids are:

(a) 'The day and night bombings are a prelude to our invasion of the Continent.'
(b) 'U-boat bases are the main target.'
(c) Some comment on our losses. These are deplored 'but considered a necessary evil'.
(d) Pleasure on 'the return of Hamm to the news'.

THE REPRISAL RAID ON LONDON appears to have been generally expected and, outside London, was not considered too high a price to pay for the bombing of Berlin. But in London itself 'isolated reports suggest that enthusiasm for bombing Berlin is getting less and less', and 'there seemed to be slightly more apprehension this time'.

There is some feeling that 'the reprisals are so poor because it's all the Germans can do'. On the other hand, people continue to believe 'in a last desperate enemy raid'. The Bethnal Green shelter accident, however, is said to have 'completely swamped discussion of other aspects'.

6. AERIAL DEFENCE

There is some criticism this week of anti-aircraft defences and of our inability to check attacks on coastal areas. At a place in the South-Eastern Region, people were reported to be 'fed up' after a raid, as 'the place was full of guns and nothing happened'. While there is said to be a certain satisfaction that some of the planes may have been destroyed, it is not 'considered much consolation' that they are brought down after having come in successfully and dropped their load.

There is also said to have been some disappointment in London after the Wednesday night raid that more planes were not destroyed: 'the barrage and the wonderful defences are all very well but the results are not very impressive – casualties in London from AA guns were greater than casualties to German airmen'.

The disappearance of the balloon barrage from Belfast is reported to have been the subject of comment. It is said (a) to have gone to Londonderry; (b) to have gone to the east coast of England; (c) to have been needed for ships in convoy.

7. RUSSIA

A slight falling off in interest and enthusiasm are reported this week, but admiration for Russian successes continues to be widespread, and sympathy for Russia remains very deep. Particular pleasure is expressed at the recapture of Rzhev – 'a great moral triumph for the Russians' – and 'the return of Timoshenko'.

People – generally 'the more cautious' – are, however, wondering 'how long the Russians can keep it up', and a good many 'believe the Red Army advance has nearly reached its limit' – it is not expected that more spectacular advances will be made. There are signs, too, that a number of people are trying to sum up 'what has happened on the Eastern front since the Russian drive began'. There is no tendency to 'discount the indisputable Russian successes' but 'it is pointed out that the Germans are still very strong', and that, 'despite their losses, they have maintained an intact front'. There continues, also, to be some 'scepticism of reported German losses'.

RUSSIA'S FUTURE ROLE: Despite the admiration and gratitude of the majority, a good deal of uneasy speculation is reported about:

(a) 'WHAT WILL HAPPEN WHEN THE GERMANS HAVE BEEN PUSHED OUT OF RUSSIA': Fear is creeping in that the Russians will become 'isolationist' then, and may make a separate peace. 'Stalin's recent words, suggesting that the Red Army's task will be ended when it has liberated Russian soil, has reinforced this.'

(b) THE RUSSIAN ATTITUDE AFTER VICTORY: The thought that Russia may defeat Germany 'all by herself' makes people fear that, 'by leaving Russia to be the European conqueror', we shall 'leave her also the right to decide how Europe shall be re-organised'. It is 'noted that Stalin is constantly referring to the fact that Russia is winning the war unaided', which 'can only mean that she is now claiming the right to dictate the peace'.

(c) RUSSO-POLISH RELATIONS: Here, though opinions and sympathies are divided, there is considerable misgiving as to the outcome of the frontier 'squabble'. It is felt that 'if Russia insists on maintaining her present attitude, harmony between the Soviets and this country may be endangered, as we began this war to defend the integrity of Poland'. In Northern Ireland, there is particular feeling about the right of self-determination of smaller nations.

8. NORTH AFRICA

There seems to have been less comment on both the military and political situation in North Africa, and there is little new to report. 'The Eighth Army's feat in withstanding and routing the German tank attacks' has relieved anxiety and 'created better feeling all round'. Admiration for Generals Alexander and Montgomery and pride in the Eighth Army are very strong.

Some feeling persists, however, that 'there is something obscure about the African fighting, and there is some surprise that Rommel had such adequate supplies'. It is felt that 'the Allies are taking the Tunisian problem too easily'. 'We have been told many times about our all-round superiority of men and supplies, yet the Axis can launch an offensive with some success.' People's chief worry is that 'precious time is being lost', and they are anxious to 'get the job over so that we can invade Europe'.

GENERAL EISENHOWER'S APPOINTMENT continues to be criticised, though less than before. He is said to be regarded now 'more as a figurehead than anything, and General Alexander is considered to be in actual command'.

THE FIGHTING QUALITIES OF US TROOPS continue to be the subject of 'unfriendly comment', though less than last week. It is believed that 'the lesson learnt will be valuable', and that 'this will give them a better understanding of British defeats in the earlier part of the war and make them realise that these were "suffered by fine men"'.

9. THE FAR EAST

DESTRUCTION OF THE JAPANESE CONVOY IN THE BISMARCK SEA: The news of this action has aroused enthusiasm in all Regions. While some felt that this was 'one up for the Americans', others stressed that it was 'an Allied and not just an American success'. It is said 'people felt they were in at the kill' because of the earlier news that 'the convoy had been sighted and planes were assembled for the attack'. There is some tendency to believe that the 'tide has turned in our favour in the East' and 'the threat to Australia has been once more removed'. The radio account of the 'shooting up of lifeboats' brought protests from two Regions – 'surely this a breach of international usage' ... 'even U-boats don't shoot up lifeboats' ... 'it may lead to reprisals on our seamen'.

GANDHI'S FAST: Satisfaction continues to be expressed at the firm action of the Government in the matter of Gandhi's release, and relief that the fast has ended is 'mingled with pleasure that it failed in its object'. It is thought that 'Congress has lost many sympathisers because of this so-called fast' ... 'Orange and lime juice – it's more than we get!'

CHINA: Interest in, and a wish that 'more might be done to help', China is expressed in six Regional reports. Madame Chiang Kai-Shek's visit to the States is again mentioned, as also is the hope that she may be able to visit this country.

BURMA: Little comment is noted on Burma, but one Region reports 'some disappointment at the way operations in Burma are hanging fire' as 'sympathy for

China inspires demands for more positive action leading to the re-opening of the Burma Road'.

MUTINY OF JAPANESE PRISONERS: The reports of the mutiny of Japanese prisoners in a New Zealand camp is said to have caused uneasiness among relatives of British prisoners of war in Japanese hands. It is felt that the publication of the facts may lead to reprisals.

10. AMERICA

Apprehension about our future relations with the United States, and fear of 'American imperialism' becoming a dominant factor in the post-war world, are reported from three Regions. It is thought that, in view of the Republican attacks on the President, the attitude of America is likely to be imperialist and isolationist after the war in matters of trade, rather than co-operative.

Resentment is now expressed at recent American speeches, appearing in the press, which criticised Britain. It is thought that some Americans have quite 'wrong-headed' views about the British Empire and that this is an obvious field for well-directed and tactful British propaganda.

Some anxiety about the bases leased to America is reported from two Regions; this is said to arise from fear that 'they will not be returned at the end of the war'.

11. THE WAR AT SEA

Mr. A. V. Alexander's speech in the House on the 3rd March (referred to by four Regions) is described as having had a 'reassuring effect', and as having caused people to take a 'more generally cheerful view of our naval situation', but the publication of our total naval losses 'proved a shock' to some people. Four Regions report less public interest in the war at sea, but in the North-East 'it is closely and anxiously watched, and there is great desire for news, good or bad, as to the actual situation'. There is 'measured satisfaction' in this Region at the recent statements, but it is realised that 'the position has been bought at a considerable price in lives and ships'.

12. MR. CHURCHILL'S RECENT ILLNESS

There is 'sincere thanksgiving by all classes' for Mr. Churchill's return to health. There is, however, 'still some anxiety lest he undertakes more than his strength allows, and he is thought to have been doing too much before he was ill'. There is, too, some concern for the risks he takes – 'Was the journey worth it?' – and 'fear of what might have happened'.

13. 'WHERE IS HITLER?'

Rumour and speculation are reported from four Regions as to why Hitler is 'dumb' and 'afraid to show his face'. Suggestions made, half-jokingly, are that he may be dead, 'mentally deranged', or in South America.

14. BROADCASTING AND PRESENTATION OF NEWS

Praise for 'the handling of the news by press and radio' is expressed in four reports, and very little criticism is reported. The restraint with which the news of the London shelter tragedy was handled is appreciated in the report from one Region, while in another its 'immediate release' is praised.

ARMY WEEK PROGRAMME: Appreciative comment on Sir James Grigg's broadcast introducing Army Week (28th February) is reported from three Regions; the Army Week programmes are said to have pleased the public – 'It's time we heard something about our own army'. While the individual programmes are thought to have varied in quality, and some were considered 'poor entertainment', *The Building of an Army* is specially praised as 'giving the public a better appreciation of the transformation in training and equipment effected by the army since early disasters'.

BBC PROGRAMMES: These are criticised for being 'too dull and too much alike', and there are various complaints of too much jazz, too much 'highbrow music', and too many gramophone records. It is suggested that there should be more plays and light entertainment.

COLONEL OLIVER STANLEY'S SPEECH AT OXFORD (5TH MARCH) does not seem to have caused much comment: two reports mention some criticism, but 'public sentiment in Northern Ireland' is said to agree with his declaration that the administration of the British Colonies 'must continue to be the sole responsibility of Britain'. Once again, the US was thought to be the target of a speech about the British Empire.

II. SPECIAL COMMENTS

15. MANPOWER

Although slightly less in volume this week, comment continues on familiar lines, and complaints reported are: (a) the number of young men in 'soft jobs'; (b) the transfer of labour; (c) hardship caused to owners of a one-man business by the call-up.

Comments on the call-up of women include: (a) both acceptance and complaint of the direction of older women into part-time work; (b) 'alarm' at the shortage of domestic labour; (c) complaints of 'the attitude of some Labour Exchange interviewers', and of 'bullying by Women's Local Appeal Board personnel'; (d) criticism of childless servicemen's wives 'still left to do as they like'.

16. CLOTHING AND HOUSEHOLD LINEN

COUPONS FOR HOUSEHOLD GOODS: Housewives still complain of the great hardship caused by the surrender of clothing coupons for household goods. People say: 'The Government statement on this question doesn't impress'; 'Does the Government realise the serious lack of towels in poor families?'

CLOTHING COUPONS: Families who cannot afford good-quality clothes or who had no stock when rationing started are said to have great difficulty with the coupon allowance. The reaction to Dr. Hugh Dalton's statement that he has not used one of his coupons yet is – 'Will people in high positions ever realise that poor people can't afford clothes that last for years and years?' Other coupon difficulties are reported over growing children, and 'infants from birth to two years who grow so quickly'.

STOCKINGS: It is said that the better-quality stockings promised have 'not yet been seen by most people', and they ask 'why so many rayon stockings should be made, which are not hard-wearing; fewer good-quality lisle stockings should be made instead'.

FOOTWEAR: The poor quality and shortage of footwear is again reported, both for adults and children. One report suggests that 'the Board of Trade should go down to some of the poorer districts and take a look at the sort of footwear the children are going about in'.

ELASTIC GOODS: Suspenders, suspender belts and corsets are said now to be 'made of material which make them useless for the purpose for which they are intended', and women complain of utility corsets which 'give no support to those who are working and have to stand about'.

17. HEALTH

The 'low state of health' of many people is commented on in three Regions and also Postal Censorship reports. The wartime diet is regarded as the main cause; and to this are ascribed skin troubles, 'flu with bronchial or pneumonic symptoms, and the inability of people to throw off chills. The lack of fruit, fats and sugar are particularly mentioned.

VENEREAL DISEASE: The campaign against venereal disease is referred to in five reports this week. Wholehearted approval of the airing of the subject and the demand for more factual information are reported. The press advertising is generally praised.

18. TRANSPORT AND PETROL

TRANSPORT DIFFICULTIES, especially for war workers, are reported from ten Regions this week. Complaints follow familiar lines: (a) inadequate bus services, especially on Sundays and in rural areas; (b) 'ill-fitting bus connections'; (c) bad manners of bus conductresses and drivers. The demand for workman's tickets for shift workers is again reported.

PETROL WASTE continues to be reported, this week from five Regions. The number of cars and taxis on the road is criticised, and there are complaints of the misuse of petrol. In the London Region, doctors are said to complain of an 'insufficient petrol allowance'.

19. FOOD

'We're not badly off at all' continues to be the general view on the food situation. Grumbles are again reported about the following:

(a) THE SHORTAGE AND DISTRIBUTION OF:

    (i) FISH: According to two reports, however, the situation is said to have improved in some areas.

    (ii) MILK: 'The compulsory change from one distributor to another' has also caused some 'bad feeling'.

    (iii) SWEETS AND CHOCOLATES.

    (iv) RABBITS.

    (v) EGGS. There is said to be some confusion over the announcement on February 27th of 'the new egg rationing period': 'Customers will never know to which allocation their last egg belonged.'

    (vi) TINNED FRUIT.

(b) THE WASTE OF BREAD.

(c) THE HIGH PRICE OF GREEN VEGETABLES: 'It's a disgrace to see food rotting because people can't pay the price.'

20. FUEL

The mild weather is again considered to have materially helped the fuel situation. People are still said to be doing their best to economise, though families working on different shifts are alleged to be having difficulty in 'making do' on their coal allowance.

The poor quality of coal is again criticised, and it is said 'to be causing trouble to housewives'. In the Northern Region it is felt that some action should be taken to overcome the presence of the large quantity of stone sold with the coal; and there are said to be rumours among miners in the North Midland Region of good seams of coal being saved by the owners for after the war, as 'anything that's black' can be sold at present.

21. SHORTAGE OF BATTERIES

A shortage of torch batteries (particularly No. 8s) is reported from six Regions, as opposed to four last week; in one report a shortage of torch cases is mentioned. A shortage of cycle batteries is only reported from four Regions this week, as opposed to six last week.

22. SHOPPING DIFFICULTIES

Food queues are still reported to be the cause of 'much wasted time'; and war workers complain that, as queueing is impossible for them, 'those who are doing least for the war effort are able to get most of the extras'. The North-Western Region reports the complaint that 'shopkeepers will not allow friends to collect for war workers'.

23. SALVAGE

Complaints of the non-collection of salvage from dumps are again made. 'The park railings are all stacked up ready to go back at the end of the war.' The collection of railings from private dwellings is still causing great dissatisfaction both because of the 'manner of demolition and because of the conviction that it should not be necessary while so many tons of scrap are lying about'. There is mention of 'a scrap dump at Sheffield where, it is alleged, metal has been lying idle since the last war'.

24. YOUNG PEOPLE

Reports from four Regions this week refer to much comment on 'the lax behaviour' of young people. This is attributed both to the high wages earned by juveniles and to lack of parental control, and takes the form of drinking. Girls of fifteen years old or even less are said 'to come in for particular censure for dressing up beyond their age and haunting camps, aerodromes and street corners'.

APPENDIX TO WEEKLY REPORT 127

THE BRITISH EMPIRE

'Some aspects of public opinion on the British Empire and, in particular, the Colonial Empire' was the subject of an enquiry recently undertaken by the BBC Listener Research Department, as a background for possible talks on the subject.

The following is a summary of the conclusions:

1. The term 'the Colonies' is still in general use among the British people to denote any part of the Empire outside the United Kingdom. The principal reason for this is a widespread ignorance of the difference between a Colony and a Dominion. In an appreciable number of cases, even where the distinction is realised, it is not observed in ordinary conversation, nor has the term 'The British Commonwealth of Nations' one universally accepted meaning. To a great many it is nothing more than an alternative name for the British Empire, to be preferred because of its freedom from imperialistic associations. Others define it as a term for Great Britain plus all the self-governing Dominions; others do not include the United Kingdom within the term and many more would not regard it as including the Colonial Empire or the Indian Empire.

2. Many, if not most, people have their own opinions on how the Colonial Empire was acquired, the greatest measure of common agreement being on the proposition that it was acquired by conquest from native peoples. Only a minority realise that substantial territories were mandated to this country by the League of Nations.

3. The need for markets and raw materials and the spirit of adventure are held by the public to be the principal causes which led this country to acquire Colonies, though it is also believed that the need for living space was an important cause.

4. The vast majority of the British public consider the Colonial Empire to be an economic asset to Great Britain – a view which the war has driven home – but there is abundant evidence of uneasiness, at any rate among that section of the public which has a sense of social responsibility, about the present state of economic and social development of the Colonial Empire. It is clear that nothing has done more to bring this about than the fall of Malaya, which caused widespread questioning of our Colonial policy.

5. These misgivings, however, have not been such as to cause wholesale condemnation of British Colonial policy in the past. By far the most typical reaction to this is a feeling that, although our Colonial record is a mixed one, containing things of which we ought to be ashamed as well as things of which we have every right to be proud, it is a record in which the good exceeds the bad.

6. A very considerable section of the public has a formulated view on what the future Colonial policy of this country should be. It is highly significant that neither the view that the Colonies should be handed over to an international administrative authority, nor the view that Colonial territories should be re-allocated among the Powers – both of which were widely canvassed in the years before the war – received any significant support at all. But a very considerable measure of agreement does exist on what future Colonial policy should be: it is felt that the ultimate aim should be the admission of all Colonial territories into equal partnership with Great Britain and the self-governing Dominions; that a thorough overhaul of the present policies should be undertaken in the light of this aim, particularly with a view to eliminating any exploitation of native labour and bringing vested interests under control. The prevailing view is that if, pending the day when a Colony is self-supporting, it is necessary for it to be subsidised by the British taxpayer, this is a burden which must not be shirked.

7. The projected talks aroused considerable interest, and suggestions for the lines which they should take covered a very wide field. But more important than these were two points relating to the policy which, it was hoped, would underlie the talks. The first was that the talks should include a frank presentation of the problems as seen through the eyes of the Colonial peoples. The second, which was even more important, was that the series should at all costs be objective. It is quite apparent that if the public came to think that past mistakes were being glossed over, or present difficulties minimised, the series would do little but engender cynicism among precisely those who might otherwise derive most benefit from it.

NO. 132: TUESDAY 6 APRIL 1943 TO
TUESDAY 13 APRIL 1943

I. GENERAL COMMENTS

1. GENERAL STATE OF CONFIDENCE AND REACTION TO NEWS

'The splendid news' from Tunisia seems to have absorbed practically the whole of public attention this week. People feel that 'whatever difficulties lie ahead, nothing can now stop the triumphant progress of the Eighth Army', and 'Tunisia may be ours even earlier than was hoped'. The advance has added to the expectation of – and speculation about – an early Allied offensive in Europe. There is, however, said to be 'little undue elation', and only a slight rise in public spirits is reported.

Reports from six Regions (five last week) refer to war-weariness; fatigue is again attributed to long hours of work, Civil Defence duties, and 'food deficiencies'.

Only preliminary reactions have been received to:

(a) The broadcast by HM The Queen. This has been praised for its sincerity and also for 'the clearness of her voice'.

(b) The Budget, 'which has caused little discussion compared with former Budgets'; it 'was much as was expected'.

2. NORTH AFRICA

'The surge forward of the Eighth Army has given deep satisfaction and pleasure', and the Tunisian campaign has again proved 'the outstanding topic of the week'. In two reports people are referred to as 'watchful and attentive', and 'avaricious to hear news of more progress'. Discussion on the future of the campaign centres on:

(1) 'The time it will take to clear the enemy out of Africa.' While the majority are forecasting an early victory, 'the more cautious believe that a lot of hard fighting still lies ahead'.

(2) 'What are Rommel's possible moves?' Can he 'stage a Dunkirk?' 'Is he already getting his men away?'

(3) 'Will the First Army be able to cut the Germans in two, and prevent Rommel joining von Arnim?'

General Montgomery and his men 'have now become national heroes' and confidence in them has reached a new high level; it is felt that 'they will triumph over all obstacles'. Particular pride and pleasure in the operations of the 51st Division are reported from Scotland, and in the Northern Region 'people are pleased that it was a north country division which held Rommel's panzers at Wadi Zigzaou'. The Americans and the First Army are also reported 'to be coming in for some praise, though rather as an afterthought to the admiration for the Eighth Army'; criticism of the Americans is still expressed in two reports.

POLITICAL SITUATION: The postponement of the meeting between Generals Giraud and de Gaulle has 'puzzled and bewildered' people, and increased concern about the political situation in North Africa. The reasons for the postponement are not understood, and it is asked 'why de Gaulle's visit should hinder or impede the prosecution of the war?' The delay in negotiations has created uneasy speculation along the following lines:

(1) The situation is due to 'American ineptitude', or to General Eisenhower's preference for 'the reactionary elements'.
(2) Our Government is 'backing Giraud and freezing out de Gaulle'.

At the same time there are 'contemptuous references' to the 'unreliable French who never have known their own minds', and there appear to be 'some doubts about the political wisdom of General de Gaulle'.

3. HM THE QUEEN'S BROADCAST

Only preliminary reports have so far been received on the broadcast by HM The Queen (11th April). In Scotland, her audience is thought to have been especially large and appreciative. Her 'beautifully clear diction' caused general comment, and the 'understanding thought behind her talk', 'her obvious sincerity and feeling' were much appreciated. 'Because it was time someone said these things' appealed strikingly to some listeners, and it was felt that 'her tribute to women was well deserved'. Many women were specially pleased 'because she did not patronise'.

There is some speculation about whether the broadcast had some hidden significance, and from two Regions there are reports of suggestions that it was designed to 'fortify the women of Britain and the Empire against news of heavy casualties which will follow a Continental invasion'. 'Is this a sign that we are on the eve of big events?'

4. THE BUDGET

BEFORE: 'A moderate amount' of speculation preceded the Budget, and the forecasts were 'on the whole, pretty accurate'. They included an increase in indirect taxation – tobacco, cigarettes, entertainment and cosmetics were specified – and no increase in direct taxation. 'A cycle tax' was, however, considered possible and according to one report 'would have been welcomed as a splendid source of revenue'.

AFTER: Preliminary reports suggest that the Budget, 'which was just what we expected', has met with approval. It is felt that 'these optional forms of new taxation are fair'.

Of the proposals themselves, the increased tax on beer, cigarettes, tobacco and 'the cinema' has aroused most comment. Good-humoured grousing is reported from the smokers and beer drinkers 'who wonder when the abstainers will have to do their bit'. Reports from five Regions refer to sympathy for 'the poor Old Age Pensioners who'll be particularly hit'. Other points which aroused interest are as follows:

(a) THE EXEMPTION OF SOME UTILITY GOODS FROM TAXATION:
Housewives are said to be very pleased, though it is suggested that 'a
coupon concession would have given even more pleasure'.

(b) THE INCREASED ALLOWANCES FOR DEPENDENT RELATIVES
AND FOR HOUSEKEEPERS are appreciated 'as a considerate and human
concession'.

(c) THE RAISING OF THE PURCHASE TAX ON LUXURY ARTICLES
is considered 'just', and people are said 'to appreciate the need to check
spending'.

(d) THAT NO NEW BURDEN HAS BEEN IMPOSED ON THE DIRECT
TAXPAYER is appreciated. Relief is reported from salary and wage earners,
and 'the fixed income sections of the community'.

THE CHANCELLOR'S SPEECH gave satisfaction and was considered
'understandable'. Interest in 'the Lend-Lease facts' is said to have been as great in
some cases as in the tax changes, and people were glad 'to hear that we give as much
Lend-Lease as we receive'. They hope that 'America is being told this'. The amount
'already allowed to Russia' has given special pleasure but, according to one report,
some people are wondering 'how much reached them'.

5. THE SECOND FRONT

Expectation of an Allied offensive in Europe continues, and 'clues such as the coastal
ban and troop movements' are widely commented on. 'Innumerable' speculations as
to 'when and where we shall strike' are again referred to.

(a) WHEN: It appears to be taken for granted that 'Tunisia has to be cleared
up first'. While some people are encouraged by our progress there to think
that 'zero hour must be drawing near', others fear that the past delay may
have held us up too long.

(b) WHERE: 'Every conceivable' part of Europe is mentioned.

6. ALLIED AIR OFFENSIVE

There are widespread reports of continued satisfaction with the news of the Allied
air raids, especially in view of the 'comparative weakness of enemy reprisals'. It
is hoped that 'there will be a real smashing of Germany this summer'. There is,
however, some increase in anxiety at the extent of our losses, and double figures
cause special regret; people would like to be able to 'assess the percentage of planes
lost'. These losses are contrasted with the small number of American Fortresses
which fail to return, and some 'wonder whether the results are worth the loss of
skilled pilots'. It is pointed out that when two successive raids are made on the same
target the losses suffered the second night are always the heavier; it is asked if the
'element of surprise is being neglected'. The heavy losses in 'dirty weather' are also
a subject of comment: 'surely raids on such nights are better postponed?'

Satisfaction is expressed with the raids on Italy and Sicily, and it is hoped that the Americans will deal 'far more ruthlessly with Italian targets than our home-based bombers are permitted to do'.

It is asked: 'What are the results of mines laid in enemy waters?'

The achievements of the US aircraft are 'watched with interest'. They are thought to be doing a 'fine job of work, but figures given of planes brought down are not wholly trusted'. It is asked why US aircraft are not used in night raids.

7. RUSSIA

The decline in comment about Russia, associated with the lack of news from that front and the interest in Tunisia, continues to be reported from the Regions and in Postal Censorship. The following quotation sums up present feeling: 'The Russians seem to be held up with the change in the weather, but I don't think they'll be pushed back like last summer. Anyway, a clean-up in Africa will give us more chance to help them out.'

8. THE WAR AT SEA

Concern about the Allied shipping position seems to be less widespread than last week, but there is still said to be 'considerable anxiety' – especially in the Northern and North-Western Regions. Uneasiness appears to have been stimulated by Colonel Knox's statement (6th April) that losses were considerably worse in March than in February, by questions in the House, and by German wireless claims. There is a continued demand for more information and further reference to confusion resulting from conflicting statements from official speakers. 'No sooner does someone state that the U-boat situation is well under control than someone else just as important describes it as more serious than ever.'

9. THE FAR EAST

'Little thought and attention' are given to the war against Japan, though some disappointment is reported 'at our recent withdrawals in Burma', and those with relatives are reported to be anxious for more information.

PRISONERS OF WAR IN JAPANESE HANDS: The written statement by Sir James Grigg (House of Commons, 6th April) about conditions in Japanese prison camps is reported to have 'considerably relieved the anxiety of relatives of prisoners'. In one Region, however, anxiety at lack of news is still reported.

CHINA: There are references in four reports this week to regret that 'our gallant ally China is not fully appreciated', and 'concern that we are not helping her as much as we should'.

10. THE JEWISH PROBLEM

Familiar allegations concerning the behaviour of the Jews in this country have been reported on a slightly reduced scale during the past three weeks, and have been supported by letters in Postal Censorship. There is, however, a demand from two Regions for the publication of statistics giving the number of Jews in this country, their present occupations, and how many are in the Forces, the war industries, etc. It is felt that this would help to combat anti-Semitism and 'would show the country what the Jews are doing for the war effort'.

THE JEWS IN OCCUPIED EUROPE: Discussion on the problem of receiving refugees from occupied Europe appears to have declined considerably, and only one report refers to some interest in the 'attitude which the Government will adopt towards Jews at the forthcoming Bermuda conference'.

11. EQUAL COMPENSATION FOR WAR INJURY

There has been little comment on the decision to pay equal compensation for war injury to women. The award is accepted by both men and women as a 'wrong righted' – 'We've got the ladies in Parliament to thank for it.'

12. ACCESS TO COASTAL AREAS

Two reports indicate that the new regulations about access to coastal areas, announced by Mr. Morrison on 30th March, are not everywhere understood. 'Strong comments' are reported from the South Devonshire coast about 'the vagueness of the regulations: these are said to have given rise to a good deal of apprehension among elderly residents as to whether they may not be turned out at a moment's notice with nowhere to go'.

'It is reported from the Isle of Wight that the re-imposition of the ban on travel to the island has led to criticism of the Government' for giving the impression that the ban is for offensive purposes. It is feared that this will lead to heavy bombing and Mr. Morrison is thought to have 'gone too far in announcing the reason for extending the prohibited coastal areas'.

13. DOUBLE SUMMER TIME

The coming of double summer time appears to have been 'taken very quietly indeed', and with little complaint. Farmers are grumbling – though less than on former occasions – about 'unnecessary interference with the laws of nature'. Early workers, particularly those 'who are really having to get up round about 2.30 a.m.', find that 'rising in the darkness is not balanced by the pleasure of light evenings'. It is thought, too, that more fuel will now be used, as the colder mornings make people more inclined to switch on gas and electric fires.

14. THE SHELTER ENQUIRY

'Surprisingly little comment' is reported on the decision not to publish the results of the shelter enquiry. The most widespread reaction is said to have been 'disappointment that the findings are not to be known, linked with acceptance of this decision, without suspicion but with regret'.

A minority, however, 'cannot see what security reasons could be involved, when only civilians and the Civil Defence Services were concerned'. They feel that silence will 'tell the enemy what he wants to know' and may also 'give rise to a crop of exaggerated rumours'. Though Mr. Morrison is thought to have 'done well to scotch the anti-Semitic rumours', a few say that 'the decision not to publish the findings is proof that the Jews did, in fact, panic'.

15. MR. EDEN'S VISIT TO THE US AND STATEMENT IN THE HOUSE (8TH APRIL)

Interest does not seem to be strong or widespread, but comments both about Mr. Eden's trip and his statement in the House are almost entirely favourable. People are pleased at 'proof of the determination to establish a basis for closer Anglo-American co-operation', but a few question the value of isolated meetings and point to 'the absence of any permanent joint machinery'.

16. THE EDDISBURY BY-ELECTION

Three reports mention some interest in the Eddisbury by-election. The result is thought by a few to indicate dissatisfaction with the Government, and some feel that 'the House of Commons is now unrepresentative of the outlook of the nation'. 'The younger generation' is said to be pleased at the return of the Commonwealth candidate and there is a desire to know 'what this new party stands for'. Incidentally, it is asked why Sir Richard Acland is sometimes described as 'Independent', sometimes as 'Commonwealth', on the radio.

17. SIR PERCY LAURIE

Little comment has been reported about the Sir Percy Laurie case. In two Regions it is said to have caused an unfavourable impression, it being 'considered deplorable that such irregularities should be committed by a person of his prestige'. 'Surprise that the fine was so high' is reported from the Northern Region where it is thought 'he was made a scapegoat'. In Wales, however, it is said 'public confidence would have been undermined if there had been no conviction or a purely nominal fine imposed'.

18. THE BEVERIDGE REPORT AND THE POST-WAR WORLD

Although 'the let's win the war first' people are said to remain 'vocal', discussion on post-war conditions continues to be fairly widespread and to follow familiar lines. The main points of comment include:

(a) Fear of post-war unemployment.
(b) The Beveridge Report. The belief that 'it has been shelved' is reported from three Regions, and the belief that it will be implemented from two. Mr. Bevin's speech at Bristol (27th March) is said 'to have removed much misunderstanding among the workers who read it'.

(c) Interest in other aspects of post-war planning, particularly housing; the position of women after the war – 'It is hoped they will play a bigger part in Parliament, and in the planning of homes'; national health; international currency plans; education and agriculture.

(d) 'What can be done with Germany when the war is over?' There is said to be 'more confidence in Russia exacting penalties from Germany after the war than in Great Britain or the USA doing so'.

(e) 'What will Russia's attitude be in post-war Europe – particularly in the case of religion?'

(f) 'What will be the future of political parties in this country?'

19. BROADCASTING AND PRESENTATION OF NEWS

Comment on news presentation is, on the whole, favourable, with 'considerable appreciation of the service rendered by the BBC'. But it is asked whether all news possible is given to the public 'after due allowance has been made for the requirements of security', as there is a feeling that 'we are only told what the Government wants us to know'. There is some criticism of war commentaries being 'inserted in the body of the news, except when outstanding events have just occurred', and of the 'rapid and monotonous manner in which the news is sometimes read'. The repetition of the headlines at the end of the broadcast is welcomed, and there is regret that 'some announcers fail to observe this practice'.

Two Regions refer to a demand for more maps and pictures in the press. The present maps are regarded in one Region as containing an insufficient number of place names.

ALLEGED INDISCRETION: 'Very strong indignation has been felt throughout the Glasgow district over the publication and broadcast of the speech made by Mr. Garro-Jones (3rd April), in which he gave details of the war production of the Glasgow district.' Criticism of this is also reported from a Welsh industrial area – 'No one in this country at present wants this information; why enlighten the enemy?'

DEBATE IN PARLIAMENT ON THE BBC: The debate was thought to be 'footling', and some of the criticism 'ill-founded and playing to the gallery'. But 'the statements made by Sir Ian Fraser and Mr. Brendan Bracken should have been given to the public freely, instead of a debate being necessary to drag them out'. The resulting 'longest news bulletin for ages, mostly about the BBC itself', is criticised.

BBC PROGRAMMES: There is again criticism of the *Brains Trust* – Professor Joad is becoming particularly unpopular as he is 'thought to show political feeling'; also of Mary Ferguson's *Calling the Factory Front, Music Hall, Workers' Playtime*, and *Country Magazine* 'which some feel has lost its charm'.

There is praise for the European News, *The Man in the Street, Into Battle, A Man Talks to Women*, the *Postscript* on the underground press in Europe, Godfrey Talbot's *Postscript*, the talks on youth by Jack Longland, on finance by Geoffrey Crowther, and on the Uthwatt Report by Mr. F. J. Osborn.

It is thought that people are taking more interest in talks, particularly those that are 'educative in some form or another'.

FILMS: *Desert Victory* is praised in four reports and Postal Censorship. It is compared with *In Which We Serve* as being the 'real thing and not mere entertainment and propaganda' – 'the public seems to be in the mood to appreciate serious war films'. The newsreels of the Mareth line are considered some of the finest war pictures, and in one report people are said to 'cheer themselves hoarse' whenever Montgomery appears on the screen.

II. SPECIAL COMMENTS

20. INDUSTRY

ENFORCED IDLENESS is alleged in six reports, particular mention being made of Metro Vickers at Trafford Park, Cowes factories, 'aerodrome construction work in Cornwall and factories in Gloucestershire'. 'Many workers, both men and women, employed at Cowes openly state that the only time the whole staff works is when the inspector comes down, and that they have to save their jobs until that occasion and idle away their hours beforehand.'

INCREASED GOVERNMENT CONTROL: The taking over by the Government of various firms and collieries does not seem to have caused widespread interest, but comment is, in the main, favourable. Criticism and apprehension are said to come mainly from 'industrialists' and 'business circles'. A Sunday evening *Postscript* is suggested as 'a good means of dispelling any rumours or thoughts that we are now ruled by a Dictator Government'. Curiosity is reported from two Regions as to 'what unsavoury facts lay behind the Government's decision in regard to Short Brothers'.

STRIKES: 'Concern at the workers' readiness to strike over trivial issues' is reported from five Regions. Those with relatives in the Forces are said to be particularly resentful and to consider that the strikers and their leaders should be put in the Forces or shot. 'Soldiers have to do what they are told, why not workers?' There is some 'ill-feeling that the Government condones strikes'.

TRANSFER OF LABOUR is a subject of complaint in four Regions. Frequently the reasons for transfer seem not to be understood. For example, 'at a certain steelworks, women, assisted by labourers, were assigned to jobs previously carried out by men working individually, with the net result that there was no saving of labour but an increase in each job of a woman's labour'.

ENGINEERS' WAGE AWARD: Dissatisfaction continues to be reported, chiefly, it is said, because 'the increases were not made retrospective'. In the North-Western Region, 'a fair amount of productive time is said to have been lost through misunderstanding arising out of the complications of the award, and the attitude and exaggeration of some newspapers are alleged to have been resented'. Largely through meetings organised through the trade unions, however, 'the details of the award are becoming better understood, but many of the men still feel they have been cheated out of the actual hard cash they expected'.

FINES FOR ABSENTEEISM are said to be resented. It is claimed that there is no point in going to work if there is no work to be done when you get there – 'production is the only thing that should count'. Ironstone miners (Cleveland,

Teesside) say that theirs is 'the hardest manual work in the country and that a man must be 100% fit for it; some men, although not ill enough for a medical certificate, are still not fit enough for work'.

THE GREENE SCHEME: Northumbrian miners are reported to be upset at the way some of the press handled the action of the Northumbrian Mineworkers' Association. They feel that they were merely drawing attention to a minor flaw in the agreement, and to accuse them in headlines of sabotaging the scheme was 'very out of place'.

21. THE CALL-UP

EVASION OF CALL-UP, both by men and women, is alleged. Servicemen's childless wives are particularly resented in the Inverness area, in Salisbury and especially in Filey, where they are 'criticised as preferring to stay in bed till noon, to stand in queues outside cake shops, and to go to dances rather than work at any time of the day'. Allegations about young men are more vague, but reference is made to 'young men hawkers who have nothing to do but sell firewood', and to butchers, whose contribution to the war effort is questioned, 'since their shops open only three days a week'.

SHORTAGE OF DOMESTIC HELP is mentioned in reports from four Regions as the cause of much hardship. Two of these also refer to the shortage of hospital staff.

22. CLOTHING

Coupon difficulties are again reported from nine Regions, and a strong demand for a separate household allowance continues. The special hardships of working-class families are once more mentioned; they had no previous stocks, and many of them are now 'down to their last towel'. The need for extra coupons for children 'while they are growing' is again stressed – many mothers are 'using all their own coupons for their children'. They say, 'What would be thought of me, if I have to go to the hospital in rags?' It is thought also that extra coupons should be allowed to newly married couples, 'especially as the man is so often in the Forces with no coupons of his own'. In one mining area there is said to be dissatisfaction among pitmen whose stockings last only about three weeks owing to frequent soaking by water in the pits – 'sixteen pairs a year entails an outlay of forty-eight coupons'.

Complaints are made of the quality of utility clothing – utility corsets are particularly mentioned – and of the difficulty of getting footwear repaired.

23. FOOD

Satisfaction with the food situation appears to be general, except on the following subjects:

FISH: There continue to be complaints of the shortage and unequal distribution of fish and of the preferential treatment of favoured customers. It is said that many people would welcome registration or rationing for fish. Nevertheless, four reports indicate satisfaction at the recent increase in supplies, but there is some comment on the 'coarse unknown fish' offered for sale.

SWEETS, BISCUITS AND CAKES are all said to be in short supply and unequally distributed.

CHEESE: There is said to be little concern at the latest cut in the cheese ration, though it is thought that, after the further cut on the 1st May, the ration will be 'a bit small'. There is 'some puzzlement as to the reason for it, now there is increased milk supply', and there is 'surprise that a baby gets the same ration as a man'. The better quality of cheese is praised.

MEAT: Some disappointment is reported at the reduction of the fresh meat ration, but a few are not sorry because 'bully beef is more like meat than some we have had on the ration'.

BREAD: Two reports indicate that 'some people would welcome bread rationing to cut out waste'. Complaints are still made of its quality and 'ill effects'.

24. HOUSING AND ACCOMMODATION

The shortage and high price of housing and accommodation is widely reported. In one Midland area, it is said that houses are overcrowded to a degree quite dangerous to health. It is common to find five or six men sleeping in a small bedroom; in one case four girls were sleeping in one bed; a particularly bad case was of three men sleeping in one bed which was immediately occupied by three others after the first three had gone to work. In this latter house, eight men, each paying 32/6 per week to the householder, were accommodated in two council-house bedrooms.

25. HEALTH

Complaints of war-weariness, fatigue and minor ailments come from five Regions this week. These are attributed mainly to long working hours, the wartime diet, and the mild winter.

VENEREAL DISEASE: There is less comment this week on the Venereal Disease Campaign. The advertisements are praised in two Regions though it is thought that more stress should be put on the moral side and on the dangers of alcohol. The desire for more publicity in the form of lectures on the subject is reported from two Regions. In Scotland, there is said to be a greater readiness among the public to discuss venereal disease; and the campaign is thought 'to be a big step forward in education on hygiene'. Talks by public health officials are said to be much appreciated and young people are said to be 'interested in the subject'.

HOSPITAL ACCOMMODATION: Two Regions this week refer to the shortage of hospital accommodation. 'Persons requiring immediate operations have to enter nursing homes and pay dearly or wait at the risk of their lives.' Young women, though willing to have more children, are said to refrain as there are not sufficient maternity beds in hospitals, and no daily help available for lying-in at home.

26. AGRICULTURE

The labour shortage is reported to be worrying farmers in three Regions. They are said to be apprehensive about the coming harvest, although volunteers are said in one Region to be coming forward readily; many would 'gladly spend their holidays farming', but it is felt that the lack of accommodation and billets will prove a serious deterrent.

HOUSES FOR AGRICULTURAL WORKERS: Disgust is reported from the North-Eastern Region at the new houses which it is proposed to build for agricultural workers. Their design and amenities are criticised and the rents considered abnormally high. In the North-Western Region there are 'already worries as to who should choose the tenants for the cottages – the farmer, the War Agricultural Committee, or the local authority'.

POTATOES: Concern and criticism at the Ministry of Agriculture's instruction to allotment holders not to grow so many potatoes is reported from two Regions. The wisdom of such instructions is said to be doubted 'if the shipping situation is as bad as is suggested'; it is thought this may lead to a shortage next winter.

27. TRANSPORT DIFFICULTIES AND PETROL

Transport difficulties are reported from seven Regions this week. Complaints are on familiar lines: the overcrowding of buses; the bus curfew; inadequate rural bus services; buses running ahead of scheduled time causing workers to miss them and arrive late at work.

PETROL: During the past two weeks eight Regions have reported the waste or misuse of petrol. The chief complaints are: the use of taxis for shopping and unessential journeys; and the alleged unfairness of petrol allocation.

28. SHOPPING DIFFICULTIES

Shopping difficulties for workers are reported from seven Regions this week. The chief difficulty is the old complaint of the lunch-hour and early closing of shops.

Queues for cakes and fish are reported from two Regions. In the Northern Region the feeling is said to be general that queues should be made illegal. Women workers in Wales are said to express the desire for fish and cakes to be rationed.

29. NATIONAL SAVINGS

While approval is again expressed for the 'Wings for Victory' weeks, there is criticism of the amount of money and paper used in advertising, and of the following transactions:

1. 'The transfer of money from bank deposits at low rates of interest to 2½% bonds, to the advantage of the lender and the bank which draws commission at a cost to the community.'
2. 'Bodies who hold "events" in connection with "Wings for Victory", and then invest the funds on their own behalf and draw interest.'

30. FUEL ECONOMY

There are reports again this week from two Regions that the announcement increasing coal allowances (1st April) is still not clearly understood, and 'people require more details'. On the other hand, the chance to 'stock-up – if we can get it' is welcomed in two reports, though a few people are asking: 'Will we be treated as criminals next winter for hoarding?'

31. RUMOUR

There is a recurrent rumour that British coal is being exported to neutral European countries – thus lightening the burden on the Axis. This story is given as a reason for miners refusing to work hard.

NOTE: The offices of the Ministry in the London and South-Eastern Regions (Nos 5 and 12) have been amalgamated under the London Regional Office.

NO. 136: TUESDAY 4 MAY 1943 TO TUESDAY 11 MAY 1943

I. GENERAL COMMENTS

1. GENERAL STATE OF CONFIDENCE AND REACTION TO NEWS

Public spirits, which had been rising steadily as the week progressed, have reached a very high level with the fall of Tunis and Bizerta. All reports speak of people being 'elated' or 'cock-a-hoop', but the feeling of the majority seems to be one of 'quiet jubilation founded upon real facts', rather than of dangerous optimism – though there are some references to this, particularly on the part of young people. If spirits are not even higher, this is thought to be because the public were already 'on their toes about the African campaign' and were 'sure it was nearing its end': according to most reports it is the surprising speed of the final blows and the suddenness of the enemy's collapse that has pleased everyone so much.

Everywhere, 'delight is mingled with eagerness regarding the next step', and already, while details of the Tunisian victory are still coming in, '"Where next?" is on everyone's lips'.

'A noticeable increase in optimism about an early finish to the war' – probably this year – is reported; but on the whole the feeling seems to be that 'we're on the last lap now, though it will be a fairly long lap', and by no means easy.

Considerable anxiety continues to be reported over the state of Russo-Polish relations.

Although 'home front grumbles have been almost forgotten in the present excitement', difficulties connected with shopping, clothing and fish supplies still arouse widespread comment. References to weariness and 'nerves', due to food difficulties and 'other war restrictions', continue to be reported, though on a smaller scale than last week.

(No reactions have yet been reported to the Prime Minister's visit to Washington.)

2. TUNISIA

'The outcome in North Africa had never seriously been doubted', but 'the sudden crumbling of the Axis defences was so unexpected that the public, which had become reconciled to a long and bitter struggle, found itself reading its papers again and again to convince itself that the news was actually true'. 'Surprise that it has happened so quickly' is the outstanding feature in all reports.

The public are overjoyed at 'this famous victory', and there is 'a general feeling that Dunkirk has been avenged, although it's taken three years to do it'.

Some sympathy is expressed, chiefly by women, for 'the trapped Germans who cannot "Dunkirk"' (an operation which 'the British alone are capable of carrying out'); and there is said to be 'little sign of any gloating over the fate of the Axis troops'.

People are delighted that 'Allied armies can out-general and out-fight the Axis', and there is an 'increase in confidence in our achievement as warriors' – 'this just shows what can be done when we have the equipment'. Particular pleasure is expressed at 'the superb co-operation between units of different nations and between land, air and naval forces'.

'Adulation for the Generals and men' concerned has reached 'a new high level', and particular comment has been reported about the following:

(a) GENERAL ALEXANDER: His generalship is considered 'an absolute triumph'. 'Up to now he has been rather overshadowed by General Montgomery in public estimation, but Tunisia is felt to have been "Alexander's show".'

(b) THE FIRST ARMY is thought to have 'shown itself as fine a force as the Eighth', and its 'prestige has rocketed as a result of its latest activities'. 'There had been a tendency in recent weeks for people to assume that the Eighth Army would have to finish the job, but the work of the new armies has dispelled this Eighth Army complex.'

(c) THE AMERICANS: 'People are gratified that the Americans, who have hitherto been somewhat of an unknown quantity, have "at long last justified their existence".' 'It is recognised that the American Second Corps has developed into a first-class fighting unit.'

(d) THE FRENCH are 'warmly praised for their part in the battle'.

(e) THE ALLIED AIR FORCES: people 'cannot praise too highly the performance of the air forces engaged, which are thought to have kept casualties down to a minimum'.

(f) GENERAL MONTGOMERY AND THE EIGHTH ARMY continue to be 'heroes No. 1'. Some people feared that heavy casualties had prevented their taking a more active part in the final operations. Others think that a considerable part of the Eighth Army has been sent back to Egypt to prepare for an attack on Crete or Rhodes. 'Relatives of men in the Eighth Army are asking whether the men will get any leave before they start fighting again.'

CASUALTIES: Considerable anxiety is expressed, particularly by relatives of the men fighting in North Africa, as (in spite of Mr. Attlee's statement in the House on 11th May) it is felt that casualties will have been very heavy. It is suggested that 'casualty lists should be published, for, although men talk of the wider issues of the war, women are more concerned with their own men out there, their safety and their chances of coming home'.

3. THE NEXT MOVE

Surprise and delight at the news from Tunisia quickly led to speculation as to what is going to happen next. Except for 'communist clamour', the agitation for a second front has almost ceased, as an Allied attack on the Continent is now 'generally taken for granted' and is thought by the majority to be imminent. There is said to be general realisation that the next step will be 'bloody and difficult' but, 'despite the possibility of heavy losses, people are confident about the future as it is felt that nowadays the Allied command make more sure of their blows before embarking on new ventures'.

Widespread speculation is reported as to when and where the attack – or attacks – will take place:

WHEN? 'The opening of a European front is expected to follow quickly', and anticipations range from 'any day now' to 'the next few weeks' – but at any rate this summer. A small minority are reported to say that 'it will never come off, it's too late now'. It is thought that criticism would start 'if the attack is delayed for another two months or so'. Many hope that 'any move we make will coincide with strong Russian pressure on the Eastern front'.

WHERE? 'The man-in-the-street is said to have wonderful ideas' on this subject. Some 'envisage more than one simultaneous attack'. Great interest is taken in our choice of bombing targets and in shipping movements, and 'German reports of concentrations of ships and barges at Gibraltar' confirm some people's suspicions that the attack will be in the Mediterranean rather than from England. Guesses include almost every country in Europe, including:

(a) ITALY, 'the idea being to put Italy completely out of the war as soon as possible'. Sicily and Sardinia are also mentioned in two reports, Pantelleria in one.

(b) TURKEY: it is thought that 'Turkey will be in the war pretty quickly now'.

(c) NORWAY: 'Then the Russians will try to drive through the northern section of their front and help us.'

(d) THE BALKANS, with 'a drive on Rumanian oil'.

(e) FRANCE: one report refers to 'the hope that an attempt will not be made through France, as it is thought to be uncertain whether the French can be trusted'.

(f) HOLLAND, 'because of the recent enforcement of martial law in that country'.

(g) SPAIN.

4. NORTH AFRICAN POLITICS

'The continued inability of the French leaders to sink their differences' is still a subject of unfavourable comment. 'It is felt that both Generals de Gaulle and Giraud are prompted by selfish motives and personal ambition.' The hope is expressed that 'with the clearing of the Axis from African territory, we shall not hand over control to a French military clique unless we have very strong safeguards'.

5. THE RUSSO-POLISH DISPUTE

This is still reported to be a subject of considerable comment, although discussion appears to have lessened since last week. The principal reaction is said to be concern, particularly at the implication of the dispute for the post-war settlement of Europe. 'If a thing like this can start in the middle of a war, what on earth will happen afterwards?' The hope is expressed that every effort will be made by the United States and ourselves to 'end the deadlock and restore the unity of the Allies'. There is a suggestion that closer co-operation on the part of the Allies would have avoided the dispute, and some comment is reported on 'the desirability of having a central consultative committee of the United Nations'.

There seems to be a disinclination to take sides in the dispute, partly because people feel that they have not sufficient knowledge on which to judge the issue. Some are said to be puzzled and to feel that 'there is more in it than meets the eye'. On balance, opinion is reported to favour Russia: 'Victory for the Allies can't come without her great aid.' Some sympathy is expressed for Poland, though there is also suspicion of the 'fascist character' of its government. There is said to be some suspicion, too, of Russia's post-war intentions, but 'a hearty welcome for last week's Russian declaration that Moscow wishes to see a strong and independent Poland'.

The view that the dispute is the result of German propaganda is reported much less this week, but some disappointment is expressed 'that Axis efforts to split the Allied nations have been successful and that German propaganda still imposes upon and weakens the war effort'.

Polish opinion in this country is said to be strongly anti-Russian, and in Scotland it is reported that the expression of this feeling by Polish troops is 'influencing public opinion almost as much as the strong pro-Russian propaganda during the last two years'.

There is criticism of the 'publications being put out in this country by the Polish Government'. It is asked 'why our Government allows some of the views expressed in them, and why the Poles are permitted such quantity and quality of newsprint?'

6. RUSSIA

There is still relatively little comment on Russia. Satisfaction is expressed with the Russian successes in the Kuban, which are said to have 'heartened the public'. People are reported to be expecting 'a major flare-up soon'; the majority seem to think that Russia will take the offensive.

The bombing of eastern Germany by the Red Air Force is said to have aroused appreciative talk of co-operation between the Allies; another report refers to 'a general feeling that there are signs of a better understanding developing between Russia and ourselves'. Against this, there is reference to 'an undercurrent of doubt as to the future activities and intentions of this country' with regard to Russia. It is reported also that 'merchant seamen back from Murmansk are – except for the left-minded – sceptical regarding Russian-British friendship'; they all, however, express admiration for 'the tremendously earnest war effort of the Russians', but most believe 'the Russians are cynical regarding our motives for helping them'.

STALIN'S MAY DAY SPEECH: Reports continue to express satisfaction with this and particularly with his recognition of the Allies' efforts.

7. THE FAR EAST

Little comment is reported on the war in the Far East, though there is said to be some concern about our withdrawal in Burma. A report from one Region says that 'explanatory communiqués and dispatches which tend to make excuses for our defeats, only add to the bitterness with which the news is received'.

Some concern is also reported over 'the whole situation on the Pacific front' and in India, and there is anxiety 'lest too much is being left to Australia'. 'More air strength is considered by a number of people to be urgently needed to smash the pending Japanese attack there.'

8. THE WAR IN THE AIR

'The Allies' vigorous air offensive' continues to meet with general approval, and the majority are anxious 'to give them more – they put us through it, now we are giving it back'. A small minority, however, particularly women, 'express humane regret that such destruction should be necessary', while others 'wonder if bombing gets us anywhere, because German industries are spread over thousands of miles'.

Concern about our losses in men and machines continues to be reported, but anxiety appears to have been considerably allayed by Squadron Leader John Strachey's highly praised *Postscript* (May 6th). 'He was able to give information on a matter which had been troubling a number of people', and his talk 'helped to combat depression and give people a more balanced view of our losses'.

The organisation of our air cover in Tunisia and 'the disappearance of the Luftwaffe from the African skies has pleased many people' and has given rise to some speculation as to the reasons for the withdrawal of German planes. While some believe it was done 'to save aircraft and protect enemy territory in the event of an invasion', others suspect that 'Hitler is saving aircraft to retaliate with a London blitz'.

AIR RAIDS ON THIS COUNTRY: It is reported from the Southern Region that the recent publication (6th May) of further details about the daylight raid on Reading (11th February) has aroused strong criticism in the town. Complaints are made that such an announcement 'merely encourages the Germans', and that to describe the raid as 'recent' is misleading and might cause anxiety to people with relatives in Reading, who would think that a second raid had taken place.

POISON GAS: Some discussion is reported on the possibility of poison gas being used. It is thought that 'when Hitler gets desperate he will use it', and that therefore publicity is needed to make people 'look for – and at – their gas masks'.

9. THE WAR AT SEA

The official US announcements (May 5th and 6th) of the low sinkings of Allied ships during April have cheered people, and though anxiety about our losses is still reported, it appears to have decreased. Conflicting reports on the shipping situation, and the lack of official British information, are still criticised, and it is asked 'why American news is more informative than ours. Are they allowed to use news which is withheld from us?'

10. RIFLEMAN CLAYTON'S DEATH

Rifleman Clayton's death in a detention camp continues to be the subject of much indignant comment. People are said to be 'horrified at the revelation of detention camp abuses', which are regarded, according to reports from seven Regions, as being 'as bad as anything the Germans can do' and are freely likened to the Gestapo.

There appeared to be a very strong feeling that an example should be made of the men responsible, that they should be tried for manslaughter, or flogged. (This was before the announcement of the verdict.) 'It is feared that, should the sergeants be reduced to the rank of private, they will be seen to have an opportunity of reaching their own rank again, and it is considered that they should be removed far away from the witnesses at the inquest', some of whom are thought to have been told to 'cover up the incident'.

The case is said to have led to 'much adverse discussion, of "glass houses" in general', as well as 'a fair amount of talk about "naval torturing", i.e. the "sand-bag punishment" which, it is stated, is still imposed in spite of what the Admiralty say'.

11. US MINERS' STRIKE THREAT

Interest remains slight, but the following reactions are again reported:

(a) Criticism of John L. Lewis: 'He will have much to answer for if men in the US army are crippled for want of supplies.'
(b) Dissatisfaction with the US: 'The American man-in-the-street doesn't realise what total war means.'
(c) Disgust with the US miners for holding up the war effort. On the other hand, 'some people have pointed out that we also have had strikes'.

(d) Relief that the miners have returned to the pits and 'faith that trouble will not develop'.

12. THE BEVERIDGE REPORT AND THE POST-WAR WORLD

Interest and discussion continue on familiar lines. The feeling is still reported, particularly among the working classes, that the Government 'does not really mean to deal with the question of social security and improved standards of living'.

Lord Croft's Manchester speech (5th May) is said to have 'met with a good deal of hostility' and, 'as a result of his words, people are said to wonder whether they had dreamt about the Atlantic Charter and the Government pronouncements on reconstruction'.

13. BROADCASTING AND PRESENTATION OF NEWS

Although people are reported to be eagerly attending to newspapers and news bulletins, news presentation does not appear to be much discussed. On the whole, it is thought to be regarded as satisfactory. There are, however, some complaints of 'padding the news' and of the repetition of unimportant items. Despite this, some people wish that 'Tunisia and other vital war news might be dealt with more fully and given sooner'. Broadcasts from war correspondents there are now said to be listened to with great interest, though there is some complaint of their indistinctness.

Praise is given to Lt. Commander Agar's *Postscript* (2nd May), which is described as 'first class', and to that of Mr. Edward Murrow (9th May). This was thought to give 'a vivid picture of the conditions in which the Tunisian campaign had been conducted, and to pay generous tribute to British soldiers'. There is further praise for Lt. Commander Peter Scott's *Postscript* (25th April).

II. SPECIAL COMMENTS

14. INDUSTRY

DISPARITY IN PAY AND HOURS WORKED:

(a) WAGES: Complaints come from 'some mining quarters at the high wages and bonuses paid to Government coal outcrop workers'. There are also complaints from Stroud, where 'holiday pay inequalities as between different factories in the same area cause understandable dissatisfaction'. Other complaints come from women, 'who are resentful that their own men in the Forces earn so little, while others in factories get so much'.

(b) HOURS: Criticism is reported of the short hours worked by: (i) local authority staffs: 'Sarcastic talk comes from Cheltenham following the County Council's decision to increase hours from thirty-eight to forty-two per week'; (ii) workers in the catering trade; (iii) printers 'who have a pre-war week of five days'.

ENFORCED IDLENESS continues 'to be talked about'. There are said 'to be grumbles from shipyard workers all over Scotland', but 'much less grumbling than recently about lack of material holding up work' in the North-Western Region. It is again suggested that workers should be given explanations whenever idle time occurs, to dispel anxiety and uneasiness. According to one report, however, 'idle time is a perennial excuse for lateness or absenteeism'.

FATIGUE OF WORKERS:

(a) WOMEN workers particularly are described as suffering from nervous debility and anaemia due to long working hours. Criticism is reported from the Eastern Region 'of the fact that many industrial insurance societies only allow sick benefit for expectant mothers during the last month of pregnancy, which is thought to be injurious to the health of mother and child, especially now that women are tackling heavy jobs'.

(b) MEN: Mention is made of 'many shipyard workers feeling the strain' and also of 'the extreme tiredness of miners; more coal could be produced, it is suggested, if men worked a five-and-a-half-day week'.

MISUSE OF LABOUR is alleged in four Regions and the following instances are given: (i) miners working on Exide batteries in the North-Western Region; they are said to be unwilling to return to the mines as their present work is lighter and better paid; (ii) skilled joiners and carpenters 'navvying' on aerodrome sites; (iii) cotton workers who are now making munitions are 'so cotton-minded' as to be of little use in any other capacity. At the same time, young women with experience in Food Offices are said to be 'put into cotton, of which they know nothing'; (iv) experienced bus drivers being called up and 'replaced by elderly drivers or mechanics who had hitherto failed to be satisfactory drivers'.

STRIKES: Concern continues about 'the number of strikes taking place'. In two reports the 'almost daily' strikes and stoppages among miners are associated in the public's mind with 'similar trouble for many years in Britain, Belgium, Northern France, and today in the United States. '"Are miners the same all over the world?" it is asked.'

ABSENTEEISM AND SLACKING OF WORKERS: Instances given are: (i) shipyard workers in Scotland: 'Pre-war workers are working all out, while new people in the same shipyards who can't be easily sacked are doing little'; (ii) young miners of eighteen 'who are keen to enter the Services and have no intention of working well in the pit'; (iii) men working on Government contract, particularly Irish labourers; (iv) waste of time 'through lack of supervision'; the Forestry Commission home-grown timber production work is mentioned in this connection.

GOVERNMENT CONTROL: Some criticism is reported about 'the Government working of the Forest of Dean Iron Mines'; reference is also made to 'chaotic conditions at Boulton and Paul Aircraft Ltd. of Wolverhampton, since the control was changed: departmental officials appear lacking in knowledge of their work, and diffident in taking responsibilities'. The May Day demonstrations in Belfast, at which demands were made that 'the British Government should take control of firms in Northern Ireland that are not producing to full capacity', are said to have been organised 'chiefly by Communists'.

15. THE CALL-UP

The main points of discussion are:

(a) The shortage of domestic help, which is 'very hard' on invalids, elderly people, and young mothers – particularly those of the middle class.

(b) The direction of women into part-time work. It is hoped that older women will be treated sympathetically, and that younger women will not continue to escape direction into war work 'by doing jobs which take only an hour or so a week'. (Some managements and shop stewards, according to the report from the South-Western Region, 'still regard part-time labour as a damn nuisance'.)

(c) 'The number of young men and women still in civilian occupations'; according to the report from the Southern Region, 'there is increasingly bitter comment about the large group of civil servants in the middle of a working-class neighbourhood, who work in a section of the Foreign Office at Bletchley Park – a bolt-hole for men and women who wish to avoid military service, and who have influence enough to do so'.

16. CLOTHING

Clothing difficulties are reported from eleven Regions this week as opposed to seven last week. Next year's clothing problems are said to be 'a bogey to most people'. The chief complaints are:

INADEQUACY OF COUPONS, particularly for: (a) household goods: the demand for a special household issue continues; (b) families with growing children: mothers 'wonder how they will be able to cover themselves and their children'; (c) very poor families who cannot afford to buy good and durable clothes; (d) miners and factory workers in dirty trades. Talk of further coupon restrictions next year is causing 'concern and dismay'; the official announcement (8th May) that next year's allowance will be only thirty-six coupons does not yet appear to be fully realised by the general public.

SHOE DIFFICULTIES, particularly (a) the difficulty of obtaining shoes for children and for workers who are not able to get to the shops before the day's quota is sold; (b) the difficulty of getting shoes repaired, for which the shortage of leather is blamed; in one Region the unwillingness of shoe repairers to mend children's shoes unless 'they are really bad' is said to be having its effect on school attendances. There are also complaints about the poor quality of leather used for repairs; (c) the high price and poor quality of shoes.

THE SHORTAGE AND POOR QUALITY OF CLOTHING, particularly utility stockings and WX and outsize corsets. There are also complaints about the poor quality and high coupon value of children's utility clothing – 'The supply of really hard-wearing utility shorts would solve a lot of problems.'

17. FOOD

Satisfaction with the food situation continues. In the Northern Region there is some speculation as to whether 'food will be less plentiful because of having to feed the large number of Axis prisoners taken in Tunisia'.

The following complaints have been reported this week:

SHORTAGE OF FISH: There are complaints about early morning queues, preferential treatment of certain customers, and of fish 'finding its way into special quarters instead of into the shops'.

THE HIGH PRICES OF VEGETABLES, especially lettuces, are mentioned in six Reports. It is suggested that 'as supply apparently exceeds demand prices could be lowered'.

THE CUT IN THE CHEESE RATION, complaints of which are mentioned in reports from five Regions.

THE MEAT SHORTAGE and the 'meagre allowance of meat', complaints of which come from four Regions.

THE DIFFICULTY OF FINDING SUITABLE FILLINGS for packed meals is reported from three Regions.

SHORTAGE OF SWEETS is reported from three Regions, 'although it is only the beginning of a ration period'.

PRESERVE RATION: Housewives are said 'to long for an increase in the preserve ration but not at the expense of the sugar ration'. A 'sugar-for-jam ration' as well as a preserve ration are wished for.

18. HEALTH

'Lack of tone', 'fatigue', 'nerves', irritability, or weariness are complained of and are ascribed to ill-balanced diet, long working hours, transport difficulties and the housing shortage. An epidemic of chills in the Peak District is attributed to the ban on central heating. (At the same time, general satisfaction is reported from there at the lifting of the ban.) In the London Region opinion is said to 'incline definitely to the view that the health of the public is not as good as official announcements state', though the report from the North-Eastern Region suggests that the past week has acted as a tonic to those who were showing signs of strain.

There is said to be 'some concern particularly among workers and middle-class elements' at the increase of tuberculosis.

VENEREAL DISEASE CAMPAIGN: Approval is again reported of the publicity being given to this 'great menace'. Its increase is said to be causing come consternation, as it is thought 'that the disease must have assumed alarming proportions for the Ministry of Health to give it such publicity'.

There is some demand for 'more and stronger' publicity, and for more specific accounts of the later stages of the disease. It is also suggested that the possibilities of 'innocent infection', e.g. from towels, cups, etc., needs explaining more carefully.

The films *Subject for Discussion* and *Social Enemy No. 1* are both praised, the first being described as 'good, clear and sensible'.

19. HOUSING ACCOMMODATION AND DIFFICULTIES OF BILLETING WORKERS

During the past fortnight there have been reports from eight Regions of the difficulties of securing housing accommodation. The 'acute shortage' is said in one report to be affecting both morale and health. In the London Region it is described as a common occurrence for three or four adults to share one room.

There are also complaints of the high price of furnished houses and rooms ('this is a racket that should be thoroughly investigated') and of the prices of houses put up for sale. To those 'who have hunted for accommodation for weeks and months' the sight of empty houses is said to cause much bitterness. Men in the Forces are said to be frequently given compassionate leave to search for accommodation for their wives and children.

In five Regions workers complain of 'the difficulty of finding digs', while landladies are worried by having to 'make the ration stretch', and by the shortage of towels, bed linen, etc.

20. SHOPPING DIFFICULTIES

'This eternal queuing' is referred to in reports from seven Regions, and is a subject of bitter complaint, not only from those who have to stand in queues, but also from war workers, who are considered to be very hard hit, as they have no time to queue 'for the unrationed extras that make the rations go round'.

The closing of shops at lunch time is said to be causing office and factory workers 'great difficulties'. Shops close before they finish work and 'the lunch hour is their only opportunity to do shopping'.

21. SERVICEMEN'S PENSIONS AND DEPENDANTS' ALLOWANCES

In the last two weeks the following complaints have been reported: (i) men discharged from the Forces as unfit for military service, being refused a pension on the grounds that their disability was not caused or aggravated by military service. It is also said that 'so many disability claims are contested', and that 'the pension appeal application forms are far too complicated'; (ii) the 'inadequacy' of pensions granted to disabled men; (iii) 'the whole question of pensions, and of dependants' allowances'. It is felt that 'this blot on our records should be thoroughly reviewed by the Government'.

22. NATIONAL SAVINGS

While enthusiasm for 'local weeks', such as 'Wings for Victory weeks', is reported from three Regions, a minority view is said to be that 'there's a lot of eyewash about the target which cities and districts set themselves, as the large amounts subscribed by large firms are not genuine savings'. Other factors said to be affecting savings adversely are: (i) 'Tuesday morning's (4th May) revelations about the big profits on warships. These have discouraged secretaries of savings groups, who now have to meet charges that the war is run for the benefit of a few.' (ii) a questioning of what money will be worth after the war 'because the present high price of many commodities is making people suspicious of inflation'.

23. US TROOPS

'A better understanding' is said to exist 'since the American successes in Tunisia', and people are now suggesting that 'the Americans are tougher than they appeared to be'. Complaints continue to be reported, however, of their alleged drunkenness, their lack of response to hospitality, their assumption that 'money buys everything' and their bad behaviour – particularly with women and young girls. At the same time, 'the behaviour of some young girls is thought to be a disgrace and to account for the American attitude'.

It is said that residents near camps would find it easier to be friendly with Americans were it not for 'the wide discrepancy in the treatment of our own servicemen compared with the Americans', particularly regarding the time they have to report back to camp. 'If they reported back when our men do, instead of at 6 a.m., they would make less nuisance of themselves.'

24. AGRICULTURE

Little comment on agricultural matters has been reported during the last three weeks. The introduction of double summer time raised a few grumbles. Fears about scarcity of harvest labour continue to be reported; and from the North Midland and Welsh Regions come complaints about the ploughing in of vegetable crops. This week there has been satisfaction at the recent rain, 'which has saved the hay crop', but 'the gales have played the devil'.

HARVEST HELPERS: While the scheme for holiday harvest helpers appears to have been welcomed by town dwellers, some scepticism about the value of their help is reported from farmers in the Southern Region: 'Unless they are strong and used to farm work, will they really be much use on a farm?' Doubts about the adequacy of billeting arrangements are reported from both farmers and prospective helpers.

THE GOVERNMENT SCHEME FOR LABOURERS' COTTAGES: A good deal of criticism of this scheme has been reported during the past three weeks. The cottages are criticised in four reports for their concrete floors, steep stairs and the 'size of the kitchen and third bedroom'. It is also thought that not enough cottages are being built and that their rents should be lower. It is rumoured in the South-Western Region that 'obstructive vested interests' are playing a part in the siting of the cottages, and that some 'uneconomic and unpleasant' sites are being chosen.

25. RAZOR BLADES

The shortage of razor blades is mentioned in reports from six Regions, one of which refers to 'complaints that the edges of blades described as "Utility" are very jagged, and easily cut the skin'.

NO. 137: TUESDAY 11 MAY 1943 TO TUESDAY 18 MAY 1943

I. GENERAL COMMENTS

1. GENERAL STATE OF CONFIDENCE AND REACTION TO NEWS

Public confidence, which rose sharply last week, is now even higher. 'Enthusiasm and thankfulness' are everywhere reported as a result of 'the spectacular end to the African campaign'. Many people are 'still in a state of rather delighted bewilderment, because it seems so odd that after all this time there should be no more African campaign news in the press'. Generally, elation has been 'self-contained and undemonstrative' and there has been no 'Mafeking spirit': 'people assess the victory as a stepping stone, and not as dry land at last'.

The coming offensive has now superseded the Tunisian victory as a topic of conversation, and the questions of the moment are: 'Where do we go from here?' and 'When?' The majority are said to have 'a grim understanding of the magnitude of the task'; but they have great 'confidence in our leadership' and now 'know with certainty that the Axis is doomed'.

'The general wave of excitement' is said to have swamped interest in other events, such as Mr. Churchill's trip to Washington, the Russian front and Burma ('the only dark spot in the picture').

Only preliminary reactions have so far been received to the bombing of the German dams, but these suggest that 'this brilliant achievement has tended to raise spirits to an even higher level than before'.

On the home front, 'the public is so heartened by good news and so tensed for big developments that minor grievances and grumbles are to a large extent forgotten'; and the good weather is credited with having done much to 'promote cheerfulness and satisfaction – even among farmers'.

A good deal of strong feeling is, however, reported about 'the numerous strikes which have occurred during the past week'.

2. TUNISIA

Intense pleasure continues to be expressed at 'our colossal victory' in Tunisia. The public appear to be chiefly impressed by:

(a) 'THE SPEED OF THE ATTACK': People are 'delighted because we have now shown the Nazis what a blitzkrieg – their own speciality – is really like'.

(b) THE 'SUDDEN COLLAPSE OF THE ENEMY': There is a good deal of speculation as to whether 'this demoralisation of Axis forces indicates that Germany may suddenly collapse, as in the last war'.

(c) 'THE COMPLETE CO-OPERATION OF THE ALLIES' and of the three arms of the Services. There is praise, too, for 'the skill of Eisenhower, back-stage, in organising the supplies and welding the many nationalities into a coherent unity'.

(d) THE FACT THAT 'THE ALLIED ARMIES HAVE PROVED THEMSELVES SUPERIOR TO THE AXIS IN FIGHTING POWER' and 'have been able to give the elite of the German panzer divisions a first-class thrashing'. There is 'unusual delight that the British army has come into its own' and there is genuine pleasure because the Americans have 'learned the battle techniques quickly after all'. There is an impression that 'the German army is not so strong as was thought'.

(e) 'THE STRATEGY AND DARING OF GENERAL ALEXANDER': The majority now 'feel that we have nothing to be ashamed about in our generalship'.

(f) 'THE ASTONISHING NUMBER OF PRISONERS': There is much speculation as to where we shall put them all and how we shall feed them. There is satisfaction that so many of them are German, but regret that more were not killed. 'Can we now do something about the chaining of our boys?' it is asked.

(g) 'THE SLIGHTNESS OF OUR CASUALTIES': 'Few appear to have scrutinised the figures at all carefully, but people had steeled themselves for much higher figures.' Some anxiety had been reported as a result of references, particularly by the BBC, to the costly nature of the offensive.

Rumours are said to be current about 'women going joyfully to meet their menfolk – and not being warned of dreadful mutilations'. According to one rumour the wife visits her husband in hospital, discovers him to be without arms, legs or sight, and dies of shock.

(h) 'THE CAPTURE OF VON ARNIM and news of his arrival in England caused particular satisfaction', but not 'the reports (in the press of 17th May, but since contradicted) that he would receive £40 a week while in captivity'. It is rumoured that he is imprisoned at the Sassoon House, Trent Park, and that comfortable furniture and supplies were being hastily brought there over the weekend; it is felt that less generous treatment, in comparison with 'what our boys get out there', should be meted out to the General.

(i) 'WILL THE EIGHTH ARMY GET SOME LEAVE NOW?' is a question
     often asked, particularly by the men's relatives. Greatly as people wish that
     the enemy should be 'hit again before his morale has time to recover', it is
     felt that those who have been fighting in Africa since the campaign began
     should be rested before they are sent to fight on a new front.
(j) LACK OF ARRANGEMENTS TO CELEBRATE THE VICTORY: 'No
     flags or outward jubilation'. The pealing of victory bells and the special
     thanksgiving services were, however, on this occasion considered justified.

3. THE NEXT MOVE

'The next step is now more talked about than North Africa', and 'on all sides
expectancy and speculation are reported'. It is generally believed that 'there will be
a bitter struggle with heavy casualties', though some say: 'No, Germany will crack
up soon. Look at North Africa.' No one appears to doubt that the attack on the
European fortress will succeed.

WHEN? 'Most people expect Europe will be invaded almost immediately',
though some think we had better wait for 'at least another fortnight, until there is
no moon'. It is hoped that we shall 'follow up as soon as possible' – 'Hitler hesitated
after Dunkirk and it proved his undoing – we do not want to do the same.'

WHERE? 'Suggestions as to the whereabouts of attack once more cover the
whole continent of Europe.' Some 'expect there will be a small landing to cover up
the real operations'; others favour 'a double assault from England and Africa, with
a consequent pincer movement'. Some speculations are more detailed – 'the Tenth
Army to Crete and the Balkans, the Eighth and First to Sicily and Sardinia, and the
Armies in England between Boulogne and Dieppe'. On the whole, Southern Europe,
with Italy predominating, appears to be first choice – Italy is expected to 'cave in
easily'. Next to Italy, the place most often mentioned is Turkey, through which it is
thought the Rumanian oilfields could be reached.

4. NORTH AFRICAN POLITICS

The main feeling is summed up in the following quotation: 'People are sick of the
flapdoodle between Giraud and de Gaulle. They want the two to get on with the job
jointly, and to leave questions of rank, status and priority aside.' Some suspicion of
the French in North Africa continues to be reported, and it is thought that we should
maintain strict supervision of the French Colonial Empire or 'we shall have trouble
with the French officials out there yet'.

5. THE PRIME MINISTER'S VISIT TO WASHINGTON

This has been greeted in the main with satisfaction, but with little surprise, because as
soon as Mr. Attlee has to 'make an important speech in the House, the country knows
that Mr. Churchill is abroad'. This time people thought he had gone to Cairo. His
trip has caused less comment than previous ones, being 'outshone' – like everything
else – 'by the North African news'. Comment is chiefly on the following aspects:

(a) MR. CHURCHILL'S 'TOUGHNESS AND COURAGE': There is 'joy on all sides that he is fit enough to make the journey, and great admiration for his willingness to go to any lengths to effect close working. It seems to be taken for granted now that if his presence is needed, he will be there.'

(b) HE 'SHOULD NOT EXPOSE HIMSELF TO DANGERS, at this turning point in the nation's fortunes'. 'We can't do without Mr. Churchill: he shouldn't leave the country.' Some wonder 'why Mr. Roosevelt can't come here for a change'. The risk to Mr. Churchill's health, as well as to his safety, also causes some concern.

(c) RUSSIA IS 'AGAIN UNREPRESENTED': 'When are we going to hear of a real Four Nation conference, with the Soviet Union and China represented?' It is particularly wished that 'Stalin could be in at such conferences' and feared that he is 'playing a lone hand'.

(d) WHY DID HE GO? Although some think he went in connection with the coming offensive, it is believed that that must all have been settled at Casablanca 'long ago', and it is generally believed that 'the subject of the conference is the Far East, rather than Europe'. 'Moves against the Japanese', it is thought, 'would explain the presence of Wavell and the absence of Russian representatives'. Minority suggestions as to his reason for going include: 'to bridge the gulf between Poland and Russia'; 'to iron out difficulties with Russia'; 'to arrange that General Alexander should take General Eisenhower's place in command of the North African forces'; to arrange 'more help for China'.

THE PRIME MINISTER'S BROADCAST TO THE HOME GUARD aroused less interest than his speeches usually do: it 'delighted the Home Guard', but most other people were disappointed. No fault is found with the speech itself – though some thought the ending abrupt – but the great majority seem to have been expecting a war speech. People were hoping for 'a paean of victory about Africa, and an assurance that we had at last passed through the era of blood, toil, sweat and tears'. 'People hope for something juicy when he broadcasts', and they were hoping to hear him say: 'I told Mussolini that we would tear his Italian Empire to shreds, and now we've done it.' Nevertheless, most people were pleased 'to hear from him – whatever he was saying – when he was so far away on an important mission'. It was generally expected that the war situation would be dealt with more fully in his Congress speech.

6. THE FAR EAST

Interest in the Far Eastern war, although still on a small scale, is reported to be somewhat greater this week, principally owing to Mr. Churchill's visit to Washington, which 'seems to presage action in the Far East'.

Disappointment and concern are again reported at the continued setbacks in Burma.

Some people in one Region are said to think that 'the Japanese are preparing a big offensive while there's time', and others wonder, as the result of General

Wavell's visit to this country and Washington, whether the situation in Burma is 'sufficiently serious to retard the opening of the coming offensive on the Continent'. There is some criticism that press reports of the Burma fighting are small and 'not explicit enough'.

Although the Far East war is felt by some people to be 'Australia's and America's affair', others express concern at the 'Jap approach to India' and it is said that 'more people are beginning to realise that 100 per cent effort is needed to defeat Japan'. A number of people are reported to feel that 'to keep the general public interested in the Far Eastern war after the collapse of Nazidom in Europe will be a most difficult task'.

CHINA: A slight increase in interest is reported; it is said that 'more people are hoping that some Allied move is to be directed at the release of China', and that the public would welcome additional news about China.

7. RUSSIA

There is still little comment reported about Russia. People are said to be awaiting developments, in some cases with anxiety about the outcome of the fighting, and in others with confidence in the Russians. A slight expectation is reported that a Russian offensive will be 'linked with some Anglo-American invasion move'. The operations in the Kuban appear to have aroused little discussion, but a feeling that the situation there 'is thought to have much improved' is reported from one Region.

Among a small minority there is said to be some speculation on 'the outcome of Britain's alliance with Russia', and some fear of her post-war policy.

8. THE RUSSO-POLISH DISPUTE

Interest is now much less. Some anxiety about the effects of the dispute, particularly as to the post-war settlement in Europe, continues, although there now seems to be more confidence that a satisfactory settlement will be reached; Stalin's statement is thought to have been helpful.

Criticism of the Poles, along the lines previously reported, outweighs sympathy for them this week. The belief that the Polish leaders are fascist in outlook is again mentioned.

9. THE ALLIED AIR OFFENSIVE

THE BOMBING OF THE GERMAN DAMS: Preliminary reactions to the bombing of the three dams serving the Ruhr-Westphalia industrial region have been received from nine Regions. This 'brilliant and daring achievement' has aroused feelings which vary from 'jubilation' to 'grim approval' – in some cases not untinged with feelings of horror at the terrible consequences to civilians: 'I wonder what it would be like to be wakened at midnight by an avalanche of water'. Many people, however, are said to feel little sympathy for the civilian victims – 'they asked for it, now they've got it'. Great praise is expressed for the RAF, and some for the Jewish refugee who was thought to have given the necessary information. It is hoped, however, that the announcement that he was Jewish will not provoke a savage anti-Semitic outburst in Germany.

There is already some speculation, and a little apprehension, as to 'what the Germans can do here in return', though 'well-informed' people do not believe that any of the dams in this country 'could be hit with comparable effect'.

THE GENERAL ALLIED AIR OFFENSIVE: Satisfaction with this continues to be reported from all Regions. It is felt that 'the undreamed-of proportions' of our air blows have now fully redeemed past promises of continuous and ever-increasing air attacks, and people are enthusiastic at the 'deadly blows we are dealing to the enemy's war production'.

Some speculation on our ability to maintain the present intensity of attack is reported; some people wonder if it is 'just a well-timed gesture', while others believe it to be a forerunner to the invasion of Europe. The bombing of German targets is specially welcomed – 'there should be a raid on Germany every night, however small' – as are also the raids on Italy; and the bombing of Sicilian ports and bases is looked upon as a prelude to early large-scale attacks on Italy herself.

There is said to be less concern about our losses, and the horror, expressed chiefly by women, 'at the necessity for such mass slaughter' is only reported from one Region this week.

10. AIR RAIDS ON THIS COUNTRY

The release of the Luftwaffe from the African skies, and Hitler's desperation, are given as reasons for a slight increase in the belief that there will be more raids on this country. The expectation that they will be heavy comes only from coastal districts, and most people are said to feel that the enemy no longer has it in his power to inflict severe blows.

SOUTH-EASTERN COASTAL AREAS: Very little comment is reported on the nuisance raids in this area, and many people are now said to be able 'to sleep undisturbed while the sirens wail at night'. At Deal, however, there are allegations that the cross-Channel shelling is affecting morale; there is some feeling of resentment that it continues, because 'Jerry only starts shelling when we do'.

LONDON: The nuisance raids do not appear to worry people very much and are referred to as 'just enough to keep us on our toes'. There are comments on the fact that bombs were dropped on Sunday night before the siren and that the continual sounding of the sirens disturbs people: 'If the general policy of the enemy is nuisance raiding, cannot the warning be given once at night, and then the all-clear sounded in the morning?'

EAST COAST RAIDS: Concentration on the two coastal towns is believed to be due to the Germans' inability to get through to Norwich. Considerable sympathy for the bombed, particularly the ATS hostel victims, is reported.

SOUTH WALES TOWN: Preliminary enquiries indicate that the attack has been taken philosophically, and very much in the spirit of the elderly lady who, searching among the rubble that was once her home, was heard to exclaim: 'Ah well, anyway this means that we shall get more coupons.'

ABERDEEN: A rumour has reached the Midland Region that five hundred Gordon Highlanders were killed in the recent raid on Aberdeen.

GERMAN LEAFLETS dropped in a Northern Region coastal district on the night of 15th May were received with amusement, because some of the ships named by the Germans as sunk are known by local seamen's families to be whole and intact.

11. THE WAR AT SEA

Less comment on the shipping position is reported this week, and anxiety seems to have decreased since the recent American statements (4th and 5th May) about the low sinkings of Allied ships during April. People are also cheered by the recent successes against the U-boats with our 'new secret device', and by the belief that owing to the Tunisian victory we shall now be able to send our ships through the Mediterranean and thus shorten our shipping routes.

The desire for 'a truer account of our shipping losses' continues to be reported, and it is felt that 'people would be more prepared to tighten their belts and work harder if the facts were clearly stated'.

12. HOME GUARD SUNDAY

The celebrations on Sunday are said to have given great pleasure and to have been appreciated. It is thought that it was about time the Home Guard got some praise, instead of the usual jokes, and some credit for 'hard work put in on top of a long day's work', as 'many are not so young as they used to be'. The smartness and 'impressive soldierliness' of the men is commented on and the women are said 'to have enjoyed the opportunity of seeing their own men on parade'.

Although the Home Guard is said to commend itself by its efficiency, and the public have full confidence in it, there are some who are doubtful of its ability to deal with a sudden major emergency. They think it would be quite inadequate against a highly-trained and mechanised German army, owing to its members being mostly raw untried youths and elderly men; though not under-estimating the spirit of the men, they fear that their age and lack of experience would prove a severe handicap.

13. RIFLEMAN CLAYTON'S DEATH

The inquest on Rifleman Clayton still seems to be 'a main topic of conversation, particularly among the working classes' and 'those in contact with the ranks'. Horror and indignation are again mentioned and, though there is 'some relief that the assailants are not likely to get away with it', a number of people think that the sergeants should be hung, or at least court martialled. 'Women with male relatives in the Forces are uneasy that this alleged policy of brutalism may be common for men undergoing detention', and 'mothers are expressing great concern about their sons in the army'.

The MO is thought to be 'just as guilty'. Women with relatives in detention, especially if they are physically unfit, are said to be anxious. It is asked whether it is possible for a man to 'ask for a second doctor's opinion, if his MO tells him he is fit'.

It is rumoured that Clayton was a notorious character in his home town of Enfield.

14. YOUTH

During the past three weeks there have been references from nine Regions to the behaviour of young people. The increase in juvenile delinquency, drunkenness, lax morals and hooliganism is said to be giving rise to anxiety. Lack of parental control, high wages, and the 'lack of sufficiently alluring counter-attractions' are thought to be the cause.

The need for 'organised play' for younger children is reported from four Regions. Even where there are public playgrounds children are said to play in the streets, and it is suggested that, where they exist, the use of these playgrounds should be made compulsory. Owing to the longer days, children are said to be allowed to stay up late; at the same time, some demand for a 'children's curfew' is reported by parents in the North-Western Region, as 'children scatter at their play and cannot be found'.

YOUTH ORGANISATIONS: Some improvement is felt to be necessary in the youth services as there are doubts whether they are fulfilling their purpose of fitting young people for future citizenship. Concern is reported in the London Region at the 'number of COs directed to do youth work by military tribunals'.

15. THE JEWS

During the past fortnight, nine Regional reports have commented on Jews in this country and two reports mention an increase in anti-Semitic feeling. The main criticisms continue to be of their alleged evasion of the call-up, black marketing and truculent behaviour.

In Brighton it is said 'to be widely felt that a countrywide check-up on identity cards is desirable' as 'there are obviously too many fit young aliens and Jews walking about the streets'.

PERSECUTION OF THE JEWS IN OCCUPIED COUNTRIES: Sympathy is expressed for the Jews in Europe; from one Region comes support for the idea that 'asylum should be found in this country or in Palestine for as many as can escape the Nazi clutches'. Though cruelty and persecution are condemned, generally speaking there is said 'to be little love lost' on those who are alleged to 'come crying for help and remain to plunder'.

16. BROADCASTING AND PRESENTATION OF NEWS

Comment on news presentation this week is mixed, the balance being favourable; in four Regions comment is said also to be not very strong and this, it is suggested, should be interpreted as 'tacit appreciation', there being 'no desire to criticise obviously good news'.

The handling of the Tunisian news, both by press and BBC, is praised in reports from five Regions; satisfaction is recorded at the 'promptness, completeness, and excellent taste' of the news bulletins, and at the prompt and frank statement of our losses. Some criticism is made, however, of the 'sketchy way' in which the first news of the Tunisian victory was given, fuller details being published only some days later, in the press. The 'matter-of-fact' tone of the announcer giving the news is also criticised. The prompt publication of photographs and details of the raids on the German dams is also praised.

Some doubts are expressed as to whether our news service is not too rigidly controlled: 'Are people being given the information they should be?'

BBC programmes are both praised and criticised. There is appreciative comment of 'brief and pungent' war commentaries and talks: 'authoritative talks by men with first-hand knowledge' are said to be always welcome.

There is praise for Commander Kimmins' *Postscript* (16th May), and further praise this week for Squadron Leader John Strachey's *Postscript* (6th May) and for the 'dual commentary' in which he took part on 13th May. There is also further praise for Mr. Edward Murrow's *Postscript* (9th May).

Satisfaction is expressed with *Marching On* and with *Into Battle*. Talks by Professor John Hilton are also praised.

II. SPECIAL COMMENTS

17. INDUSTRY

STRIKES: Irritation at strikes is again reported, especially among servicemen and their relatives; according to the report from the Northern Region, 'bitterness has been much stronger the last few days'. There is a further demand for 'the Government to do something drastic, and for strikes to be made illegal for the duration of war'. Disgust is said 'to override any question of sympathy for the contending parties, because whatever the rights or wrongs may be, our men fighting victorious battles abroad are being let down'. Only in the North Midland Region is mention made of some sympathisers with the strikers; they cite cases of 'transport workers and factory girls at Players Ltd., Nottingham, who, with deductions, are now receiving a net wage regarded as being lower than pre-war'. Particular reference is made to the strike of transport operatives in Yorkshire 'which has made it very difficult for many people to reach essential work', to a bus strike in the Thames valley, and to a rumoured munitions strike in Coventry.

ENFORCED IDLENESS: Stories continue to be reported of idle time in factories; this is variously attributed to 'the overstaffing of large firms', 'overproduction of certain munitions, so that production has now had to be stopped', and to inefficiency: 'A craftsman may wait two days for a part that can be bought retail at 4/6d. – meantime other men are waiting for the job.'

SLACKING OF WORKERS: There are further references to 'workpeople not pulling their weight'. Some workers feel, it is suggested in the North Midland Region, that 'if they produced more work, piecework rates and bonuses might be cut'.

FATIGUE: Although fatigue is believed in two Regions to be responsible for some absenteeism, it is suggested in others that 'the good news is bucking people up and signs of strain among war workers are less obvious'.

WAGES: Dissatisfaction is reported at the high wages of munition workers compared with servicemen's pay. On the other hand, transport employees and engineers in heavy industry are said to grumble about 'wages and conditions of work in general'.

18. THE CALL-UP

Comment continues to be reported about: (i) the number of young women, 'usually soldiers' wives with no apparent obligations', who evade the call-up. It is suggested that when such women, living in hotels or lodgings, 'are called up before the Ministry of Labour, they tell the authorities they are only staying in the town temporarily and may have to leave any day, but remain for months and are apparently lost sight of'; (ii) the direction of older women into part-time work. The only grumbling reported is when they see younger women apparently evading national service; (iii) the number of young men still in civilian occupations. Mention is also made of 'young men hawking logs and plants in the streets', and of pavement artists.

19. CLOTHING

CLOTHING COUPONS: The inadequacy of clothing coupons continues to be reported – particularly for (a) renewing household goods, (b) working clothes for workers in heavy industries, (c) poorer families, and families with growing children.

A belief (and consequent concern) that next year's coupon allowance will be smaller continues to be reported; some people are said 'to have decided that the allowance will be thirty-six, and are gasping ...'.

FOOTWEAR DIFFICULTIES: Difficulties in getting shoes repaired are reported from seven Regions (as opposed to four last week), and the high prices charged, and poor quality of leather used, are both commented on. There is again reference to the shortage of footwear, particularly of Wellingtons, large sizes in boots, children's light shoes and plimsolls. Leather laces and large nails and studs for farmers' boots are also said to be scarce.

UTILITY CLOTHING: The poor quality of utility socks and stockings is criticised again: complaints of (i) poor quality of utility corsets, (ii) utility shirts, (iii) the bad cut of men's underpants (short style), (iv) the poor quality of workers' overalls, and (v) the small hem on children's dresses, are all received from one Region each.

BLACK MARKET: The obtaining of coupons by illegal means, and the thieving of coupons and clothes, are reported from three Regions this week. In Rugby, it is alleged that unworn but 'deliberately soiled' clothing is sold on the market coupon-free.

LAUNDRY SERVICES: The struggle of women war workers to find time and soap to do their washing is reported from two Regions this week, and there are demands for communal laundries in the London Region. Complaints of the laundry zoning scheme come from the Southern Region, and from another Region the 'transport-soiling' and wear and tear of laundered clothes is adversely commented on.

NOTE: We much regret that under the section headed Clothing in our last Report (No. 136) a statement about the new issue of clothing coupons was inaccurate. Through a misunderstanding, it was said to have been officially announced on 8th May that the allowance of coupons for next year would be thirty-six. No such statement was made, and in fact on 14th May the Board of Trade announced that no decision had yet been taken, but that the total number of coupons would not fall below thirty-six.

20. TRANSPORT

Transport difficulties are referred to as 'a perpetual grouse'. Complaints, which continue on familiar lines, include (i) the overcrowding of buses, particularly in rural areas; special mention is again made of short-distance passengers crowding out long-distance ones; (ii) the difference between train and bus fares, 'which places a heavy burden on road transport leaving the trains running half empty'; on the other hand, the overcrowding of suburban trains 'by floods of week-end visitors' is referred to in the London report; (iii) the curfew, 'which doesn't give people a chance to go out for an hour after they've worked till 6 or 7 p.m.' (iv) crawling buses in London – 'a pernicious and unnecessary factor of wartime transport'.

There are again requests for additional transport facilities at weekends and for holidays. To quote from Postal Censorship: 'We are asked not to travel, but people are more in need of a holiday than ever, what with war strain and blackout winters.'

PETROL: Complaints continue about waste of petrol through (i) lack of co-ordination in transport; (ii) private cars run on unnecessary journeys by farmers, Government officials, US soldiers and others; (iii) the use of taxis for pleasure purposes.

In the Northern Region, employees of bus companies are said to be criticising 'the storing up by some companies of relatively new fuel-oil-driven buses that do twelve to fourteen miles to the gallon, and their replacement by old and worn-out petrol-driven buses that only do five miles to the gallon'.

21. FOOD

Satisfaction with the food situation, and faith in Lord Woolton's administration, continue. It is said 'present restrictions are bearable so long as supplies are fairly distributed and black markets controlled'.

There is, however, some grumbling about:

(a) THE SHORTAGE OF FISH: Reports of preferential treatment of customers continue. In one town there is said to have been a hostile demonstration when a man called to collect his telephoned order while a queue was waiting to be served.

(b) DISTRIBUTION OF FRUIT: Complaints that greengrocers are issuing cards to their best customers and only serving their own customers are reported; they thus stop war workers and those who grow their own vegetables from getting their fair share. The disappearance of rhubarb from the shops since its price was controlled is also complained of.

(c) THE REDUCTION IN THE CHEESE RATION: This is said to be causing difficulty, especially to those who take packed meals.

(d) PACKED MEALS: These continue to be a source of difficulty to wives. Miners' wives are said 'to be going without their own rations in order to give their men food'.

(e) THE SHORTAGE OF DRIED FRUIT: Housewives in the North Midland Region rural areas say they 'never see a sight of figs or dates'.

(f) THE SHORTAGE OF MEAT.

(g) THE SHORTAGE OF SOFT DRINKS: The warm weather is said to have caused people to complain of the shortage of soft drinks.

22. THE NEW RATION BOOKS

'Angry and bitter comment' from rural dwellers at the prospect of a five- or seven-mile journey to collect their new ration books is reported from five Regions. 'Have they given much thought and consideration to local conditions and local working hours?' it is asked, and Isle of Wight residents complain that 'this is not the way to encourage people not to travel'.

23. SHOPPING DIFFICULTIES

Shopping difficulties are reported from eight Regions this week. Complaints of queuing come from six Regions. Preferential treatment of customers 'who ignore queues and just walk in to have their orders handed to them', the waste of time spent in queues, and leisured women who can 'comb the shops' are mentioned.

The early and lunch-hour closing of shops and the irregular business hours of butchers' shops are reported to be extremely unpopular. Workers in full-time jobs are said to be 'worried out of their lives to get their rations'.

24. HEALTH

Tiredness and strain, particularly among women workers and older men and women, are reported this week from seven Regions. In the Southern Region, however, the signs of strain among war workers are said to be less than a few months ago – 'summer, and the news, having bucked people up'.

Fears of the increase of tuberculosis are reported from three Regions; stories of 'dirty milk being put into dirty bottles', the 'bad ventilation of buses and the dirty condition of the streets' are said to give rise to talk that these are possible causes of the increase. It is suggested that sufferers should be 'compelled to go into isolation as they are a menace to other people'.

The 'worry and difficulties connected with obtaining beds in maternity homes' are complained of in reports from two Regions; they are said to be having a bad effect on expectant mothers.

THE VD CAMPAIGN continues to be spoken of in complimentary terms, though it is said that much has yet to be done. Recent posters and newspaper advertisements are thought to be more 'pungent' than earlier ones, but there is some complaint that the repetition of the advertisements causes lack of attention.

25. HOUSING ACCOMMODATION AND THE DIFFICULTIES OF BILLETING WORKERS

The difficulty of obtaining housing accommodation, the high rents charged, and the high prices of houses are mentioned in reports from eight Regions this week. People who seek accommodation are said to be reluctant to take action through the local authority in respect of excessive charges for rent, and Government action is asked for. In the London Region much dissatisfaction is said to be felt that houses are left empty when they are so badly needed.

Hard cases of 'notice to quit' furnished houses and lodgings are complained of. Expectant mothers are said sometimes to be asked to leave their lodgings and to be unable to find others.

Billeting problems are reported from three Regions; 'better working-class billets' are said to be very scarce.

RURAL HOUSING: The desire among country people for better housing conditions is reported from three Regions, but the cottages to be erected under the Government scheme continue to be criticised for their concrete floors and small bathrooms, and because it is thought that an insufficient number will be built.

26. NATIONAL SAVINGS

WINGS FOR VICTORY WEEKS: The good news is said to have stimulated enthusiasm for Wings for Victory weeks and people are 'saving as much as possible to help reach the target'. Disappointment is reported among some Newcastle people 'that only a Hurricane was exhibited; they thought they were at least entitled to a bomber, as their target was seventy-five Lancasters – let alone the importance of the city'.

THE OXFORD COUNTY COURT DECISION AWARDING A WIFE'S SAVINGS TO HER HUSBAND is said to have had an adverse effect on group savings and to have aroused widespread indignation: 'If this is the law, it should be amended at once.'

THE NATIONAL SAVINGS CAMPAIGN 'is still not as effective as it might be', it is felt in one Region, as it does not draw a response from all members of the public. Examples given are (i) a working-class woman's remark: '£14 a week takes a lot of getting through'; and (ii) 'the appalling amount of money spent by children: they buy anything eatable, even stomach tablets, and go two or three times a week to the pictures'. It is suggested that more competitive schemes should be introduced.

27. SERVICEMEN, THEIR PENSIONS AND DEPENDANTS

Comment continues on the lines reported last week; the main criticism is of 'the low rates' of all Service pensions and dependants' allowances. 'Very great uneasiness' is reported from the Northern Region because 'men discharged from the Forces are compelled to seek public assistance; it's something the Government ought to attend to at once'. In Scotland, some bitterness is mentioned among the discharged soldiers themselves because of alleged inattention to their needs: 'One soldier, recommended for outdoor work only, was given a job as a clerk, and it is asked if there is any organisation to see to this kind of thing.' The new pensions tribunals are welcomed.

28. BIRDSEED IN THE NORTH-WEST

Workers in the North-West are great bird fanciers and there is indignation at the rise of the price of birdseed to as much as 15s a lb. Some are making it a class question: 'The rich can keep their canaries, but the poor man's pet must die.'

29. RUMOURS

There appears to be a slight increase in the number of rumours circulating, apart altogether from speculation about the opening of the European front. Typical examples are as follows: the Germans landed at Pegwell Bay at the beginning of the month (Sandgate); a German plane surrendered in the air and was escorted into Dyce by four Spitfires – it had a high German official on board (Aberdeen); Swindon's barrage balloons have been removed now that the local 'Wings for Victory' week is over. Some rumours are falsely attributed to BBC bulletins – that Turkey is in the war; and that 6s. in the £ is to be deducted from everybody's Post Office savings.

Careless talk by members of the Forces, mainly in trains, is also said to be increasing. Allegations of mention of shipping movements and shipping losses are made.

NO. 139: TUESDAY 25 MAY 1943 TO TUESDAY 1 JUNE 1943

I. GENERAL COMMENTS

1. GENERAL STATE OF CONFIDENCE AND REACTION TO NEWS

The level of public confidence remains high. People are expecting 'big things' to happen at any moment, and the Allied non-stop bombing offensive – which gives satisfaction in itself – is regarded as preparing the way for our invasion of Europe.

Other feelings making for optimism are 'the recollection of the African victory' and 'high hopes of the practical results of the Washington Conference'.

A number of people appear to think that the war may be over this year, but there are many who are 'not quite so cock-a-hoop and are afraid it will be a long and hard business yet'.

Comment on the home front is again slight, though criticism continues about the distribution of ration books and the shortage or poor quality of children's shoes. Many workers say they want a good holiday this summer – adding that they intend to travel; 'fatigue and the fine weather have made them long for a change of scene from the industrial set-up'.

2. THE ALLIED AIR OFFENSIVE

The Allied air offensive seems to be 'the main topic of conversation in most quarters'. 'The round-the-clock bombing of Germany, the mighty raids on the Ruhr and the persistent heavy attacks in the Mediterranean command the admiration and the wholehearted approval of the great majority of people.' It is felt that 'every bomb delivered is shortening the war'. People are delighted at 'the proof given every day that our air strength is constantly growing', and at 'the inability of the enemy to check us or retaliate effectively'.

There is overwhelming approval for speeches by Mr. Attlee, Mr. Eden, and Air Chief Marshal Sir Arthur Harris, in which they make it clear that the Allies will not be diverted from their bombing policy. 'The Government is just beginning to talk the only language that Hitler can understand.' Particular pleasure is expressed at the 'unequivocal answer' to Spanish suggestions for the restriction of aerial attacks – General Franco, it is thought, 'should be the last one to squawk: Nazi propaganda through Spain deceives nobody'.

THE PURPOSE AND EFFECT OF OUR BOMBING: 'The main feeling seems to be that the heavy bombing everywhere is a prelude to something bigger', and 'will be followed at a fairly early date by the landing of troops'. There are fewer reports this week of the feeling that the air offensive may be a substitute for a land invasion, but people are beginning to wonder whether 'increased and incessant attacks may render it unnecessary'.

There is reported to be great speculation as to whether 'the morale of Germans and Italians will soon show signs of cracking'. Those who doubtingly point out that German bombing in 1940–41 did not make our morale crack, meet with the reply: 'We in this country cannot imagine what an RAF raid is like: they are terrifyingly heavier than any we have experienced.' A few, however, persist in 'raising serious doubts of the efficacy of our raids': they say that 'the fact that the last raid on Dusseldorf was the fifty-second proves that previous damage inflicted could not have been as high as we had been led to believe – otherwise it would have been totally unnecessary to visit that city again'. Much the same is said about Essen.

THE PUBLIC'S ATTITUDE TO 'RELENTLESS' BOMBING: Unqualified approval of relentless air bombing, with little or no thought of enemy civilian casualties, appears to be the attitude of the majority, some of whom 'say freely that it is a good thing to kill the Germans, not so much from vindictiveness as from policy'. It is felt that 'none too soon are Germany and Italy being given the same battering which, in the past, they have given other countries'.

What appear to be a large minority, however, regard the bombing as 'horrible but necessary'. They 'don't enjoy the news because they realise the suffering produced', but they 'warmly approve the policy as a right means towards winning and ending the war' and 'have no wish to see the raids reduced in number and intensity'.

RAF LOSSES: Comments are reported on the loss of planes, and 'considerable sorrow is expressed for the loss of the gallant young airmen'. Reference is made to 'a feeling that the sons of widows should not be used as air crew personnel'.

THE BOMBING OF THE DAMS continues to be much discussed. There is great praise for 'the audacity of its conception and execution' ('Gibson VC is Hero No. 1 at present'), and the great majority agree that 'it was perfectly justified and may mean the shortening of the war by several months'. As a writer quoted by Postal Censorship says: 'I feel that this one episode has done more to shorten the war than any single effort to date.'

There are still, however, a considerable number – by no means only women – who 'express sympathy with the German civilian victims, even while they regard the raid as a valuable step towards victory'. 'Many people do not like to probe into their minds too deeply to discover their attitude to the drowning of civilians by floods' – 'Were not the people living around the path of the floods farm folk, not taking an active part in the war?' A small minority regard the bombing of Dortmund, so soon after the floods, as an instance of 'unnecessary brutality', or as at any rate 'unsporting'. The question is raised as to whether it was 'a breach of international law to bomb the people's water supply'. It is also still asked 'whether British prisoner-of-war camps would suffer from floods from the burst dams'.

Intense adverse criticism continues to be reported of the story that the attack on the dams was inspired by a Jewish refugee. Reprisals on Jews in occupied countries are still expected, in spite of the official contradictions of the Jew story.

THE BOMBING OF ITALY: Particular satisfaction is expressed at 'the air onslaught on the Italians'. Many seem to think that Italy 'may be forced into submission by bombing alone'. Some people are 'surprised that no ultimatum, coupled with a terrible threat, has been sent to that country – as, for example, that 1,000 bombers will go for Rome if total surrender does not come within a definite time'. There is much talk of possible raids on Rome, of which many people are said to be in favour. People say 'Italian planes helped the Germans to bomb us and our King in 1940; why should we not bomb the Pope?' On the whole, the majority feeling is said to be that 'Rome should be bombed, if it is necessary for the war effort'.

3. THE NEXT MOVE

Many people expect 'to wake up one morning soon and find a landing has been made on European shores', while others think 'it may take some time yet' either because 'it'll take so much organising', or because 'we may be waiting for Mr. Churchill's return'. The majority are patient, however, and confidently leave the decision as to how, when and where, to 'those in command'; yet it is hoped that our offensive 'will be timed in co-operation with Russia'.

Realisation is very general that 'the battle is bound to be hard, and casualties heavy, but people are grimly determined we must go through with it'.

Only a small minority feel that 'we may be leaving things too late', and much less comment is reported this week about 'the air offensive being all we shall see this year'.

SPECULATION:

(a) The most commonly held theory now is that Italy will be invaded, probably via Sicily and Sardinia. She is, it is fairly widely felt, on the verge of collapse, and people wonder whether the pounding she is getting from the air 'will do the trick by itself' – or whether 'she will wait until she's attacked before throwing up the sponge'. On the other hand, one report suggests 'this is an under-estimation of Italian fighting qualities; she may put up a stiff resistance for a short while'.

(b) OTHER THEORIES: It is again suggested that the next moves 'will probably be at a number of points simultaneously', and the Balkans – perhaps through Turkey – are in some cases coupled with Italy.

Far behind these possibles come France, Norway, Holland and Belgium, and, according to two reports, 'people are wondering what help we will get from the subjugated countries'.

Every theory has its rumour or rumours 'to back it up': 'Troops and war material are leaving from all African ports' ... 'A British raiding party dropped by parachute in France found feeling overwhelmingly in favour of the Allies' ... 'Flat-bottomed boats have gone north, it is rumoured on Teesside, which indicates Norway will be attacked.'

CRITICISM OF MR. LYTTELTON'S 'I KNOW' PRONOUNCEMENT continues to be reported. Opinions about it include: (i) 'I don't believe he knows at all.' (ii) 'Even if he does, he shouldn't say so; it's not a good example of keeping silent.' (iii) 'Several men in the Government', it is felt, 'must know but they do not appear in public like schoolchildren saying "I've got a secret but I'm not going to tell you"'.

4. THE PRIME MINISTER'S VISIT TO WASHINGTON

Whole-hearted approval continues to be reported and is confirmed in a Special Postal Censorship report where every one of over three hundred writers mentioning Mr. Churchill's visit echoes the sentiment: 'Our Winnie is away again to arrange final Victory'. Although his presence in America is thought to be having 'a tonic effect on Anglo-American relations', people will be glad to hear of his safe return, as 'they're anxious till he gets back'. There is some speculation as to his present or future whereabouts: 'Is he in Gibraltar, as the Axis say, or is that only a "kite"?' 'Will he visit Stalin after Washington?'

THE CONFERENCE: It is felt that 'big things are being brewed', and the public 'await with full confidence either news of the decisions reached, or, if that is not possible, their results'. Two Regional reports mention some regret that M. Stalin was not present.

THE SPEECH TO CONGRESS is again praised as masterly – some say 'his best yet' – and warm appreciation is unanimous. Its reception by the Americans has also given pleasure.

'The chief value of the speech is felt to lie in Mr. Churchill's assurances to the Americans that Britain has no intention of quitting, as far as Japan is concerned.' Comment on the fact that this part of the speech aroused the greatest applause in America – greater than that for Russia – is that 'the war nearest home concerns one most'.

5. TUNISIA

Talk is dying down, but deep satisfaction at 'a splendid job well done' continues; one of the effects of 'the great victory' is to have 'inspired confidence in our war direction, our generalship, our men and our arms'.

The publication of photographs of the 51st Highland Division entering Tunisia has given great pleasure to Scottish people: 'They were cut out and pasted up in shipyards and factories and many admiring comments were passed on the proud bearing of the soldiers.' In Cornwall, 'the recently arrived air mail which has brought Cornish families great news of the Cornish regiments' part in enabling the armour to go through in the final campaign' has had a heartening effect.

LEAVE: There is again reference to hope, and in some cases belief, that 'our lads who have been fighting in Africa will be given home leave as soon as possible'.

HONOURS: It is hoped that our Generals will not be forgotten; otherwise it would be considered 'rather a shame to award GCBs to Generals MacArthur and Eisenhower and nothing to reward Generals Alexander and Montgomery'.

6. NORTH AFRICAN POLITICS

Full reports of reactions to the meeting between Generals Giraud and de Gaulle have not yet been received, but the first stages of the negotiations do not appear to have aroused a great deal of comment. Since the Allied victory in Tunisia, feeling about French political differences has been much reduced.

Satisfaction is recorded, however, that matters seem 'well on the way to being settled', although mingled with this is the feeling that it's 'about time too'. There is still some criticism of 'French politics', at which 'people throw up their hands in horror', and some suspicion of the French in general. In one Regional report the fear is mentioned that 'we shall probably have more trouble with the French than with the Germans after the war'.

Some sympathy is expressed for General de Gaulle: 'after all he was first to make the effort to free the French' … 'he has been rather badly treated by the Allies'. But there is a division of opinion about him: he is thought to 'have made a lot of fuss about the Algerian visit'.

THE FRENCH FLEET AT ALEXANDRIA: Mild pleasure appears to be the main reaction to the 'coming over' of the French ships. The tonnage of the ships gained is looked on as of 'secondary importance to the knowledge that more of France is behind us'.

In one Region there is said to have been some amusement at the 'few old crocks', while in another the incident has served as 'a rude reminder' that the fleet had refrained from joining our cause for so long.

7. THE FAR EAST

Although it is universally agreed that 'Hitler is public enemy No. 1' and our first concern is Germany, Mr. Churchill's renewed assurances that we are 'in to the hilt with the USA in the war in the Pacific' have increased interest in the Far Eastern war and given much satisfaction. It is hoped that the Japanese may soon be 'bombed on their homeland ... Tokyo as heavily as London' – and that the Americans may be able to use the Aleutian Islands as a base for this purpose. It is said that 'Japan is no longer looked on as an enemy that will be easily defeated'; some think 'a tougher nut even than Germany', and 'people want full vengeance'. On the other hand, one Regional report says there is still a tendency to 'leave it to the Americans'; and some people do not yet realise that the Far East war will not end with the collapse of Germany.

PRISONERS OF WAR: Relatives of prisoners take the war against Japan very seriously. It is thought that the 'withholding of names by Japan for nearly a year and a half was the most pronounced cruelty that man could devise'. It is feared that should the Allies bomb cities under Japanese control 'prisoners will be put in places more vulnerable to attack'. There is also some concern among the relatives of serving men who may have to fight the Japanese.

BURMA: It is hoped that we shall soon make progress in this area, both in order to help China and to remove the danger to India. The work of the Commandos in Burma is spoken of with admiration.

8. RUSSIA

Again, comparatively little comment is reported on the Russian military situation. There is some speculation about 'developments expected shortly', and many hope that 'Russia and the Allies have planned to strike simultaneously'. Confidence in the Red Army remains high, and those who anticipate a German move feel that Russia will be 'able to deal with the blow', but 'we must do something to take the strain from her shoulders'.

DISBANDMENT OF THE COMINTERN: Satisfaction is again expressed at the decision to dissolve the Comintern. But a 'right-wing minority' think 'Stalin has simply removed a "propaganda front" to his shop, business inside being unchanged'; and 'it will be unfortunate if people here believe too open-mindedly that the Russian leopard is changing his spots'. Some interest is reported in the religious aspect and a possible 'closer unity between the Eastern and Western Churches'.

There is speculation about the attitude of the Labour Party towards affiliation with the Communists. It is thought that 'the responsible men' will not want any truck with the Communists 'who are definitely undemocratic in outlook'; although some 'left' opinion suggests that there is 'now no real bar to affiliation'.

THE RUSSO-POLISH DISPUTE now arouses little interest. A special Postal Censorship Report suggests that 'blame is about equally divided'. Poland appears to be losing some sympathy; workers describe it as a 'capitalist stronghold with reactionary tendencies'. This feeling appears to have been stimulated by the belief that the 'Polish press has too much freedom in Britain to publish anti-Semitic and anti-democratic papers' which are 'against the ideals we are fighting for'.

9. AIR RAIDS ON THIS COUNTRY

Recent raids on this country, though not apparently affecting morale, have resulted in criticism of our defences and rumours of exaggerated damage and casualties.

(a) CRITICISM OF DEFENCES:

SUNDERLAND AND NEIGHBOURING COASTAL TOWNS: Indignation is reported at (i) the weakness of the AA fire, coupled with allegations that the Home Guard were not up to the mark ('now that the Home Guard have taken over, the fire has deteriorated'); (ii) the absence of night fighters, a smoke screen, and, in Sunderland itself, a balloon barrage: 'Sunderland and South Shields have been sacrificed to Newcastle.' Sunderland people are now said to be 'pleased that balloons have gone up though some would like even more'. Rumours of more AA guns also give satisfaction.

CARDIFF: There are continued complaints about 'inadequate defences during the raid' ... 'a general remark is that "if the defences were considered efficient, then Heaven help us in any future raids"'.

BOURNEMOUTH: The recent raid is 'reported to have had some effect in Poole and Weymouth, where the question of fighter patrols over coastal towns has again been raised'. Some Weymouth people 'feel that with the great expansion of the RAF a few fighters might patrol to destroy the raiders *before* they drop their bombs, not after'.

SOUTH-EAST COAST: 'Inhabitants of Rye are apprehensive because the AA guns in their area have been reduced.' They find the situation difficult to understand 'at a moment when this coast is nearest to the Hun of anywhere in the world'.

ABERDEEN: 'Bitter feelings are still reported regarding the alleged inadequate defences.'

(b) RUMOURS: There are rumours of:

    (i) EXAGGERATED DAMAGE at Sunderland, Cardiff, and Brighton.

    (ii) EXAGGERATED CASUALTIES at Cardiff, where they were multiplied by three in the town itself, and by ten in a town twenty miles away. 'Greatly exaggerated figures of casualties to RAF personnel at Bournemouth' were said to be current in Portsmouth, Southampton and Winchester.

The delay in giving news of local damage and casualties is said to give rise to discontent and anxiety, and to cause the 'exaggerated and fantastic rumours'. It is 'wondered whether more details could be given without their being of service to the enemy'.

10. WAR AT SEA

Comment remains slight. It is felt that the shipping position is improving, and the news of U-boat losses is said to have 'gratified' people. Confidence is reported in our 'ability to counter successfully the U-boat menace'. The improved shipping position in the Mediterranean is also 'a cause of much satisfaction'.

People are reported to be full of admiration for the work of the Royal Navy in all waters, but especially for 'the splendid support given to the Allied Armies in North Africa', and for 'the small craft that operate round our shores, particularly in the North Sea and Channel' ... 'Dash, intrepid command, combined with superior seamanship and tactical skill, remain the characteristics of British naval forces, officers and men.'

11. CHURCH BELLS

There is further appreciation this week of the removal of the ban on the ringing of the church bells, particularly of the decision to raise the ban completely.

The ringing of the bells is said to 'sound like peacetime' and to bring an optimistic feeling that we are 'over the worst'. It is also taken as 'some indication' that there is now no fear of invasion.

12. BROADCASTING AND PRESENTATION OF NEWS

Comment on the presentation of news is slight this week. Four Regions report that 'the recent handling of the news has been satisfactory', though it is said 'the fact that the news has been good has saved the BBC from its previous habit of amplifying and glorifying minor incidents'.

It is thought by some that 'too much gloating and unnecessary detail' about the bombing of the Ruhr dams was given by both press and BBC. There is again 'condemnation of the stupidity of releasing the German Jewish refugee story'. 'What is a censor for anyway?'

Praise is reported this week for the *War Commentary* by Major Lewis Hastings (May 20), for his joint *War Commentary* with Squadron Leader John Strachey

(May 13) and for Mr. Edward Murrow's *Postscript* (May 9). The *Postscript* by a Polish refugee has been both praised and criticised. It is said to have been considered 'ill-timed and in bad style' – 'just right to create a bad impression about the Poles'.

II. SPECIAL COMMENTS

13. INDUSTRY

STRIKES: Unrest among transport workers is still reported in the Northern, North-Eastern, North Midland and North-Western Regions; in the Sheffield area it is partly attributed to 'unreasonable delay in arbitration proceedings'. There is said to be a good deal of sympathy for the employees 'who are not as well paid as they should be', but strike action is nevertheless strongly condemned, and it is felt that 'strong measures should be taken to stamp it out'. In the North Midland and North-Western Regions, miners are also criticised for using, or threatening to use, 'the strike weapon'.

14. NEW RATION BOOK DISTRIBUTION

The difficulties of obtaining new ration books continue to be a major topic of discussion. Complaints, which follow the lines indicated last week, are chiefly of time wasted in obtaining the new books, and come from all Regions except Northern Ireland, where the distribution has only just begun. Employers and workers particularly resent the loss of working hours, and in the latter case loss of pay has been an added irritation. Time is said to have been chiefly wasted through:

(1) TRANSPORT DIFFICULTIES: Long distances and inadequate transport are the chief complaints of country dwellers, who also resent the money, sometimes as much as 2/- or 2/6, spent on fares to the Food Office.

(2) QUEUEING AT THE FOOD OFFICES: Stories are reported of people queueing for three or four hours, of expectant mothers fainting, and of the difficulties of mothers with small children.

(3) THE INNACURATE FILLING IN OF APPLICATIONS for the new books.

The distribution is criticised as 'one of the most badly organised schemes of the war – just another Civil Service muddle', and in rural areas is alleged to have caused 'much resentment and contempt for officialdom'. The grumbling is said to have been all the worse because 'the Ministry of Food was regarded as one of the best managed Ministries, and Lord Woolton was very much looked up to before'. The headquarters of the Ministry is more blamed 'for the mess' than the local offices, 'who should have been given more discretion in making local arrangements'. It is also asked why the help of the WVS was not invoked at once, 'as it has been on previous occasions'.

GOOD LOCAL ORGANISATION, resulting in no complaints of delay, is reported from many districts, chiefly urban areas. In one area this is attributed to good local publicity about times of attendance; in another, the unofficial help of the WVS is highly praised. In the Southern Region, where the 'block collection' of books from factories has been undertaken, it is said to have worked well.

THE ADVERTISEMENTS IN THE NATIONAL PRESS are praised in two reports, but it is suggested that they may not have been understood by ignorant people.

LORD WOOLTON'S BROADCAST (May 28) was welcomed: 'it eased the situation when things were heading for a real mess'. His 'frank admission of miscalculation' is praised, and his concessions are reported to have 'removed a great deal of resentment'. 'What a pity he didn't make it ten days ago' is the only critical comment.

PRESENT POSITION: Six Regions report that the situation is improving in many areas, and 'though feeling is still strong and bitter in some places', the improved organisation 'is beginning to subdue criticism'.

15. FOOD

The only respects in which the food situation appears to differ from that reported last week are with regard to:

(a) THE REMOVAL OF HOME-PRODUCED TINNED FRUITS FROM POINTS: This is reported to have given great pleasure to many housewives, and 'almost a feeling of getting something for nothing'. For many, however, satisfaction was tempered by the fear that 'these goods would now be unobtainable in the shops' or 'resentment that they had already disappeared'. There are 'allegations of large-scale under-the-counter sales' and comments such as: 'It'll all go to shop assistants and their friends.'

Housewives who bottle their own fruit are said, in one report, to be asking 'why the Ministry of Food is telling the public that English canned plums and damsons should be eaten before the end of June, while home-bottled fruit can be kept for two or three years'.

(b) FRUIT: A 'great and growing longing for fruit' is mentioned in three reports. Annoyance is expressed at 'the disappearance of rhubarb, just when it should be plentiful'. People are anxious for 'plenty of fruit to be released at reasonable prices for eating and bottling'. Some are asking 'why we don't bring back lemons and oranges from Algiers', instead of prisoners: 'Why let our sailors risk their lives and use up valuable shipping space? – we're short enough of food here as it is.'

(c) TOMATOES: 'The advent of tomatoes is eagerly awaited.' People are already asking where they are and familiar comments are heard about commodities disappearing when the price is controlled.

(d) BREAD: There are complaints that bread is 'deteriorating in quality' and 'drying more quickly than previously'; that 'housewives on full-time work cannot obtain bread either at lunch time or in the evening'; and that 'bakers are not making 1 lb loaves, with the result that much is wasted in small families who have to take the 2 lb loaf'.

(e) 'A NO-COUPON HOLIDAY' is reported as 'a new racket from Brighton and Worthing'. It is alleged that people stay at one hotel just long enough to escape giving up their ration books before moving on to the next.

16. FIRE GUARDS

Complaints about some aspect of fire-watching come from seven Regions this week. The complaints, mostly from one Region each, are as follows:

(a) 'Fire-watching in many districts has become a farce, because of the very remote chances of any raids, yet people still carry on just in case.' It is suggested that 'in smaller and less populous districts the manning of Fire-Guard posts at business premises on an alert would be more effective than the present system'.

(b) Lack of uniformity of duties. 'Some firms start half an hour before blackout – others at 6.00 p.m. or later. Let there be a definite ruling: fire-watchers do not know where they are.'

(c) People are 'getting out of fire-watching'. 'A number of women who wanted exemption did not register, because they were unaware that they should have registered in any case.'

(d) 'Old and established volunteers resent taking orders from new group leaders.'

(e) Women object to having to act as Fire Guards 'in those areas of the town (Weymouth, in this case) most vulnerable to attack, especially when these areas are already demolished by previous raids'.

MISS ELLEN WILKINSON'S address to representatives of local authorities in Leeds does not appear to have been very well received.

17. AGRICULTURE

Criticism of the Government scheme for rural housing continues along familiar lines.

Two reports this week refer to criticism of the publicity about harvest helpers, and to demands for a clear statement to prospective helpers about the work available and particularly the correct place at which to make application for holidays. Kent farmers are reported to be very worried about labour for the coming harvest; they also fear that petrol restrictions will make it difficult for holiday workers to reach the farms.

18. RUMOURS

The story of a woman dying of shock on discovering, on a visit to her husband in hospital, that he had lost both his arms and legs in Tunisia has again been in circulation – in Nottingham; this is apparently a rumour current in the last war. The old story of the salvaging of the *Ark Royal* is once more reported from Merseyside. Hess and von Arnim are said to be confined in a mansion near Abergavenny.

It is rumoured that 900 gallons of petrol were issued for the Newark by-election.

NO. 145: TUESDAY 6 JULY 1943 TO TUESDAY 13 JULY 1943

I. GENERAL COMMENTS

1. GENERAL STATE OF CONFIDENCE AND REACTION TO NEWS

Until Saturday morning, people were inclined to be 'bored and apathetic' and concerned rather with their own affairs than with the war. Impatience at the delay in launching our expected offensive had increased when activity on the Russian front 'flared up into a large-scale offensive'.

Saturday's news of our invasion of Sicily, however, has 'changed the scene, and revitalised the public's confidence and interest'. Many people were openly excited at the news of the landings: 'The war has begun at last – what a thrill!' A few even thought we should be 'through Sicily in a couple of days'. But the majority seem to have received the news 'with profound but undemonstrative relief' and without great excitement; they 'hope it's going to bring us a bit nearer to the end' and are glad at the thought that the offensive may relieve pressure on Russia. Most people realise that 'the invasion of Europe is a colossal task' and that the invasion of Sicily is only the beginning. Nevertheless, confidence is steady, but comment is reserved while more news is eagerly awaited.

The news from Sicily has put other war fronts to the back of people's minds, but home front topics continue to be of great interest. Of these, 'holidays is the only one which can compete with Sicily', but there is also much talk of pensions, clothing problems (stimulated by Mr. Dalton's forecast of coupon reductions) and the shortage of fresh fruit and tomatoes. There are still reports of war strain, particularly among women workers.

2. SICILY

Excitement, pleasure, relief and some surprise are reported at the news of the Sicilian landings. The Prime Minister's 'autumn leaves' reference had indicated that our offensive was certain but not necessarily imminent, and people were growing restive and anxious at our inactivity in face of the strong German attacks in Russia. The report of heavy air attacks on Sicily during the days preceding invasion had prepared some people for the news of a landing, though others felt it was too obvious a choice.

There is general satisfaction that the lull has been brought to an end. Opinion is, however, divided between those who look on Sicily as just another Mediterranean island which has to be cleared up before we can start upon a European offensive, and those who regard this as the beginning of the major offensive itself.

The size and 'thoroughness of the combined operations' are greatly admired – 'If Sicily is a nut, we are using a sledgehammer to crack her' ... 'and quite right too'. 'The news that Generals Alexander and Montgomery were in charge gave everyone an additional lift', and so did the presence of the Eighth Army. Many were surprised that we 'landed so easily'; the operations are thought to be going 'excellently' and their success seems to be taken for granted. The majority, however, 'appreciate the immensity of the task and are not prepared to underestimate the enemy' – particularly if there are many Germans among them. Only a few are said to have thought that Sicily would be overrun in a couple of days; its fall was actually rumoured last Saturday night and announced from a theatre stage in Newcastle.

People are prepared for heavy casualties sooner or later, and 'some apprehension among wives and mothers of serving men is noted'. The report that initial casualties were slight has been received with thankfulness and has raised hopes that 'it isn't going to be so bad after all'.

THE NEXT MOVE, AFTER SICILY, is the subject of much speculation. Among a great variety of suggestions, the most popular seem to be that, once Sicily is ours, we shall attack Italy proper, the Balkans, or both.

3. RUSSIA

There is general confidence in the Russians' ability to hold the new German attack: 'Germany is wasting her time battering at an iron and concrete wall that will never fall.' The present fighting is thought to be 'a madman's last desperate gamble'.

There is, however, surprise at the strength of the German offensive. People are asking 'where such numbers of tanks are produced by the Germans, if we have smashed their industrial centres'. It is also regarded as 'a salutary reminder to the over-optimistic' and has 'killed some talk of German morale cracking'.

Comments on the Sicilian front are coupled with satisfaction that 'at last we are starting an offensive which will help the Red Army'.

Doubt as to accuracy of the figures of German losses in men and materials given by the Soviet High Command is reported from seven Regions: 'The loss of 185 planes in one day caused the Nazis to give up in the Battle of Britain. Why do not their alleged colossal losses in Russia bring about a similar result?' There is equal doubt about the German figures of Russian losses.

4. GENERAL SIKORSKI

Widespread and genuine regret outweighs all other sentiments at the death of General Sikorski. The effect of his death on future Polish policy, particularly in connection with Russo-Polish relations, is the cause of some speculation. He is felt to have been a 'moderate man' and to have had a 'fairly sound policy', though the Polish government is criticised 'for being too right-wing and illiberal'. The hope is expressed that 'the leaderless Poles will not fall to squabbling like the French'.

Speculation as to whether his death was due to sabotage is reported from six Regions. 'It is felt his death is a mystery which is still unsolved' and 'it is considered necessary that an inquiry should be instituted to discover how four engines could "cut out at once"'. It is hoped that the German version 'that we bumped him off to get the Polish and Russian affair straight' is not believed by other countries.

Again this week it is pointed out that air travel is dangerous for important persons, and it is hoped that the King and Mr. Churchill 'will not risk further journeys by air'.

COLONEL VICTOR CAZALET: Regret is reported from three Regions at the death of Colonel Victor Cazalet. In south-east Kent special interest was taken because of the popularity of the Cazalet family there. Sincere sympathy and regret for 'the loss of a likeable personality' are reported from his constituency in the South-Western Region.

5. AIR OFFENSIVE

Less comment about our air offensive is reported this week. Satisfaction 'with our overwhelming strength in air power', however, continues to be widespread, although many people 'now take our big Ruhr raids for granted' and are said to be 'bored by BBC raid recitals'. At the same time, a minority are reported to be disappointed at 'the recent lull', particularly 'as it coincided with a spell of good weather'. Distaste for 'gloating' continues, as also does 'severe criticism' of Dean Inge for his article on bombing (July 2), which is described as 'a gift to German propaganda'.

OUR LOSSES: Many people are still concerned over our losses, and some ask if a percentage of losses could be published, weekly or monthly. In the South-Eastern district, however, the recent explanations in the press and BBC are said to have had a good effect.

THE BOMBING OF ROME continues to be strongly advocated, 'even if it does mean bombing the Vatican'. The 'restraining hidden hand' is still suspected. A minority of 'educated people' – mainly Catholic – 'consider the bombing would be an act of vandalism to be avoided at all costs'.

6. AIR RAIDS ON THIS COUNTRY AND CIVIL DEFENCE

Air Marshal Sir Trafford Leigh Mallory's Birmingham speech (June 26) has aroused a good deal of discussion on the possibility and probability of heavy reprisal raids. The Air Marshal is severely criticised for his 'over-optimism', which is thought to have 'led to apathy and indifference' and to 'have discouraged Civil Defence workers'; the Home Secretary is praised 'for ticking him off' (House of Commons, June 30). But 'such contradictory statements by high-up officials' are said to irritate and confuse the public.

While many do not believe Germany will again be able to make heavy raids on this country, others, though not apprehensive, think 'they may have another go at us when a European front is established'.

CIVIL DEFENCE DEBATE (June 30): Some interest is reported, together with suggestions that 'a general overhaul of the Civil Defence organisation is much needed'. The new raid warning system has aroused great interest in the South-Eastern 'front-line area', where there is some anxiety because 'no definite news has yet been communicated to the Civil Defence officials who will be called on to operate the system'. Miss Wilkinson's reference to 'the dangers to the health of some workers' has been well received, and is thought to apply particularly to women with home responsibilities.

EAST GRINSTEAD RAID (July 9): In spite of the heavy loss of life incurred by the bombing of the local cinema, 'the morale of the people' is described as 'sound'. 'The tragedy is accepted, albeit sorrowfully as an unlucky chance.' The Civil Defence workers and the local troops who helped to clear the debris are praised, and there is said to have been 'no criticism of the defences or anyone else'.

'The most painful scenes were at the improvised mortuary where the difficult task of identification was proceeding.'

LOW-FLYING PLANES: Criticism of low-flying planes 'which worry and upset the population' continues to be reported.

7. THE WAR AT SEA

Great satisfaction is felt over the shipping position and people are confident that all possible measures to combat the U-boat are being taken. 'The Navy and the RAF have now got their measure.' It is, however, realised that 'the Allies still have a long way to go'. There is pleasure 'that even Hitler's most ardent liar, Goebbels, has been forced to admit that the U-boat is not the power it was intended to be'.

The announcement that news of the battle against the U-boats will in future be given in a joint monthly statement is welcomed – 'provided sufficient details are given to enable the public to appreciate the size and complexity of the problem'.

8. NORTH AFRICAN POLITICS

Comment continues without much change. General de Gaulle – whatever criticism there may have been of him during the Algiers negotiations – has throughout remained the more popular of the two generals. Even those among whom he is not popular feel 'he is the more worthy of trust'.

The anti de Gaulle movement in the American press is 'watched with concern', and there is some feeling that not only is America 'backing Giraud, but we are weakening towards de Gaulle'.

THE 'MARSEILLAISE': People are confused about why a Free French newspaper should be banned. 'As this coincides with Giraud's visit to the USA', they wonder whether it is further proof of de Gaulle 'being pushed aside in favour of Giraud'.

9. FAR EAST

Satisfaction with the offensive in the Pacific continues. At the same time, some wonder whether 'too much is being made of very small successes against the Japs – as compared with their victories in the past'.

Interest in this theatre of war is still limited to a few – particularly relatives of men serving there; it is looked on as 'so remote', and 'anything east of Cairo seems beyond the average man's imagination'. 'Not one in twenty know where Munda is.'

CHINA: Admiration for the Chinese continues, and people are worried that we are not doing more for them.

10. THE PRIME MINISTER'S GUILDHALL SPEECH (JUNE 30TH)

Many expressions of approval for Mr. Churchill's recent speech are again reported, on exactly the same lines as last week.

'Of the Prime Minister himself praise is widespread, one comment being that "he will go down to posterity as one of the greatest leaders this world has ever produced".'

11. HOLIDAYS

There is the same intensity of desire 'to get away for a few days' change; belief that a holiday away is necessary, particularly for housewives and all workers – certainly those who have been working a seven-day week; and finally a widespread determination to get away'. Few are deterred by transport, accommodation and feeding difficulties.

Stories of trippers and week-enders and long queues at stations continue to be reported.

TRANSPORT: Industrial workers feel that they have special claims on transport, whether in their capacity as workers or holiday-makers. Thus, though they themselves complain of holiday-makers crowding them off trains and buses on their way to and from work, they also resent any criticism of their own 'hard-earned jaunts'.

Some people think 'the Government should assist by providing additional transport to enable tired workers to spend a real holiday away; otherwise the health of the nation is bound to suffer next winter'.

On the other hand, railway companies are criticised for 'their lack of principle, and shilly-shallying policy'. It is felt that 'they don't practise what they preach'; particular objection was taken in Wales to an announcement that 'the LMS ran a special train for their staff to Blackpool'.

HOLIDAYS AT HOME: In the 'general scramble' to take holidays away, there is little reference to holidays at home. In some areas satisfaction is reported with 'the municipal arrangements provided in parks', but in others it is felt these could have been developed much more. In Belfast, however, parents in one area of the town are threatening to boycott the amusements 'because of the exorbitant charges for children and adults on the "dodgems" and flying chairs'.

12. DETENTION CAMP DEATH

Uneasiness about detention camps in general, and Rifleman Clayton's case in particular, continues to be reported. Considerable blame is felt to attach to the medical officer, but at the same time, the sentences imposed on the two NCOs are considered 'ridiculously light'.

13. YOUTH

During the past seven weeks, ten Regional reports have referred (most of them more than once) to the behaviour of young people. Public concern is increasing about:

(a) THE GROWTH OF JUVENILE DELINQUENCY. 'Children and young
people don't seem to know right from wrong.'
     The present methods of treatment are considered inadequate:
'The position needs serious consideration and careful and sympathetic
investigation.' In Wales, 'calls are made' for younger magistrates and for
teacher magistrates.

(b) THE UNRULINESS AND DESTRUCTIVENESS of children and youths.
Particular mention is made of their destruction of produce in allotments
and of bombed property. Instances are also given: (i) from Isleworth, of
'small boys who started fires which gutted a church, the police station, and
two fire stations'; (ii) from Battle, of boys who 'slashed and tore a marquee
especially erected for the feeding of troops and broke up the tables inside'.

(c) THE IMMORALITY OF YOUNG GIRLS, particularly those in their early
teens. Stories are reported from the Eastern Region of 'innumerable girls
being pregnant by US soldiers, whether black or white'; and in the North
Midland Region the conduct of young girls with black troops is felt to call
for better surveillance.

(d) EXCESSIVE DRINKING by lads and young girls, 'the girls being tempted
by the Forces'.

Lack of parental control is felt in all these cases to be 'the root of the evil' ...
'mothers having to work and fathers in the Forces'. Some people feel that 'mothers
of young children should not be encouraged to work', and the absence of mothers is
particularly regretted 'just when young girls are at an age to need them most'.

High wages paid to juveniles, and cinema-going, are considered as contributory
factors.

JUVENILE LABOUR: From Scotland and the Midland Region come complaints
of 'increasing disciplinary troubles with juvenile labour'. The difficulty of 'sacking
the lads' is said 'to make them cheekier than ever'.

YOUTH ORGANISATIONS: There has been some praise for youth clubs and
organisations – 'which are taking children off the streets' – and people regret that
'a large number of boys and girls are not touched by them – particularly those most
needing guidance and control'. 'Young people on leaving school', some feel, 'should
be compelled to join some youth organisation for at least two years, just as they are
compelled to attend school'.

There is concern about the waste of food in youth hostels and clubs. Some people
feel that to supply food to them is merely encouraging 'social evenings'. At the same
time, it is thought 'to be unfair that voluntary organisations such as Scouts and Guides,
which were doing good work in pre-war days, are omitted from such a scheme'.

Alarm among a few is reported from two Regions at 'the secularising of the
Sabbath', and protests have again been made against youth parades during hours of
divine service. Opinion is divided as to young people's attitude to religion: some feel
that it needs to be thrust upon them, while others remark on a spontaneous desire
for religious knowledge among the GATC, and on 'the earnest support given to
Chippenham's Religion and Life week'.

14. BROADCASTING AND PRESENTATION OF NEWS

There has been much greater eagerness to hear the news since the announcement of the Sicilian landings. More information would be welcome, but 'security problems are fairly well realised' – though it is said that 'there is more on the European and American news'. With regard to press treatment, it is felt that 'with news yet sparse, editors are wise in not raising hopes too high'.

Broadcasts from Italy and Germany are receiving more attention, mainly to 'see what sort of a tale they will make'.

COLOGNE CATHEDRAL: Radio counter-propaganda and the publication of photographs are again reported to have been appreciated.

BBC PROGRAMMES: There is again praise for Mr. Priestley's *Make it Monday* series. He is thought to be 'homely and direct', although some think broadcasts of this type 'make no contribution to national unity'. There is praise also for John Hilton's *Postscript*, July 9; Sir Stafford Cripps' broadcast, July 9; *The Radio Doctor*; Thursday evening *War Commentaries*; also *The Radio Padre*; Dr. Evatt (July 4); talks by Colonial speakers; and the *Red on the Map* series.

There is some desire for more talks on current affairs in the style of *The World Goes By*, and for more discussion on post-war agricultural and industrial policy.

'Impatience' is expressed with talks by men on fuel, cookery and household management, and there is criticism of 'too much heavy classical music' and 'too much jazz'.

II. SPECIAL COMMENTS

WEEKLY SUMMARY

15. PENSIONS AND ALLOWANCES

Comment is reported from ten Regions this week. The pension question 'looms large in people's minds' and is thought by many to be the most discussed subject on the home front. Criticism is on similar lines to last week.

It is felt that 'the Government got a jolt on the pensions debate', but 'if there's warmth in the House of Commons it is nothing to the tropical heat in the country'. There is condemnation of the 'grudging spirit' with which pensions are granted, and general 'irritation with the Government, and the Minister of Pensions in particular, that there should be all this fight to get a just bill passed'. 'No one wants abuse of privileges', but it is felt 'far better that some should be granted pensions who do not deserve them, than that others should be left with grievances like running sores'. Middle-aged people have 'bitter recollection' of treatment after the last war and are anxious this should not happen to their children. Discussion is reported on the chances of a pension for the family of Rifleman Clayton, as it is felt that the Government must take responsibility for faulty diagnosis.

Some people are anxious about the new tribunals. They fear that the Ministry of Pensions tribunals may have 'the same disadvantages as present Ministry of Labour ones'. It is thought that the new tribunals should contain members 'who have had actual experience in war' and who can 'thus really appreciate the factors involved'.

16. THE POSSIBLE REDUCTIONS IN CLOTHING COUPONS

Mr. Dalton's forecast (July 7) of a probable reduction in the number of clothing coupons has been greeted with widespread concern – rising even to 'consternation'. Some people had even expected an increase in the allowance.

Particular alarm is reported from: (i) families with young children; (ii) 'working people, who claim that the present allowance is inadequate for present replacements'; (iii) housewives, who are 'already called on to provide, out of their own allotment, coupons for such things as curtains and towels'; (iv) 'women who live in very cold and exposed places (Northern Region) and are finding their coupons insufficient for warm underwear'.

'Shopkeepers are now complaining that they can get more stocks than there are coupons available', according to the North Midland Region report: 'the public interprets this as meaning that the proposed reduction is unjustified'. From the Northern Region comes a rumour that 'coupons are to be suspended for a period in order that shopkeepers may get down their overstocks'.

Comments on other aspects of clothes rationing follow familiar lines and will be summarised in the next report.

17. FOOD

SOFT FRUIT: The shortage and uneven distribution of soft fruit and tomatoes continue to be reported. Complaints follow the familiar lines of conditional sales, favoured customers, and the inability of war workers to obtain supplies. In Birmingham, there are allegations that Lewis' Stores get larger supplies because 'Lord Woolton is connected with them'.

JAM-MAKING: Pleasure at the increased sugar ration, but irritation because the necessary soft fruit is unobtainable, continue to be reported. In fruit-growing districts, housewives resent the bulk of the fruit going to the manufacturers, particularly 'in view of the bad quality of manufactured jam'. At the same time, there are housewives who feel that the increased sugar ration should have been given earlier and over a longer period, and suggest that sugar should have been made available in lieu of sweet rations.

INCREASED RATIONS FOR EXPECTANT MOTHERS, announced by the Ministry of Food on July 6, have been warmly welcomed.

NEW POTATOES: There are complaints of 'a muddle in the marketing of new potatoes'. Growers feel that they should have been allowed to market their new potatoes earlier, and there are complaints of 'price cutting', particularly from the South-Eastern district where it is alleged that potatoes from the Scilly Islands were sold at lower rates. Householders growing their own new potatoes are thought to have added to producers' marketing difficulties.

REDUCTION IN THE PRICE OF DRIED EGGS: The reduction in price continues to be welcomed; though shopkeepers complain that they are losing 2d.

on every packet, and some housewives are suspicious that the decreased price is 'an inducement to buy before the powder gets too bad'.

INCREASED POINTS VALUE FOR BISCUITS continues to be criticised.

MILK SUPPLIES: The Government's encouragement to producers of TT milk (announced July 8) has been welcomed, though small farmers in the South-Western Region fear that 'they may be cut out'.

18. AGRICULTURE

CROPS AND HARVESTING: Farmers in Cumberland, Northumberland and the South-West are pleased with the hay crop this year. There is much talk of harvesting prospects for different crops, and a hope that this year's harvest will be 'the best ever'. At the same time the apple crop in the North is expected to be poor, and reference is made to storms and blight having ruined rhubarb and gooseberries in the North-West.

The following points – some of them contradictory – are made about harvest helpers (none of them has been reported from more than two Regions):

(a) Sufficient publicity has not been given to the scheme, and there is a shortage of helpers.

(b) Applicants have come forward 'only to find there is insufficient work for them, or that it is non-existent'.

(c) The helpers have made a favourable impression on farmers. On the other hand, 'some farmers don't want amateur helpers'.

(d) The holiday-makers are glad to help and are very pleased with the labour camps.

FARM SUNDAY: This 'passed off quietly'. A few familiar 'grouses' about the waste of time and petrol continue.

19. STRIKES

TRANSPORT WORKERS: Discontent about wages and working conditions among transport workers is reported from the Northern and North-Eastern Regions, and particularly from the North Midland. To quote from the latter: 'Busmen and woman feel they are being unfairly treated, and probably there will be another strike unless they get a rise following the new talks. They are in sympathy with the railway workers and are co-operating with them.'

MINERS: In Scotland, the taking over of the Priory pit by the Government continues to excite a good deal of comment. 'The public are quite uncertain as to the rights of various parties, but very much hope that this will mean the end of trouble there. These collieries have an unenviable reputation as being the centre of continuous strife.'

THE FLEETWOOD FISHERMEN: Strong condemnation of this strike is reported from South Devon.

20. RUMOURS

Rumours are circulating in the Northern Region that anti-personnel bombs, in the form of explosive cigarette cases, fountain pens, and watches, were dropped at Hull. At Bradford, it is rumoured that the damage at Hull is 'terrific'.

A Methodist minister in Monmouth claims he is a cousin of Mr. Chenhalls, one of the victims of the Lisbon air liner disaster; he states his cousin bore an unusual facial resemblance to the Prime Minister; spies may have mistaken him for Mr. Churchill and thus brought about the attack on the air liner.

NO. 146: TUESDAY 13 JULY 1943 TO TUESDAY 20 JULY 1943

I. GENERAL COMMENTS

1. GENERAL STATE OF CONFIDENCE AND REACTION TO NEWS

A further rise in spirits is reported this week. The public appears 'more than satisfied with the first week's operations in Sicily', while the Russian counter-offensive and good news from the Battles of the Atlantic and the Pacific have all added to the feeling that 'we are on the road to victory'. At the same time, little excitement has been reported. The prevailing mood seems, rather, to be 'quiet satisfaction that we are on the offensive with a well-trained army and adequate equipment'.

Preliminary reports indicate that the bombing of Rome has caused widespread satisfaction, the only criticisms being that we did not do it sooner and that we 'bother to apologise'.

There is considerable discussion as to when the war in Europe will end. 'The optimists' say it will end this year; the majority say 'this time next year'; a few think it will last three or four more years. The feeling that we are 'within sight of the end' is said to be the cause of increasing discussion of post-war plans.

War-weariness is again reported, particularly among women, who dread another winter of blackout. 'Holiday hunger', and the determination to satisfy it, is the most widely discussed home front topic. There is also much talk of clothing problems (particularly the threatened coupon cut, and children's shoes), the shortage of fresh fruit and tomatoes, pensions, and the housing shortage.

2. SICILY

There is general satisfaction with the planning and progress of the Sicilian offensive, and complete confidence in the outcome. The general view seems to be that the island will be overrun 'within a very few weeks', or sooner. The public is particularly impressed with:

(a) 'THE REALITY OF COMBINED OPERATIONS': Each separate service of each separate nation has been highly praised, but the greatest satisfaction is reported at their co-ordination.

(b) THE 'EASE AND RAPIDITY' OF OUR PROGRESS AND THE LACK OF OPPOSITION: Many are said to be 'surprised at our easy landings and the lack of coastal defences and immediate opposition'. 'The absence of adequate measures of defence along the Sicilian coast is taken as a glaring exposure of Axis limitations' and has led to 'optimism about the results of possible landings elsewhere'. 'Reports of stiffening by Axis troops as the fighting moved north' – particularly 'the present battle of Catania' – have now resulted in a 'growing realisation of the difficulties'.

(c) THE 'LIGHTNESS OF OUR CASUALTIES' SO FAR has given great satisfaction, though there are still fears that they may yet be heavy.

MR. CHURCHILL'S AND PRESIDENT ROOSEVELT'S MESSAGE TO THE ITALIANS: There is widespread speculation on the possibility of an Italian collapse or capitulation in the near future; many people hope that Mr. Churchill's and Mr. Roosevelt's message – combined with the bombing of Rome – will help to bring this about. The terms of the message and its timing are considered very good, and 'it is welcomed as putting the onus of possible sufferings on the shoulders of the Italian people'.

Nevertheless, 'action rather than appeals is what the average man feels is wanted', and the message is criticised by those who are suspicious of any attempt to spare Italy; they feel that the Italians were wholeheartedly behind Mussolini when things were going well for them and badly for us, and that we should not now try to 'wheedle Italy out of the war by propaganda'.

There is some comment on the attitude of the civilians in Sicily, accounts of which are 'tempting people to hope that it may be an indication of the feelings of the whole Italian people towards the Allies'. But, though stories of the Sicilians' 'friendly attitude' are welcomed by many, others are sceptical and ask how friendly we should be if the Germans landed here.

3. THE BOMBING OF ROME

The bombing of Rome came as a surprise. It has been 'thoroughly approved of' by the great majority. Some, particularly Londoners and working-class people in Scotland, expressed delight and jubilation at the news; and there is a widespread feeling 'that what has long been needed, has been done, and about bloody time too'. Those who had not previously realised the military and strategic importance of Rome are particularly of this opinion.

The bombing is felt to be fully justified. Rome, it is said, is the capital and Mussolini's headquarters, and should be treated in the same way as Berlin, as a military objective. Workers particularly have 'no time for people who want to spare Rome – take a look at London'. Others who have not forgotten the bombing of English cathedrals ask: 'Be the objects of culture in Canterbury or Rome, what is the difference in their being destroyed?' A very small minority, however, feel 'that our stock would have been enhanced had we carried out the attack on Italy without resort to this act of vandalism'.

THE CULTURAL MONUMENTS: Among those who consider Rome as a cultural and religious centre, there have been some doubts and genuine regrets, particularly as it was realised that the strength of the attack would necessarily entail some damage 'on the fringe of targets'. Plans of the city are said to have been anxiously studied to see what historic buildings could have been destroyed, and relief is expressed that 'none were near the three main objectives'.

THE CAREFUL PLANNING OF THE RAID and the choice of targets has been approved, though surprise is expressed at the insistence on precision bombing 'when all raids are supposed to be carefully made on military objectives'. On the other hand, there is some adverse comment on the 'extra risks American airmen are reported to have had to take, to avoid bombing cultural monuments'.

In the London Region the alleged choice of Catholic airmen is thought to have been 'an astute move'.

THE DROPPING OF THE LEAFLETS beforehand is praised by many who thought the effect of the explanation to be worth while, but a considerable body of opinion criticised 'this unnecessary risk to airmen's lives'. 'Why should we bother to tell them? We don't need to apologise or explain our actions; they've asked for it!'

ROMAN CATHOLIC OPINION: On the whole, Catholics are reported to feel that the bombing is justified, particularly those who realise that Catholic churches in this country have been bombed. 'Catholic opinion', it is said, 'will be satisfied if the Vatican remains unscathed'. Resentment among Catholics is reported only from Northern Ireland.

4. THE NEXT MOVES

Although people are delighted with the invasion of Sicily, many appear to have expected, 'not an isolated movement in an obvious place, but a big-scale invasion in three or four parts of the Continent, including France, the Balkans and Norway'. Though welcomed as a sign that 'the war has started again', and as a diversion to help Russia, the Sicilian attack is 'not thought to qualify for the second front'. It is regarded, rather, as 'the first step in the invasion of the Continent', and there is much speculation about the successive steps. As before, suggestions range round the whole coast from Norway to Turkey. Many take for granted that the next step will be 'the immediate invasion of the Italian mainland'. This, it is thought, may lead to 'wholesale desertions by Italian troops' and the 'early collapse of Italy, followed by the break-up of the German army', thus making other invasions unnecessary.

5. THE ALLIED AIR OFFENSIVE

There is less comment on the air war this week, though satisfaction with the 'rising strength of our air power' continues. The bombing of Italian towns is highly praised, but before the news of the bombing of Rome was received, there was some demand for 'more intensified operations against Italy'. 'Why can't some of the bombers that go to Germany be switched over to Italy?' Disappointment is again expressed that our raids on Germany 'are now so spasmodic'. 'Why haven't they been kept up – is the weather bad over there?'

There is less concern about our losses, though people in the North Midland Region who have been to Grimsby since the recent raid are asking 'why it is necessary for such large numbers of our planes with such heavy loads to go to one German city many times, when so much damage can be done in Grimsby by a few planes'. On the whole, however, people are aware that our sustained bombing 'may ultimately save thousands of lives', and that it cannot be undertaken without casualties.

6. RUSSIA

Great satisfaction is reported with the events on the Russian front, and confidence in Russia remains steady. 'As the situation has developed from the Germans being held, to their being pushed back and finally to the Russians' own successful assault, the public's satisfaction has grown.' The German offensive is now considered 'to have slackened if not expired', and is regarded as 'Germany's last possible effort in this direction'. There had been some fear that 'the Germans might, in a final desperate offensive, be stronger than we have liked to believe'.

The accuracy of Russian figures of German losses in men and material continues to be doubted, though in two Regions some people are said to 'believe and relish the Russian reports'.

7. FAR EAST

Although events in the south-west Pacific are overshadowed by those in Sicily and Russia, there is slightly increased interest in the Pacific fighting. There is, however, still little detailed following of events on this far distant front.

There is praise for the efforts of the US troops and naval forces who are thought to be doing 'all that can be expected'. 'We don't expect startling events, but the tide has changed.'

A certain amount of discussion on 'how long the war in the East will last after the war in Europe has ended' is reported from four Regions. Some people are said 'to consider that after the destruction of the main enemy Germany, Japan will be an easy matter'. It is felt that 'Government propaganda should be working now to educate "these optimists"'. Some speculation as to when men serving in India and other parts of the Far East 'will be able to come home on leave' is also reported.

8. THE WAR AT SEA

'Recent assurances of decreases in shipping losses and increases in U-boat sinkings' continue to give general satisfaction, and there is much praise for the Royal and the Merchant Navies. 'The revelation of the seriousness of our shipping position two years ago has shocked some people', but everybody now seems 'satisfied there is nothing much to worry about'; some even think that 'the Battle of the Atlantic is won, and that we shall never again be in such dangers in this respect as in the past'. There is particular pleasure at the thought that the destruction of U-boats will 'ease the shipment of supplies when the major attack on Europe takes place'.

The proposal to issue monthly statements on the position is thought likely to be satisfactory.

9. NORTH AFRICAN POLITICS

Comment comes from six Regions only this week, but there is still anxiety at the lack of unity between the French generals, and some doubts about the French Committee for National Liberation.

All the reports express sympathy with General de Gaulle, who 'trusted Great Britain in 1940' and has been 'honestly and openly pro-British from the start', whereas General Giraud is thought to 'need watching'.

There is criticism of the attacks made on de Gaulle by the American press at the time of Giraud's visit to Washington; and the suppression of *La Marseillaise*, said to be 'bitterly resented in some quarters', has 'strengthened the belief that the US is calling the tune to which we dance'.

Some people wonder what is going on behind the scenes and hold the opinion that 'if de Gaulle has been difficult', there may have been other causes for this, more justifiable than personal ambition.

10. GENERAL SIKORSKI

There is little comment this week on the death of General Sikorski. His loss is generally regretted and deplored. Speculation continues as to the cause of the crash, and there is resentment in Plymouth, where the General's body was landed, at the German insinuations.

The resignation of the acting Prime Minister over differences in connection with the choice of the new Commander-in-Chief has inclined some to remark 'how these continentals love one another'. It is hoped that General Sikorski's successor will realise the importance of keeping his government on good terms with Russia.

11. THE EDUCATION WHITE PAPER

There is said to be considerable interest in the question of education, and preliminary reactions to the Board of Education's White Paper are highly favourable. The plan is thought to 'display vision' – 'a difficult problem admirably handled' – and particular approval is expressed for the proposal to raise the school-leaving age to 15.

A minority, while reserving their views 'until the details are fully considered', are asking if we can afford it. Two reports refer to sceptical teachers, their view being that 'the ideas are all very well, but they just won't work' – 'high-sounding ideas about curricula are no good for children who haven't the brain to benefit'. It is feared, too, that 'the shortage of teachers alone would cause considerable delay in putting the scheme into operation'.

12. HOLIDAYS

'At no time has the desire for a holiday been so apparent as this year.' People feel they must get away for a change and are determined to do so. 'Any qualms of conscience' are outweighed by the feeling that 'they're entitled to a holiday now after four years of war, with so many extra duties for housewives and workers'. In any case, 'it's in the national interest that our health shouldn't suffer; and we've got the money, and the war has taken a decided turn in our favour'.

People remain undeterred by the accommodation and supply difficulties, even by the increasing transport difficulties – which will be 'unimaginable by August'. In fact, workers, 'who discuss no other subject, have such a longing for the sea, that they're going to get a smell of it if they have to walk'.

Stories continue of thousands of people travelling and of 'enormous queues' at main line railway stations; of overnight queues again at Edinburgh, Glasgow and Aberdeen; of 40,000 leaving Belfast, many of them for Dublin.

Such queueing is considered 'all right for grown-ups, but it's a crime to expect children to stay in them overnight'.

There is increasing talk of residents and workers, particularly in rural areas and resorts, being ousted from trams and buses by holiday-makers and day trippers.

HOLIDAYS AT HOME cannot, it is felt, take the place of 'a real change – not even such amusements as the Big Top in Birmingham'.

THE GRANTING OF HOLIDAYS TO WORKERS: Resentment has been reported over:

(a) Failure of some firms to revert to full-scale holidays on a pre-war basis.
(b) Delay 'of a firm engaged on Government work to let their employees know when they were to get their annual week's holiday'. They only did so the day before the holiday was due.

HOLIDAY OPENING OF SCHOOLS: In the North-Western Region, there is some criticism of the continued opening of schools during holidays as the scheme is thought 'to have proved itself dead over and over again'.

13. BROADCASTING AND PRESENTATION OF NEWS

'A marked increase in eagerness to hear the news' has been widely reported since the Sicilian landings and the bombing of Rome. The Sicilian news is thought on the whole to have been very well handled both by press and BBC – 'sensibly and without undue optimism'. People have particularly enjoyed the 'eye-witness accounts' by men in the Forces and correspondents on the spot.

COMMANDER KIMMINS' BROADCAST ON THE SICILIAN LANDINGS (July 15) has been highly praised, the 'human and personal touch' being particularly liked.

THE JULY 14 PROGRAMMES have been the subject of favourable but not widespread comment. Criticism has been on the grounds that they were 'much overdone – occupying both programmes and most of the evening', and that they were 'out of touch with British opinion on France, which is by no means favourable'.

MR. J. B. PRIESTLEY: The *Make it Monday* series is said to be popular; Mr. Priestley 'appeals to the straightforwardness of the British people'. At the same time, some people just 'don't like him', or find his talks 'too left-wing'. 'His broadcast on "I'm going to get lit up" was thought by some to be a little harsh, as "what young folk sing in their dance songs is never intended as a blueprint for what they are planning for the future".'

MR. JOHN HILTON'S SUNDAY POSTSCRIPT (July 11) on his journey to North Africa was much enjoyed, 'as are all talks that give first-hand news'. Blood donors were 'delighted at his appreciative reference, and glad to know what the service had meant to the fighting men'.

MR. NOEL COWARD'S SONG (July 19) 'Don't Let's be Nasty to the Nazis' has been both praised and criticised by some as 'being bad taste at the present time'.

THE KITCHEN FRONT is thought to be 'played out' and no longer as 'amusing as in Gert and Daisy Days'. There is criticism of foreign speakers describing 'messy' foreign recipes, of Mr. Grisewood being 'affected', and of the facts given 'being redundant and what every woman knows'.

THE WISH FOR MORE PLAYS, and for less swing, crooning and jazz, comes from two Regions.

THE FILM 'WORLD OF PLENTY' was highly praised after a showing at Cheltenham. It was followed by the audience 'with close attention'.

II. SPECIAL COMMENTS

MONTHLY REVIEW

14. THE POST-WAR WORLD

Discussions on post-war problems have been continuously reported during the past four weeks, but the feeling 'that we are on the road to victory and the end is in sight' has increased public interest in the post-war world. The majority consider that 'the time is now ripe for far-reaching plans to be made; and the failure of the Government to produce one simple positive large-scale plan for any single post-war problem' is thought to be partly responsible for the fairly widespread pessimism on this subject. Working-class people in particular continue to be sceptical of 'promises of a better and fuller life'.

The minority of 'anti-planners' continue to fear 'post-war control of industry and of people's lives', and to feel that 'a Whitehall-planned England would at best be dreary'.

The post-war problems which receive the most attention are:

(a) EMPLOYMENT: Anxiety about the prospects of post-war employment
     is widely reported among working-class people, particularly from areas
     which suffered a high rate of unemployment in pre-war years. There are
     widespread fears of heavy unemployment after the war – 'It will be just the

same as last time, only worse for getting jobs' – and the position of the men in the Forces and their absorption into industry continues to be anxiously discussed.

(b) THE BEVERIDGE REPORT AND SOCIAL SECURITY: Hopes and fears regarding the implementation of the Beveridge Report have, if anything, increased with the renewed interest in post-war problems. Whilst there is anxiety to know 'what the Government's intentions really are', numbers of working-class people are said to be growing increasingly sceptical of the 'Government's sincerity'. 'It's a piece of propaganda machinery to keep us quiet, and it will never be adopted.' It is suggested that Welsh voters 'will sweep the Tories out of existence at the next general election if they don't toe the line on Beveridge'.

(c) HOUSING: 'Will there be anywhere for us to live?' is becoming as frequent a topic for discussion as the problem of 'social security', particularly among young people who wish to make their homes after the war. 'Feeling is running high on the lack of present and future housing accommodation', and it is felt that the Government 'should make a bold plan which can be put into operation when the war ceases'. Even those 'who dislike controls' believe that the Government should take over post-war building 'to stop the jerry-builders and speculators from "exploiting the ignorant public"'. The delay over the rural housing scheme, however, has given rise to apprehension and doubt as to the Government's 'ability and intention' to plan post-war housing.

Strong feeling against the building of flats continues to be reported.

'The County of London Plan' exhibition has as yet excited little comment. There is some belief that 'the plans will never be realised', though people who know about the exhibition are said to be interested.

(d) EDUCATION is reported to be quite a favourite 'post-war topic', and better educational facilities for all are advocated. People are anxious to eliminate 'dead-end occupations', and for this reason some advocate 'apprenticeship at fourteen rather than staying at school till sixteen'.

Some people feel that after the war unskilled youths who are earning very high wages, and youngsters who are 'running wild' while the parents are on war work, will present very difficult problems.

(e) AGRICULTURE: Discussion about the position of agriculture after the war, and the desire that it should be placed 'on a sound basis', continue to be reported from rural areas. Houses with modern amenities, and adequate wages for agricultural workers, are strongly advocated.

(f) POST-WAR TRADE: Fears about our position in the world market have been reported during the past four weeks. There is a feeling 'that we are losing to the Americans', and the future relations between ourselves and the US and the USSR give rise to anxiety. The suggestion of 'a permanent World Council after the war is welcomed'.

(g) HEALTH: Less comment on health matters has been reported this month. On the question of a state medical service, doctors are said to be awaiting the Government scheme 'with interest and apprehension', while poorer sections of the population, critical of 'the arbitrary treatment of patients by doctors', hope for better results from a state medical service.

A SPECIAL POSTAL CENSORSHIP REPORT ON POST-WAR RECONSTRUCTION, which is believed chiefly to reflect middle-class opinion, states that the two outstanding views expressed are:

(i) Fear of the abolition of private enterprise in the future.
(ii) Fear that the working class will be exploited and down-trodden.

The report adds that 'a despondent note pervades much of the correspondence, optimistic comment being couched only in vague and inconclusive terms denoting hope, rather than conviction'.

15. CLOTHING

Contrasts are drawn between the Government's handling of the food and clothing situations.

The 'consternation' which greeted Mr. Dalton's statement of a probable reduction in the coupon allowance is again generally reported. 'The minimum has already been reached.'

The Government is felt, particularly, to show 'no sign whatever of understanding the difficulties of the growing child'; 'it would be interesting to know whether there are any real family men in the administration of this sphere'. Mothers who have already been sacrificing their coupons for their children's clothing 'have no idea how they will manage in future'.

The problems of the 'ordinary' man and woman without surplus suits and other reserves are also thought not to be properly understood. Those who had only a small wardrobe before the war are wondering 'how to cover their nakedness'.

It is feared that the present coupons might suddenly become invalid. Some statement about them would be welcomed.

Wholesalers and retailers are finding themselves with stocks of cheap goods which they cannot sell. The public consequently see large amounts of clothing in the shops and cannot understand why the number of coupons has to be reduced. Poor-quality goods are deplored; 'utility', particularly, 'is rapidly becoming synonymous with inferiority'.

During the last four weeks there have been widespread and repeated complaints on the following lines:

FOOTWEAR DIFFICULTIES: The poor quality, shortage, high price, and difficulty of replacing footwear, especially for children, have become a 'major problem'. 'Shoes are responsible for more parental worries and grey hairs than all the air raids.' Children are being kept from school, or else are arriving with 'saturated' shoes; in Newcastle 'they are to be seen running barefoot in the streets, after a lapse of twenty years'.

The materials used in the make-up of shoes are described as 'no more than brown paper'; 'it is scandalous to have to give coupons for such rubbish'.

THE INABILITY TO HAVE REASONABLY QUICK REPAIRS DONE INCREASES THE PROBLEM: In some cases, they take up to three months, and repairers are 'at their wits' end'.

THE SHORTAGE OF BOOT POLISH is also criticised: 'It is useless to ask the public to take care of footwear if no cleaning materials are available.'

Wooden clogs, however, 'might provide the solution, provided they are well made'. 'People were very scornful to start with, but are now delighted to find them very comfortable and practical.' It is wondered, however, why shoes with wooden soles should have such 'fancy' prices.

THE 'QUOTA' SYSTEM: The difficulty of buying shoes, particularly for workers and people in rural districts, is complained of. 'Some of the shops open at ten and have sold their day's quota by eleven.'

RUBBER BOOTS: Land workers are becoming anxious about rubber boots for next winter.

COUPONS FOR HOUSEHOLD GOODS: The demand for household coupons continues and it is hoped that a special allowance will be made in the next period. 'Members of the household will not *now* give up their coupons and will be much less inclined to do so after September.'

The poor quality and high price of household linen are also criticised.

STOCKINGS AND SOCKS: The poor quality of stockings and socks is deplored. 'Since nothing seems to be done about their quality', it is thought that their coupon value might be reduced. The drain of coupons for stockings is one of the greatest problems for women. It is feared that older women, now going stockingless, may contract rheumatism.

COUPONS FOR INDUSTRIAL WORKERS: Workers in many industries are 'getting desperate for clothes'. Steel workers, building trade employees and agricultural workers, particularly, feel that they are being unfairly treated. Supplementary coupons are much discussed, 'whether by those who are not eligible for any, or those who think they are getting too few'. Many doing 'dirty' jobs complain of being technically excluded from the larger issues.

Uniformed workers, particularly nurses, who have to give up coupons for their uniforms, also complain of unfair treatment.

CORSETS are 'quite unsatisfactory', especially for the larger and older women. Good ones are thought particularly necessary in view of the extra or unaccustomed work many women are now doing.

16. PENSIONS AND ALLOWANCES

Until the announcement of the new pensions plan, criticism had been on the lines indicated last week. There is now widespread pleasure that 'some progress has been made in the fight for better pensions', coupled with very considerable regret that the 'Government could not be more generous while it was about it'. There is again appreciation of the stand taken by the MPs.

Criticisms of the new proposals are as follows:

(a) People are still concerned about the number of men discharged without pension. '"Fit for service, fit for pension" is likely to become almost a slogan.'

(b) It is not understood why the Government can accept the service of a man to fight anywhere, and yet disown him if he sustains injury while on leave.

(c) More could be done for the widow ... 'The supplement of 12/- per week for rent and rates does not cover childless widows, who may not be able to work through ill health'; parents' pensions are 'vague'; criticism is made of children's allowances; doubts are expressed as to whether the pension is sufficient for the totally disabled ... 'Those who have been totally disabled in the service of their country should be assured from want.'

Some people wonder whether the concessions 'will not react to the disadvantage of the Beveridge Report', while a few working-class people say: 'Why doesn't the Government put the Beveridge Report into operation instead of bluffing with niggling measures?'

It is felt that 'more publicity is needed on the subject of pensions concessions', and some of the more thoughtful say: 'People imagine the state reserves are limitless.' It is suggested that 'much good might be done by a description in the press of hypothetical cases, with analogies, where pensions should not be granted'.

17. OLD AGE PENSIONS

Sympathy with the difficulties of the old age pensioner has been fairly widely reported during the last four weeks. The Government's attitude is said to be causing concern. It is felt that 'old people are not being looked after' and that the basic rate should be raised to meet the extra cost of living. 'We are striving for a better world; why not begin to put a little into practice?'

Old people are said to be bitter about supplementary allowances. They feel that 'thrift is penalised ... A working man who saves carefully all his life has no claim, while a squanderer has his claim granted.' It is thought that the raising of the basic rate would 'obviate supplementary allowances in a number of cases'.

18. INDUSTRY

STRIKES: Criticism of strikers is again reported this week, and it is suggested that 'organisers of lightning strikes should be summonsed for sabotage'.

There is also little sympathy with the workers of the Thames Valley Companies who struck July 8 to 12, but people feel that 'the perpetual differences over rates and conditions should have been straightened out by now'. Some feeling is reported among housewives, who feel they are war workers too, that during the strike they had to struggle up the steep hills out of High Wycombe to do their Saturday morning shopping – while war workers were transported by military vehicles.

THROUGHOUT THE LAST FOUR WEEKS comment has been reported on the following (they are arranged in order of the frequency of reports):

WAGES: The main complaints include:

(a) DISPARITY of pay between:
   (i)   SKILLED AND UNSKILLED WORKERS: The resultant friction is thought adversely to affect production; and according to one report 'discontent is aggravated by the Essential Work Order, as it prevents movement to more remunerative work'.

   Skilled workers particularly complain of the high pay of men on piece rates 'who by long hours can earn much more than they can'. The fact that the skilled workers set the machines is regarded as 'adding insult to injury'. Another 'grouse' is that, in many cases, 'a father is now bringing in less money than his son or even his daughter'.

   Miners and transport workers are also 'dissatisfied with their present wages compared with those of workers in other industries'.
   (ii) SERVICEMEN AND WAR WORKERS: 'Bitterness is even greater now that thousands of our men are at actual grips with the enemy.'
   (iii) WOMEN AND MEN: Women complain about their low wages, and part-time workers refer to their 'shilling an hour being less than a charwoman earns'.

(b) HIGH WAGES OF (i) munition workers, (ii) juvenile workers, (iii) men on Government construction work, and (iv) Irish labourers. In Lincolnshire it is rumoured that the lowest wage paid them is £7 a week with additional lodging allowance of 24/6d.

MISUSE OF MANPOWER is alleged in nine Regions (several more than once). The main complaints include:

(a) Idle time in factories, which is variously attributed to:
   (i)   Overstaffing.
   (ii) Muddle and lack of co-operation between Government departments in the change-over from defensive to offensive weapons.
   (iii) Overproduction: 'We've more stuff than we want.' An example quoted is that 'there are enough stockings to clothe the ATS for twenty years'.

(b) The direction of skilled workers to unskilled work.
(c) Women 'footling away' time in the Civil Defence Services.

THE TRANSFER OF LABOUR: The whole question, particularly as it affects women, is still 'a sore point', and feeling continues to be reported that 'the Ministry of Labour hounds girls from place to place even when there are no vacancies to fill'. It is felt that it would be a great help if 'a little more time were spent explaining the position to the women and girls'. 'Some have never left home before, and some cannot get used to the idea of being treated like men and are inclined to feel that there is a personal animus behind an order of direction.' Special objection is taken to:

(a) People being directed to work in another area when there is work in their own area. Two forms of this 'general post' are complained of:

    (i) Girls being transferred from Scotland to England and from England to Scotland; from London to the North, from the North to London; from Flint to Llandudno Junction, and from Llandudno Junction to Flint.

    (ii) Sending girls further away from home than is necessary. To quote from Postal Censorship: 'Peggy's works are closing down in a fortnight or so ... they want girls at Fieldings and also at Vulcan Street; they are both home. She asked to go to one or the other but they said "No". I think it's a shame to send her to work a distance from home when she could get work so near'.

(b) Transferring people from useful work to less useful work, or to a place where 'they have difficulty in finding enough to do'. An example quoted is of a carpenter, drafted to the aircraft industry at Easter, who 'has done no real work since'.

(c) The difficulties of finding billets. It appears, however, that some transferred workers fail to approach their billeting officer.

(d) The financial difficulties of girls who have to contribute to the upkeep of their home.

PRODUCTION: There is considerable satisfaction with production, and a feeling that 'in the main we are doing splendidly'. There is, however, some talk of workers being 'stood off while industry is reorganised'.

SLACKNESS OF WORKERS: There are a few stories of slackness, particularly in shipyards and steel factories. It is felt that in many cases 'less work is done on Sundays though the men are paid double time'. Slackness of workers, however, is sometimes blamed on the management, for lack of supervision or for 'the small amount of work they demand from their employees'.

FIRMS PREPARING FOR POST-WAR: 'A careful watch', it is suggested, should be kept on firms who are said to be (i) hindering production by developing for after the war; (ii) building up on taxpayers' money. According to the report from the North-Western Region, 'much new machinery is requisitioned, then officially scrapped in favour of a similar but slightly more powerful kind – and the scrapped machinery is stored by the firms for use after the war'.

19. THE CALL-UP

During the last four weeks, references have been on the following familiar lines:

GENERAL: Many accept the call-up as necessary, and 'do not complain'; with others, however, 'its apparent lack of consistency still rankles'. They particularly resent middle-aged people being called up when younger men and women evade their duties. Childless servicemen's wives, and young men sheltering in soft jobs, are especially mentioned.

SHORTAGE OF STAFF:

    (a) The shortage of domestic help is 'an acute and widespread problem'. Not only is it causing hardship to women with young children, expectant mothers, invalids and old people, but farmers' wives, 'who have more work than they can deal with, wonder how they can ever manage to cook for all the extra people who will come for the harvest'.

    (b) In small firms, the staff situation is said to be getting very difficult. The call-up of owners of one-man businesses is also causing concern and is believed by some to prove 'it's the Government's policy to destroy the small trader'.

20. FOOD

This week there have been comments about:

    (a) INCREASED RATIONS FOR EXPECTANT MOTHERS (July 6) continue to be well received and are looked on 'as a move to encourage the birth rate'. The extra amount of meat ration is, however, queried, as many doctors advise expectant mothers not to eat it.

    (b) THE ANNOUNCEMENT OF CHOCOLATE AND SWEETS CHANGES IN THIS COUNTRY (July 13): The reservation of vitaminised chocolate for post-war food relief in Europe has been welcomed by those 'who are conscious of, and uneasy about, our better standard of living compared with occupied Europe'. On the other hand, some resentment is reported – 'What about my kids? It's about time that they got vitaminised a bit.'

    (c) NEW POTATOES: The glut of new potatoes in Northern Ireland is said to have 'involved the farmers in heavy losses and to have prevented the planting of catch crops'. In the Southern Region, however, where the crop is said to be poor, people feel that 'official advice to grow less this year was foolish and may lead to a shortage later on'.

ORANGES: During the past two weeks, there have been several comments about the distribution of oranges. People believe that children over five are suffering from a lack of vitamins, and, in view of the fact that orange juice is allowed to children under five, the allocation of fresh oranges to children over this age is again advocated. Since there is believed to be some unfair discrimination in the distribution of oranges, it is suggested that they should be distributed through the schools and clinics. There is still some feeling that oranges and lemons could be brought to this country in ships which return from North African ports.

DURING THE PAST FOUR WEEKS satisfaction with the food situation 'at this stage of the war' has been again reported, though 'eulogy is rather less'. There have been complaints of:

(a) THE SCARCITY OF FRESH FRUIT AND TOMATOES, which continues to be widely reported along familiar lines.

(b) THE FISH SHORTAGE – though recently some improvement in supplies has been reported.

(c) HIGH PRICE OF GREEN VEGETABLES AND FRESH FRUIT, particularly lettuces, tomatoes and rhubarb.

(d) RATIONS FOR INDUSTRIAL AND AGRICULTURAL WORKERS: There is a growing feeling that the rations for heavy workers, particularly miners and land workers, are insufficient. Land workers complain that the harvest rations are not big enough, and in the South-Eastern district communal feeding centres for agricultural workers are advocated. Wives of land workers and industrial workers, who have no access to canteen facilities, are also faced with the difficulty of finding fillings for sandwich lunches; they complain of the decrease in the cheese ration.

(e) FOOD DISTRIBUTION: There are complaints of the unfair allocation of food supplies. They are alleged 'to be worked out on a pre-war basis', and to take no account of the increases and decreases in the wartime population. Holiday centres, particularly, complain of shortage of supplies during their season. It is also felt in the Northern Region that the south is better served with soft fruit, and northerners are dissatisfied: 'We think we deserve some soft fruit for living in the bleak north! After all, south country folk have a better chance of growing their own fruit in their gardens.'

(f) MILK SUPPLIES: Complaints of the delivery of poor-quality, sour, and dirty milk have been reported from different parts of the country, and there are allegations from the North-Eastern Region that graded milk 'is all mixed up before distribution'. Other complaints are:

  (i) THE RATIONALISATION OF MILK DISTRIBUTION: Some customers complain that they cannot now get the same grade of milk with which they were previously supplied.

  (ii) THE REDUCTION IN THE MILK RATION: People wonder why it should be cut in midsummer. In the South-Western Region, 'milkless days are most unpopular, because the milk from the previous day doesn't keep to see us through'.

  (iii) PASTEURISATION: There is still reported to be a good deal of opposition to pasteurised milk, and there is a demand for more information 'on the pros and cons of pasteurisation'.

(g) NATIONAL BREAD AND FLOUR: Complaints of the poor keeping quality of bread are still reported, and there is some feeling that bakers do not always put in the full 80% wholemeal flour. Gastric troubles are still attributed to national flour.

(h) ALLOTMENT GROWERS: There is an increase in complaints from allotment holders that they are unable to get soft fruit, tomatoes and vegetables in short supply, because greengrocers will only sell to regular customers.

21. SHOPPING DIFFICULTIES

Shopping difficulties, particularly for war workers and country women who are not regular customers in their market town, have been reported continuously during the past four weeks. Queues are still the outstanding complaint, but the following have also been repeatedly commented on:

(a) PREFERENTIAL TREATMENT OF CERTAIN CUSTOMERS, especially those who receive 'under-the-counter sales'. The placing of orders by 'phone is felt to be particularly unfair: 'Isn't our money as good as theirs?'

(b) EARLY AND LUNCH-TIME CLOSING OF SHOPS.

(c) CONDITIONAL SALES: 'Goods in short supply are only sold to regular customers, but you become a regular customer if you buy spuds.' Another complaint is that 'the rich buy out-of-season produce – grapes and peaches – and are then given a good supply of tomatoes and fruit'.

22. TRANSPORT

Increased transport difficulties, due to 'holiday-makers and pleasure seekers', have been reported during the last four weeks.

Inadequate bus services, particularly in rural areas, are also criticised. Villagers complain of being unable to board buses running between towns. Complaints of 'dangerous' overloading of buses are also made.

The cessation of late buses is still deplored. In rural areas it means that farm workers are not able to get to town at all during the busy month. Transferred workers also find the curfew a great irritation.

WASTE OF PETROL: There have also been increased complaints of waste of petrol; the Civil Defence, farmers, the Services and the 'official and semi-official badge of Government departments' being chiefly blamed. There is also 'a good deal of suspicion that privileged people get advantages denied to others'.

The misuse of taxis is complained of. Taxis running on 'drinking tours', and 'shuttle services running between Cambridge and Newmarket for the races', are alleged: 'Surely their petrol could be more usefully used to run a few more buses.'

23. HOUSING AND BILLETING

There have been widespread complaints of the shortage and high price of housing accommodation during the last four weeks. Criticism is becoming stronger, and in the Scottish Region it is pointed out: 'after all, we are fighting for a home; it is time a start was made'.

Serious feeling is said to be developing in the Forces about the position. Men on leave from the Middle East say 'they aren't very keen on going back to fight when they find their wives and children living in such terrible conditions'.

It is thought that there must be many empty shops, and flats over shops, that could usefully be requisitioned, and that houses kept empty for an 'emergency' could now be used to relieve congestion. Local authorities are thought to be not very willing to do much in this way and it is suggested that the Ministry of Health might 'wake them up'.

The shortage of houses is thought to be adversely affecting the birth rate. There are complaints of people being turned out of their houses on the advent of children. 'The Government's anxiety to increase the birth rate is considered farcical in view of housing difficulties'; 'let's look after the children who are already here'.

People who 'keep on' houses, though not living in them, and 'week-end cottage' owners are criticised.

AGRICULTURAL WORKERS: Agricultural workers want better and more modern houses. 'Sons say their wives shall not be allowed to live under the conditions their mothers had to put up with.' It is thought that some migration into the towns would be prevented were a substantial agricultural housing programme carried out after the war.

GOVERNMENT RURAL HOUSING SCHEME: Criticism has continued over 'the muddle made by officialdom'. It has become a 'bad joke'. The design of the cottages 'continues to be discussed with warmth in rural communities'; there is some feeling that they will be 'mediocre and uniform'. The high price and the delay in building them are sharply criticised: 'They are like the Beveridge Plan – too old to be useful.' Some say that if the building trade had been given a free hand, all three thousand would have been built by now. Others blame a 'ramp' in the trade for the high price and delay.

BILLETING: Billeting difficulties continue to be complained of, particularly in the small home where the housewife 'often has enough to do to look after her own family'. Evasion by the well-to-do causes additional grievance. Lodgings for workers are difficult to obtain and prices too high.

24. MINERS AND MINING

Considerable anxiety concerning the coal situation has again been reported during the past four weeks. Some people blame the miners for not pulling their weight, while the miners blame the owners, 'who care little for their welfare', and the Ministry of Fuel and Power. People urge a 'thorough clean-up of the coal industry', and it is again suggested in one report that production would be higher if better seams were worked.

While some express sympathy with the miners, 'who should have fair play and be paid the same or more than munition workers', others feel that the 'Government mollycoddles them', and that 'action taken regarding strikes is not strong enough'.

It is felt there is still a 'large number of men with mining experience in the Forces and factories who should be transferred to the pits' ... 'If engineers can be seconded from the RAF why cannot miners be seconded from the Forces?' On the other hand, the restriction whereby young men working on the surface are no longer allowed to join the Forces when called up, but are directed underground, is said to be causing very strong resentment among the miners ... 'Everyone is very bitter about it', and there is also much ill-feeling on account of the fining and imprisonment of lads who refuse to go into the pits. They would willingly enter the Services and it is thought that this aversion to colliery work is deep-rooted. Unless the mining industry is made more attractive, and the men given a better status and some share in the organisation, the 'difficulty of getting boys into the collieries will be one of the major problems of post-war Britain'. It is often said that 'no sons of bosses are to be found at the coal face'.

ABSENTEEISM is said to cause anxiety, but it is felt that a fairer method should be found to deal with the trouble: 'Some have days off without having to appear before a Board, while others who lose perhaps a day per quarter are hauled up.' Some people think it is the young miners who do not realise their responsibilities who are 'getting the industry into bad odour, while older men in the pits are killing themselves with work'. Others say the miners have no sense of brotherhood when their wages are concerned, and that, having earned the amount free of income tax, they feel 'only a fool would continue'. Enforced idleness in factories is also thought to encourage absenteeism among miners.

The initiation of pithead courts in the South-Eastern district is described by some as 'just what is wanted to obtain 100% effort without delinquents having to go before the magistrates and thus be made embittered'; but others think 'the real system of dispensing justice will be prejudiced if the practice is allowed to grow'.

JOINT PRODUCTION COMMITTEES: In the North-Western Region miners are thought to distrust Joint Production Committees on the grounds that members are elected from 'managerial stooges'. On the other hand, employers are reported to be afraid of the Committees because they think they may encourage nationalisation.

TARGETS: Two reports say that miners would prefer to work to a pit rather than a county target, as the former is more 'tangible and personal', and they would 'welcome competition'.

In the North Midland Region, it is felt that in the direction of men into the Home Guard, special regard should be given to men working full time at the coal face – also that these men should not be expected to fire-watch.

25. FUEL AND DOMESTIC COAL

Considerable anxiety about the fuel position has been reported during the past four weeks, and the apparently contradictory statements by people in authority are said to have 'created doubts as to whether the Ministry have any real policy' ... 'Who are we to believe?' This view is strengthened by many complaints that people cannot follow Government instructions to stock fuel now because coal merchants have no supplies for the purpose: 'Some orders placed in April are not yet delivered.' There is also complaint of the poor quality of coal supplied and of permit difficulties. Appeals to the public to stock fuel 'do not mention limitations'. 'One woman on being refused a licence to stock coal for the winter because she had more coal than the "limit", burnt most of her extra coal so that she would be able to apply for a licence.'

Some comment is made concerning the wisdom and method of stocking coal, as 'it is impossible to judge whether one gains or loses thereby'. In spite of Government statements to the contrary, some believe that external storage causes fairly rapid deterioration, particularly in the poor-quality coal which is being supplied now. Poor people say they could not afford to buy ten bags at a time even if they could get them, and those with little storage space 'rely on the Government's promise to supply them during the winter'.

People living in country districts who are dependent on coal and paraffin for all purposes think the present system of fuel allowance most unfair. They contrast their lot with those living in towns who, by using gas and electricity now, can save their present allowances for the winter. The North Midland Regional report mentions a request from the Peak District for an increased fuel allowance, and a similar request from shift workers.

26. AGRICULTURE

HARVEST HELPERS: Comment is still very varied this week and none of the points raised below have been reported from more than two Regions:

(a) A demand for more information as to where to apply for enrolment, billets and transport – also as to opportunities for schoolboys aged 14 to 16.

(b) Disappointment of some volunteers at finding that their help was not wanted by local farmers – as happened at Winchester. In parts of the Northern Region, things were worse: 'People who had made all arrangements for their farm holiday found it cancelled at the last moment because of the ill-behaviour and drunkenness of previous helpers.' In Bradford, however, potential volunteers are more wary about offering their services because 'the organisers are unable to guarantee work for them'.

(c) Interest in the scheme among farmers. In Leicestershire, they are said to be counting on voluntary help. At the same time, farmers in the Peak District show no interest, and in the North Midland Region they feel that 'amateur help does more harm than good – and the public have not been educated not to trample down crops'.

(d) Regret that more agricultural holiday camps were not prepared in Kent and West Sussex. 'The Duke of Norfolk's much advertised tour, to inspect such camps, was criticised because they do not exist in his own county of West Sussex.'

(e) Some feeling about 'the poor pay', which 'provides little beyond mere subsistence'. 'In the event of a few wet days, the worker will suffer a loss.'

In the North Riding and in Carmarthenshire, farmers complain about the shortage of labour for harvesting their crops: 'I've got a hundred acres of the finest corn I've ever seen, but how I'm to get it in with only two men and myself I don't know.'

GARDENS AND ALLOTMENTS: Stories have 'cropped up again' this week of allotment thieves; and bitterness is reported among the allotment holders. Two further troubles are:

(a) A maggot which attacks cabbages and other brassicas. Many gardeners say it is not worth growing these crops.

(b) The 'poor quality' of seeds sold to the public at present. A case is mentioned of 'only five leeks coming up out of ample seed – the rest growing into grass'.

ITALIAN PRISONERS OF WAR are this week referred to in reports from four Regions. The recent incident (July 11) in which one of them killed a guard and wounded a woman has led to some uneasiness – particularly in the immediate district and among women – and there are stories of (i) guards armed with 'nothing more than a wooden club, with their rifles supporting a nearby wall and accessible to the criminal minded'; (ii) two prisoners who live alone in a cottage and who have been provided by the farmer for whom they work with a gun to shoot rabbits. In the Eastern Region, however, the prisoners are generally thought to be well behaved and the incident mentioned above 'is assumed to be an isolated case of a man running amok'.

It is felt that 'a closer watch should be kept on the prisoners'; people 'resent them being allowed to walk unguarded along roads'. On the other hand, there is some criticism of waste of manpower and petrol when guards and lorries are provided. An example given is of a three-ton lorry making a daily journey of fifty miles to take seven prisoners to and from their work in a quarry – 'and then the Italians only work for five hours'.

DAMAGE TO CROPS has been reported from four Regions during the past month. From Lincolnshire and the East Riding come complaints of 'military manoeuvres causing unnecessary damage'. Rabbits and other vermin – which cannot be destroyed because of the shortage of cartridges – are blamed for spoiling food production in Northants and in the Carlisle area.

27. SALVAGE

Reports of non-collection or irregular collection of salvage have again been received from ten Regions during the past four weeks. There are many complaints of railings and other metal left lying about in dumps for months – some of it now useless – and of the unfairness of removing small gates etc., whose weight is insignificant, while hundreds of tons of collected scrap metal are still lying untouched.

Housewives complain of uncollected salvage harbouring vermin, and also of the indiscriminate loading and mixing of carefully separated salvage.

Although it is suggested that some people are inclined to become slack, it is stressed that the enthusiasm for the collection of all kinds of salvage is damped by bad collection and the sight of unused dumps.

28. INCOME TAX

During the past four weeks there has been a fairly consistent demand for the 'pay as you go' scheme for income tax payment; the difficulties are recognised but thought to be 'not insurmountable if the Government is willing'. The system of deducting tax based on the previous six months' earnings is thought to be very hard on workers whose pay and hours of work are variable. Some workers say they would 'prefer to be on normal time and wages and not to earn big money intermittently with no guarantee that it will continue'. They also think there should be a special rate for overtime, as it 'involves the expenditure of extra energy, and the bulk of the additional receipts has to be paid back as tax'. Because of this some are said to decline to work overtime when they have the opportunity.

Many people think that pensioners of all kinds bear a very heavy burden with the higher cost of living and suggest they should have a bigger personal allowance.

29. HEALTH

There have been frequent references this month to complaints of tiredness and strain, which are attributed to the lack of vitamins in the wartime diet, the lack of fresh fruit, and the need for a holiday. The alleged increase in minor skin diseases and sporadic epidemics are also attributed to the wartime diet. 'There is some inclination to believe that although we are not actively unhappy, a wartime diet causes low resistance to and slow recovery from any illness which may be about.'

The Government statement that 'we are healthier now than in peacetime' has been commented on with some scepticism, though the general health of children is acknowledged to be good.

HOSPITAL ACCOMMODATION: The shortage of hospital accommodation, especially of maternity beds, continues to cause concern. Expectant mothers are said to feel that 'the Government is showing a lack of interest in maternity welfare'.

TUBERCULOSIS: Concern is reported at the increase in tuberculosis. This is thought to be due to long hours and work in artificial light. It is suggested that there should be an X-ray machine in every works.

30. VD CAMPAIGN

Approval for the VD advertisements continues to be expressed, although it is sometimes wondered whether they are reaching the right people or merely terrorising and confusing the innocent. There is praise for the film *Subject for Discussion* which is said to be encouraging people to discuss VD more freely and making them realise the dangers. There continues to be a steady demand for more lectures on sex education in schools and elsewhere.

Although the campaign is considered to be doing good work, a minority fear that there is a danger of 'too much publicity' on this subject: 'one or two lewd jokes' are said to be 'in wide circulation; and concern is felt that these may be a prelude to others, which, if widely repeated, will nullify the effects of the campaign'.

NO. 147: TUESDAY 20 JULY 1943 TO
TUESDAY 27 JULY 1943

I. GENERAL COMMENTS

1. GENERAL STATE OF CONFIDENCE AND REACTION TO NEWS

The high level of public spirits reported last week has risen even higher with 'the best news yet – the sudden downfall of Mussolini'. People are delighted at this sign of Italian 'shakiness', but many are curbing their excitement until they are certain this is the first step to Italy's capitulation, and not 'only a new name on the old shop front'. Intense discussion as to its cause and possible effects is general, and the bombing of Rome and the Allied progress in Sicily have taken second place. Satisfaction with these, however, continues, and is also reported for the very heavy bombing of Hamburg and Essen, the Russian counter-offensive and 'the good news from everywhere'.

Forecasts on the length of the war in Europe are very optimistic this week: 'Italy, in any case, will be out of the war any day now or within a month ... and then for Germany!' Some expect 'we'll have another armistice on November 11'. The more cautious still give it a year and criticise the over-optimistic.

HOME FRONT: Holidays – with the struggle against all difficulties – continue to be the main topic. The strain and tiredness resulting from four years of war are thought to have made a change of air and scene essential.

Housewives still complain of clothing difficulties (particularly footwear) and of the shortage in towns of fresh fruit and tomatoes.

2. MUSSOLINI'S RESIGNATION AND
THE CHANGE OF GOVERNMENT

This news came as a great surprise. It is widely and excitedly discussed and pleases everybody. To the majority, it indicates that the Italians are disorganised and demoralised, particularly by our invasion of Sicily and the bombing of Rome. They see in it the end of fascism and 'the beginning of the end of Axis resistance'. Italy is expected to be out of the war soon, and rumours that she has already surrendered are widespread.

A minority, however, for various causes, are less optimistic:

(a) Some are waiting to see what will happen and whether the new administration is any different from the other.

(b) A few fear that Italian resistance, far from being weakened by the new administration, will be strengthened by 'a Government containing army leaders'.

(c) A few others feel 'it's a put-up job arranged by Hitler – possibly at his recent meeting with Mussolini – who will now be running the show with Victor Immanuel and Badoglio as figureheads'.

A SEPARATE PEACE: Many think that Badoglio will negotiate for a separate peace with the Allies and, having thrown over fascism, will expect considerate terms of surrender. It is hoped that 'whatever happens, we will insist on unconditional surrender, and will be just as tough with him and the King as with Mussolini'. Badoglio is considered 'no better than the rest', and his Abyssinian cruelties, particularly the use of poison gas, are widely remembered. Another reason 'for refusing an easy peace' to Italy is that Germany may expect it too, and 'this time the war must be finished off properly'.

People wonder what Hitler will do if Italy sues for peace. 'It will mean endless new headaches for him.'

MUSSOLINI: People think that 'he must have been in a very tight spot to resign, as he'd have paid almost any price to hang on to his dictatorship'; some are astonished that 'a dictator could resign'.

There is considerable speculation as to his whereabouts; Spain and Germany are suggested – while 'the rumour that Mussolini has sought sanctuary within the Vatican is angrily discussed'.

REACTIONS IN OTHER COUNTRIES: Events in Italy are expected to have the following effects:

(a) Greatly to encourage people in the occupied countries; there is 'some anticipation of repercussions in the Balkans'.
(b) Effectively to prove to the Allies that the Axis facade is vulnerable.
(c) To give the Germans food for thought: 'If Musso can get the push like that, then what about Hitler?'

3. SICILY

Satisfaction with the speed of Allied progress is widespread, as is the belief that Sicily will soon be ours. Only a few complain of 'our slowness' or suggest that the Germans may be able to put up a prolonged defence round Mount Etna.

Praise continues for 'the grand job' of planning and carrying out 'this model of combined operations'. It has given people the highest confidence in the Allied leaders, Forces and equipment.

CATANIA: People feel that the Eighth Army has been given the toughest job – 'which is to be expected and is right. The Americans are less seasoned troops and should be given the Wops on a plate, while the best army in the world attends to the really dangerous enemy.' There is, however, some feeling that 'the Eighth Army ought to get more credit for it – all the praise seems to go to the Americans and Canadians'.

CASUALTIES: Some fear that casualties in the Catania sector may be heavy and are 'anxiously waiting for news'.

4. THE BOMBING OF ROME

'So they have bombed Rome at last – I'm glad!' seems to have been the reaction of all but a very few. This is usually followed by: 'Why have we waited so long?' and:

'Why apologise?' The raid is thought by many to have been 'the finishing touch, the final push that toppled over Mussolini'. Many hope it will be 'followed up by others, which, in the view of some people, need not be preceded by leaflets and can include the Vatican City'.

ROMAN CATHOLIC OPINION, with a few exceptions – notably in Northern Ireland – is said to 'approve of the bombing, if it is really necessary for the war effort'. Some, indeed, are described as being 'all for it'. Many Catholics 'point to the destruction of the churches of Britain and ask: "Why should the Axis shelter behind our Catholic churches?"' The general feeling among Catholics seems to be – 'We are British first.'

THE PLANNING AND EXECUTION OF THE RAID are more criticised than praised this week. Although the care taken in preparing and carrying out the raid is again commended, many people are very critical of 'the unjustifiable risks to the airmen' involved by:

(a) THE DROPPING OF WARNING LEAFLETS: There is sarcastic comment on the lines of: 'How decent it was to warn the Italians! No one sent me a warning the night before my home was destroyed.'

(b) PRECISION BOMBING: Airmen's lives are 'worth more than historic monuments'.

(c) CARRYING OUT THE RAID IN DAYLIGHT: It was thought 'foolish to arrange for valuable pilots to present a clearly seen target to well-prepared defences'.

THE AIRMEN TAKING PART: There is comment on the fact that only Americans took part in the raid, and some regret that there were no British airmen. It is even said by a few that 'our men refused to do it'. Others think it was a shrewd move, 'to counter US Catholic opinion' and 'cause less trouble with the Pope'. People were interested that Roman Catholic pilots took part. A few suggest that it is now the turn of the British to bomb Rome, to show the Americans we have not left them 'to face the dirtiest piece of propaganda this war has yet produced'.

THE ANCIENT MONUMENTS in Rome are the cause of some apprehension, which has been greatly relieved by details of 'the accuracy of our bombing and our care not to injure historic objects'. Nevertheless, a minority regret the damage to the Basilica of San Lorenzo. 'Those who had thought that all of Rome was stuffed with places of antiquity welcomed the maps, which relieved them of the fear that air raids could not fail to destroy much that was of historic interest.' It is clear, however, that the general public do not understand why there should be any cultural reasons for distinguishing between Rome and London, Canterbury or Coventry.

THE POPE: The Pope's letter to the Vicar-General of Rome has caused considerable comment, most of it adverse. There is said to be no sympathy for the Pope and some sardonic comment at his claims to be impartial. There is impatience at his protests, which are thought to have come 'rather late in the day'. Many people believe that the Pope 'condoned the terrible attack on one of the oldest Christian peoples' – the Abyssinians. It is also asked why the Pope should 'cry out when one Roman Catholic church suffers partial damage and remain silent when 4,000 religious edifices in this country – including St. Paul's and other cathedrals – have been attacked'. There is also some comment that 'he made no mention of the loss of life, but only of buildings'.

5. THE NEXT MOVES

The next move now most eagerly awaited is that of Italy rather than of the Allies.

Many continue to look on Sicily as 'a preliminary' to our invasion of Europe and think that 'there are more surprises in store for the Axis'. A small minority still complain that Sicily is a 'flea-bite', and that they want 'a real second front'.

SPECULATION goes on; but the Balkans, via Crete, have now replaced Italy – which may capitulate without invasion – as 'the best bet'. Turkey, it is again suggested, may come in on our side. Norway, France and Belgium are all once more mentioned as 'possibles'.

6. HOLIDAYS

The desire for holidays, and 'the grim determination to get away whatever the difficulties', are again reported to be strong and widespread. Holidays are believed to be a necessity, to overcome the war strain from which so many are said to be suffering. Most people, workers especially, feel that they must 'get away for a change of air and scenery after four years of war' and 'before facing another blackout'. Many, regarding it as a right, 'no longer feel guilty about going away' – especially now that the war has taken such a turn in our favour. Workers 'ask why their one week's holiday a year should be "cluttered up with restrictions", while members of the Forces get regular leave and are able to travel'. The chief drawback to holidays at home is that they 'give no rest to the housewife'.

HOLIDAY TRAVEL: The 'tales of terrific congestion' which are circulating seem to have done little to deter would-be travellers but have led to much criticism of the Government (for not 'doing something about it'), of the Ministry of War Transport (for 'not making up its mind'), and of the railway companies (for 'vacillating'). It is suggested that 'the Government should have made some determined attempt to stagger holidays to avoid the congestion arising from the concentration of holidays in August'. 'Trouble is anticipated at Bank Holiday weekend, if the Government and the railways don't do something' – Blackpool alone is said to be expecting a quarter of a million visitors.

War workers complain of being crowded off the trains by holiday-makers; they say that appeals to police regulating queues to give them priority are without avail, as the police explain that they 'have no instructions and that the Ministry of War Transport is the body responsible'.

The patience and good behaviour of huge queues at London termini is commented on.

CONDITIONS AT HOLIDAY RESORTS: There are complaints of holiday-makers buying up food in short supply; residents think that visitors should bring their own food with them. One report refers to difficulties arising from 'refusals to honour emergency cards both for the public and the Forces'.

There are also complaints from workers at 'the exorbitant prices charged for apartments at seaside hotels', while people obliged to go to such places on business resent having to pay 'exorbitant charges of 25/- a day in hotels normally charging much less'.

7. ALLIED AIR OFFENSIVE

The excellent news from other war fronts and the raid on Rome have diverted much of people's attention from the continued air offensive on Germany and Italy. Satisfaction, however, continues.

HAMBURG RAID (July 25): People were both pleased and awed by the raid on Hamburg. 'Comparison with the London raids has given some idea of the weight of the attack; it proves that our strength must be great indeed, if we can do this while maintaining operations in the Mediterranean.'

THE ESSEN RAID (July 26) further increased people's satisfaction. The damage to Krupps was 'eagerly discussed, especially by war workers in large factories' in Scotland.

At the same time, much of our air offensive is now taken for granted. The routine questions are now: 'Where did we go last night?' and 'How many did we lose?' 'Many people expect every raid to be bigger and heavier than the last, and so remain unexcited; others feel that the number of planes taking part is more real than the weight of bombs dropped, and the absence of the former information is regretted and the reason not always appreciated.'

FLYING FORTRESSES: The armament of Flying Fortresses, as compared with that of our planes, is a subject of discussion; people compare RAF losses with the Flying Fortresses that fail to return home and wonder 'if our machines are sufficiently well protected'.

8. RUSSIA

As with the air offensive, so with Russia. Mussolini and Sicily have put Russian news in the background, but satisfaction and admiration continue to be general. Further Russian advances are expected and Germany is considered 'up against it'. 'As Russia is doing so well during the summer, many are hoping for great things from her in the winter.'

The timing of the Red Army offensive is taken as evidence that 'the strategy of the United Nations is now co-ordinated'. In London, however, 'while many feel the Sicilian campaign has been of great assistance to the Russians, it is asked by others whether in fact there really is co-operation, and whether Russia really is receiving all the help the Allies can possibly give'.

Russian figures of German losses in men and material are still treated 'with reserve'.

9. FAR EAST

There is no change in public comment about the war in the Far East. Relief continues as the news of British prisoners in Japanese hands comes in. Sympathy for China is again mentioned.

10. NORTH AFRICAN POLITICS

Comment continues in moderate volume along the same lines as in the past three weeks.

11. THE WAR AT SEA

Thanks to the anti-U-boat successes and the work of the Royal Navy in the Mediterranean, general satisfaction with the situation continues to be expressed. Praise for the Merchant Navy is again voiced.

12. THE EDUCATION WHITE PAPER

The increasing interest in education, and approval for the proposals outlined in the White Paper, are again reported. 'In mining and quarry districts it is said that education has been popularly discussed in quarry cabins and pubs for the first time. People are asking: "Will it really mean that my son will have the same chance as the Works Manager's son?"'

The proposal to raise the school-leaving age seems to be the point most often discussed. Most people are said to be in favour of this, many favouring 'education till 16 and over, with part-time continuation to the age of 18'; but a few suggest that 'some children do not benefit from the education given and would be better apprenticed earlier to suitable trades'. A small minority fear that we may become too educated and wonder 'who will do the labourers' jobs'.

Other points approved are the proposals to introduce more nursery schools, to abolish examinations at 11, and 'the attempt to solve the system of dual control'. It is hoped that provision will be made for teaching such things as 'the necessity and machinery of local government, the incidence of rates and taxes and why they are levied'; also the functions of social services and public utility undertakings.

A minority are critical, mainly on the grounds that 'half the new ideas are impractical and too expensive'. Teachers, in particular, are said to consider the proposals 'handsome on paper, but unlikely to make any real changes in the present position'.

13. THE BIRTH RATE

There has been little comment on the discussion in the House of Commons on the trend of the birth rate. In London, a typical remark is: 'I don't know what all the fuss is about; every young woman I see seems to be in a state of expectation.'

Two factors working against pregnancy at present are mentioned:

(i)   The lack of domestic help for mothers who have their babies at home.
(ii) The refusal of house and flat owners, and those who let furnished rooms, to take people 'when they hear there are, or are going to be, children.' The complaints of servicemen's wives are particularly bitter.

Two long-term factors are said to be:

(i)   'Lack of guarantees against future wars.' 'People resent losing their children at 18 just when they have reached an interesting, useful, and profitable age.'
(ii) Among the middle classes, clergy, etc., 'the very high cost of the education these parents are anxious to give their children'.

14. RESIGNATION OF MPs FROM THE HOME GUARD

There have been cynical comments at the announcement that a number of MPs have resigned from the Home Guard. Their lot is contrasted with that of the 'ordinary man, who, though working far harder, is gaoled for non-attendance at parades'.

Penalties against workers who miss Home Guard parades are increasingly resented. It is thought that 'training is too arduous for many on top of a full day's work' ... 'especially as there is now so little chance of the Home Guard having to fight'.

15. BROADCASTING AND PRESENTATION OF NEWS

News bulletins are eagerly listened to, and newspapers 'snapped up as soon as they appear'; but, although the news is thought, on the whole, to have been well handled by both press and radio, there is criticism of over-optimistic statements about Catania; of too much apology for the Rome bombing; and of the BBC's 'habit of jeering at the re-formed 15th Panzer division'.

There is special admiration for the work of the war correspondents and the 'risks they take to get their stories from the front line'. Photographs from the battlefront are also much appreciated and 'do an extraordinary amount of good'. More are asked for. The *Sunday Chronicle* (July 11) is criticised in one report for 'presenting an artist's impression of a landing scene in Sicily, which gave a harrowing impression of our troops on the beach under gunfire; this was at variance with the facts and unnecessarily distressing to relatives of men there'.

THE EUROPEAN SERVICE news bulletins are again reported to be far more interesting than those in the Home Service.

PROGRAMMES:

J. B. PRIESTLEY'S 'MAKE IT MONDAY' series has, on the whole, been much liked, though some think he is not necessarily constructive and true to life. His final broadcast was considered 'specially good'. 'They really should have a young serviceman giving his views as Priestley suggests.' It is thought that 'another Sunday night series might revive the interest once taken in the *Postscripts*'.

COMMANDER ANTHONY KIMMINS' BROADCAST (July 15) on the Sicilian landing is again widely praised. 'Talks by the men who do things are the highlights of the news.'

AIR-MARSHAL SIR PHILIP JOUBERT'S WAR COMMENTARY (July 22) is praised. Such broadcasts 'have greater weight because of the avoidance of any tendency to over-statement'.

PROFESSOR JOHN HILTON'S TALK ON NORTH AFRICA was also much appreciated, though 'some think him too patronising'.

Praise is also reported for: Douglas Houghton's *Can I Help You?* series; and for *ITMA*, *The Radio Padre*, *Marching On*, and Mr. Elmer Davis' (July 25) *Postscript*.

BBC ANNOUNCERS: Maurice Shillington's voice is said not to be liked and is described by some as 'nasal and American'. There is regret that Joseph Macleod is no longer an announcer.

II. SPECIAL COMMENTS

WEEKLY SUMMARY

16. CLOTHING

Complaints of the inadequacy of clothing coupons continue on the same lines as last week and at about the same level. Concern at the proposed cut is widespread, particularly in view of the 'shoddy' quality of much of the utility clothing and footwear available. It is felt that 'the Board of Trade has "fallen down" in not ensuring better standards'.

Some shops are said to be taking utility labels out of clothes so as to sell them at exorbitant prices.

The chief difficulties are: (i) shortage and poor quality of children's shoes; (ii) length of time taken to get repairs done – 'often with leather of such poor quality that the labour is wasted'.

According to a report from the North-Western Region, 'Manchester bus conductresses express resentment at the Board of Trade's demand for the surrender of twelve clothing coupons from the new book, which the women say is "not yet legally in use". Friday, July 16, was the date assigned for surrendering coupons, under threat of prosecution. Many have refused to comply. The conductresses also consider it unfair that their uniform (unlike that of postwomen) is not free but has to be hired at the rate of 2/6 a week – according to a regulation left over from the last war – and they are "not allowed to keep it at the end".'

17. MINING AND MINERS

Mr. Bevin's statement that boys of 16 will be directed to work in the pits has aroused strong feeling and is said to be 'not too well received in the mining industry'. It is, however, said that 'no one in the mining industry will seriously object if the labour is really necessary' provided 'such a call-up is not confined to mining families' and 'the children of the well-to-do are taken'. Otherwise, it is thought that the call-up would cause 'a storm in the industry'.

The boys themselves are said to be against it: 'They would rather wangle their age and join the army as the mines are too dangerous.'

It is felt that 'the large number of men' in the army and working in factories and quarries, who have had mining experience, should be returned to the pits before any further action is taken. From Scotland comes the suggestion: 'Why not put Italian prisoners of war in the mines and put the boys on the land?'

COAL FOR ITALY: The recent statement by Mr. John Armstrong at the Mineworkers' Federation conference (July 21) to the effect that coal will be needed in Sicily and Italy has caused slight comment on the lines of: 'Why should we spoon-feed enemy countries?' and: 'The miners don't seem anxious to provide coal for their own kith and kin, and they will be much less likely to buckle down to provide coal for Italians.'

18. PENSIONS AND ALLOWANCES

Further reactions to the new pensions plan have been 'very mixed'. While some are delighted at the new concessions, many people 'are still not satisfied and press for more generous treatment'. The concessions to the Services have made old age pensioners the more bitter.

Criticisms of the new plan are as follows:

(a) 'FIT FOR SERVICE, FIT FOR PENSIONS': 'No matter what the Government says.'
(b) THE PENSIONS PROPOSED ARE STILL NOT ENOUGH: Ex-servicemen 'expect more security than after the 1914/18 war'. The totally disabled, particularly, 'will still be the poorest section of the community'.
(c) THE TAXATION OF WAR WIDOWS' PENSIONS: 'It should be recognised that a wife's commitments are not much reduced by the death of the husband.'

It is said that 'there is much ignorance and emotion' about the whole subject, and that the Government should put out publicity about the true facts of the situation.

19. FOOD

Satisfaction over the food situation continues to be general except for THE SHORTAGE OF SOFT FRUIT AND TOMATOES, complaints of which are reported from ten and eight Regions respectively. Comments about this, though on familiar lines, are strong, particularly in the Northern Region and in Scotland where 'housewives who have no time to queue have never seen fruit'; in Scotland 'housewives are beginning to cry out for some system to be devised to do away with queues'.

ALLOTMENT HOLDERS are said to be unable to get any fruit at all: having 'loyally tried to grow their own food, they have to watch women who have made no effort at gardening carry home good quantities of fruit'.

The other outstanding food topics this week are:

THE PROMISED INCREASE IN THE JAM RATION: This is looked forward to with great pleasure but – as was the case with the dried eggs – there are some who say that this means 'it must be going bad'. Others say: 'Marvellous ... but it depends on the jam.'

THE ANNOUNCEMENT THAT STORES OF CHOCOLATE ARE BEING BUILT UP FOR OCCUPIED EUROPE has again caused varying reactions, mostly approving. Some are pleased for altruistic reasons, others are glad if it means more boiled sweets instead of chocolate; others, again, are content so long as 'our own children don't go short in consequence'.

THE ANNOUNCEMENT THAT INCREASED SUPPLIES OF BLANCMANGE AND CUSTARD POWDER ARE TO BE ON SALE has caused varied comment. There is pleasure; annoyance that, in spite of the announcement, people still cannot get it; and surprise that increased supplies should coincide with the reduction of the milk ration.

CANTEEN FOOD: Complaints about the food in canteens come from three Regions. It is not the food that is complained of, but the way it is cooked, particularly 'in factories where canteens are run by catering firms'. At Findlay's Shipyard, Old Kilpatrick, however, it is the food itself which causes dissatisfaction, according to the Scottish report; workers describe it as 'poisonous' and say that it 'comes from Ministry of Food dumps'.

THE ALLOWANCE OF SUGAR FOR JAM is again the subject of pleasure, mixed with the feeling of: 'What's the use, when you can't get fruit?'

CEREAL ZONING is criticised, particularly by those who regard Kellogg's 'All Bran' as a medicine and can no longer get it.

THE INCREASE IN RATIONS FOR EXPECTANT MOTHERS is again praised, but some people feel that 'there should be a monetary allowance to enable servicemen's wives to take full advantage of it'.

THE IMPORTING OF AFRICAN WINE is again criticised, as it is felt that fruit should have been imported instead.

20. AGRICULTURE

CROPS: Pleasure at 'the excellent hay crops' is again reported this week, as well as talk about the good prospects for corn, potato, apple and pear crops.

HARVEST LABOUR: Farmers in the Northern and North Midland Regions complain of a labour shortage, and 'harvest helpers' in Kent are worried at the small number of volunteers for harvest work.

From the Southern Region this week comes a demand for more general publicity as to 'facilities and amenities at harvest helpers' camps, and where to enrol'.

PLOUGH LAND: Small farmers in the North Midland Region complain of the amount of land they are expected to plough in, and in the North-Eastern Region of the delay in the payment of ploughing subsidies.

NEW POTATO CROPS: 'The big muddle over the potato business' continues to be criticised in Lincolnshire. In the North-Eastern Region there are complaints that hardship is being caused to small farmers through the delay in the acreage payment for delivered potatoes.

ALLOTMENT HOLDERS in the Northern Region are reported to be very uneasy 'lest they should be summarily evicted from their holdings at very short notice after the war, because their land is required for building sites'. Apprehension is said to be greatest among older men 'who remember what happened after the last war'. Allotment holders would like to know 'what provisions, if any, have been made to safeguard their interests'.

21. STRIKES

TRANSPORT WORKERS: The recent strike of women transport employees in Leicester, though condemned in principle, is said to have been looked on sympathetically by many people. The girls, who were asked to do a nine-hour shift, complained that they are handling dirty money all day and have no facilities for washing their hands before they eat their sandwiches. Lavatory accommodation is also lacking. 'Their objections were considered justified.'

Unrest is reported among the drivers of the Yorkshire Traction Co. because income tax, which would normally have been deducted during the recent strike period, is being deducted now, in addition to current income tax deductions. As a result, pay packets are reduced.

22. CIVIL DEFENCE AND FIRE-WATCHING

FIRE-WATCHING remains 'an unpopular duty', and adverse comment has been continuous though not widespread during the past eight weeks. Official criticism, directed at the less painstaking, is resented, particularly by 'those who are really pulling their weight'.

Other complaints have been as follows:

(i)   'THE STRAIN OF FIRE-WATCHING IN CONJUNCTION WITH OTHER DUTIES': Particular reference is made to the hardships of married women with household responsibilities in full- or part-time jobs; of those working long hours; and of shift workers.

(ii) THE 'DODGERS': Suspicion that 'many able-bodied men are not pulling their weight' continues, and women are particularly resentful. Compulsion for all is advocated, though there is some belief that 'press-gang watchers do not carry out their duties properly'.

(iii) ALLOWANCE RATES: There is some dissatisfaction with the varying rates of pay and allowances, and demands for 'a national scheme'.

(iv) UNFAIR ALLOCATION OF DUTIES, particularly 'too much weekend fire-watching'.

THE NEW FIRE-GUARD REORGANISATION which has been coming into operation since the beginning of the year has aroused some adverse comments on the lines of:

(i) The orders are 'badly phrased and complicated' and 'too numerous'. 'The public', it is alleged, are 'reduced to apathy by the repeated Fire-Guard orders, and there comes a time when people can be over-organised'.

(ii) The plan for closer working arrangements between the Fire Guards and the NFS is disliked in some places, and there are doubts of its practicability in rural areas.

THE CIVIL DEFENCE DEBATE (June 30): Comment continues to be very slight. Some doubts about 'the new warning system' are reported from the Hull area, where 'feeling is still strong at the delay in sounding sirens' in recent raids (see Home Intelligence Weekly Report No. 143, July 1). In Wales the reduction in Civil Defence personnel is welcomed, but some people in London fear that 'a twelve per cent cut at this stage in the war is not in the public interest': 'the air-raid lull may only be temporary'.

23. MISCELLANEA

PLAGUE OF MOTHS: A plague of clothes moths is reported both in London (Ealing, Kentish Town, Hampstead, Kensington, Chelsea) and in Bristol. More official guidance is asked for on how to deal with these pests.

BLOOD TRANSFUSION: Comfortably-off women in Merseyside dormitory areas are reported to be slow to come forward as volunteers for blood transfusion. 'Thousands of them, when approached, said they were anaemic and so their blood would be no good.' Some people object to giving blood because 'it removes the sugar from the blood and leaves a craving for sweet things'.

NO. 152: TUESDAY 24 AUGUST 1943 TO TUESDAY 31 AUGUST 1943

I. GENERAL COMMENTS

1. GENERAL STATE OF CONFIDENCE AND REACTION TO NEWS

Confidence remains high as a result of the Russian successes, the air offensive – particularly on Berlin – and the evidence of unrest in occupied countries. In spite of the good news, however, there appears to have been a slight drop in spirits since last week, showing itself in:

(a) Widespread uneasiness over British and US relations with Russia; this has increased since last week.

(b) Impatience at Allied inactivity, both in not invading the Continent 'to give more concrete help to the Russians', and in 'not driving Italy out of the war'.

At the same time, there continues to be a good deal of expectation that 'something big is brewing', though speculation is less than a week ago.

Although there are still many optimists who think the war will be over by Christmas, there is an increasing tendency to put back the date of final victory to next year, and a minority say that 'the war is only beginning now'.

HOME FRONT: The hope that this will be the last winter of the war appears to be reducing dread of the blackout, but dislike of it is very strong; people are asking whether blackout conditions could be modified and whether cycle and torch batteries will be in reasonable supply this year. The greatest home front worry still appears to be footwear.

2. RUSSIA AND THE OTHER ALLIES

Suspicion and anxiety that all is not well between Russia and the English-speaking Allies, already widespread last week, have increased. Russia's apparent lack of appreciation of our war effort and our help to her, the recall of MM. Maisky and Litvinov, and, above all, the absence of any Russian representative at Quebec, are 'linked as evidence that friction exists between Russia on the one hand and USA and ourselves on the other'. Talk of the possibility of Russia making a separate peace with Germany is reported from six Regions.

On the causes of disagreement, two main viewpoints are apparent (apart from a minority who blame both sides or neither):

(a) THOSE WHO CONSIDER THAT RUSSIA HAS EVERY REASON TO BE DISSATISFIED, because:

(i) We have not started a large-scale Continental landing to relieve German pressure. Even many who are 'far from friendly to Russia' say we have had ample time to build up and plan a major offensive, and that 'to offer Sicily as our contribution is an affront to Russia and a dishonour to ourselves'. They add that 'if we don't do something big soon to divert Axis forces from Russia, we shall have only ourselves to blame if she takes the view that we are hoping to win the war at her expense, finishing up fresh and powerful while she is exhausted and weak'.

(ii) There is little sympathy with Russia among 'highly-placed officials and influential people', and still less appreciation of what she has done. This view is held by workers especially. There are 'rumours of a whispering campaign against Russia' and it is feared that 'the reluctance of the high-ups – but not Mr. Churchill – to work with Russia will lead to a breach and actual war with her later on'. In Orkney, 'it is firmly believed that the defences being constructed there are designed for future conflict with Russia rather than Germany'.

(b) THOSE WHO, WHILE APPRECIATING ALL RUSSIA IS DOING, FEEL THAT SHE IS UNREASONABLE because:

    (i) The Russians have not given enough credit to the other Allies for their help – by providing supplies, sometimes to our own disadvantage, by our heavy bombing policy, and by holding troops in the west to meet the invasion threat. People particularly feel that the Russians don't understand naval power or 'the difficulty of transporting troops and material by sea'.

    (ii) Stalin is 'cynically indifferent to everything but Russian ambitions'. It is pointed out that Russia left us alone in 1940 while she had a pact with Germany, and is still at peace with Japan while we have to fight her.

Whatever reasons are suggested to account for lack of co-operation, its possibility is almost universally deplored. It is widely hoped that:

(a) A conference between the three powers can be arranged to take place at an early date, to bring about 'open and friendly co-operation and ensure peaceful European settlement hereafter'.

(b) Mr. Churchill would throw some light on the subject in his speech and make it clear that 'we are really one with Russia in the present struggle'.

3. THE RUSSIAN OFFENSIVE

General pleasure is reported at the capture of Taganrog, following on that of Kharkov. Admiration for the Red Army, already great, is said to be increasing, and there is gratitude for 'all she is saving us' and 'restlessness that we are doing so little to help'.

Many expect further advances; some think 'the Ukraine may be captured by the end of the summer campaign', or even that, 'during the next few months, the Russians may be able to free most of their country'.

There is also speculation as to what Russia will do then. Some think she may stop at her borders and negotiate a separate peace, others that she will march through Poland into Germany; it is asked 'what will happen in this country if Russia gets to Berlin first?'

4. THE NEXT MOVES

Expectation that an Allied invasion of the Continent is imminent continues, but there appears to be less certainty about it this week, and, in view of Russia's need, more impatience.

Discussion is, however, not quite as widespread as it was, but the majority still find plenty of evidence to support their belief that it will take place before long, many thinking that 'the balloon will go up when the Prime Minister returns'.

There is considerable disappointment that 'We have reached September without any large European front being opened'. People are impatient that 'the Sicilian success was not followed by a quick attack on Italy', and fear that our delay is allowing the enemy to strengthen his defences. There is impatience at the apparent lull after each new move we make. Some suspect that the USA is more interested in the Far Eastern than the European war and may 'insist on the second front being against the Japanese'.

At the same time, most people, whether confident or disappointed, seem 'content to leave it to our leaders', feeling that 'further preparations are worth waiting for if these are essential to a more complete success'.

Speculation as to 'where' is on exactly the same lines as last week.

5. THE ALLIED AIR OFFENSIVE

(No reports have been received since the Berlin raid of August 31/September 1.)

Satisfaction with our 'massive raids' on enemy territory continues, and so does praise for, and pride in, the men of the RAF. It is felt that our 'terrific pounding' of Germany must be having its effect on German morale, and it is thought that 'signs of demoralisation and defeatism are already beginning to appear'. Demands for harder and heavier blows are again reported, and people are particularly anxious to see Italy 'hammered into submission'. Some believe that the RAF blows, particularly on southern Italy and the French aerodromes, are a prelude to invasion.

THE BERLIN RAID (AUGUST 23/24) was greeted with great satisfaction, though 'pleasure was modified at first by surprise and regret at the high losses'. However, it is felt they were probably not disproportionate to the numbers of planes involved or 'the effect achieved, and insignificant compared with those of a land offensive'. Demands for more and heavier bombing of Berlin continue ... 'let them go night after night – give 'em all we've got'.

USAAF: Comparison is made between the bomber losses of the USAAF, their claims of fighters shot down, and our own losses. People doubt if our own bombers are as well defended, and there are demands for their better equipment.

ROME: The general view is still that we should reject the proposal to make Rome an open city and that we should put no faith in Italian claims. 'Badoglio cannot be relied on to clear out military objectives.' People would like to see the bombing continued; and the Pope is criticised for his 'squeamishness' about possible damage to religious buildings. It is again pointed out that 'he did not appeal to the Germans to refrain from bombing London churches'.

6. GERMANY'S DIFFICULTIES

Although a few people are 'reluctant to be optimistic about it', many consider Himmler's appointment as 'a clear indication that German morale is getting shaky'. Some go so far as to hope that the bad news from the war fronts and our terrible air onslaught 'may break it more suddenly than appearances suggest'.

The unrest 'all over occupied Europe' – 'which must be increasing Germany's difficulties' – is watched with interest; as is also 'the changing attitude of neutral countries'. All this is felt to show that 'confidence in, and fear of, Germany are fading'. Specific reference is made to:

(a) DENMARK: There is admiration for the courage of the Danes in revolting against Nazi oppression and people hope that 'we may be able to help them very soon'. There is a tendency to interpret trouble here as a sign either that we intend to invade Denmark or that the Germans fear we will do so.

(b) DEATH OF KING BORIS: Little is known about Balkan politics and people cannot tell whether 'his removal will improve matters or not'. There is no sympathy for King Boris, but a good deal of speculation about how he died: 'Most people are convinced it was not a natural death.'

7. THE QUEBEC CONFERENCE

Speculation and comment about the Quebec Conference are less this week; some people are described as 'indifferent'. Decline in interest is variously attributed to lack of information, to people being 'tired of talk' and anxious for action, and to disappointment that the war against Japan was the principal subject of discussion. Nevertheless, many welcomed the Conference as 'foreshadowing a more active West Front offensive' and are 'hoping for big announcements'.

THE LACK OF RUSSIAN REPRESENTATION continues to be the cause of widespread regret and much anxiety (see section 2).

MRS. AND MISS CHURCHILL: Comment continues.

THE PRIME MINISTER'S SPEECH (to which no public reactions have yet been received) was eagerly awaited by most people, many of whom hoped it would shed light on the various questions that are exercising their minds. Its postponement caused disappointment and much speculation as to the reason. Some thought it indicated 'political awkwardness' and a failure to 'make up their minds'; but most people thought it implied some new development, such as the end of Italian resistance, which Mr. Churchill was to announce.

PRESIDENT ROOSEVELT'S SPEECH AT OTTAWA (August 25) is said to have aroused some 'mildly favourable' comment but not a great deal of interest.

THE REVELATIONS ABOUT HESS have been criticised on two grounds:

(a) Scouts and their parents are indignant, in spite of the explanation. As a Welshman observes: 'We take great news in a matter-of-fact way, while one remark out of place causes widespread discussion – we truly are a mad people.'

(b) 'The answer to the Hess mystery' was 'refused to the House of Commons' but was given in Canada.

THE PRESS HANDLING OF THE CONFERENCE is criticised. It is thought to have been 'singularly contradictory and confusing' and is also blamed for giving prominence to 'the holiday atmosphere at a time when people are anxious about Russia and want decisive action'.

8. ITALY

There is less talk this week about the political situation. A growing conviction that 'only military pressure will drive Italy into submission' is allied to restlessness at our delay in invading it. People wonder if this delay is 'yet another example of our being too kind to the Wops' – 'like the mistake we made laying off giving it to them when Musso fell'.

While the majority are in favour of 'nothing but unconditional surrender', a minority feel 'such severe terms are likely to make them fight on'.

BRITISH PRISONERS OF WAR: Anxiety continues at reports of their transfer from Italian to German hands.

9. SPAIN

There continues to be some speculation about the reasons for the Hoare-Franco talks: 'Does it mean better relations with Spain, or has Franco been acting on behalf of Italy?'

10. AMGOT

Some distrust of Amgot continues to be reported. It is described as 'an undemocratic body'; people wonder why it is necessary and where in the future 'the exiled Allied Governments and their peoples will come in'.

11. THE FRENCH COMMITTEE FOR NATIONAL LIBERATION

There has been satisfaction but very little comment at the recognition of the French Committee for National Liberation: 'There is not much interest in the French at present.'

'The lukewarm declaration by America' has caused comment, and she is also blamed for having caused the delay in giving this recognition.

12. FAR EAST

There continues to be little interest in the Far East, although some people wonder whether 'there is to be a new offensive as a result of the Quebec Conference'.

THE APPOINTMENT OF LORD LOUIS MOUNTBATTEN to the post of Supreme Allied Commander in South-East Asia is generally thought a good one: 'People expect fireworks when he gets going.' A minority doubt his being the right man for the post, however.

The appointment has been taken to show that we may be about to make a definite move, possibly towards the recovery of Burma and Malaya. Some 'puzzled' comment is recorded, however, that 'such leaders are needed against Germany, before bothering with the Far East'.

CHINA: Sympathy for China and the desire to help her are reported from six Regions this week.

PRISONERS OF WAR IN JAPANESE HANDS: Names of missing relatives continue to be welcomed but it is asked whether 'Geneva cannot do more to get information?' Gratitude is expressed for the broadcast about prisoners of war in the Far East given on August 24th.

13. WAR AT SEA

There is again little comment on this subject, but satisfaction and pleasure continue at the successes against the U-boat menace.

The fine work of the Royal Navy, especially during the Sicilian campaign, is praised and there is great confidence 'in its ability to deal with any situation'.

14. HOLIDAYS

There is less talk of holidays this week. People continue to believe in 'the necessity of holiday travel'; they feel that those workers who have gone away have been wise to do so. 'Those who did not go away, wish they had.' Some criticism of the 'Government's weakness and lack of foresight' and of the policy of holidays at home is again reported on familiar lines.

15. THE COASTAL AREA BAN

Interest and speculation continue as to the significance of the ban imposed on the south and south-east coast. It is still believed that preparations for invasion are being made in the area. It is again suggested that it may be a bluff designed to cover activity elsewhere – or even a double bluff.

Uncertainty as to the exact areas banned to visitors has been the cause of much telegraphing and telephoning. In the Southern Region, it is said that 'the restriction notices are so worded as to be incomprehensible to the general public'.

Rumours of troop movements come from the Regions involved in the ban.

16. BROADCASTING AND PRESENTATION OF NEWS

Satisfaction with news presentation by the BBC and in the press is reported from four Regions. 'People appear content to accept such official news as can be given at the moment.'

Sensational press headlines are criticised in two Regions. Although qualified by the following news paragraphs, 'they remain in the reader's mind' thus conveying the wrong impression. People are, however, said to be 'on guard against press misrepresentation'.

The BBC is again criticised for the repetition of news.

EUROPEAN NEWS SERVICE: Praise is again reported: 'It is given with more colour than the Home News'.

PRAISE this week for: Commander Kimmins' *Postscript* on the King's visit to the Fleet, August 22; the *Russian Commentary* by Alexander Werth, August 21; the *Into Battle* series; *War Commentaries*; the talk describing the construction of Mosquito planes, August 24.

DR. J. J. MALLON'S POSTSCRIPT (AUGUST 29) is criticised in three Regional reports. It is thought to have been an 'irritating pro-American advertisement' and 'too sloppy'. In one Region, however, it is thought 'likely to arouse real interest in American troops here'.

II. SPECIAL COMMENTS

WEEKLY SUMMARY

17. MANPOWER

THE PROPOSED REGISTRATION OF WOMEN: There is a further decrease in comment, but opposition is still said to be very strong and on the lines previously reported:

(a) IT WOULD BE UNNECESSARY 'IF MANPOWER WERE NOT BEING WASTED': Specifically mentioned are the many young people, particularly girls:

    (i) With little or nothing to do, in the Civil Service – including Labour Exchanges and Food Offices – factories, large businesses, and HM Forces.

    (ii) Doing jobs which older women could do.

    (iii) 'Who wriggle out of doing anything at all.'

(b) THEIR CALL-UP WILL SERVE NO GOOD PURPOSE because:

    (i) 'They won't be able to stand factory work.' Labour, it is suggested, should be recruited from those physically more fit, such as men and women discharged from the Forces, retired men in good health, and 'the many men on the dole'.

    (ii) 'All the older ones who are good for anything did not need calling up and have been doing their bit for ages.'

    (iii) 'What will happen to the voluntary work they are doing?' Many have been looking after their grandchildren, thus freeing younger women for the factory. Also, 'who's going to get the men's food and stand in queues for it?' Some of the work of the voluntary services, the WVS and National Savings movement in particular, 'will have to be curtailed'.

(c) 'WOMEN ARE CARRYING MORE THAN THEIR SHARE OF THE BURDENS OF WAR.'

RECRUITMENT TO THE WOMEN'S AUXILIARY SERVICES AND LAND ARMY: There is some disappointment among girls that no more recruits are wanted for the Forces and that 'they now have to go into munitions'.

In Dorset, farmers are said to be 'very perturbed at the restriction on recruiting for the Women's Land Army, especially as some of their male workers have only a short reservation'.

CHANGES OF PRIORITY IN MEN'S CALL-UP: Little comment is reported except in some mining areas where miners 'object to unskilled men being allowed to "opt" for mines when it requires years of training to become a useful worker'.

18. CLOTHING

Clothing continues the subject of much concern – footwear problems, in particular, in view of the coming winter months.

INCREASED COUPON VALUES FOR LEATHER-SOLED SHOES: (No reactions have been received to the announcement of extra coupons for children with big feet.) During the past two weeks there has been widespread criticism and resentment at the increased coupon values for leather-soled shoes. Parents of growing children who take adult sizes, and who are not tall enough to qualify for extra coupons, are especially upset: 'Boy's size 5 only require three coupons, but size 5½ now require nine coupons.'

People are said to have felt that even the old number was too high in view of the poor-wearing qualities of present-day shoes. It is claimed that a reduction rather than an increase in the coupon value of adult leather-soled shoes should have been made.

19. FOOD

Satisfaction with the food situation continues, although there is again some grumbling about the distribution and prices of certain commodities. The shortage of fruit and of tomatoes, and the high prices of vegetables and of fruit, are particularly criticised. People are asking 'where is the bumper crop of plums?'

From Scotland, it is reported that 'public anger is strong concerning the dumping of herrings at Clydeside ports last week. Press reports of conferences on the subject only increase the anger. "It's a pure scandal" is one of the milder comments on the situation. People are talking about this everywhere.' From Co. Durham it is also reported: 'There is a glut of fish, but here we have a famine.'

20. AGRICULTURE

The bumper harvest is praised this week in three Regional reports and Postal Censorship. In Wales, Devon and Cornwall, however, farmers complain that 'the weather has been against them'.

Though some farmers still report shortage of labour, others speak of voluntary help 'willingly and enthusiastically given'.

21. AMERICA

During the last four weeks, increasing appreciation for 'the great effort made by our American ally' in providing us 'with the food, the weapons, and the men' has been noted – though 'Russia's effort still overshadows them'.

'Doubts' still reported about America are as follows:

(a) America desires to dominate the world after the war. Some people ask 'how much of the Empire has already been ceded to America, and will we ever get it back?'

(b) There is some resentment and distrust of American claims of losses inflicted on the enemy: 'The Americans are assuming all the credit for present victories.'

AMERICAN TROOPS IN THIS COUNTRY: There has been little comment on American troops during the last four weeks. Some praise their 'niceness'; but the following familiar criticisms continue to be reported:

(a) Their behaviour with women and especially with young girls. 'Due to their efforts children of fourteen and fifteen are with child'; it is thought that 'American troops are amenable only to American law'. The girls themselves are, however, much blamed.

(b) Their high pay – as a result of which they are accused of ostentation, and of 'buying up' everything available including labour. The 'palatial premises' and 'lavish provision' provided for them are also criticised.

(c) Their waste of food and of petrol, their dangerous driving, rowdy behaviour, and excessive drinking.

In London, people are puzzled about the ribbons worn by American troops in this country.

NO. 153: TUESDAY 31 AUGUST 1943 TO TUESDAY 7 SEPTEMBER 1943

I. GENERAL COMMENTS

1. GENERAL STATE OF CONFIDENCE AND REACTION TO NEWS

The invasion of Italy – while 'taken for granted as the obvious next step after Sicily' – has cheered people; and satisfaction continues at Russian successes and our air offensive, particularly the bombing of Berlin. Confidence remains high, therefore, in spite of:

(a) Continued uneasiness over our relations with Russia. Though this has been partly allayed by the Prime Minister's speech, 'only the promised Conference with Stalin can prove we are in complete agreement'.

(b) A feeling that our landing in Italy 'is not an adequate contribution to Russia'. There is still considerable speculation as to where 'the real second front' will be.

(c)   Disappointment that Mr. Churchill did not make 'a really big announcement' in his Quebec speech.

The majority continue to expect the war to be over 'sometime in 1944', and an optimistic minority, by Christmas. People in any case 'do so hope this'll be the last blackout; it's like being buried alive'.

Footwear is again the main home front grumble.

2. ITALY

'The invasion of Italy, though a foregone conclusion after Sicily', gave people 'quite a thrill'. This has now given place to quiet satisfaction, to relief that 'our delays about Italy are over', and to interest in our progress.

People are expecting the Allies – most probably the Americans – to invade at another point further north in the next few days and cut off the Axis armies in the south. Some, indeed, are disappointed we have not already done so; and there is a slight fear 'we may have to work up the whole length of Italy'.

Many are wondering how long Italy will last, and most think 'not long'. A minority continue to feel that our insistence on unconditional surrender has prolonged matters, as 'it gave her no option but to carry on'. At the same time, there is some questioning as to whether we want her to collapse: 'it wouldn't be much good, as she'd become a liability just as she is now to the Germans'.

THE EIGHTH ARMY: A feeling that the Eighth always get the hard and dangerous jobs is again reported; but there is also satisfaction that it is the Eighth, as they can be relied on for a successful campaign. The absence of the Americans has led to some cynical comment, as well as speculation as to what they are going to do.

BADOGLIO'S GOVERNMENT: People 'aren't too sure' that fascism is really dead in Italy. This suspicion was increased by Badoglio's appointment of a new ambassador to Berlin (September 1).

BRITISH PRISONERS OF WAR: Much anxiety, particularly among relatives, continues at their transfer from Italy to Germany; 'Some people have already received news from men so transferred.' It is asked 'why can't the Government do something about it?'

3. THE PRIME MINISTER'S SPEECH (AUGUST 31)

Disappointment is widely reported, because:

(a)   His own voice could not be heard. 'People missed his personality.'
(b)   'We were not told anything new.' The postponement of his speech, and 'the false lead from the press', are blamed for making people expect striking news, such as Italy's capitulation or the start of our invasion of the Continent.

There was, however, great interest in, and satisfaction with, Mr. Churchill's statement on Russia, particularly with:

(a) His explanation of why Russia was not represented at the Quebec Conference. Many thought it wise to remind us that Russia and Japan are not at war and agree it would have been tactless and embarrassing to invite Marshal Stalin. Some, however, are uneasy that the war against Japan was a major topic at the Conference: 'Is our policy of dealing with Germany first being whittled down?'

(b) His wish for a threefold conference between President Roosevelt, Marshal Stalin and himself. This was much appreciated and people hope 'it will be speedily fulfilled'.

(c) His tribute to Russia.

Some adverse comment is reported from Wales and Scotland on Mr. Churchill's praise of France: 'So unnecessary after their miserable record'.

MR. CHURCHILL: There is anxiety for his safe return; and it is felt that 'he ought to be tethered at home for the sake of his own safety'.

4. RUSSIA, THE OTHER ALLIES, AND THE SECOND FRONT

Although Mr. Churchill's speech has helped to clear the air, uneasiness still continues about the relations between Russia and the English-speaking Allies. Blame for the disagreement is again placed on:

(a) A belief that there is anti-Russian feeling in the USA and also in high places in this country (but not Mr. Churchill or Mr. Eden).

(b) 'Russia's lack of appreciation of all we are doing.'

The cure is felt to be:

(a) 'The promised meeting' between the heads of the three powers.

(b) 'A proper second front which will divert sufficient German divisions from Russia.' Many do not accept the landing in Italy as a real second front and are ashamed we are not doing more for Russia.

THE SECOND FRONT: Though 'more and more fear we will have to wait for 1944 for our big move', many still expect that we shall invade either Western Europe or somewhere in the Eastern Mediterranean this autumn.

5. THE RUSSIAN OFFENSIVE

Admiration for the Russian advances increases. Some hope they will get to Germany first ... 'Russia will deal more effectively with war criminals.' Others think the Germans are carrying out a 'well-conducted withdrawal, directed now by military leaders and not by Hitler's intuition'; they fear the Germans may be able to get a firm hold on a shorter line before we can divert any large part of their forces.

Doubt continues of figures given in Russian communiqués. 'Anyone taking the trouble to keep totals will realise their impossibility.'

6. THE ALLIED AIR OFFENSIVE

Satisfaction continues, as does praise for the RAF and USAAF. While people hope for even greater and more frequent raids in future, there is concern at our losses; although many accept them as inevitable, it is felt 'an occasional reference to percentage losses might alleviate anxiety'.

Comment, some of it sceptical, is again made on the disparity between the number of fighters shot down by our own planes, and by American bombers.

Though no adverse comment is made, there is some tendency to believe that RAF targets 'are not all military now', and that the aim is to 'wipe out whole cities'. This view is based on the continual revisiting of bombed cities and the alleged lack of reference in the press to damage done to military objectives.

Special mention is made of:

(a) THE BERLIN RAIDS: These have given special satisfaction, as do all raids on the German capital.
(b) THE BRENNER-BOLOGNA RAID: This has also been greatly admired, though there is some feeling that this area should have been attacked before.

ROME: People still hope that we will 'bomb Rome and then bomb her again', disregarding all suggestions of making her an open city.

7. GERMANY'S DIFFICULTIES

People hope that the 'recent outbursts in occupied Europe', the internal difficulties in Germany (partly it is hoped due to our heavy raids), and the 'stiffened attitude of Sweden', are seriously weakening German morale; some feel that 'we should take advantage of the situation to make the vital diversion'.

Countries specifically mentioned are:

(a) DENMARK: People are full of admiration for the resistance of the Danes – particularly the actions of the Danish Navy – but there is some fear that they 'acted prematurely'. People wonder whether the outbreak was engineered by the Allies, either to 'keep the Germans on the jump', or as part of an invasion plan.
(b) BULGARIA: Interest in King Boris' death continues, as does the assumption that he died 'unnaturally' – either at the hands of a 'patriot' or of German agents. Some hoped that his death might 'improve the situation', and there is regret that it does not appear to have done so.
(c) SWEDEN: As a result of the recent friction between Sweden and Germany, people are wondering if 'she will be drawn into the war' or whether we shall invade Scandinavia.

8. THE FAR EAST

Interest remains limited (except for those with relatives out there). Nevertheless, news of Japanese air losses and of US Forces 'paving their way through territory held by the enemy' gives great satisfaction.

THE APPOINTMENT OF LORD LOUIS MOUNTBATTEN as Supreme Allied Commander in South-East Asia is again mentioned with pleasure. He is thought to be 'efficient and a good man for the job'. It is hoped an intensified attack on Japan will result from his appointment, bringing substantial relief to China.

PRISONERS IN JAPANESE HANDS: Concern continues over Japanese treatment of prisoners and their refusal to admit representatives of the International Red Cross.

CHINA: People ask for more news of China, and think she is not sufficiently acknowledged by Britain and the USA. 'The country which made the first stand seems to be last on our books.'

9. AMGOT

Criticism of Amgot is reported from two Regions. It is accused of 'suppressing democracy in Sicily', and people fear that if introduced into the liberated European countries, 'we shall see our military forces used to stabilise the fascist administrations we are setting out to destroy'.

10. HESS

There is still some criticism that the Hess story was told in America first.

Attempts in the press to 'write Hess off as insane' are looked on as possible excuses for avoiding punishing him.

The 'Boy Scout' discussion continues; a minority hold the view that it is 'much ado about nothing' ... 'an obviously unintentional slip of the tongue'.

11. NATIONAL DAY OF PRAYER

Reports from six Regions give news of services 'well attended'. There were queues outside a Manchester church where 'services were held every twenty minutes during the day', and enthusiasm at Cheltenham where, on the previous day, General Dobbie had spoken to packed audiences.

12. MR. LEARIE CONSTANTINE

Strong indignation has been reported at the refusal of a London hotel to accommodate Mr. Constantine and his party. Discrimination against any coloured men, but 'especially against those from the Dominions' (sic), is deplored: 'If they are good enough to fight for us, they are good enough to live with us.' In the Southern Region, people are said to feel that the matter cannot be left where it is, and in Scotland 'a number suggest that Mr. Constantine should be invited to lunch with the Royal Family at Buckingham Palace'.

Mr. Constantine's broadcast was appreciated and is said to have been very sympathetically received.

13. HOLIDAYS

Comment goes on along familiar lines. It is believed the press and BBC exaggerated stories of crowded stations so as to make people stay at home.

14. BROADCASTING AND NEWS PRESENTATION

Satisfaction with news presentation by press and radio continues.

There is, however, criticism of speculation and guesswork by the news services. Specific instances quoted are the sensational expectations aroused about the Prime Minister's speech, and the speculation on the reason for the recall of M. Maisky and M. Litvinov.

Some think there is too much detail in reports of air raids on enemy countries. They are said to resemble the 'Boche gloating of 1941'; people are 'getting weary of hearing the pilot's story of his experiences during raids'.

Criticism of press photographs is reported from two Regions. 'The press photographs of emergency feeding in Berlin have not convinced people that Berliners are worried and dejected.'

EUROPEAN NEWS SERVICE: Praise continues.

JOHN HILTON'S DEATH: 'Sincere regret' is expressed at the death of John Hilton. 'After listening to a man for ten years it is a great loss. He was, I am certain, very popular.'

PRAISE THIS WEEK FOR: Dr. J. J. Mallon's *Postscript*, August 29; Sir Philip Joubert's *Postscript*, September 2.

THE CHANGES IN THE DIRECTORATE OF THE BBC have aroused very little comment, but some hope of improvement in programmes and news editing.

THE EFFECT OF BATTERY SHORTAGES ON LISTENING HABITS

A BBC Listener Research Report, August 31, reveals the extent to which listeners are at present compelled to restrict their listening because of difficulty in getting batteries. The position for Great Britain as a whole, and for urban and rural areas within Great Britain, is shown below.

	In GB as a whole	In urban areas	In rural areas
	%	%	%
% of listeners whose sets are –			
– mains driven	78.6	82.4	64.0
– battery driven	21.4	17.6	36.0
	100.0	100.0	100.0

% of listeners who, because of battery shortages, cut down their listening –

– to little more than the news	3.3	2.2	8.0
– to a limited extent	9.9	7.8	17.7
% of listeners who, despite battery shortages, do *not* cut down their listening	8.2	7.6	10.3
Total battery-driven sets	21.4	17.6	36.0

In Great Britain as a whole more than 13% of the listening public is having to restrict its listening because of the shortage of dry batteries or the difficulty of getting wet batteries recharged. As will be seen, the position in country districts is very much more serious than in towns. Battery sets are relatively twice as frequently used in rural as in urban areas. In both types of area rationed listening is a majority practice by battery-set users, but it is much more common in rural areas where three battery-set owners in every four curtail their listening because of the shortage. (These figures may somewhat overstate the frequency of mains-driven sets in Great Britain, but there is no reason to believe that the relative positions of urban and rural areas are seriously misrepresented.)

II. SPECIAL COMMENTS

15. MANPOWER

THE PROPOSED REGISTRATION OF OLDER WOMEN: There has been a further decline in comment, but criticism continues on familiar lines:

(a) IT WOULD BE UNNECESSARY IF MANPOWER WERE NOT BEING WASTED. Specific mention is made of:

    (i) Younger women who are not pulling their weight in the Forces – 'they are openly boasting that they have nothing to do and are having the time of their lives' – in Government and local authority offices, and in the retail trade.

    (ii) Fit young men who are left in jobs which could be done by women. In the Midland Region it is felt to be a 'disgrace for older women to be called up so long as there is a conscientious objector allowed to evade war service'.

(b) MANY OLDER WOMEN ARE ALREADY FULLY OCCUPIED BY HOME CARES: 'Some long to be called up to be sure of a holiday.'

(c) THEY COULD NOT STAND THE STRAIN OF FACTORY WORK.

Some people feel that 'the proposal will come to nothing'.

16. CLOTHING

Clothing and footwear problems continue as main topics on the home front.

INCREASED COUPON ALLOWANCE FOR CHILDREN WITH LARGE FEET: The announcement of extra coupons for children with large feet has been welcomed. It is, however, said that the increased allowance 'doesn't promise the shoes will be there to buy' and 'doesn't solve the repair problem'. In the North-Western Region, there have been large queues to collect the additional coupons; because, it is thought, publicity 'has not been sufficiently clear and simple' and the general public are not aware that they have twelve months in which to collect them.

17. FOOD

General satisfaction with the food situation continues, as do the following complaints: the shortage of fruit and tomatoes, and high prices of vegetables. While the 'sugar instead of jam' scheme is again praised, it is asked 'what is the good without fruit?'

THE ANNOUNCEMENT OF THE REMOVAL OF CORNED BEEF FROM THE MEAT RATION has been greeted with satisfaction. People in the South-Western Region, however, 'didn't mind a bit of corned beef; it was useful for sandwiches'.

18. NEW FIRE-GUARD ORDERS

During the past two weeks there has been fairly widespread criticism of the Fire-Guard Orders, which are thought too complicated to be generally understood. There continues to be satisfaction with the concessions to women and the 'tightening of loopholes by which many escaped'. In the North Midland Region, it is said 'up to now few women have been released, and men appear hardly affected'.

19. YOUTH

During the past four weeks, references have again been made to concern about:

(a) The lack of home influence on young children, due to both parents being either at work or in the Forces. This is felt to result in much juvenile delinquency, including wanton damage and theft.
(b) The bad behaviour of adolescent girls 'throwing themselves at the troops', and the rowdy behaviour of adolescents of both sexes in public houses.

YOUTH ORGANISATIONS: Reference is again made to the importance of youth organisations in preventing the growth of juvenile delinquency and adolescent bad behaviour, and to the need for these organisations to find new methods of tackling these problems.

20. RUMOUR

In spite of denials, it is rumoured in three Regions that the basic petrol ration is to be reinstated.

NO. 154: TUESDAY 7 SEPTEMBER 1943 TO TUESDAY 14 SEPTEMBER 1943

I. GENERAL COMMENTS

1. GENERAL STATE OF CONFIDENCE AND REACTION TO NEWS

The news of Italy's capitulation raised people's spirits to a very high pitch and there was great enthusiasm and rejoicing at 'the biggest and most definite good news of the war'. There appears, however, to have been little of the 'Mafeking spirit'; and elation has since been steadied by the realisation that heavy fighting will be needed to beat the Germans in Italy, and by uncertainty about the present position there. On the whole, the public are said to be taking 'a steady and well-balanced view' of the situation; while Italy's collapse is thought to have brought the end of the war 'appreciably nearer', the majority still think it will not be before 1944 – though a minority say 'it will all be over by Christmas'.

The Italian news has overshadowed all else, but there is continued admiration for Russian successes and a slight decrease in uneasiness over her relations with the other Allies.

Though home affairs are 'taking very much of a back seat' at the moment, there continues to be much grumbling at footwear difficulties, and at the blackout. Many people think the blackout might be 'relaxed without undue danger, especially where the war effort would be aided'.

The change-over in war production is causing increasing comment.

2. THE CAPITULATION OF ITALY

The delight which greeted 'the best news of the war' found expression in flag flying and, in Northern Ireland, bell ringing. Some women wept with relief; many people hearing the radio announcement could not believe their ears and 'rushed from their homes to confirm if they had heard rightly'. There was a 'great eagerness to talk to strangers about the news'. Most people had believed that Italy would 'give it up' sooner or later, though few had expected it so soon. But even in the first flush of exhilaration, there seem to have been few celebrations, many thinking 'the time is not ripe for general thanksgiving'. The capitulation was rather looked on as 'a major step towards getting at the real enemy – Germany' – giving us control of the Mediterranean, and opportunities of invading the Balkans or southern France, and later bombing Germany and south-east Europe.

The first wave of excitement quickly subsided as it was realised that 'Italy is not to be ours till we have won it', and that there is strong German opposition to overcome. There is a feeling that, somehow or other, 'we have missed the bus', and have not got the initial advantage we appeared to have. People are 'disappointed that the Germans were allowed to get such rapid control of Rome and the rail and postal communications'. There is concern, too, at the progress of the present fighting, particularly in the Salerno area. Many are beginning to suspect that they had been 'unduly elated about a battle that had not been fought'.

THE PUBLIC'S ATTITUDE TO ITALY AND THE ITALIANS appears to be mixed. Some are bitter against Italy and 'regret that she hasn't been thrashed', and Rome 'Hamburged'. Others now regard the Italians as 'almost allies' and expect them to fight on our side. The most general attitude seems to be unsympathetic and distrustful: their capitulation is regarded as 'another stab in the back to their friends', while Italy's willingness to become active on our side is attributed to her 'wish to be on the winning side in the hope that some plums, even if very few, will be hers when settling day arrives'. Many feel that we must not be too lenient, nor 'forget Italy's evil doings'.

Anxious discussion is reported about the political side of Italy's surrender. People are insistent that, whatever the fate of the Italian people, 'Fascist leaders and accomplices must receive just punishment' and that there shall be 'no more Darlan episodes'. Distrust and disapproval of Amgot are reported, chiefly because it is believed to be 'bolstering up the fascist elements in Italy'.

The Badoglio government, as such, is little discussed.

THE ARMISTICE TERMS have not been talked of much; but there is 'pleasure at Eisenhower's statement that Russia approved of them', as the general impression had been that Russia was being left out.

THE SURRENDER OF THE ITALIAN FLEET has given great pleasure. The fleet is thought by many to be the most valuable result of the capitulation, particularly as 'it will free a useful number of warships for use against Japan'. There has, however, been 'some irritation at the sudden transformation in official judgment of the Italian fleet from a useless to a beautiful and powerful fleet'.

The description of the ships' arrival at Malta caught people's imagination, and there was 'sympathy and pleasure at the joy of the people of Malta' who 'so well deserved this cheering sight'.

BRITISH PRISONERS OF WAR IN ITALY: There has been much discussion about the return of British prisoners in Italy. Many people's first thought was that they would soon be home; their relatives were 'overwhelmed with joy'; some were asking if they could now send better parcels to their menfolk and if the old address would find them; a few even said: 'He'll be home before our parcel would reach him.' Disappointment and worry have now returned; it is beginning to be assumed that no immediate repatriation is probable and that many prisoners will be in German hands by now. There is great anxiety to know how many may already have been sent to Germany, and some desire for a Government statement.

ITALIAN PRISONERS OF WAR IN THIS COUNTRY: People – Scottish farmers, among them – are asking if they are to be returned to their own country or kept here. Their agricultural help will be missed.

MUSSOLINI'S 'RESCUE' is viewed with some scepticism, and it is questioned whether he was ever in Badoglio's hands. At the same time, people feel that, if the German version is true, then we have 'allowed them to make a propaganda scoop' and have ourselves 'slipped up, in not getting Mussolini into our hands earlier'. It is not expected, however, that he will be of much use to the Germans, though it is feared he may rally some Italian troops to the new Fascist government. Some people regret we have lost this opportunity of showing how war criminals would be dealt with.

SUPPLIES FOR ITALY: People are not pleased at the idea of our having to supply Italy with coal and wheat, while Germany will now be freed from this burden. They feel 'the Italians may get more than they are accustomed to, while we at home get less', and they fear 'we shall see further cuts in various commodities to provide the Italians with the necessities of life'. One widespread suggestion is that Italian prisoners of war should be sent down the mines to hew coal for Italy.

3. RUSSIA AND THE OTHER ALLIES

Uneasiness at Russia's relations with USA and ourselves continues, but is rather less than during recent weeks. This appears to be due to the Prime Minister's explanation of Russia's absence from the Quebec Conference. But the desire for a three-power conference as soon as possible is again widely expressed.

The wish to give all possible help to Russia remains strong, and many feel we are not yet doing enough. Nevertheless, there is said to be 'a hardening attitude towards Russia's implied criticisms and "immediate second front" demands'. People feel increasingly that Russia refuses to recognise what we have done in Africa and Italy, and by bombing the Germans and 'pinning down an army in France and elsewhere'; and there is a growing belief that 'Russia could not have sustained her gigantic offensive without the vast quantities of war materials poured into her by Britain and America'. There is increasing irritation at 'Russia's insistence on the opening of the one kind of second front they happen to visualise', and there has been great praise for Sir Walter Citrine's 'sane speech' on the subject, 'particularly his reminder that Japan is also our enemy'.

4. THE NEXT MOVE

Further landings on the Continent in the near future – not just in another part of Italy – seem to be generally expected and hoped for; people still find many portents to support their belief. Speculation remains varied, both as to place and time, but people persist in thinking that invasion of the west of Europe is the shortest way to Berlin, and the sooner the better – though at our time, and not Russia's.

5. THE ALLIED AIR OFFENSIVE

Though overshadowed by other events, considerable satisfaction continues at our air offensive. Comment follows familiar lines. Some feel we should have bombed Berlin while German morale was still affected by Italy's capitulation.

The recent invasion exercises in the Channel were thought by some to be a prelude to invasion; others thought they were 'a bluff to get the Luftwaffe into the sky' and are wondering why 'they did not play'. A rumour that France had actually been invaded on September 9 circulated quite widely in two Regions.

6. THE PRIME MINISTER

HIS QUEBEC SPEECH (AUGUST 31): Comment continues on the same lines as last week.

THE SPEECH AT HARVARD (SEPTEMBER 6) seems to have caused little comment, though some discussion of Basic English has resulted among educated people, particularly in Scotland.

7. THE RUSSIAN OFFENSIVE

Admiration continues, but there seems to be a growing assumption that 'the Germans are retreating intentionally to a line nearer their frontier' and are 'not sustaining the succession of calamitous defeats the Russians are making out'.

Doubt continues of figures given in Russian communiqués.

8. HITLER'S SPEECH (SEPTEMBER 10)

A little contemptuous comment is reported. 'He knows he is beaten and must do something to camouflage it with heroics.'

9. THE TRADES UNION CONGRESS

There has been considerable interest in the Congress this year and in the presence of members of the Russian delegation. Great praise is reported for the speeches by:

(a) MR. BEVIN: By far the most comment aroused by the whole conference was about his statement on demobilisation. While many think it only fair that 'first in should be first out', it is also felt that the following claims should be considered:

    (i)   Key men in industry who have most probably been called up late. It is felt that the quickest way to get post-war employment going is to release these men and others with jobs waiting for them.

    (ii) Family men.

    (iii) Those serving abroad.

(b) SIR WALTER CITRINE: His reply to M. Shvernik is felt to have put Anglo-Soviet relations in their right perspective.

(c) MR. JARMAN (Seamen's Union): Some refer to his speech as 'the gem of the proceedings'.

10. RAIDS ON THIS COUNTRY

During the past three weeks comment on the expectation of raids on this country has declined. There is some fear that 'Germany will have a last fling when she is desperate', but otherwise little expectation. It has been rumoured in London that a large bomber force was discovered assembled in northern France for reprisal raids; this was attacked by Fortresses and completely destroyed.

Criticism of the air-raid warning system is reported from three Regions. At Bognor and Portsmouth, the 'All Clear' is said to have been given 'while planes were still in the vicinity and gunfire in progress'. In Plymouth 'bombs were dropped as the "All Clear" was sounding'.

11. MR. LEARIE CONSTANTINE

Indignation continues about 'this most abominable business'. It is said that the manager of the Imperial Hotel 'should have invited the complainant to leave if he did not wish to be in the same hotel as a distinguished coloured guest' … 'Talk about Hitlerism, it exists in this land of ours and must be rooted up.' It is again suggested that Mr. Constantine should be invited to dine with the Royal Family. His broadcast was heard with sympathy and appreciation.

12. BROADCASTING AND PRESENTATION OF NEWS

Interest in news has greatly increased. Criticism of its presentation remains slight.

The playing of the national anthems of Britain, America and the USSR in the 9 o'clock news on September 8 gave pleasure and satisfaction. Wales is pleased that the 5 o'clock Welsh news on September 8 was the first to announce Italy's capitulation.

PRAISE THIS WEEK FOR: the broadcast made from a bomber over Berlin, September 4.

MR. DALTON'S POSTSCRIPT SEPTEMBER 7: This received a mixed reception but was praised for its frankness.

II. SPECIAL COMMENTS

MONTHLY REVIEW

13. INDUSTRY

DURING THE LAST FOUR WEEKS there has been an increase in comment. The main topics have been:

PRODUCTION: A fairly general belief that 'things are not as good as they might be' is attributed to widespread stories of:

(a) ENFORCED IDLENESS: Specifically mentioned are Woolwich Arsenal, Plessey's of Walthamstow, ROF Aycliffe, the British Overseas Airways Corporation at Hythe, Southampton, and aircraft factories in Dorset. At Sherborne, irritation has been increased by press advertisements for part-time and other workers for factories where both men and women already employed 'are sick of hanging about with nothing to do'.

It is also suggested in the Northern Region that shipyard workers think 'the powers that be are not anxious to have the building of merchant ships accelerated, as reliance is being placed on US output'.

(b) SLACKING OF WORKERS: This is variously felt to be due to:

(i)   'A considerable lack of honest effort.' At the Ordnance Depot,
      Tongham, near Aldershot, women on part-time work complain of
      well-paid men workers asleep during their working hours.

(ii) Income tax.

(iii) A feeling that the war is nearly won. Thus, in Croydon,
      managements are complaining that 'in some instances workers have
      slacked off following Admiral Sir Edward Evans' statement to Civil
      Defence workers (Sept. 8) that the war will be over by March 3.
      This statement received wide publicity as it was 'splashed' in the
      local papers.

(iv) Lack of interest in their jobs because of talk of over-production.

(v)   Lack of sympathy between workers and management, in some cases
      allied to a belief that firms are working for post-war.

(c) THE CLOSING DOWN OF SOME MUNITION WORKS: Workers are
     said to be nervous about the loss of work and wages entailed, or likely to
     be entailed, by the change-over in production; Clydeside is described as
     'seething with talk about the change-over'. The decision that women, 'who
     will thus become redundant, should go into machine shops to replace men
     who will be called up for the Services has led to the formation by some
     shop stewards of a "Campaign Committee" to protest against the proposed
     redundancy of the women'.

WAGES: Criticism continues of:

(a) THE HIGH WAGES paid to munition workers and to juveniles.

(b) THE DISPARITY OF PAY between:

(i)   People doing the same jobs in different factories. Those in
      Government and those in private firms, for instance.

(ii) Munition workers and, variously, agriculture workers, transport
      workers, servicemen and miners.

TRANSFER OF WORKERS: The two main complaints are still of billeting
difficulties and of transfer to less well-paid jobs.

The transfer of Scottish girls to England continues to be highly unpopular and
many bitter comments are heard.

LONG HOURS: It is felt that too much overtime is harmful to the workers –
particularly juveniles – and to production. On the other hand, workers would not,
it is surmised, 'welcome any reduction in wages'.

14. MANPOWER

THE PROPOSED REGISTRATION OF OLDER WOMEN continues to be
unpopular; again, mainly because 'it's a shame to raise the age from 45 before all
the 20s and 30s are weeded out'. Evasion and overstaffing both 'need a complete
overhaul'. Other objections are:

(a) These women are already doing as much as they can, 'what with the time now taken housekeeping, with shopping and transport difficulties'. Too severe a strain on their health is feared.
(b) Many of them are looking after young children while the mothers are at work.

Among the women themselves, some agree with the general condemnation, others have accepted the proposal philosophically, and yet others 'are worrying themselves sick about it'.

In London, it is suggested much of the hostility is based on a misunderstanding of the position: 'Registration is thought to mean immediate call-up and women do not realise they have a right to appeal.'

DEFERMENT CUTS FOR MEN UNDER 39: In Scotland, 'while men and Civil Servants are on the whole considering their threatened call-up calmly, key men in industry are annoyed'. In the Midland Region fuller details are asked for of trades, industries and professions likely to be affected.

DURING THE LAST FOUR WEEKS – in addition to the proposed registration of older women, evasion of national service, and overstaffing – there has been criticism of:

(a) THE LACK OF DOMESTIC HELP: The difficulties of expectant mothers and invalids are particularly mentioned: 'Not only can they get no help at home, but they can also get no accommodation at nursing homes and hospitals.' It is felt that 'there should be an organised scheme for home helps for those with legitimate needs'.

Two reports refer to the high pay of domestics, 'out of all proportion to the services rendered'. Hotels and boarding houses are blamed for forcing prices up, by paying, for instance, 15/- a day all food found, or, in another case, £1 for half a day only.
(b) THE MISDIRECTION OF MANPOWER: Stories are reported of labour being directed to factories where there is insufficient work, and of skilled workers being put on unskilled work.
(c) SHORTAGE OF STAFF: Firms of all kinds, particularly small ones, 'are finding it difficult to carry on with the staffs left to them'. They resent 'the direction of members of their staff to jobs where there is little work to do'.

15. THE POST-WAR WORLD

DURING THE PAST FOUR WEEKS, discussion has continued along familiar lines. The great majority of people remain anxious for plans to be made now, 'to avoid a repetition of the chaos after the last war', and there are persistent demands for 'less talk and more action' on the part of the Government. In London particularly, 'the prospects of early victory' are thought to have increased interest in post-war problems, and less people are said to be advocating the 'plans can wait, let's win the war first' policy.

The desire for social security, particularly the implementation of the Beveridge Report, remains as strong as ever, especially among working-class people who feel that 'the Tories and the vested interests are doing their best to torpedo any social security plans'. Cynicism and apprehension as to the Government's intentions are still widely reported; it is feared that 'they do not mean business as far as Beveridge is concerned'. A small minority still feel that 'social security must depend on the state of post-war trade' and fear that 'we may be unable to afford Beveridge'.

Other problems discussed include:

HOUSING: Anxiety and concern – particularly among servicemen – at the housing shortage continue. People are asking: 'If it's like this now, what will it be like when the boys return?' and they demand that the Government 'face up to the issue at full speed'. The need for control of land speculation, and more definite pronouncements of Government policy on the Uthwatt, Barlow and Scott Reports, is also expressed.

The desire for modern 'non-jerry-built' houses with all labour-saving devices is said to be strong among working people.

EMPLOYMENT: Discussion about the prospects of post-war employment continues along familiar lines. Concern is particularly expressed by servicemen, who wonder if 'there will be a job waiting for them after demobilisation', and by war workers whose jobs close at the end of the war.

EDUCATION: Discussion on the White Paper continues along familiar lines (see Home Intelligence Weekly Reports Nos. 146–149).

AGRICULTURE: Farmers continue to express concern at the lack of official statements on post-war agricultural policy, and some fear that the Government means to 'let them down again'. Others dread their markets will be undercut after the war by an influx of cheap imported food.

16. MINERS, MINING AND COAL

THE AWARD OF THE NATIONAL TRIBUNAL (THE PORTER COMMITTEE) ON PIT YOUTHS' WAGES: Seven Regions refer to criticism and irritation at this award. 'No wonder the mining families send their boys into any work except mining – this is much less than office boys or factory hands are getting.' In Scotland, while a small minority are said to be pained at the 'contemptuous manner' adopted by the miners' leaders, the public generally are thought to agree with them.

There is 'malicious amusement that the award should have coincided with the Government's appeal for recruits'. 'The announcement of the award has killed the appeal.'

THE GOVERNMENT'S CAMPAIGN TO OBTAIN LABOUR FOR THE MINES: During the past two weeks there has been considerable criticism of this campaign and 'sceptical doubts' on the possibilities of its success. It is thought that its success will be hindered by the following beliefs:

(a) 'MINING IS A "GHASTLY" LIFE': Bad conditions, low wages, the nature of the work, 'the long history of injustice in the mines', are thought to make the present appeal 'almost frivolous, it is so superficial'. 'Parents would rather go to prison than allow their sons to go down the mines.'

(b) INEXPERIENCED MEN IN THE MINES ARE WORSE THAN NONE AT ALL: 'The "pit sense" and skill acquired by the miner are not attained in the short space of eight months.'

(c) MEN WILL PREFER SERVICE IN THE FORCES.

The following suggestions for tackling the problem are made:

(a) The return of skilled men from the Forces. In six Regions this 'is felt to be the solution'. 'It should have been foreseen that the strong young miners being called to the Forces would reduce production.' 'Boys should enter the Services and skilled miners now in the Forces should return to the pits.'

(b) Italian prisoners of war should be employed in the mines, 'as Germany used our prisoners last time, and is no doubt doing again'.

(c) 'Some guarantee of permanent Government control.'

In the Southern Region, the advertisements in the *Times*, the *Observer*, and the *Daily Telegraph* are thought to be a waste of money, 'since no readers of those papers could possibly be expected to volunteer as miners'.

COAL FOR ITALY: DURING THE LAST FOUR WEEKS resentment at the possibility of coal being sent to Italy has been reported, 'particularly since our own needs are far from being met'.

The fact that 'boys of sixteen may be forced into the pits to send coal to the Italians' is particularly resented. Miners, it is also thought, cannot be expected to produce more coal if at the same time large quantities are being shipped to Italy. 'Bring the Italians over here and let *them* do the digging.'

It is suggested that 'there has been some confusion of propaganda in this direction'. Recent statements are thought not to have sufficiently emphasised that the coal will be needed to keep essential services going, in Allied interests.

FUELS AND DOMESTIC COAL: DURING THE LAST FOUR WEEKS anxiety about the coal situation for the coming winter has increased. It is felt that the need for stricter economies needs stressing.

There have also been complaints of the difficulty of stocking up coal – largely because of transport difficulties. 'Ordering of coal in response to fuel advertisements is a farce when orders placed in June have not yet been completed.'

THE PARAFFIN PRIORITY SCHEME: Complaints of the inadequacy of the paraffin ration come from three Regions. People with no other means of heating and lighting, or with very large houses, are said to be 'loud in their grumbles'.

It is thought that people are overstating their needs on the application form in the belief that they will be allocated only a proportion of their needs.

17. CLOTHING

DURING THE PAST FOUR WEEKS clothing and footwear problems have remained as major topics on the home front. The various complaints may be summarised as follows:

FOOTWEAR: This is the principal difficulty of housewives and causes more comment than any other clothing item. Apprehension about the footwear position in the coming winter has increased during the past month.

THE POOR QUALITY of shoes, particularly children's, is the main cause of complaint: 'It is feared that shoes as at present available will be poor protection in bad weather.'

THE SHORTAGE of children's boots and shoes is also causing increased concern. Parents in Scotland are saying: 'What is the use of providing cod-liver oil and orange juice at one end while the other end is exposed to the rigours of our devilish winter?'
    Other comments on footwear include:

(a) SHOE REPAIRS: Complaints of the difficulty and length of time taken to get shoes repaired are very widespread. 'In some areas the position is so serious that repairs cannot be effected under six to eight weeks' ... 'In Coatbridge the leading shoe repairer had a queue of over 100 with repairs, on opening after the holiday period.' The shortage of shoe leather for home repairs and the 'rubbishy nature' of leather used in repairs are complained of. The call-up of repairers 'who are directed to national service of some kind' is deprecated.

(b) INCREASED COUPONS FOR SHOES: Criticism has continued during the past two weeks and people think 'it would have been better to add two coupons to suits and dresses'.

(c) WOODEN-SOLED SHOES: It is thought a campaign is needed if the Government want people to wear wooden-soled shoes. Their price is thought to be too high.

CLOTHING COUPONS: These remain a major topic of discussion. The difficulties of the poorer sections of the community whose pre-war incomes never permitted a good stock of clothes are stressed. 'Even the most careful insist that the present ration does not allow them to buy the necessities unless they were fortunate enough to have heavy pre-war stocks.' The problem of keeping pace with the demands of growing children is again stressed. Specific mention also continues to be made of:

(a) COUPONS FOR HOUSEHOLD LINEN: The demand for these continues. 'Householders' stocks of linen are getting lower and on the coupons now allowed there is no prospect getting replacements.' The unfortunate position of newly marrieds is particularly mentioned.

(b) COUPONS FOR INDUSTRIAL WORKERS: Heavy industrial workers are said to be in a desperate position: 'The coupon allowance covers only working clothes and leaves nothing for best.'

UTILITY CLOTHING: The poor quality of utility clothing continues to be alleged. It is again argued that 'utility goods should be dependable', as many articles sold today are a waste of material and labour: 'Men complain of shirts and collars shrinking in the first wash.'

SAM BROWNE BELTS: It is hoped that their abolition will mean more leather for children's shoes and repairs.

18. HOUSING

DURING THE PAST FOUR WEEKS, the shortage of housing and accommodation has remained acute. It is alleged that many large houses have been held by Government departments and never used, and it is thought that these would be better employed as dwelling-places. The high price of housing is also much commented on: 'Rents are likely to remain high when people pay over £1,000 for an agricultural cottage.'

AGRICULTURAL HOUSING: The slowness in the erection of agricultural cottages and their high rental are criticised.

LOCAL AUTHORITIES' NEW POWERS TO REQUISITION EMPTY HOUSES are thought to be a very short and inadequate step in the right direction; there is some cynicism about their effectiveness.

19. FOOD

There is less comment on the food situation this week. Complaints of the high prices of vegetables, and of the shortage of fruit, vegetables and tomatoes, continue, however.

THE ANNOUNCEMENT THAT THE JAM RATION WILL BE DOUBLED during the twelve weeks beginning September 19 has been welcomed.

DURING THE LAST FOUR WEEKS satisfaction with the food situation and praise for Lord Woolton, 'the country's best doctor', have been general. This has been qualified, however, by the grumbles already reported about the shortage, distribution and high price of fruit, vegetables, and tomatoes. In addition, the following topics have been the subject of complaint.

MILK SUPPLIES: There have been reports of dissatisfaction about:

(a) THE SHORTAGE OF DRIED MILK.
(b) MILK GOING SOUR: 'It's a full day old before we receive it.' The long distances involved in distribution, 'wholesale mixing' at depots, dirty milk bottles, and the poor quality of milk are all blamed.
(c) THE REDUCTION OF THE RATION: There is also anxiety about the milk position for the coming winter.
(d) IRREGULAR DELIVERIES: There are again complaints of the milkless day; in some cases, there are said to be no Saturday or Sunday deliveries.
(e) RATIONALISATION OF MILK DELIVERIES: There are still grumbles about not being able to choose the milkman and that the Co-operative Wholesale Society is not affected by the scheme.

FISH: While there is some satisfaction at improved supplies, complaints of shortage, distribution and poor quality continue. There is still some bitter discussion about the dumping of fish back into the sea.

BREAD: There have again been complaints of the poor keeping quality of the National Loaf. Some council pig-food bins are said to be 'full of half-used National Loaves'. There are also complaints of the poor quality of flour.

SWEETS AND CHOCOLATES: Inadequate supplies are reported.

INADEQUACY OF RATIONS is complained of by the following:

(a) Workers in heavy industries.
(b) People living alone, whose difficulties in obtaining goods with higher points value are stressed.

MINISTRY OF FOOD 'FOOD FACTS' ADVERTISEMENTS are praised, particularly the advice on the bottling of fruit and vegetables. 'They are thought to take the place of the family recipe book, which speaks for itself.'

20. SHOPPING DIFFICULTIES AND FOOD QUEUES

Complaints have been widespread during the last four weeks. There is much concern at the anticipated earlier closing of shops and the possibility of goods being in short supply during the coming winter.

Chief complaints are from the following:

(a) HOUSEWIVES ON WAR WORK: They complain that even now they find it extremely hard to do their shopping and have, in any case, no time for queuing 'for the tit-bits which are scooped up by the leisured'.
(b) COUNTRY DWELLERS who, having to cope with transport difficulties, often find things sold out by the time they arrive.
(c) RESIDENTS AT HOLIDAY RESORTS: Complaints continue of goods being bought up by visitors.

21. CIVIL DEFENCE AND FIRE-WATCHING

THE NEW FIRE-GUARD ORDERS continue to be criticised for their complexity. It is felt that there are 'too many orders which override one another'.

THE BLACKOUT: During the past four weeks, some dread of the winter blackout, and persistent demands for its relaxation, have been reported. People feel that this winter 'it could be modified without due danger', and dwellers in the provinces ask for 'an improved lighting system, the same as London'.

In three Regions, people, especially in the poorer districts, are thought to be growing careless over their blackout.

CIVIL DEFENCE WORKERS: During the past three weeks there has been occasional reference to slackness of Civil Defence workers owing to the absence of bombing. Difficulties are being encountered in getting them to take their training seriously. Fire-Guard personnel – especially women – object to exercises as a waste of time.

22. AGRICULTURE

During the past four weeks 'bumper crops' have been reported, in some cases safely harvested, but there is also much anxiety about the weather, particularly over grain crops. In the Lake District the 'fine wheat crops are becoming rapidly spoiled by the heavy and increasing rainfall'. 'Grain is wasted in Keswick as the weather is not suitable even if the soil is.'

People note with approval that 'more land than ever before' is under cultivation and it is hoped that 'we shall not let England go to waste again'. But farmers in Berkshire and Wales fear it may not be realised how much is being taken out of the land by constant cropping, now that the usual rotation cannot be practised.

LABOUR shortage is reported, and there is doubt whether some farmers have taken full advantage of volunteer labour available. In some cases it is warmly welcomed, but it is also said that 'with the exception of a few, holiday-makers make no serious efforts except under direct supervision'. Many farmers prefer soldiers, and appreciation is expressed in the Southern Region of help given by the army, particularly by troops from wheat-growing districts of Canada. In the North-East, some farmers grumble because more troops have not been allocated to them, as 'owing to the bad weather many more helpers are needed on the occasional fine days if crops are to be saved'. Schoolboys have done 'good work in harvest and potato lifting'. There is both criticism of 'sketchy and tardily planned' accommodation for volunteers and appreciation of arrangements made.

AGRICULTURAL MACHINERY AND IMPLEMENTS: The more general availability of machinery is said to have a 'stimulating effect on the tempo of the workers', and a census of all implements is suggested with a view to their being fully used. One of the most serious handicaps is the lack of spare parts – 'sometimes it is necessary to get in touch with twenty firms before finding the required part'. It is suggested that agriculture should have a fair share of priority in manufacture of these spares, and records kept of where they can be obtained.

ITALIAN PRISONERS: There are again complaints of 'too much liberty' and of 'association with English girls'. It is thought that cautions given to girls should be enforced by 'something more stringent than pious advice'.

WOMEN'S LAND ARMY: It is said that the WLA does not, in some places, receive the same consideration and facilities for canteens, etc., as other Women's Services; and it is felt that the WLA should have the same treatment as the ATS when on leave.

POTATOES: There is comment on the shortage of feed potatoes. Some farmers complain they cannot get a licence from the Ministry of Food to sell potatoes damaged by wireworm for animal food, and they fear these will be wasted. Others say that because of transport regulations potatoes are being dug in as manure by growers.

FARM REPAIRS AND UPKEEP OF TOOLS: Farmers comment on the difficulty over repairs owing to the removal of small country builders to other work, and of the distance (sometimes a five-mile walk) to the nearest blacksmith for horse-shoeing and sharpening of implements.

DOMESTIC HELP ON FARMS: Farmers' wives complain that home helps are still not available and labour is getting shorter and shorter.

PAY FOR AGRICULTURAL LABOURERS: The proposed 5/- increase to farm labourers is thought by some farmers to be unnecessary, as they have many privileges such as cheap or rent-free cottages, milk and other commodities, and 'the average farm labourer is now earning £5 with overtime'.

Further comments, each from one Region, are:

(a) Criticism of the taking over by the Government of the County Veterinary Services. Some farmers say the only result has been a definite increase in sheep scab and higher costs.

(b) Praise for the generous treatment of small poultry owners by some farmers, in giving facilities for gleaning.

(c) Criticism of the Ministry of Food in expecting the incentive of ½d. per gallon for an increased supply of milk to operate in two or three weeks' time: 'It takes a long time to produce a milk cow.'

(d) Uneasiness caused by the report of successful action taken by a landlord against a tenant who had been ordered by the WAEC to plough land. On giving up tenancy after two years he was sued for ploughing and leaving land contrary to agreement.

(e) In Maidenhead, the Temple golf links, with huge acreage of meadow land, are 'reserved for a few gentlemen to play golf', while Pinkneys Green common has been cleared, at enormous expense, for corn.

23. TRANSPORT DIFFICULTIES

Complaints of transport difficulties continue to be widespread, particularly:

(a) OVERCROWDING OF BUSES AND TRAINS by (i) holiday-makers, though during the past two weeks complaints have decreased; (ii) short-distance travellers crowding out long-distance travellers; (iii) shoppers travelling at rush hour.

(b) RESTRICTION OF BUS SERVICES, particularly at weekends and in the evening.

(c) THE INADEQUACY OF:

   (i) BUS SERVICES IN RURAL AREAS.
   (ii) TRANSPORT FOR WORKERS, particularly buses at rush hours. There are demands for the priority badge system from districts where it has not been introduced; and, from districts where it has, complaints that it does not always ensure transport for workers.

(d) Time wasted queuing and failure of buses to stop at recognised stopping places.

24. WASTE OF PETROL

Complaints of waste of petrol continue to be fairly widespread. There is still some feeling that petrol allowances are not fairly allocated and that the 'wangling of allowances still goes on'. There are complaints of petrol wasted by:

(a) TAXIS AND PRIVATE CARS, particularly for holiday-making, greyhound racing and pub-crawling.
(b) PLEASURE FAIRS, 'who use as much petrol as a convoy', and HORSE BOXES bringing horses from long distances to agricultural shows.

The following are particularly accused of wasting their petrol allowances: farmers, Government officials, works managers, cinema proprietors, the Services and the Home Guard.

During the past two weeks three Regional reports have referred to rumours that the basic ration is to be reinstated for those whose cars are now taxed.

25. SALVAGE

Complaints of non-collection of household and other salvage have continued during the past four weeks. Bones are specially mentioned: 'Bones salvaged by housewives are reasonably clean, but whole heads sent by butchers become a nuisance when they cannot be collected daily.'

Some people think that interest in salvage collecting is flagging and 'the time may be opportune for a general boost', but the 'iron salvage collected in school playgrounds' and the 'dumps of old tins' are likely to have a detrimental effect on any appeal.

There is complaint of iron salvage removed for which no compensation has been paid, and of the rates of compensation. It is thought that the Government should pay reasonable prices, and the fact that only 3% of the public have claimed compensation is no indication of their willingness to give up their railings, but is due rather to the feeling that it is not worth while to claim a few shillings for what will cost pounds to replace.

PAPER SALVAGE AND BOOK DRIVES: There is comment on the waste of paper both by the public and by the Government. 'The Government tells us there is a shortage, yet who wastes paper as much as Government departments?' It is thought there is great room for economy in posters and leaflets. Continued good response to the appeal for books in the North-Eastern Region is reported.

26. HEALTH

DURING THE LAST FOUR WEEKS, there have continued to be many complaints of tiredness and ill health, particularly among women workers. This fatigue is variously thought to be due to long hours of work, 'the additional drain on energy' of Civil Defence duties, insufficient fresh air or daylight in factories, wartime food, and 'the harassing problems of housekeeping on top of it all'.

'A whole crop of minor ailments' such as shingles, boils, rashes, festering fingers and varicose conditions are reported in some factories.

Two Regions refer to concern over the spread of impetigo and 'the carelessness of people who have an infectious disease in the house in spreading germs'.

27. VENEREAL DISEASE

There has been little comment on the venereal disease campaign during the last four weeks. Praise has been accorded the 'more vivid press advertisements', as a result of which more people are thought to be seeking advice, but some belief is reported that the letters in the advertisements are merely 'made-up stuff'. There is also some fear that the campaign is not 'cutting much ice among the ordinary people or hitting the mark where it is needed'.

28. INCOME TAX

The widespread demand for 'pay as you go income tax' continues. There is much dissatisfaction with the present system, particularly among workers who:

(a) Are working fewer hours than previously because of the production change-over.
(b) Are transferred to less-well-paid jobs.
(c) Return to work after a period of sickness.

29. PENSIONS AND ALLOWANCES

Comment has been less during the past four weeks. People feel that further improvement is still needed, but the increased pensions for widows with children 'is another nibble in the right direction'. It is thought widows' pensions should not be taxed and that parents who have lost a child on war service should rank for pension without a means test. The Pensions Tribunals are welcomed but there is some impatience at the delay in their operation.

Other points raised are:

(i) Servicemen's wives with families have difficulty in living on the Government allowances. Expectant mothers need more than their allowance.
(ii) The unnecessary hardship caused to servicemen's wives whose grants are reduced following an increase in their husband's pay. If the man is abroad nobody informs him of the cut, and 'in the time that elapses before he can hear from her she gets into difficulties'.

OLD AGE PENSIONS: There have been few references during the past four weeks, but criticism of the inadequacy of pensions and the delay in applying a remedy continues.

NO. 155: TUESDAY 14 SEPTEMBER 1943 TO TUESDAY 21 SEPTEMBER 1943

I. GENERAL COMMENTS

1. GENERAL STATE OF CONFIDENCE AND REACTION TO NEWS

Elation over Italy's capitulation gave way to anxiety at the news of 'the precarious struggle' for the Salerno bridgehead, which in turn was followed by relief when the position was saved. Spirits have not, however, returned to their previous high level, because of:

(a) Disappointment that Italy will have to be fought for instead of being 'the piece of cake at first imagined'.

(b) A feeling that 'our dilly-dallying with Badoglio' has been responsible for:

    (i) The stiff opposition put up by the Germans at Salerno.

    (ii) The Germans' strong foothold throughout Italy.

    (iii) Mussolini's escape.

The Russian victories have been a consolation throughout.

There is not quite the same tendency this week to forecast an early end to the war.

Although attention has mostly been focused on war news this week, there has been grave and widespread concern about the Nottinghamshire coal strike.

Footwear difficulties are still 'a real domestic worry'.

2. ITALY

SALERNO: People 'held their breath' during 'the terrific battles' for this bridgehead and excitedly watched 'the lessening space' between the Eighth and the Fifth Armies. There was profound relief when the position improved and the two armies joined.

The difficulties encountered at Salerno have given rise to the following reactions:

(a) Criticism of 'our slowness off the mark'; this is thought to have given the Germans time:

    (i) After Mussolini's fall – to entrench themselves throughout Italy.

    (ii) Between Italy's capitulation and the landing of the Fifth Army – to dig into the strongest positions at Salerno.

        'If we'd gone in and risked it', some think, 'we'd have made much better progress.'

(b) Surprise at German strength and a feeling 'there is bitter fighting ahead'.

(c) Doubts about the fighting qualities of American troops; there has been some comment about 'our having to help them out again'.

(d) Some slight criticism of the American command. 'Alexander and Montgomery, proved British generals', it is once again suggested, should be in control.

(e) A feeling that the invasion of Italy is 'the biggest thing we've done'; and
deep satisfaction that we've proved that, in spite of the dangers and
difficulties of large-scale amphibious operations, we can land as and where
we like.

MUSSOLINI: The 'apparent careless loss' of Mussolini has amused some people
but annoyed the majority: 'The Germans have been too smart for us again.' 'His
immediate handing over should have been one of the terms of the armistice'.

His 'resurrection' is not expected to do much harm, as 'he is now a spent force'.
He is, however, thought to be good propaganda value for the Germans.

There is some fear that war criminals will never be brought to trial; 'they will be
allowed to live comfortably after the war, in spite of what has been said'.

THE SURRENDER OF THE ITALIAN FLEET is frequently mentioned with
great delight. It has removed 'a nuisance in the Mediterranean'; and if 'in spite of
what we said in the past the ships are some good, their acquisition will help us'.

FEELING ABOUT THE ITALIANS: There is some pleasure at the 'Ities standing
up to the Germans' in Sardinia and Corsica, but in one Region Italian war guilt is
again referred to: 'Let's hope we shall not forget barbarities like Abyssinia and the
bombing of London.'

AMGOT: Criticism and suspicion continue; one reason for this is the belief that
'the figures behind Amgot are all persons in big business and finance'. At the same
time there is said to be general ignorance of what Amgot is, and of what it is really
meant to do.

3. THE PRIME MINISTER'S RETURN

This has caused great pleasure and relief. Many were feeling he 'had been away
quite long enough' and were uneasy on account of his safety and his 'absence from
the helm'. Some fear 'his tying us up so closely with USA may cause some anxiety
in Russia'. His statement in the House (to which no public reactions have yet been
received) was eagerly awaited; people think 'things will begin to happen now that
he's back again'.

4. RUSSIA

With the continued successes, there is more belief this week that the Germans are
being chased out rather than voluntarily withdrawing. Apart from this, reactions to
the military and political situations are on the same lines as those reported last week.

THE NEXT MOVE: There is less comment this week and less speculation. The
two most favoured theories are again an invasion from this country, or an attack on
the Balkans.

THE NEW PRIVILEGES ALLOWED TO THE RUSSIAN ORTHODOX
CHURCH: The meaning of the Russian Government's permission to establish a
Holy Synod and elect a Patriarch has been variously interpreted. Many take it as a
sign that the Russians have 'gone back to religion' and are pleased; some ask if it
is genuine, while others are puzzled as to its meaning and ask if there is religious

freedom in Russia. Whether regarded as genuine or due to 'expediency', however, the move is widely welcomed as 'an answer to the many who still regard Russia as godless'.

The reasons for the granting of the privileges are variously thought to be: (i) 'Stalin's desire to make friends with us'; (ii) an astute move on his part to placate the USA; (iii) 'a natural development, following the destruction of the corrupt Czarist Church and the re-establishment of the Church on a cleaner basis'; (iv) a political move to get a hold over the priests in German-occupied territory.

THE ARCHBISHOP OF YORK'S VISIT TO RUSSIA has caused little comment. Some are pleased, as his visit is thought likely to help in dispelling the 'bogey that our ally is anti-religious'.

5. FAR EAST

Slightly more interest in the Far East is reported this week. There is pleasure that 'things appear to be going well' and some expectancy that 'things will be hotted up there' even more soon, 'particularly when Lord Louis Mountbatten has had time to organise his forces'. Some expect a campaign in Burma.

FOOD SHORTAGE IN BENGAL: From Scotland and Wales some concern is reported at the food situation in Bengal. Though some people admit that they don't know enough about it 'to apportion blame', it is asked 'how we can plan to feed Europe when our own people in Bengal are starving'.

6. ALLIED AIR OFFENSIVE

Satisfaction with the work of the RAF and the American Air Force continues to be reported, but there is some comment on the 'lull' in heavy air attacks on Germany. People hope that during the coming months attacks on Berlin and German industrial centres will increase as a prelude to invasion. At the same time, people are anxious about air losses, both of men and planes, and wonder if the bombing can be kept up. There is speculation about the effect of air bombardment on Nazi morale and production ... 'It is the only language the Germans will ever understand.'

Raids on airfields and communications in France, while regarded as a necessary preliminary 'softening-up', do not give the same satisfaction as those on Germany, and there is sympathy for the civilian population.

7. MR. BEVIN'S 'DEMOBILISATION SPEECH' AT THE TRADES UNION CONGRESS

This has aroused great interest and has been very well received. Most – particularly working-class people – are said to favour the 'first in, first out' policy. Many, however, while considering it reasonable in principle, argue that to state this without reservation may cause discontent later if exceptions have to be made with members of the building trades, teaching professions, etc. They take the view that 'the demands of post-war industry and reconstruction will be better served by releasing experienced men from the Forces, even though it is not their turn'. Some think that married men should be released first.

8. MR. LEARIE CONSTANTINE

Indignation at this incident is again reported. Mr. Constantine's action in suing the hotel is approved and 'it is hoped he will get big damages'.

There are again expressions of appreciation for his broadcast.

9. BROADCASTING AND PRESENTATION OF NEWS

There has been increased comment on news presentation this week. Satisfaction, generally, continues, but the following criticisms have been made:

(a) MISLEADING STATEMENTS AND EXAGGERATION, particularly about the announcement of the armistice with Italy. 'They lead us to think the battle is all over bar the shouting, then comes the little snag.'

(b) TOO MUCH PROMINENCE GIVEN TO GERMAN REPORTS. 'German accounts being given at great length lead people to think we are being prepared for bad news.'

In Ireland there is criticism that while 'considerable attention has been paid in BBC feature programmes, celebrating the collapse of Italy, to English, Scotch and Welsh regiments which have taken part in the fighting, no mention has been made of the Ulster regiments which, it is known, gave a good account of themselves. This omission is interpreted by some as evidence of "prejudice in high places against Ulster".'

THE EUROPEAN NEWS SERVICE continues to be praised.

THE FOLLOWING BROADCASTS HAVE BEEN PRAISED this week:

COMMANDER ANTHONY KIMMINS ON THE LANDING AT SALERNO, September 15, is described as 'vivid, lucid and moving'. 'Arrangements ought to be made at whatever cost and trouble to give more broadcasts by people who have actually been on the spot. They do more good than anything.'

RT. HON. A. V. ALEXANDER'S WAR COMMENTARY, September 16, 'brought home forcibly the perils which beset us and the debt we owe to those who got us through those difficult times'.

SIR STAFFORD CRIPPS' BROADCAST, September 14: 'His warning against any easing-up in production was welcome.'

THE POSTSCRIPT BY A VAD, September 19, had a 'mixed' reception. Some thought it 'terrible – a neurotic lot of nonsense', but others found it 'arresting'.

The return of the *Brains Trust* has been welcomed.

II. SPECIAL COMMENTS

WEEKLY SUMMARY

10. MINERS AND MINING

THE NOTTINGHAMSHIRE STRIKE has been widely discussed.

MANY PEOPLE 'AWAY FROM THE PITS' have strongly condemned the strike: 'Our men in the army can't strike'; they feel that 'at present there should be no strikes, whatever the circumstances', and that stronger action should be taken to stop them. These feelings appeared to override the sympathy they nevertheless feel with miners for:

(a) 'The raw deal they had between the two wars.' It is, however, also asked: 'What about the Merchant Navy? And look how they've responded.'

(b) 'Their rotten job.' The present appeal for volunteers seems to have brought it home to people that 'no one would ever be willing to take up such work'.

THE MINING COMMUNITY, however, and some other industrial workers are in sympathy with the strike and point out that it is an indication of the trouble attendant on compelling boys to go into the mines.

SYMPATHY FOR THE YOUTH, PAGE, and a feeling that it is wrong to imprison him for 'his understandable dislike of going underground', is reported from seven Regions, and a belief that he should not work in the pits from two, 'since a person afraid of a pit constitutes a danger to other men'. In Scotland, however, 'there are sarcastic comparisons with the possibility of soldiers packing up because of seeing wounded comrades'.

Four Regions report regret that the Government gave in too easily. As 'the legal decisions had been issued in the national interest and approved by both sides', the Government 'has interfered with the course of the law'. 'Is justice to be decided by mob law?'

There is some feeling that 'such strikes could be avoided by more careful handling by the authorities'.

Discussion of the following topics appears to have been stimulated by the Nottinghamshire strike:

(a) DIRECTION OF YOUTHS INTO THE PITS: Opposition continues to this proposal, particularly because miners and other workers fear that there will be a differentiation between their children and the 'better-to-do': 'If there is compulsion it must apply to all sections of the community.' Miners' wives, according to reports from the North Midland and Welsh Regions, say they are not going to have their sons compelled to go to the pits: 'Young boys of call-up age prefer active service to life underground.'

(b) PROSECUTIONS: There is strong feeling among the working classes at prosecutions for lateness, absenteeism and refusal to go underground. It is variously said that:

    (i) 'No one should be sent to prison for private enterprise.'

    (ii) 'It is unfair for miners to be imprisoned for these offences when the managements are not prosecuted for bad organisation.' There is still some talk of working bad seams because 'managements have an eye to post-war'.

    (iii) Such cases should not be brought to civil courts but should be settled inside the industry by a mining court composed of miners and owners.

MANPOWER, AND THE GOVERNMENT CAMPAIGN TO SECURE LABOUR FOR UNDERGROUND EMPLOYMENT IN THE MINES: It is felt that 'the manpower problem has been bungled from the start' and that the whole problem of increasing coal output is now bristling with difficulties. Few think the campaign will be any solution. What is needed, it is felt, is:

(a) THE RELEASE OF MINERS FROM THE FORCES AND OTHER OCCUPTIONS: Many feel this to be the only solution. Unskilled labour may even retard output, as the skilled workers would have to spend time training them.

(b) BETTER WAGES: The recent award to youths 'hasn't helped any': some consider it 'totally inadequate if we are to get young men to go coal mining'. On the other hand, some think miners are highly paid and that the award to youth is 'too high for youngsters'.

(c) CERTAINTY OF CONTINUITY OF EMPLOYMENT AFTER THE WAR: 'If it hadn't been for the shabby treatment after the last war, there would have been no coal problem now.'

(d) ADEQUATE GUARANTEED COMPENSATION FOR INJURIES, AND SOME FORM OF SOCIAL SECURITY.

(e) WORKING CONDITIONS IN THE MINES MADE AS SAFE AS POSSIBLE.

COAL FOR ITALY: 'It would be a good idea' for Italian prisoners of war to work for the coal that is to be despatched to Italy.

11. INDUSTRY

PRODUCTION: Talk of factories not working at full pressure and of enforced idleness is again reported this week. This is variously attributed to 'over-production coupled with Lease-Lend'; to 'bad organisation or lack of co-ordination'; or to the managements' wish to 'keep up the appearance of production and gain the Government's 10%'.

STRIKES: There is said to be widespread concern at the number of strikes taking place and at what is described as the 'industrial malaise'. Some say it is inevitable in wartime and that we have been lucky to avoid more trouble before this; others attribute it to 'the better news' or to 'the continual praise given to the industrial workers, which has set their minds on wage increases, better working hours and a tendency to try and get peacetime grievances settled in wartime'. Many are said to feel that 'we are too easy and that stronger measures should be taken against strikes'.

THE CLYDESIDE SHIPWRIGHTS' STRIKE, which started in Scott's Yard, Greenock, over a week ago and has now spread to the upper reaches of the Clyde, is referred to in the Scottish report. The shipwrights consider their time rate of £4. 7. 6. 'scandalous', particularly when compared with 'the earnings of unskilled workers in the yards and also in nearby war factories, where £10–£12 a week is a common wage'. They claim that 'their grievance has been at arbitration for over nine months, and greatly resent the delay in negotiation'. 'Clydeside workers generally are sympathetic to the shipwrights' point of view, and the management and the Government are blamed for their slowness and their parsimony – the Government especially. Middle-class opinion is against all strikes, and some scathing comments are being uttered about the shipyard workers.'

12. THE REGISTRATION OF OLDER WOMEN

The idea of calling up older women continues to be criticised on familiar grounds: 'Nothing appears to convince the public that younger people are being fully used, and while this is the case, it remains the chief cause of the resentment at the call-up of the 46–50s.' Conditions connected with the present changes in production programmes also prompt workers to ask: 'Why call up more women when overtime is being stopped in some factories and others are being closed down?'

The strongest criticism is said to come from men, and from the families of the women concerned, while, according to two reports, 'the only people not upset are the women in question'. Some of them are said to have been 'rather bucked about having to register – they felt it gave them status'. It is believed, too, that many elderly domestic workers may be thankful of an opportunity to change their occupation.

13. INCOME TAX

The wish for a 'pay-as-you-go' scheme continues, interest having been strengthened by the news that the Chancellor of the Exchequer was considering it. The need is felt especially by those transferred to less-well-paid work. Married women, too, are concerned at the 'awkward position' they may be in at the end of the war, with their job at an end, a year's income tax owing – and, in some cases, a husband demobilised from the Forces and out of work as well.

It is hoped that, if the pay-as-you-go scheme is introduced, 'the conditions will be set out so that the average individual can understand them'.

14. CLOTHING

Comment continues unabated and unchanged. Footwear difficulties, especially for children, still predominate.

CLOTHING COUPON THEFT: There has been little comment reported on this. The Board of Trade's 'knock-out blow' in countering the theft was admired, but there was surprise and concern that such a large quantity of coupons should not have been more carefully guarded.

15. FOOD

In addition to general satisfaction with the situation, this week's outstanding food topics have been the distribution, insufficiency and poor quality of *milk*, and 'the fantastic prices' being charged for *vegetables*, particularly beans, lettuce and marrows – people do not understand why their price cannot be controlled.

THE INCREASED JAM RATION has given great satisfaction, and there is pleasure at the new varieties offered.

16. HOP-PICKING

A report from the South-Eastern district states that there has been as large a response of pickers as in normal times, and many pickers now in the Forces have spent their leave in this way.

The use of mobile and gas-cleansing units for giving baths to the pickers has been tried with great success in several camps – as many as 100 baths being provided in one evening at Faversham. Health inspectors are reported to find this scheme particularly helpful, and in one camp alone three cases of scabies were detected and treated immediately.

NO. 159: TUESDAY 12 OCTOBER 1943 TO 19 OCTOBER 1943

I. GENERAL COMMENTS

1. GENERAL STATE OF CONFIDENCE AND REACTION TO NEWS

Spirits continue at the slightly lower level reported last week. The news from Russia, the Allied air offensive, 'the diplomatic victory in the Azores' and – to a less extent – steady Allied progress in Italy all give satisfaction; yet it is said that few are entirely satisfied with the present position and there are many references to:

(a) Continued uneasiness about the political situation in Italy, which Italy's acceptance as a co-belligerent seems to have intensified.

(b) Continued uneasiness over the coal situation, which the debate in the House appears to have done little to allay.

(c) Concern about post-war conditions and scepticism about the Government's intentions about them.

(d) Increasing war-weariness, fatigue or ill-health.

(e) Longing for 'a speeding up of events', for 'one grand slam to get it all over as quickly as possible'.

HOME FRONT: Footwear is again the main domestic complaint.

2. ITALY

ITALY'S DECLARATION OF WAR ON GERMANY has been greeted with much ridicule and very little pleasure. It is described as 'Gilbertian' and as 'something to laugh at', and there are many sarcastic comments about Italy trying to save her own skin. Most people doubt if Italian help at this late stage can possibly be of any value to the Allies. Some, however, welcome the possibility of using the Italian fleet and a few – women especially – hope it will 'help our armies along a bit' and shorten the war; but others consider that Italy's entrance on our side has 'put months on the war' and are full of sympathy for 'unfortunate British regiments who may have to go into battle alongside the Italians'.

THE ALLIES' ACCEPTANCE OF ITALY AS A CO-BELLIGERENT has caused little or no approval, and considerable bewilderment and dislike. There is said to be much confusion as to Italy's present position – 'What on earth does a co-belligerent mean?' – and the following reactions are reported:

(a) DISLIKE OR DISTRUST OF THE ITALIANS: People say they are 'a treacherous lot' ... 'have always been opportunists'. It is thought that 'a nation which has ratted once would do so again if it paid them' ... 'after all, they've turned traitor to their own allies'. The public's attitude to the Italian people is said to have hardened since Mussolini fell, though a few pity them.

(b) DESIRE THAT THE GUILTY SHALL NOT ESCAPE PUNISHMENT: While many feel strongly that the Italian people as a whole must not be released from their share in responsibility for the war and their support of fascism, it is particularly desired that war criminals and 'ex-fascist rogues' should not escape punishment. Roatta's appointment to a post under Badoglio's government is especially criticised and is taken by some as 'a pointer to the insincerity of all talk of punishment of war criminals'.

Many are uneasy at accepting our late enemies as friends and think we are overdoing the 'let's forget the past' attitude. 'Are our enemies jolly good fellows after all, and the war just a grand game?' 'Isn't it time we made friends with Germany?' Older people say: 'It's the Kaiser all over again.'

THE KING OF ITALY, BADOGLIO AND HIS GOVERNMENT continue to arouse strong and widespread dislike and distrust. People are very uncomfortable at our having anything to do with 'the old gang' and at the 'apparent whitewashing of Badoglio's government'.

THE MILITARY SITUATION: There is general satisfaction at the progress of the Fifth and Eighth Armies but much comment on its slowness, which is contrasted with the rate of the Russian advances, and also with the speed with which the Germans were driven back across the North African desert. Some, however, consider progress good in view of the difficult country and weather, and the strength of German opposition. Nevertheless, many people continue to believe that 'someone blundered badly at the beginning' and that 'had we been quicker at the time of Mussolini's downfall our job now would have been much easier'.

OUR PRISONERS OF WAR IN ITALY: Anxiety and the wish for news continue.

3. THE COAL DEBATE IN THE HOUSE OF COMMONS (OCTOBER 13)

Many – particularly miners and other industrial workers – have been disappointed by the debate; they feel that 'the Government is shirking the issue and is not prepared to examine the root cause of discontent in the mining industry or to offer an adequate remedy'. The problem of increased coal output is, therefore, thought to remain unsolved.

Although the whole debate was followed with interest, discussion has centred round the Prime Minister:

(a) HIS INTERVENTION: People generally agree that 'this saved a difficult Parliamentary situation', and they admire his statesmanship. There is amused appreciation of how Mr. Churchill can 'talk folk into or out of anything'.

(b) HIS SPEECH had a mixed reception, with nationalisation of mines the main controversial point. Opinion is divided between:

(i)   'Left-wing' people and workers generally who think nationalisation is the only way to solve the problem.

There is some feeling that the decision not to nationalise 'indicates the Government's attitude towards all major reorganisation proposals: the shelving of reforms till after war'. 'Tory pressure', 'vested interests' are thought responsible.

(ii) 'Right-wing' people, some businessmen and 'those who wish for a return to the status quo after the war', are pleased at the firm stand made against nationalisation. At the same time some 'non-Socialists and Old Tories' feel nationalisation must come in the end.

People are not convinced of the need for a general election before nationalisation can be introduced: 'If we can decide to enter the war without a general election, and can nationalise lives without one, why can't we nationalise the mines?'

4. THE AZORES

General satisfaction with the agreement with Portugal comes from eleven Regions, though comment is limited. It is considered 'an astute step by the Foreign Office' and 'a pointer to what neutrals think about Germany's chances of winning'. Portugal, it is thought, must now consider her position safe, though a few fear that she may suffer for her action.

People criticise 'all the stuff about the alliance of 1374' and believe the old treaty had nothing to do with the agreement. They would have preferred a plain statement without 'the dope'.

EIRE AND OTHER NEUTRALS: There is much speculation as to the effect of the agreement on the other neutrals, particularly Eire, and it is hoped that others, such as Turkey, may 'display similar boldness'.

Many ask why Eire cannot follow Portugal's example, but the comment from Northern Ireland is that no one 'believes de Valera will do anything of the kind'. According to the Scottish report, the Azores agreement 'has again stirred up antagonism against Eire and a feeling that we should deal hardly with her after the war'. An example of this animosity is given – that of 'an Eire boat which came up the Clyde last week – the first for a long time – and the crew complained bitterly that dockers and shipyard workers hurled abuse at them all the way up the river, taunting them with cowardice and with their neutrality'.

5. THE ATTACK ON THE *TIRPITZ*

This has 'seized the public's imagination' and evoked great admiration, as 'worthy of the tradition of the Royal Navy'. The 'great bravery' of the crews is particularly stressed. There is some concern about our casualties.

Some criticism is, however, reported of:

(a) The account of the raid. People want more details and think these should be given to counter German reports. They want to know how many submarines were used and the proportion of our losses to the forces engaged.

(b) The exceptional risks taken for the results achieved: 'the *Tirpitz* can be easily repaired'.

6. RUSSIA

Admiration for Russian progress continues, but 'their successes are so commonplace that people don't trouble to talk about them'. The anticipated 'autumn lull' is now thought unlikely to materialise and the Russians are expected to 'drive ahead until the Germans are pushed out of their country'.

Familiar fears as to what Russia will do when she reaches her frontiers – particularly as regards Poland – are again reported. Her post-war attitude is also causing some concern.

THREE-POWER CONFERENCE: 'Hopeful interest' is the general reaction. 'The need for absolute unity' is recognised, and people are 'most anxious that nothing should separate us from the Soviets'.

7. THE NEXT MOVE

There is slightly more comment this week. Some 'have given up all hope', but others are increasingly discontented that another front has not yet materialised.

Some – particularly relatives of fighting men – are indignant with those who express desire for another front: 'Experience in Italy has shown it will be no walk-over.'

8. YUGOSLAV PATRIOTS

Admiration for the Yugoslav patriots continues, as does fear that 'the fruit of their heroic work will be thrown away'.

9. ALLIED AIR OFFENSIVE

Great satisfaction with the Allied air offensive continues and 'no praise is too high' for the RAF.

More and heavier attacks are still asked for, some people feeling that the war may thus be shortened. People in one Region express 'a grudging admiration' for the Germans.

There has been some 'dismayed comment' at our heavier losses though they are compared favourably with those in land fighting. A few, however, ask whether such losses are 'worth it?'

USAAF: 'Warm admiration' is expressed for the achievements of the USAAF, which are reported to be 'increasingly recognised'. However, people still take US claims of enemy fighters destroyed with 'a large grain of salt'.

Concern is expressed at the heavy US losses in the Schweinfurt raid, which some interpreted as meaning the German defences are 'immensely strong'. People are very impressed by such raids as this.

10. RAIDS ON THIS COUNTRY

Little comment has been reported this week, and little expectation of renewed heavy raiding, though there is some nervousness in the South-West.

Criticism continues of 'the poor shooting by Home Guards and others on the AA guns' during the raid on London on October 7.

11. FAR EAST

There is little general comment, but the defeat of the Japanese at Rabaul has 'quickened public interest' and it is felt that the war in the Pacific has 'started in earnest'.

PRISONERS OF WAR: 'Greater concern' is reported from one Region about the fate of men missing in the Far East. It is thought that a recent *Postscript* (October 1) by a civilian recently returned from a Shanghai gaol was 'terribly harrowing to those with relatives in Japanese hands'. Some feel that the Government is not doing all it could on behalf of prisoners of war and their relatives.

12. BENGAL FAMINE

Although most people continue to hold the Government responsible for the situation, a large minority blame the local authorities and the Indians, 'who have had too big a hand in the government of Bengal'. People ask why prices of foodstuffs were not controlled, and feel that 'whatever local conditions prevail, our administration should be responsible for alleviating the famine, which should not have reached such terrible proportions'.

13. COS

There has been less comment this week, though disappointment is still reported. People are surprised that the Germans can still make even a small attack by sea. 'Scanty news' is again complained of.

14. THE HEREFORD CASE

Fairly widespread discussion has been aroused by this case, and considerable indignation is reported. The magistrates concerned are generally condemned; a few, however, excuse them on the grounds either that 'the Clerk of the Court should have seen that the correct legal procedure was adopted', or that 'they have been blamed for things for which the police were responsible'.

The case is thought to have demonstrated the need for a review of juvenile court administration. 'Closed' courts are condemned, and the need for younger and 'more suitable' magistrates is thought to have been proved.

15. THE FIVE AMERICAN SENATORS

Though interest does not appear to be widespread, their charges have caused resentment and pained surprise and seem to have stimulated anti-American comment, some of it rather bitter. This is particularly deplored now that 'there are signs that Americans and British are becoming friendly'.

Some uneasiness is also reported that there may be grounds, however slight, for the charges, and it is hoped that 'the matter may speedily be cleared up'.

16. THE NATIONAL CONFERENCE OF WOMEN

Comment continues on the same lines as were reported last week, but the greatest emphasis is now on the question of expense. Some people consider the expenditure of £17,000 'outrageous', and it is suggested that 'the Prime Minister could have addressed a much larger and more comprehensive audience of women over the wireless, and at much less expense'.

17. BROADCASTING AND PRESENTATION OF NEWS

General satisfaction with news bulletins continues, and the European Service is again commended. On the other hand, there is some criticism of 'dullness', 'repetition' and 'padding'; one complaint of padding refers specifically to Russian news.

Bad reception of the Forces programme, except on powerful sets, is complained of by Sunderland people. There is a further complaint from Penzance of bad wireless reception, particularly at night.

THE BRAINS TRUST: Opinion is divided, though on the whole it is adverse. Questions are still thought 'silly' and some people want Donald McCullough back.

THE CHINESE STUDENT (October 10): This *Postscript* was liked and was thought to be of the type which 'helps people to understand the outlook of other nations'.

BBC: The following are praised this week: Dr. Garbett's *Postscript* on Russia, October 17; *ITMA*; and BBC drama. Adverse comment on the VAD's broadcast continues.

PRESS: The increased supplies of newspapers are welcomed.

II. SPECIAL COMMENTS

WEEKLY REVIEW

18. POST-WAR CONDITIONS

Uneasiness, scepticism and cynicism, on the lines summarised in the last Home Intelligence Report (No. 158, Section 14), continue to be reported. There is said to be a widespread desire to know more of the Government's intentions; it is believed that people's spirits and enthusiasm – and also production – would be greatly raised by an authoritative statement of the Government's plans for 'achieving that better standard of living for the people which, in the minds of most, is the major object for which we are fighting'.

19. MINERS AND MINING

Uneasiness about the coal industry continues. People again express sympathy for the miners – for 'their raw deal' in the past and their conditions of work – but at the same time they condemn 'strikes in wartime', particularly unofficial ones.

SOLUTIONS to the problems are felt to be:

(a) NATIONALISATION OF MINES.
(b) THE RELEASE OF MINERS FROM THE FORCES: The statement that some are now to be recalled is welcomed.

Neither APPEALS FOR VOLUNTEERS nor CONSCRIPTION are thought likely to be effective, and opposition to conscription is generally reported, as 'the idea of forced labour for mines is repugnant'. Particular opposition is reported:

(i) Among miners, who think the employment of inexperienced workers will endanger lives; also that 'it will only be our sons who are directed into the mines'.
(ii) Among people in non-mining areas, who 'are worried at the possibility of their own sons being drafted into the pits'. Some non-miners say 'they will not go down – not for £5 a day danger money'.

20. INDUSTRY

STRIKES: There is less talk about strikes, but concern about 'the general unrest in industry' continues.

Blame is again, variously, laid on:

(a) THE STRIKERS: Many people – particularly those with relatives in the Forces – think 'strikes at the present time amount to sabotage and should be treated as such'.

(b) THE GOVERNMENT, both for not taking a firmer line with strikers in the beginning, and for 'not interfering with business interests'.

(c) THE PRESENT MACHINERY for negotiations between the interested parties. Some think 'it needs drastically overhauling'.

(d) TRADE UNION OFFICIALS 'for sitting on grievances till the pot boils over, by saying "we must not embarrass the Ministers"'.

TRANSFER OF WORKERS: Perturbation about actual and proposed transfers both of men and girls is reported from Clydeside. Workers from a particular factory are said to be 'trying to work up public opinion in the matter by delegations to the local town council and Labour party'; they claim this method was effective elsewhere.

In Aberdare, people 'resent the fact that numbers of workers have either to cease work or be transferred to other areas'. They also complain of 'unfair treatment of applicants before the local tribunal'.

21. 'PAY AS YOU EARN' INCOME TAX

Praise for the new scheme continues: 'Up to the present there seem to be few snags.'

Sir John Anderson's statement that salaried workers earning up to £600 per annum will also be included in the scheme has been equally well received, though the feeling remains that 'this method of calculation should apply to salaries whatever the amount', or 'at least to salaries up to £1,000 per annum'.

22. FOOD

Satisfaction with the general food situation continues. The chief complaints this week are: (a) shortage of biscuits; (b) shortage of fish; (c) high price of green vegetables.

Pleasure is reported at:

(a) The promised distribution of oranges and specially the inclusion of children up to 16 years.

(b) The likelihood of more dried fruit. Housewives are said to be worrying about dried fruit for Christmas.

(c) The reduction of the points value for canned meats.

23. CLOTHING

Complaints continue on familiar lines, and footwear difficulties, particularly for children, still predominate. There are also complaints of the need to surrender clothing coupons for household goods.

24. ALARM CLOCKS

During the past two weeks a shortage of alarm clocks has again been reported and there is 'increasing demand' for permits by workers other than those employed in the transport services. At the same time, representatives of the bus and railway men are concerned about the number of permits applied for by employees, as the number granted to the companies is said to be quite inadequate.

In the North-Eastern Region it is reported that 'large firms advertise alarm clocks as available to all on essential work'.

25. THE CENTRAL HEATING BAN

Prior to the relaxation of the ban, there were reports of colds and other ailments attributed to lack of heating. The ban was felt to be false economy.

26. HOME GUARD

Home Guards are reported to be 'fed up' with the number of duties and parades they have to perform. Particular complaint is made of three parades a week, and of Sunday duties and parades especially during the harvest season. There is some talk in two Regions of the possibility of easing the demands on Home Guards, especially the older men, in view of the improved outlook.

27. ANTI-SEMITISM

During the past eight weeks there have continued to be few but fairly regular reports of anti-Semitic feeling.

The chief allegations made against Jews have been:

(a) They are capturing trade and markets – particularly the drapery and tailoring trades – to the detriment of the non-Jewish trader. 'Jewish syndicates' are said to buy up any kind of business and to back 'shady' business ventures. There is some fear also of refugee Jews building up businesses here.

(b) 'They have too much control in this country.'

There continue to be familiar complaints of the association of Jewish names with black market offences; of the 'bad manners and arrogance of Jews'; of their escaping the Services; and of their 'buying up luxuries'.

At the same time sympathy for those who have suffered in occupied Europe continues to be expressed.

NO. 164: TUESDAY 16 NOVEMBER 1943 TO TUESDAY 23 NOVEMBER 1943

I. GENERAL COMMENTS

1. GENERAL

There has been a widespread and, in some cases, considerable drop in spirits from the previous high level of last week; and less optimistic talk about an early end to the war. The fall in spirits is attributed to the loss of Leros, the situation in the Lebanon, the continued slow advance in Italy, and, to a less extent, the Russian setbacks at Zhitomir and various home front matters. The only cheering factors mentioned are Russian successes on other fronts and Thursday's raid on Berlin.

The release of Sir Oswald and Lady Mosley has caused a storm of indignation and all but unanimous disapproval.

HOME FRONT: THERE ARE COMPLAINTS OF: war-weariness and tiredness, accentuated by Home Guard and Civil Defence duties, the prevalence of colds and flu, and the onset of winter weather; footwear and housing difficulties; unauthorised strikes; shortage of milk and fish; and lack of supplementary industrial coupons.

Widespread anxiety about post-war prospects continues.

2. THE RELEASE OF SIR OSWALD AND LADY MOSLEY

The following reports were received before the Home Secretary's statement in Parliament.

Widespread indignation is reported at the release of the Mosleys. In many cases feeling appears to be intense and bitter; and what is described as a howl of rage is reported from Scotland. The subject is said to be discussed in every queue, shop and factory, by friends and strangers alike.

Disapproval of their release is reported as almost unanimous; nor is it confined to any particular section, though people in industrial areas and those with relatives in the Forces or prisoners of war are especially vocal.

The reasons given for this indignation are somewhat confused. Few people fear Sir Oswald will be a danger to the country when released, and the majority of objections are on quite other grounds. The Government is accused of letting down the Forces who are 'fighting to break what Mosley stands for', of softness, of temporising with fascism, and of giving our Allies cause to doubt our sincerity. Comments on the case itself are extremely varied, but may be summarised as follows:

(i) 'ONE LAW FOR THE RICH, ANOTHER FOR THE POOR', with particular anger at what are believed to be the luxurious conditions of the Mosleys' life in gaol.

(ii) DISBELIEF IN THE GENUINENESS OR SERIOUSNESS OF SIR OSWALD'S ILLNESS: Some regard it as 'a wangle' or an excuse; others doubt its being serious enough to warrant his release.

(iii) IF HE IS REALLY ILL, WHY CAN HE NOT BE TREATED IN THE PRISON HOSPITAL?

(iv) WHY KEEP HIM ALIVE, WHEN HE WOULD BE 'BETTER DEAD'?

(v) WHY WAS HE LIBERATED WHEN PARLIAMENT WAS NOT IN SESSION?

(vi) WHY RELEASE LADY MOSLEY AS WELL? Her release is an almost greater source of aggravation to some.

A SMALL MINORITY are willing to await the Home Secretary's statement, approve the Government's action in 'allowing Mosley to fizzle out and not become a martyr by dying in prison', and point out that 'he has been charged with no crime and cannot be treated like a convict'.

3. DODECANESE ISLANDS

Increased and widespread criticism and disappointment are reported at the fall of Leros. It is asked why we occupied it if we could not send adequate forces to hold it. Those responsible for our strategy are blamed for the unnecessary sacrifice of men and for the failure to provide the necessary support – particularly air support. It is thought that the island should have been evacuated. Relatives of troops are particularly concerned at this 'cruel and unnecessary waste'.

There was little hope of retaining Samos.

The defeats in the Dodecanese Islands are compared with those in Crete and Norway: 'too little and too late all over again'.

General Maitland Wilson's statement is thought weak and unconvincing, and a further official explanation is considered necessary.

There are fears of the effects on Turkey's policy and on our prestige in the Balkan states.

It is also feared that the Germans have again been under-estimated; people thought their air power in the Mediterranean was broken and are uneasy that they can still develop so much strength to attack so strongly.

4. THE LEBANON

Criticism of the 'high-handed' French action in the Lebanon has increased, though the situation is still little understood. There is now growing disappointment in General de Gaulle and distrust of the French National Committee. It is thought that if the Lebanon was promised its independence, it should get it; and it is hoped that we will take firm action.

There is some fear that the situation in Lebanon is a portent of the future difficulties we will have with France when she is liberated.

5. ITALY

MILITARY: Less interest, but otherwise little change. There are again comments that bad weather in Russia seems to have much less effect than in Italy. There is some fear that our original plan of campaign has misfired and that this is in part due to poor supreme generalship.

POLITICAL: Less comment, but criticism continues.

6. RUSSIA

The Russian setback at Zhitomir has caused surprise and has detracted from news of gains elsewhere. It has also made some people realise that the Germans can still produce plenty of men and material, and is thought to have had a salutary effect on over-optimists. Nevertheless, the majority remain full of confidence and admiration.

7. POLAND

Continued minority uneasiness over Russia's intentions about Poland. The remark made by the Russian Ambassador to Mexico, that the Russians were not 90 miles from the Polish frontier – but over 200 – has caused some discussion; people wonder if the remark was made with the approval of Moscow.

8. ALLIED AIR OFFENSIVE

Little comment has yet been received on the last two attacks on Berlin, but the renewal of heavy raids, particularly on Berlin and Ludwigshafen (November 18), has given much satisfaction. Our smaller losses are also noted with pleasure.

There is praise for the USAAF raids on Norwegian targets and for the way their crews have pressed home daylight attacks.

From one Region, there are reports of some grudging admiration of the way the Germans are standing up to our bombing: 'Germany can certainly take it.'

9. CABINET CHANGES AND POST-WAR PROBLEMS

Pleasure at Lord Woolton's appointment and regret at his leaving the Ministry of Food continue to be general.

Despite his appointment, however, anxiety and scepticism about the Government's post-war policy are still very widespread; feeling follows closely the full review given two weeks ago (Report No. 162 Section 14), with particular stress on unemployment and demobilisation, housing, social security, and post-war controls.

10. THE PRIME MINISTER'S MANSION HOUSE SPEECH
(9TH NOVEMBER 1943)

Comment mainly follows last week's lines. The quiet confidence and realism of the speech are appreciated, although some are cast down at the reference to hard times ahead – particularly those with relatives in the Forces. Some confess to feelings of dismay when Mr. Churchill emphasised that he was no socialist: 'Does this mean no clear-cut Government policy, and a return to party politics?'

11. NEXT MOVE

Not much talk, but continued disappointment that it is taking so long to come, and impatience to give more direct aid to the Russians and the Yugoslavs.

12. RAIDS ON THIS COUNTRY

Although no great concern is reported, the recent raids on London have made some people realise the possibility of attacks in other areas and the need to be prepared. In London, morale is thought not to be as high as in 1940/1.

Raids on Plymouth and the South-West were looked on as an unwelcome proof that Germany still has power to strike. Morale in Plymouth itself is said to have been better than ever before; though rumours of excessive damage and casualties were fairly common in the South-West. Anxiety about defence against sneak raids is reported from one or two south-western coastal places.

13. GERMANY'S SECRET WEAPON

Mild speculation about a new enemy secret weapon comes from six Regions; reports from four of which mention slight uneasiness (not London or the South-East). Gas warfare, new bombs, bacteria or 'some vague evil' are thought possible.

14. FAR EAST

Interest in operations in the Pacific continues slight. Hope of a large-scale offensive from India are again reported.

15. FAMINE IN BENGAL

Comment follows familiar lines and continues to dwindle.

16. BROADCASTING AND PRESENTATION OF NEWS

Apart from local criticism of press publicity about American battle training areas, and some feeling that optimism was falsely aroused over Leros, there has been little comment on news presentation. People would welcome a simple explanation of the background to the Lebanon crisis.

THE BRAINS TRUST is still criticised, though the December 16 broadcast was considered the best for a long while.

BROADCAST PLAYS are said to be liked and more are asked for. *The Barretts of Wimpole Street* and *Appointment with Fear* were specially appreciated, though some are said to dislike the latter type of play. .

GENERAL: Appreciation of *The Radio Doctor*; Lord Winster's *War Commentary*, November 11; and *The Fifth Freedom* and *Marching On*.

II. SPECIAL COMMENTS

BRIEF WEEKLY REVIEW

17. HOUSING

Housing continues a major problem: for many, the situation is described as 'absolutely desperate'. Russia's 10,000 houses since Stalingrad are contrasted with the situation in Britain.

18. STRIKES

Comment has increased slightly, disgust and resentment being the reaction of the great majority. Among the few in industrial areas who feel sympathy for strikers, some nevertheless condemn strikes in wartime.

Many feel it is 'high time the Government stepped in and took firm action'.

Apart from familiar suggestions as to the cause of strikes, the following are also made:

(a) THAT STRIKES ARE INCITED BY ENEMY AGENTS.
(b) THAT STRIKES ARE ENCOURAGED BY INDUSTRIALISTS:

   (i)   As they are 'raking off' too much to want the war to end yet.
   (ii) So that they can say after the war that the workers sabotaged the war effort.
   (iii) To slow down aid to Russia.

STRIKES IN THE COAL MINES: There is slightly more sympathy for the coal miners than for other strikers, though they too are criticised by the majority.

19. DOMESTIC FUEL

DURING THE PAST TWO WEEKS there has been a fair amount of comment about the fuel campaign.

It seems that although people generally feel they are not wasteful, they are not so fuel-conscious as last year because of:

(a) The lack of a 'serious attempt to get under the public's skin' over fuel economy ... 'Ordinary warnings are like water off a duck's back.'
(b) Mismanagement and stoppages in the coal-mining industry.

SUPPLIES OF COAL: Some people wonder how they will get through the winter on the present allowance, especially if supplies are irregular. Particular anxiety is felt by people with small storage space who were unable to get in supplies during the summer; by people with large houses; those who have to keep fires going all day because of shift workers; and those who live in outlying districts.

The poor quality of coal – 'all dust' – is commented upon.

MAJOR LLOYD GEORGE'S STATEMENT, 9 NOVEMBER. Many people feel resentful of his reproaches because he omitted all reference to strikers, who, it is thought, are more blameworthy than consumers.

A few felt the Minister was 'trying to turn his failure on to the public'.

Some comment that housewives who now work are unable to look after coal fires, and therefore cannot help but use gas and electricity more than previously.

In one Region the statement is said to have had some effect.

20. CLOTHING

Comment continues on lines similar to last week. Particular concern is felt about:

(a) Footwear difficulties, especially where there are children. It is feared their health will suffer; country children's need for rubber boots is stressed.
(b) Insufficiency of coupons, especially for replacing household goods.
(c) The lack of information about the expected issue of industrial coupons.

21. HOME GUARD, FIRE-WATCHING AND CIVIL DEFENCE

FIRE-WATCHING DUTIES: Lack of enthusiasm is reported, and some feeling that duties could be relaxed, particularly in less vulnerable areas, without impairing general efficiency. There is criticism of the number of lectures workers are asked to attend, and of the 'Prussian attitude' in the wording of many Fire-Guard orders. On the other hand, a considerable minority are alarmed at the prospect of any relaxation of duty.

HOME GUARD: Complaints are made of 'incessant drill and ceremonial parades'. It is thought that tiredness is very evident and that once Home Guards are trained, drill and parades might be further reduced. One Regional report mentions comment that there are two separate Home Guard organisations – the men who voluntarily gave themselves to the service of their country, and the superimposed body of paid officers whose 'overbearing attitude is at times extremely irksome'.

SIR WALTER CITRINE'S SPEECH AT MANCHESTER, November 6: Comment is rather less, but follows the lines reported last week.

UNIFICATION OF SERVICES is suggested in two reports as a solution of manpower difficulties and in the interests of economy. It is thought that much could be saved by designating areas as 'dangerous', 'liable to attack', and 'comparatively safe', and arranging duties by merging the three Services.

22. FOOD

General satisfaction – but some tendency to blame lowered powers of resistance onto deficiencies of wartime diet. Continued complaints of insufficient milk and fish.

CHRISTMAS FOOD occupies an increasing place in people's thoughts.

There is anxiety, particularly in the smaller towns, about turkey and chicken supplies. People fear that these will go to hotels and restaurants, which can afford to buy in quantity, and to the wealthy and influential.

People variously yearn for an extra allowance of cooking fat, suet, sugar and sweets, and for mincemeat and oranges. It is thought that concessions would give a fillip to spirits. Disgust and envy are reported from one Region at the published menu for US troops.

JAM: Approval for the 'sugar or jam' scheme, but complaints of lack of variety and prevalence of plum. Some suspect the good varieties are kept under the counter.

23. SPECIAL REGIONAL MATTERS

EVACUATION FOR AMERICAN BATTLE SCHOOLS: In the South-West, the people concerned are 'being very good about it', but there is widespread and strong condemnation of press publicity; indeed recent raids in the South-West are attributed to it. Rumours and fears that many other areas are to be evacuated are also thought to have been stimulated by the press announcements. In the North-East, the press is also criticised for being indiscreet in this connection.

In the Southern Region, it is asked why the Americans could not use moors instead of good agricultural land. In the Newbury area, rumours of impending evacuation for the same purpose are leading to strong comments that it is not really necessary.

The effects of evacuation plans in rural areas in northern Scotland are described in a special report from the Scottish Intelligence Officer. The farmers, smallholders and other people concerned are taking it very well. A typical remark is: 'If it will end the war even a few days sooner, or save men's lives, we are willing to leave our homes.'

No grousing has been heard though there have been many questions, mainly about compensation, addressed to the Information Centres and to the speakers at public meetings held to explain the reasons for the move.

SCOTTISH-POLISH RELATIONS (SCOTLAND)

In spite of the development of Scottish-Polish cultural projects, there is said to be obvious tension and a good deal of ill-feeling about the Poles at present stationed in Scotland. In the Borders it is claimed that the Poles are inefficient in the military sense – that they recently failed ignominiously in a tank test and have been ordered to do this training again. Housewives in Border towns complain too of the difficulty of getting clothes dry-cleaned: 'Polish uniforms have priority, and we never can get our own things done'. Recently some workers in a printing works were angry at having to show their processes to a visiting party of Poles and expressed their anger furiously. The Poles are said to be voicing strong anti-Russian sentiments – by calling the Moscow agreement 'another Munich' and to be expressing great bitterness at suggestions that the Russians should be allowed to retain their 1941 boundaries. In the face of the present popularity of Russia these sentiments are ill-received, especially among Scottish workers.

SHORTAGE OF BEDDING (NORTHERN REGION)

The shortage of sheets and blankets is said to be a growing problem in the Northern Region, and the plight of the working classes increasingly more difficult. 'At the beginning of the war, the bedding of the majority was, as a result of the depression, of extremely poor quality – if it existed at all. The position is steadily deteriorating and complaints are reported from most of the working-class areas in the Region about the impossibility of buying sheets and blankets.'

SHORT SUPPLY OF UNRATIONED GOODS (NORTHERN REGION)

People in the Northern Region are frequently reported to consider themselves unfairly treated over supplies of unrationed goods in short supply. In the late summer there were many grumbles over lack of fruit. Tynemouth and North Shields are convinced that their corner of the Region is given a particularly raw deal, and Sunderland people maintain that their city has had a very poor choice of extra jams by comparison with other towns.

THE 'USHERETTE MURDER' (SOUTH-EASTERN DISTRICT)

Strong public feeling is reported from Folkestone at the acquittal of the soldier alleged to be responsible for the murder of the local cinema usherette. Many townspeople believe the soldier concerned to be a sexual maniac and fear that now he has been set free there is a danger of the crime being repeated. Some advocate an alteration of the law so that 'a person, obviously guilty according to the evidence, does not escape justice on a technical point of law'.

THE BAN ON VISITORS (SOUTH-EASTERN DISTRICT)

Folkestone people are said to be anxious that the ban should be lifted for a fortnight in order that people may visit their friends and relations in the town. Failing the complete lifting of the ban, it is wished that permits might be granted to 'sweethearts, many of whom will not otherwise have a chance of seeing their girls or men in the Services before they are drafted overseas'.

III. PERIODIC REVIEWS

24. AMERICAN TROOPS IN THIS COUNTRY

During the past four weeks there has been some increase of comment – particularly of favourable comment – on American troops.

Recently arrived troops are described as a 'pleasant surprise' – quiet, courteous and friendly. People are thought also to be more tolerant, and more willing to be favourably impressed; unfriendliness towards American troops is criticised, and exploitation by retailers, landladies, and taxi drivers strongly condemned.

At the same time familiar complaints have continued. These are of their:

(a) BEHAVIOUR WITH WOMEN, PARTICULARLY YOUNG GIRLS, the association of coloured troops and young girls causing special concern. Late leave passes are criticised and stricter control over the troops thought necessary. At the same time, there are complaints of girls 'besieging' the troops – both white and coloured. Among women there is some fear of being molested by American troops in the blackout. 'Sexual crimes' by Americans are quoted; and there is also anxiety because it is thought that British administration has no control over them.

In one area, decent American troops are described as 'fed up with the sexual exploits of their colleagues'.

(b) HEAVY DRINKING.
(c) 'SLOVENLY' APPEARANCE.
(d) 'OVERBEARING AND BRAGGART MANNER'.
(e) HIGH SPENDING POWER.
(f) ATTITUDE TOWARDS THEIR COLOURED TROOPS.
(g) CARELESSNESS WITH THE BLACKOUT AND WITH TORCHES.
(h) Wasting petrol on pleasure trips; speeding; crowding local people off buses; their medals; and careless talk.

BILLETING: Complaints of having to billet American troops are reported from the South-West and Wales. Criticism chiefly is that 'it must be absolutely necessary' – 'no empty reserved buildings should remain available'.

THE UNFRIENDLY ATTITUDE OF BRITISH SERVICEMEN TOWARDS AMERICAN TROOPS is mentioned in reports from five Regions. A special report from the Midland Region illustrates what is believed to be the British serviceman's attitude:

(a) The Americans have too much money.
(b) They have no respect for British girls: 'They think they can buy them body and soul, if they take them into a pub and buy them a drink.'
(c) They carry themselves badly: 'Doesn't look like a soldier' ... 'wants his hair cut' etc. Their attitude to British officers and to their own junior officers also comes in for criticism.
(d) 'Dunkirk' stories still linger.

25. NATIONAL SAVINGS

There has been little comment about National Savings in the past four months.

Enthusiasm seems greater for small local savings groups than for big, nationwide campaigns, and there is some comment on the popularity and success of street schemes and of enthusiasm among group workers.

A number of people, however, question the use of saving. They feel that after the war savings may be found not so safe as some had supposed.

CAMPAIGNS IN GENERAL: Opinion is divided as to their effectiveness. Some appreciate the publicity; others 'deplore its fatuous tone'. Some feel campaigns increase interest in savings; others that the expense is not justified because much of the money 'saved' is really only transferred, and therefore does not represent an extra saving. They feel 'consistent' saving is of greater value.

Boredom with the Sunday night recital of War Savings is reported from three Regions, though a few find it 'most interesting'.

CAMPAIGNS IN PARTICULAR: During the last five months, there has been comment on the following campaigns:

(a) THE 'SQUANDER BUG': It is regarded by many as 'unnecessarily unpleasant' and is thought to have become 'tiresome'. Some feel that, in the fifth year of war, the public needs few injunctions of this type; others suggest that careless spending advertisements should be replaced by careful spending hints.

(b) THE 'RAISE THE STANDARD' CAMPAIGN: This is thought by the majority to be dull and to lack the 'potency' of 'Wings for Victory'. Consequently, even collectors are said to feel little enthusiasm about it.

NO. 166: TUESDAY 30 NOVEMBER 1943 TO TUESDAY 7 DECEMBER 1943

I. GENERAL COMMENTS

1. GENERAL

Public satisfaction with war events has increased this week, thanks to the new offensive in Italy, the raids on Germany, Russian advances and the meeting at Teheran 'between the three great men'.

Nevertheless, spirits have risen only a little: the flu epidemic is the chief topic for most people, and general tiredness, ill-health and the blackout are the cause of some depression.

The release of the Mosleys continues to be widely discussed, but with less vehemence – though much resentment is still simmering.

The ballot scheme for securing labour for the mines has had a mixed, but on the whole favourable, reception.

DOMESTIC FRONT: Much talk of Christmas, chiefly about the prospects of getting a turkey, and the price and quality of toys. Post-war prospects, housing and footwear continue to be anxiously discussed.

2. THE ALLIED CONFERENCES

The news of the two conferences has given much satisfaction, but so far there has been only limited comment. This is thought to be because people are waiting for more precise information before expressing opinions, because the news did not come as a complete surprise, and because there is some impatience with so many conferences which talk of the final assault.

THE CAIRO CONFERENCE: The first reactions were surprise and pleasure at the presence of General Chiang Kai-Shek, and disappointment at the absence of Marshal Stalin. This disappointment largely disappeared with the news of the Teheran conference, though there was still some regret and failure to understand why the Russian and Chinese leaders can never meet. Most people are glad to have China once more 'in the picture' – as with many, workers especially, she comes second in popularity only to Russia – and there is great satisfaction at the comprehensive plans for fighting the Japanese.

The declaration of punishment to be meted out to Japan went further than some had expected but has met with very wide approval. There is, however, minority criticism from (a) those who are tired of 'fist-shaking' and want to see words translated into action, (b) those who feel that the problem of Japan's expanding population will still have to be solved, (c) those who fear that threats will only stiffen her resistance and may provoke her to atrocities.

THE TEHERAN CONFERENCE: Only preliminary reports have been received so far, but people appear to be far more interested in this than in the Cairo conference. There is great satisfaction – and some enthusiasm – that at last the three great leaders have come together; though Marshal Stalin has been criticised for 'only going 60 miles out of his own country', while the other two had to go so far. People hope that all misunderstandings between the western democracies and Russia have now been smoothed away, that the future of Poland has been satisfactorily settled, and all arrangements made for the final assault on Germany. Meanwhile they are pleased at the apparent friendliness of the proceedings and eagerly await further information.

There is so far little comment on the joint declaration, but, according to the Scottish report, 'the fact that Stalin's signature appears on it gives evidence to many – especially workers – that the document will be honoured. Greater faith is placed in Stalin's word than in any other statesman's.'

THE RELEASE OF NEWS: Criticism of 'the mishandling of publicity' is mentioned in reports from eight Regions, two of which, however, suggest that it comes largely from press circles or the 'more informed'. Nevertheless, many people seem annoyed that other countries, and especially the USA, should have heard the news before we did; and the fact that the Cairo conference to some extent 'fell flat' is thought to be because news came through first from enemy and neutral sources.

3. THE MOSLEYS' RELEASE

Excitement has subsided considerably, and many are now speaking of 'a storm in a tea-cup', and asking: 'Why all the fuss?' But there are still many, particularly working people, who feel strongly that the Mosleys should not have been released. There is no change in the arguments they use:

(i) ONE LAW FOR THE RICH AND ANOTHER FOR THE POOR. Mosley would not have got out had he not been a rich man.

(ii) PHLEBITIS IS NO EXCUSE. Holloway is ideal for its treatment.

(iii) IT IS A COMPROMISE WITH FASCISM.

Among the growing number who approve the Home Secretary's action are some who nevertheless think that the timing was inappropriate.

Mr. Morrison is now fairly widely praised for acting courageously, according to his convictions in the face of popular clamour, and for his skilful speech in the debate. There is more comment that opposition was deliberately whipped up to spite the Home Secretary.

In the East End, there are fears of a recrudescence of fascism and rumours that the British Union of Fascists has taken an old hall in Paddington for meetings.

18B is again criticised, though the majority appear to have no understanding of it.

4. ITALY

The news that we are again moving forward is generally described as heartening. It is thought we still have a stiff job on hand, and the most optimists hope for is Rome by Christmas. There is much sympathy for the troops, and it is feared casualties may be heavy. More details of conditions under which fighting is going on are asked for.

The political situation is little mentioned. There is disgust at stories of Italians being allowed to fleece our men.

5. ALLIED AIR OFFENSIVE

There is again great interest in the raids on German territory, especially Berlin. They are looked on as a 'gruesome necessity' to make future land operations less costly; there is much speculation as to their effect on German morale. Though there is some sympathy for civilians, people generally are thought to display 'neither tenderness nor exultation' over the victims; any tendency to 'gloat' over their sufferings is disliked.

Concern is reported over the number of bombers lost, especially in the raid of December 2nd.

6. REPRISALS AND SECRET WEAPONS

In London, it appears that a majority are now giving some thought to the possibility of a retaliatory secret weapon. Indeed, many are anxious about it, though there are still a large number who laugh at the idea. 'Frightening tales' are repeated 'on good authority'. It is rumoured that rockets have already fallen on London – in Park Lane, the Borough High Street, and somewhere in the West End. There appears to be some confusion between rockets of British and German origin; thus, rockets are said to have been fired at Civil Defence practices. It is also rumoured that the Government is expecting large-scale gas attacks, and huge stocks of bleach powder are said to have been delivered at decontamination centres. Evening theatre and cinema attendances are thought to have declined.

In the rest of the country, there is a good deal of discussion about reprisals, though much less anxiety and more scepticism. Secret weapons are less discussed, though a large-scale gas attack on London is thought conceivable. Anything much anywhere else is not expected.

7. RAIDS ON THIS COUNTRY

The recent raid on Plymouth is still producing comment on the lack of defences.

In Deal, it is said that people have noticed with dismay the removal of AA defences from the town, and in view of threatened reprisals would feel much happier if they could be returned.

8. GENERAL SMUTS' ADDRESS (NOVEMBER 25)

This has provoked much thought and discussion. On the whole it has been very highly praised, especially for its candour and realism, though a number of people have been disturbed and feel this is not the moment to throw explosives about.

Disapproving comment is more detailed than approving and has particularly centred round his references to:

FRANCE: Though the realism of his references to post-war France is praised, they have caused some surprise and regret, and are thought to be rather ill-timed and a 'rich plum' for German propaganda. It is thought that the ardour of the French – whether fighting or otherwise – will be damped.

RUSSIA, THE 'COLOSSUS': This, too, was considered ill-timed by some and likely to pave the way for still more distrust of Russia.

'BRITAIN WILL BE POOR': Some anxiety and failure to understand the reason for this. A few ask what is to come of the 'grandiose' post-war schemes, if we are to be so poor.

SPLITTING UP THE EMPIRE INTO ZONES: Some suspect an attempt to secure native territories of South Africa for the Union and consider that coloured peoples are likely to be less well treated under the Dutch or South African flag than under the British.

9. RUSSIA

Admiration of the Russian successes and her continued progress continues, though the slight withdrawals caused some anxiety. The feeling is again expressed that the 'Russians are winning the war for us' and it is time we relieved them.

10. THE LEBANON

Comment continues on familiar lines and has decreased.

11. LEROS

Comment continues on familiar lines and has decreased.

12. TURKEY

(No reports since the news of the second Cairo conference.)

Speculation as to Turkey's possible entry into the war has recurred – in London it was recently rumoured that she had come in, with resulting intense satisfaction.

There is still some feeling, however, that our loss of the Dodecanese Islands has prejudiced the possibility of Turkey becoming our ally.

13. WAR AT SEA

DURING THE PAST FOUR WEEKS general satisfaction with our successes against the U-boats has been reported. The figures of U-boat losses have acted 'as a tonic'.

14. BROADCASTING AND PRESENTATION OF NEWS

Apart from references to the release of news of the Allied Conferences (q.v.) there is little comment on news presentation; but there is still some complaint of inaccuracy and repetition. Some people feel that the BBC bulletins have been 'soft-pedalling' on Russian withdrawals.

PROGRAMMES: The improved standard of drama productions is appreciated and more plays are asked for. More light music is wanted and people are thought to tune in to foreign stations to get it. There is comment on the poor quality of variety programmes.

SIR NORMAN ANGELL'S POSTSCRIPT, November 28, was appreciated. It was thought to be 'brilliant, logical, and needing to be said'.

GENERAL: Praise for Major Hastings' *War Commentary*, December 2; *The Air is Our Concern*; *Brains Trust*, St. Andrews's night; Theodor Broch's *Postscript*, December 5.

II. SPECIAL COMMENTS

FULL MONTHLY REVIEW

15. POST-WAR

DURING THE PAST FOUR WEEKS comment on post-war matters has continued widespread. Uneasiness seems to be deepening; in some cases, anxiety has become pessimism. The appointment of a Minister for Reconstruction, the Prime Minister's promise of 'food, work and homes for all', and the emphasis on post-war matters in the King's speech, although serving temporarily to raise hopes, have had no appreciable lasting effect.

Cynicism about the possibilities of a 'better and brighter' world after the war is increasing. The 'shelving' of the Beveridge and other Reports and White Papers, the 'lack of definite proposals' and the 'nebulousness' of promises are criticised, and are taken as evidence that the Government is really little interested in post-war matters ... 'All this talk is merely window-dressing.' 'Definite action' is called for and is considered by many to be the only likelihood of reassuring people.

Increasingly pessimistic comparison is being made with 'what happened last time'.

HOUSING: Post-war housing continues to arouse widespread concern, particularly among those married since the war and so far dependent on relatives, or living in furnished rooms. A 'wild scramble' when the war ends is feared to be likely.

The delay in announcing plans for housing is strongly criticised. Apart from impatience that building is being held up, it is feared that lack of guiding policy will result in 'jerry-building coming into its own again', in speculation in land, and 'the same shameful exploitation which took place after the last war'. The buying up of land and premises 'more or less surreptitiously going on at present' is already causing some concern.

There is little detailed comment on the kind of home wanted, though women are becoming increasingly interested and are demanding more say in the planning of houses. The preference for small houses rather than flats is mentioned.

EMPLOYMENT: Fears of post-war unemployment are widespread, particularly, it is said, in the Forces. 'Flooding' of the labour market after the war is dreaded and there is much discussion of the prospects of those in the Forces and armament industries, and of women.

In the mining, cotton and heavy industries generally, there is acute anxiety about another 'slump' ... 'Prospects of a return to normal conditions mean to the people in the coalfield, and in heavy industry generally, a return to unemployment and the dole.' In the Northern Region, the introduction of light industries into the district is demanded, to ease the employment problem after the war.

EDUCATION: Discussion of educational reform has continued and has become rather more general, though still chiefly limited to those professionally interested. The raising of the school-leaving age – which it is hoped will help to lessen unemployment – the need for educational apprenticeship, and the 'religious side', all arouse interest.

Opposition to the White Paper from religious bodies is criticised, and it is hoped 'the Government will be ruthless in its determination to make no concession'. Some minority fears are entertained, however, that 'under the cloak of improving education, plans are afoot to educate all in a common mould'.

POST-WAR CONTROLS: Post-war controls continue to arouse discussion though on a reduced scale. The public are prepared to admit that some controls will be needed after the war, and in some cases urge them as a means of preventing speculation and 'racketeering'. Nevertheless, they are tired of 'continual interference and form-filling', and 'there will be trouble if this is not kept within reasonable bounds'.

It is felt that some definite official statements should be made about post-war control, because at present it is not clear if the utterances of Ministers are expressions of the Government's views.

AGRICULTURE: Anxiety about post-war farming continues. Farmers and labourers are said to be equally concerned about the Government's future attitude. Better wages and housing for agricultural labourers are urged as means of keeping men on the land.

LOCAL AUTHORITIES: The future of local authorities is the subject of some discussion. There is said to be some uneasiness about Whitehall's 'increasing control' over local affairs.

16. HOUSING AND BILLETING

DURING THE PAST FOUR WEEKS the shortage of all kinds of housing accommodation has continued to be the cause of considerable anxiety. In many cases it has become 'one of the most immediate and pressing problems on the home front'. The Government's delay in 'getting a move on' is criticised and it is feared that a chaotic position would result if the war were to end soon.

Particular reference is made to the difficulties experienced by:

(a) WAR BRIDES: Many of them who have remained at home with their parents already have children and are becoming increasingly anxious to set up homes of their own.

(b) FAMILIES OF SERVICEMEN: There are again complaints that landlords will not let to them for fear of 'bad debts'.

(c) COUPLES WITH CHILDREN.

(d) OLD PEOPLE.

THE HIGH RENTS OF HOUSES, FLATS AND ROOMS – furnished and unfurnished – continue to excite bitter comment. It is again urged that rents for furnished rooms should be controlled.

The 'ramp' in the buying and selling of houses at exorbitant prices is also criticised. A 'ceiling' on the price of houses, based on pre-war values, is urged.

REPAIRS: Difficulties in getting repairs done are complained of. Even where repairs have been carried out, they are said not to stand up at all well to the rain.

In London there are also complaints of the delay in repairing bomb-damaged houses 'until an investigation has been made by the council'.

LOCAL AUTHORITIES' REQUISITIONING POWERS: Disappointment continues to be expressed: 'Either there is nothing to requisition, or all talk and no do' results.

AGRICULTURAL HOUSING: The delay in the building of the agricultural cottages continues to arouse comment.

BILLETING: In the Eastern and Southern Regions billeting difficulties are said to remain a source of dissatisfaction. In the Southern Region particularly, it is felt that the housewife is sufficiently harassed without having people billeted on her, and that after four years of war hostels should by now have been provided.

In the South-Western Region and in Wales there have been some complaints at the thought of having to billet American troops.

17. MINERS AND MINING

THE BALLOT SYSTEM: Comment has been considerable and reactions have been as follows:

APPROVAL: The majority among both miners and the general public think it is a good idea because they feel it will be fair to all.

DISAPPROVAL: An appreciable minority disapprove or qualify their acceptance, because they believe:

(a) There will be 'loopholes' by which the rich will gain exemption, e.g. by reason of their 'education'.
(b) It would be better to withdraw trained miners from the Forces. Miners, in particular, feel that 'green' labour will be of little use for many months.

There is some sympathy for those who are chosen and parents are said to be 'aghast'. It is reported that young men in the Northern Region say they would rather go to gaol than down a mine; they are said to be volunteering for air crews and the Navy.

Nothing but disapproval is reported from the Midland Region, where it is thought that it will only result in more square pegs in round holes. Simpler folk wonder how they will get all the names into one hat.

DURING THE PAST FOUR WEEKS concern about the coal-mining situation has continued.

THE FOLLOWING ARE THOUGHT CHIEFLY TO ACCOUNT FOR TROUBLE AND DIFFICULTIES:

(a) Unpopularity of Government manpower measures, in particular:
  (i)   The introduction of 'green labour', which miners in particular feel will increase accidents.
  (ii) The direction of young boys to the mines and their prosecution for absenteeism.
       (Since the announcement of the ballot system there has been less criticism on these lines.)
(b) Miners' remembrance of the way they were treated after the last war and their concern about the future of the industry.
(c) Conditions of work in general, and particularly the lack of up-to-date machinery in some mines.
(d) Disparity of wages between mining and other industries.
(e) 'Subversive influences' in the coalfields.

REMEDIES: Many feel that NATIONALISATION is the only solution. EXTRA FOOD RATIONS and a SHORTER WORKING WEEK are other suggestions.

18. DOMESTIC FUEL

SUPPLIES OF COAL: People in the Northern, North-Eastern, North Midland and London Regions wonder how they will manage on the coal allowance this winter. Supply difficulties are reported from Norfolk.

ECONOMY CAMPAIGN: There is little interest in the campaign. Opinion is divided as to the effort being made to economise. There is some feeling that people resent exhortations and feel rather that firmer action against strikers and greater economy in large organisations is needed.

WASTE OF FUEL is alleged in London stores, offices – especially American premises, and fun fairs.

19. INDUSTRY

Press accounts of the action taken by the Ministry of Labour against Desoutters, for ignoring a direction, has heartened work-people, who think that 'at last' the Essential Work Order is being used impartially.

DURING THE PAST FOUR WEEKS comment has been mainly on the following topics:

(a) TIREDNESS AMONG WORKERS, especially the young – thought by the majority to be due to excessively long hours.

(b) ENFORCED IDLENESS AND OVERSTAFFING: There are a number of complaints of idle and wasted time in war factories, particularly in the Northern Region. Complaints are also made of needless work (e.g. building a wall and pulling it down again), due, according to workers, to the employers' desire to swell costs and thus obtain the added percentage of profit.

(c) SLACKNESS OF WORKERS AND ABSENTEEISM: This causes some concern and is thought, in part, to be due to illness and the lack of the stimulant of intense military activity; though also to indifference, particularly among youths.

(d) DISPARITIES IN WAGES: Again this month particular mention is made of the disparity between skilled and unskilled workers' wages. It is said that skilled workers in the North Midland Region try for this reason to get work on unskilled operations.

(e) HIGH WAGES: Complaints are mostly of the high wages paid to factory workers compared with the Forces and workers still on peacetime salaries.

(f) DISMISSAL OF WORKERS AND UNEMPLOYMENT: There is a considerable amount of talk of the dismissal of war workers and of unemployment, particularly in the Northern and Midland Regions and Wales. Rumours are also reported of the closing down of war factories.

(g) CHANGES IN PRODUCTION: Reports speak of preparation for post-war production already being made and of fears among workers of a 'return to soulless industrial competition'. Even where the change-over is to work in preparation for relief in occupied countries, workers are said to lose their feeling of urgency and to feel they are no longer needed to win the war.

(h) TRANSFER OF WOMEN: This causes complaints and is considered a sign of bad management of labour.

(i) OVER-PRODUCTION: Some believe that output has exceeded requirements in many directions.

20. STRIKES

A slight decrease in comment this week, though the great majority continue to condemn strikes in wartime; a small number still feel that workers have no other means of improving conditions.

DURING THE PAST FOUR WEEKS various suggestions as to the cause of strikes have been made:

(a) Lack of firm action on the part of the Government.
(b) Failings on the part of employers.
(c) Tiredness and war-weariness.
(d) Inability of trades unions to control their members.
(e) The inefficient functioning of negotiating machinery.
(f) Paid agitators and Fifth Columnists.
(g) Communists and 'Trotskyites'.

21. MANPOWER

DURING THE PAST FOUR WEEKS comment has decreased. However, the main topics have been:

(a) THE REGISTRATION OF OLDER WOMEN: Some criticism has again been reported but on a very reduced scale, dying away to nothing the last week.

The chief ground of criticism was that many young people are not yet fully employed. It is also believed by a few that some factories have idle time; also that the women's health will be affected. Others complain of the tactless manner of Ministry of Labour interviewers.

Women in the South-East are reported on the whole to have welcomed the registration and to be impatient with the attitude of some male MPs.

(b) MISUSE OF LABOUR: The view persists that labour is still not being used to the best advantage and reference is again made to:

(i) YOUNG UNMARRIED MEN STILL NOT COMBED OUT: This is thought unfair to the older men, especially those with one-man businesses or with families.

(ii) OVERSTAFFING, especially in the Civil Service.

(c) EVASION OF CALL-UP by some women, especially young marrieds.

22. DOMESTIC HELP

DURING THE PAST FOUR WEEKS there have been continued references to the shortage of domestic help. The difficulties of elderly people, invalids, mothers with several young children, farmers' wives, and doctors, are particularly mentioned. The flu epidemic is said to have brought the question of domestic help to a head. Men are said to have had to stay away from their work when their wives have been ill.

There has been some criticism of Mr. Bevin's 'New Deal for domestic servants'. It is feared that many middle-class homes will be quite incapable of paying his rates.

23. AGRICULTURE

THIS WEEK much concern is reported at the revised farm prices announced by the Minister of Agriculture. Farmers feel these will not meet the increased wage charges and that the Ministry is guilty of a breach of faith. Some are said now to be becoming apprehensive about the future and to compare the present action with the repeal of the Corn Production Act after the last war, when the first step was made towards sending the industry into a state of depression.

DURING THE PAST FOUR WEEKS the main topics have been:

LAND CULTIVATION: Farmers are beginning to fear for the continued fertility of the soil under the present policy of intensive culture. They feel the peak has been reached and that it is useless to grow further cereal crops unless the land has been rested. Some consider the loss of fertility is already apparent.

It is thought also that suitability of land and climatic conditions should be carefully considered when extra cultivation demands are made. Grain matures so late in the North that much is wasted, and some farmers think they have ploughed to the limit and that the time has come for concentration on milk, and cattle for meat.

LABOUR AND WAGES: Concern is reported at the serious shortage of skilled labour, particularly cowmen and dairy hands. Farmers say that since their employees now pay income tax, they are not so keen on working overtime and it is also very difficult to get men to work on Sundays. A case is reported of one farm being forced to close down its dairy section on that account. Some feeling is reported that the new minimum wages rate of £3. 5. 0 compares unfavourably with wages paid on local aerodrome sites and causes discontent among the workers. At the same time there is praise for the land workers and appreciation of their 'long hours and no indulgence in unpatriotic strikes'.

Concern is reported also at the shortage of rural craftsmen, such as thatchers.

WAR AGRICULTURAL EXECUTIVE COMMITTEES: Some feel these Committees tend to become composed of 'groups of men all in with each other', and there is criticism of mismanagement and the dictatorial attitude of some junior officials. It is reported from the Southern Region that 'although no publicity is given to the methods of ejection of "bad husbandmen" by the Hants WAEC, their activities are causing a little alarm and their apparently unlimited powers are considered to savour of the Gestapo'. On the other hand, in the Eastern Region, 'the work of these Committees is, in the main, appreciated'.

HOUSING: Hardships over tied cottages and the shortage of agricultural cottages continue to be reported, and there is complaint that farm workers' cottages are being made of poor materials, e.g. cardboard door panels.

WOMEN'S LAND ARMY: The vital work which the women are doing for the country is praised, but there is comment on the proposed rise in wages by 3/- a week. Some employers consider the beginning of the winter an inopportune time for this and fear it may lead to some land girls being paid off.

24. HEALTH

DURING THE PAST FOUR WEEKS there have been increasing references to the EPIDEMIC OF COLDS AND FLU, which this week is said to be a widespread topic of discussion. The epidemic is attributed mainly to lowered powers of resistance due to lack of vitamins in the national diet. Other causes mentioned are:

(a) The poor quality of leather shoe soles.
(b) War-weariness.
(c) Germs dropped by the enemy.
(d) A germ rumoured to have been brought back by members of the Eighth Army.

There is a desire that some simple precautionary measures should be issued by the Ministry of Health, and there is some discussion about Patulin. Some anxiety is reported among those who remember the flu epidemic of the last war.

GENERAL HEALTH: There have again this month been several references to war-weariness and strain. This continues to be attributed to long hours of work, wartime food and lack of holidays.

Government statements about the good health of the nation continue to meet with criticism. In the Southern Region it is pointed out that statistics cannot take into account the number of people who, although not fit, are conscientiously at work, whereas under normal conditions they would be away under doctors' orders.

TUBERCULOSIS: Concern continues at the increase in tuberculosis. It is thought that the exclusion of chronic TB sufferers from the Government allowance will cause hardship and that it is 'a blot on a civilised country'.

SHORTAGE OF HOSPITAL ACCOMMODATION: Concern continues, especially at the lack of maternity beds in hospitals.

SHORTAGE OF DOCTORS: Doctors are reported to be overworked and to have too many patients to be able to watch each one carefully. It is thought too many doctors have been called up.

25. VENEREAL DISEASES CAMPAIGN

DURING THE PAST FOUR WEEKS approval for the campaign has continued. The posters and publicity are praised, though it is thought that even stronger measures are needed. More lectures and films on the subject would be welcomed.

The increased amount of drinking, especially among young girls, is deplored as it is thought to pave the way for VD. It is again suggested that the 'no treating order' should be reintroduced.

26. CLOTHING

There has been some appreciative comment in Northern Ireland and the South-Eastern district on the reduction in coupon value of wooden-soled shoes (November 22) and cheaper shoes (November 25). In four other Regions, however, opinion is more critical: 'Two pairs of rotten ones at ten coupons not worth one good pair'. It is suggested this was done to enable manufacturers to get rid of shoddy goods; also, that wooden-soled shoes are 'simply a flop' because they wear out too quickly.

DURING THE LAST FOUR WEEKS the following familiar topics have been reported:

(a) FOOTWEAR: 'Most people's greatest clothing worry'. The main complaints are:

  (i) POOR QUALITY OF SHOES ON SALE, particularly children's. 'Even in new shoes children have wet feet within fifteen minutes of leaving home.' Mothers say they will have to keep the children away from school.

  (ii) REPAIR DIFFICULTIES: Reference is made to: the very long time repairs take; the poor quality of leather used for repairs – 'compressed cardboard is not suitable for mending shoes'; the poor quality of the repairs – 'patching of soles is no good'; the lack of leather for home repairs.

  (iii) SHORTAGE OF FOOTWEAR: Specifically mentioned are: hob-nailed boots for farmers; workers' heavy nailed boots; children's shoes, sizes 7 to 13; men's shoes, size 8½.

  (iv) LACK OF RUBBER BOOTS for country people, particularly children. To quote from Postal Censorship: 'Ronald has a cold just now, his feet got wet going to school and we can't get rubber boots for him.'

  (v) THE NUMBER OF COUPONS REQUIRED.

  (vi) HIGH PRICE.

(b) INSUFFICIENT CLOTHING COUPONS: It is said essential clothes cannot be replaced and that some people 'cannot keep even reasonably warm'. Specifically mentioned as suffering from insufficient coupons are:

  (i) OUTDOOR MANUAL WORKERS, particularly AGRICULTURAL WORKERS.

  (ii) INDUSTRIAL WORKERS: Blast furnacemen and workers in heavy chemicals feel their coupon expenditure on working clothes is not sufficiently allowed for.

  (iii) CHILDREN: Many, it is suggested in one Region, 'are without warm underwear in order to keep them tidy in top clothes'.

  (iv) PEOPLE NEEDING UNIFORMS, such as Scouts, Guides, members of the GTC and children at schools where uniforms are worn.

  (v) EXPECTANT MOTHERS: Some complaint is reported about Mrs. Anne Edwards' reference in her broadcast (November 27) to a baby needing only a dozen or a dozen-and-a-half napkins: 'It is generally assumed that two or three dozen is a minimum, and accordingly sixty coupons do not go far.'

(c) THE SURRENDER OF PERSONAL COUPONS FOR TOWELS, CURTAINS, ETC.: The demand for a special household allowance is said to be greater now that stocks are getting depleted.

(d) SHORTAGE AND POOR QUALITY OF CLOTHING GENERALLY, particularly WOMEN'S STOCKINGS: It is suggested in one Region that 'far too much labour is expended on cheap and shoddy goods'.

(e) HIGH PRICE OF CLOTHING, particularly hats.
(f) DELAY IN ISSUING WORKERS' SUPPLEMENTARY COUPONS.
(g) TIME TAKEN BY LAUNDRIES: It is suggested they have been told
       'nothing matters but the soldiers; don't concern yourselves about civilians'.

SHORTAGE OF BLACKOUT MATERIAL: 'People think it unfair they should be prosecuted for blackout offences when it is impossible to buy sufficient material in the shops.'

BOARD OF TRADE PUBLICITY: 'Make Do and Mend' classes continue to be popular, particularly in the South-Western Region; they are also creating a great deal of interest in South-Eastern villages. THE DOMESTIC FRONT EXHIBITION is spoken of appreciatively in Swindon.

27. TOYS

Strong complaints continue of high prices and often very poor quality of toys. Some people are disappointed that there was not a greater number of toys available following the announcement of the lifting of the quota restrictions (December 1). Fantastic prices of second-hand toys are bitterly criticised: £10 or more for a doll's pram is thought ridiculous.

28. ALARM CLOCKS

DURING THE PAST FOUR WEEKS there have again been complaints of the shortage of alarm clocks, and requests for permits from many workers not entitled to receive them.

THIS WEEK it is reported from Wales that many workers are pleased with the new regulation concerning the issue of alarm clocks, as they will now be eligible to receive them.

29. FURNITURE

DURING THE PAST FOUR WEEKS there have again been complaints of excessive prices demanded for both new and second-hand furniture. Utility furniture is also thought to be expensive.

30. FOOD

General satisfaction with the food situation is tempered by comment on the particular items set out below. There is, too, a growing feeling that wartime food is not sufficiently nourishing to give the necessary resistance to illness and tiredness, and some people connect the flu epidemic with the quality of the present food.

CHRISTMAS FARE is again a subject of much interest and some anxiety, and many people are worrying about what they are likely to eat for Christmas and drink on New Year's Eve. People on the whole do not seem very hopeful of getting a turkey – 'we shall be lucky if we get a rabbit' – and some are resentful and suspect that the matter is not being fairly dealt with. It is suggested that turkeys could be cut up and sold in portions.

The shortage of dried fruit is greatly deplored; so is absence of suet.

DURING THE PAST FOUR WEEKS there has been comment on:

MILK: There have been continuous complaints of the smallness of the present ration. Particular sufferers are:

(a) Small households, who complain of the arbitrary imposition of milkless days. Some one-person households have only two deliveries a week, owing to milkmen refusing to deliver half pints.
(b) Elderly people and invalids.
(c) Children of 5–14: 'What happens to all the school milk during the holidays?'
(d) Those who never get a meal away from home.

There are also complaints of distribution, and there is a persistent belief that 'other places' – whether the next street or a different locality – have plenty, or at least a bit over the ration.

ORANGES: Distribution has been criticised on two grounds:

(a) THEY SHOULD BE MADE AVAILABLE TO MORE PEOPLE, particularly (i) children over five – 'as the sixes and sevens long for them when the little ones get them'; (ii) the sick and aged.
(b) THEY AREN'T ALWAYS FAIRLY DISTRIBUTED: Some children failed to get any of the last allocation and there is a feeling that oranges sometimes go to favoured customers instead. One report mentions people with time to queue getting oranges from two or three different shops. It is suggested that they should be distributed through schools and clinics or that shops should be compelled to display notices when an allocation is available.

THE INADEQUACY OF THE COOKING FAT RATION, particularly at Christmas time.

CANADIAN APPLES have been looked forward to with pleasure; and there is some impatience at their non-appearance, particularly in the Northern Region where it is asked: 'Why should they go to the South where they have plenty of English apples and can grow their own?' Supplies were greatly appreciated in Scotland, but 'control of sale would have been welcomed, as supplies often went to shop-crawlers before workers could get them'.

THE DIFFICULTY OF GETTING INVALID FOODS: Ovaltine is particularly mentioned and so is whisky which, even when ordered by the doctor, is often unobtainable for other than regular customers.

THE 'NASTINESS' OF WARTIME CAKES.

31. SHOPPING DIFFICULTIES AND FOOD QUEUES

DURING THE PAST FOUR WEEKS complaints have been fewer, but on familiar lines, and very strong in the London Region where shopping is described as 'a nightmare for the working woman'. The lunch-time and earlier winter closing of shops still seems to be the greatest cause of difficulties, and workers are still the section of the public to suffer most. People grumble that shopping is very tiring and wastes so much time.

There are again complaints of:

(a) The quota system whereby goods in short supply are put on sale at 10 a.m. or later and are sold out before lunch time.
(b) The comparatively poor stock of food in rural shops, which involves rural housewives in travelling to the nearest town, where they often find that goods on points or in short supply have already been sold.
(c) The ordering of goods by telephone, to the detriment of personal shoppers.

32. OLD AGE PENSIONS

The improved standard of supplementary pensions, which will come into force on January 17 if approved by Parliament, has been welcomed, though many people feel that an increase in the basic pension is needed.

DURING THE PAST FOUR WEEKS there have been repeated references to the inadequacy of old age pensions, in view of the increased cost of living, and to the wish for their increase. Some feel that, in addition to an increase, there should be an extra food allowance – especially milk – and 'less probing into the most intimate conditions of a pensioner'.

33. INCOME TAX

DURING THE PAST FOUR WEEKS approval for the 'pay-as-you-earn' scheme has continued. There are still many people who would like a clear and simple explanation of it, and a broadcast on the subject (December 3) was praised.

Managements continue to complain of the extra amount of work for their staff that will be involved, and some fear they will have to engage extra accountants. Those not concerned with operating the scheme, however, hope it will not be shelved because of the extra labour needed.

POST-WAR CREDITS: Some people fear that post-war credits will merely be credited to them against income tax and not paid in cash.

IRISH WORKERS: Bitter comment is reported about Irish workers who return to Eire after six months, without paying tax.

SLACKING TO AVOID PAYING TAX IS STILL REPORTED: The case is mentioned of a nurse who said she was obliged to take far longer holidays than she used to, as otherwise she would be liable for tax.

34. SERVICEMEN'S PENSIONS AND DEPENDANTS' ALLOWANCES

DURING THE PAST FOUR WEEKS there have again been complaints of the inadequacy of Service pensions – whether for dependants or for the men themselves – and of dependants' allowances. There is, however, some feeling that the general treatment of cases has improved and there is praise for the work of the Pensions Appeals Tribunals; it is thought that more publicity about them might do good. There is, too, appreciation of the grant to widows for rent.

Specific complaints mentioned are:

(a) Employers are discouraged from making up the pay of their employees who join up, because the amount allowed by the firm will be deducted from the war service grant.
(b) The hardship incurred, due to the time lag between the reduction of a woman's war service grant and the increased allotment made to her husband.
(c) The reduction in a dependant's allowance if she takes paid employment.
(d) The inclusion of a widow's Service pension for income tax.

35. HOME GUARD, FIRE-WATCHING AND CIVIL DEFENCE

FIRE-WATCHING DUTIES: During the past two weeks criticism has continued on lines previously reported, though the recent announcement of some alleviation of duty in areas where this can safely be made has given satisfaction. There is disappointment in some districts where no release is possible. One report states 'the present increase in illness has brought fresh grumbles, and in industrial areas there is strong evidence of the deplorable effect of fire-watching on miners, heavy workers and housewives'.

HOME GUARD: Complaints have continued of the amount of duty required, particularly from workers already employed for long hours and those who have already trained for many months. But keen members of the Home Guard again criticise Sir Walter Citrine's speech as implying a doubt of the value of their services and providing wavering members with an excuse for shirking. They advocate a greater insistence on attendances. It is thought that the 'browned-off' feeling persists probably because it no longer seems evident that the Home Guard has a function to perform. One report suggests that what is wanted is not a cutting down of the Home Guard but more time off, and that one Sunday a month would have a tremendous effect.

CIVIL DEFENCE: It is suggested in one report that full-time CD personnel could be detailed for work in shops and offices near their headquarters.

36. BLACKOUT

DURING THE PAST FOUR WEEKS there has again been comment on the depressing effect of the blackout, which some think might now be modified, especially in inland areas. Some people ask why side roads cannot have star-lighting like main roads. In London it is thought that grumbles have died down sharply since the raid on Putney.

On the other hand, laxity of blackout is criticised in some quarters and it is thought that torches used by people leaving buildings must show up more than scattered lights. Pedestrians, motorists and cyclists all complain of the dangerous flashing of torches, and of the blinding effect of headlights with badly adjusted masks. Drivers who adhere to regulations are often at a disadvantage.

37. TRANSPORT DIFFICULTIES

DURING THE PAST FOUR WEEKS transport difficulties have continued to be widely reported on familiar lines:

(a) INADEQUATE RURAL BUS SERVICES: In some areas bus services are almost 'non-existent' ... 'buses only twice a week'.

(b) THE EARLY EVENING BUS CURFEW: Workers complain they have no chance for recreation. The difficulties of people arriving by train after the last bus has gone are also mentioned.

(c) OVERCROWDING: Excessive overloading is said to cause tiredness and irritation to workers.

(d) LONG WAITS IN BUS QUEUES: Workers complain that buses arrive in groups with long intervals in between.

(e) BUSES FAILING TO STOP AND PICK UP PASSENGERS: Bus drivers are said to pass 'request' stops and to put on a spurt if they see people running to catch the bus.

(f) INCIVILITY OF TRANSPORT EMPLOYEES.

(g) WITHDRAWAL OF RETURN BUS FARES: This continues to cause indignation in the Northern and North-Eastern Regions.

(h) BUSES PULLING AWAY FROM STOPS BEFORE PASSENGERS ARE READY: There is said to have been an increase in minor accidents in the North-Western Region due to conductresses ringing the bus off before the passengers are ready.

HOLIDAY TRAVEL: Some people in the South-Western Region are said to be intending to travel over Christmas; heavy holiday traffic is also expected between Northern Ireland and Eire.

38. PETROL

DURING THE PAST FOUR WEEKS there have been several complaints of waste and misuse of petrol. Unequal distribution of petrol is alleged and it is asked where private car owners get their petrol. Complaints are chiefly of petrol wasted by:

(a) WVS.

(b) Civil Defence, particularly the NFS.

(c) Taxis used for pleasure purposes.

(d) The Forces.

(e) Farmers, Government officials, Home Guard.

The restoration of the basic petrol ration rumour has reappeared this week in reports from the North-Eastern and North-Western Regions.

39. SALVAGE

DURING THE PAST FOUR WEEKS, inadequate collection of salvage has been reported from four Regions. This, coupled with the alleged waste of paper by (a) Government departments in sending out circulars, and (b) the display of commercial advertisements, is considered to be the reason for the falling off of public interest in salvage.

IV

January to December 1944

19 JANUARY British, Indian and African troops of the Fourteenth Army launch a fresh campaign on the Arakan front. The following month a Japanese counterattack is defeated at Ngakyedauk Pass. The front subsequently stabilizes along monsoon positions.

22 JANUARY The US Sixth Corps lands at Anzio, south of Rome, to outflank the enemy. The Germans mount a determined defence around the beachhead.

27 JANUARY The German siege of Leningrad is lifted after a two-and-a-half-year blockade.

15 FEBRUARY US aircraft bomb the Benedictine abbey of Monte Cassino in central Italy on the assumption that the Germans are using it for defence. The raid kills 230 Italian civilians who had taken refuge in the abbey. German parachute troops subsequently occupy the ruins.

17 FEBRUARY The government publishes a white paper on the establishment of a National Health Service.

7–8 MARCH Japanese forces in Burma launch an offensive against Imphal and Kohima in north-east India. The Fourteenth Army fiercely resists.

8 APRIL Soviet forces reach the Czechoslovak border.

18 MAY Polish troops of the Eighth Army raise their national flag over the abbey of Monte Cassino after storming the Cassino heights.

23 MAY The US Sixth Corps breaks out of the Anzio beachhead.

26 MAY The government publishes a white paper on employment policy.

4 JUNE The US Fifth Army enters Rome.

6 JUNE D-Day. American, British and Canadian troops land in Normandy as part of Operation Overlord. By the end of the day, some 150,000 Allied airborne and seaborne troops are ashore at a cost of 10,000 casualties.

13 JUNE The Germans launch a campaign of V1 flying-bomb attacks from northern France against London and the south of England.

15 JUNE US marines mount an amphibious assault on Saipan in the Mariana Islands. Japanese forces doggedly resist for three weeks.

18 JUNE A new Italian government under Bonomi replaces Badoglio's regime.

19–20 JUNE US carrier forces inflict heavy losses on the Japanese fleet in the Philippine Sea.

22 JUNE The Fourteenth Army lifts the Japanese siege of Imphal-Kohima. It then proceeds to drive the Japanese out of north-east India.

22–23 JUNE Soviet forces begin a major offensive in Belorussia. Over the weeks that follow, the Germans are pushed back into Poland.

26 JUNE Britain's Second Army launches an attack to envelop Caen in Normandy. The Germans put up determined resistance.

26 JUNE The US First Army captures the port of Cherbourg in Normandy.

5 JULY In the face of the V1 attacks, the first organized parties of mothers and children are evacuated from London. Between July and September nearly one million people are helped by the government to escape the target zones.

9 JULY The Second Army takes northern Caen, with the southern suburbs secured ten days later. Allied bombing has devastated the city, killing some 1,700 French civilians.

18 JULY The Second Army attacks southwards from Caen. The Germans fight staunchly to contain the thrust.

18 JULY In the face of Japanese military reverses, the prime minister of Japan, Tōjō, resigns.

20 JULY A German army officer, Colonel Claus von Stauffenberg, attempts to assassinate Hitler by planting a bomb at his headquarters in East Prussia. The bomb only lightly wounds him. Stauffenberg and his chief accomplices are swiftly executed.

21 JULY US Marines mount an amphibious assault on Guam in the Mariana Islands. Japanese forces fight tenaciously for three weeks.

25 JULY The US First Army unleashes an attack from around Saint-Lô in Normandy. The German defences are soon breached and an Allied breakout from Normandy begins.

1 AUGUST With Soviet forces approaching Warsaw, the Polish resistance launches an uprising in the city to drive the German garrison out. Over the weeks that follow, the Germans ruthlessly crush the resisters.

3 AUGUST The government's education bill receives royal assent.

15 AUGUST American and British forces land between Toulon and Cannes in southern France, with a French corps coming ashore shortly afterwards. There is limited opposition to the landing, and German forces withdraw north up the Rhône valley.

16–21 AUGUST The remnants of the German forces in Normandy escape eastwards through the Falaise 'gap' as the advancing US, British and Canadian armies converge.

25 AUGUST After an uprising by the French resistance against the German garrison in Paris, the US First Army, spearheaded by the French Second Armoured Division, arrives to liberate the city.

3 SEPTEMBER The Second Army liberates Brussels.

8 SEPTEMBER The first German V2 rockets strike London and southern England from launch sites in the Netherlands.

12–16 SEPTEMBER Quebec conference. Roosevelt and Churchill agree on the division of post-war Germany into zones of occupation.

13 SEPTEMBER The US First Army attacks the Siegfried line near Aachen and the fighting crosses into western Germany. The Germans put up stern resistance which stalls the advance.

17–26 SEPTEMBER The Allies undertake a combined ground and airborne operation to outflank the Siegfried line and secure a crossing over the lower Rhine at Arnhem in the Netherlands. Paratroops of the British First Airborne Division capture the north end of the road bridge at Arnhem but are overwhelmed by the Germans before the advancing Second Army ground forces arrive. The survivors of the operation at Arnhem are forced to withdraw.

21 SEPTEMBER The Eighth Army captures Rimini in north-east Italy after breaching the Gothic line. Progress is then hampered by deteriorating weather and difficult terrain.

22 SEPTEMBER The government publishes a white paper on demobilization. This is followed by a white paper on social insurance (26 September) and on industrial injury insurance (27 September).

2 OCTOBER The Warsaw uprising ends as the Polish resisters surrender to German forces amidst the ruins of the city. During the uprising some 17,000 resisters have been killed, along with 150,000 Polish civilians.

16 OCTOBER As the Germans withdraw from Greece, a British expeditionary force lands at the port of Piraeus to ensure the safe arrival of the Greek government-in-exile.

16 OCTOBER Soviet forces launch an attack on East Prussia and take the war onto German soil in the east. The advance soon grinds to a halt in the face of strong German defences and counterattacks.

20 OCTOBER The US army undertakes an amphibious assault on Leyte in the Philippines. The Japanese contest the island for two months.

21 OCTOBER The US First Army takes Aachen in western Germany.

23–26 OCTOBER The Japanese navy tries to destroy the US landing at Leyte but suffers irreparable losses at the hands of the US fleet in the battle for Leyte Gulf.

12 NOVEMBER The German battleship *Tirpitz* is sunk by RAF Lancaster bombers off Håkøya island near Tromsø, Norway.

14 NOVEMBER The Second Army in the Netherlands attacks eastwards to clear the west bank of the river Meuse. Meanwhile, further south the US First and Ninth Armies press forward at Aachen, and the US Third Army at Metz, in a general offensive along the western front.

2 DECEMBER East African troops of the Fourteenth Army occupy Kalewa on the Chindwin river as the Japanese fall back from north-east India into central Burma.

3 DECEMBER Civil war erupts in Greece. British forces in Athens intervene to prevent a Communist takeover by the Greek National Liberation Front (EAM-ELAS). British troops find themselves fighting Greek resistance groups that had battled the Axis occupiers.

14 DECEMBER Fifteenth Indian Corps renews the campaign against the Japanese in Arakan.

16 DECEMBER German forces launch a counter-offensive in the Ardennes, south of Aachen. The Allies are taken by surprise and the Germans drive a wedge into the US First Army's front.

24 DECEMBER V1 flying bombs aimed at Manchester hit the north of England after being air-launched from German aircraft off the east coast.

25 DECEMBER Churchill arrives in Athens to try and bring about a negotiated settlement to the Greek crisis.

NO. 171: TUESDAY 4 JANUARY 1944 TO
TUESDAY 11 JANUARY 1944

I. GENERAL COMMENTS

1. GENERAL

There is little change in public spirits this week; they are maintained at a high level by the Russian successes, expectations of invasion, the naval victories, and our air offensive. At the same time, there is some uneasiness about Russo-Polish relations; also some dread of casualties when we do invade.

The conviction remains that this is the last year of the European war.

ON THE HOME FRONT tiredness and war-weariness are again widely reported. Other main topics are the reduction in the domestic coal allowance, the clothing coupon allotment for the next six months, and post-war prospects.

2. RUSSIA

The news of the Red Army's advance across the Polish border aroused widespread admiration and delight. People are amazed at the speed and magnitude of the achievement, and many hope the Russians will sweep right through into Germany. It is hoped Polish partisans will not hinder the Russian advance.

RUSSO-POLISH RELATIONS: The crossing of the 1939 Polish frontier has aroused considerable concern over Russo-Polish relations. Though opinion is divided most people appear to support the Russian point of view. It is felt that the Red Army is doing all the work, and that, but for Russia's entry into the war, Poland would now be part of the Reich. People consider Poland was not a democracy before the war and there is some distrust of the Polish government here, and dislike of their 'stiff attitude'.

On the other hand, many sympathise with the Poles. They are apprehensive lest the USSR should insist on holding on to the land she occupied in 1939; whatever the original merits of the Curzon line, they maintain that Britain went to war to guarantee Polish integrity.

Whichever side they take, everyone hopes a solution of the frontier problem may soon be found and that nothing will occur to hamper the main issue – the defeat of Germany. Some think tension might be relieved if the Poles are offered an extension of boundaries westwards.

3. THE SECOND FRONT

Speculation, especially about place and time, remains widespread and varied. France or the Low Countries are favourite guesses; opinion as to time varies from a few days hence to next May.

Many regard the systematic air attacks on Germany and France as preliminaries and hope they will mean reduced losses when it does take place. However, there is great concern at the thought of casualties; but confidence remains high.

A few believe the second front may not be necessary in view of Russian successes and the allied air offensive. A small number think the second front talk is all bluff.

THE COMMANDERS: There is still much comment, but it is on almost exactly the same lines as last week. However, two reports mention minority criticism of General Montgomery, on the grounds that he has too much press publicity.

THE EIGHTH ARMY: Expectation that returned Eighth Army men will bear the brunt of the early fighting has increased; relatives especially do not like the idea. 'Our 25 per cent are sure to go in first.'

4. THE AIR WAR

ALLIED AIR OFFENSIVE: Continued satisfaction, particularly with the Berlin raids – though some now take big raids for granted. Most people are pleased with the systematic destruction of Berlin and want it kept up 'for practical and psychological reasons'. A number, however, regard it regretfully 'as a job which just has to be done', while a few feel that the Allies are sinking to the level of the enemy and that the raids are terror raids. A minority still express sympathy for German women and children.

Our losses continue to cause comment and some concern. However, most people think that, considering the size of the raids and the damage done, they are not excessive.

REPRISAL RAIDS: Many think there will be heavy raiding here immediately the invasion of Europe starts; some think it will be as heavy as anything previously experienced, especially in the South. The bombing of Merseyside is expected by people in the North-West, in view of its importance as an intake port. Some nervousness is reported in London and the South-East, chiefly among women.

A considerable number, however, do not expect large-scale reprisals, believing that the Germans either have not the planes, or that they will need them for dealing with our attacks.

There continues to be a little speculation about the rocket gun.

THE JET-PROPELLED FIGHTER is the subject of widespread interest and speculation. In at least two areas, the news came as no surprise, however. There is great admiration for Group Captain Whittle's ingenuity and perseverance. On the whole, though people are delighted that we have stolen a march on the Germans, few expect that there will be time to use the new plane on any considerable scale against Germany. Some anxiety is reported among aircraft workers as to whether it will adversely affect production of other types and, therefore, their own future.

There is some surprise that so many details are published at the present time. Criticism is reported from a Royal Aircraft Establishment in one Region at the published claim that the tests were carried out without a single accident, 'because workers know this is untrue'.

5. ITALY

Disappointment continues at our slow progress. There is, however, some gratification at the local successes of the Fifth Army. Greater appreciation of the bad conditions and difficulties which our men have to face is reported, though comparison is again made with the Red Army, which can advance in any weather. It is still felt that something went wrong with the Italian campaign at the outset.

There is praise for General Montgomery's farewell speech to the Eighth Army. It is thought to have moved civilians as much as his own men.

Surprise at the appointment of General Maitland Wilson continues. General Leese's appointment has excited little comment.

6. WAR AT SEA

General delight with the victories over the *Scharnhorst* and the German destroyers continues on familiar lines.

7. THE BALKANS

Interest in Yugo-Slavia and admiration for the people's resistance continues, stimulated by press rumours of Allied landings there.

People want more help for Tito and vaguely criticise Allied policy towards Yugo-Slavia and Greece; but they remain mystified at the 'eternal intricacies' in both countries.

8. THE SKIPTON BY-ELECTION

So far, this is mentioned in three reports only. People appear pleased at the return of the Common Wealth candidate. His success is variously thought to be due to his party's 'definite' programme, to dissatisfaction among farmers, and to the Government's handling of post-war affairs.

9. BROADCASTING AND PRESENTATION OF NEWS

This week there is criticism of the tendency to 'soft pedal' Allied reverses while giving great prominence to successes, and of 'harping too long on our victories'. People also complain that American and Dominion troops get much more publicity than those from this country.

PROGRAMMES GENERALLY are criticised as too Americanised, dull and monotonous. People would like better variety and more light music.

PLAYS are liked and more are asked for, but *Appointment with Fear* is thought 'unduly gruesome'.

BRAINS TRUST: The attack on Professor Joad by another member of the *Brains Trust* (January 4) is criticised as childish and rude.

HOWARD THOMAS: The breach between the BBC and Howard Thomas has aroused comment and some feeling that there are uneasy relations between the BBC and their staff.

PRAISE FOR: *ITMA*; Alistair Cooke, January 8; Thursday evening *War Commentaries*; *Can I Help You?*

II. SPECIAL COMMENTS

SHORT WEEKLY REVIEW

10. POST-WAR

Post-war problems continue to be very widely discussed. The Government's 'dilly-dallying' is criticised; concrete plans and the implementing of promises are urgently wanted, particularly in relation to housing, employment, social security, and education.

11. AGRICULTURE

Dissatisfaction with the revised prices is again widely reported from farming circles. The Minister of Agriculture's attitude is felt to be a 'red light in regard to post-war prospects', and his broadcast is not thought to have eased matters. While some of the general public appear to feel the farmers have done very well, others are sympathetic.

12. DOMESTIC FUEL

Grumbles and concern continue at the reduction in the coal allowance, particularly:

(a) In rural areas without gas or electricity. Transport is an additional difficulty quoted.
(b) In homes with no storage space for coal. On the other hand, in the Southern Region, people who took official advice and stocked up feel the reduction will operate against them.
(c) In homes with invalids.
(d) In homes where workers are on different shifts.
(e) In the Peak District of Derbyshire, where quarry workers complain that when they arrive home at night 'wet with rain and snow, there is not sufficient fire to dry clothes before morning'.

Non-mining families in mining areas in the North Midland Region consider it unfair that the ordinary householder should be restricted to 5 cwt. of coal per month, while a miner's family is still able to have a ton.

13. MINERS AND MINING

The reduction in the domestic coal allowance seems to have overshadowed the mining situation – which, however, continues to be discussed on familiar lines.

14. CLOTHING

The announcement of the clothing coupon allowance for the next six months has had a mixed reception. While some are relieved that the ration has been maintained, others are disappointed that it has not been raised. All, however, continue to complain of the insufficiency of the present allowance.

Some misunderstanding of the announcement seems to exist, for in the Eastern and South-Western Regions, pleasure is expressed that coupons have been 'slightly increased'.

15. MISCELLANEA

WATER SUPPLY: A serious water shortage in rural areas is reported from two Regions. Some springs and wells are very low or quite dry. Though it is realised that the shortage is primarily due to the long drought, it is thought to be aggravated by the opening of aerodromes and camps in the vicinity, and by the large amount of draining carried out lately.

GERMAN SURVIVORS INTERNED IN EIRE: News that 162 German naval officers and men have been landed in Eire and interned caused some mild excitement in Northern Ireland, where it is asked what would happen if a batch managed to escape. It is believed they could easily contact IRA leaders, penetrate into Ulster, gather valuable military information and communicate it to German diplomatic representatives in Dublin.

PRICE OF WHISKY: In Scotland, dissatisfaction and resentment at the prices charged for whisky continue strong. People do not accept assurances that there is no black market in the trade. They know what they are being asked to pay for their bottle or their 'half' and see little difference between black market and gross profiteering. They consider that the man who takes a 'half' is entitled to get it without being robbed, and it is not understood why the authorities do not fix a maximum price. It is stated that the price of whisky ranks with housing as the chief morale problem with working-class men.

THEFTS OF AMMUNITION: Recent court cases, showing that explosives have been stolen and used (e.g. in efforts to wreck the ICI offices in Glasgow), are causing anxiety. People ask why Home Guard and army ammunition stores are not better guarded.

SLEEP FOR THE NIGHT SHIFT: Night workers ask for further propaganda to make the general public show more consideration for those who have to sleep by day. They are not only disturbed by the radio, but by general noisiness. They ask for more messages on the BBC, at times when everyone is listening.

III. PERIODICAL REVIEW

16. YOUTH

DURING THE PAST FOUR WEEKS there has been rather less talk about the behaviour of young people; but there is still serious concern about the following:

(a) THE INCREASE IN DRINKING, particularly among young girls. Approval is reported of the steps taken at Morley to prevent young people under 18 from obtaining drinks.

   (b) PETTY DELINQUENCIES such as pilfering, and GENERAL
       INDISCIPLINE among children, as well as young people.
   (c) THE 'LANDSLIDE' IN MORALS, especially among young girls.
   (d) YOUNG GIRLS ASSOCIATING WITH MEN, especially troops. It is said
       that the steps taken to prevent young girls attending military dances in the
       Colne Valley have been approved locally.

Factors largely responsible for the above are thought to be:

   (a) LACK OF PARENTAL CONTROL – 'father in the Forces, mother at
       work'.
   (b) ABSENCE OF A 'NO TREATING ORDER'.
   (c) TOO MUCH MONEY, EARNED WITH LITTLE EFFORT.
   (d) NEED FOR 'WHOLESOME AND CHEERFUL' MEETING PLACES,
       in the country as well as in towns, where young people can spend their
       evenings without the necessity of consuming intoxicants.
   (e) BOREDOM AND FATIGUE.
   (f) LAX POLICE SUPERVISION.
   (g) INADEQUATE SCHOOL DISCIPLINE, due to the large classes and
       teachers being overworked.

YOUTH ORGANISATIONS: Some feel these should be further encouraged and
developed, to counteract bad influences and teach young people their responsibilities.
The need to get leaders of the right type, with a genuine understanding of young
people, is stressed. A few feel the older organisations are suffering at the expense of
the pre-Service corps.

    THE ESSENTIAL WORK ORDER is criticised for preventing young people from
advancing in their careers, and also for sometimes operating against parental control.

APPENDIX TO WEEKLY REPORT NO. 175

AMERICA

17 FEBRUARY 1944

A BBC Listener Research Report on the changes in the state of British
public opinion on the USA during 1942 and 1943

Two years ago, a survey of the attitude of the British public towards the USA was
made by Listener Research for the guidance of the New York office. The enquiry
was based on the observations of over 1,000 local correspondents and was carried
out very shortly after Pearl Harbour. The fact that since then American troops have
become a familiar sight in Great Britain was felt, apart from anything else, to be
a justification for a repetition of the enquiry on broadly similar lines. A second

enquiry was, therefore, made in January 1944, and nearly 900 local correspondents supplied evidence for it. Throughout the analysis a division was made between the observations of correspondents from areas where there had been considerable opportunities for people to meet or observe American troops, and those from areas where no such opportunities had occurred. The following is a summary of the results.

THE AMERICAN PEOPLE

Two years ago, the prevailing view in this country was that the Americans were a 'mixed lot' in which, however, the British strain predominated. This is still true, the experience of having met American troops in this country having tended to confirm it. It is very noticeable that among those who have not met American troops and who must, therefore, rely for their evidence upon second-hand sources, the view that Americans of British descent are now in a small minority is very common. There is a notable tendency for alleged defects in the American character, political institutions, or war effort to be attributed to the ethnographical complexity of the United States.

THE AMERICAN CHARACTER

The vast majority of the British people refuse to subscribe to the wholesale statements about the American character, whether they declare it to be in all fundamental respects very like the British, or in all fundamental respects different from it. This was the conclusion arrived at after the enquiry in 1942, and it still holds true today. It is noticeable, too, that it is among people who have met American troops that wholesale judgments about the American character are least common. Among the minority, however, it must be noted that, whereas two years ago the tendency was to say that the American character is in all fundamental respects very like the British, today the minority take precisely the opposite view.

AMERICAN POLITICAL INSTITUTIONS

Two years ago, comparatively few people in Britain considered that American political life was less democratic than our own. This view, however, though still that of a minority, is much more widespread than it was, particularly among those who have met American troops. In the same way, there are fewer people today than there were two years ago who declare that American political institutions are more truly democratic than our own, though this view is still prevalent. It should be remembered that it is only within the last two years that many people have actually seen the colour bar in operation, and this has made a profound impression in some quarters. There seems, too, to have been a growth in apprehensiveness about the power of 'big business' in the United States, and it is certainly true that many people find American politics extremely bewildering. The tendency to equate Congress with Parliament and party divisions in America with party divisions here, is increasingly recognised to be misleading, though what the precise functions of the House, Senate and Administration are, and what the real differences between Republicans and Democrats are, remain for many, if not most, people a profound mystery. It may be mentioned here that admiration and even adulation of President Roosevelt is still very common, anyone who opposes him on domestic issues tending to be automatically dubbed reactionary.

AMERICAN INTERNATIONAL POLICY BETWEEN THE TWO WARS

The British people, looking back over the period between the two wars, are much more inclined than they were two years ago to take a harsh view of the American contribution to international peace during 1919–1939. Those who have met American troops tend to be considerably less critical than those who have not; but taken overall there is reason to believe that at least half the British people believe that America made fewer contributions to international peace and order between 1919 and 1939 than any other democratic country.

AMERICA'S ENTRY INTO THE WAR

In January 1942, in the first enthusiasm of welcoming so powerful an ally as the USA, most people declared that America would have entered the war eventually on the side of the United Nations, even if she had not been attacked first. Today this view is much less prevalent. Indeed, the view that America would never have come in on our side if she had not been attacked first is almost as frequently held, and there is little difference between the views of those who have, and those who have not, met American troops here. It is not doubted that the President would have endeavoured to lead America into active participation by the side of this country, but it is feared that opposition to entry into the war was, in fact, far stronger than the ordinary man here thought it was at the time.

THE AMERICAN WAR EFFORT

Very nearly 80% of the reports received show that the ordinary man's opinion is that the American people are still not wholeheartedly in the war, and that, man for man, their war effort is on the average not as great as our own. This view is even more prevalent among those who have had personal contact with American troops than among those who have not. Domestic disunity, whether in the form of political or labour opposition to the President, and the absence of comprehensive rationing systems, are cited as evidence of this. Politics, it is pointed out, still come first. There seems to be a belief that the physical remoteness of the American people from the areas of combat, and their freedom from air raids and from the threat of invasion, are enough to account for any defects in the American war effort.

AMERICA AND THE POST-WAR PERIOD

Opinion is very much divided over the role America will play in international politics after the war. Most people think she will work in co-operation with Great

Britain, but a substantial proportion of these doubt whether she will be prepared to work in equal partnership with the USSR as well. A substantial minority believe that she will not work in equal co-operation with any other great power but will bid for world leadership, while another minority, almost as big, believe that she will revert to isolation. People who have met American troops tend to be more hopeful of co-operation in the post-war period from America than do those who have not made contact with Americans. Here again, stress is constantly laid upon the position of the President himself. It seems to be generally believed that all will be well if the President is returned for a fourth term, but that if he is not, 'big business', which is not interested in international co-operation, will have its head unrestrained.

AMERICAN TROOPS IN THIS COUNTRY

Correspondents in districts where American troops have been stationed were asked to say whether or not these troops are generally popular. Very few reported that the prevailing attitude was an extreme one: that American troops were very popular indeed or highly unpopular. The vast majority were almost equally divided between saying that American troops were quite popular and rather unpopular. Opinion is also sharply divided on the American soldier as a fighting man. But on this point there is a significant difference between those who have, and those who have not met American troops. Those who have not met American troops incline to the view that once they have acquired experience the 'American is as good a fighting man as the British', whereas those who have met them incline to the view that the 'American fighting man will never be equal to the British'.

From the comments it is obvious that the sorest point is the difference in pay between the American and British soldiers. Though the American troops themselves are not blamed for this, it is felt to be the source of much ill-feeling. There are complaints that they are boastful and overbearing, but these are much less frequent than might have been expected. It is clear, however, that many people are shocked by the sight of so much drunkenness among American troops, by what they regard as undisciplined behaviour and slovenly dress, and that these, probably as much as anything else, have led many to doubt the efficiency of the Americans as soldiers. There were statements that the coloured troops are preferred because they appear to have better manners, though others deplored their wild outbursts as reported in the press. The attitude of white American troops to their coloured compatriots was mentioned only to be condemned and used as evidence against the reality of American democracy. The behaviour of American troops with women was severely criticised though the blame was not always laid exclusively on the man. Comments which said they were 'really decent chaps when you got to know them' were perhaps as revealing as any, implying that many of the adverse criticisms came from people who had not, in fact, taken the trouble, or had not the opportunity, to make personal acquaintance with the American troops, and certainly the generosity of the Americans, particularly towards children, and evidence of their warm-heartedness and gratitude for hospitality have made a favourable impression.

SUMMARY

Two years ago, the sight of an American soldier anywhere in this country would have been a source of immediate comment and interest; today the United States uniform is, in many parts of Great Britain, as familiar as, if not more familiar than, our own. How are these American soldiers regarded in this country? There would appear to be no basis for alarmist statements to the effect that American troops are universally unpopular, though their much higher pay is a source of considerable ill-feeling. In general, they are accepted as including, like all large groups of men, both good and bad. Inevitably it is the behaviour of an obtrusive minority which is noticed, however unrepresentative that behaviour may in fact be, so that drunkenness or an overbearing attitude of white to coloured troops creates a bad impression far out of proportion to the real incidence of such occurrences. The British people are, too, somewhat shocked by what they feel to be a slovenly appearance or bearing of American troops, and this makes a very great many doubt whether the American soldier will ever be the equal of the British. It is only fair to add that American soldiers' generosity, to children for example, is quickly appreciated, and such significant comments as 'they are really decent chaps when you get to know them' were not infrequent. In a word, bearing in mind the potentialities of misunderstanding and discord, the relationship between American troops and British civilians is more satisfactory than many sanguine observers might reasonably have expected.

There have been certain other modifications in British opinion about America which are not necessarily greatly affected by, or at any rate not exclusively due, to the presence of American troops here. It is not unfair to say that two years ago British opinion about the USA was a little naive. It is less so now. There is more readiness to be sceptical about the superiority of American to British ideas of democracy, more doubts about the likelihood that America would have participated in the war had she not been attacked first, and a harsher judgment on American international policy between the two wars.

The prevailing view here is that the American war effort is not, man for man, equal to our own. The spectacle of domestic strain and continued internal political warfare is cited as evidence of this, yet this judgment does not seem to cause any marked degree of bitterness or ill-feeling. People feel that the remoteness of America from the scene of the conflict must inevitably mean that the American people cannot feel the compulsion to total war as it is felt here. Opinion about America's attitude to the post-war world is clearly much divided. Hopes tend to be fixed on the President, the average man feeling that if he is defeated anything might happen to the prospect of American co-operation with Great Britain and the USSR after the war. It is difficult for the British not to read an exact parallel between the position of President Roosevelt today and President Wilson in 1920. Admiration for the President and bewilderment at the workings of American political machinery seem to be as widespread as ever.

LISTENER RESEARCH DEPARTMENT

NOTE: The findings of this investigation confirm those of Home Intelligence Division over the past year.

NO. 177: TUESDAY 15 FEBUARY 1944 TO
TUESDAY 22 FEBRUARY 1944

I. GENERAL COMMENTS

1. GENERAL

Spirits remain at the lower level of last week, though long-term confidence continues high. Anxiety about the Anzio bridgehead was partly allayed by the statement from 10, Downing Street (February 12), but considerable misgiving persists and there is disappointment at the general slow progress in Italy. The Italian situation continues to make people feel that invasion of the Continent may be 'a tougher proposition' than they had thought, and there is an increasing suspicion that the war in Europe may not, after all, finish this year.

Satisfaction at our air offensive is coupled with anxiety at the loss of seventy-nine planes on the Leipzig raid. The Bishop of Chichester's speech continues to be almost unanimously condemned.

HOME FRONT: There has been keen interest in the Derbyshire by-election and some pleasure at the result. Criticism of the Government continues, chiefly over post-war plans and the mining situation – both the subject of much anxious discussion. Housing and clothing are also much discussed. The White Paper on the National Health Service has not been widely commented on, as yet.

War-weariness or strain are reported from seven Regions, but there has been much less talk of complacency.

2. ITALY

Widespread anxiety and depression about the whole campaign, and particularly the 'stalemate' on the Anzio beachhead, are again reported; though the statement from 10, Downing Street (February 12) and latest reports are said to have relieved some people. A few still fear the beachhead landings have been a failure.

Detailed criticism of the campaign has declined, but comment is largely on the following lines:

(a) THE ABBEY OF MONTE CASSINO: The destruction of the abbey has met with the emphatic approval of the vast majority, including Roman Catholics; though some call it 'a regrettable necessity'. There is, however, widespread annoyance at our 'hesitancy' and 'reluctance'; some hope 'we shall not be like that' over Rome. There is also some suspicion of 'over-tenderness' to the Roman Catholics and of papal influence on Allied policy.

A number praise the BBC treatment of the incident, and the recording of a statement by the Abbot of Downside was thought 'a clever propagandist stroke'; a few think all the explanations 'another example of British hypocrisy'.

(b) RUSSIA: Comparison is again made with the Russians' progress, and some wonder what they must think of us.

(c) SECOND FRONT: Many continue to feel the Italian campaign is not a good portent ... 'How can we expect to make headway on a strongly fortified front, when we couldn't where our landing was a surprise?'

(d) OUR STRATEGY: A number still feel that we failed to exploit our initial advantages.

(e) THE AMERICANS are blamed by a few for our setbacks.

NEWS PRESENTATION: Many think news, especially the more serious, is being withheld; their anxiety is increased by this feeling of 'being in the dark'. 'Let us have news, good or bad, so long as it is true.'

Some blame the censorship for 'clamping down restrictions' on correspondents; others ask 'Why was the press allowed to mislead us?', and correspondents are blamed for creating over-optimism and subsequent disappointment.

STATEMENTS BY PUBLIC MEN: A number comment on pronouncements which do not tally and say these increase uncertainty. Statements by Mr. Churchill, Mr. Mackenzie King, Mr. Roosevelt and General Montgomery are given as examples of this inconsistency.

3. THE SECOND FRONT

Continued speculation, but reduced comment – on the same lines as last week.

4. ALLIED AIR OFFENSIVE

Admiration for the scale of British and US raids continues; there is particular satisfaction with the recent heavy one on Berlin. The loss of seventy-nine aircraft in the raid on Leipzig was greeted with a gasp of horror.

4A. THE BISHOP OF CHICHESTER'S STATEMENT ON ALLIED BOMBING POLICY

Widespread condemnation continues. The great majority are convinced that bombing must go on, however deplorable the necessity.

5. RAIDS ON LONDON AND THE SOUTH-EAST

These are being closely followed outside London; great sympathy is reported from Scotland – where the raids are 'bringing home the possibility of raids on Scotland'.

IN LONDON there are reports of some people being 'windy' and of others taking the raids calmly and in good heart. The former are apprehensive after each raid on Berlin; the latter 'don't mind them at all as long as they know Berlin has been raided'.

While some regard the raids as inevitable in view of our own activities, there is a tendency, particularly in poorer districts, to resent the raids: 'We should not have to "take" them again ... the Government should do something.'

There is criticism of (a) the NFS for alleged lack of efficiency ... 'press reports of rapid handling of fires are inaccurate'; (b) insufficient co-operation between the NFS and Fire Guards; (c) insufficient help given to people in salvaging their possessions.

PUBLICITY: Three Regions, including London, report a feeling that the raids are being played down and that casualties and damage are greater than announced. The expression 'scalded cat raids' is said to annoy Londoners.

6. RUSSIA

MILITARY: Admiration for Russian successes – particularly the 'liquidation' of the trapped German divisions – is again general. Some doubts as to the accuracy of Russian communiqués and figures of German losses continue, however.

POLITICAL: Fears of Russia's post-war position and of her dictating the peace settlement are slightly increased this week. There is again some comment that the recent constitutional changes were meant either to help 'pack' the peace conference or to help the 'assimilation' of neighbouring states.

RUSSO-POLISH DISPUTE: Comment is once more on a diminished scale, but concern continues. Sympathy is divided on familiar lines.

7. FINLAND

Expectation of Finland suing for peace is fairly widespread, though interest seems to be limited. People are described as 'rather uncomfortable' about her.

Some suspect the Russian peace terms may prove to be too severe. Others feel that the Russians will not 'make the same mistakes in Finland that we are making in Italy'.

8. THE WEST DERBYSHIRE BY-ELECTION

There has been a good deal of interest in the West Derbyshire by-election, and the result – which has caused some pleasure – is attributed to:

(a) People in a democracy wanting to feel they are free to vote as they wish.
(b) People blaming the Government for (i) not hurrying on with post-war plans; (ii) the housing and mining positions.
(c) The choice of Conservative candidate.

9. FAR EAST

Increased interest in American and Australian activities in the Far East is reported. The American landing in the Marshall Islands and the attack on Truk, following so soon after the revelation of the Japanese atrocities, gave great pleasure; further news is eagerly awaited. Some people wonder whether the war with Japan will drag on after Germany's defeat, or whether the odds will be too great and Japan will stop fighting.

BURMA: Slightly more interest is reported and people would like more news of this campaign.

10. JAPANESE ATROCITIES

Comment is less this week but anxiety and distress, particularly among relatives of prisoners, continue. People are strong in their hatred of the Japanese and in their determination that they 'need expect no mercy'. Doubts as to the advisability of making the disclosures, and speculation as to the reason, are again reported.

11. SPAIN

The desire for firmer action against Spain continues to be reported. There is bitter comment about her neutrality.

12. WHITE PAPER ON NATIONAL HEALTH SERVICE

Preliminary reactions have been received from nine Regions. The general public are said to welcome the proposals and to comment favourably, though as yet there has been little discussion. The ability to choose one's own doctor is regarded as particularly satisfactory, though some middle-class people in London think their relationship with their doctor will not be so 'intimate' under the proposed National Health Service.

13. BROADCASTING AND NEWS PRESENTATION

Comment this week is chiefly on the presentation of news from Italy (see Section 2). Apart from this there is little discussion. Criticism continues of repetition in news bulletins, and doubts of the veracity of news published by the press are reported.

ENTERTAINMENT PROGRAMMES: Criticism continues.

PRAISE FOR: the *Postscript* by a Dutch officer, February 13; Major Lewis Hastings' *War Commentary*, February 17; *ITMA*; broadcast plays.

BRAINS TRUST: Opinion continues to be divided.

II. SPECIAL COMMENTS

BRIEF WEEKLY REVIEW

14. MINERS AND MINING

The whole mining situation continues to cause great anxiety, and many people are 'fed up with the coal muddle', or completely cynical about it. Comment centres round the following:

THE GOVERNMENT, and in particular the Ministry of Fuel and Power, are strongly criticised for their handling of the coal situation both now and in the past, and for lack of foresight and firmness. The Government is particularly blamed for having taken experienced men from the pits in the first place. It is widely felt that their return is the only solution, though some favour nationalisation.

THE MINERS are widely criticised for their 'grasping and unpatriotic attitude' in using the war situation to 'force a decision in their favour'. Criticism is particularly strong from the relatives of those in the Forces, also from farmers and agricultural workers, who think the miners get greater consideration than they do. A considerable minority, however, and especially working-class opinion, sympathise with the miners, maintaining they 'wouldn't strike without good reason' and 'have been badly treated for years'.

THE PORTER AWARD: The ordinary public cannot understand why production goes down when wages go up. On the other hand, those people who, though not miners themselves, are connected with the industry or interested in it, think the award can only have the effect of still further reducing output, as not offering sufficient stimulus to the piece-worker.

Miners criticise the award chiefly, it is said, for (i) failing to give a rise in piece-rates – as a result 'unskilled workers will benefit more than skilled' – and (ii) making insufficient differentiation between surface and underground workers, 'having regard to the risks run by the latter'.

BBC and press publicity are blamed, both for confusing the men and 'putting wrong ideas into their heads', and for 'eliciting sympathy with the miners by stating the wages of the lowest paid' – 'All the facts about all the earnings should be made public.'

THE BALLOT FOR THE MINES continues to cause comment; most of this is adverse, on the familiar grounds that it is simply putting square pegs in round holes – 'lads without a pit background can never become good pitmen' – and that the war will be over before they are of any use. Relatives of eligible boys continue hostile to the scheme, middle-class mothers, and parents who have made sacrifices in school fees, being especially indignant. Some anxiety is expressed, too, on the grounds that there is no guarantee that after the war the boys will be free to return to their intended careers.

Some cynical or envious comment is reported from miners at all that is being done for the trainees in the way of medical examination and hostels.

BILLETING THE BEVIN BOYS: Some difficulty in finding billets is again reported, and it is asked why boys are in some cases sent far afield to train when there are training centres near their homes.

15. DOMESTIC FUEL

Continued complaints of bad distribution and slow deliveries, of the inadequate allowance and of the poor quality and high price of coal.

16. POST-WAR

LORD PORTAL'S STATEMENT IN THE HOUSE OF LORDS ON HOUSING (February 8) has aroused little comment this week. It is thought to be a step in the right direction, but 'action is required'. There is some doubt about the wisdom of building temporary houses.

RECONSTRUCTION PLANS GENERALLY are discussed on familiar lines, with interest and anxiety. There is some wish for Lord Woolton's powers and duties to be more clearly defined.

17. HOUSING

Widespread complaints of the 'desperate' shortage continue. Immediate action is asked for.

18. 'PAY-AS-YOU-EARN' INCOME TAX

Many people continue to welcome the scheme. The very helpful talks given to workpeople by income tax officials are much praised, but the need for further explanation is emphasised. In Scotland some firms are arranging special interviews to explain the coding system to their workers, and this is much appreciated.

Some grumbling is reported from employers – including farmers – about the extra work entailed by the scheme.

Other comments are:

(a) The concessions with regard to bonuses are appreciated.
(b) Superannuation and contributory pensions should not be included in tax returns.
(c) It is felt that the awkward period at the change-over will be made more acceptable because of the debt forgiveness that will occur.

POST-WAR CREDITS: Some lack of understanding and scepticism about repayments are reported. Some workers wonder whether these credits will be subject to some kind of means test, or whether the amount they are excused paying during the change-over period will be deducted from their credits.

19. CLOTHING

COUPONS: Widespread complaints continue of the difficulty of supplying personal needs, clothing growing children, and replacing household goods on the present coupon allowance.

SHOES AND SHOE REPAIRS: Poor quality, particularly of children's shoes, and 'endless repair difficulties'.

MEN'S SUITS: Satisfaction with the removal of austerity regulations continues; in one Region it is said that 'traders who were formerly concerned about stocks appear satisfied with Government action'.

20. FOOD

ORANGES: Complaints of unfair distribution have increased this week, though much satisfaction continues to be expressed by those who have received oranges. Complaints are chiefly of inequalities due to:

(a) TRADERS NOT MARKING BOOKS.
(b) BOOKS BEING MARKED IN PENCIL so that markings could easily be rubbed out.
(c) RURAL AREAS BEING PENALISED by oranges being on sale only in towns.

III. PERIODICAL REVIEW

21. ANTI-SEMITISM

During the past eighteen weeks intermittent criticism has continued. In two Regions, anti-Semitism is said to be particularly apparent among workers.

Much criticism is not specific; otherwise, it is mainly on the following lines:

(a) BLACK MARKET: Many believe that Jews are largely responsible for black market offences; this belief is said to be encouraged by Jewish names seen in the press in this connection.
(b) INDUSTRY AND BUSINESS: There is some feeling that the Jews 'have a finger in every pie' and are trying to monopolise industry and business.
(c) POST-WAR: Some belief that the Jews will make money at other people's expense in the post-war period.
(d) WASTE OF PETROL; ESCAPING THE SERVICES, HOME GUARD AND CIVIL DEFENCE; BUYING UP PROPERTY AT EXORBITANT PRICES.

NO. 180: TUESDAY 7 MARCH 1944 TO TUESDAY 14 MARCH 1944

I. GENERAL COMMENTS

1. GENERAL

The main topic of the week has been the miners' strikes, which have caused widespread anger and disgust – and in Wales, some shame.

The debate on Service pay and allowances, the shortage of domestic fuel, and post-war problems have also been widely discussed.

Preliminary reports about the Eire situation show anger at de Valera's refusal to meet US demands, a desire for strong action, and a feeling that 'it's high time something was done'.

Apart from this, spirits remain about the same as last week, with:

(a) Great satisfaction at the intensity of the Allied air offensive and Russian advances – particularly in the Ukraine; (b) tension about the second front; (c) disappointment at our slow progress in Italy; (d) war-weariness, fatigue and irritability, together with some continued criticism of the Government.

2. ALLIED AIR OFFENSIVE

THE USAAF DAY RAIDS, particularly those on Berlin, have been the highlight of the week in the air war and have aroused tremendous enthusiasm. Small minority reactions are: (i) too much publicity and credit given to the Americans; (ii) doubt of US claims of enemy planes brought down; (iii) 'Is night bombing on its way to being superseded by day bombing?'

RECENT SMALL LOSSES have caused particular interest.

THE INTENSIFIED AIR OFFENSIVE is widely regarded as 'the preamble to invasion' or as the beginning of it. Some think the Luftwaffe fighter strength is rapidly diminishing and that the damage now being done will make a second front unnecessary – 'except as a spectacular parade'.

OUR BOMBING POLICY continues to have almost unanimous public approval. The apparently considerable minority who regard it as a regrettable necessity, and who express sympathy for German women and children, are nevertheless in favour of its being kept up. People wonder how much longer Germany can take it.

2A. AIR RAIDS ON THIS COUNTRY

(No reactions yet reported to the raid on London on March 14.)

The general view is still that the recent bombing of London must have been more devastating than the press or BBC indicated and that people have not stood up to bombing as well as they did in 1940/1. Both these suspicions are confirmed by the arrival of evacuees in various parts of the country.

3. EIRE

(From some Regions, only preliminary reports have as yet been received.)

People are indignant and disgusted at Eire's refusal to remove Axis consular and diplomatic representatives; relatives of merchant seamen and naval men are especially angry. While the US request is generally approved, there is at the same time a feeling that something should have been done years ago about the menace to our war effort of Eire's neutrality. Eire workers in this country have long been distrusted.

Only a small minority in Scotland, mainly Eire workers, express sympathy with Mr. de Valera's point of view, 'usually raking up past history as justification'. In

Northern Ireland, however, Nationalists and Roman Catholics 'hesitate to express in public approval of Mr. de Valera's action'.

THE BAN ON TRAVEL: Reactions have as yet been received only from London and Northern Ireland; strong approval is reported in both places.

It is appreciated in Northern Ireland that on the eve of invasion the Allies must tighten up their precautions against a leakage of information to the enemy. In fact, the sternest measures to counteract Eire's attitude would be accepted and approved by the majority of the Ulster people. Although people in Northern Ireland realise that many there will have to suffer from the ban, the prevailing opinion is that, owing to the impossibility of closing the Ulster-Eire border, the British authorities could not make any distinction between Northern and Southern Ireland without making the ban entirely inoperative.

THE PRIME MINISTER'S STATEMENT (March 14) defining British-American policy as designed to isolate Southern Ireland from the outer world during the critical period now approaching has been widely approved in Northern Ireland – except among Nationalists and Republicans. (No reactions to the Prime Minister's statement from other Regions yet.)

There is, indeed, a considerable volume of opinion in Northern Ireland in favour of more drastic measures; it is argued that the closure of the border should be attempted, even if it were only 50% effective. Many Belfast industrial workers, in particular, favour the strictest form of border control – even to the extent of forbidding the thousands of Eire workers employed in war factories there to go to their homes for weekends. Londonderry businessmen, however, are apprehensive at the possibility of a border closure as there is a big volume of cross-border traffic and trade between Londonderry City and County Donegal. The same attitude is taken in Newry and other border towns, though the difficulty there would be less acute.

4. SECOND FRONT

Comment, speculation, expectancy and tension have again increased this week. Some expect it any day now. More are inclined to give it till the end of April. While most people view the venture with fear, especially the fear of heavy casualties, others are longing for action and are said to be 'tired of the repetitive publicity'. It is pointed out that while it may be part of the war of nerves against Germany, it is also acting against people here.

Comment otherwise is on familiar lines: (a) the bombing and shelling of the French coast is the prelude to invasion; (b) rumours of movement of troops and CD personnel, evacuation, etc.; (c) the minority view that it is all bluff; (d) the anticipated repercussions on civilian life.

5. ITALY

Disappointment continues widespread, but there is rather less discussion and less anxiety this week. People appear more inclined to accept the situation; in some cases, they are pleased and thankful we are still holding on to the Anzio beachhead and appreciate our men's tenacity. They are also more ready to believe we are merely conducting a 'holding' operation and console themselves with the thought of the number of enemy troops we are pinning down. Our 'defensive mentality' continues to be deplored, however.

The following criticisms are again made:

(a) COMPARISIONS WITH RUSSIAN ADVANCES: Their achievements, 'under worse conditions than ours', are thought to reflect very badly on us.
(b) OUR STRATEGY is still thought to have 'slipped up' somewhere.
(c) THE SECOND FRONT: 'If this is the sort of progress we make from a beachhead', people fear for our chances.
(d) THE BOMBING OF THE ABBEY OF MONTE CASSINO does not seem to have improved our position. 'We were led to believe that only an old monastery stood between us and Rome.'

OUR POLITICAL POLICY IN ITALY is said to be disliked. There are still some complaints that we were let down by the Italians.

OUR AIR OFFENSIVE IN ITALY: There is thought to be little sympathy, except among Roman Catholics, for pleas to spare Rome and other Italian cities. 'This is not a moment to be squeamish.' A few, however, ask if air attacks are limited to military targets and if care has been taken over ancient monuments in Rome; also, if Florence is a necessary target.

6. RUSSIA

MILITARY: Admiration and satisfaction – particularly at the successes in the southern Ukraine – continue general.

POLITICAL: There are again some fears of Russia's future intentions.

RUSSO-POLISH DISPUTE: Comment has almost ceased but some concern is still reported.

7. RUSSIA AND FINLAND

The armistice terms continue to be approved as generous, and it is again hoped that Finland will soon make up her mind to accept them. There is surprise – in some cases concern – that she has delayed so long. Some think she is merely trying to gain time for the Germans; others excuse her as being so strongly in the Germans' grip.

Minority sympathy for her continues.

8. FAR EAST

The continued American successes in the Pacific are greeted with satisfaction. Pleasure also continues over the successes in Burma, but there is some disappointment that a larger campaign has not started.

Among a few, Japan's recent shipping losses, and our Burma successes, have led to a feeling that when Germany collapses Japan will be ready to crumble up. On the other hand, many people think the struggle will involve years of warfare.

Once again, there are requests for better maps of the Pacific area.

9. TURKEY

Some bewilderment over Turkey's attitude is reported, and it is thought she is playing a double game. The action taken by the Allies is approved. Some, however, say Turkey cannot be blamed for her reluctance to enter the war unless adequately supported by the Allies.

10. WAR AT SEA

Mr. A. V. Alexander's statement (March 7) on the naval situation has been received with satisfaction. Great satisfaction is also reported at the news of the successes against the U-boats.

11. BROADCASTING AND PRESENTATION OF NEWS

Radio news bulletins are criticised for padding the Italian news and for over-frequent references to the number and weight of bombs dropped over Germany.

GENERAL FORCES PROGRAMME: This continues to be criticised by the majority on various grounds. It is, however, said 'if the Forces like it, let them have it – but we don't want it'. Criticisms of the programmes are: (a) too disjointed and 'bitty'; (b) too much jazz; (c) poor quality; (d) the use of women announcers. It is said that the BBC has robbed civilians, as they now have no alternative programme.

A minority in nine Regions are, however, said to appreciate the change.

PRAISE FOR *ITMA*; Emlyn Williams' *Postscript*, February 27; Major Lewis Hastings' *War Commentaries*; radio plays.

WELSH BRAINS TRUST is again criticised.

ALVAR LIDELL'S RETURN is welcomed.

LISTENING TO THE NEWS: Two special Listener Research investigations were made on this subject during February.

1.   In the week beginning Sunday, 13th February, a special study was made to find out how much of the 9 o'clock news had been heard by those who claimed to have listened to it. The following were the results:

     14%   heard the headlines only.

     17%   heard the headlines and the principal news items.

     66%   said they listened to the whole bulletin, though how much attention they gave to it is not known.

     3%   gave unclassifiable answers.

2.   An analysis was made of the listening to news bulletins on Monday, Tuesday and Wednesday, 7th, 8th and 9th February; that is, three weeks

before the new General Forces Programme began. The results were as follows:

79% of the whole adult population heard some news every day.

18% heard the whole or part of one bulletin.

The remaining 61% heard the whole or parts of two or more bulletins.

II. SPECIAL COMMENTS

BRIEF WEEKLY REVIEW

12. MINERS AND MINING

The most discussed topic of the week has been the miners' strike. Feeling on the subject is stronger and more widespread than ever. BLAME IS LAID ON:

(a) THE MINERS: The great majority of the public bitterly condemn the men for striking at a critical moment when the second front is imminent, and in defiance of their leaders. Many people have felt all along that there must be another side to the question, and that the miners may have genuine grievances, but it is their resort to strike action instead of arbitration which is so strongly condemned; many who formerly sympathised with the miners have lost patience with them now.

Criticism is particularly strong from people who are short of coal, from relatives of servicemen, from farm labourers and people in rural areas, from middle-class people, and from those who resent anything which may prolong the war. Strong indignation is expressed by many at 'miners bargaining for money while their comrades are dying', at their 'blackmail' and lack of patriotism. It is variously suggested that all miners should be put under martial law, that a few of the ringleaders should be shot as an example, that miners' rations should be stopped, or that miners of military age should be put in the Forces if they refuse to return to work. Miners' pay and conditions are frequently compared with those of men in the Forces.

Sympathy for the miners continues, however, to be felt by a minority, mainly working-class people, particularly those in mining areas, and those in iron and steel.

(b) THE GOVERNMENT, INCLUDING THE MINISTRY OF FUEL AND POWER: It is not a question of blaming the miners or the Government; many people blame both. The Government is criticised for: (i) its weak handling of the mining situation – comparison is made with Mr. Roosevelt's firm handling of coal strikes in USA; (ii) 'allowing' strikes in war time; (iii) being over-partial to the owners and, alternately, (iv) placating the miners at any price. The Ministry of Fuel and Power is blamed for not having foreseen the troubles which would result from the

Porter Award, which 'must have something wrong about it' to induce so
many miners to strike.

(c) THE OWNERS: Blame of the owners is far less widely reported than of
the miners or Government. They are, however, criticised for: (i) putting
dividends first – in Scotland, communist speakers point to increased
profits of coal companies as a proof that owners are really to blame, and
people who pay £4 a ton for coal think they know where the money goes;
(ii) interpreting awards in such a way as to make miners strike.

Owners are also in some cases accused of (i) keeping the good seams till
after the war; and (ii) victimisation.

(d) THE MINERS' REPRESENTATIVES: According to the North Midland
Regional report, 'unrest among the miners is blamed partly on the fact that
in some areas the men have no faith in their leaders who are said to be more
for the owners than the men'. Welsh miners think that the Government and
the coal owners, being better educated than their representatives, are able to
twist the latter when costing and figures are discussed.

THE PORTER AWARD: No reactions have been reported to the Government's
new wage proposals for piece-rate workers. Unfavourable comment on the Porter
Award continues from mining areas, in some of which it is criticised by men, owners
and managements alike.

Press handling of the award in the first place is criticised in reports from Wales
and the Northern Region. The miners did not realise that deductions were to
be made for house or rent allowance and coal. They also blame the papers for
statements such as 'Miners get big pay packets this week' and allege that 'no paper
stated that men earning over £5 a week before the award would get nothing out of
it'. The inclusion in the minimum wage of the house coal and the special allowance
for working in abnormal places has been particularly resented.

NATIONALISATION OF THE INDUSTRY is the solution most widely
advocated this week.

13. FUEL

Complaints of the shortage of fuel come from twelve Regions. Much hardship is
alleged, particularly to the old and sick; many housewives in Scotland are said to
have received only 1 or 2 cwt during the last month. A great deal of the shortage is
thought due to delivery difficulties.

Miners' strikes are said to have an adverse effect on fuel economy ... 'Why should
we bother, while miners continually strike?' ... 'If fuel economy really mattered,
something would be done about the stoppage at the mines.'

14. POST-WAR

Anxiety about post-war matters continues. There is still felt to be too much talk and
too little action. Minorities, however, are again said to be fearing that too much time
is being given to post-war planning at the expense of the war effort.

Housing and employment are again the main preoccupations. The Government's post-war housing scheme has attracted some attention. Some are approving but others remember the agricultural cottages and are cynical. It is also felt that '30,000 built now would be better than hearing 300,000 will be built after the war'.

THE EDUCATION BILL is again arousing considerable interest. It continues to be approved.

15. HOUSING

Complaints of housing difficulties continue unabated. In the North Midland and Southern Regions, evacuees from London are making the situation worse. In London, difficulties have been accentuated by recent raids.

The 'shocking racket' in the price of houses is causing concern and anger. It is thought that prices should be controlled.

In the North-Eastern Region, the Matthew Nasmith case is said to have aroused disgust and anger.

16. SERVICE PAY AND ALLOWANCES

The debate in the House (March 2) has worried people; and they criticise the Government for refusing to grant any increase in basic pay. Fear of inflation is thought inconsistent with the high wages paid to munition and other workers: 'No such bogey is held up when miners strike.'

Most people – workers particularly – support the demand for increased rates of pay and even more strongly the demand for increased allowances to dependants.

There should, it is widely felt, be greater equality between civilian and Service pay; some suggest 'the Forces should have more pay and war workers less, to balance'. Civilians' savings for the post-war period are also compared with the Forces' inability to save. The 'Salute the Soldier' campaign is not thought to fit in with the present attitude of the Government to Service pay.

Isolated references are nevertheless made to servicemen not being so badly off as appears at first glance. A few people think insufficient stress is laid on allowances, grants, reduced prices and expenses, which 'make the pay compare favourably with industrial workers after all'.

Adverse comment continues on the small number of MPs present at the debate.

17. PRODUCTION

DURING THE PAST TWO WEEKS reports from eight Regions referred to comment suggesting an increase in industrial uneasiness. There has been talk of enforced idleness and reduced hours of work in factories; unemployment; workers being transferred from aircraft factories to work of less importance; a slackening in the demand for hitherto vital supplies; over-production; factories 6 months ahead of schedule; factories about to cease production of war materials. Various explanations are hazarded: that war material can be produced more cheaply in America, and so is no longer being made here; that the jet-propelled plane is the reason for slowing up production of other types; that the war must be nearly over.

The need for explanation to put workers' minds at rest is stressed in three reports.

UNEMPLOYMENT IN THE NORTHERN REGION: Concern is reported. Widespread consternation is said to have been caused on Teesside by the paying off of 700 iron and steel workers at one establishment – much larger figures had been rumoured. 'Men and their families wondered what would happen to them – "Will it be the dole or transfer to the Midlands?" – and were saying that even if they got a job it wouldn't be at their old trade and would mean less money. "If it is like this now, what's it going to be like in peace?" Particularly keen resentment is expressed that no explanation was given, and there was much speculation as to the cause. Rumour was rife of thousands being paid off at other concerns.'

17A. THE MINISTER OF PRODUCTION'S STATEMENT
(MARCH 8)

Mr. Lyttelton's statement giving figures of production has created a very favourable impression and it is hoped that, security permitting, more details may be given by the Ministry of Aircraft Production.

18. FOOD

Again, there is general appreciation for our fortunate food situation after four-and-a-half years of war. The chief comments this week have been about:

ORANGES: People are pleased with the supplies, but there are complaints of unequal distribution, the difficulties of those who have no time to stand in queues, and, from retailers, of the high percentage of damaged fruit. In Scotland many of the bitter oranges are still unsold.

CHEESE: The cut in the cheese ration has caused some dismay, particularly among housewives who depend on it for 'quick, nourishing snacks' and as a filling for sandwiches.

FATS: Professor Sir Jack Drummond's statement that the wartime consumption of fat is only 15% below pre-war is again criticised.

POINTS RATIONING: The increase has been welcomed.

19. WHITE PAPER ON NATIONAL HEALTH SERVICE

Comment is again slight; the proposals are generally welcomed, though as yet little detail is known about them. People are waiting to learn more and to see what will be done; a few are 'sceptical of the proposals ever getting to the statute stage'. Special comments are:

(a) The scheme is felt to be too much of a compromise – 'a boiled down version of Beveridge'. Some feel complete state control would have been better.

(b) It is feared that the retention of private practices may result in better treatment for those who can pay most.

(c) It is doubted if the voluntary hospitals will be able to give adequate service.

(d) There is speculation about where the money is to come from; and some annoyance at such a costly scheme being described as free ... 'If all the services are free who is going to pay for them?'

It is thought that some country dwellers may be unwilling to pay increased rates for 'amenities which are only enjoyed in local towns'.

20. THE NEWCASTLE ENQUIRY

This is still much discussed and the subject of many crude jokes among all classes, not only in Newcastle, but up and down the whole Northern Region. In some quarters it remains the chief topic of interest.

While some continue to treat it as rather a joke and look on the matters under investigation as trivial, others who had earlier taken this line and said it was much ado about nothing are growing increasingly disgusted and disquieted by 'the criminal slackness' and want of integrity among public officials. It is said that only the fringe of the affair has been touched on and that even if the enquiry goes on for weeks more, all the irregularities will never come to light. People think the time is ripe for prosecutions; some say 'shoot the lot'. Criticism is levelled not only at individuals but at the whole corporation, and the enquiry has destroyed some confidence in the police. It is felt that their word is not good enough for them to be called as witnesses.

Concern continues at the slur cast on the city and lest confidence in local government generally be impaired. This seems to be warranted by such comments as: 'They are all alike, these councillors.' People wonder how far a similar state of affairs exists in other cities. There is much cynicism on this point, and it is said that Manchester and Glasgow are getting 'quakey'.

People in the North-Eastern Region are said to be aghast at the revelations. There are further references to the need to make similar enquiries into the affairs of other councils.

III. PERIODICAL REVIEW

21. DOUBLE SUMMER TIME

DURING THE PAST FOUR WEEKS unfavourable comment has been reported at the announcement (February 24) that double summer time is to be reintroduced.

Criticism comes chiefly from:

(a) AGRICULTURAL AREAS, where farmers and cowmen complain of having to get up at what is in fact 3 a.m. to attend to the stock. They say that the proposal for them to work one hour behind the rest of the country is not practicable, as their children have to go to school on double summer time, etc. Some farmers complain that 'last year they had to pay three hours overtime on occasion, that men would not work in the evening, and that consequently much hay was wasted'. Some people suggest, however, that the grumbling is partly traditional and the report from the South-Western Region says that a 'surprising number of farmers have become reconciled to the idea'.

(b) PARENTS, who say their children will not go to sleep while it is light.

22. US TROOPS IN THIS COUNTRY

DURING THE PAST FOUR WEEKS comment has again been increasingly approving. 'We are beginning to understand one another better.' American generosity and friendliness are particularly praised.

Some sympathy is expressed for the way in which the US troops are over-charged. Criticisms, however, are on familiar lines:

(a) BEHAVIOUR WITH WOMEN AND GIRLS – particularly the youth of the girls and the 'poor type' with which they associate.
(b) UNMILITARY APPEARANCE: 'They don't look as though they are doing anything vital for the war effort.'
(c) APPARENT LACK OF DISCIPLINE.
(d) TOO MUCH MONEY.
(e) HEAVY DRINKING: This is particularly criticised when it is believed to cause local shortages of beer.
(f) DANGEROUS DRIVING.
(g) US TRANSPORT: The waste of petrol in collecting dance partners and in 'shopping expeditions' also comes in for criticism.
(h) 'DAZZLING' HEADLIGHTS AND OVERBRIGHT TORCHES.
(i) THE ATTITUDE OF WHITE TROOPS TO COLOURED: In some cases, people like the black troops more than the white.
(j) BOASTFULNESS, particularly about winning the war.
(k) NOT TURNING UP AFTER INVITATIONS.

BRITISH AND AMERICAN SERVICEMEN: The disparity in their pay, and the better treatment American troops are believed to receive, are the cause of much criticism and some anxiety. These are blamed for lack of fraternisation between the men, and this, it is feared, may have unpleasant repercussions when the second front starts.

22A. AMERICA

POLITICAL: There is some interest in the forthcoming presidential election. It is hoped that Roosevelt will again be returned.

POST-WAR: Some anxiety about our future trade relations with America is reported from two Regions.

23. WATER SUPPLY

DURING THE PAST EIGHT WEEKS growing concern about the serious water shortage has been reported. Many wells are now almost dry and the water is unfit for drinking purposes ... 'In certain rural areas houses and farms have been without water for almost a year.' Factors contributing to the shortage are said to be:

(a) The building of aerodromes in some districts.
(b) Waste of water by the troops ... '60,000 gallons used in one day for washing one hundred vehicles even to the undersides of mudguards'; and waste of water at American aerodromes.
(c) Recent agricultural drainage schemes, and the diversion of water from surface wells to deep gravel pits dug during the war; these now resemble lakes.

People hope that consideration of the water situation may be one of the Government's first efforts of post-war reconstruction.

NO. 185: WEDNESDAY 12 APRIL 1944 TO TUESDAY 18 APRIL 1944

I. GENERAL COMMENTS

1. GENERAL

Spirits continue at the low level of recent weeks. The expected second front is uppermost in everyone's mind and is the subject of increased tension and impatience this week. War-weariness is widely reported – even among those who are doing well out of the war – and there are many references to people feeling tired, irritable or depressed.

There is great rejoicing over the news from Russia, but concern over our position in Italy and Burma.

HOME FRONT: Satisfaction at the return of most of the strikers is tempered by doubts as to whether the agreements reached will be permanent. Housing, both present and post-war, is widely discussed.

2. THE SECOND FRONT

The imminence of the second front has been the most widely discussed topic of the week ... 'in everyone's mind, and on nearly everyone's tongue'. The prevailing emotions appear to be tension, suspense, impatience and anxiety. There is no tendency to think that invasion will be other than a tough proposition, but many people find the strain of waiting almost unbearable; apprehension about casualties and a grim time ahead is outweighed by the desire to make the final push to end the war. The Forces' wives and mothers are said to be the most nervous and anxious section of the public, and even the men themselves are believed to be feeling the strain of waiting.

Talk centres round the following points:

'WHEN?' It is variously thought that the second front will start:

(a) ANY DAY NOW: This belief finds support in a great number of events reported in the press, observed locally, or rumoured; e.g. the coastal ban; the cancellation or stoppage of Service and NFS leave; the suspension of diplomatic rights; increased allied raids, particularly on the Pas de Calais; the disappearance of US troops from various localities; inspections of identity cards; the issuing of the Home Guard with equipment; civilian evacuations; etc., etc.

(b) DURING THE NEXT FEW MONTHS: August is the latest date mentioned, but many suggest the end of May.

(c) NEVER: This is still the view of a considerable minority who maintain either that all second front talk is bluff, calculated to keep German divisions inactive in the West, 'while the Russians do the kill', or that our bombing and the Red Army will defeat Germany between them.

'WHERE?' The Balkans remains a popular alternative to the west, and some think the idea of an impending western invasion is merely a ruse to cover a move somewhere else. People who observe certain pointers suspect Norway may be the objective.

'WHY THE DELAY?' The fact that the second front has not yet started is attributed by various minorities to strikes, particularly in the mines; 'miscarriage of plans'; disunity among the French; lack of discipline among the US forces; disagreement between the USA and Great Britain as to how it is to be carried out; and 'cold feet' following our experiences in Italy. In the Midland Region some people think we have already attempted to open a second front somewhere on the French coast, have failed to land, and have had to withdraw.

'WHAT WILL HAPPEN HERE?' People variously expect increased enemy raids, particularly in coastal districts; interference with civilian transport and food supplies, if not a complete travel veto; and evacuation of coastal areas – Midlands people in particular fearing they may be asked to receive the evacuees. It is hoped that Mr. Churchill will give warning of possible civilian dislocations and some guidance as to behaviour.

3. THE COASTAL BAN

Reduced comment on familiar lines. This week uncertainty as to what is, or is not, allowed under the travel ban is reported only from the South-Western Region, where it continues to produce 'multitudes of enquiries'.

4. RUSSIA

MILITARY: General delight at the progress of the Russian armies is only tempered by feelings of shame and disappointment that Russia is winning the war for us while we are at a standstill in Italy. The speed of the Russian advance is the subject of astonishment; and jokes on the possibility of the Red Army's arriving at Calais before us have a wide currency. A minority persist in wondering if Germany is not making an orderly retreat in order to put up a more concentrated stand on her own borders.

This week there is a marked recurrence of the feeling that Russian advances would have been slower but for British and US help, and that Russia says far too little about our contributions to her success, particularly our bombing operations. But some people are at least relieved that 'the Russians haven't told us to get on with the second front'.

POLITICAL: Uneasiness and suspicion regarding Soviet policy, both now and post-war, continue to be reported, with particular reference to:

(a) The 'initiative' taken by Russia in recognising the Badoglio government without the general approval of the United Nations.
(b) The possibility that, not being at war with Japan, Russia will be free to carry out her plans in Europe undisturbed, while we are still occupied in the Far East. A few fear she may ally herself with Japan.
(c) Russia's dominating influence in the Balkans.

5. ALLIED AIR OFFENSIVE

Satisfaction with our raids and those of the USAAF is again general. They continue to be welcomed as the prelude to invasion or – by a minority – as likely to make invasion unnecessary. There is particular appreciation also for raids on the Balkans, as being of direct help to the Russians.

Comment otherwise is again of:

(a) LOSSES: Concern continues.
(b) DOUBTS ABOUT THE EFFECTIVENESS OF BOMBING: Some think the 'softening up' process is taking longer than expected and that results should have been more apparent by now. There is surprise at recent statements about Germany's increased air power.
(c) GERMAN MORALE: Speculation continues as to the effects of our raids.

6. ITALY

MILITARY: Anxiety and disappointment continue general, though in some cases comment is less, as 'little happens to attract attention'. Comparison with Russian advances and criticism of leadership and strategy continue ... 'Things have not gone so well since Montgomery left.'

Bewilderment at the deadlock, doubts about the whole campaign and fears for the success of the second front are again reported, though some continue to think we do not intend to advance, but merely to pin down enemy divisions.

The importance of having air bases in southern Italy from which to bomb the Balkans is thought to be 'the bright spot'.

POLITICAL: The news that King Victor Emmanuel is to retire when Rome is taken has aroused little interest but is welcomed. Some ask – 'Why wait till then?'

7. FAR EAST

BURMA: Anxiety and bewilderment over the position in Burma and the Japanese thrust into India are widespread and are thought to have been increased by the scarcity of news from this front. People fear that something is wrong and that we have 'suffered a bad knock in Burma'.

Air Marshal Sir Philip Joubert's broadcast talk (April 13) on the Burma campaign was welcomed as 'making the scene real and alive'.

PACIFIC: Appreciation of American operations continues.

8. NEUTRAL COUNTRIES

MR. CORDELL HULL'S WARNING TO NEUTRALS (April 9) has aroused considerable interest and approval, though a few are critical on the grounds that it was 'a veering away from the Atlantic Charter to power politics'.

The public are growing increasingly impatient with the neutral countries. Some are satisfied at the Allied governments' recent moves regarding the supply of war materials to Germany; others would like stronger pressure applied to neutrals, even though it might be inconsistent with 'academic neutrality'.

Annoyance is expressed with all the neutrals except Switzerland. People are particularly puzzled and annoyed over Turkey. Although some suspect we have mishandled the situation, special disgust is felt that Turkey should 'let us down, after we supplied her with arms'.

9. FRENCH POLITICS

Impatience is expressed at the news of the troubles between Generals Giraud and de Gaulle. Opinion is divided over the dismissal of General Giraud. While there is some sympathy for him, majority feeling is said to be on the side of de Gaulle; Giraud is thought to be too old and his military ideas out of date.

Fears are reported that 'the rot that caused the downfall of France has again set in at Algiers'.

10. ALLIED RELATIONS

People continue to have an uneasy feeling that all is not well between the USA, USSR, and ourselves, without being specific as to what they think is wrong. (See also Section 4, Russia, political.)

11. US PRESIDENTIAL ELECTION

There has been some discussion on the forthcoming election. Hopes are expressed that Mr. Roosevelt will be re-elected. The withdrawal of Mr. Willkie is said to have left people in a 'fog' ... 'If it has to be a Republican, Mr. Willkie would have been preferred.'

12. BROADCASTING AND PRESENTATION OF NEWS

GENERAL FORCES PROGRAMME: Criticism continues, though apart from 'choppiness', few specific reasons are given. The only praise is for its additional news items and for its suitability for serving soldiers.

A BBC LISTENER RESEARCH REPORT states that at the end of the fifth week of the GFP, public opinion about the new programme appears to have settled down. The programme is widely disliked by those civilians who used to find the old Forces programme provided them with a continuous cheerful background noise. Such listeners are numerically a very large number. On the other hand, civilian listeners to whom the Forces programme did not mean a great deal do not find the new programme unacceptable and many think it an improvement on the Forces programme. The main complaint of Forces programme lovers is the choppiness of the new programme, which makes it unsuitable for continuous listening.

In the Home Forces, however, the majority think that the new programme gives them a better service than the old. This appears to be due largely to the conditions of listening in which most members of the Forces find themselves – usually in canteens.

PRAISE FOR: *ITMA*; *The Man Born to be King*; Air Marshal Sir Philip Joubert's *War Commentary*, April 13; *Radio Doctor*; Lord Vansittart's broadcast, April 11; Raymond Gram Swing's *American Commentary*, April 13; Commander Kimmins' broadcast on the bombing of the *Tirpitz*, April 7; Alan Moorehead's *Postscript*, April 2; *To Start You Talking*; radio plays.

II. SPECIAL COMMENTS

BRIEF WEEKLY REVIEW

13. MINERS AND MINING

STRIKES: There is general relief at the miners' return to work. People hope there will be no further trouble, but many fear that the underlying problems have not been solved and that disputes will break out again soon.

Despite the resumption of work, the miners are still bitterly criticised, particularly for choosing such a time as the present to strike. People in rural areas and those with relatives in the Services are especially indignant.

Minority sympathy with the miners is again reported and has increased since last week – 'now they have the whip hand, it's their only chance of making grievances heard'. Some, while sympathising with their grievances, nevertheless condemn their strike action.

Criticism of the Government and the Minister of Fuel and Power – and also, in smaller measure, of the owners – continues; but relief is reported that strong steps have been taken at last. Mr. Bevin's firm stand is specially commended.

Nationalisation is again advocated by some.

14. SUBVERSIVE INFLUENCES AS A CAUSE OF STRIKES

Comment continues on the same lines as last week. Some people ridicule the idea of Trotskyist agitators instigating strikes, either in mining or other industries; others accept the idea – at the same time asking why, if the Government knew about their activities, it did not stop them a long time ago.

15. INDUSTRY

STRIKES: Concern and indignation at the recent strikes continue. People are relieved that the strikers have now returned to work and that Mr. Bevin has reached agreement with employers and the TUC as to new methods of dealing with strikes, but many are not confident that the causes of strikes have really been dealt with.

PRODUCTION: Comment has considerably increased since last week. Reports from six Regions refer variously to shortened hours in factories, enforced idleness, abolition of overtime and/or night shift, and factories closing down. Where this means a drop in wages, workers are discontented; others are merely bewildered; others, again, put the changes down to fuel restrictions.

FROM THE NORTHERN REGION continued concern is reported at the 'ca canny' policy of Tyneside riveters. 'It is wondered if the Ministry of Labour realise how seriously their attitude is holding up production and that the cumulative effects, over many weeks, are now becoming very marked.'

16. FUEL

Complaints continue of shortage of coal; delayed deliveries and inadequate allowance – 'while the miners who have been on strike get good supplies'; poor-quality coal and shortage of coke.

Warmer weather is said to have resulted in fewer complaints in the Southern and South-Western Regions.

THE HEATING BAN: It is said that people in the North and North-East have 'not taken kindly' to this, because of the cold weather and the muddle in the mining industry; also because of stories that some offices, including Government and local authority, still have coal fires.

Some misunderstanding is also reported. CD personnel in London do not know whether the ban applies to wardens' posts; some employers think coal fires are still allowed.

17. SERVICE PAY AND ALLOWANCES

The demand for increases continues.

18. FOOD

EASTER FISH: Complaints of the non-materialisation of the promised Easter fish continue widespread. In the North-Western Region, and in parts of the Eastern, London and South-Eastern Regions, however, satisfaction is expressed at improved supplies.
THE CUT IN THE CHEESE RATION: Complaints continue.

19. HOLIDAYS

DURING THE PAST TWO WEEKS there has been some comment on the need for holidays away from home this year, though many feel that this will be impossible in view of the demands of the second front on transport. Holidays at home are, however, not considered satisfactory.

NO. 186: TUESDAY 18 APRIL 1944 TO TUESDAY 25 APRIL 1944

I. GENERAL COMMENTS

1. GENERAL

Once again, the second front is the public's chief, and almost exclusive, interest. The great majority appear to be even more tense and impatient than last week; many are said to be thoroughly 'browned off' with waiting. People want invasion to start, to bring the end of the war nearer.

War-weariness, tiredness and irritability are still widely mentioned, and there is a great longing for the war to end. Nevertheless, it is thought that as soon as the second front opens, this 'dull patch' will disappear, together with the present industrial unrest. Despite the increased tension, reports from four Regions say that people are more cheerful than they were.

Discussion of the Italian front has much declined, though it is on the same lines.

HOME FRONT: The industrial situation is widely discussed; criticism of strikers continues and the Government's new anti-strike regulations are welcomed.

There has been very little speculation about this year's Budget.

2. THE SECOND FRONT

'The same as last week – only more so' sums up the general feeling. The increase in anxious talk about expected casualties has been especially marked; people 'dare not think of what will happen to the first 10,000 who land'.

'Any day now' has become, for the great majority, 'any moment now', though as various prophesied dates (e.g. St. George's Day) pass without invasion, prophets are commanding less belief. To the familiar list of signs that the second front is imminent are added the suspension of diplomatic rights, the ban on all foreign travel, and the censoring of home-based Forces' mail to other parts of the country. (The diplomatic restriction is entirely approved, particularly in Northern Ireland where it is thought by some to have been primarily directed against Eire.) A few think that no one will know the second front has started until it is an accomplished fact, even until at least a week afterwards.

There continues to be a substantial minority who think that, for one reason or another, invasion will never take place.

Though some people think further warnings against careless talk are needed, on the whole security measures are considered to have been very successful ... 'let's hope that Hitler knows as little as we do'.

EXPECTED REPERCUSSIONS IN THIS COUNTRY are the subject of increasing discussion. It is thought that the public has very little idea how it will be affected, but that, once the second front has begun, people will accept any hardships willingly.

Discussion chiefly centres round:

(a) TRANSPORT: Many envisage the sudden closing of the railways to civilians, and some are postponing their holidays for fear of being stranded. Some think all holidays will be cancelled.

(b) FOOD: Relief that the Minister of Food stated that supplies are adequate, but a few think we shall be 'foodless' when invasion starts.

(c) THE PROBABILITY OF HEAVY AIR ATTACKS, possibly with gas.

(d) THE POSSIBILITY OF COMPULSORY EVACUATION, especially of coastal towns.

(e) POSTAL AND TELEGRAPHIC COMMUNICATION, which, it is thought, may be denied the public at first.

2A. THE COASTAL BAN

Familiar comment, with continued complaints of the inconvenience resulting from lack of definite information, and irritation because police interpretation of the regulations varies, so that one traveller may be turned back and another on similar business allowed to proceed.

There is annoyance too in the Havant, Hants., area at the neighbouring city of Chichester being placed out of bounds, because this has become the shopping centre since so many Portsmouth shops were bombed.

From the Midland Region come tales of friends who have been able 'to walk about unchallenged for a week in a banned area and can get in merely by saying they have a relative there who is ill'.

3. ALLIED AIR OFFENSIVE

Satisfaction with our intensified attacks and those of the Americans is again general. They are increasingly considered to be integral to invasion – either as a preparatory 'softening-up' process or as constituting, in effect, the actual beginning of the invasion. A few think they are our 'second front'.

There is also much pleasure with the help the air offensive is giving Russia – particularly the bombing of the Balkans from Italian bases.

Some doubts of the effectiveness of bombing continue, however – partly as the result of statements about the Luftwaffe's continued strength. Speculation continues as to the actual state of German morale.

4. RUSSIA

MILITARY: Comment is the same as last week with the addition of:

(a) Speculation about how swift future Russian advances may be.
(b) Some suggestion that the Russians have been meeting less opposition than our armies in Italy.

POLITICAL: People continue to fear that Russia's greater efforts and sacrifices will enable her to dominate the peace talks. On the other hand, some 'see no danger in this' and feel 'she deserves all the political advantages she can get through her successes'.

FINLAND: Some disappointment is reported that the Finns have finally turned down the Russian terms. People are said to be indifferent to Finland's fate now.

5. ITALY

MILITARY: Comment is again less; in the absence of any change, people are said to be losing interest. Anxiety and disappointment remain the chief reactions; for the rest, opinions, critical and hopeful, continue unchanged.

POLITICAL: Little interest is reported, but there is both satisfaction at the changes in the Italian cabinet, and some mistrust.

6. FAR EAST

BURMA: Concern and misgiving over the situation in Burma and the Japanese advance are again reported, although recent news has caused some slight increase in confidence. The uneasiness felt is largely attributed to reports of censorship of news by the South-East Asia Command, and the conflicting British and American news. People fear bad news is being kept back, and ask … 'Why did the correspondents protest over the censorship? What we want are more reports and fewer conflicting statements.'

PACIFIC: Satisfaction with successes continues. People hope we shall soon be in a position to bomb Tokyo.

7. NEUTRALS

People have welcomed the strong stand made by the Allies against neutrals who are helping Germany.

TURKEY: There is general satisfaction that Turkey is substantially to reduce her exports of chrome to Germany. Some people, however, were surprised to hear that

Turkey – 'whose sympathies were supposed to be pro-Allied' – should have exported chrome to Germany in the first place.

SWEDEN 'should immediately stop supplying the enemy with ball bearings'.

SPAIN continues to be distrusted.

8. WAR AT SEA

The release of the news of the 'human torpedoes' has caused much interest; unbounded admiration for the men who ride them is reported. While some criticise the Admiralty for keeping it secret for so long, others question the wisdom of revealing the particulars now. The fantastic nature of the weapon is said to have stirred the imagination, but it is thought to have a limited value only.

A minority are said to consider it a 'terrible weapon'.

9. DEBATE IN THE HOUSE ON IMPERIAL UNITY (APRIL 20)

Not much comment, but warm appreciation for the Prime Minister's speech – 'worthy of its great theme' – and some praise for Mr. Shinwell's. Though the general trend of the debate evoked appreciative comment, young working-class people are said, in one report, to have made fun of the talk of 'wonderful achievements' and to have quoted the Indian political situation and the Bengal famine.

MR. CHURCHILL'S REFERENCES TO IRELAND were not received with complete satisfaction in Northern Ireland, 'at any rate in Unionist circles', according to the Northern Ireland report. 'Although the Prime Minister used the word "lamentable" in regard to Eire's refusal to come into the war, other phrases in his speech created an uneasy feeling that he was hinting at some new effort to placate Eire on the border question at Ulster's expense. The opinion was expressed in many quarters that Mr. Churchill appeared to be paving the way for the re-opening of the Ulster-Eire question in the post-war settlement. The Unionist attitude is that this question must on no account be re-opened, having regard to the important part which Ulster has taken in the war effort in contradistinction to Eire's neutrality.'

10. USA

Some fears for Anglo-American relations – both present and post-war – have been reported. It is felt that an unfriendly attitude towards us is being fostered, and people fear that American post-war plans are going to be very unfavourable to us … 'America is going to make us pay dearly after the war for the favours she has extended us.'

11. BROADCASTING AND PRESENTATION OF NEWS

Praise for BBC news presentation this week.

GENERAL FORCES PROGRAMME: Unfavourable criticism continues, with 'bittiness' again the main cause of complaint.

PRAISE FOR: *Desert Highway*, April 15; *ITMA*; G. V. Keeling's *Postscript*, April 16.

II. SPECIAL COMMENTS

FULL MONTHLY REVIEW

12. MINERS AND MINING

STRIKES: Comment has declined, though indignation and condemnation continue. People are relieved the miners have gone back to work and hope for a period of peace; some fear, however, that the present settlement is only temporary.

THE GOVERNMENT is again criticised for its past 'policy of appeasement', and some think it is afraid of the miners and would have taken more drastic action with another industry. However, the new strike regulations are warmly welcomed (see Section 13).

FOUR-YEAR PLAN: Miners in Scotland and the Northern Region are sceptical and reticent; in the North Midland Region, they are said to welcome it.

AMERICAN MACHINERY is generally liked in the Lothians, safety measures such as enclosed machinery being warmly commended.

DURING THE PAST FOUR WEEKS, apart from subjects dealt with weekly, comment has mainly been about:

(a) THE BEVIN BOYS AND THE BALLOT: From two Regions there are reports that the boys are settling down in both pits and 'digs'. MINERS object because the boys are said to get as much pay or more than those who train them. Some volunteers and optants speak bitterly of the preferences given to the boys, who receive equipment etc. free. Some miners object, too, to the number of boys each man has to train – said to be nine. They think the boys are 'a positive menace' and that one each is quite enough to train. They also feel care should be used in directing boys to mining, 'for any showing signs of nervousness in an emergency might constitute a danger to themselves and others'. THE BOYS THEMSELVES, particularly those with pre-Service training, or those who want to join one of the Services, remain critical, though some are surprised at the easy training. Some resentment is reported at conscription without any guarantee of a return to previous jobs after the war. THE GENERAL PUBLIC remain sympathetic with those who want to join the Services and critical of conscription by ballot for private pits. They think, too, that the boys will not make much difference to production.

(b) THE PORTER AWARD: Comment has been almost entirely adverse. Miners are reported to be confused and 'still smarting under the knowledge that it has meant no advance to them'. They feel particular anger that deductions are made for coal allowance, that the skilled worker gets 'no more than the raw recruit', that local conditions are not considered, and that the award was enforced before a general wages agreement was arrived at.

13. STRIKES (OTHER THAN MINERS')

Widespread condemnation of strikes, particularly on the eve of the second front, continues. Some again suggest strikers should be put in the Forces; though others believe unrest will disappear when invasion begins.

THE GOVERNMENT'S NEW STRIKE REGULATIONS are widely commended, though many wish they had been made long ago. Others doubt their effectiveness unless applied firmly. A few object to the regulations because they 'dislike the imposition of Government orders without explanation or discussion'.

THE LONDON BUS STRIKE: Little comment except from London, where, despite some indignation, the majority accepted the strike 'philosophically', with little bitterness against the strikers. Everyone wanted to ride on 'a soldiers' bus', and the variety imparted to the daily routine was welcomed.

MANCHESTER GAS STRIKE: The majority in the North-Western Region condemned the strike. However, it was alleged that the Manchester Town Clerk had 'persistently refused to ameliorate the condition of gas employees and that this, not the conditions of the award, was the real cause of the strike'.

14. FUEL

THE HEATING BAN has caused annoyance and complaints, especially in the North and North-East – and among people in sedentary jobs. Annoyance is said to be due to the belief that (a) the ban is precipitate; (b) some people have gained exemption or are not complying with the ban; (c) people cannot stand cold as they did before the war, and sickness will result. People in the Northern Region maintain that the North-East of England is colder than many parts of Scotland which are not yet affected by the order, and do not understand why it has not been included with Scotland, as it was last year.

DURING THE PAST FOUR WEEKS comment has been chiefly about:

DOMESTIC SUPPLIES: Complaints have been less widespread, though they persist, particularly in the North and North-East, and have been on the following lines:

(a) SHORTAGE OF COAL: Some put this down to THE ALLOWANCE BEING INADEQUATE, others to DELAYED DELIVERIES. Cases are reported of houses, in towns as well as rural areas, which have been without coal for more than a fortnight. People complain, too, of losing a month's supply when the merchant does not deliver within the period and will not leave two months' supply the next month.
(b) POOR-QUALITY COAL: 'Five hundredweights of pre-war quality was worth double the present muck and dirt.'
(c) SHORTAGE OF COKE.
(d) POOR-QUALITY OIL, AND SHORTAGE.

Those thought particularly hard hit are people with no alternative form of cooking or heating; those who do a lot of washing at home because the family is large or because of laundry difficulties; shift workers and those who could not lay in stocks.

The miners are said to be 'the only people who can keep a decent fire going' and this is resented, particularly by their non-mining neighbours, and by those who blame them for the supply situation.

THE INDUSTRIAL FUEL CUT: Some uneasiness is reported as to how the cuts can be effected without reducing production.

STOCKS AND DUMPS OF COAL: People complain of 'long unused' coal dumps deteriorating, and think they should be used in the present emergency.

ECONOMY CAMPAIGN: Very little comment. Some think most people are being economical because of the coal shortage; others that people are not doing all they can to economise in gas and electricity. The miners' strikes and Government's 'failure' to deal with the situation are thought not to have encouraged people to 'take kindly' to the restrictions.

15. POST-WAR

DURING THE PAST FOUR WEEKS there appears to have been less discussion of post-war matters (with the exception of housing); this is partly due, it is thought, to preoccupation with the second front. While there continue to be widespread concern and uneasiness about post-war prospects and considerable lack of faith in the Government's intentions, there are two schools of thought on the subject of planning now:

(a) An apparent majority who are anxious that plans should be made immediately to prevent 'a repetition of the muddles after the last war', and who criticise the Government for not producing definite clear-cut plans now.

(b) A growing minority who advocate winning the war first. These people feel that too much time and energy are expended by the Government and others in considering post-war plans now ... 'Arrange for houses to be built, but get on with the war.' A few ask 'What can our Allies think of our concentrating on reorganisation of practically all our social services at the climax of the greatest war in history?'

There is continued uncertainty as to how all the money is to be found.

Most reported comment has been about:

(a) HOUSING: This still takes precedence over all other post-war preoccupations, in spite of a slight increase in confidence after the Prime Minister's broadcast. The Government's short-term housing programme seems to have excited little general comment. People ask for an 'adequate long-term housing scheme with concrete proposals' and say that housing plans should have come before health or any other schemes.

Aspects of post-war housing particularly discussed are:

(i) PREFABRICATION: The public's ideas about prefabricated houses are very vague, but there is great interest in the possibility and people are very curious to see them. The models displayed in Manchester, and press accounts of Coventry's prefabricated houses, aroused interested discussion, and people ask that one should be exhibited in every large town, or that a film be made showing what they are like.

Though the idea of prefabrication is not generally popular, it is said to be gaining increasing acceptance. People object on the grounds that these houses will continue in use long after they should have been replaced and will develop into slums, and that they are too poky ever to be real homes. People say they want houses, not hutments, to live in, though it is conceded that prefabricated houses might be 'all right for retired couples', or for young people who have not yet made up their minds what they want.

(ii) HOUSING AND LAND DEVELOPMENT: Complaint, some bitter, continues at the apparent shelving of the Uthwatt and Scott Reports. Local authorities are said to be impatient to start on their housing developments without delay – especially the preparing of sites by laying down sewers and gas – and dissatisfaction is reported on the grounds that they are without the necessary information to enable them to begin. There is particular complaint at the delay in sanctioning sites selected by the local authorities and in deciding on a policy regarding the purchase values of land required for building. It is thought that the rejection of the Hull Bill will retard local enterprise.

(iii) RURAL HOUSING: People in rural areas are keenly interested in the prospect of having piped water, improved sewerage, and electricity after the war. The Government's proposals about water supplies have been welcomed; though 'nationalisation' is considered the ultimate remedy for present difficulties.

(b) EMPLOYMENT: Fear of unemployment comes second now to the fear of having nowhere to live after the war. People are sceptical over the Government's plans to provide work after the war and are anxious to know how work can be found for all the people on munitions or in the Forces. Fears of widespread unemployment are reported from the Northern Region, particularly among those in heavy industry and on Teesside, where many steel workers are now out of work.

(c) INDUSTRY AND TRADE: The change-over from war to peace industry is the subject of some speculation and anxiety, and there is comment on the future of certain areas, e.g:

(i) TEESSIDE AND CLEVELAND, where the decision of the Board of Trade to exclude these areas from the North East Development Board is said to have aroused intense indignation.

(ii) WALES, where there is concern in some districts over the future of the tinplate trade.

(iii) MIDLANDS, where there is said to be much grumbling over a recent Government project to establish factories in South Wales and Scotland for the production of aluminium hollowware.

'The industry has been developed over a number of years in the Midlands by local enterprise and it is felt to be unfair that the fruit of this endeavour should be dropped into the laps of South Wales industrialists and workers by the Government, to the detriment of Midland workers and employers.'

(iv) CAMBORNE-REDRUTH area of Cornwall, where the future of the tin-mining industry continues a matter of anxious concern.

Interest is also reported in the future of small firms and shopkeepers, in the Government scheme for renewing apprenticeships interrupted by service in the Forces, and in the TUC's proposals for a 40-hour working week.

(d) AGRICULTURE: Continued uneasiness among the agricultural communities over the future of the farming industry. Farmers, though doing well now, are said to have little faith in the future when unrestricted supplies from abroad become available. Farmers are wondering how they are to go on paying their labourers at the present rate, unless present prices are maintained.

One suggestion for helping farmers after the war is the removal of death duties on privately owned farms.

(e) DEMOBILISATION: 'First in, first out' appears to have most support, though the points scheme and priority for essential workers both have their advocates. 'Let it be soon' sums up all opinions, however.

16. HOUSING

DURING THE PAST FOUR WEEKS complaints of the housing situation have been reported from all Regions save Northern Ireland; and every week from Scotland and the North Midland, London and South-Eastern, and Midland Regions. Dissatisfaction with present conditions appears to be aggravated by a feeling that the Government is not tackling the problem vigorously enough. 'If the position is so serious now, what will happen at the end of the war? We shall be in rooms and lodgings for ever.' In London, houses available for requisitioning are said still to be empty 'due to legislative loopholes, which the owners have been quick to exploit'.

Particular hardships mentioned this month are those of newlyweds having to share homes with their parents, and of discharged disabled soldiers who want to get married and cannot get decent accommodation within their means.

Though as strong and as widespread, recent comment has been less detailed than last month's; the chief complaints are still of:

(a) SHORTAGE OF ACCOMMODATION OF ALL KINDS: This is said to be the cause of bitter discontent and, in some areas, of serious overcrowding. Again, the problem is said to have been increased by evacuees from London.

(b) HIGH RENTS AND PRICES: It is alleged that some houses are being offered at prices 400% above 1939 levels, and restriction of prices and further restriction of rents is asked for.

AGRICULTURAL COTTAGES: The Government cottages are still said to be unpopular; the rents are considered too high for the accommodation offered and also for the farm labourers' wages. It is suggested that there should be some legislation to prevent farm workers' cottages being bought up, over-improved and let at high rents to people who are not agricultural workers.

PREFABRICATED HOUSES (see Section 15, POST-WAR).

17. EDUCATION BILL

DURING THE PAST FOUR WEEKS interest in the Education Bill has been stimulated by the Government defeat and subsequent vote of confidence. As before, reactions have been mainly favourable, though some people ask anxiously 'where all the money is coming from' and fear a rise in rates. Though interest is shown, people do not seem to be discussing the bill in much detail and, except for the question of EQUAL PAY (see below), comment has been mainly on familiar lines:

(a) RAISING THE SCHOOL-LEAVING AGE: Opinion divided, but mainly favourable. Disappointment that no date has yet been irrevocably fixed has led a few to say that 'now that victory is nearer, the Government is going back on its promises more and more'. On the other hand, a few say 'Keep the leaving age at 14, but improve the education.'

(b) ROMAN CATHOLICS: Lack of sympathy with their point of view is reported, and some slight opposition to granting them loans at low interest.

(c) TEACHERS: People fear there will not be enough teachers. It is hoped that their pay will be improved, 'to put the profession on its proper level and attract the right kind'.

18. EQUAL PAY

DURING THE PAST FOUR WEEKS, as a result of the debate on clause 82 of the Education Bill, the principle of equal pay has been widely discussed – in some cases, with strong feeling. According to the Scottish report, women are less interested in the subject than men.

Opinion, though divided, is mainly in favour of equality. Some, while accepting the principle as fair – 'if the work really is equal' – consider many adjustments would be necessary. People are glad to know the subject is to come up for further discussion, though a minority feel such controversial matters should be left till after the war.

19. WHITE PAPER ON A NATIONAL HEALTH SERVICE

DURING THE PAST FOUR WEEKS the scheme has continued to meet with general approval, and only doctors are thought to be disapproving. There is, however, some fear that the standards of the national service will be lower than those of private practitioners, and that people who are able to pay may still get better treatment. Relief is reported from two Regions at the retention of the free choice of doctor.

20. SERVICE PAY, ALLOWANCES AND PENSIONS

The promised statement in the House was eagerly awaited, and increases were hoped for, but no reactions have yet been received to the Government's decision (April 26).

DURING THE PAST FOUR WEEKS there has been continued and widespread support for increased dependants' allowances and – to a lesser extent – basic rates of pay.

Resentment is again reported at the disparity between United Kingdom servicemen's pay and (a) the pay of US, Dominion and Colonial troops; (b) war workers' wages.

There has also been some comment about:

(a) PENSIONS TO MEN DISCHARGED ON HEALTH GROUNDS: People are said to consider that an adequate pension should be paid to any man or woman who was admitted to the Forces A1, no matter on what grounds they are later pronounced medically unfit.

(b) WAR SERVICE GRANTS: Dissatisfaction is again reported that these are reduced when the husband receives an increase in pay: 'If grants are to decline as a soldier's proficiency pay increases, there is no encouragement to a man to be a better soldier.'

21. INDUSTRY AND TRADE

DURING THE PAST FOUR WEEKS bewilderment and uneasiness among workers have again been frequently reported. This is thought to be because people cannot reconcile the imminence of the invasion and official appeals for maximum output with the slacking-off they see at work or hear about.

PRODUCTION: There have been many references to: (a) reduced hours and abolition of overtime; (b) enforced idleness and overstaffing – 'Women workers find knitting useful for filling in the time, for which they are paid'; (c) staff cuts, factories closing, and unemployment. However, the recent industrial fuel cut is thought by some to explain the changes, but others think this explanation 'phoney'.

WORKERS' ATTITUDE: There is some talk of apathy and slackness among workers – 'the spirit of Dunkirk is missing' – though it is felt that this is partly due to overstaffing, and to the fact that 'this "all out for the second front" idea has been pushed at the workers for about two years and they are all bored with it'. A marked feeling of tiredness among workers is also reported.

ESSENTIAL WORK ORDER: This is said to annoy. Workers think employers use it as a means to pay inadequate wages and to retain men needlessly.

SMALL TRADERS: Some feeling is reported that small traders, particularly shopkeepers, are unfairly treated by the Government and Ministry of Labour, whereas people would like them encouraged. A few feel that co-operative societies are 'swallowing them up'.

22. INCOME TAX

PAYE: The scheme is said to be running fairly smoothly and to be generally approved, particularly by black-coated workers. It is thought that many people will be properly assessed for the first time and that there will be a substantial increase in taxpayers.

There has been some grumbling, however, that it has 'taken the gilt off pay packets'. Manual and casual workers seem to have taken less kindly to the scheme than anyone, though most criticism is based on bewilderment and misunderstanding.

Employers, including farmers, complain – some bitterly – of the extra work entailed, especially in view of depleted clerical staffs.

Comment otherwise is mainly about:

(a) THE EFFECT ON ABSENTEEISM AND OVERTIME: Many feel PAYE will encourage absenteeism and mean that workers will avoid overtime. It is said that 'the working man is getting to know where he stands', and that many, including farm labourers, are saying they will only work up to income tax point. Some women are already refusing to work full time any more.

Some people think overtime earnings should be exempt from taxation.

(b) METHODS OF ASSESSMENT, ETC.: Workers are said not to understand the coding system, nor how the deductions are arrived at. As a result, many think they are 'being done' and that they will have to pay more under the new system. The fact that deductions vary from week to week adds to the confusion. Casual workers, those working in gangs, and those, including miners, whose wages are paid a full week in arrears, are particularly bewildered.

(c) EXPLANATORY TALKS, THE PAYE BOOKLET ETC.: Appreciation of talks continues, though it is regretted that farm workers cannot have things explained to them in the same way as factory employees. More broadcast talks would be welcomed. The PAYE booklet is 'sought after' but found to be 'full of mysteries'.

More explanation is wanted, especially about the discharge of tax which would normally be paid this year, as many do not understand why there will still be arrears to pay, nor why the proportion of arrears to be paid is not the same for everyone. Government employees feel hardly done by in this respect.

POST-WAR CREDITS: Doubts about their value are again reported and it is said that they are still not understood, some thinking the period of remission of income tax will 'swindle them' out of their post-war credits.

FARMING SUBSIDIES: Farmers are said to think ploughing subsidies should not be taxed as 'they are a capital item'. Non-farmers, however, think it is fair, 'because other bonuses are taxable'.

23. WAGES

DURING THE PAST FOUR WEEKS comment has greatly decreased, though it has been on familiar lines:

(a) DISPARITIES IN PAY, especially between our servicemen and (i) US troops, (ii) Dominion troops, and (iii) civilians; between miners and munition workers; between skilled and unskilled workers.

Resentment is also caused by the wages alleged to be paid to Irish workers. Irish navvies working on roads in Hampshire are paid 2/0½d an hour, which is more than the local rate; also, 'because they are Irish, it is apparently free of income tax'. Irishmen working on the railways are also said to get extra allowances.

(b) HIGH WAGES, particularly of unskilled workers, young people and war workers. The wages paid to some young people are said to cause discontent to relatives of servicemen and to the young people's own parents – 'How would you like it if your young girl were bringing home as much as yourself and you could hardly call your home your own?' Some think unskilled war workers' high wages are one of the chief causes of strikes.

(c) LOSSES OF PAY: Anxiety and discontent are reported at loss of wages where hours have been cut down or overtime stopped. Hardship caused to women who are directed to leave their jobs for others carrying smaller pay is reported; other women complain that they now only get 1/- an hour for the same job for which they got 2/6d last year.

24. FOOD

DURING THE PAST FOUR WEEKS satisfaction with the general food situation has continued, with appreciation of the way the Government has organised the feeding of the nation through four-and-a-half years of war. Other comment has been of:

ORANGES AND LEMONS: People have been very pleased with the supply – and some are hoping for more. On the other hand, complaints of unfair distribution still come from 'the unlucky ones'. Housewives with jobs – who have no time to queue – are thought to have suffered particularly; ration books, it is suggested, should have been cut, not just marked in pencil which can easily be erased.

THE CUT IN THE CHEESE RATION continues to be much regretted, particularly by workers who need lunch sandwiches.

In the North Midland Region, 'some miners who are told they can get supplies at their canteens point out that workers' buses will not wait while they call at the canteens for the food and so they have to break into family rations'.

GREEN VEGETABLES:

(a) High price, particularly of (i) lettuces and other salad ingredients; (ii) cauliflowers. Retailers are thought to be making excessive profits: 'A cauliflower costs 1/9d in shops, and yet the grower only thirty miles away gets 4d each for the best.'

(b) Shortage.

FISH: Complaints continue of a shortage in some areas, but pleasure at improved supplies is reported from others. Complaints of the high price come from the Northern Region, and of 'nothing but cod and that not fresh' from the Midlands.

THE LACK OF VARIETY, which is 'irking' people. In the Northern Region, for example, they complain of 'mutton reaching almost saturation point', and in London and the South of 'eternal pork'. On the other hand, oranges and lemons have added 'colour and spice', and fresh fruit and salads are looked forward to and, in London, ice-cream is hoped for in the summer.

COMPARISONS are made between:

(a) People living in the country and those in towns; the latter are 'much better off with their canteens and British Restaurants'.

(b) Old people and children. It is said that while the Government has done much for the welfare of the children, nothing has been done for the old. Old people are often unable to obtain fish, fruit, etc. because they cannot queue; they are often not well enough to supplement their rations by visiting British Restaurants; they find it difficult to manage on the milk allowance.

THE ADDITIONAL FOUR POINTS for the present ration period are welcomed.

TINNED MEATS: Complaints of shortage come from four Regions.

CAKES, BISCUITS AND CONFECTIONERY: A shortage is reported from the Northern and South-Western Regions. In the latter, supplies are believed to be 'far more plentiful in the north'.

BREAKFAST CEREALS: Two Regions report a shortage.

TINNED FISH: Satisfaction with the lowering of the points value and complaints of shortage.

BRITISH RESTAURANTS: People want them to open in the evenings – particularly for the young.

24A. SHOPPING DIFFICULTIES

DURING THE PAST FOUR WEEKS complaints have continued of:

(a) QUEUES – particularly for unrationed foods. Housewives who go out to work, and rural housewives with buses to catch, complain they have no time to queue and are therefore unable 'to get their fair share'.

(b) EARLY AND LUNCH-HOUR CLOSING OF SHOPS.

(c) THE 'QUOTA' SYSTEM IN SHOE SHOPS.

25. CLOTHING

DURING THE PAST FOUR WEEKS comment has continued on familiar lines. Complaints are again chiefly of:

COUPON DIFFICULTIES:

(a) Having to give up personal coupons for household linen. Housewives complain that the need for the replacement of linen is becoming increasingly acute and that they find it impossible to spare their personal coupons. A special allocation – particularly for towels – is felt to be needed.

(b) The inadequacy of coupons for the general public and for children.

(c) Too high coupon value of some articles, particularly footwear – especially children's; coats; mackintoshes; women's suits; fully-fashioned stockings; and curtains.

There are complaints of trafficking in coupons – particularly in children's.

FOOTWEAR DIFFICULTIES:

(a) Repairs, particularly the long time taken.

(b) Poor quality, particularly of children's.

(c) Shortage of children's footwear.

SHORTAGE OF HOUSEHOLD LINEN AND BEDDING, particularly sheets.

UTILITY CLOTHING: The poor quality of corsets, stockings and socks, and the 'skimpiness' of skirts, are alleged.

HIGH PRICES of non-utility clothing generally and household linen, women's hats, shoes and children's clothes.

DIFFICULTIES FOR WORKERS IN HEAVY INDUSTRIES: They feel that reconditioned battle dress should be made available for them.

25A. FURNITURE

DURING THE PAST FOUR WEEKS complaints of the high price of furniture have continued, particularly the 'exorbitant' prices charged by second-hand dealers.

POINTS SCHEME FOR UTILITY FURNITURE: There are complaints of the inadequacy of the points allowance for newly married couples, and of the delay before the furniture is available.

26. DOMESTIC HELP

DURING THE PAST FOUR WEEKS complaints of the difficulties arising from lack of domestic help have continued widespread. Those particularly affected are again said to be:

(a) OLD PEOPLE.
(b) INVALIDS: Even in cases of serious illness it is said to be impossible to obtain help.
(c) MOTHERS WITH YOUNG CHILDREN.
(d) HOSPITALS AND NURSING HOMES.

It is again complained that what help is available is not fairly shared but usually falls to the less needy.

27. FIRE GUARDS, CIVIL DEFENCE, NFS AND HOME GUARD

DURING THE PAST FOUR WEEKS there has been comment about:

FIRE GUARDS:

(a) THE FIRE-GUARD ORDER: Dissatisfaction and difficulties over the new order have continued to be reported.
(b) EVASION OF DUTIES, especially by conscripts. It is complained that men who refuse to fire-watch are not proceeded against; some factory workers think it unfair that they have to do more than workers living in the country.
(c) LACK OF INTEREST IN FIRE-GUARD DUTIES, thought to be due to absence of raids in the areas concerned.
(d) VAGUENESS OVER GENERAL FIRE-GUARD DUTIES: Some Fire Guards are said not to know what to do or where to find equipment.

CIVIL DEFENCE AND NFS: Comment continues slight. Although keener interest in duties has been reported in some places as a result of the London raids, it is thought in the Northern and North Midland Regions that an alert or two would be very beneficial to CD workers.

In the London Region, wardens are anxious that persons moving house, or having additional people to live with them, should notify the wardens' post; they would like the BBC to 'make constant reference to this'.

HOME GUARD: Complaints are reported – especially by heavy workers after night shifts and long hours of work – of the number of parades and duties which have to be done. Home Guards in the North Midland Region are said to be enjoying their unusual exercises and expecting active work very soon.

NEWCASTLE ENQUIRY: Comment in the Northern Region has died down, but the forthcoming report will, it is thought, rapidly revive public interest.

28. CALL-UP

DURING THE PAST FOUR WEEKS there has been very little comment. Still a few complaints of young women not being called up; of unnecessary deferments; of girls being trained for factory work and afterwards no work being available; and of hardships caused in offices where 'the few remaining personnel' are called up.

29. HEALTH

DURING THE PAST FOUR WEEKS the prevalence of tiredness, war-weariness, nervous strain, and minor ill-health has continued to be reported. This is attributed to:

    (a) LACK OF GOOD FOOD: To this is also attributed the difficulty of throwing off minor complaints.
    (b) LONG HOURS OF WORK.
    (c) LACK OF HOLIDAYS.
    (d) FIRE-WATCHING.

Official assurances of the good health of the nation continue to be doubted and to cause irritation. It is, however, thought that the health of babies and children is good.

    TUBERCULOSIS: The increased amount of tuberculosis, particularly among young girls, causes anxiety. A Government campaign to combat this increase is suggested.

    SHORTAGE OF DOCTORS: Workers complain that they now have to wait such a long time in doctors' surgeries that they do not visit them as often as they otherwise would.

    SHORTAGE OF HOSPITAL ACCOMMODATION: This continues to be a difficulty, especially for maternity cases.

30. TRANSPORT

DURING THE PAST FOUR WEEKS transport difficulties have been reported from twelve Regions, the chief complaints being:

    (a) INADEQUATE SERVICES GENERALLY, PARTICULARLY IN RURAL AREAS.
    (b) OVERCROWDING: Workers complain of being crowded out at peak hours by women shoppers and children travelling short distances; country shoppers living in villages lying between bus termini find the buses overloaded on arrival.
    (c) CURTAILMENT OF EVENING SERVICES: Complaints are made in one Region that people without permits to travel after 9 p.m. have to walk, while half-empty buses pass them; and in another, that servicemen are not

allowed on late workers' buses, even when these are the last buses for areas where the men have to report for duty.

(d) INCIVILITY OF TRANSPORT EMPLOYEES – AND DRIVERS FAILING TO STOP AT RECOGNISED POINTS.

(e) WORKERS' BUSES RUNNING HALF EMPTY: There is also some resentment against priority travel for workers … 'We are all in the front line now'.

(f) INADEQUATE SUNDAY SERVICES.

(g) LACK OF CO-ORDINATION BETWEEN DIFFERENT TRANSPORT SERVICES.

30A. PETROL

DURING THE PAST FOUR WEEKS comment has been reported on:

(a) USE OF TAXIS FOR PLEASURE AND SHOPPING, with particular criticism of the large number of taxis taken by racegoers from London to Windsor on Easter Monday.

(b) WASTE OF PETROL by the army, NFS and Civil Defence Services.

(c) MISUSE OF OFFICIAL CARS, which is described as 'a ramp'.

(d) THE NUMBER OF PRIVATE CARS IN USE, 'while petrol for bus services is thought to have been further curtailed'.

Some people continue to feel that petrol is not distributed fairly; businessmen think more could be spared.

31. HOLIDAYS

Many people feel they need a change; some are afraid of being stranded when they are away if the second front opens, but others are going ahead with their plans.

32. AGRICULTURE

DURING THE PAST FOUR WEEKS concern about the future and resentment at the Minister's Tonbridge speech, March 16, have continued. It is thought that he is out of touch with the practical difficulties, particularly of the small farmer.

LABOUR: Shortage of labour is felt to be a very serious problem, particularly for the smallholder, though one report refers to complaints of 'too many men sheltering from call-up under the disguise of farming for the duration'.

In one Region it is hoped that seasonal labour demands can be met if adequate provision is made for camps and hostels. Clear details in the press concerning accommodation, pay, and districts where help is needed, are asked for.

There are complaints of:

(a) THE AMOUNT OF CLERICAL WORK entailed in continual form filling.

(b) TOO MANY YOUNG MEN EMPLOYED BY WAECs, and the 'regimentation and inquisition' farmers have to suffer from these committees.

(c) THE MINING OF OPEN-CAST COAL in fields that have already been sown with wheat and turnips.

(d) THE SERVING OF 'NOTICES TO QUIT' on allotment holders because land is required for building. The holders want to know if all is being done to ensure they are not penalised unless absolutely necessary, as it is thought other land is equally suitable for building.

DOUBLE SUMMER TIME is disliked in farming circles. Farm workers complain they cannot start work so early because of the heavy dews.

32A. WATER SUPPLY

DURING THE PAST SIX WEEKS concern about the water shortage, especially among farmers, has again been reported. Recent rain has been greatly welcomed, but it is feared that even in areas where heavy rain has fallen the problem may soon be serious again, as springs and wells have completely dried up. Difficulties due to labour shortage on farms are being increased by the lack of rain.

In the North Midland Region, people blame the shortage not only on the two years' drought, but on the excessive use of water in camps and by Civil Defence units for cleaning vehicles.

It is felt that 'water should be laid on everywhere after the war'.

33. 'SALUTE THE SOLDIER' CAMPAIGN

DURING THE PAST FOUR WEEKS interest and enthusiasm have been reported, although there is some minority feeling that people are getting tired of these special savings campaigns and that 'the National Savings Committee expects too much of the public'.

34. SALVAGE

DURING THE PAST FOUR WEEKS complaints of inadequate collection have continued. Again, this is cited as affecting people's response to the salvage campaign.

There have been some complaints of waste of paper – particularly in Government departments.

NO. 191: TUESDAY 23 MAY 1944 TO WEDNESDAY 31 MAY 1944

I. GENERAL COMMENTS

1. GENERAL

The second front remains in the forefront of people's minds, and tension and impatience continue. Spirits have again risen slightly, mainly because of the good news from Italy, but also because of the Whitsun break and fine weather. Nevertheless, war-weariness is reported from nine Regions.

The Prime Minister's war review in the House has been generally praised, apart from the references to Spain.

HOME FRONT: Familiar criticism of the ballot scheme for the mines has increased. There is also again considerable anxiety among workers – about short time, idle time, stoppage of overtime, and paying off, particularly in shipbuilding and engineering.

Discussion of housing – shortage, high price and prefabrication – continues; so do complaints of insufficient clothing coupons.

2. SECOND FRONT

Feeling is on familiar lines, with tension continuing – particularly among relatives of those likely to be involved. Two Regional reports, however, refer to a decline in 'invasion fever'; and it is said that news from Italy is easing, to some extent, the strain of waiting. Although some people now say that any speculation about the date may as well be abandoned, suggested dates again range between 'Any moment now' (the majority view), and 'Never … it's all bluff.'

2A. THE CANCELLATION OF TRAINS

Resignation to a necessary discomfort is the chief reaction. Some continue to welcome the cuts as a sign that the second front is really imminent.

There is some criticism, however, because

(a) NO NOTICE IS GIVEN: It is felt that some kind of short notice would help a lot, without giving information to the enemy.
(b) THE RESTRICTIONS COULD BE BETTER HANDLED: There are complaints that in some cases workers have been particularly affected, for instance by early morning instead of mid-morning trains being removed.

People continue to ask for a lead from the Government about holiday transport; this comes particularly from those who have already booked accommodation.

3. ITALY

There are widespread satisfaction and relief at the news from Italy. Many look on the renewed offensive as a 'curtain raiser' to, or the actual start of, the second front.

The fall of Cassino and the linking-up of the beachhead troops with the main forces give particular pleasure … 'Cassino is a symbol of restored prestige.'

Many hope we shall now soon reach Rome, but there is no tendency to minimise the difficulties ahead, and people realise the campaign will have to be 'fought bitterly inch by inch'. Some are concerned about the fate of Rome, but while it is hoped that the city may be spared as far as possible, most people feel that 'historic and religious reasons' must not be allowed to hamper operations or endanger Allied lives. In Scotland, it is said that Roman Catholics, especially Eire workers, strongly hope Rome will be by-passed.

Confidence in General Alexander is increasing, and admiration for the troops is reported, with special praise for the Poles and French.

Delay in mails is causing anxiety among relatives of fighting men, and fears of heavy casualties continue.

4. THE PRIME MINISTER'S REVIEW OF FOREIGN POLICY

Mr. Churchill's review has been generally well received, apart from his references to Spain and the French National Committee. The speech contained more information, covered more ground, and was more frank than people expected. Comment has centred chiefly round his references to:

SPAIN: There is widespread criticism of the remarks about Spain and about General Franco, who is greatly distrusted and regarded as 'an out-and-out fascist'. Some are bewildered by Mr. Churchill's 'conciliatory' attitude and cannot understand what good it can do; others speak of appeasement and fail to see why, if fascism is to be eliminated from Italy and the world generally, Spain should be excepted. Others again feel Mr. Churchill must have been speaking with his tongue in his cheek.

Nevertheless, a minority approve, feeling either that the Prime Minister has 'superior inside knowledge' and that diplomacy demanded such an attitude, or else that his references to Spain showed that she had, in fact, done something to help the Allies.

FRANCE: Though opinion is divided, most people seem in favour of recognising the French National Committee, at any rate as a provisional government. There is, therefore, some disappointment at the line Mr. Churchill took, and a feeling that on this point our foreign policy is dictated by Washington. Nevertheless, some feel he may be right and that we made mistakes over the Yugoslav and Greek governments and are not going to risk repeating them.

TURKEY: Mr. Churchill's plain speaking to Turkey has been generally approved, but a few were surprised, either being unable to see what good it would do, or thinking it was unmerited.

POLAND: Some are pleased at the hint that relations between Russia and Poland may not be as bad as was feared; others are dubious and wonder how this squares with the setting up of a rival Polish government in Moscow.

GREECE: There are uneasiness and bewilderment at Greek disunity and at the story of the mutiny. Some think the mutiny was caused by the actions of the King and his government. A few do not like the idea of British troops having been used to put down the mutineers.

YUGOSLAVIA: Admiration for Tito, satisfaction at the aid given to him, and at the visit to this country of his representatives. A little criticism of the royal Yugoslav government, and a feeling that in throwing over Mihailovitch, their only object was to ensure their own survival.

WORLD ORGANISATION FOR PEACE: A little approving comment.

5. ALLIED AIR OFFENSIVE

Satisfaction continues. The raids are looked on as a prelude to the second front, especially those on enemy rail communications. Again, some take the raids for granted.

Losses are accepted calmly. The accuracy of press statements of damage is doubted by some.

Surprise continues at the way the Germans stand up to the bombing. There is some sympathy for them and also regret at the killing of French civilians.

6. GERMAN SHOOTING OF AIR FORCE OFFICERS

Comment is on similar lines to last week's. Indignation and horror are general, and people want to see those responsible punished. A few again urge reprisals; others fear the risk to our other prisoners. The results of the enquiry are anxiously awaited.

A small number share Lord Vansittart's view that it was a 'deliberate massacre'. Some think it may have been in reprisal for our raids.

7. RUSSIA

Again, very little comment. Most people think the lull is due to preparations for a new assault when the second front starts. A small minority believe that Russia is now deliberately waiting for us to do our share.

8. FAR EAST

Interest continues limited.

Better maps are again asked for; people complain that the poor maps in the press make the campaigns incomprehensible.

BURMA: The situation continues to be looked on as more satisfactory, but still causes some bewilderment.

CHINA: There is less comment. Concern for her, and the desire to help her more, continue.

PACIFIC: Satisfaction with successes continues.

9. THE GOVERNMENT WHITE PAPER ON EMPLOYMENT POLICY

Little discussion as yet, and many think that more publicity is needed. Most reported comment is highly favourable ... 'Lord Woolton's stock, as Minister of Reconstruction, has risen as a result of its publication.'

A number, while favourably disposed, will be even more pleased when the proposals become Acts of Parliament ... 'We must see this paper does not get Beveridged.'

Others are sceptical or cynical; but the Scottish report states that on being pressed for their reasons, the cynics are generally found not to have read the report and only to have glanced at the press accounts.

10. SHELLING IN THE SOUTH-EASTERN DISTRICT

THE SHELLING INCIDENT AT STEYNING is said to have caused considerable local uneasiness and some angry comment. It is hoped that steps will be taken to prevent any recurrence of 'an incident whose effect on morale was more serious than the damage done'.

People hope that 'the high proportion of ineffective shells' was exceptional.

CROSS-CHANNEL SHELLING: The feeling in Dover towards the men of the RA batteries is said to have improved since the publicity given to the sinking of a German ship in January.

It is said that if Folkestone were to be mentioned by name, instead of as 'in the vicinity of Dover', it would compensate to a slight degree for anxious nights.

11. BROADCASTING AND PRESENTATION OF NEWS

There is more praise for correspondents' eye-witness accounts, especially of the battles in Italy.

GENERAL FORCES PROGRAMME: Criticism continues on familiar lines.

PRAISE FOR: *ITMA*; *War Commentaries*, especially those by Squadron Leader John Strachey; plays; Sir Walter Layton's *Postscript*, May 21; *Into Battle*; *Monday Night at Eight*; *The Empire Speaks*, May 24.

II. SPECIAL COMMENTS

BRIEF WEEKLY NOTE

12. THE NEW RATION BOOKS

There is general satisfaction with the distribution of the new ration books. Only from Darlington are there complaints of queues.

In the Southern Region, however, there are complaints about having to carry identity cards in security areas; this means workers cannot have their books collected for them.

III. PERIODICAL REVIEW

13. SALUTE THE SOLDIER

DURING THE PAST FIVE WEEKS interest in forthcoming Salute the Soldier weeks and/or enthusiasm for them while in progress have been reported. Both interest and

enthusiasm are, however, said to be waning ... 'People hope this will be the last of
these campaigns.'

Though a little praise is reported for Salute the Soldier publicity, there is a good
deal of criticism of these special weeks on the grounds that:

(a) THE PUBLISHED TOTALS DO NOT REPRESENT REAL SAVINGS
     because a proportion is thought to consist of:

    (i) Sums of money contributed in bulk by various organisations
     or private individuals to swell the local totals. These bulk
     contributions are not looked on as genuine savings, but merely
     as a transfer from one account to another for the purpose of
     achieving an impressive figure.

    (ii) Stamps, which are bought for the same purpose, but cashed again
     almost as soon as bought – sometimes the same day. It is suggested
     that certificates should be less easily converted into cash and that
     a minimum of, say, three months should be enforced.

(b) WASTE OF MONEY, PAPER, PETROL OR LABOUR ARE INVOLVED.
     Specifically mentioned are the waste of paper in printing so many posters
     and taking so much space in the press, and the extra burden on village
     postmistresses. It is particularly thought that considerable waste of time,
     paper and effort are involved by the cashing of stamps bought only a short
     time before (see a, ii).

(c) MONEY THAT WOULD HAVE BEEN INVESTED IN SAVINGS
     EARLIER IS HELD BACK, in order that it may be invested in the local
     'week'.

(d) LACK OF HONESTY ABOUT THE OBJECT OF SAVINGS WEEKS.
     People are 'beginning to realise that the money has nothing to do with
     providing weapons' and say that these will be produced in any case ... 'If
     the idea is to take surplus purchasing power away from people, then let's be
     honest about it.'

WAR SAVINGS GENERALLY are thought to be adversely affected by the
following:

(a) THE BELIEF THAT 'THE MORE WE LEND, THE LONGER THE WAR
     WILL LAST'.

(b) PAYE: Some workers take the line that, 'now they are paying income tax,
     there's no need to save as well'.

(c) DOUBT AS TO WHETHER CERTIFICATES WILL BE HONOURED
     AFTER THE WAR.

(d) REDUCED EARNINGS.

(e) MANY PEOPLE NOW HOLDING THE MAXIMUM NUMBER OF
     SAVINGS CERTIFICATES: An increase in the maximum is suggested on
     the grounds that there is too big a gap between the interest allowed on
     these and on war bonds.

(f)   RELUCTANCE TO INVEST LARGE SUMS, owing to a belief that they are more difficult to withdraw if required at any time; farmers are particularly mentioned.

(g)   THE RUMOUR THAT POSTMASTERS AND SUB-POSTMASTERS GET COMMISSIONS ON THE SALE OF SAVINGS CERTIFICATES.

14. YOUTH AND MORALS

DURING THE PAST FOUR WEEKS comment has again been on familiar lines. There has been some increase in the volume of complaints, however – particularly of the immorality of young girls and the behaviour of children. There is particular concern about the damaging of property: breaking of windows, slashing cinema seats, smashing electric light bulbs in trains, and damage to parks and gardens are all alleged.

FACTORS BLAMED are:

(a)   LACK OF PARENTAL CONTROL, particularly where mothers are at work. Women, it is suggested, should not be allowed to take full-time jobs unless they are able to satisfy the authorities that their children will be looked after in their absence.

(b)   THE IRRESPONSIBILITY OF PARENTS, particularly of working mothers 'with money to spare' who spend their time in pubs and cinemas.

(c)   LACK OF SUPERVISORS FOR CHILDREN when they are not in school.

(d)   LACK OF 'WHOLESOME' AMUSEMENT for children and young people, including lack of recreation grounds, games equipment, and toys.

(e)   CINEMAS: More films suitable for children are felt to be needed.

(f)   TOO MUCH MONEY TO SPEND.

Suggestions are

(a)   MORE WOMEN POLICE: It is felt, however, that great care must be exercised in their choice – the wrong type would do more harm than good.

(b)   OPENING BRITISH RESTAURANTS IN THE EVENINGS.

(c)   A CURFEW.

(d)   STRICTER TREATMENT of offenders by juvenile courts, more remand homes, and less 'gentlemanly' treatment by policemen. It is also suggested that 'difficulties in the way of adequate correction in schools' should be removed.

YOUTH CLUBS: Some interest in these continues. On the whole, they are approved and are thought to need more encouragement. There are some complaints, however, of their inability to hold young people's interest.

MORALS: In addition to anxiety about the behaviour of young people, concern has been reported at the increase in moral laxity generally – particularly of married women, whose husbands are abroad, with Dominion and US troops ... 'There will be mass murder unless the Government gets them out of the country before our men come back.'

15. ANTI-SEMITISM

DURING THE PAST FOURTEEN WEEKS criticism has continued at the same low level. There was a slight increase at the time of the reports of anti-Semitism in the Polish forces – though this was condemned – but comment now seems to have reverted to its previous level.

Criticisms are on familiar lines:

(a) BLACK MARKET ACTIVITIES: Some continue to think 'Jews are at the back of all the black market'. They are blamed for the 'ramp' in the price of houses, and for the whisky and poultry 'rackets'. They are also alleged to deal in ready money and so evade income tax.

(b) EVADING NATIONAL SERVICE: It is also complained that they held all the best positions before the war, and that they will get jobs which ex-servicemen should have after it.

(c) OBTAINING GOODS IN SHORT SUPPLY.

(d) EVACUATING TO SAFE AREAS, BEING ABLE TO RUN CARS, USING TAXIS FOR PLEASURE AND SHOPPING, and GAMBLING OFFENCES.

In the North-Eastern Region there are complaints that Jews foment industrial unrest and that Jewish communist agitators were concerned in the recent coal strike.

Complaints of the above matters have not, however, been confined to Jews.

NO. 192: WEDNESDAY 31 MAY 1944 TO WEDNESDAY 7 JUNE 1944

I. GENERAL COMMENTS

1. GENERAL

News of the Allied invasion of France has caused profound relief after weeks of waiting and tension.

Restrained excitement and sober confidence seem to be the feelings of the majority. People realise the immensity of the task and the possibility of heavy casualties but are relieved that such a good start has been made. There is little sign of over-optimism, but this is thought to be the beginning of the end and there is a tendency to hope that 'now we've started, perhaps it won't be so long before the war is over'.

The invasion news has overshadowed everything else, but earlier in the week our advances in Italy had given great satisfaction, followed by delight at the fall of Rome.

HOME FRONT: Housing, clothing coupons and the ballot scheme for the mines had all continued as topics of discussion earlier in the week.

2. THE INVASION OF FRANCE

(Latest reports cover the period up to the morning of June 7 inclusive.)

'At last ... Thank God it's started!' sums up the general feeling of profound relief from the tension and the strain of waiting.

Many were surprised when the news first broke, having expected a more sensational start, more 'fuss' and dislocation of civilian life; some cheered; some wept hysterically; some felt 'flattened out' ... 'sick in the stomach'. The great majority, however, are described as confident, calm and steady, and excitement – even when intense – is usually restrained. 'Everyone is inwardly thrilled', but people are undemonstrative, and there are few signs of jubilation. Many are said to be awed, both by the magnitude of the operations and the issues at stake. There is, too, much anxiety for the safety of those taking part, relatives – and especially women – being particularly fearful. Nevertheless, spirits have greatly lifted, and the 'browned-off' feeling of recent weeks completely vanished.

The hunger for news is intense, and many people are said to keep the wireless on permanently. People hang round every available radio in offices, shops and houses. Some complain they cannot get on with their work for excitement and interest in the bulletins. There are queues for papers, which are soon sold out. But now that some of the initial surprise has worn off, people are said not to be talking about it much, at any rate in public; many find it 'too big to talk about'.

REACTION TO THE ACTUAL OPERATIONS: People are deeply impressed by the scale of operations – the immensity of which makes many gasp – by the planning, organisation and execution and, above all, by the number of planes and ships involved ... 'I simply can't visualise 11,000 planes'.

Mr. Churchill's announcement that losses were lighter than expected and that events were moving satisfactorily has caused great relief and satisfaction. Women are said to appreciate that our leaders seem to be doing all they can to spare our men's lives.

THE LACK OF GERMAN OPPOSITION, particularly in the air, is widely discussed, and people are variously pleased, surprised, puzzled and uneasy. Many feel 'German non-resistance' is ominous and wonder what they are saving up for us; some wonder if our troops are being led into a trap and fear that the Germans are waiting till we have got an immense quantity of men and material well into France before counter-attacking. People cannot understand why they are not bombing our invasion ports.

POSSIBLE REPERCUSSIONS HERE are fairly widely discussed, especially the likelihood of raids, whether in reprisal or in attacks on embarkation ports. Many are surprised that there were no raids on Tuesday night; people in London and on the eastern and south-eastern coasts had expected to hear the sirens. Dover people say that if retaliation starts, Dover will get the worst of it, and some fear of reprisal raids is reported from Hull. A few Londoners ask if there is to be any order about carrying gas masks.

THE BBC'S PRESENTATION OF THE NEWS has given great and widespread satisfaction, with particular praise for eye-witnesses' accounts and for the 9–9.45 p.m. programme on Tuesday, in which Howard Marshall's contribution was especially liked.

The advantages of the radio over the press for vividness and up-to-the-minute news has been remarked on.

THE EFFECT ON THE WAR EFFORT: Invasion is thought to have had a stimulating effect in war factories, in spite of frequent interruption of work to listen to news bulletins. The intense interest of miners and the efforts of managements in coal mines to stimulate miners to greater efforts are also referred to. The Fife Coal Co. fitted up loudspeakers in their pits and had posters ready printed with the slogan: 'The second front opened today, we are backing them up.'

At Slough, the news resulted in filling the blood transfusion centre with people wishing to give their blood.

HM THE KING'S BROADCAST has pleased many people, who found it comforting and inspiring. The religious note was especially appreciated by women, for whose guidance and help the talk was thought to be particularly intended. Some men, it is said, would have liked something more stirring, but it is pointed out that 'Churchill gives the news, His Majesty the steadiness'.

NOTE: The rest of the report covers the week up to and including June 6.

3. ITALY

Allied progress in Italy was received with widespread pleasure and relief. Admiration for General Alexander and the troops is widespread, the French and Poles again being specially mentioned. People realise that the 'going' will still be hard … 'a slogging match all the way up the Peninsula' … but there is optimism about the outcome. Fear of heavy casualties is again reported.

BEFORE THE CAPTURE OF ROME there was much speculation whether the city would be devastated or by-passed, and while people hoped it might be spared, they also felt strongly that Allied lives must not be risked. General Maitland Wilson's statement that, if the Germans chose to defend Rome, the Allies would be obliged to take appropriate military measures to eject them, was approved. The statement from enemy headquarters that withdrawal was ordered to prevent destruction is ridiculed, and people wonder if this was an attempt to gain Roman Catholic sympathy, when Hitler knew he would lose Rome in the end.

THE POPE'S APPEAL to save Rome and for 'a peace without revenge' aroused little sympathy and some strong indignation. People remember his 'blessing Mussolini's banners', and the papal attitude to the Abyssinian War is recalled. In Northern Ireland people comment on the need for drastic treatment of Germany after the war, not for vengeance but for the safety of other nations.

THE NEWS THAT ROME HAD FALLEN was received with much pleasure at the speed of the victory; and much relief, particularly in Roman Catholic circles, that the city had been spared. The success was looked on as a good omen for the coming invasion.

4. ALLIED AIR OFFENSIVE

Comment has continued with little change from that reported in the past few weeks.

US AIR BASES IN RUSSIA: The landing of US planes in Russia has been approved as evidence of the unity of the strategy of the United Nations. Some people are said to have thought for a long time that a shuttle service of this kind would be a good idea.

AIRCRAFT PRODUCTION: The recently published figures of aircraft production in this country have caused pleasure.

5. RAIDS ON THIS COUNTRY

Recent raids on coastal towns are said to have had no ill effects on people's spirits. There is relief that there has been so little raiding, and more people are concluding that the enemy can no longer carry out serious raids on Britain.

6. THE PRIME MINISTER'S REVIEW OF FOREIGN POLICY

Until the invasion monopolised everyone's attention, there had continued to be a good deal of discussion of Mr. Churchill's speech, and particularly of his references to Spain, France, and world organisation for peace.

SPAIN: Widespread criticism on the same lines as last week's continued. Many people were concerned as to what Russia would think. A small minority, however, felt there was probably a good reason for the Prime Minister's attitude.

FRANCE: The majority appeared to favour recognition of the French National Committee and were disappointed or critical at the continued non-recognition of the Committee and of General de Gaulle. Many felt we were yielding to American pressure in this matter. (Pleasure is now expressed at General de Gaulle's visit to this country; many still hope that the Government will recognise him and the French National Committee.)

WORLD ORGANISATION FOR PEACE: This was far less discussed than the references to Spain and France, but comments were mainly approving.

7. RUSSIA

Comment continued without substantial change.

8. FAR EAST

Comment about the fighting has continued unchanged.

PRISONERS OF WAR IN JAPANESE HANDS: Anxiety and concern continue to be reported.

9. GERMAN SHOOTING OF AIR FORCE OFFICERS

Comment has again been on familiar lines, with indignation and horror continuing general.

A complete statement is awaited.

10. THE GOVERNMENT WHITE PAPER ON EMPLOYMENT POLICY

This appears to have aroused little interest. It is suggested that some kind of simplified statement is needed as people have still only a 'hazy' impression of the proposals.

What little comment there is is again chiefly favourable. It is thought to be a step in the right direction. Some, however, regard the proposals as 'a pious hope' only and doubt whether they can or will be fulfilled.

11. EIRE ELECTION

Outside Northern Ireland, the results of the Eire election excited almost no interest. Even there, interest has been comparatively slight, though there was some surprise at Mr. de Valera's increased majority.

12. BROADCASTING AND PRESENTATION OF NEWS

(See also Section 2, Invasion of France.)

Satisfaction with news bulletins has continued. Radio news is thought cautious and reasonable. Reports by war correspondents are praised, especially Godfrey Talbot's broadcast on the occupation of Rome (June 5). Our news reporting now is thought to be of a higher standard than at any time during the war.

GENERAL FORCES PROGRAMME: Criticism continues. The frequent news bulletins are, however, said to be appreciated and some like their 'chummy tone'.

PRAISE FOR: *ITMA*; *American Commentary*, June 2; H. Robson's *War Commentary* on the Pacific, June 1; *Heaven and Charing Cross*, June 3.

II. SPECIAL COMMENTS

BRIEF WEEKLY REVIEW

13. THE NEW RATION BOOKS

Satisfaction with their distribution continues general. Again, the only complaint comes from the Northern Region – this week Stockton-on-Tees.

Complaints of the difficulties involved through having to carry identity cards in protected areas come from both Southern and South-Eastern Regions this week. Workers, in some cases, do not know how they are going to manage to collect their books.

14. THE CANCELLATION OF TRAINS

The chief reaction has again been one of resignation but there was some increase in criticism. This was again on the grounds that:

(a) THE CANCELLATION COULD HAVE BEEN BETTER HANDLED,
    particularly so that business and workpeople would have been less affected.

(b) SOME NOTICE SHOULD HAVE BEEN GIVEN, or at least a timetable of trains still running should be issued.

A lead from the Government about holiday transport continues to be asked for.

15. AMMUNITION TRAIN INCIDENT AND MUNITIONS EXPLOSIONS

In the Cambridgeshire town involved, there is high praise for the men who gave their lives to save the town. Home Guard and black troops are also praised for the speed with which they cleared the debris and got the line working again.

Both in the Eastern and North-Eastern Regions, there are suggestions that the explosion, as well as others recently reported, may have been due to sabotage. A local rumour attributed the Cambridgeshire explosion to German parachutists, while in Northern Ireland it is suggested it may have been due to a bomb from an enemy plane.

16. FLOODS

HOLMFIRTH: The North-Eastern Regional report states that the flood at Holmfirth has been the major topic of conversation during the week in the Huddersfield area.

NORTH DERBYSHIRE: The following report has been received from the North Midland Region:

A very heavy thunderstorm on Monday, May 29, caused serious flooding in North Derbyshire. Small mountain streams became raging torrents, bursting their banks and causing widespread damage. Houses and cellars were flooded to a depth of several feet, and floors were left covered with slime and filth (sewers burst in a number of places). Areas affected included the towns of Glossop, New Mills, and Hayfield.

The behaviour of the public during the floods is described as 'in every way admirable'. There was no suggestion of panic, but a general willingness to help the victims. This help was difficult because of rationing, for people had no stocks of food.

In New Mills and Glossop, rest centres were opened and meals served. In many cases people requiring temporary shelter went to relatives and friends, the Food Officer issuing emergency cards. Disinfectant and soap were supplied to householders to enable them to clean their homes. Air-raid wardens gave valuable help and the military are assisting with the clearing of the debris. In Hayfield, no rest centre was opened, and there is widespread public discussion because no steps were taken to replace food which was washed away or rendered unusable by the water. The comments made are on the lines of: 'Red tape should not be allowed to stand in the way of alleviation of distress.'

Farmers have suffered damage to growing crops – fields of wheat and roots have been lost. It is felt that this, so late in the season, is a serious loss of winter-feeding stuffs. Poultry, poultry cotes, greenhouses and many allotments and gardens have been washed away completely. It is hoped that in these circumstances the allotment of fruit and vegetables to the district will be on a more generous scale.

Works have been enormously damaged; plant and machinery, including electric motors, have been deep in water and mud. Employees have worked hard to clean up the mud and it is said that fourteen days will be needed to get going again.

Many people have lost working clothes and boots, bedding, furniture and floor-coverings, and immediate replacements are essential. Although a Relief Fund has been opened its publicity must be restricted because of censorship regulations, so prompt help through Government departments or local authorities is hoped for.

Two matters on which public opinion has been expressed have been:

(a) That much could be done to improve drainage generally and water courses in particular – 'iron railings at bridges being better than walls with small draining holes'.

(b) Wood at Turnell Mill should be stored above flood level as the washing down of many logs of wood was the cause of considerable damage and flooding.

III. MONTHLY REVIEW

US TROOPS IN THIS COUNTRY

DURING THE PAST FOUR WEEKS the public's increasingly kindly feeling towards US troops has in the main continued. Praise considerably outweighs criticism, though the latter is usually given in greater detail.

This improvement in relations is attributed to:

(a) The fact that people are getting to know the Americans better. It is stated that most of those who have worked with them for some time like them very much. Particularly good relations are reported between the troops and those on whom they are billeted. People are described as 'beginning to realise that the majority have been slandered for the deeds of the few'.

(b) Growing appreciation of the part that US Forces, and in particular the USAAF, are playing in the war.

Only in the Northern and Midland Regions is comment said to be largely unfavourable (though from both come a good deal of appreciation), while in parts of the Southern Region and in one place in Northern Ireland, some deterioration in the previous good relations between the US troops and the local inhabitants is noted.

Reported comment has chiefly centred round:

(a) BEHAVIOUR WITH WOMEN AND GIRLS: The whole question, particularly the relationship of young girls with US troops, white and coloured, continues to be widely discussed and to cause much anxiety. PEOPLE ARE CRITICAL OF:

    (i) THE WOMEN AND GIRLS CONCERNED, who in many cases are said to make most of the running. Blame of the girls is more widespread, and sometimes stronger, than of the men. Their predatoriness is particularly censured; some girls are said to be dunning as many as three or four US soldiers to provide for their coming child.

    Some people are very concerned at what the Americans are going to say about British girls when they return home.

More women police are advocated; satisfaction is expressed where their number has been increased.

(ii) THE TROOPS, who are variously blamed for accosting, making love in public, having intercourse in telephone booths, leaving contraceptives about, and for 'indiscriminate' choice of women.

According to the North Midland Region report, 'Mr. Kendall's speech in the House is considered to have been unfortunately worded but, nevertheless, many feel that there was truth in his allegations.'

(iii) THE GIRLS' MOTHERS. However, some parents say they cannot have the same amount of control over their daughters as formerly because of difficult working hours; they would welcome some outside help from the authorities, such as a curfew.

(b) COLOURED TROOPS: These are praised. In some cases, they are said to be better behaved and 'less sloppy' than the whites; also, in the Huddersfield area, better behaved than the British troops.

People deplore the association of coloured troops with white girls, but it is the latter who are censured. At the same time, it is suggested that the negroes might be provided with a contingent of coloured Auxiliaries, or more camp amenities so that they should spend less time out.

There is some concern at the relations between the white and coloured troops and at reports of friction between them. Recent cases of coloured men being condemned to death for rape have aroused strong local protests on grounds of colour discrimination (South-West Region). In Norwich there is resentment that certain restaurants will not serve negroes.

(c) HIGH PAY: Comment on this differs little in volume or detail from that reported last month. Nevertheless, there is high praise for the Americans' generosity, especially to children (whose cadging is deplored).

(d) DRIVING AND TRANSPORT: Familiar allegations of dangerous driving and waste of petrol. People are specially indignant when they think petrol wasted on pleasure trips has been brought over by our merchant seamen.

(e) HEAVY DRINKING: Some realise this is confined to a minority, however.

(f) LACK OF RECREATIONAL FACILITIES: Many are said to realise that one of the difficulties is that the men are often bored and lonely, with nowhere to go and nothing to do, particularly in the smaller places without amusement amenities.

(g) CONSUMPTION OF CIVILIAN SUPPLIES: There is a good deal of complaint of civilian shortages being aggravated by US troops. People believe the Americans have plentiful and varied food and drink in their camps and consider it 'a shame they can buy up everything in short supply'. While references are made to cakes, fish and chips, whisky and dry-cleaning services, the most prevalent complaints are in connection with beer. The complaint about drinking up all the beer comes particularly from rural areas, where it is said that the result of an 'influx of a few hundred US troops into a small country village having only one or two public houses, which are already shut on several days a week, can well be imagined'. This is said to be an increasing grievance in the Southern Region, though elsewhere some people blame the brewers rather than the Americans.

Two Regional reports mention allegations of wastefulness of food, fuel and paper in US camps, billets and canteens, and the resultant impression that the Americans are indifferent to British shortages and difficulties. References are also made, however, to the tactful moderation displayed by individual Americans when accepting private hospitality.

(h) RELATIONS BETWEEN US AND BRITISH TROOPS: The impression continues that relations are not as cordial as they might be; this is generally attributed to differences in pay and conditions. A few, however, believe relations are improving and speak of English soldiers who have trained with Americans as saying they are 'excellent fellows'.

(i) APPEARANCE AND DEMEANOUR: Continued comment to the effect that some of the US troops give a slovenly and undisciplined impression.

(j) BILLETING: Relations between American soldiers and the people on whom they are billeted are said to be excellent. A little talk is, however, reported of varying rates of payment for the same accommodation; householders in Stockport are alleged to receive only 2d a day to billet US soldiers. In the South-Western Region there is also some talk of unfair billeting allocations, e.g., 'one household having three successive lots, the next door people none; influential people are much suspected of wangling out of such obligations'.

(k) DAMAGE: References are made to allegations of damage of various kinds by US troops, e.g. to crops, hedges, game birds and their eggs, nesting swans, and spawning beds; and also, as a result of careless driving, to 'old bridges and historic features'.

NO. 194: TUESDAY 13 JUNE 1944 TO TUESDAY 20 JUNE 1944

I. GENERAL COMMENTS

1. GENERAL

The prevailing mood remains one of calm and hopeful confidence. There is great satisfaction over the progress of the Normandy, Italian and Russian campaigns, but most people are described as guardedly optimistic, realising that a colossal task still lies ahead.

The pilotless aircraft has for the time being taken first place as a topic of conversation; it has given rise to a good deal of anxiety and speculation, and, in those parts of southern England most affected, to considerable nervousness and tiredness.

There is increasing discussion of the French National Committee; most people seem to favour its recognition.

Much hopeful talk about war ending this year, encouraged by Allied successes, optimistic remarks by General Montgomery and Mr. Arthur Henderson, and by the Prime Minister's affirmative nod on being asked whether the blackout would be done away with before Christmas.

HOME FRONT: Grumbling continues to be on a much reduced scale, though there is a good deal of talk about post-war conditions – particularly housing and employment – and some talk of clothing and housing now.

2. PILOTLESS AIRCRAFT

Since Friday, the arrival of the pilotless plane has been a major topic of discussion throughout the country; in most places, it has displaced the invasion as the main subject of conversation. News that something unusual was happening spread rapidly. There were stories of an exceptionally long alert in London; and talk of paratroops landing and even of gas having been used. First stories of a flying bomb were greeted with shocked horror. Then came Mr. Morrison's statement. Most people found this distinctly reassuring, though some felt it was unduly alarming. Since the statement the more fantastic rumours have vanished, but everywhere there has been much discussion and speculation – about the mechanism of the device and about ways of countering it, and many stories of extensive damage in London and of considerable evacuation.

The general view appears to be that our technical experts will soon find an answer to it. A considerable minority, however, are less certain; and there is some criticism because no answer was ready beforehand despite our advance knowledge of it.

As to its military value, there is general agreement that it will have no effect on the course of the war as a whole. It is thought to have arrived too late. It is looked on as a morale weapon against the people of the south of England, or as a propaganda weapon, primarily for German home consumption.

It is variously spoken of as 'Hitler's last kick' ... 'his last desperate fling' ... 'the worst he can do' ... 'his last patch of awfulness'. There appears to be no discussion of any other possible secret weapons.

LONDON: Most Londoners confess to feeling considerably shaken, despite their calm behaviour. Only at the scene of some incidents has there been anything approaching panic. The main feeling is one of 'incredible tiredness' from lack of sleep, coupled with nervous anxiety, arising in part from the 'weird and uncanny' nature of the device, and in part from the strain of listening for and to their approach. Aerial reprisals had been expected, but nothing quite like this.

DEFENCES: The stopping of the AA guns was generally welcomed for two reasons:

(a) They were disturbing in themselves, and appeared to do little good, while effectively preventing sleep.

(b) The cessation of firing was taken as a sign that fighters were after the flying bombs, and this was regarded as a better way of tackling them.

It is now believed that many of them are being brought down before they get to London, either in the country or over the Channel, though whether this means we are on the way to mastering them appears to be little discussed. Indeed, Londoners appear too tired to speculate much on methods of dealing with the bombs; and there is less talk in London than elsewhere about confidence in our technical experts being able to master them. There is beginning to be some talk about the necessity for inflicting pilotless planes on the Germans.

SIRENS: It is felt that the sirens should be sounded only in the areas lying along the course of the bombs.

SHELTERS: Shelters are said to be more crowded than ever before. Mr. Morrison's advice on seeking shelter was welcomed, and many are following it, getting off the streets quickly when they hear the noise approaching, and quicker still when it stops. On the other hand, many cannot resist looking from windows etc., to get a glimpse of the machines.

Some wonder if surface shelters are adequate; and mothers are keeping their children from school because of doubts about school surface shelters.

There is some demand for the opening of the deep shelters mentioned by Mr. Morrison early this year. They are looked on as 'London's own'.

Some tube shelterers are worried about the risk of vermin and about the risk of catching VD from the seats in the tube shelter lavatories.

Owing to the crowding of the platforms, some regular tube travellers are taking to buses.

EVACUATION: There appears to have been a small amount of evacuation of women with children – mainly upper- and middle-class. But many more people are trying to make up their minds whether or not to evacuate. Among poor people, women with children under three are inclining towards evacuation, but do not know how to set about it. Those with older children are inclined to stay, for two reasons – the existence of deep shelters in London, and memories of the unhappy times they had when previously evacuated.

FIRE-WATCHERS: Fire-watchers are bitter in their complaints. They point out that the bombs do not cause fires but do kill people in exposed positions. They therefore feel that fire-watching is both useless and dangerous, and that they are simply losing more sleep than the rest of the population. Some revision of the scheme is felt to be urgently needed. A late report states that the relaxation of the regulations 'has given a certain amount of relief'.

UNDER-RIVER TRAFFIC: The cessation of underground traffic beneath the Thames during alerts is the cause of some irritation; it is thought not to be necessary, as the penetrating power of the flying bombs is considered relatively slight.

NEWS PRESENTATION: Feelings are divided. Some would like to see more news of London's ordeal in print; others regard the censorship as a wise move.

Servicemen's relatives are wondering how they are getting on for accurate news and are hoping they are not being kept in the dark.

THE SOUTH-EAST: People in the South-East had specially expected retaliation, though not in the form it has taken. Their main problem is sleeplessness, due to the noise of the bombs passing overhead and guns in action. The work of the fighters is much appreciated. Earlier statements about the relatively slow speed of the bombs were treated with incredulity. On the whole, people in the South-East appear considerably less shaken than Londoners.

THE REST OF THE COUNTRY: Apart from the general points mentioned above, the main reactions are as follows:

THE RANGE OF THE BOMB: In Scotland and the North people feel safe. In Wales and the Midlands, people wonder if its range can be increased. In the Midlands, it is asked if there is any truth in the German story that it got as far as Daventry.

GENERAL STATE OF FEELINGS is to some extent determined by views on the range. In the Eastern and South-Western Regions and Wales, an uncomfortable feeling is said to be pretty general. Many in the Midland Region were inclined to wash their hands of the thing, when they heard about the line from the Wash to the Bristol Channel. Further north, there has been much sympathy for Londoners and considerable anxiety over relatives and friends in the South.

BIG BEN: The substitution of gramophone records for the original chimes has led to a number of rumours that the clock has been damaged by a flying bomb.

ADMIRATION FOR THE WEAPON: There have been isolated examples, both in London and elsewhere, of admiration for German inventiveness.

3. THE INVASION OF FRANCE

There is great satisfaction at the Allied progress so far, but a fairly general realisation that there may be big battles ahead. Few expect any spectacular developments at this early stage.

Praise for all concerned, particularly for General Montgomery, is widespread and unbounded. The planning and organisation, and the co-operation of the different Services and Allies, are the subject of special admiration. The public's opinion of the Americans has gone up and there are said to be many admiring references to their 'fighting spirit and success' in the Cherbourg peninsula.

Comment on the operations is not detailed. Attention is now mainly on the fight for Cherbourg, which people expect will soon be taken.

The Channel Isles continue the cause of much speculation, and there are rumours that paratroops landed there and were wiped out to a man. Alternatively, some people ask why we have not tried to capture the islands.

The situation round Caen had also caused uneasiness earlier in the week. Some people believe we intended to capture Caen as an early objective and that here, too, paratroops were landed only to be wiped out.

CASUALTIES: Relatives' anxiety about casualties remains very strong, though there was great relief that they were fewer during the first assault than had been expected. Some treated this news with reserve, however, and rumours of heavy casualties persist. There is, too, a feeling that statements have been contradictory. People ask why details of US casualties were given, while British losses are withheld; it is hoped that some announcement will soon be made.

There is much appreciation for the care that is being taken of the wounded, particularly the organisation of air transport, though one report mentions surprise at a rumour that both killed and wounded are being conveyed home in the same ship. A few, too, are resentful that 'German wounded – even the arrogant ones – are treated just like our own men'.

Dissatisfaction continues at the thought that relatives may not be able to visit the wounded if the hospitals are in banned areas.

The postal services continue to be appreciated.

THE PEOPLE OF NORMANDY: Great surprise is felt that they are so well fed and clothed; it had generally been assumed that everyone in countries overrun by the Nazis was starving and in rags ... 'Has our Government fooled us with stories of short rations in Europe?'

The attitude of the French to their deliverers is also the cause of considerable surprise, suspicion or resentment. 100% co-operation had been expected, and the news of sullen reception in some places and of girl snipers has astonished people and stirred up anti-French feeling. Some people are afraid that fifth columnists will once more be active.

An article in the *Sunday Pictorial* (June 18) by Rex North has caused some concern as it is feared it will have made the general public less sympathetic to the French than ever.

There are rumours of evacuees from Normandy expected at any moment. Some Londoners resent the idea of their 'coming here and eating our food'.

WOMEN SNIPERS: There is surprise, considerable interest, and some difference of opinion as to how they should be treated. The majority view, however, is 'Shoot them on sight.' People ask why we brought back Myra alive, silk stockings and all. If the Russians had captured her, 'her fate would have been sealed – What a soft-hearted lot we are!'

VISITS TO THE BEACHES: The fact that HM the King and the Prime Minister visited the beaches is taken to show how strong our hold is, though some people's blood ran cold at the thought of Mr. Churchill and Generals Eisenhower and Smuts all being in one spot where a single German bomb could have finished them all off together. There is great admiration for Mr. Churchill's spirit and for his determination to see everything for himself, and it is thought that his visit must have been a great tonic for the troops and also for their relatives here. Captain Cunningham Reid's solicitude is resented and Mr. Bracken's reply thought excellent.

Nevertheless, a minority fear the Prime Minister takes too many risks; and some object on the grounds that the generals in the field and other service personnel should not be employed in conducting tours of the beaches – 'Monty has something better to do than show people round France'. Another minority consider that General de Gaulle should have accompanied Mr. Churchill, rather than General Smuts, whose comments on France in a recent speech are remembered.

NEWS PRESENTATION: Approval continues almost unanimous, and reactions generally do not differ from those reported last week. The only new points are:

(a) Some of the recordings by BBC observers in the nightly war reports are hard to hear.

(b) Eye-witness accounts sometimes conflict with press and BBC announcements, e.g. Robert Barr on the West Wall; Roger Greene, AP, on the reaction of the French population.

(c) The attention given to the US army in the newsreel of the invasion; in Falkirk, during the showing of the film, cinema patrons are said to have called out: 'Where is the British army?'

STALIN'S tribute to the Allied invasion has been greatly appreciated.

3A. THE NEXT MOVE

Further landings are generally expected in due course.

4. GENERAL DE GAULLE AND THE FRENCH NATIONAL COMMITTEE

Comment has increased but is mostly on familiar lines. There is considerable uneasiness at the present situation, and people are unable to understand what is wrong.

Many are very concerned that if things are left as they are, our men's lives may be sacrificed for political reasons. They feel we cannot wage war in France unless we have the confidence of the French people; it is thought we should explain to the French the reasons for our attitude in order not to antagonise them, both now and in the long run.

The majority feel that General de Gaulle stood by us 'in the darkest days' and embodies the spirit of the Fighting French, that the French National Committee should be fully recognised – at least until elections can be held, that the USA stands in the way of agreement and that we are weak in giving way to them. Various sinister motives are suggested by a few to account for the present situation.

A minority, however, have considerable reserve about recognising General de Gaulle and the Committee, believing the former to be ambitious and dictatorial and the latter unrepresentative.

On the whole, people were pleased that General de Gaulle visited France; they noted with interest the enthusiasm with which he was received in Bayeux.

5. ITALY

Although still overshadowed by events in Normandy, progress in Italy is followed with great pleasure. High praise for General Alexander and the troops, and pleasure at the freeing of Rome, continue. The news of the landing of the Fighting French in

Elba is welcomed. People feel we are getting somewhere at last and hope Italy will soon be cleared of the enemy.

POLITICAL: Pleasure at the retirement of King Victor Emmanuel and Badoglio continues, and people hope the political situation will soon be cleared up. Some are inquiring about the 'trend towards communism in Italy'.

6. RUSSIA

Satisfaction with Russian successes against Finland is qualified to some extent by surprise that her offensive did not take place further south; it had been expected 'to link up more closely with our invasion'. A further attack somewhere else is, however, expected – in some cases impatiently.

Little or no sympathy is said now to exist for the Finns. Their early capitulation is expected.

7. FAR EAST

THE BOMBING OF JAPAN has given satisfaction. People are pleased that 'a new phase of the Far Eastern war has begun'.

ADVANCES IN THE MARIANA ISLANDS have also been greeted with pleasure.

Interest otherwise remains limited and comment is on familiar lines.

8. TURKEY

Her action in allowing enemy ships through the Dardanelles has given rise to strong resentment and suspicion. It is thought that after the way she has been favoured by our Government, she is not playing the game; some hold she would just as soon link up with Germany. There are a few satisfied comments that we have taken a firm line; it is hoped that now the Turkish foreign minister has resigned, her policy may alter.

9. PARLIAMENTARY DEBATE ON REGULATION 18B

Very little comment or interest. However, Mr. Morrison's firmness is approved, though opinion is divided as to the merits of the regulation.

10. BROADCASTING AND PRESENTATION OF NEWS

(See also: Invasion of France and Pilotless Aircraft.)

There is little general comment this week. It is thought there is too much publicising of the American contribution to the Allied cause and not enough of the Russian, Chinese and our own efforts.

PROGRAMMES: There are thought to be too many dance bands and too much crooning. Opinion is divided over the General Forces programme; some say it has improved lately.

II. SPECIAL COMMENTS

FULL MONTHLY REVIEW

11. POST-WAR

During the past four weeks great and widespread discussion have been reported, though it is said in some cases to have been less detailed and more vague than previously. There are some who still think the war should be won before planning begins; others have had their interest 'pushed into the background' by the invasion news.

Doubt and trepidation about post-war prospects, and cynicism about the implementation of the various White Papers, continue. The Government is variously accused of slowness, vagueness, and making promises which are beyond either its intentions or its powers. Some are tired of 'proposals', which are thought to be 'mere talk', and want the schemes passed into law, so that they cannot easily be repudiated in the future.

A small minority accept the Government's plans as signs of 'serious preparation'.

'PAYING FOR THE SCHEMES' is discussed on a reduced scale. Some, particularly those with money, doubt whether it will be possible to defray the cost, though a few of these people fear it will be done at their expense. Some workers, on the other hand, want 'the whole thing at any cost'. It is suggested that an outline of how it is proposed to finance the plans should be made public; or, on the other hand, 'if we are to be very poor', schemes should not be 'dangled before our eyes'.

As regards specific subjects of discussion, housing and employment are people's main preoccupations, dwarfing all other subjects.

Comment has been on the following lines:

(a) HOUSING: It is the dominant interest and worry of many and is discussed by all sections of the population. Particular anxiety is felt about the prospects of people with children, and demobilised servicemen and women.

The Government is criticised for slowness – 'so much is said, so little done'. Some think plans should come into operation immediately; local authorities are said to await a lead on the financial aspects of planning, and builders on the Government's long-term policy. Women want to be consulted more about plans.

RURAL HOUSING is much discussed by country people and others. The need for improvements on present 'lamentable' conditions is frequently stressed, and some fear that all thought and effort will be concentrated on the urban aspect of the housing problem.

Country people stress first and foremost the need for an adequate water supply; though electricity, modern sanitation and gas are also hoped for.

(For 'Prefabricated houses' see Section 13.)

(b) EMPLOYMENT: Discussion is second to that on housing, and among many workers, particularly in the industrial areas of Wales and the north, the desire for a guarantee of work overshadows everything. A post-war slump, especially in heavy industries, is feared and expected. (Building is excepted.) It is asked what work there will be for demobilised and disabled Service people, and for transferred workers, on their return home. People want a plan which will assure them that there will be no more depression or distressed areas.

THE GOVERNMENT WHITE PAPER ON EMPLOYMENT POLICY (dealt with in our Reports of 2nd and 8th June) still arouses little interest. Few people know anything about it, and more exposition is asked for. Opinion is now about equally divided between those who find it reassuring and those who either have little faith in the plans proposed or in their being carried out.

EMIGRATION as a solution to the employment problem continues to appeal to some, particularly young people.

(c) TOWN PLANNING AND LAND DEVELOPMENT: Interest is reported, especially in town planning and the plans published for the rebuilding of specific towns. Discussion of the Scott, Barlow and Uthwatt Reports continues, and people hope for Government control in order to avoid jerry-building.

(d) THE BEVERIDGE PLAN AND SOCIAL SECURITY: Desire for the implementation of the Beveridge Plan, coupled with scepticism, continues.

(e) GOVERNMENT CONTROLS: It seems generally to be realised that controls will have to remain, both as they affect industry and the individual, but it is nevertheless hoped they will be removed as early as possible. 'People want to co-operate rather than be ordered by officials.' Employers want many present controls discarded 'to give private enterprise a chance', and, in the case of the Essential Work Order, so that they can get rid of redundant workers.

(f) AGRICULTURE: Anxiety among both farmers and laymen, and fears of 'another slump', continue.

(g) TRADE AND COMMERCE: There continue to be fears that we shall not regain our export markets and, to a lesser extent, concern about the re-establishment of peacetime industry.

(h) SMALL TRADERS V. COMBINES: Concern is reported lest small businesses are unable to get started again after the war, through being squeezed out by large combines. A few feel that the latter are powerful enough to be able to suggest controls which suit their own interests but hit smaller businesses.

(i) LOCATION OF INDUSTRY: Interest in this subject comes largely from former depressed areas in Wales and the Northern Region, where great importance is attached to new light industries being established locally. People in the south-east view with concern the prospect of a further drift of industry to the south.

11A. EDUCATION BILL

DURING THE PAST FOUR WEEKS pleasure at the passing of the Bill has continued, though interest is said to be limited, and there is some fear that the Bill may be impracticable for some years.

Discussion is chiefly of:

(a) THE SUPPLY OF TEACHERS: Some fear the shortage will prove the chief stumbling block to making the Bill effective. Conditions generally, and especially low salaries and large classes, are thought to militate against recruitment, and a number, including some teachers, believe the question of supply will not be solved until improvements are effected. A few criticise the quality of present teachers, think more specialisation is wanted, and fear the emergency training scheme may lower standards.

(b) RAISING THE SCHOOL-LEAVING AGE: Some, including elementary school teachers, think the children will not benefit unless the curriculum is adapted, the need to introduce more 'practical' work being emphasised. Some workers and farmers continue to disapprove of the change because it postpones the time when their children start earning money.

(c) SCHOOL BUILDINGS: These are felt to be quite inadequate and to be a further impediment to implementing the Bill.

(d) RURAL SCHOOLS: Country women want less disparity between conditions in country and urban schools. They resent, for instance, 'one teacher, in one room, being responsible for 24 children aged 5–14 years'.

12. HOUSING AND ACCOMMODATION

DURING THE PAST FOUR WEEKS, although complaints about the housing position have continued widespread, they appear less violent than last month.

Criticism has again been chiefly of:

(a) SHORTAGE OF ALL TYPES OF ACCOMMODATION: People's resentment is increased by the belief that the situation could be eased if all the available accommodation were used. It is thought that many houses are permanently shut up, the owners living elsewhere; that there is plenty of unused room in many large houses; that rooms over empty shops, which could easily be made habitable, are left unoccupied; that some people are still allowed to keep weekend cottages; and that houses requisitioned by the War Office are now empty. People think local authorities should see that such accommodation is used.

Those particularly hard hit are (i) families with children; (ii) young married couples, who 'have never had a chance to live a married life under decent conditions' or who have to live with parents; (iii) war workers, some of whom are said to travel up to three hours a day because of shortage of accommodation near their place of work; (iv) discharged soldiers.

(b) HIGH PRICES AND RENTS: Resentment continues. Especially outrageous are thought the prices of houses for sale, particularly those with vacant possession; rent of furnished accommodation generally; lodgings.

Some continue to urge price control; others 'daren't complain for fear of being turned out'; others, again, are 'so desperate they will pay anything'.

(c) REPAIR DIFFICULTIES AND DELAYS: Some feel the position would be eased if repairing and reconditioning, particularly of blitzed properties, were speeded up. There are also complaints that local authorities are 'stymied' by the long delays of Government departments in answering queries about reconditioning empty premises, and by the apparent inability of various departments to work together.

AGRICULTURAL COTTAGES: There are some complaints of delays in building these cottages, and it is also felt that the rents are too high for agricultural workers ... 'If the Government is going to charge a big rent, it is not much good raising farm wages.' There are complaints from one county that 'one in every four' of the cottages is being reserved by members of the WAECs.

BILLETING: This is said still to be a problem in some areas; some have been upset to find they have to give up a room they have kept for their son or daughter in the Forces when on leave.

13. PREFABRICATED HOUSES

DURING THE PAST FOUR WEEKS, widespread and detailed interest in THE PORTAL HOUSE has continued, and there are many requests for specimens to be on show in all parts of the country, and for a chance to see over the house; Londoners complain they cannot get tickets. The erection of a house in Edinburgh has aroused great interest there.

CRITICISM is more widespread and much more detailed than approval. It is objected that:

(a) THE CEILINGS ARE TOO LOW ... 'Even factory roofs have to be 9 ft. 6 ins.'

(b) THE HOUSE WILL BE HOT IN SUMMER AND COLD IN WINTER; AND UNSUITABLE TO THE CLIMATE, PARTICULARLY IN THE NORTH.

(c) IT IS NOT SUCH AS TO ENCOURAGE PEOPLE TO HAVE CHILDREN, mainly because it is so small, but also because it is 'flimsy'.

(d) IT IS TOO EXPENSIVE, especially in view of its size and short life. At the same time, some are confused about the cost, not knowing how inclusive it is, or whether the houses will be rented or not.

(e) THERE IS NO BACK DOOR.

(f) IT IS UNATTRACTIVE TO LOOK AT – 'a glorified shed'. Some think this may prove detrimental to the value of surrounding property.

(g) THE HOUSE AS A WHOLE IS TOO SMALL, AND ALSO THE INDIVIDUAL ROOMS; the kitchen is particularly mentioned – 'all right for working and eating, but no good for living in'.

(h) WASHING FACILITIES ARE INADEQUATE.

(i) THE LAYOUT COULD BE IMPROVED: People do not like the bedrooms leading out of the other rooms, or the lavatory being opposite the front door.

APPROVAL: Despite the criticism, many approve the house and an even greater number accept the scheme 'as a temporary measure' because 'it would at least be a place of our own' and 'better than lodgings'. Many are, however, apprehensive lest the houses be allowed to remain permanently and degenerate into 'slums'. Women particularly like the kitchen, with its labour-saving devices; the fittings, especially the built-in wardrobes; and the sound-proof walls.

The only reference to the fact that alterations are to be made is a suggestion that this should be given more publicity.

THE TARRAN HOUSE: Some prefer this type of house, because of the back door and the fact that it has two storeys.

14. INDUSTRY

The invasion has acted as an incentive to industrial workers, who are now 'going to it'. 'Now real fighting has started, very few will seriously consider striking.'

Nevertheless, DURING THE PAST FOUR WEEKS comment has again been about:

REDUCED PRODUCTION 'at a time when an all-out effort is asked for'. Tales continue of:

(a) Workers in factories – aircraft factories particularly – and in shipyards with little or nothing to do.

(b) Reduction or stoppage of overtime.

(c) Workers being paid off. This is felt to be a bad sign for post-war industry – workers on Clydeside and Tyneside are particularly anxious and 'greet with derision statements that there will not be a recurrence of mass unemployment'. Rumours are also reported of forthcoming wholesale discharges in large works in the North Midland Region and in a Wearside shipyard.

(d) Production being at saturation point, e.g. the finishing of war contracts, demand for production slacking-off, war factories no longer busy.

(e) Unemployment. Both ex-servicemen and redundant workers are said to be on the dole.

TRANSFER OF LABOUR: Apart from the fact that 'finding digs away from home is not a pleasurable matter now', there are allegations of:

(a) Local people transferred from certain works while workers from other districts are being directed to these works.

(b) People directed to factories where there is little to do, although in some cases 'firms near to their homes are in urgent need of staff'.

(c) People transferred to work where their wages are lower than at their previous work. Young girls, particularly, 'find it difficult to manage on their pay'.

(d) Men who have been directed into various industries because of the slackness in their own, not being allowed to go back to their own trade when it revives.

TIREDNESS AND ILL-HEALTH: Some workers still complain of long hours. Women workers with household responsibilities, particularly those with children, are suffering from the strain. Reduced hours or reduced overtime have for this reason been welcomed in two specified factories: 'Some consternation was caused by smaller pay packets, but workers appreciate the extra leisure.'

On Teesside there was 'dissatisfaction over the fines imposed on welders (who suffer badly through constant breathing of fumes) for being a few minutes late each morning while nothing is said to foremen or managers who are late'.

SLACKING OF WORKERS AND ABSENTEEISM: Young girls and lads are felt to be the chief culprits.

REGULATION 1AA: Talk is dying down. Opinion remains divided between the general public, who accept it as a necessary evil, and many workers, shop stewards and left-wingers who oppose 'this piece of British fascism'.

There is some criticism among workers of the TUC for its action in the matter.

STRIKES, which continue to be strongly condemned.

SHORTAGE OF LABOUR, particularly in the cotton trade.

14A. MANPOWER

DURING THE PAST FOUR WEEKS comment has decreased, but allegations continue of:

(a) Evasion of call-up by young women and able-bodied young men. Workers doing long hours and older men and women on war work are particularly resentful.

(b) Unsympathetic treatment by Ministry of Labour interviewing officials. One mother, called up for an interview about part-time work, with 7 children at home, including twins of 5 weeks old, is said to have been asked, 'Well, what do you do in your spare time?'

(c) Delay in call-up.

14B. DOMESTIC HELP

DURING THE PAST FOUR WEEKS complaints of hardship due to shortage of domestic help have continued, but latterly on a reduced scale. Those chiefly affected are:

(a) Old people.
(b) Mothers with young families.
(c) Expectant and nursing mothers.
(d) Sick people and invalids.
(e) Hospitals and maternity homes.

There is again criticism that available help is not fairly shared ... 'One household of three adults, with eight indoor servants and three gardeners, who, furthermore, refused to billet officers'.

15. MINERS AND MINING

Miners – those in the Forest of Dean possibly excepted – are now said to be 'whole-heartedly behind the lads in the army'. An increase in output in important mining areas in Wales is reported; some pits have for the first time reached their target.

DURING THE PAST FOUR WEEKS comment has been about:

THE PIT BALLOT SCHEME: People generally continue to criticise the scheme, and the youths concerned continue to dislike it. There is particularly strong feeling against the direction of pre-Service-trained boys to the mines. This is considered uneconomic, very hard on the boys 'who are eager to fight', and unlikely to produce good miners as 'their hearts aren't in it'. Much sympathy is still felt with those who refuse to go to the pits, and there is indignation at recent court cases.

The view persists that it would be better to recall all ex-miners from the Forces and industry.

ACCOMMODATION FOR THE BEVIN BOYS: It is believed that in some cases landladies exploit the boys, but landladies also complain of their difficulties. In Rotherham, for instance, people are pleased that huts are being built for the boys as 'they do not like billeting them in their homes'.

In the Northern Region there is 'much resentment at hostels for the Bevin boys because they are so elaborately and extravagantly fitted out. They are said to cost £50,000 to £100,000, and miners and their wives contrast them with their own miserable hovels, and say "If they can build for the lads, why can't they do something for us?"'

STRIKES: Condemnation continues, even where it is felt that miners have a grievance. There is particular resentment against miners in Scotland because of alleged incidents such as the following: a colliery bus broke down near East Linton, five minutes from the pits; the miners would not get out but waited until repairs were effected.

THE MORE SETTLED STATE OF THE MINING INDUSTRY is again referred to with satisfaction.

WAGES: Discussion is dying down about the four years' wage plan, but there is some dissatisfaction at its interpretation. Some miners consider their earnings of £5 or £6 a week are only a fraction of what they should be receiving under the agreement. On the other hand, pleasure at wages, and at advances for pieceworkers, is also reported.

15A. DOMESTIC FUEL

DURING THE PAST FOUR WEEKS comment has been mainly about:

(a) THE DIFFICULTY OF OBTAINING COAL SUPPLIES, both for use now and for laying in supplies for next winter. Households with no alternative fuel are particularly worried. People ask, 'what is the use of urging us to stock up now for winter if we don't get enough to do us now?' Bad distribution and irregular or delayed delivery are considered chiefly responsible, but the small allocation is also blamed. There is particular annoyance with 'the absurd announcement' that the maximum allowance for the north would be 15 cwt 'when the authorities must have known that the retailers would scarcely have enough coal to give their customers 10 cwt'. In Barrow, householders have so far only had 3 cwt for April and 3 cwt for May.

(b) POOR-QUALITY COAL.

(c) THE OTLEY CASE, where a householder was fined for borrowing coal: 'In times of acute shortage borrowing and lending in the interests of children or invalids should be encouraged as Christian charity, and not penalised.'

16. WAGES

DURING THE PAST FOUR WEEKS, comment has continued about:

DISPARITY OF PAY between:

(a) Our servicemen and (i) industrial workers, (ii) US, Dominion and Colonial troops.

(b) Black-coated workers and munition workers.

(c) Skilled men in their regular trade and unskilled and semi-skilled workers in war industries.

HIGH WAGES paid to young people, and to unskilled men and women in industry.

LOW WAGES paid to non-industrial workers, such as shop assistants, waitresses and nurses, all of whose wages are said not to have risen with the cost of living; also agricultural workers and foresters, colliery clerks, workers in the building trade and in basic industries, and girls and women in factories. Some of the latter say that 'with fares, meals out and income tax it is not worth working'.

16A. PAYE

DURING THE PAST FOUR WEEKS approval for the scheme in general has continued. There have, however, been references to workers being puzzled, and in particular failing to understand why the deductions should vary on a wage that is the same each week.

There are also a few complaints from people who think they are paying more tax under the new scheme than they did before. It is also alleged that holiday pay is taxed as unearned income.

It is thought there is a need for more explanation and that tax tables should be more accessible, though the official booklet is appreciated.

Some workers, both agricultural and industrial, are said to watch their earnings and decline to do Saturday work or overtime in order to keep the income tax down. They resent having overtime taxed and believe that the rate is 10/- in the £. Agricultural workers are said in some cases to work in private gardens in the evening for payment from which tax is not deducted, instead of doing overtime at useful agricultural work.

National Savings are said to be affected in some works by PAYE. Workers regard their income tax deductions as their share of the war effort and no longer put money into savings.

17. CLOTHING

DURING THE PAST FOUR WEEKS complaints about insufficient coupons have continued at the increased volume reported last month. There appears, however, to have been a slight decline in complaints about footwear difficulties, while about other aspects of the clothing situation complaints appear to be much fewer than they were a month ago.

Detailed comment has been reported about:

INSUFFICIENT COUPONS for:

(a) GENERAL CLOTHING REPLACEMENTS: Complaints continue on the same lines as last month, and there are the familiar references to the sad plight of people with clothing worn to shreds after nearly five years of war and without either reserves to fall back on or coupons to buy more. Some people are said to be very bitter. Men are said to be particularly hard hit, as a suit uses up an allocation; so, too, are the lower-paid workers who cannot afford the best quality.

Some concern is reported over alleged trafficking in coupons. In Scotland, the scarcity is such that the price is now said to have reached 1/9 apiece.

There is great keenness to know how many coupons there will be in the next allocation; some hope for and expect an increase, and it is suggested that if people knew more about the next allowance, they could plan better.

(b) HOUSEHOLD REPLACEMENTS: Many and familiar complaints of household textiles worn and torn, and of lack of coupons for replacements. The provision of towels is said to be the greatest difficulty. Some parents say they are already sacrificing their coupons for their children and cannot spare any for household goods. Householders feel they are unfairly treated as compared with women who have not got homes to keep going, and newlyweds are thought to need a special allocation of coupons. The wish for special household coupons persists.

(c) CHILDREN.

(d) WORKERS.

FOOTWEAR:

    (a) POOR QUALITY:

        (i) CHILDREN'S: It is said to be especially difficult to keep children shod, particularly country children who have to walk two or more miles to school. Mothers particularly resent having to pay such high prices and give up so many coupons for shoes which are, in many cases, unrepairable. Some people ask that they should be a lower coupon value or even coupon-free ... 'No mother in her senses is going to buy more than she needs when the kiddies grow out of them so quickly.'

       (ii) ADULTS'.

    (b) REPAIRS – particularly the time taken and the poor quality of leather used. Newcomers to a district are said to find difficulty in getting footwear accepted for repairs.

    (c) SHORTAGE.

HOUSEHOLD LINEN:

    (a) SHORTAGE – particularly of the utility kinds – made more acute by laundry delays and in households which have had lodgers for a long time. Pleasure is expressed that priority to buy linen is to be granted to holders of permits for utility furniture.

    (b) HIGH PRICE, particularly of non-utility ... 'Working-class women can't afford £3–£4 a pair for non-utility sheets.' In one area poor people are said to be sleeping under old coats and dirty carpet felts because they cannot afford the expensive sheets and blankets, and there are none available at controlled prices.

HIGH PRICES of clothing generally, with particular reference to hats ('Why no utility hats?') and shoes. Uncontrolled prices are said to be a serious problem to those whose incomes have not increased during the war.

POOR QUALITY of clothing, with particular reference to utility clothing, socks, stockings, corsets, brassieres and vests.

SHORTAGE AND POOR QUALITY OF ELASTIC: Some people think that such articles as suspenders and braces are now of such poor quality, it is a waste of labour and material making them.

LAUNDRIES AND DRY CLEANERS – chiefly delay or difficulty in getting things accepted. Also, a little uncertainty about the customer's due when the laundry loses things.

OUTSIZE GARMENTS, and the difficulty of obtaining them.

COUPONS FOR UNIFORMS: Complaints that Scout uniforms require coupons, that wardens have to give up so many coupons for their uniforms, and that 'full-time NFS personnel have to surrender a quota of coupons annually, whether they get replacements or not'.

17A. FURNITURE AND PERAMBULATORS

DURING THE PAST FOUR WEEKS there have been a few references to the high price and scarcity of new and second-hand furniture, and approval for the price of the latter being controlled.

There are some complaints of the small number of units allowed for utility furniture. It is thought, too, that families whose numbers are increasing should get utility furniture permits.

PERAMBULATORS: Shortage, poor quality and high price. It is alleged that utility prams do not stand up to country roads.

18. TRANSPORT

DURING THE PAST FOUR WEEKS, in addition to comment on train cancellations, complaints have been on familiar lines. There was some surprise, however, that the invasion caused so little disruption of transport services.

Comment has been of:

(a) INADEQUATE BUS SERVICES, particularly in rural areas.
(b) THE CROWDING OUT OF WORKERS by (i) shoppers at rush hours; (ii) holiday-makers; (iii) schoolchildren.
(c) LACK OF LATE EVENING SERVICES, particularly during the light nights. It is suggested that later buses would help holidays at home.
(d) RUDENESS OF BUS EMPLOYEES.
(e) QUEUES.
(f) NEED FOR BETTER SUPPLIES OF CYCLE PARTS since cyclists help to relieve the strain on transport.
(g) LACK OF SUNDAY BUSES – particularly for churchgoers.
(h) WORKERS' BUSES NOT PICKING UP PASSENGERS when they have room.
(i) ROAD DEATHS: Excessive speed and careless driving – especially by the military – are thought responsible.
(j) MEMBERS OF THE GOVERNMENT TOURING THE COUNTRY IN SPECIAL TRAINS.

HOLIDAY TRANSPORT has been the subject of considerable speculation. Some are reconciled to doing without holidays away from home, but others think they are entitled to them and in some cases mean to take them. A definite lead from the Government continues to be asked for.

18A. PETROL

DURING THE PAST FOUR WEEKS complaints have continued on familiar lines as follows:

(a) PETROL WASTED ON 'JOY RIDING', including trips to cinemas, dances and races. Allocation of petrol for race meetings is thought absurd.
(b) UNECONOMIC USE OF PETROL by Civil Defence, army, Home Guard and farmers.
(c) CARS BEING USED when buses are available.
(d) UNFAIR DISTRIBUTION: It is complained that while some waste it, others find it difficult to get for legitimate needs.

19. FOOD

DURING THE PAST FOUR WEEKS satisfaction with the food situation has continued widespread and there has been praise for the Ministry of Food. The smooth working of the ration book distribution has also been the subject of much satisfaction.

Comment has been of:

(a) THE CHEESE RATION: Earlier there were complaints of the inadequacy of the ration – particularly from agricultural workers. The prospect of an increase has given pleasure, however, though some think three ounces would still be too small.
(b) FISH: Complaints of shortage are fewer and some pleasure at increased supplies has been reported. Some country districts still feel they do not fare as well as towns; and hotels and restaurants are thought to have preferential treatment.
(c) MILK: The prospect of a milk cut is causing some disappointment, particularly as prior to the announcement of the impending cut, there had been pleasure at the extra milk received and at the prospect that rationing might be done away with. There is some criticism of the Ministry of Food for its alleged inconsistency. A few, however, think the cut may be caused by milk going to the hospitals or to the Forces.
(d) MEAT: Complaints continue of (i) too much pork; it is said that children, old people and invalids cannot eat it; (ii) the poor quality and toughness of meat.
(e) FRUIT: The longing for fruit, and regret at the damage to the fruit crop, continue. There is pleasure at the prospect of more fruit being imported.
    It is hoped jam manufacturers will not get all the soft fruit crop.
(f) THE HIGH PRICE OF GREEN VEGETABLES AND SALADS – 'rampant profiteering'. Shortage is also referred to in reports from four Regions.
(g) JAM: The promise of extra sugar for jam continues to be welcomed, as does the promise that the quality of the jam will be improved – 'it can do with improvement'.
    There continues to be some confusion over the sugar or jam scheme.
(h) DRIED FRUIT: The shortage – particularly of prunes – continues to be complained of. Some are pleased with recent supplies, however, and particularly with the promise of more.

(i) TOMATOES: People are grumbling at the difficulty in obtaining them and are wondering whether more will be made available. It is hoped they will be distributed more equitably this season.

(j) POOR DISTRIBUTION of off-the-ration goods. Country districts, and towns with large influxes of visitors for shopping or holidays, are thought to do very badly compared with other places.

(k) RECENT SUPPLIES OF 'OFF-THE-RATION' HAM AND BACON: Pleasure continues.

(l) MONOTONY OF DIET.

(m) INADEQUACY OF RATIONS FOR HEAVY WORKERS – particularly agricultural workers.

(n) BEER SHORTAGE: In the South-West, however, supplies are thought to have improved since the invasion.

(o) DIFFICULTIES OF SMALL FAMILIES AND PEOPLE LIVING ALONE.

20. SHOPPING DIFFICULTIES

DURING THE PAST FOUR WEEKS complaints have continued on familiar lines. Comment has been chiefly of:

(a) PREFERENTIAL TREATMENT AND UNDER-THE-COUNTER SALES, particularly fruit and tomatoes. People growing their own vegetables are becoming anxious that they will find difficulty in buying fruit again this year.

(b) SHOPPING DIFFICULTIES OF WORKERS, largely as a result of lunch-time and early evening closing. Women complain of being unable to get off-the-ration goods and extras. There are also complaints of the difficulty in buying shoes when shops impose a quota system.

(c) QUEUES, chiefly for cakes, fish, and tomatoes. Some think goods in short supply should be rationed, to give everybody a fair chance.

21. SERVICE ALLOWANCES, PENSIONS AND PAY

DURING THE PAST FOUR WEEKS very little pleasure at the recent INCREASES IN PAY AND ALLOWANCES has been reported. There has been increased adverse criticism, as well as considerable confusion and disillusionment from dependants who are bewildered to find themselves 'pretty much where we were'.

COMPLAINTS ARE CHIEFLY THAT:

(a) The increases in both pay and allowances are meagre and inadequate, especially in view of the wages earned by many civilians.

(b) It is unjust for dependants to suffer financially because a man is killed.

(c) The Government promised extra pay for wives of servicemen and then 'deducted from the men's pay'.

(d) The increase is nullified where it is offset by a corresponding reduction in the war service grant.

(e) Wives and widows are liable for income tax.
(f) Childless wives do not get the same increase as those with children.
(g) The disparity between the pay of our men and that of Dominion and Allied troops continues.
(h) Servicemen will be discouraged from trying for promotion.

RAF: There are complaints that very few wives of RAF men will benefit from the increases, and some (without children) 'are from 1/9 to 7/- worse off'.

DURING THE PAST FOUR WEEKS there has been little comment about SERVICEMEN'S PENSIONS. People are, however, anxious that disabled men should have 'decent' pensions – 'we can find millions a day to run this war and ought to be able to find it for the lads when they come back'. It is felt Pensions Tribunals are sometimes unfair and that 'fit for service, fit for pensions' should be the principle acted upon by the Ministry of Pensions.

22. PENSIONS (OTHER THAN SERVICE)

OLD AGE PENSIONS: DURING THE PAST FOUR WEEKS comment has declined. However, complaint continues of the inadequacy of old age pensions, particularly the basic rate; a few believe old age pensioners cannot afford to get enough to eat.

Both old age pensioners themselves and other people think there should be an adjustment to meet the present cost of living.

More sympathetic consideration of claims is suggested; and there is some resentment that when an old age pensioner works his pension is taxable.

PENSIONS GENERALLY: News of wages and salaries being increased 'all round' is said to make 'bitter reading' for elderly people 'struggling' to live on pre-war pensions; and there is resentment, also, at the taxing of pensions.

23. HEALTH

DURING THE PAST FOUR WEEKS complaints of war-weariness, tiredness, strain and general debility have continued, though the volume has appreciably declined since the invasion of France.

Causes mentioned are:

(a) LONG HOURS AND CONTINUOUS OVER-WORK OVER A LONG PERIOD: Particular reference is made to the effect on elderly workers and women with household responsibilities.
(b) WARTIME DIET.
(c) GENERAL STATE OF HEALTH: While some feel that the nation's health is fairly satisfactory, it is 'thought absurd to say that health has never been so good'. People find it particularly difficult to throw off illness.

SHORTAGE OF HOSPITAL ACCOMMODATION FOR MATERNITY CASES: This again causes anxiety and deep concern.

SHORTAGE OF DOCTORS: It is thought that consequent over-work is lowering the efficiency of doctors.

24. WHITE PAPER ON A NATIONAL HEALTH SERVICE

DURING THE PAST FOUR WEEKS comment has again been limited. Approval in general continues, as does resentment at the doctors' opposition to it. People would like to know if pride and prejudice are their real motives, or if they have a genuine complaint. People hope that hospital and medical services will be fully and equally available to all.

VOLUNTARY HOSPITALS: Opinion is divided on their future. Some hope they will retain their individuality. Others are against them and think that doctors and specialists have a vested interest in them.

25. CIVIL DEFENCE, FIRE GUARD AND HOME GUARD

DURING THE PAST FOUR WEEKS reported comment has again consisted mainly of grumbles about duties and parades, variously regarded as tiring, excessive or completely unnecessary.

CIVIL DEFENCE AND FIRE-GUARD DUTIES are both the subject of complaint on the grounds that they are a waste of time, money, manpower and energy. This feeling is particularly reported in Scotland and the Northern, North-Eastern and North-Western Regions, where heavy raids are thought by many to be a thing of the past. Apathy and, in some cases, irritation are reported in consequence. Some people, particularly in the Northern Region, feel that relaxation of duty might be made in less vulnerable areas and take particular exception to daylight fire-watching.

Other complaints are of: (i) people evading or refusing to do duty; (ii) waste of money and material in providing chevrons, badges and clothing; (iii) anomalies in the hours and conditions of duty; (iv) Fire Guards being compelled to attend lectures which turn out to be 'mere revision of a very simple procedure'.

The Home Secretary's circular about the position of members of local authorities in relation to the Civil Defence Services is said to have caused some annoyance.

HOME GUARD: Complaints of (i) unnecessary drills and parades, e.g. fully-trained men being paraded on Whit Sunday; (ii) farmers and allotment workers being too busy for HG duties during the summer months; (iii) the tiring effect of parades and duties on top of a day's work – elderly men are said to be unfit for work after a night on duty following a 10 or 11 hours' shift; (iv) parades ending too late for men to catch the last bus home, due in some cases to those in charge turning up late for parade.

The Home Guard had expected to be called on to take a more active part when invasion started; it is feared there will be much disappointment if their four years' work is completely wasted.

26. AGRICULTURE

DURING THE PAST FOUR WEEKS comment has been chiefly about:

LABOUR: Shortage of labour is causing anxiety. Farmers say they will need all the help they can get, and hope camps will be set up wherever possible; though, even with volunteer help, some fear they will not be able to cope with the coming harvest. Some agricultural workers feel they should be released from Home Guard duties and hope their officers will be very tolerant at harvest time. In the Northern Region, the loss of Italian prisoner-of-war labour is deplored.

Some interest is reported in the HOLIDAY HELP SCHEME, though a few workers feel too tired this year to take part, and they want a real holiday. In the North-Eastern Region 'war workers feel they are being frustrated in efforts to volunteer because some ROF centres and various officials take the view that workers cannot be released'. Farmers are said to appreciate the Help from Schools scheme.

DROUGHT AND FROST DAMAGE: Farmers and smallholders are concerned about the effect of the drought on all crops, but particularly the hay, and the consequent problem of feeding livestock in the coming winter. Anxiety about frost damage to potato and fruit crops is again reported, though in some areas the loss is believed to be less than was at first anticipated.

FOOD AND DRUGS (MILK AND DAIRIES) BILL: Though a few say it is time something was done, much resentment is reported at the bureaucratic methods proposed.

FOUR-YEAR PRICE GUARANTEE: Mr. Hudson's 'unexpected' announcement about the stabilisation of prices until the summer of 1948 has given considerable pleasure and is thought to have made farmers more contented.

FORMS AND PERMITS: Farmers again complain of continual form filling and plead for fewer forms and more simple wording of those which are essential.

WAGES: While some people feel that small farms cannot support the fixed wages, some workers are said to want an increase and to be growing dissatisfied with the attitude of the farmers. It is thought that men will not be attracted to farming as a career while the basic wage is only sixty-five shillings.

SEED POTATOES: Some complaints are reported about seed potatoes, many of which have had to be thrown away.

PESTS: A plague of rabbits and other farm pests is said to be adding to farmers' difficulties in the Southern and South-Western Regions.

27. GOVERNMENT WATER SCHEME

DURING THE PAST FOUR WEEKS difficulties caused by the drought have been constantly reported. The Government Water Scheme has aroused pleased interest, and people in rural areas look hopefully for improved supplies. The only fear expressed is that some local authorities will fail to take action without Government pressure.

28. SALVAGE

DURING THE PAST EIGHT WEEKS there have again been complaints of non-collection or careless collection of salvage, with consequent 'slumps' in enthusiasm for the salvage campaign. Some householders are uncertain whether tins are still required for salvage.

RAILINGS AND SCRAP METAL: Complaints are again made of metal lying about in dumps, often of long-standing, while railings are still being taken down. A case is given of a woman having to pay to get rid of some scrap metal, yet a month or so later her house railings were removed.

PAPER: People are thought to be getting careless about paper and cardboard, and there is also criticism of non-collection, and of paper wasted in advertisements and posters. In two Regions, book drives are said to create interest.

NO. 195: TUESDAY 20 JUNE 1944 TO TUESDAY 27 JUNE 1944

I. GENERAL COMMENTS

1. GENERAL

Confidence and spirits are high. Encouraged by successes on all fronts and by Mr. Churchill's 'unusual optimism' in his Mexican Embassy speech, people are beginning to be increasingly hopeful about the end of the war; many think it will certainly be over this year, possibly by the autumn.

The pilotless plane has introduced the one stern note, but – except in target areas – seems to have done little to damp spirits. There is anxiety for relatives and sympathy for sufferers, but no one thinks it will alter the course of the war. Londoners, however, are weary, strained and anxious.

Mr. Eden's statement on the shot prisoners has combined with 'the most beastly weapon of the war' to stimulate hatred of the Germans.

HOME FRONT: Grumbling is again at a minimum, but post-war conditions, housing and clothing coupons are still much discussed.

2. THE INVASION OF FRANCE

Great and widespread satisfaction continues, coupled with sober confidence in future developments – 'there is no exuberance, because five years of war have taught caution, but there is great hope'. People are prepared for tough fighting ahead and possible setbacks.

Unqualified praise for all concerned and for the feats of planning and organisation continues. There is complete confidence in the leaders, especially General Montgomery; and all the Services, both British and American, are a source of great pride and satisfaction – many prejudices against the Americans are said to have been cleared away.

Interest has been fixed largely on Cherbourg during this week, and its fall gave great pleasure. With proper port facilities, people feel we shall now be able to maintain progress, if not to accelerate it. A very small minority are impatient at the slow advance south of Tilly, though others are glad the British stand there has contributed to the fall of Cherbourg. There is a little anxiety on behalf of the troops because of the weather.

Anxiety about possible CASUALTIES continues, particularly among relatives, though there is great relief that they have so far been unexpectedly light – 'not like the last war'.

Before the publication of the figures of British casualties on June 28, people were asking why this had not been done.

THE ORGANISATION OF THE CARE OF THE WOUNDED wins great admiration and appreciation; a few ask for more details about arrangements for visiting relatives in military hospitals.

People are grateful for the good MAIL SERVICE to and from Normandy, though a few think press and radio have exaggerated its rapidity, thus raising false hopes.

A RUMOUR THAT GENERAL MONTGOMERY HAS BEEN SHOT BY A SNIPER comes from several districts of Scotland. Press and radio 'silence' about him during the past few days is said to have favoured the spread of the rumour.

WOMEN SNIPERS: Rumours of French women snipers continue widespread and cause angry comment. People think they should be shot.

There has, as yet, been no comment reported on the SHAEF denial of these rumours (June 26).

VISITS TO THE BEACHES OF THE KING AND PRIME MINISTER: Comment continues as last week.

THE PEOPLE OF NORMANDY: Reports in the press, and stories said to have been brought back by the wounded, have aroused considerable perplexity and doubt as to the attitude of the French. People ask: 'Are they really with us?' Some accuse them merely of lack of enthusiasm about their liberation – 'they don't want us there at all' – and of not cooperating with our armies; others, of hostility, and of being anti-British, and say they are not to be trusted. Prominent among the latter are ex-Servicemen from the last war, and it is said that stories of 'the sullen French' dating from then have revived. A few sympathise with the French because of all the destruction in their country.

Surprise continues at the good food and clothing of the people. Many people ask what they can believe of all they have been told about conditions in occupied countries. It is said 'the French are better off than we are'.

A number feel unless an explanation is given both for French 'antagonism' and for the comfortable circumstances of the inhabitants of Normandy, people will not take kindly later on to rationing of food and clothing in order to send supplies to Europe.

Rumours about refugees being sent to this country continue. It is hoped there will not be too many, but some Ulster housewives ask whether any women will be available for domestic work.

THE NEXT MOVE: Further landings are generally expected. Belgium and Norway are the only specific guesses.

NEWS PRESENTATION OF THE INVASION: Approval of the handling of the news of the invasion continues general. Comment is again on familiar lines. There is, however, some increase in criticism this week and also evidence of a slight decline in interest in the news ... for some people 'headlines are beginning to suffice'.

Criticism is of:

(a) COMMENTATORS TREATING THE NEWS 'TOO MUCH LIKE A SPORTS EVENT'.

(b) ACCOUNTS BEING TOO REALISTIC OR 'MORBID': Others, however, dislike any 'toning down'.

(c) EYE-WITNESS ACCOUNTS: There is some division of opinion. Some like them; but others criticise their repetitiveness and also the fact that recordings are hard to hear.

(d) THE AMERICANS BEING GIVEN TOO MUCH LIMELIGHT at the expense of our troops.

MOI NEWSREELS: In Scotland, the 16 mm version of the invasion newsreels, at present being shown in remote areas by MOI film units, has come in for special praise. 'Probably the most up-to-the-minute newsreel ever shown in the Islands; the inhabitants are delighted.'

MOI SPEAKERS FROM THE BEACHHEADS are also highly praised.

3. FLYING BOMBS

THE COUNTRY AS A WHOLE

The pilotless plane continues to rival the invasion of Normandy as a topic of conversation. Much anxiety is expressed; but this seems chiefly on account of those living in danger areas, particularly friends and relations. The use of the flying bomb is thought to indicate Germany's weakness and her need to bolster up home morale at all costs, and it is variously described as 'Jerry's last kick' and 'the product of despair'.

The general feeling is that flying bombs cannot affect the outcome of the war, but people's estimates of them vary widely. Some think them a flash in the pan, too expensive to last long; others are beginning to take them more seriously than at first, regarding them as by no means a passing phase.

The habits and effects of the bomb are the subject of widespread and exaggerated rumours. These are said to be aggravated, and often caused, by: (i) lack of information resulting from security measures, (ii) the tales of evacuees from – and visitors to – London, (iii) letters and telegrams from Londoners, in many cases frantically seeking accommodation in safe areas, (iv) German radio accounts, (v) cancelled outside broadcasts.

RUMOURS chiefly relate to:

(a) DAMAGE, which is said to be worse than in the 1940/1 blitz ... 'London a heap of rubble'. Damage to Big Ben, House of Commons, Buckingham Palace, Westminster and Waterloo Bridges; to St. Pancras, Waterloo,

Victoria, King's Cross and Charing Cross Stations; and to Regent Street and Oxford Street. Boards are said to be displayed at railway stations indicating which stations have been closed due to damage. A particular chapel is named in reports from six Regions. Various London suburbs are named. 'You've only to look at the deaths column in *The Times* to see where they've fallen.'

Portsmouth, Plymouth, Southampton and Bristol are also said to be badly damaged.

(b) CASUALTIES, which are said to be immense, e.g. 1,200 in Ruislip alone; 600 dead in one area in one day; 1,000 in one dance hall; 300 killed by a bomb near Buckingham Palace, etc., etc. The number of obituary notices in the press of people killed by enemy action in southern England is said to give the impression that casualties must be heavy.

(c) LONDONERS' REACTIONS AND BEHAVIOUR: The uncanny nature of the bomb, the length of the alerts and the lack of sleep are thought to be making people very nervy, more so than during the heavy blitzes. Some people feel that morale in London may be low, that Londoners are scared or actually panicking. Railway stations are said to be crowded, and train-loads of women and children leaving London. Tube stations are said to be 'jammed every night', and 'no one enters London without a tin hat'.

Alerts are said to last as long as 36 hours, during which time Londoners remain in their shelters, sometimes not undressing for a week.

(d) THE HABITS AND CAPACITIES OF THE PILOTLESS AIRCRAFT: Stories of 300 falling at once; 283 in the Croydon area in one night; 12 going over every 2 minutes all night; raids every quarter of an hour, etc. One bomb is said to have reached Leamington and another to have dropped near Wigan.

PUBLICITY ABOUT THE BOMB AND THE RAIDS: In view of the widespread rumours, it is thought that more details should be published. A number of people appreciate that the enemy should be allowed to know as little as possible of the effects of the raids, but many blame official reticence for leaving the way open for exaggerated accounts, for leading people to accept German claims and for causing uneasiness in other parts of the country. People in target areas, and elsewhere, are critical of official and press accounts which appear to tone down the raids and the damage they cause. People ask for 'less secrecy and more true information'.

THE HOME SECRETARY'S two statements, and particularly the second (June 23) about casualties, have done something to reassure people, but some would like still more details and a few say his casualty figures 'obviously didn't include military'.

DEFENCES AND COUNTER-MEASURES: The majority continue confident that our experts will succeed in finding means of countering the bomb, though a minority fear it may take some time. Press diagrams of the bomb inspire confidence that, now we know its mechanism, we have a better prospect of overcoming it. A good many believe, however, that the menace will only definitely end when Allied troops have occupied the whole north coast of France. A number think we should land in the Pas de Calais area as soon as possible, though some women workers in London are reported as saying 'We don't want our men's and boys' lives risked to stop it – we'd rather "take it" than have massacre.' Though some, in London particularly, are critical of the Government for not having been better prepared 'since they knew about the plane for the past 2 years', most people are satisfied with the measures taken so far.

Particular reference is made to:

(a) THE CONTINUOUS BOMBARDMENT OF THE LAUNCHING PLATFORMS, which is thought most encouraging, though some Londoners doubt if it is as effective as represented. Regret is also expressed in other parts of the country at the RAF having to divert its attention from invasion targets for this purpose.

(b) DESTRUCTION OF THE BOMB BY FIGHTERS: The fact that the enemy appeared at one stage to be concentrating more on night attack was thought to show how many we were bringing down by day; some believe 75% have been destroyed.

(c) BALLOONS: There is some talk of balloons being moved from various places to the south coast. In Hull there is said to be disgust at the removal of its barrage balloon, 'after all it has gone through'.

EVACUEES: There are many references to the arrival of self-evacuated people – full of tales of damage and casualties and of their own sufferings – and to the efforts of Londoners to find accommodation in the provinces. In Wales the very sight of evacuees returning is taken as an indication that this form of attack is more than a nuisance. People in the North-Western Region anticipate considerable voluntary evacuation. In Nottingham, where the chief CAB is said to have been inundated with refugees, and in Oxford and Aylesbury, there is a feeling that official arrangements should be made for the reception of evacuees. St. Albans people are said to be apprehensive at the idea of having to billet evacuees.

LOCALISED REACTIONS

A. LONDON: The raids have completely swamped all other war news for the great majority of Londoners, many of whom find it impossible to think of anything else. Nervousness, anxiety, strain and weariness are widespread. Sleepless nights account for much of the increased jitteriness and lowering of morale. Some people can 'scarcely believe the raids have only been going for ten days'.

Descriptions of the raids range from 'sheer terror' to 'a very nasty nuisance but not so bad as the blitz'.

Among the more severely disturbed, a few go so far as to say that unless a remedy is found, 'people are not going to stand for it'; they dread another winter if no solution is found.

A considerable number, however, remain calm, regarding the raids with interest, being more disturbed by the atmosphere of uncanniness than by their possible effect; they feel the anxiety expressed is greater than the damage warrants. They think, too, that people are beginning to adjust themselves to the raids.

SHELTER: Some are undecided what to do about sheltering. Others pin their faith to shelters – street and otherwise. Overcrowding in tube and other shelters is reported, as well as unpleasant conditions, smell and behaviour in the tube shelters; as a result, people are deterred from travelling by train in the evenings, and some nervous people are even reported to be willing to do anything rather than go to a public shelter.

Some people are anxious about children and think they ought not to be allowed to leave the school premises during an alert.

EVACUATION: As yet, there is apparently no general outcry for evacuation, though people in some areas are demanding it (Bethnal Green, Ilford, Sutton); others ask for Government direction in the matter. Many of those able to do so have already evacuated with their children. In the East End, it is said that if the raids continue the Government will have to face up to a new evacuation scheme. Long queues, some members of which are obviously evacuees, are reported at main line stations, with people losing train after train owing to the crowds.

BOMBED AREAS: Rescue squads and hospital services are said to be working marvellously, but first-aid repair parties are criticised for their tardiness in getting to work on damaged property. More mobile canteens are said to be wanted at the damaged sites, both for CD workers and for the blitzed, who are sometimes too dazed and tired to go any distance to a meal centre. Relatives arriving at the sites after the WVS have gone for the night complain they are unable to locate the whereabouts of their homeless relations.

DEFENCES: Londoners appear to be rather less satisfied than people in other parts of the country with the measures so far taken to counter the flying bomb, and less sanguine that it will be speedily overcome. A few are now said to feel less safe since the AA fire has been discontinued and ask why this course has been adopted.

B. SOUTH-EASTERN DISTRICT: Feelings range from dislike to fear and dread, the latter particularly among those who have seen the damage caused; women are said to be particularly nervous. In some places, 'people fly for shelter when one comes over, chased by a fighter'. There is no suggestion of morale being lowered, however, and on the whole people clench their teeth and carry on, 'finding it a nuisance but getting used to it'. Here, too, lack of sleep is regarded as one of the most trying features and some diminution of output is said to be noticeable among workers. AA gunfire is particularly blamed for disturbing rest, and there is some complaint that it is inefficient; but the sight of fighters engaging the planes is said to have done people good.

C. EASTERN REGION: In areas where the bombs have dropped, people are thought to be taking things fairly calmly and carrying on as usual, though suffering from lack of sleep. Nervousness undoubtedly exists, though people were glad to be told by the Home Secretary what they ought to do, and the streets are said to be cleared immediately the siren goes. Confidence has been expressed in the alerts, because their duration has been short and an incident has invariably followed the warning.

D. SOUTHERN REGION: Some alarm, particularly among women, at the possibility that they may drop anywhere and at any time. People's nerves are said not to be standing up to them so well after five years of war. The general view, however, is that the new weapon is a nuisance but not nearly as bad as the raids which people expected to start when invasion began.

E. SOUTH-WESTERN REGION: Much apprehension of attacks reaching into the West Country, with something approaching scare among a minority in places possibly vulnerable. However, there is great satisfaction, particularly in sea-board towns like Plymouth, at the capture of the PAC bases in the Cherbourg peninsula.

F. THE REST OF THE COUNTRY: People in Scotland and the North are glad they are out of range, while being full of sympathy for the sufferers further south.

Though only a minority think it conceivable that the flying bomb could ever reach the Midlands, people there appear to be less certain of their own immunity, at the same time expressing less sympathy for southerners.

The capture of the Cherbourg peninsula is thought likely to have saved South Wales, though the possibility of their arrival is not dismissed in the Principality.

People in other parts of the country are said to be cancelling visits to London where possible but coming back full of stories when they have been.

3A. FURTHER REPRISALS

The possibility of other reprisals is being discussed, poison gas in particular. A few wonder if the enemy may send gas in flying bombs. Some concern is reported in London where, in addition to gas, flying incendiaries are feared by a few.

So far there is no reported comment on the possibility of rocket bombardment.

4. ITALY

Although still much overshadowed by events in Normandy, there is very general satisfaction with our advances in Italy and considerable praise for General Alexander.

A few think the attention devoted to Normandy by the BBC and press is unfair to our troops in Italy. In Scotland 'people are quoting letters from soldiers in Italy expressing bitterness at the tendency to overshadow events there'.

POLITICAL: Satisfaction with Badoglio's retirement continues. There is some approval of the Bonomi government, but more information about it is wanted.

5. RUSSIA

News of the launching of the latest Russian offensive in the central sector has given great satisfaction, and progress both here and against Finland is followed with much interest. Earlier in the week there had been some surprise that Russia was concentrating her efforts on the northern front, though many people had considered this to be only preliminary to advances on the main front directly against Germany. 'Big things' are expected of the new offensive; some people again express the hope that the Soviet armies will be the first to reach Berlin ... 'They'll know how to deal with the Germans.'

Only a very small minority express sympathy for the Finns, who are felt to have had their chance. It is expected they will soon capitulate.

Praise for the spirit of the Russian people continues; also some distrust of Soviet intentions in the post-war world.

6. GENERAL DE GAULLE AND THE FRENCH NATIONAL COMMITTEE

Concern and mystification at the present situation continue on familiar lines. Many people deplore the failure to recognise General de Gaulle and the French National Committee and feel we are being dominated by US interests in this matter.

Despite some feeling that General de Gaulle may be 'difficult' and 'uncompromising', many feel he is the only possible French leader and would be a 'rallying point for French resistance'. They fear repercussions in France if the situation is not cleared up, and that delay may cause the unnecessary sacrifice of men's lives.

While some are prepared to accept Mr. Churchill's view that the situation is a delicate one and should not be debated in Parliament, there is a minority feeling that the time is overdue for some authoritative statement to be made.

7. SHOOTING OF AIR FORCE PRISONERS

Mr. Eden's statement that the prisoners were murdered caused horror, and hatred of the Germans has hardened. Some suggest retaliatory measures on German prisoners now; the majority are prepared to wait till the criminals are caught.

The deed is looked on as 'sheer butchery'; the public has noted the round number of fifty, that there were no wounded and no bodies – only ashes, and that the recaptured prisoners were unarmed. Some think that those who were shot were first tortured.

In the London Region some relatives of prisoners of war are anxious about their men, despite the statement that this is an isolated incident.

8. FAR EAST

There has been an increase in interest in the Far Eastern war this week, as a result of the news of the American naval battle in the Pacific. The result has given much satisfaction, though there is slight disappointment because the Japanese 'bolted and wouldn't take it'. There is also some doubt of the American account and figures of aircraft shot down.

The bombing of Tokyo continues to give satisfaction, and more is hoped for.

The situation in Burma is regarded as satisfactory, though it is said still to be a mystery to most people.

There is a desire for more news of the Far Eastern fighting and for an improvement in the maps published.

PRISONERS OF WAR: The lack of news continues to arouse anxiety among relatives. It is suggested that regular broadcasts to relatives might offset the fear that the Government has forgotten the prisoners.

9. MR. LYTTELTON'S REMARKS ABOUT AMERICA AND JAPAN

The general view appears to be that, although Mr. Lyttelton admittedly 'dropped a brick', it was ridiculous for the American press to make such a fuss. It is thought the cause may be 'presidential election nerves'; and it is hoped the American papers will not go on trying to create unnecessary bad blood.

10. BROADCASTING AND PRESENTATION OF NEWS

There is little comment apart from that on news of the invasion and the pilotless plane.

BBC PROGRAMMES: There is again criticism of too much jazz. More light music is asked for.

PRAISE FOR the *Brains Trust* and broadcasts of the Proms.

II. SPECIAL COMMENTS

BRIEF WEEKLY SUMMARY

11. THE GOVERNMENT WHITE PAPER ON EMPLOYMENT POLICY

Discussion of the White Paper remains limited, and people do not go into detail. The Government's declared intention to maintain a high level of employment is appreciated. People hope slumps will be prevented but remain fearful: 'If it is so easy, why didn't they cure the 1931 slump?'

Mr. Bevin's speech in the House of Commons (June 21) has aroused favourable comment – also on a limited scale only.

In Northern Ireland, there is some hope that it may be treated as a development area.

12. HOLIDAYS

People are doubtful about how bad holiday transport is going to be, and again ask for a Government lead in the matter. Many are planning to get away if they possibly can, and accommodation is now said to be almost unobtainable. People hope that the ban on some of the restricted areas will soon be lifted.

Holidays at home remain of limited popularity, especially as people find difficulty in travelling to local events.

Workers hope that adequate travelling facilities will be provided for local wakes weeks, to enable those who have booked rooms to be sure of reaching them. They feel they have earned a holiday in better air.

13. FOOD

FRUIT AND TOMATOES: People are longing for fruit, and shortage is complained of, especially of gooseberries and strawberries. There is said to be much queuing for them, and for tomatoes; unfair distribution is alleged. Under-the-counter and conditional sales are also reported, and it is said that as soon as the price of fruit comes down, bringing it within reach of the less well-off, the fruit disappears entirely.

III. PERIODICAL REVIEW

14. SALUTE THE SOLDIER

DURING THE PAST FOUR WEEKS interest in Salute the Soldier weeks and satisfaction with successes have continued; in some cases, interest is thought to have been much stimulated by the invasion. However, enthusiasm is again said to be on the wane.

The following criticisms have also continued:

(a) THE TOTALS DO NOT REPRESENT 'REAL' SAVINGS, because
    (i)   Money is only transferred from one account to another.
    (ii) Investments by banks and insurance companies are included.
    (iii) Money in many cases is withdrawn almost immediately after the 'week' is over.
    (iv) Savings fall off for some time afterwards.
(b) THE WASTE OF MONEY and PAPER.

PUBLICITY AND ADVERTISEMENTS ARE PRAISED, particularly the POSTERS.

15. YOUTH AND MORALS

DURING THE PAST FOUR WEEKS comment has differed little in either tenor or volume from last month's. However, complaints of sexual immorality among young girls, mainly with US troops, have decreased. There is a slight increase in comment about infidelity among women whose husbands are overseas. Reports of hooliganism among children and adolescents, of juvenile delinquency, and of heavy drinking among women and young people, continue.

Factors blamed and remedies suggested are almost unchanged since last month.

NO. 196: TUESDAY 27 JUNE 1944 TO TUESDAY 4 JULY 1944

I. GENERAL COMMENTS

1. GENERAL

Good news from all fronts has maintained confidence at the same high level as last week and has further encouraged belief in victory this year.

The flying bomb is 'the only black spot in the picture'. Exaggerated rumours of damage and casualties are widespread, and there is a great demand for factual information with which to counter them. While concern is general, only in London are spirits really affected – they are lower now than at any time during the last two years.

Familiar HOME FRONT grouses are again at a minimum.

2. FLYING BOMBS

THE COUNTRY AS A WHOLE

In most parts of the country, flying bombs are more discussed than anything else. Though hardly anyone appears to think that they can alter the course of the war, people everywhere are taking them more seriously; some feel the Germans have definitely scored over us with them.

The reappearance of evacuees in many parts of the country, each with a lurid story to tell, has created a widespread impression that the raids are far more severe than indicated by press and radio. The request for volunteer wardens for duty in the affected places has also stressed the seriousness of the situation.

There is much sympathy for Londoners and great concern for relations and friends living in the danger areas.

PUBLICITY ABOUT THE RAIDS: There is a widespread demand for more news to allay rumours and anxiety. The Government is criticised, in some cases very strongly, for withholding definite information about casualties, damage and the number of bombs destroyed.

There is some appreciation of the reasons for censorship, but it is thought that the Germans must have a good idea where the bombs are going, and that something is urgently needed to check the wild and exaggerated talk which is circulating.

People ask why the papers are allowed to publish German claims ... 'people who read that the enemy claim that Southampton is in flames may not believe all of it, but they think there may be some basis in fact'. There are reports of increased listening to German broadcasts.

RUMOURS, most of them fantastically exaggerated, are circulating in all parts of the country and are reported in considerable numbers from every Region. These are attributed to evacuees, letters, travellers returning from the south, false deductions, German claims, and to the lack of official information with which to counteract them.

Rumours chiefly relate to:

(a) DAMAGE, which is thought to be tremendous. The list of places damaged or razed to the ground includes most well-known London buildings and railway termini and a number of Thames bridges. Whole streets are said to be devastated by the bombs, each one of which 'demolishes everything in a mile radius'. Thousands are homeless – 7,000 in Beckenham alone.

Southampton, Portsmouth, Liverpool, Luton, Bristol, Guildford,

Reading, Worthing and Littlehampton are all thought to be more or less damaged.

(b) CASUALTIES, also believed to be tremendous. The highest total rumoured – 250,000 – comes from London, where people 'delight in scaring their neighbours with casualty figures'. Two of the Prime Minister's daughters are rumoured killed.

(c) LONDONERS' REACTIONS: Many stories of 'everybody leaving London', trains packed to suffocation, Londoners worn out under the continuous strain, in their shelters day and night and unable to leave them even long enough to cook a meal. Evacuees have given the impression that these raids are far worse than the blitz. There is some fear that Londoners' morale may give way under the strain of incessant alerts and continuous sleepless nights – if it has not done so already.

(d) THE BOMB ITSELF: It is variously rumoured that:

    (i) Bombs have reached a number of distant points, the furthest being Corby (near Kettering), Penarth and Treforest.

    (ii) Bombs come over in hundreds in the daytime, and every two minutes all through the night.

    (iii) Some of the bombs have been filled with gas. In the St. Pancras area and elsewhere in London the bombs of the last few days are rumoured to be different from the first – variously, gas bombs, rocket bombs or merely bigger.

    (iv) Spain has had a good deal to do with the production of these bombs – tungsten, chrome and wolfram being supplied as necessary components in their manufacture.

(e) FUTURE FLYING BOMB ATTACKS:

    (i) There has been a spate of rumours that Haw-Haw has named various places shortly to be attacked. In London these rumours are particularly numerous and persistent and are said to circulate specially in areas which have been bombed, and more noticeably near to the damaged sites.

    (ii) In London it is rumoured that Eire is loaning the Germans bases in Southern Ireland from which to launch the bombs.

(f) SERVICEMEN'S REACTIONS: In London it is rumoured that:

    (i) Some servicemen are so anxious that they are refusing to return to their units after the three days' compassionate leave allowed when their families have been bombed out – until they have managed to send their families out of London.

    (ii) The Germans are horrifying prisoners of war with ghastly tales of flying bomb damage.

DEFENCES AND COUNTER-MEASURES: Many think we shall soon overcome the flying bomb as we did the magnetic mine, but people seem about equally divided as to the success – or otherwise – of the counter-measures taken so far. The bombing of the launching bases satisfies some; others think it ineffective, some suspecting the RAF is wasting time bombing dummy sites.

People want to know how many bombs are destroyed ... 'If the percentage is as high as is claimed, facts would improve morale.'

However, whatever people think of counter-measures, it is generally felt that the only infallible cure will be the military occupation of the area in which the bases are situated.

REPRISALS: Opinion is divided. Though some want us to reply by using gas or flying bombs, most people seem opposed to reprisals of this kind, if only because it might mean diverting our air power from military objectives. However, no one would object to even heavier bombing of German cities, it is thought.

EVACUATION: Self-evacuated people in considerable numbers are arriving in many parts of the country and causing a great problem in places which are already overcrowded. The fact that they are 'unofficial evacuees' is said to make the problem of billeting them even more difficult; the need for organised official evacuation is mentioned in reports from four Regions. It is felt that unless there is compulsory billeting, good-natured people will bear the brunt.

People from London are said to be willing to pay anything and to sleep anywhere for the sake of a night's rest, and unscrupulous people are charging high prices just for accommodation on the floor.

In general, people are said to be sympathetically inclined towards the evacuees, though some resentment is reported against Jews whose behaviour is criticised, people who 'arrive fecklessly without prior arrangement', and those who are shirking responsibilities by coming. Particular evacuation problems relate to:

(a) RESTRICTED AREAS: There is some demand that these areas should be opened for reception of the friends and relations of the inhabitants. A case is mentioned of a man, anxious to move his mother (aged 81 and living alone) out of London, being refused permission. It is said, too, that within these areas the regulations are being enforced differently in different places in face of the present influx.

(b) EVACUEES ARRIVING WITHOUT MONEY OR CLOTHING: One reported difficulty is that 'evacuees without money may be given an authorisation by the Assistance Board for an emergency grant by the Ministry of Labour, but this does not apply to Forces' wives or old age pensioners; this is thought very unfair'.

(c) FOOD: In the Eastern Region there is concern at the scarcity of food, particularly in restaurants. Many evacuees have found beds but must 'eat out', and in Hertford it is said to be difficult even to find a sandwich: 'Rest Centres can only feed the bombed-out and the British Restaurant has insufficient staff.' It is hoped that the Ministry of Food will lose no time in sending extra supplies to reception areas.

LOCALISED REACTIONS

A. LONDON: Reports from all parts of the London area mention the adverse effect the raids are having on Londoners, both in bombed and unbombed areas. Strain, weariness, fear and despondency are widely reported, particularly among women with children, those whose husbands are away, and the old and middle-aged.

Many think these raids worse than the blitz, both because of their continuity and their uncanniness.

A minority say, 'it's impossible to stick them much longer' and are said to be ready for 'peace at any price' ... 'After five years of war, there is a limit to what people can stand.'

A considerable number want retaliation and feel that nothing is too bad for the Germans. In Lambeth, Southwark and Deptford they are said to be demanding retaliation by gas 'to bring a sense of horror to the sadistic Germans'.

Nevertheless, a good many people are becoming adjusted to the raids and are standing up to them well.

Lack of sleep is one of the effects most generally complained of and is said to be causing much absenteeism and lateness among workers.

ATTITUDE TO THE GOVERNMENT: A good deal of criticism of the Government is reported – some of it rather unspecific – with particular reference to the Home Secretary and the Prime Minister. The chief complaints seem to be that: (i) figures of the casualties, damage and the number of bombs destroyed are not published; (ii) we were not better prepared beforehand against the bomb; (iii) it is not being more effectively dealt with now.

The belief that there is no official evacuation scheme is also causing some criticism of the Government.

SECURITY AND PUBLICITY: General dissatisfaction that the raid news has been completely mishandled, with particular reference to:

(a) LACK OF INFORMATION about damage and casualties leading to:
    (i) RUMOURS, London rumours being no less 'fantastically exaggerated' than those in circulation in other parts of the country.
    (ii) ANXIETY on the part of relatives and friends of Londoners. Service wives believe that men now going to Normandy will spread stories of the raids and make the men already there very anxious.

(b) 'THE OFFICIAL SUGGESTION THAT MORALE HAS NOT BEEN AFFECTED', which irritates some people considerably: 'Why are the Government telling people that the Germans have failed to upset morale, when everyone who knows people in bombed areas knows this is a lie?' General Smuts' reference to the bomb as a damp squib was not thought a happy one.

(c) THE RAIDS BEING DESCRIBED AS 'OF NO NATIONAL IMPORTANCE': This is said to have annoyed servicemen particularly, as they are 'fighting to secure the safety of their homes and families'.

DEFENCES: The majority appear to be critical on the various grounds that (i) no panacea has yet been found; (ii) the bombing of the launching bases seems useless; (iii) the absence of AA fire leaves people feeling unprotected and without the extra warning that danger is imminent.

A considerable minority, however, think that the defences are adequate, and all possible measures are being taken to stop the raids.

SIRENS: The continual sounding of the sirens is thought ridiculous by some people and is blamed for holding up work. Others dislike the strain of waiting and listening for the bomb after the siren has gone and would prefer some form of local warning. Others again say that the sound of traffic drowns the approach of the bomb and causes anxiety to people in the street after the siren has gone.

EVACUATION has taken place on a considerable scale among those who could get away, particularly women with children, who are said to be crowding the main line stations all day. Urgent enquiries as to how to get out of London are reported from many WVS and CAB centres.

There is reported to be a growing demand for an official evacuation scheme, particularly for children. People are angry, in the belief that no plan has been put into operation, and attempts to get away are, in a few instances, said to be 'verging on panic'.

Servicemen's wives want their fares paid; and people who have relatives in non-reception areas want billeting allowances paid if they go to stay with them.

SHELTERING has become 'the next best thing to evacuation' for a great many Londoners. In some parts there is a general rush to the shelters when a bomb is heard, and men are said to show little signs of the 'women and children first' spirit.

Many more people are sleeping in shelters, both public and private, than was noticed in the blitz, and some are said to refuse to leave shelters day or night.

The tubes and some big public shelters are 'packed and unpleasant'. Children are running about dirty and uncared for, wetting on the floor unchecked; they appear to get little or no sleep and to need more supervision.

There is a demand for more public shelter accommodation – people in Euston and Peckham shelters having been obliged to sit or stand all night – and for more medical care in public shelters.

CHILDREN: Parents, teachers, and members of various organisations express great anxiety for children who can be seen 'playing about in the streets' during alerts. Some lead by educational authorities is demanded about the question of school attendance during the raids. Some children go, others are kept at home, others again are on their way to school when an alert is sounded and are uncertain as to what to do. Many women have stopped going to work owing to the desire to be with their children. This and other causes are said at a big Greenwich factory and elsewhere to have made attendance 'go all to hell'.

Parents are very critical that school examinations are being held at this time.

Husbands working away from home are anxious about wives and children.

THE BOMBED OUT in some areas south of the river are 'very angry' about the lack of consideration shown them by the authorities. They feel that insufficient is being done to rehouse them and protect their goods and property when it has suffered from blast.

Compensation is said to be 'insufficient for necessities' and some people complain that they are having to give up their clothing coupons for household linen replacements. The damage done to property is said to be much discussed and considerably exaggerated.

CD WORKERS are warmly praised by the public. They themselves say they were ready for this emergency. They prefer dealing with these incidents to those during the blitz. They think the casualties are light.

SECRET WEAPON NO. 2 is the cause of growing fear. People wonder anxiously 'What next he has up his sleeve'. People are incredulous but uneasy at the idea of a rocket bomb; some believe it could wipe out a whole borough.

B. SOUTH-EASTERN DISTRICT: Reactions vary considerably according to the areas from which they are reported. People seem about equally divided between:

(a) Those who are carrying on as usual and getting used to it. A few even laugh at the raids and say that 'if Hitler thinks he can win like this, he's got to guess again'.

(b) Those who are nervous, shaken and unhappy and who find these raids worse than any in the past. Many are very tired, and their morale is said to be lowered. People in areas which have suffered feel that a small additional ration of tea would be a great help.

DEFENCES: Praise of the fighters is widespread ... they are said to 'bring them down in hundreds'. AA gunfire is, however, criticised as futile, costly, damaging to property and preventing sleep, though a few find it helpful as indicating the route taken by 'the little devils'.

Barrage balloons are felt to be effective in Tunbridge Wells, and some Canterbury people are anxious at having lost theirs.

In Haslemere it is complained that several bombs have gone over without an alert being sounded.

C. EASTERN REGION: In areas where the missiles have fallen, people are said to be suffering from sleeplessness and strain. In other areas where the alerts have sounded, there is said to have been no undue alarm but a noticeable shelter-consciousness and tendency to get up at night when the siren goes. There is some dissatisfaction reported at too many sirens being sounded during the night at Watford and Welwyn. There is also concern at crash warnings in factories while people in the streets and in schools are unaware of any danger.

D. SOUTHERN REGION: Generally, the continuance of the raids, and stories spread by the increasing number of evacuees, appear to be leading to more nervousness, although in the south-western part of the Region people are thankful for the capture of the bases in the Cherbourg peninsula and consequent removal of danger. At Slough people are said to be disturbed at the lack of public warnings during the day, particularly for children in the schools, whilst war workers in factories are ordered to the shelters; weariness of Civil Defence workers is noted here.

E. THE REST OF THE COUNTRY consider themselves out of range, though a little uneasy speculation is reported at the possibility of the range of the flying bomb being ultimately extended.

The disappearance of their balloons is, however, causing a little uneasiness in a working-class quarter of Newcastle, where people are suggesting that the Germans are using the flying bomb as a means of getting the balloons away to clear the sky for bomber attacks.

3. THE INVASION OF FRANCE

There is intense and widespread satisfaction with our progress, together with continuing relief that our armies are now firmly established in France, and great confidence in our maintaining progress. However, 'ups and downs' and stiff fighting ahead are fully expected.

Great praise continues for the organisation and planning; the leaders and generals, especially General Montgomery; the troops, British, Canadian and American – people's opinion of the latter has risen by 'leaps and bounds'; and for the teamwork between the three Services, and between the British and Americans.

The fall of Cherbourg was greeted with great enthusiasm, and the Americans widely praised, particularly for the speed with which they did the job. Some ask whether it will be possible to land supplies direct from America.

Most people are satisfied with progress in the Caen sector, though a minority are anxious. The British and Canadians are praised for their 'doggedness'. A few suggest we are going slow here before a big push, possibly to coincide with a second landing.

Bad weather has caused exasperation; in one agricultural district, though the recent rain was needed, it was said 'we are all praying for fine weather and a good harvest for our bombers'.

A few people think the German tanks are better than ours.

THE STATEMENT ON BRITISH CASUALTIES (June 28) was appreciated, and accepted by the majority with relief. But apprehension continues, especially among relatives, that as the campaign develops, and possibly even now in the Caen fighting, there may be a very different story.

Confidence in the medical care given to our wounded, which is much appreciated and is said to have reduced anxiety about casualties.

A few complain about MAILS, though others are satisfied. Some people who believe their relatives to be in France are extremely worried, having been without news for three weeks.

THE RUMOUR THAT GENERAL MONTGOMERY IS DEAD, captured, or wounded, is this week reported from four Regions.

PRISONERS OF WAR: From one Region each it is reported that (a) the news of our men being marched through the streets of Paris has made people think the same should be done to German prisoners here; (b) stories of the Germans murdering parachute troops have resulted in a surge of hatred; (c) people are surprised at the number of non-Germans captured and ask if they are press-ganged or collaborators; (d) people dislike the saluting etc. accorded to high-ranking prisoners arriving in this country.

WOMEN SNIPERS: Intense indignation at stories of women snipers is again reported, but also some confusion because of conflicting information. It is again said that these women should be shot, and anger at the 'soft' treatment meted out to Myra continues. The official denial about the snipers (June 26) is only mentioned in one report; it is said to have been welcomed, though people ask who sent the earlier reports.

THE PEOPLE OF NORMANDY: There is confusion as to the attitude of the French, and feelings range from puzzlement to uneasiness and indignation. Reports are thought to have conflicted with each other, and more official information is wanted, rather than journalists' reports. Most people apparently think the French are on the whole unfriendly.

However, there is some sympathy for those in battle areas, and press pictures of devastated French towns make people hope this will not be necessary all the way to Berlin.

The well-fed and well-clothed appearance of the French continues to arouse considerable comment and surprise – they are thought to look better off than we are, and there are questions as to why we should feed them. It is again suggested we have not been told the truth about conditions in Europe.

There is little talk about the possibility of French refugees arriving here. However, in one east coast town 'the fact is an "open secret", and much bitterness is felt at the preparations made. Houses were quickly requisitioned for these refugees, yet servicemen's wives are living in totally inadequate rooms. Paid wardens are engaged as cooks for communal feeding centres, yet servicemen's wives having babies can get no home help.'

NEWS PRESENTATION OF THE INVASION continues to be widely praised on familiar lines.

Mention is again made of:

(a)   The popularity of the *War Reports* after the 9 p.m. news. Only a small minority find some of the eye-witness accounts 'too harrowing'.
(b)   Some feeling that too much publicity is given to the Americans at the expense of our troops.

3A. THE NEXT MOVE

Further landings are generally expected. Some think these will be in the Pas de Calais area; Londoners hope so. Other suggestions are Norway, the Low Countries, the south of France, and the Balkans.

4. RUSSIA

There is widespread admiration and pleasure at the Russian successes, and the Russian news is once again to the fore in public comment – in some cases second only in military interest to the Normandy campaign. An increasing number hope the Red Army will reach Germany and Berlin first, for fear we shall be too soft.

Some doubt is expressed about the accuracy of Russian figures of German losses.

FINLAND: Very little sympathy, though small minorities feel she has been for a long time 'between two fires'. The government rather than the people are blamed for the situation. It is thought the campaign will soon be over.

The news of the break in US diplomatic relations with Finland has been well received.

5. ITALY

People are very satisfied with our steady progress and are confident it will continue – some expecting that the whole of Italy will soon be in our hands.

The fighting in Normandy, however, continues to overshadow this campaign, and there is criticism that both press and BBC are not giving our men there 'a fair show'.

GENERAL ALEXANDER is widely praised.

BRITISH SERVICEMEN HAVING TO SALUTE ITALIAN OFFICERS: Keen exception is taken; the men themselves are said to be particularly bitter.

6. FAR EAST

Interest in the Far Eastern war is less this week, events nearer home overshadowing this theatre.

Satisfaction continues with progress in Burma and the Pacific, and with the recent naval success. People hope for more air attacks on Japan.

The desire for more news and better maps is again reported.

7. SHOOTING OF AIR FORCE PRISONERS

Horror and anger against the Germans continue. Some fear we shall be too soft with the criminals.

8. GENERAL DE GAULLE AND THE FRENCH NATIONAL COMMITTEE

People continue uneasy and puzzled and would like a clear statement about the present position. Feelings reported about General de Gaulle are:

(a) He and his provisional government should be recognised. American policy is again blamed for our failure to do so.
(b) His proper place is in his own country. He should be there, 'not as a politician but as a soldier to rally the French and enlist them in a new French army'.

9. BROADCASTING AND PRESENTATION OF NEWS

See under Section 2, The flying bomb; Section 3, The invasion of France; and Section 5, Italy.

THE DEBATE ON THE MINISTRY OF INFORMATION: Slight comment only. It is generally thought the Minister made a good case.

II. SPECIAL COMMENTS

BRIEF WEEKLY REVIEW

10. FOOD

MILK RATION: The cut is deplored; particularly as it renews the hardship to old people who need extra milk.

FRUIT AND TOMATOES: Complaints continue, on the same lines as last week, of the shortage and unfair distribution of fruit and tomatoes.

11. HOLIDAYS

Many are hoping to get away and are disappointed that rail services to popular resorts are not being extended. Workers feel they need a change of air and environment, and that facilities for holiday travel should be allowed.

From restricted areas in Scotland there are 'cries of distress' from people who normally let rooms or take boarders; many hope the ban on some of the holiday resorts may soon be lifted.

In the North-Western Region, though holidays at home are thought well organised, it is felt the country would 'get the dividends' on extra travelling facilities, as holidays at home are no substitute, particularly for women.

In the North Midland Region, it is suggested that in view of transport restrictions, waters hitherto the monopoly of distant clubs and individuals should be made available for local anglers.

In London people ask for more transport to open spaces during holidays-at-home times.

12. THE GOVERNMENT PROPOSALS FOR THE CONTROL OF LAND

Little interest as yet.

Disappointment is reported that the Government has rejected the Uthwatt proposals for balancing compensation and betterment. It is feared that vested interests and speculation will remain, and the public interest be subordinated to them.

Cynicism about post-war conditions generally is said to have been confirmed.

However, some right-wing people are pleased that control of the land will only be enforced where essential for the public good, and not merely to please 'doctrinaire planners'.

13. THE GOVERNMENT WHITE PAPER ON EMPLOYMENT POLICY

Interest and discussion remain limited. Workers are said to be sceptical, though some interest among businessmen is reported. The Government's acceptance of responsibility for the maintenance of employment at a high level is again welcomed.

14. HOLMFIRTH FLOOD

Tradespeople in Holmfirth who lost stocks during the flood disaster are well satisfied with the way the Board of Trade officers have handled the job of providing them with replacements.

There is still concern about putting in order the River Holme. Local people feel that this ought to be a national charge.

III. MONTHLY REVIEW

US TROOPS IN THIS COUNTRY

DURING THE PAST FOUR WEEKS, friendly relations have increased 'as the Americans are better understood'. US achievements in Normandy have contributed to this improvement. Nevertheless, substantial minority criticism has again been reported, and continues in the Northern Region to outweigh praise (though to a lesser extent than last month). Many people think that much criticism comes from those who have not personally contacted the Americans, and that some tend to argue from the particular to the general, condemning all Americans because one or two are seen behaving badly.

PRAISE is particularly accorded to:

(a) US SOLDIERS' PARTICIPATION IN 'SALUTE THE SOLDIER' AND OTHER SAVINGS WEEKS.

(b) THE KINDNESS TO CHILDREN OF BOTH BLACK AND WHITE TROOPS; though the children's begging habits are deplored and it is thought that in some cases parents encourage them by dressing the children up in rags.

(c) THEIR GENEROSITY.

(d) THEIR FRIENDLINESS.

OTHER COMMENT has centred chiefly round:

(a) ATTITUDE TO AND BEHAVIOUR WITH WOMEN AND GIRLS: Much the most criticism of US troops still comes under this heading. At the same time, many continue to feel the girls themselves, and their parents, are at least as much to blame; it is thought the Americans' money is the chief explanation for the girls' behaviour.

Wives of British servicemen and 'undesirable' women are also thought partly responsible.

More police vigilance and more policewomen are asked for.

THE QUESTION IN THE HOUSE BY MR. KENDALL, MP (25 May) has aroused some comment. The majority view is that the 'stifling' of Mr. Kendall was 'another example of the official attitude that the Americans must not be criticised'; however, a few think Mr. Kendall was wrong in 'blaming all the Americans for the sins of a few'.

(b) COLOURED TROOPS: The attitude of white Americans is again condemned, as is the attitude in some cafés etc. to which coloured soldiers are refused admission. Some continue to think they are better behaved than white troops, though with others their popularity is declining because of their behaviour with women and girls.

General Eisenhower's recent action in commuting the death sentence on a black soldier for alleged rape caused great relief.

(c) HOSPITALITY: People are said to be anxious to give the Americans a 'very warm welcome'; and where hospitality has been extended there have been 'very happy results'. However, there are continued complaints of their neither turning up, nor sending an apology, after accepting an invitation.

Some feel more clubs and canteens are wanted, particularly of the Welcome Club type, because in this way the Americans meet 'the nicer type of girls'.

(d) APPEARANCE AND DEMEANOUR: Allegations of unsoldierly, slovenly appearance continue, also of 'profusion of non-fighting medals'. People also find the Americans 'bumptious'.

(e) TRANSPORT: Reckless driving is again alleged.

(f) COMPARISONS BETWEEN CONDITIONS FOR OUR TROOPS AND THE AMERICANS: Comment about disparity of pay has decreased considerably, although there is still some resentment. It is also thought the Americans are better off for clothing, clubs, food, 'luxuries', restrictions on leave and regulations; e.g. 'our soldiers' wives cannot visit Colchester for the weekend, but the Americans' girlfriends can'.

(g) SHORTAGES: Some people feel the Americans buy up tomatoes and other fruit; others blame them for the beer shortage.

(h) INSANITARY HABITS: Complaints continue of leaving contraceptives lying about and of using doorways as lavatories.

(i) DRINKING: There is felt to have been much more moderation of late.

(j) WASTE: People still feel petrol is being wasted. In the South-Western Region there were widespread and vigorous protests against the alleged destruction by departing US troops (at the time of D-Day) of large quantities of equipment, stores and commodities, including furniture, clothing, books, food, tobacco, spare parts, packing cases, paper, equipment of all kinds, and even live ammunition. It is said to have aroused horror among people badgered for so long into being thrifty and salvage-minded.

NO. 197: TUESDAY 4 JULY 1944 TO TUESDAY 11 JULY 1944

I. GENERAL COMMENTS

1. GENERAL

Spirits remain high – with a slight rise in some Regions; in London people are steadier this week. Optimism about an early end to the war in Europe continues, due again to the good news from all fronts – particularly Russia.

The flying bomb is still the main topic, but the Prime Minister's statement has eased the situation considerably; casualties are lower than most people had expected, and fewer rumours are now reported.

On the HOME FRONT there is much talk, in the areas affected, about the influx of evacuees from London and the south.

2. FLYING BOMBS

THE COUNTRY AS A WHOLE

THE PRIME MINISTER'S STATEMENT has on the whole been received very well – though soberly. Only in London is much disappointment reported. It has done much to clear the air, relieve tension and dispel rumours – 'Consternation at the unknown has to a great extent given way to concern for the sufferers.' There is, however, some regret that the statement was not made earlier, before evacuees had started to spread their stories round the country. Comment has mostly been about:

(a) THE CASUALTIES, which are regarded by most people as surprisingly low. A minority, however, think that 10,000 casualties is a very high figure in such a short space of time. Some people suspect the casualties were greater than Mr. Churchill stated. A few East Anglians are under the impression that each bomb launched on London has killed only one person.

(b) COUNTER-MEASURES: Some were disappointed that Mr. Churchill was not more reassuring about defeating the flying bomb; they had hoped he would announce an effective solution. Gratification that our Secret Service found out about the flying bomb so long ago has been somewhat counteracted by regret that the Government could not have made even more effective use of their knowledge.

(c) THE ANNOUNCEMENT OF THE OPENING OF DEEP SHELTERS AND OF EVACUATION PLANS, which has caused some satisfaction.

GENERAL REACTIONS TO THE BOMB remain very much the same as last week. It is still more talked about than anything else. Rumours are fewer and, for the most part, less fantastic – largely thanks to the Prime Minister's statement.

There is much sympathy and admiration for Londoners. The general impression seems to be that they are undergoing ordeals worse than the blitz, an impression which evacuees are tireless in spreading. People visualise 'old people wandering round, homes totally destroyed and with no evacuation scheme to help them'.

There is considerable diversity of opinion as to how the ordeal is being borne, and there continue to be many tales of Londoners panicking, living in the shelters day and night, and having to be turned out by the police in order that the shelters may be aired.

It seems to be generally believed that Londoners are more nervous over these raids than over any in the past. The possible effect on production of workers' lack of sleep is also causing some concern. On the other hand, people are told by returning visitors how well Londoners are taking it, working steadily, and carrying on as usual.

Some believe that, once the children are evacuated, Londoners will find it easier to carry on.

RUMOURS OF CASUALTIES are notably fewer than last week. RUMOURS OF DAMAGE have only slightly decreased; it is said that the recent press stories of the damage, and those told by evacuees, visitors to London, and air-raid wardens have to some extent offset the good effect of Mr. Churchill's speech. RUMOURS OF THE BOMB ITSELF continue on the same lines, but fewer than before.

DEFENCES AND COUNTER-MEASURES continue to be discussed on the same lines as before, the majority hopeful that a solution will eventually be found and satisfied that everything possible is being done in the meantime. A minority feel that what we are doing now is not very effective and are not very hopeful about the future. Almost everyone seems agreed that the only certain cure is occupation of the area of the launching sites; though a few fear the bomb's range is greater than we suppose, that the launching sites can be progressively withdrawn towards Germany, and that we shall go on being bombed after we have occupied the coastal strip.

REPRISALS are increasingly discussed and appear to be increasingly favoured (particularly by Londoners), though opinion remains divided. Those in favour mostly advocate threatening Germany with the systematic obliteration of her cities unless she stops the flying bombs, and in London there is said to be some support for John Gordon's articles on the subject in the *Sunday Express*; a few want 'retaliation by the most vile weapon possible'. Those against retaliation object that this would only lead to a competition in terrorism and would be playing Hitler's game, besides distracting our air power from military objectives.

'WORSE TO COME': There is a good deal of speculation about:

(a) A POSSIBLE EXTENSION IN THE RANGE OF THE BOMB, which is the subject of minority concern in some parts of the country apparently well out of range at present. Bombs are already rumoured to have reached Bristol, Weston, Worcester, Birmingham, Coventry, Leicester and Northampton. In the Eastern Region there is some uneasiness at the possibility of there being launching platforms in Holland from which East Anglia can be bombed.

(b) SECRET WEAPON NO. 2: Gas and rockets are both feared; rocket shells of 20 tons are discussed with awe, and there are alarming pictures of the damage they are likely to inflict. Some anticipate a development of the flying bomb with oil bombs, land mines and incendiaries attached.

EVACUEES

Discussion about the problem of finding accommodation for the 'constant stream' of both official and unofficial evacuees has greatly increased in many parts of the country. Some people are sympathetic and willing to house evacuees wherever possible, but on the whole there is felt to be less readiness to billet them than in 1940/41. This is attributed to:

(a) The already serious accommodation difficulties.

In the Eastern Region, satisfaction is reported that the War Office have released a number of empty requisitioned houses; people hope more will be released. Hostels, it is suggested in another Region, should be used for evacuees.

(b) Unhappy recollections of evacuees in the past.

(c) The many women who now go out to work; they are anxious about the additional housework and food problems involved, and do not like having to leave strangers alone in their homes.

(d) The difficulty of supplying and replacing bedding and household linen.

(e) A feeling that people in large houses with few occupants get out of billeting, while small houses are crowded out.

There is criticism of unofficial evacuees 'who make no plans', and of Jews, who are said to be 'the first to rush to safety'.

FOOD: There is again some concern over supplies in reception areas; people hope food allocations will not lag behind arrivals of evacuees. A shortage due to evacuees is reported from areas in the Southern and South-Western Regions.

LOCALISED REACTIONS

A. LONDON: The great majority continue to find the raids a severe trial, but first fears have to some extent died down, and there are now fewer references to terror or great anxiety. The continuity and inhumanity of the attacks have resulted in nervousness and strain and much lack of sleep, added to the shock of finding that the war is as yet by no means over. A few doubt if Londoners can stand a long bombardment.

Fear and anxiety do not appear to vary much as between bombed and unbombed areas, though they are slightly more pronounced among people in central and south-east London, mothers with young children, and women who are at home all day. Men working away from home, too, are anxious for their families.

On the other hand, a growing number have become more or less adjusted to the raids; many of them feel, moreover, that it is their contribution to the war effort and that 'our boys in Normandy are getting it worse'. Military successes have also done much to help.

THE PRIME MINISTER'S STATEMENT appears to have disappointed most Londoners; they had hoped for more reassurance about the future and more information about the present. A few disbelieve the casualty figures, pointing out that no reference was made to the number of persons missing.

A good many, however, consider the speech all that could be expected and think that it has had a good effect. They are glad that he 'refused to sugar the pill'.

Mr. Churchill's statement appears to have had the effect of discouraging rumours; far fewer have been reported since he spoke.

ATTITUDE TO THE GOVERNMENT: This is a little less critical since the Prime Minister's statement; but there are still complaints that the Government should have been better prepared, that it should have overcome the flying bomb by now, and that it should give more information about the raids.

Anything in the nature of a 'we can take it' speech is resented ... 'We do, because we must!'

DEFENCES: Opinion seems about equally divided: some consider everything possible is being done and that the raids will not last much longer; others question the effect of Allied bombing and fear that little can be done to stop the raids, which will go on for some time.

SIRENS AND WARNINGS: Some people find the sirens very 'trying to the nerves', and an increase in the local warning system is asked for.

EVACUATION is widely discussed. Everyone who mentions it agrees that children, mothers with children, and pregnant women should be evacuated at the earliest possible moment. At the same time, old and sick people, it is thought, should be urged to go away – even though elderly people 'are taking the raids well on the whole'. While in some cases it is husbands who are insisting on wives and children leaving London, a great number of the women themselves want to get away and are inundating CABs and similar offices with requests. In Finchley and Pinner there are reported to be difficulties in meeting evacuation demands as they have not been designated evacuation areas.

A greatly increased demand for facilities to leave London followed the Prime Minister's reference to evacuation.

More people are said to be making their own arrangements this time than during the blitz.

SHELTERS are increasingly used; many who did not use them during the blitz are sleeping in them now.

Public shelters are said to be very overcrowded; some are thought unhealthy and not fit to sleep in. Particular concern is expressed at the danger to children's health, 'sleeping side by side with the aged and diseased in the Tubes'. Some people are reported to remain in the shelters day and night, regardless of work, shopping or meals. Some prefer to risk the bombs rather than lice and germs in the shelters.

There are complaints of lack of sub-surface shelters and of inadequate bunk accommodation; and there is mention of fights between regular bunk-holders and 'newcomers'.

But people are pleased that the big deep shelters are being opened.

POST-RAID SERVICES: There is now warm praise for the swift removal of furniture from blasted premises.

In the East End, there has been a little criticism of inadequate rest centre facilities; and, elsewhere, of inadequate rehousing for the bombed-out.

There are isolated references to 'fictitious claims' being made for air-raid damage compensation, and to 'petty looting'.

An extra ration of tea would be welcomed by Londoners.

US TROOPS: Their assistance during raids is warmly appreciated.

'SECRET WEAPON NO. 2' causes rather more concern this week, a greater number of Londoners speaking fearfully of 'worse to come'. The press is blamed for frightening people with stories of 15-ton projectiles. Some wish to know how devastating the threatened weapon is likely to be, and also what precautions are being taken against it.

B. SOUTH-EASTERN DISTRICT: As in London, people appear to be growing a little more acclimatised; though many – women and the less educated particularly – remain very scared. Folkestone, however, is said to prefer flying bombs to shells.

Loss of sleep is still the main difficulty, for which AA gunfire is largely blamed. People are very tired and in some cases work has been noticeably affected.

Most people in the south-east feel very sympathetic towards Londoners, as most of the bombs seem to get through. A few, however, accuse 'the Authorities' of not caring where the bombs drop, so long as it is short of London.

DEFENCES: AA batteries are criticised by many on the grounds that the gunners fire over built-up areas, causing damage from shrapnel and any bombs they may succeed in hitting. Others say the guns never destroy any bombs, and merely chase away – or hit – the fighters. A joke, said to be current in Tunbridge Wells, is to the effect that the 'bag' of one battery was 'two Spitfires, two Tempests, and a Typhoon'.

SHELTERS: More people are sleeping in shelters or downstairs; the demand for Morrison shelters has increased. Unhealthy conditions are reported in the cave shelter in Kenley, where people are said to have been living night and day for three weeks.

EVACUATION: Desire for the evacuation of women and children is reported from Caterham, districts near Sutton-at-Hone, and Egham. In Guildford, it is said far too many Londoners are arriving there and that they should be advised to go north instead.

C. EASTERN REGION: Most people are seriously concerned; some are nervous and despondent. Some are afraid the range of the bombs may be extended; and those in places without military importance, who formerly thought themselves safe, now fear they may be hit. A growing shelter-consciousness is reported from most districts.

SIRENS: It is asked whether something can be done about the warnings in coastal districts, where the bomb either coincides with or precedes the siren ... 'It is very trying to hear the siren wailing away and covering the sound of the bomb, so that people cannot judge when to take cover.'

Some nervousness is also reported as a result of the sounding of too many sirens, particularly at night; though the present system is said to satisfy the people of Luton. In St. Albans a strong feeling is reported that schools should have the same crash warnings as factories.

D. SOUTHERN REGION: There is still considerable nervousness; and a renewal of references to war strain is attributed to the flying bomb.

3. THE INVASION OF FRANCE

Widespread satisfaction and pride continue, coupled with confidence in the campaign's future development. Appreciation is again expressed of the strength and obstinacy of German resistance; heavy fighting ahead is anticipated.

At the same time, considerable disappointment has been reported this week at our rate of progress, especially in comparison with Russian successes. Some, however, think the campaign is playing an important part in the Russian victories.

The fall of Caen caused pleasure and relief; people hope it will speed progress. Satisfaction continues, also, at the fall of Cherbourg; there are widespread hopes of its usefulness as a port and base.

Praise for, and confidence in, our men, our leaders, and our planning continue; General Montgomery is particularly mentioned – there is great faith in his ability to outwit and outfight Rommel.

There is increased comment and anxiety about THE POOR WEATHER, which is thought to have been a great handicap and the main cause of any delays.

Comment about CASUALTIES AND MEDICAL CARE does not differ materially from last week.

Field postcards are said not to be arriving, and 'not to convey much' when they do.

THE RUMOUR THAT GENERAL MONTGOMERY has been captured, killed, or wounded is this week reported from six Regions.

Suggestions made by the public to account for the origin of the rumours are that (a) a French village with a name somewhat similar to Montgomery was announced by the Germans as captured; (b) a newspaper correspondent named Montgomery was wounded, captured or killed.

THE PEOPLE OF NORMANDY: Comment has decreased this week, though not distrust; this is thought to have been made worse by letters from servicemen in France. Tales are said to circulate that 'there were definitely French snipers'. Some blame the press for earlier wrong impressions; others are not surprised if the French dislike us, because of the devastation inflicted on their country. A few think hostility has been the exception in France.

Very little comment about conditions, though people continue to believe that the French have by no means suffered privations.

NEWS PRESENTATION OF THE INVASION: People are thought to be giving rather less attention to the news this week, but praise for its presentation continues.

While the BBC *War Reports* are still appreciated, it is suggested by a few that 'now people have got the atmosphere of the battlefield, this item should be cut down'.

Four Regions report some feeling that too much prominence is given to the Americans.

3A. THE NEXT MOVE

Speculation continues. Some think we shall land next in the south of France; others favour Holland, north-west France, or Belgium. Londoners continue to hope we shall capture the flying bomb bases.

In Brighton it is rumoured that airborne troops are being returned from France, and this is taken to portend another invasion soon.

4. RUSSIA

Widespread praise for the sweeping victories of the Red Army continues, and there is much admiration for the organisation of the campaign and for the High Command. People are amazed at the speed of progress and optimistic that it will be maintained

... 'The mileage from East Prussia is carefully noted after each communiqué.' An increasing number still hope that the Russians will be the first to reach Germany and Berlin.

Some wonder whether Germany is beginning to crack on the Russian front and will be 'finished off' from the East. A few say that if hostilities do finish this year, it will be largely because of Russian efforts now.

There is again some doubt about the accuracy of casualty figures given by the Russians.

FINLAND: Comment is less; there is still little sympathy. The news of the break in US relations is again welcomed. Some people cannot understand the Finnish attitude 'unless it is one of fear of what the Germans will do before they are driven out of the country'.

5. ITALY

Though still overshadowed by other fronts, our progress in Italy continues to give widespread satisfaction; there is again praise for our Forces there and for General Alexander.

There have been no reports of reactions since the news of stiffening German resistance. Previously people were pleased that 'we had them on the run'; some expected the Germans would soon abandon Italy entirely. A few, however, were even then disappointed at our slowness.

Complaints – particularly from relatives of those fighting there – of the small amount of publicity received by this theatre of war continue.

6. GERMANY

INCREASINGLY BITTER FEELING AGAINST GERMANY and a growing desire for the punishment of her war criminals and for the 'rigorous administration' of her territory after the war have been widely reported. The use of flying bombs, and – to a lesser degree – the treatment of Hungarian Jews, are both thought to have contributed.

Stories of gold being sent from Germany to Portugal are said to have stimulated fears that many war criminals will get away.

There is increasing SPECULATION AS TO HOW MUCH LONGER GERMANY CAN LAST. Some think she must soon succumb; recent speeches by Hitler and Goebbels, the belief that Germany does not want to fight on her own soil, and the capitulation to the Danish strikers are all cited.

7. FAR EAST

There is again little interest this week. People continue satisfied with the progress being made. This, together with the bombing of Japan by Super-Fortresses and the recent naval victory, have increased the hope that the Japanese will be beaten soon after the collapse of Germany.

CHINA: There is some concern over the Japanese advances in China and some apprehension at rumours of political disunity.

8. GENERAL DE GAULLE AND THE FRENCH NATIONAL COMMITTEE

People continue puzzled and uneasy at the official attitude to General de Gaulle and the French National Committee. General de Gaulle's visit to America has roused little interest, but there is some hope that it will 'clear the air'.

The desire that the Committee should be recognised as the provisional government continues to be reported.

II. SPECIAL COMMENTS

BRIEF WEEKLY REVIEW

9. FOOD

SUGAR FOR JAM: The announcement of the extra issue of sugar for jam has given pleasure. Some people, however, are disappointed at the small allowance, but a few are optimistic that more will be released later on. Disappointment is also reported on the grounds that, by the time the sugar is released, it will be too late to make use of any soft fruit that may be obtainable.

FRUIT AND TOMATOES: Complaints of the shortage of fruit and tomatoes have increased slightly this week. People do not believe that the fruit shortage can be entirely accounted for by the frost. Unfair distribution, queues and under-the-counter sales continue to arouse complaint. Workers who cannot queue are said to be especially badly off. The high price of fruit is also commented on.

MILK RATION: The cut continues to cause disappointment. It is asked whether more powdered or condensed milk could be released to make up for the cut.

10. HOLIDAYS

Comment is less, but there is still some demand, particularly among indoor workers, for facilities to get away for a holiday. Some think the Government should either ban holiday travel or make adequate arrangements. There is also some complaint of the difficulty of arranging accommodation.

In the North Midland Region, it is said that the progress of the war has reconciled most people to the thought of spending yet another holiday at home; and there is some feeling because 'those who are going away have done so each summer and are not affected by the national need'.

In Scotland 'short-distance holidays are the fashion' and accommodation is fully booked everywhere. Day trips are causing a rush on transport and restaurants.

In Northern Ireland booking to seaside resorts is said to be very heavy.

11. THE GOVERNMENT PROPOSALS FOR THE CONTROL OF LAND

Interest continues limited. However, what comment there is is now entirely adverse. People are dissatisfied with the rejection of the Uthwatt proposals for balancing compensation and betterment and feel the Government's proposals are inadequate and piecemeal.

The Land Bill is said to be a blow to many hopes and to have strengthened people's cynicism about the Government's intentions.

NO. 199: TUESDAY 18 JULY 1944 TO TUESDAY 25 JULY 1944

I. GENERAL COMMENTS

1. GENERAL

The troubles in Germany, described as the sensation of the week, and Russian advances, have combined to raise spirits yet higher. People are increasingly optimistic about the end of the European war; the majority think it certain by Christmas; while a good many expect it much sooner.

There is still disappointment that progress in Normandy has not been faster.

Except in London and the South-East, the flying bomb is now less discussed than the arrival of evacuees. Evacuation problems are the chief home front topic.

An early relaxation of the blackout is widely hoped for.

2. THE CRISIS IN GERMANY

On Friday, people were wildly excited by the news, and there was much speculation about possible dramatic developments. There were widespread rumours of civil war in Germany, and of Hitler being dead or a prisoner in the hands of the plotters. Since then, the majority, though keenly awaiting further information, have become more cautious. Even so, no matter what view is taken of the crisis, everybody feels it indicates a crack inside Germany and is the beginning of the end.

Detailed discussion has been on the following lines:

THE AUTHENTICITY OF THE PLOT: Opinion is divided between:

(a) The majority who think there really was a plot. They believe that the rebel generals, seeing defeat before them, wanted to get rid of Hitler, so as to negotiate an early peace; the German army 'could then live on to fight a third world war another day'.

(b) Those who think the whole thing a frame-up on the part of the Nazis, primarily to liquidate the disaffected military leaders. A few think it a propaganda stunt to idolise Hitler or to distract attention from Germany's present plight.

THE FAILURE TO KILL HITLER: Opinion is again divided:

(a) Some think it a great pity he was not killed, as it would have brought the end of the war much nearer.
(b) Others feel it was a good job the bomb did not get him; it would have been too easy a death; or, according to a few, it would have made him a martyr in the eyes of the Germans.

THE NEED TO DEFEAT THE GERMANS MILITARILY: People are unanimous that there must be no negotiated peace, no matter what moves are made inside Germany for the overthrow of the Nazis. They feel that now is the time to be most careful, or the Germans will trick us again; the German generals are as dangerous as the Nazis; and our best line is to go on hitting hard again and again. Only a complete military defeat of Germany can convince the German people they have really lost the war.

2A. HATRED OF THE GERMANS

The hatred reported last week due to the flying bomb, the French village and Hungarian Jew massacres, and the shooting of British prisoners of war, has increased with the news of further shootings.

People are heartily sick of German militarism and brutality, and want rigorous 'Vansittart' terms imposed on them when they surrender. Fear continues, however, that the British and Americans will be too lenient, and also that 'some elements in this country are prepared to be kind to the Germans'.

3. EVACUATION

In the country as a whole, evacuation is now even more widely discussed than the flying bombs. On the whole, it is thought to have gone off fairly well. Discussion is chiefly about:

ATTITUDE TO EVACUEES: In general, people have been sympathetic and helpful, particularly towards unaccompanied children – many of whom have pleasantly surprised their hosts.

Women with children, and pregnant women, have been far less welcome and are said to be very difficult to billet – still more so, of course, when mothers refuse to be separated from large families of children. Women do not want another woman in the house, either getting in the way or, alternatively, expecting to be waited on hand and foot. It is said to be a heart-rending job hawking unwanted evacuees from door to door.

A minority are unsympathetic, some producing doctors' certificates, others shutting up their houses and going away. Previous unfortunate experiences are not forgotten.

Disgust is reported at cases of householders refusing to accept evacuees or freezing them out by unpleasantness. A night or two in London is thought the best punishment for them. It is suggested, however, that press publicity about such cases has been both unfortunate, in not fostering a helpful attitude of mind among people in reception areas, and also unfair to the localities pilloried for the unkindness of a few.

CLASS DIFFERENCES are frequently alleged. It is thought both that better-off people living in larger houses are less ready to take their share, and that less pressure is put on them than on smaller and poorer households.

THE BILLETING ALLOWANCE is considered by many people to be much too small and consequently unlikely to encourage volunteers. The higher billeting rates of US officers is said to make them much more acceptable.

THE POLICY OF PRIVATE BILLETING, which is regarded most unfavourably, at least until other alternatives have been tried. The Government is criticised on the grounds that, knowing in advance about flying bombs, they should have prepared hostels and camps, and not asked the general public to shoulder the responsibility. It is widely thought that, before sending evacuees to private houses, the Government should organise camps and hostels, taking over for the purpose large mansions – whether partially occupied or not; vacant property – furnished or unfurnished; empty hotels (e.g. three in Stratford, the 'Royal' at Scarborough); houses requisitioned, but not used, by the War Office; vacant army camps; Cambridge colleges, etc. etc. It is also thought that the time has now come when provincial business firms, using private houses in the suburbs as offices, could give them up and go back to their quarters in the city centre (e.g. in Newcastle). Women say they would be quite willing to go and provide domestic help if the evacuees were accommodated in hostels.

BEDDING AND HOUSEHOLD LINEN: The shortage of household linen has for some time been a subject of widespread public complaint. The difficulty is now said to be seriously aggravated – particularly in working-class homes – by the incursion of evacuees. People ask if the Government cannot make provision or at least insist on evacuees bringing their own.

FOOD: There is some praise for the way the food position has been adjusted; though the shortage of points goods is said to be a difficulty. In other parts of the country, the promise of more supplies to evacuation areas has relieved anxiety on this score. Only in the South-Western Region are acute food problems reported, aggravated in resort towns by the arrival of trippers, but in the Midland Region report there is also reference to 'a party of women with young children in the train returning to London, saying that they had been unable to buy enough food'.

THE LIFTING OF THE BAN IN THE SOUTH-WEST, which is appreciated, though many people continue to think that the re-opened areas should have been fully utilised for evacuees before the general public were allowed to enter. As it is, in the Dorset coastal area, holiday-makers are said to be crowding out unofficial evacuees.

HOLIDAY RESORTS: Some seaside resorts fear that evacuees will take accommodation which would have been available for holiday-makers and so reduce the income of residents. Scarborough boarding-house keepers, 'who have lost money steadily throughout the war and are in arrears with rent and rates, ask why they should be expected to take in evacuees just at a period when, for the first time since the war, they are beginning to make up leeway. Scarborough people say that Blackpool landladies are in a different position as their business has not suffered to anything like the same extent.'

4. FLYING BOMBS

THE COUNTRY AS A WHOLE

Widespread discussion continues, although the flying bombs are no longer the main topic except in London and the South-Eastern district. Anxiety and concern persist, and people are disappointed that the intensity of the raids does not appear to have lessened. There is much sympathy and admiration for those in target areas, especially Londoners; though a few regard the raids with indifference – 'like reports from occupied Europe'.

INFORMATION ABOUT THE RAIDS: There is still considerable criticism of the meagreness and vagueness of bulletins. They are thought to treat the raids too lightly, to cause unnecessary anxiety about friends and relatives, and to encourage rumours. People find it difficult to reconcile official statements with stories brought by evacuees.

Nevertheless, rumours, although still widespread, are fewer.

COUNTER-MEASURES: Most people are confident the bombs will eventually be mastered – if only by the capture of the launching site areas; equally, they are disappointed at the lack of success so far.

Some continue to think the Government should have made more preparations before the raids began.

FUTURE EXPECTATIONS: Widespread anxiety about the possibility of the range of the bomb being extended, or of the enemy using new, more deadly weapons, continues; rocket or gas bombs are the most popular suggestions. In the Northern Region, a rumour that men attending CD lectures have been told that the bombs may be expected in the north-east in a few weeks is said to be causing uneasiness, though it is not thought to fit in with the influx of evacuees and requests to give up Morrison shelters.

REPRISALS continue to be advocated by many, the systematic bombing of German cities being the favourite suggestion. A few suggest the use of flying bombs.

Some, however, feel reprisals might achieve nothing, diverting our planes from battlefields and giving the Germans the excuse for further murders of prisoners of war.

REACTIONS IN TARGET AREAS

A. LONDON: Although anxiety and strain continue, more people are becoming adjusted, looking on the raids as part of the daily routine. There is still some mention of work being upset by disturbed nights and repeated sheltering during the day.

ATTITUDE TO GOVERNMENT: Criticism again predominates – on the grounds of lack of preparation and an unsympathetic attitude: 'they take our endurance for granted'.

CIVIL DEFENCE WORKERS: High praise continues; sightseers at incidents are criticised.

LOOTING: Much indignation. People favour heavier sentences.

DANGER WARNING: A uniform method of imminent danger warning is asked for – but not anything which will mask the sound of the bomb as the siren sometimes does.

DEFENCES: Though the RAF is praised, there is little comment. People dislike our planes 'buzzing about' during alerts.

SHELTERS: People think some areas have too few; and that Morrisons should be available for everyone.

CHILDREN: Anxiety continues about children, particularly those whose mothers are working; they are not attending school and are playing in the streets during alerts.

POST-RAID SERVICES: There is still some dissatisfaction over compensation for raid losses and the slowness of repair work.

EVACUATION: Criticism of details continues to be reported in greater volume than does approval of the principle. At the same time, some feel the Government should be congratulated for moving so many children so quickly.

The points made are:

(a) The scheme should cover a wider area.
(b) Old people should be included. Servicemen are said to be particularly anxious about their aged relatives.
(c) Camps would have been better than private billeting; at the same time, people who refuse to billet children should be severely dealt with.
(d) The prices charged to voluntary evacuees are too high; anyhow, these people should be given travel vouchers.
(e) Some mothers going with children are only going for a holiday and intend to come back in a week or two.

B. SOUTH-EASTERN DISTRICT: Tiredness remains the most prominent feature, owing to disturbed nights and lack of respite by day. Those in 'established bomb lanes' are nervous; but the majority are calm.

DEFENCES: The fighters continue to be preferred to AA fire and people are pleased where guns have been removed.

POST-RAID SERVICES: Appreciation.

SHELTERS: More Morrison shelters are wanted in some areas.

CHILDREN: Many parents are said not to be sending their children to school because there are no shelters at the schools.

EVACUATION: Discussion is on the same lines as in London. More people, however, feel evacuation is unnecessary, or that 'it will be a failure as before', and are said not to be sending their children away.

C. SOUTHERN REGION: People in affected areas, though calm, are suffering from lack of sleep.

There is continued high praise of Civil Defence workers; but again complaints that warnings coincide with bombs.

5. THE INVASION OF FRANCE

(No comments have yet been received on Mr. Churchill's visit.)

Satisfaction and confidence continue; but there is increased disappointment with our progress this week – chiefly because of the non-materialisation of the much-expected 'breakthrough'. Comparisons with Russian advances are again widely made, though some continue to point out the contribution to Russian successes that our campaigns are making. The weather, geographical difficulties, and the fact that the Germans are using some of their best forces against us are also cited.

Praise for British and American troops and confidence in our planning and leadership continue.

POSTAL SERVICES: Some continue to complain of slowness, but others express pleasure at improved deliveries.

THE PEOPLE OF FRANCE: Some are pleased that the French are helping our Forces, but others remain suspicious of them.

NEWS PRESENTATION: Satisfaction with news presentation continues, though there are a few more complaints this week. The BBC and press are accused of misleading the public by premature announcements of a 'breakthrough'; consequently, Howard Marshall's commentary warning against anticipating this is said to have confused some people.

The broadcasts of the parade service from Normandy and of the bombardment of the Caen sector are both praised.

General Montgomery's broadcasts have apparently done something to squash the rumour of his capture or death; the rumour continues to be reported, however.

5A. THE NEXT MOVE

Speculation about another landing continues. Some are surprised it has not yet taken place.

6. RUSSIA

Widespread admiration and astonishment at the rapid advance of the Red Army continue. A great majority hope and expect that the Russians will be first in Berlin ... 'They will show no mercy to the Nazis, as we might.' There is speculation about the effect the Russian entry into East Prussia will have on German morale.

Again, some fears about the Russian attitude in the post-war world; though working-class people in Scotland say that if we play the game by her, she will play it by us.

RUSSO-POLISH SITUATION: Uneasiness continues.

7. ITALY

Satisfaction with progress continues, particularly with the capture of Leghorn and Ancona; there is much praise for General Alexander's leadership and for the troops 'doggedly pushing over difficult country'. Some still feel not enough publicity is given to this campaign and that there is a tendency to forget what is being done, in view of the more spectacular events on the Russian and Normandy fronts.

A minority are disappointed at the continued enemy resistance; some, however, regard it as 'Kesselring's swan song' and think the Germans will soon clear out, in order to make a last determined stand on their home front.

Little comment has as yet been received about the visit of HM the King to the Italian front.

8. FAR EAST

Interest in the fighting continues to be overshadowed by events in Europe, but the attack on Guam has caused some appreciative and hopeful comment. People are beginning to think that the Far Eastern war will not last long after Germany is defeated.

THE RESIGNATION OF TOJO AND HIS CABINET has aroused some interest and is generally taken as another step in the right direction and as evidence that the Japanese are not doing so well and know it. Only a few seem to think that this move is intended to throw dust in Allied eyes.

9. GENERAL DE GAULLE AND THE FRENCH COMMITTEE OF NATIONAL LIBERATION

DURING THE PAST TWO WEEKS pleasure has been reported at the success of General de Gaulle's visit to the USA, and the recognition of the French Committee of National Liberation as the de facto authority for civil administration under Allied military control. It is felt this step forward will strengthen the French resistance movement. Some minority concern about Anglo-American-French relations still persists, however.

10. POLISH TROOPS

Polish troops who have been stationed in the East Riding have made a very good impression as being quiet and well behaved, contrary to first expectations. People in the area generally have taken them to their hearts, and compare them very favourably with our own troops, who had been stationed previously in the district. There is genuine regret at the departure of Polish troops from the area.

II. SPECIAL COMMENTS

BRIEF WEEKLY REVIEW

11. CLOTHING

The announcement that the ration for the next period will be 24 coupons continues to cause little comment – mainly in the nature of disappointment and renewed complaints of the inadequacy of the allowance.

There is said to be resentment that children's new coupons cannot be used before August 1, 'as the BBC and press gave the impression they could'; mothers clothing their children for evacuation are said to find this very difficult.

12. FOOD

FRESH FRUIT: People complain of shortage and uneven distribution and of the prevalence of queues. Some housewives ask why it is not possible to ration fruit in order to distribute it more evenly.

SUGAR: While the extra sugar for jam-making is appreciated, disappointment is again reported that it was not made available in time for preserving soft fruit. It is feared some garden fruit may have been wasted.

FOOD FOR RECEPTION AREAS is dealt with under 'Evacuation'.

13. HOLIDAYS

Some people are spending their holidays at home, either because they are discouraged by crowded trains and the difficulty of finding accommodation, or because they would feel guilty using transport needed for war.

In Scotland, however, all holiday accommodation has been booked up as far as the middle of September, and hotels and boarding-houses are being inundated with requests from disappointed holiday-makers and evacuees. Day trips are common, even though the trippers often have to spend most of the day in queues – for trains, buses and for food. In London, more people than ever want to go away for holidays – 'the flying bomb raids have stopped holiday-at-home resolutions'.

HARVEST HELPERS: In Scotland, those who filled up forms are said to be anxiously awaiting further information regarding farms, hostels etc., as their holiday 'has been fixed accordingly and no holiday accommodation is available now'.

It is suggested that many people would help with farming if they could take their children with them.

III. PERIODICAL REVIEW

14. YOUTH AND MORALS

DURING THE PAST FOUR WEEKS uneasiness and criticism have continued on the subject of moral delinquency. Though it tends to be social workers, the elderly and 'more thoughtful' who complain most about the wild behaviour of young and irresponsible people, the general public are not slow to criticise when the offences affect them directly.

The complaints are the familiar ones, of:

(a) SEXUAL IMMORALITY, specially of young women and girls with servicemen of every available nationality and colour. The unfaithfulness of married women, particularly those whose husbands are on active service, is also a subject of concern; public indignation against specific instances is said to be very strong, especially where child neglect ensues. A little sympathy is, nevertheless, reported towards servicemen's wives living in the country ... 'Plenty of entertainment is provided for the troops, but nothing for the women left in isolated villages; is it any wonder they get into trouble!'

(b) DRINKING, again particularly by young people. 'Working men, by no means teetotal enthusiasts, complain bitterly about the number of young girls who frequent pubs night after night and cause disgraceful scenes. They say that, after a long day's work, they want to be able to have a glass of beer in peace.' But it is recognised that it is difficult for publicans to know the age of their young customers.

(c) JUVENILE MISDEMEANOURS OF VARIOUS KINDS, including petty crimes – which are thought to be increasing – damage to property, thefts from gardens, hooliganism, rowdiness, rudeness and foul language.

FACTORS BLAMED are the familiar ones: (a) lack of parental control – whether because of irresponsibility or absence on war work; (b) lack of harmless recreational facilities, particularly for transferred workers in uncongenial lodgings; (c) too much money and nothing suitable to spend it on. As a result, adolescents frequent the pubs, and younger children the cinemas. Some elementary school children are given 10/- a week – or more – pocket money, and in some cases go to the pictures 'regularly four times a week'. One small boy, asked why he brought fly papers to school, claimed it was because there was nothing else in the shops to buy.

YOUTH CLUBS AND ORGANISATIONS are the subject of miscellaneous comment, mostly favourable. They are praised, said to be well supported, and more are thought to be needed, but there is a feeling that they do not attract those who would benefit from them most. Youth clubs are criticised from opposite points of view, either as being too sectional and religious, with too much uplift, or alternatively, as concentrating on entertainment and dancing at the expense of cultural activities.

Club leaders and social workers feel their work is handicapped by:

(a) The need for members to give coupons for uniforms.
(b) Lack of accommodation, particularly in remote areas, where Forces are stationed and the halls all requisitioned.

15. ATTITUDE TO THE JEWS

ANTI-SEMITISM: DURING THE PAST EIGHT WEEKS comment has still continued at a low level. In some areas, however, apparently as a result of discussion of German atrocities against Jews and of evacuation difficulties, there has been some increase.

Criticisms have chiefly been on the grounds of:

(a) JEWS BEING THE 'FIRST OUT' WHEN THE FLYING BOMB RAIDS STARTED.
(b) WEALTH AND OSTENTATION.
(c) EVADING NATIONAL SERVICE: 'No Jews appear to be drawn out of the ballot for the mines.'
(d) BLACK MARKET ACTIVITIES.

GERMAN ATROCITIES AGAINST JEWS: Horror at their treatment and sympathy with the victims are reported.

NO. 202: WEDNESDAY 9 AUGUST 1944 TO TUESDAY 15 AUGUST 1944

I. GENERAL COMMENTS

1. GENERAL

Spirits have risen higher still. Continued progress in Normandy and the Prime Minister's speech are mainly responsible; preliminary reports suggest that the Allied landings in the south of France have increased still further the general mood of optimism.

'WHEN WILL THE WAR BE OVER?' appears to be the chief topic of discussion. The general feeling is that 'it can't be long now', and sometime in October seems the most popular guess; many think it may only be a few weeks. However, a minority think we may be in for another war winter, as the Germans are both tenacious and resourceful.

HOME FRONT TOPICS are evacuation, transport and holidays. Post-war prospects are becoming a matter of more urgent concern, now that the end of war seems so near.

2. FRANCE

THE SOUTH COAST LANDING: So far only preliminary reports have been received. These show great elation ... 'the Nazis are now really on the run'; some are speculating on the possible directions – Italy or Paris.

Previously, there had been some reports that the move was expected – chiefly because of our heavy bombing of the area, and Mr. Churchill's visit to Italy.

GENERAL DE GAULLE'S STATEMENT that a French army would soon be in operation had been welcomed and had dispelled some previous disappointment that the French were not being used.

NORTHERN FRANCE: Great satisfaction with progress and much speculation as to what will follow on present successes; many expect the capture of Paris, some the complete collapse of German resistance in France. Londoners, particularly, hope for the capture of flying bomb and rocket sites.

The Americans are very generally praised, but there is considerable jealousy that they have had a spectacular role, while British and Canadian troops faced the 'sticky bits'. At the same time there continues to be considerable disappointment at what is thought slow progress on our part.

The planning and strategy of the campaign, and the leaders and men, are again praised; there is also much satisfaction with the air support given to the ground troops.

GENERAL EISENHOWER'S recent 'go to it' speech is said to have been much appreciated.

GENERAL EISENHOWER'S MOVE TO NORMANDY was thought a good sign.

THE CHANNEL ISLANDS: Some concern for the inhabitants is expressed, and it is hoped they will soon be freed.

3. EVACUATION

A little less comment than last week – but still a great deal – and all on familiar lines (see Home Intelligence Weekly Reports, 3rd and 11th August).

4. FLYING BOMBS

THE COUNTRY AS A WHOLE

Except in London and the South-East, where the raids continue a main topic, discussion has declined very considerably. At the same time, people remain concerned; sympathy and admiration for those in London and other target areas 'who make a joke of the doodlebugs' are widespread. An increased number believe the present ordeal worse than the blitz, and there is considerable talk of heavy damage.

Many continue irritated with official reticence – thought to result in rumour-mongering and exaggeration, and in ignorance in non-target areas of what is being endured.

DEFENCES AND COUNTER-MEASURES: Progress in France has quickened hopes that we shall soon capture the launching sites; this is increasingly thought the only certain means of ending the attacks. Disappointment with present methods, and with our 'apparent helplessness', continues, though more people now think all possible is being done.

FUTURE EXPECTATIONS: Comment continues as last week.

REPRISALS: Widespread desire for reprisals continues on familiar lines.

CIVIL DEFENCE AND REPAIR WORKERS FOR LONDON: It is alleged (a) that wardens and repair parties from the Midlands who go to help in London only get their normal pay, although those they work with receive much higher pay; (b) that no proper arrangements have been made for the reception of the workers on arrival in London.

REACTIONS IN TARGET AREAS

A. LONDON: The majority are now 'adjusted', although a few remain nervous, particularly at the possibility of raids next winter. The lack of sleep is the worst part, and many people are said to be very tired.

EVACUATION: Criticism of the Government is on almost exactly the same lines as in the past two weeks.

People in reception areas are again criticised. It is said that they think the dangers exaggerated, and that children are badly treated and want to go home. A few, however, think no one should be compelled to take evacuees.

People again criticise evacuees for 'coming and going at the public expense'.

POST-RAID SERVICES: The difficulty of getting accommodation for bombed-out people and the 'slackness' of men doing repairs cause comment. People wonder whether adequate compensation will be paid for their losses.

Civil Defence workers are again praised; some think more personnel should be drafted from elsewhere to relieve them.

DEFENCES are 'better appreciated'; a few think 'effective measures' have been taken.

INFORMATION ABOUT THE RAIDS: It is still thought people elsewhere are not told enough.

B. SOUTH-EASTERN DISTRICT: Strain and tiredness are again reported, though nervousness only among a small minority.

EVACUATION: Comment on familiar lines. There is also some pleasure at the welcome given in reception areas to evacuees.

LONDON: Some still resent 'so much propaganda' about the effect of the bombs on London, as, they say, 'only a small proportion get through now'.

DEFENCES are praised.

SHELTERS: The distribution of Morrisons has helped combat nervousness in some areas. Folkestone people want more street shelters.

C. SOUTHERN REGION: Morale has been good where there have been incidents. Great appreciation of the Civil Defence Services, 'who constantly prove their sterling worth'.

D. EASTERN REGION: Feeling is thought to have steadied, despite some continued anxiety.

Bombed-out people, especially those who invested all their savings in a house, are worried lest they only receive 1939 value for their property.

5. THE PRIME MINISTER'S WAR REVIEW IN THE HOUSE OF COMMONS (AUGUST 2)

People have been heartened by Mr. Churchill's confident tone: 'If he can be optimistic, then our prospects must be good.' Detailed comment, again slight, is on Mr. Churchill's references to: (a) the large number of houses destroyed by flying bombs – a shock to many; (b) the rocket bomb ... Londoners are somewhat apprehensive; (c) the Far Eastern war. People continue pleased at the possibility of an earlier defeat of Japan than was expected.

6. RUSSIA

Widespread admiration continues, as does the hope that the Russians will reach Berlin first. Their entry into German territory is eagerly awaited.

While many people say they are not surprised at the comparative lull on the Eastern front, a minority think that if Warsaw had been a Russian city it would have fallen by now. Some people feel that the Polish patriots fighting in Warsaw have been deliberately 'let down' by the Russians.

6A. RUSSO-POLISH RELATIONS

Uneasiness continues. People are uncertain as to the progress of the talks between Russia and Poland. While some think them satisfactory, others are disappointed that no solution has yet been reached. Sympathy with the Polish government in London is limited; it is thought the people on the spot should make the government they desire.

6B. FINLAND

Disappointment among a minority at her apparent intention to fight on. Peace prospects are, however, discussed.

7. ITALY

Quiet satisfaction with the campaign and confidence in the leaders continue. The movement of General Maitland Wilson's headquarters to Italy has been welcomed as a sign of progress.

8. GERMANY

THE CRISIS: The killing of experienced German generals is considered a good thing for us likely to lessen the efficiency of the German army. Otherwise comment, which has again declined, remains on familiar lines.

HATRED OF THE GERMANS continues, and there is considerable discussion as to how we are to deal with Germany and mete out punishment after the war.

9. TURKEY

Comment has decreased but is on similar lines to last week's. Turkey continues to be regarded as 'a fair-weather friend' and people do not think her break with Germany will be of much value at this stage of the war.

10. FAR EAST

THE PACIFIC: Praise continues for 'the superb job' the Americans are doing.

BURMA: People are pleased at our excellent work but regret that news from here is 'always put into a small corner'.

11. NEWS PRESENTATION

Praise for news presentation continues, but there is slightly more criticism this week – chiefly of prematurely optimistic statements. The press is thought a worse offender than the BBC.

Complaints continue that the Americans are given too much publicity, at the expense of our troops.

II. SPECIAL COMMENTS

FULL MONTHLY REVIEW

12. POST-WAR

DURING THE PAST FOUR WEEKS comment has again been considerable: belief that the war will now very soon be over has quickened people's already keen interest. The only exceptions are those who are too absorbed in present war news to be interested in anything else; those who urge that planning must wait until we have won the war; and a few who are so sceptical about the future that they have become apathetic.

ANXIETY about future prospects and SCEPTICISM as to the likelihood of anything being done to improve them continue the general reactions; only a small minority appear in any way hopeful. Government plans and promises are thought unlikely to materialise; for the most part they are thought to be intended merely 'to keep people quiet'; the 'shelving' of various reports – particularly Beveridge – continues to be instanced, and there are increasing references to 'vested' and 'sectional' interests. Plans, in any case, are considered inadequate and nebulous. Some fear they are unlikely to be anything else under the present Government; others that a different Government would be unlikely to carry out the plans of the present one.

Minorities continue to point out the cost of the various proposed schemes; and they complain that people expect everything to come from the Government and are not prepared for the hard work which will have to be faced if the schemes are to materialise. A few criticise the public's confusion and general lack of understanding of the various Government proposals.

Housing and employment are again the chief topics of interest.

Comment has been on the following lines:

HOUSING: Anxiety is widespread that the present shortages will continue or become even worse. The urgency to make a start is stressed; Government plans are criticised both for being so long delayed and for not being bold enough. Local authorities especially complain of the lack of any kind of a lead, and of being held up by uncertainty as to what the Government will decide about finance.

Even if houses are built, it is feared they will be beyond the means of working-class people. Fixing a ceiling for house prices, ensuring that building sites will be available at an 'honest price', and controlling the prices of building materials are all urged.

RURAL HOUSING: 'Decent', comfortable homes for rural dwellers and good water supply and sanitation are hoped for.

PREFABRICATION: People continue to dislike the idea of 'tin' houses but are reconciled to accepting them as a temporary measure. Criticisms continue, however, that they are likely to become permanent or that permanent housing will be neglected because of them; that their cost is too high; that they will be unsuitable for certain climates – particularly in the north; that they may prove to be shoddy; and that they are too small.

The demand for examples to be built in various parts continues.

THE WEIR HOUSE for rural areas is said to meet with approval in Edinburgh, where it is being inspected.

THE TOWN AND COUNTRY PLANNING BILL: Interest is limited – confined for the most part to local authorities – and is chiefly critical. It is thought to be both inadequate and an anti-climax to the Scott, Barlow and Uthwatt Reports.

Some hope for compulsory acquisition of land for building purposes or for complete nationalisation of the land; others think the state should at least prevent private ownership from interfering with town planning.

EMPLOYMENT: Fear of unemployment is widespread; there is particular apprehension about what is going to happen to the demobilised. Some think a serious slump inevitable; and a few say, even if it can be avoided, it will still happen. In the Northern Region and Scotland any paying-off of workmen is looked upon as a very bad augury.

Workers in shipbuilding, munitions, iron and steel, and coal, iron ore and Cornish tin miners, particularly, are reported to be anxious.

THE ESSENTIAL WORK ORDER: Relaxation of this is hoped for, so that people can again choose their own jobs; though a few hope that 'unreasonable' dismissal of employees will be prevented. A few, however, are said to realise 'people will have to give up a certain amount of liberty to solve the problem of employment'.

THE WHITE PAPER ON EMPLOYMENT POLICY: Little discussion has been reported. Some express satisfaction, but others 'do not believe the promises of "employment for all"'.

LOCATION OF INDUSTRY: In the Northern Region and in Wales there continue to be anxious hopes for the establishment of new industries.

CONTROLS: The early lifting of restrictions is asked for by some; others realise they will have to stay for some time.

INDUSTRY: Employers, particularly, are said to be anxious about the change-over to peacetime production, and to be asking for some practical guidance now so that they can make arrangements for tiding over the immediate post-war period.

AGRICULTURE: Farmers are very doubtful about their future and dread the prospect of the industry again being neglected. Few have any confidence that anything will be done for them; some are already preparing or intending to get out 'while the going is good'.

SMALL SHOPKEEPERS: There is considerable anxiety that they may be superseded by the big combines. The treatment Lord Winster's Bill received is said to have been a blow to some.

EXPORTS: There is some concern – particularly on the part of businessmen – about the future of our export trade. Some think that if our high standard of wages remains, we cannot hope to recover our markets. Commercial competition with the United States is particularly feared.

EMIGRATION: Quite a few are said to be interested in prospects of emigrating to the Colonies.

12A. THE EDUCATION ACT

DURING THE PAST FOUR WEEKS satisfaction with the Act has continued; it is thought to be a definite move in the right direction.

There continues, however, to be some fear that shortage of teachers and buildings may hold up the scheme. Teachers fear that the easy entry into the profession, which will result from the planned emergency courses, will mean merely a lowering of the standard of the profession.

A few country people continue to criticise the raising of the school-leaving age.

THE FLEMING REPORT has aroused only limited interest. Some, who think public schools should be open to all, criticise the proposals for not going far enough, 'though perhaps they are as much as can be hoped for at present'. Others prefer to see the public schools remain as they are.

12B. NATIONAL HEALTH SCHEME

DURING THE PAST FOUR WEEKS interest has again been limited. While the need for a comprehensive medical service is acknowledged, opinions differ about the Government proposals, and many find it difficult to make up their minds 'until the medical profession agree among themselves'. Some think doctors will not be given a sufficient share in the running of the scheme and that this may result in people not being able to choose their own doctor; also that the views of young doctors in the Forces should be obtained.

13. TRANSPORT

DURING THE PAST FOUR WEEKS transport difficulties have become a major topic on the home front, as a result of the very considerable strain placed on services by evacuees and holiday-makers. Complaints are about:

(a) OVERCROWDING of:
    (i) TRAINS: Gross overcrowding is causing hardship to those who have to travel on business or to work. Mention is made of 25 people in a compartment. People are also said to have to give up hope of reaching the lavatory once they entrain. It is thought more facilities should be provided, especially for holiday-makers and those wishing to visit evacuees, or else steps should be taken to prevent unnecessary travelling. The railway companies are criticised for poor organisation of queuing – York railway station, for example, being held in awe as a 'terrible place'. It is thought they should not issue tickets beyond what the trains can reasonably accommodate. Train cuts are considered to have been too drastic, and the Government is criticised for this and for raising the coastal ban and the ban on 48 hours leave for the Services. Businessmen feel that more petrol should be issued in view of the difficulties in rail travel.

    (ii) BUSES: Rural services are said to be more seriously overcrowded than those in towns. Village shoppers and local workers are experiencing great difficulties, as buses pass through towns full. It is urged that more buses should be put on to cater for the evacuees, who flock to the nearest town at every opportunity. Stories are told of people waiting three or more hours in bus queues.

(b) LACK OF PRIORITY FOR WORKERS: In view of overcrowding there are demands for priority for workers on buses and trains, to ensure seats and prevent waste of time in queues.

(c) LACK OF LATE EVENING BUS SERVICES: Last buses are considered to be too early for summer evenings.

(d) BUS QUEUES.

(e) FAILURE OF BUSES TO PICK UP PASSENGERS.

(f) DISPARITY IN RAIL AND BUS FARES.

SATISFACTION: In London, the Southern Railway is praised for its handling of evacuation transport.

13A. PETROL

DURING THE PAST FOUR WEEKS comment, which has slightly increased, has been about:

(a) MISUSE AND WASTE OF PETROL by (i) businessmen, who use their cars when a bus is available, and who take their families out for pleasure on Sundays, (ii) the Forces, (iii) taxis used for pleasure, (iv) voluntary organisations. It is thought that the police do not check up sufficiently by stopping motorists on the roads.

(b) ALLOCATION OF PETROL: In view of the present public transport situation, people are hoping petrol restrictions may be eased and possibly the basic ration re-introduced. Farmers feel they should be allowed more petrol for business purposes.

14. HOLIDAYS AND HOLIDAY TRANSPORT

There appears to be general agreement that people are right in insisting on having a holiday away from home this year. They feel that rest and relaxation are necessary after five years of war and are willing to risk the bad travelling conditions. Most people, too, are anxious for a glimpse of the sea. It is again pointed out that housewives get no benefit from a stay-at-home holiday. In Scotland it is said that although accommodation seems impossible to obtain, this has led to no diminution of travel.

Nevertheless, holiday-makers complain about transport conditions; they blame the Government for muddled, confused and weak official and semi-official statements about holiday travel.

14A. THE PARLIAMENTARY RECESS

DURING THE PAST TWO WEEKS there has been some critical comment on the length of the parliamentary recess, mostly on the lines that 'the gentlemen who appeal to us to spend our holidays at home, and to make a hundred and one other sacrifices as well, have just voted themselves a seven weeks' vacation with pay'.

15. HOUSING

DURING THE PAST FOUR WEEKS complaints of the housing situation have been even more widespread; evacuation to the provinces and damage to property in London have made the position even more acute.

Complaints have again been chiefly of:

(a) SHORTAGE now 'worse than ever'; there are growing demands for building to begin immediately. In London, particularly, people are said to be 'living in Andersons' because of the lack of accommodation, and it is felt that prefabricated houses, or at least wooden huts, could be built to house the homeless.

Complaints continue of mothers with young children and expectant mothers being refused accommodation and of expectant mothers being turned out of their lodgings. There are also continued complaints of 'appalling' conditions produced by overcrowding.

Demands for the requisitioning of all empty property are again made.

(b) HIGH PRICE AND RENTS: The prices of houses for sale and the rents of furnished rooms, flats and houses are thought particularly outrageous. There is increasing demand for more price control for all kinds of accommodation.

(c) REPAIR DIFFICULTIES as a result of shortages of labour and materials.

16. INDUSTRY

DURING THE PAST FOUR WEEKS reference has again been made to 'things going on satisfactorily'. Nevertheless, comment has increased about REDUCED PRODUCTION. It is attributed to a sufficiency of war supplies and in a few cases to change-overs in production. It is alleged to be causing:

(a) ENFORCED IDLENESS: Familiar stories are told – that at one aircraft factory men are told to report every morning at 7 a.m. and are then sent home. In a North-Eastern Region factory workers complain that both the National Service Officer and their employer conceal the fact that they, the workers, only work about two hours a day; those on night shift say they sleep most of the time.

(b) ABSENTEEISM AND SLACKNESS OF WORKERS: Workers are said to feel the slackening in war production heralds the early end of the war. (Other reasons, however, for workers' slackness are said to be PAYE, the reaction after the invasion thrill and the holiday season. In Scotland, holiday-makers are making 'a rather tired return to work'.)

(c) DISCHARGES, particularly in the shipyards. Workers in this industry on the Clyde and Tyneside are alarmed, and there is widespread fear of long-term and post-war unemployment: 'The slump is coming much quicker than we expected.' Rumours are that EWO will be withdrawn this month – widespread in the Northern and Scottish Regions – and that shipyards are to be released from Admiralty control.

There is also talk of present and future discharges in munitions.

(d) THE TRANSFER OF WORKERS: Workers feel that, skill being equal, single rather than married men should be transferred. There is also a certain amount of grumbling at the difficulty of finding accommodation. In the Otley area, men and women are alleged to be moved to work elsewhere, while others from outside come into the town to work.

(e) REDUCED HOURS, including overtime, 'causing a drop in wages while the cost of living continues high'.

(f) POST-WAR PRODUCTION: People gossip about firms already producing goods for post-war markets. Some are alleged to be making them of materials supplied for munitions, etc.

WOMEN DOING MEN'S JOBS: There is some ill-feeling among men that, while they are being discharged from the shipping industry, women are being retained. At the same time, stories of the discharge of all women in this industry are pleasing the men as 'men should have priority for such jobs as there are in heavy industry'. There has been similar comment about the unofficial strike resulting from women being put on textile machine processes 'that have been men's for 80 years or so'.

17. MANPOWER

DURING THE PAST FOUR WEEKS comment has again been on a reduced scale. Allegations continue of:

EVASION OF CALL-UP: Relatives of killed servicemen feel particularly strongly about all evasion. There are acid comments about:

(a) Young able-bodied men dodging the Forces by working in industry, on farms and in local authority offices, 'when sufficient numbers of servicemen are being discharged to fill their positions'. Reference is also made to hawkers who escape all duties, including Civil Defence.

(b) Young married women who follow their Service husbands about, give young children as their excuse although the children are at boarding school, or receive unjustified certificates from doctors. It is also suggested that 'better-off' women's reasons for exemption are never tested and that deferments are not checked sufficiently.

(c) Too many people of both sexes employed in non-essential work. Reference is made to the swollen staffs of the Civil Service and the manpower wasted on unnecessary advertising.

SHORTAGE OF LABOUR: Talk is about the strain of continued long hours in under-staffed businesses and non-war industries. The printing trade is specified; also, in several areas in the north-west, cotton mills, where youths are especially badly needed. Employers are angry to hear of workers with little or nothing to do being retained in munition factories.

A shortage of dock labour is reported from Liverpool.

ONE-MAN BUSINESSES: Complaints are of 'the over-strict' call-up of small businessmen, such as cobblers – much needed by the civilian population.

17A. DOMESTIC HELP

DURING THE PAST FOUR WEEKS complaints of hardship and strain, due to the shortage of domestic help, have continued. Particular mention is made of:

(a) ELDERLY AND INFIRM PEOPLE.
(b) MOTHERS WITH YOUNG CHILDREN.
(c) FARMERS' WIVES AND COUNTRY WOMEN.
(d) HOSPITALS AND INSTITUTIONS.

The suggestion is again made that as female labour is being dispensed with in some factories, this might usefully be directed into 'home helping', to cover all forms of domestic emergency.

18. WAGES

DURING THE PAST FOUR WEEKS comment has been on a reduced scale. There are, however, again complaints of:

THE 'FANCY' WAGES paid to young people and to unskilled workers in munition factories.

Some people are alarmed at the continual increase in wages, and fear inflation and a still higher cost of living. A few workers too – who foresee a drastic reduction in wages after the war – say they would prefer a standardised cost of living to increased wages.

DISPARITY OF PAY BETWEEN:

(a) Skilled and unskilled workers. Cotton workers, whose wages are very much lower than those of munition workers, are dissatisfied at being directed back to the cotton industry.

(b) Women and men for the same work. Female workers, grumbling at their rates of pay, are said to be leaving the trade unions.

(c) Servicemen and civilian workers. Particularly mentioned are munition workers and Irish workmen; and in one Northern Region area, comparison is made between the wages of agricultural workers and soldiers, 'working side by side in the same harvest field'.

19. INCOME TAX

DURING THE PAST FOUR WEEKS there have again been familiar complaints about having to pay income tax. Though PAYE is in the main approved, it is the cause of a certain amount of grumbling and incomprehension. Workers are constantly discussing the amounts deducted from their pay packets, are unable to understand the reasons for weekly fluctuations in tax on static wages, and grumble that their wages are smaller since PAYE started. The Northern Region report refers to a miners' lodge secretary being 'snowed under' with men wanting interviews to find out if their deductions are correct, and workers ask if at the end of the year they will get a statement of the total sum they have paid in tax.

There has again been much comment about THE EFFECTS OF PAYE ON WORKERS' ATTITUDE AND OUTPUT. It is alleged to cause:

(a) REFUSAL TO WORK OVERTIME OR AT WEEKENDS ... 'Why should I work just to give money to the Government? Why not have a day off?' Workers are said to make up any loss to themselves by undertaking overtime jobs for other employers, who do not deduct tax on such work (e.g. wireless and clock mending, cherry picking, etc.).

(b) ABSENTEEISM, particularly in order that workers can get back some of the tax they have paid on a full week's work. Miners are said to take a whole week off sometimes – 'medical certificates are easy to get'. In fact,

PAYE has been described by some workers as 'the best sick club they have ever belonged to'. It is suggested that publicity is needed to bring home to them that, though they are getting something back, they are losing a good deal more by having stayed away from work.

(c) SLACKING AND 'CA CANNY'.

THE INCIDENCE OF INCOME TAX: There is some criticism of the deduction of income tax from:

(a) HOLIDAY PAY (both in the sense of a paid holiday and also of pay earned during the holiday, e.g. on the land).
(b) SERVICEMEN'S PAY.
(c) THE PAY OF TRANSFERRED WOMEN WORKERS, who have many extra expenses living away from home and may possibly not earn more than 50/- or 60/- a week.
(d) THE PAY OF WOMEN WHO GO OUT TO WORK TO KEEP THE HOME GOING, e.g. office cleaners.
(e) PENSIONS: Complaint of the hardship of workers having had to pay tax on earnings and then again on their pensions. It is thought, too, that pensions, annuities and the interest on savings should not be taxed as unearned income.

20. MINERS AND MINING

DURING THE PAST FOUR WEEKS disappointment and concern have continued at the DECREASED COAL OUTPUT: 'The average man cannot understand why it should decline in spite of improved wages.'

While the industry as a whole is described as being in 'bad odour', people variously blame:

(a) THE GOVERNMENT for being helpless, or for their handling of the situation. A few suggest that the withdrawal of 'Government interference' would put things right, but more – particularly miners – feel the only cure is nationalisation. 'Nothing', it is said, 'will convince the miners otherwise'.
(b) THE MINERS: Strikes and the rise in the price of coal have renewed their unpopularity. There are also allegations of absenteeism and slackness.
(c) THE OWNERS: Miners still accuse them of withholding the best seams for use after the war – against the advice of their mining engineers.
(d) THE PORTER AWARD: Some on both sides of the industry consider the increased wages no spur to production: 'A pitman can earn all he wants in five days; why should he work six?' There is also some dissatisfaction at the award among certain classes of mechanics, and hewers and putters 'don't like the increased wages to stonemen and others; hewers regard themselves as cocks of the pit and don't like the idea that their wages are on a par with those who in their estimation do inferior work'.
(e) MINERS' FOOD: Supplies of food at pit-head canteens in East Durham are alleged to be inadequate. In addition, some miners complain that they

cannot afford the 'great cost' of canteen meals; they want more food at home, particularly 'real bait' fillings for their sandwiches, saying they cannot do a full shift on what they get.

BEVIN BOYS: Talk is of:

(a) THE BALLOT: A few grumbles continue at the 'injustice and waste' of sending pre-Service-trained boys to the mines.

  In Northumberland and Durham discontent is reported at the alleged discharge of miners over the age of 65 and their replacement by Bevin boys: 'They've got good work in them for several more years.' Twenty men are said to have been paid off from the Morrison pit.

(b) THEIR VALUE: Miners variously think that the boys are 'a wash out'; that 'it's a pity they've been brought to the north to work they don't like – they'll never become effective producers and will never stay in the industry'; and, in Wales, that they are getting on well. It would be better, it is again suggested, to get ex-miners back from the Forces.

(c) THEIR PRIVILEGES: Miners resent the fuss being made of them – their training and hostel accommodation – in comparison with the treatment of local lads who go into the pits. It is alleged with bitterness that they are also assigned better work than the sons of local pitmen.

(d) BILLETING: Desultory talk only is reported. Some local indignation where a miner's wife whose son was recalled from the pit to the army was asked to take in two Bevin boys. In the Oswestry area, some difficulties of billeting the boys due to lack of pit-head baths at the local pits: 'Housewives would be quite willing to take the trainees if they came home clean.'

(e) TRADE UNIONS: Some suspect that miners' associations insist on the boys joining trade unions, under the threat that if they do not, they will not receive the industrial concessions obtained by the associations.

OPEN-CAST COAL: Comment continues about the high working costs of obtaining open-cast coal ... 'one of the scandals of the war'. The wholesale destruction of well-developed grain crops is also criticised as 'sabotage'.

MINERS' HEALTH: Reference is made in the Northern Region to a new kind of disease caused by using pneumatic picks; the men using them are said to develop upset nerves, blinking eyes and shaking arms. 'There is no compensation for this yet; there will have to be so many cases before it is scheduled.'

20A. DOMESTIC FUEL

Indignation at the increased prices of coal and coke is again reported. Old age pensioners and other poor people are felt to be very badly hit.

DURING THE PAST FOUR WEEKS comment has continued about:

(a) THE DIFFICULTY OF BUILDING UP COAL STOCKS: 'How can we stock up when we can't even get enough for the summer months?' In addition to the shortage of supplies, difficulties are said to have been increased by the cold summer weather, and, in households without gas or electricity, by having to use coal for cooking.

There is anxiety about the fuel situation next winter – increasing anxiety in cold areas such as the Peak District of Derbyshire.

(b) THE POOR QUALITY OF COAL: 'Much of it is merely stones, so extra has to be used.' Housewives in one area in the North Midland Region are annoyed at having to take 30% of open-cast coal 'for which 2/5½d per cwt is barefaced robbery', while neighbours with different merchants are receiving all deep-mined coal.

(c) THE INADEQUACY OF THE COAL ALLOWANCE.

WASTE OF GAS: It is alleged that people are leaving a low gas alight all the time on account of the shortage of matches.

21. CLOTHING AND HOUSEHOLD LINEN

DURING THE PAST FOUR WEEKS familiar complaints have continued, most of them at about the same level as last month.

THE MAIN DIFFERENCES have been considerably LESS CRITICISM of: shoe repair difficulties; the poor quality of clothing; trafficking in coupons; laundry and cleaning difficulties; and shortage of coupons for industrial workers.

Comment has chiefly been about:

THE INSUFFICIENCY OF COUPONS for:

(a) CLOTHING REPLACEMENTS GENERALLY: People say the allowance is entirely inadequate after five years of war. Those thought particularly hard hit are:

   (i)   CHILDREN: Bigger children and boys who have recently left school present the most difficult problem.

   (ii) WORKERS IN HEAVY AND DIRTY INDUSTRIES: Miners and foundry workers complain they cannot manage and that the method of allotting the iron ration pool is unfair. Some plating workers, whose clothing is often burnt by acid, say they should either be allowed more extra coupons in addition to the 'industrial ten' or some form of protective clothing.

   (iii) MEN who 'cannot get a new suit without borrowing coupons from their wives'.

   (iv) POORER PEOPLE: 'The wealthy don't need so many coupons, as they can buy better clothes.'

   (v)   THOSE WHO WANT TO GO INTO MOURNING.

A few, however, think that, 'despite the perpetual grumbles', people seem to manage very well.

(b) REPLACING HOUSEHOLD LINEN: 'The housewife's biggest grumble is the provision of linen from personal coupons.'

FOOTWEAR PROBLEMS:

(a) CHILDREN'S: Vehement, sometimes bitter, protests continue. They are on familiar lines:

    (i) POOR QUALITY.

    (ii) REPAIR DIFFICULTIES.

    (iii) SHORTAGE: Some sizes and types are more difficult to get than others; in particular, sandals; rubber boots, which people hope will be more easily obtainable in time for the winter; small sizes; and schoolgirls' shoes.

    (iv) HIGH PRICE.

        The following two reports give a more detailed picture of these complaints.

        A School Attendance Officer in the Northern Region states that recently during one week in one town, out of 800 children absent from school, 200 had no footwear at all or were waiting for repairs; in addition, 25 boys were at school in their bare feet. Repair difficulties, poor quality and coupon shortage all apparently contributed to this state of affairs.

        In Plymouth and Bristol, people are very disquieted; they feel the likely effect on the foot-health of children and the risk of other illnesses are not fully appreciated. Grievances concern: 'the famine' in certain sizes; poor quality – 'many shoes made from offal and substitutes are at the repairers within a matter of days after purchase'; type of shoe made – the chief complaint is that vast quantities of girls' sandal-type shoes are produced, made of trash on slipper lasts; repair problems, particularly the difficulty of delay and the hardship of frequent expense.

(b) ADULTS': Complaints, though much less strongly voiced, are also of:

    (i) POOR QUALITY.

    (ii) REPAIR DIFFICULTIES, particularly the poor quality of leather, the time taken, the difficulty of getting shoes accepted and the high cost of repairs.

    (iii) SHORTAGE, especially of good-quality women's shoes.

BEDDING AND CURTAINS:

(a) SHORTAGE: Complaints are chiefly about sheets, particularly utility and other less expensive ones; and blankets. Difficulties have been further aggravated in many cases by the arrival of evacuees.

(b) PRIORITY PERMITS: There is some dissatisfaction because it is believed that cases of real hardship are often refused permits; on the other hand, some say curtain permits are useless because retailers cannot get curtaining. It is suggested that the present application form is most confusing to less educated people.

(c) HIGH PRICE of sheets and pillow-cases; and linen.

TOO HIGH COUPON VALUES, particularly of children's coats, since the recent increase; footwear, especially children's, and wooden shoes; men's suits; women's coats.

POOR QUALITY OF CLOTHING, especially corsets, including utility; stockings; men's socks, still thought too short; utility clothing generally.

HIGH PRICES OF CLOTHING, men's, women's and children's all being mentioned.

SHORTAGE of: elastic, blackout material, corsets, stockings, men's socks, utility clothes, wool and men's underwear.

TRAFFICKING IN COUPONS: Said to be widespread in a few districts.

LAUNDRIES: Chief difficulties are (a) delay and (b) loss of garments without adequate compensation.

21A. FURNITURE, FURNISHINGS AND PERAMBULATORS

DURING THE PAST FOUR WEEKS complaints of the high price and scarcity of furniture have continued.

There is also some complaint of long waits for deliveries of utility furniture; and of the difficulties bombed-out people experience in getting furniture.

The new price control has aroused little comment. Some wish it were 'stricter', others think it will mean closing down many retail businesses.

People complain, too, of the shortage of (a) linoleum and oilcloths, and (b) carpets and rugs.

Complaints continue about the shortage of perambulators; in areas where evacuees have arrived, the difficulties are said to have been accentuated.

21B. TEATS FOR BABIES' BOTTLES

During the past four weeks complaints about the 'acute' shortage have grown; in some areas people think the scarcity has been aggravated by the influx of evacuees. The position is thought to be very grave and is causing disquiet; mothers are particularly bitter. In some cases, they have to buy bottles they do not need in order to get a single teat.

Anger is all the greater because 'they ask us to increase the population', and because of the plentiful supplies of contraceptives.

21C. COMBS

DURING THE PAST FOUR WEEKS complaints about the shortage of combs – 'and those obtainable almost useless' – have increased considerably. Some fear verminous heads will result. People again say that kerb vendors 'go on gaily selling these goods at well over the controlled prices'.

22. AGRICULTURE

DURING THE PAST FOUR WEEKS comment has been chiefly about:

HARVEST PROSPECTS: Much comment, hopeful or otherwise, according to the locality, the weather and the nature of the crop – but the chief concern among farmers at the moment is how to get the harvest in. The main difficulty is shortage of labour; some farmers are at their wits' end. Another problem is the feeding and housing of holiday labour where camps are not available; farmers' wives 'can't cope with the catering', and much of the accommodation normally available for holiday workers is now full of evacuees.

FARM LABOURERS:

(a) WAGES: A good many farm labourers still seem dissatisfied with wages and conditions, and in some agricultural areas the general public think wages should be raised. Farm labourers in a mining area contrast their pay with that of miners; they think their work is just as important and that they should be paid accordingly.

(b) INCOME TAX: The Northern, Eastern and Southern Region reports mention farm labourers' unwillingness to incur extra income tax by working overtime. This makes difficulties for dairy farmers: as all work from mid-day Saturday till Monday morning counts as overtime, the labourers' reluctance to work during this period means that it is difficult to get the animals milked and fed. Meanwhile the labourers undertake evening or weekend work for other farmers, provided they do not deduct tax on the money earned. Some agricultural workers are convinced that 10/- in the £1 is deducted from all overtime pay.

(c) COTTAGES: There are some complaints of excessive rents. Two agricultural cottages recently erected in the South-Western Region are criticised on the grounds that the extensive use of cement means that the floors throw up dust, hooks cannot be fixed, nor stair carpets tacked down.

(d) HOLIDAYS WITH PAY: Pleasure at this.

WAECS: Some farmers continue to grumble about WAECs and their 'dictatorial' powers; others admit they have their uses. People in the New Forest wonder how the WAEC is going to make some of the forest land, now being ploughed up, a paying proposition.

GRASS SHORTAGE: Some worry is reported at the scarcity of grass and the consequent difficulty of feeding dairy cattle and horses. In the Eastern Region, it is thought there will be no grass till late September and that there should be a special issue of rations.

FARMERS: Non-farming people in agricultural areas persist in thinking that the farmer is being spoilt by the Government and is growing too prosperous at the public's expense. Farmers themselves sometimes complain about EPT.

22A. RURAL WATER SUPPLY

DURING THE PAST FOUR WEEKS concern over the water supply in country districts has continued; in some places, shortage has been aggravated by an influx of evacuees and holiday visitors. Some consider the Government far too slow in taking action. It is said that often there is enough water in privately owned local wells, and people deplore the impotence of local authorities to take them over for public use.

23. EXTENSION OF DOUBLE SUMMER TIME

Farmers continue to complain very strongly; early morning workers and parents of young children also complain, but to a lesser extent. People generally, however, remain pleased about it.

24. FOOD

DURING THE PAST FOUR WEEKS widespread satisfaction with the general situation and praise for the adjustment of food supplies to meet the influx of evacuees have been reported, though 'minor grumbles persist'. Comment has been mainly about:

(a) FRUIT AND TOMATO SHORTAGES, particularly the non-appearance of promised fruit supplies.

(b) SUGAR: While appreciation of the extra allowance for jam-making has continued throughout the month, many regret that more was not available early enough to save soft fruit from being wasted, and a few complain of the smallness of the weekly ration.

(c) UNEVEN DISTRIBUTION of goods in short supply, particularly fruit, tomatoes, fish, and other unrationed foodstuffs. Comparisons are made between town and country facilities and between the north and south. Extended rationing is again advocated, and it is also suggested that a greater check should be made on wholesalers who are also retailers, to avoid preferential treatment of their own retail branches. Some say that hotels seem able to obtain large proportions of the better type of food.

(d) MILK: Complaints are made of the smallness of the milk ration, particularly with 'no compensating allowance of dried milk'. It is suggested that extra milk might be made available for old people. There is also some complaint of quality.

(e) BEER, WHISKY AND SOFT DRINKS: The shortage of beer and consequent closing of some public houses is a source of strong complaint. It is thought unfair that some licensed houses should sell out by mid-day to people with leisure, leaving nothing for workers in the evening. The high-handed attitude of some publicans is criticised. Shortage and high price of whisky are also complained of – particularly in Scotland where feeling remains bitter. On the other hand, some fear the shortage of soft drinks may lead to increased drunkenness.

(f) BACON: Pleasure at the increased ration has continued throughout the month, although there are also complaints of quality.

(g) CHEESE: More cheese is asked for, and there are complaints about quality. Some people would prefer more cheese to more bacon. It is said that 'farmers and their sons working on the land harder and longer hours than those they employ are annoyed they cannot draw the extra cheese ration'.

(h) MEAT, particularly the monotony of continual pork, and the quality of meat generally. It is thought there are 'not enough meals' in the meat ration and that meat on points is beyond the means of poor people.

(i) BREAD: A few complaints of shortage and quality; and welcome for the proposal of improved bread – though there is one criticism of the 'Government's proposal to make flour of all wheat in place of the finest loaf flour we have ever had'.

(j) FISH: Shortage, particularly in rural areas. There are also complaints of lack of variety, quality and high price.

(k) INADEQUACY OF THE FAT RATION.

(l) RATIONING DIFFICULTIES OF SMALL FAMILIES, OLD PEOPLE, AND THOSE LIVING ALONE.

(m) HIGH PRICE OF VEGETABLES.

(n) 'OFF-THE-RATION' BACON AND HAM: Appreciation is reported, but some who deal at small shops have difficulty in getting their share, because the shopkeeper has no facilities for cooking.

(o) TEA: Smallness of ration. It is asked whether the allowance for old people could not be increased to 3 ozs.

(p) HIGH PRICE AND POOR QUALITY OF JAM.

(q) LACK OF VARIETY OF FOOD.

(r) INADEQUACY OF POINTS ALLOWANCE.

24A. SHOPPING DIFFICULTIES

During the past four weeks familiar complaints – to some extent increased by the influx of evacuees – have been about:

(a) FOOD QUEUES: Women complain bitterly of food queues, particularly for fruit, fish and other unrationed goods ... 'that's where all the time goes'. Holiday-makers, evacuees and women with little to do, go out early from shop to shop in search of food in short supply ... 'evacuees queue while the householder does the work'. Some think that shopkeepers prefer queues in order to crowd a day's business into a few hours.

(b) CONDITIONAL AND UNDER-THE-COUNTER SALES: Favouritism is alleged, and allotment holders are said to be penalised because they have no regular greengrocer.

(c) WORKERS' DIFFICULTIES: Working women who have no time to queue ask for some provision to be made for the allocation of goods in short supply. They feel also that shops should be open during the dinner hour and urge the staggering of shop hours.

(d) RURAL TRANSPORT DIFFICULTIES for village shoppers.
(e) INCIVILITY OF SHOP ASSISTANTS.
(f) QUOTA SYSTEM IN SHOE SHOPS: People complain that the daily quota is sold out early in the morning before workers and rural housewives can reach the shops.

25. THE BLACKOUT

Great hopes that 'the most disliked wartime measure' will be relaxed this winter, if not already rendered unnecessary by the end of hostilities. The thought of another winter of blackout is said to be more depressing than any possible food or fuel shortage. Farmers especially view with dismay the prospect of screening lamps in barns and byres, and cycling and driving with inadequate lights for another winter.

26. HOME GUARD, FIRE-WATCHING AND CIVIL DEFENCE

DURING THE PAST FOUR WEEKS the familiar complaints of wasted time, money and manpower have continued, and have tended to increase slightly.

HOME GUARD: Members of the Home Guard are 'getting very fed up'; the opinion is fairly widespread among them, and also the general public, that duties could be relaxed and even that the Home Guard could be disbanded altogether – 'Hitler can't possibly invade us now, even if he wanted; so why should we be forced to play soldiers?' Some modification is thought especially desirable in the case of agricultural workers.

In one Region, although the men in the infantry sections are very fed up – 'they mostly volunteered in the early days and have done the same monotonous drill for four years' – those on AA guns are stimulated by constantly learning new techniques, and want to get a crack at the enemy.

FIRE-WATCHING: Many people feel the present system is a 'ridiculous waste of time and money'. Daylight fire-watching is thought specially 'infuriating', but many people consider it is unnecessary at any time, day or night, except on an alert. Those who live in areas where, it is believed, raids will not recur feel particularly strongly; for instance, Tyneside workers say 'if this is a safety zone and all the guns and balloons have gone away, why must we sleep in a dirty old warehouse all night?'

CIVIL DEFENCE: Personnel are 'fed up with nothing to do', and people think much time and money could be saved by reducing the number of paid wardens and relaxing duties all round. Here again feeling is particularly strong in less vulnerable areas.

Civil Defence workers are anxious to transfer to flying bomb areas; however, some complain their employers will not release them; others, again, say part-time CD workers should not be appealed to, when 'NFS people are still able to sit around and do nothing'.

26A. NFS PERSONNEL

The news of a prospective comb-out has been welcomed, particularly in view of the long inactivity of many NFS personnel.

27. ALLIED PRISONERS OF WAR

DURING THE PAST FOUR WEEKS concern has been reported about prisoners in:

(a) FAR EAST: Scarcity of news causes great concern and people are eager for more information about conditions. While some hope that the 'uncertainty of the outcome of the war may improve the Japanese treatment of prisoners', others fear they may 'imitate the German shootings'. The Prime Minister's recent reference to the Far Eastern war has given more hope of an earlier release of prisoners than was expected.

(b) GERMANY: The recent shootings have increased anxiety among relatives of men in German hands. Some wonder what the treatment will be 'when the enemy know they are beaten'. Relatives are worried also about the recent hold-up in the mails.

27A. ITALIAN AND GERMAN PRISONERS OF WAR

DURING THE PAST FOUR WEEKS there has been comment about

(a) ITALIAN PRISONERS: Some are said to behave badly. People think more control should be exercised over them. The attitude of some girls and married women towards these men has aroused disgust.

   Farmers who employ individual Italians are said to find them highly satisfactory, but when working in gangs they are 'dreadfully lazy'. The effort to draft Italians into industry in one Region has been met with resentment by the workers. Some think they should be used for work in the mines.

   In the Northern Region, the friendliness and hospitality shown by some local people to Italian co-operators is much resented.

(b) GERMAN PRISONERS who are thought to be treated too leniently in this country. People dislike the comfortable railway travel provided for them, and there is resentment at stories that, while in hospital, they receive the same or even better treatment than our own wounded.

28. SERVICE PENSIONS, PAY AND ALLOWANCES

DURING THE PAST FOUR WEEKS there has been comment on the following: SERVICEMEN'S DEPENDANTS' PENSIONS, COMPLAINTS OF INADEQUACY, and of:

(a) Treatment of parents who have lost sons in the war – particularly the 'means test'; also the reviewing of the supplementary allowance, when a pension is granted for the loss of a son.

(b) The fact that a widow and orphan get less than a wife and child. It is thought particularly hard that a child's education is liable to suffer just because his father has been killed.

(c) The delay in granting pensions to war widows, which is said to be 'nearly always two months or more'.

SERVICEMEN'S DEPENDANTS' ALLOWANCES: Pleasure at increased allowances, though some still consider them insufficient.

SERVICEMEN'S PAY: Pleasure at increased pay but a little talk of the increases being misleading if they are 'cancelled by the withdrawal of various grants'.

DISABLED SERVICEMEN'S PENSIONS: Thought insufficient; some concern, too, at the number who are denied pensions.

29. OLD AGE PENSIONS

DURING THE PAST FOUR WEEKS there have continued to be complaints that the old age pension is inadequate. Some people advocate an increase in the basic rate. Rumours that old age pensioners may get more under the new Government social insurance scheme than even the Beveridge Report proposed have given satisfaction, particularly to older men in industry who think they may be displaced when the war is over.

There is particular comment about:

(a) The 'means test' in connection with applications for supplementary pensions – 'disliked by applicants and deplored by others'. It is thought that many thrifty independent old people, though eligible for a supplementary pension, refuse to apply in consequence.

(b) The fact that supplementary pensions are reduced if pensioners earn more than 10/6 a week. It is felt that a useful source of odd labour (e.g. cleaning, gardening, etc.) is thus lost.

(c) The fact that those who have never been in insured occupations cannot claim a pension till they are 70; this is thought hard, particularly for 'respectable middle-class people'.

(d) Income tax being payable on old age pensions.

30. THE TRANSFER OF MEN TO THE ARMY FROM OTHER SERVICES

DURING THE PAST TWO WEEKS disappointment has continued among ATC boys and RAF recruits at their transfer to the army. Some fear is again reported that much dissatisfaction will be caused by the continuance of RAF rates of pay in the army.

31. HEALTH

DURING THE PAST FOUR WEEKS complaints of tiredness, war strain and minor illnesses have continued on a reduced scale. General health is thought to be fairly good on the whole.

Ill-health is mainly attributed to long-continued overwork, lack of holidays, bad ventilation caused by the blackout, and to the wartime bread; also, in London, to sleeping in shelters.

It is thought, too, that health is endangered by the shortage of 'Flit' and fly papers, by the less frequent collection of refuse in towns, and by the water shortage.

Other comment has been of:

HEALTH OF CHILDREN: It is felt that the Government is to be congratulated on the care taken of young children ... 'babies were never bonnier' ... but people regret that facilities for obtaining orange juice and cod liver oil are not available for school children, especially when they begin school and need extras of this kind.

VD CAMPAIGN: Some feel this is 'too delicate in approach' and should be more forceful, while others think 'brutal frankness is overdone'. A few are in favour of compulsory notification.

HOSPITALS: The need for more accommodation for maternity cases and difficulties experienced by the public in getting attention in hospitals are reported each from one Region.

TUBERCULOSIS: Anxiety is reported about the treatment of TB patients and about the question of suitable employment for those who have spent long periods in sanatoria.

BLOOD TRANSFUSION SERVICE: It is thought that the response to appeals is fairly good, as people regard this as a means of showing their gratitude to the Forces. Some, however, who have volunteered have never heard anything further. It is suggested that small centres should be set up to avoid transport difficulties which arise when country donors have to visit large towns.

NO. 203: TUESDAY 15 AUGUST 1944 TO TUESDAY 22 AUGUST 1944

I. GENERAL COMMENTS

1. GENERAL

Spirits continue to rise, thanks chiefly to the sweeping advances in northern France and the new landings in the south. There is a wave of optimism, which General Eisenhower's cautious words (August 15) have done little to curb. Those who are certain the war will be over by Christmas are now counted among the cautious; and October, or even earlier, remain popular guesses. Some fear that such optimism may lead to complacency and slacking-off – if it has not, indeed, already done so.

HOME FRONT TOPICS are, once more, evacuation and holidays and the cognate subjects of accommodation, transport, shopping, and food and beer supplies.

The approaching end of the war brings increasing anxiety about post-war conditions – many fear unemployment as soon as hostilities cease.

References to war-weariness and tiredness are creeping back.

2. FRANCE

NORTHERN FRANCE

People are delighted with the speed of Allied progress. The fall of Paris was eagerly awaited; so, too, is the occupation of the flying bomb sites.

Most people seem to think that the Germans are on the run everywhere; many do not expect them to make a real stand till they reach their own frontier ... though hardly able to believe that 'the aggressive, pompous bullies are being hunted like rats out of France'.

There is, however, some disappointment because the total number of enemy troops liquidated in the Falaise pocket seems to have been less than at first predicted.

THE RELATIVE ROLES OF THE US AND BRITISH FORCES have caused much discussion, mainly on two points.

IT IS WIDELY MAINTAINED THAT:

(a) THE BRITISH AND CANADIANS HAVE BEEN GIVEN THE LESS SPECTACULAR, BUT MUCH TOUGHER, PART OF THE FRONT THAN THE AMERICANS: While there is great admiration for the swiftness of the American advance, many feel that it has only been made possible by the 'holding action' of the British and Canadians round Caen. In spite of disappointment that the British are not taking part in the drive for Paris, however, there is great pride and some comfort in the belief that our men have had to face much stiffer opposition owing to the enemy's determination to prevent a breakthrough in the Pas de Calais area.

(b) A DISPROPORTIONATELY LARGE AMOUNT OF PUBLICITY IS GIVEN TO THE AMERICANS AT THE EXPENSE OF OUR OWN TROOPS (see also Section 11, News Presentation): There is said to be considerable resentment that the British, 'who seem to have the hardest job', are scarcely mentioned, and relatives of our men in France are particularly bitter. One report even mentions 'an uncomfortable undercurrent that British troops are not fighting as they should ... Poles, French, Canadians, not to mention Americans, get all the headlines'.

GENERALS MONTGOMERY AND BRADLEY: Some resentment and confusion appear to have been caused as a result of the announcement that General Bradley was in command of the American forces in north-western France. However, annoyance at the idea of General Bradley being on an equal footing with General Montgomery seems to have been dissipated by the subsequent announcement that General Montgomery is overall commander of all Allied ground forces under General Eisenhower.

THE MAIL SERVICES TO AND FROM THE FORCES IN NORMANDY seem now to be thought on the whole good.

THE ORGANISATION, equipment, feeding and entertainment of the troops are praised, with a special word for the attention to the wounded. The Scottish report says: 'The wounded themselves are spreading stories of their excellent treatment on the battlefront, in transit and in hospitals here.'

SOUTH OF FRANCE

The landings were generally welcomed but caused only momentary enthusiasm. Further landings had been widely expected and the preliminary air bombardment, combined with Mr. Churchill's presence in Italy, had suggested to many people a landing in the Riviera. Many would, however, have preferred a landing in the Pas de Calais; some are critical that a landing should have been made so far from the 'main scene of action'.

There is great satisfaction at the speed of advance, the lack of German opposition and the small losses involved.

THE FRENCH: There is great interest in, and praise for, the work of the French underground movement. The extent of the help given by the French, particularly in the south, has surprised people and erased some of the bitterness and distrust felt about them. Doubt and suspicion still, however, remain, stimulated in some cases by the stories of returned soldiers.

3. FLYING BOMBS

THE COUNTRY AS A WHOLE

Discussion has again declined, except in London and the South-East. Concern about the damage and casualties, and sympathy and admiration for the sufferers – especially Londoners – are, however, again widely reported.

There are again a few complaints of insufficient publicity. Lord Halifax's statement, that on the average 700 houses an hour are damaged, has strengthened some people's conviction that the devastation is worse than the authorities would have them believe.

DEFENCES AND COUNTER-MEASURES: Capture of the bases is increasingly believed to be the only solution, and it is generally hoped this will soon take place.

Opinion is now divided as to the success of the present methods of combating the bombs. Some feel we are doing everything possible and are getting the better of them; others feel just as many as ever are getting through.

FUTURE EXPECTATIONS: Comment, though limited, is again on familiar lines; some begin to think if V2 is not used soon it will be too late.

In London, rockets are rumoured already to have fallen, 'flattening 200 houses'.

REPRISALS: The demand for them continues, though with no clear suggestions as to methods to be used.

REACTIONS IN TARGET AREAS

A. LONDON: The majority continue to take the raids philosophically; a minority are still fearful, strained and tired and, in a few cases, resentful at having again to face raids.

EVACUATION: Criticism of the Government scheme now only slightly outweighs praise.

Government camps and a scheme for the evacuation of the aged continue to be asked for.

People in reception areas are again criticised, particularly those with ample room to spare who refuse to take evacuees.

DEFENCES AND COUNTER-MEASURES: Londoners are divided; some attributed the recent lull to fine weather; others to better defence – a figure of 80 per cent destroyed being mentioned.

POST-RAID SERVICES: There are complaints that repairs to damaged property are both inadequate and delayed; though a few express satisfaction with their promptness.

The work of the Civil Defence, of soldiers, marines and the Home Guard is praised.

Sterner measures against looting are urged.

B. SOUTH-EASTERN DISTRICT: Increasing tiredness and some continued nervousness, but on the whole people are believed to be steadier.

EVACUATION: Some satisfaction with the organisation, and pleasure that so many have left the danger areas.

There is a little criticism that more is not done for old people.

LONDON: Continued complaints that too much publicity is given to London, at the expense of the South-East.

SHELTERS: Delay and unfairness in the distribution of Morrisons are alleged; also it is thought unfair that some have to pay.

C. SOUTHERN REGION: Morale continues good among those who have experienced incidents.

D. EASTERN REGION: Some division of opinion; some have 'settled down', while others still think 'it's worse than the blitz'.

4. EVACUATION

There is again slightly less comment this week. On the whole evacuation is thought to be working fairly smoothly, and a considerable measure of sympathy exists for evacuees. Unaccompanied children continue welcome; mothers with children unpopular.

At the same time criticisms have continued that the smaller and poorer home is the worst sufferer, and that communal rather than private billeting should have been the rule.

In addition, complaints have been of:

(a) THE BEHAVIOUR OF EVACUEES: They are criticised for:
  (i) 'Only coming for a holiday' and returning when they have had enough, or if they find the country dull.
  (ii) Their unwillingness to co-operate: refusal to help in any way with the housework; 'high-handedness' to their hostesses ... 'telling them they are paid to look after them'; shiftlessness and dirtiness.

(b) INTENSIFICATION OF THE FOLLOWING DOMESTIC FRONT
PROBLEMS as a result of evacuation.
  (i)   Food shortages and shopping difficulties.
  (ii) Transport difficulties.
  (iii) Household linen shortages. In the South-Western Region the
        promised coupon-free towels are said not yet to have materialised.
  (iv) Accommodation shortages.
  (v)   Water shortage.
  (vi) Education difficulties, since the numbers of teachers and the
        school accommodation available are limited.

5. ITALY

Satisfaction with progress continues, though there is some disappointment that the
rate of advance is not quicker. Comment is limited as this campaign is overshadowed
by those in France.

People are thankful that Florence has been saved from destruction and that loss
of life has been so small.

Praise for General Alexander and his masterly conduct of the campaign continues.
It is, however, thought that he does not get his fair share of praise and attention
from the press.

MR. CHURCHILL'S VISIT has given pleasure and been welcomed as 'an
inspiration for our neglected men'; though some are anxious for his health and
safety. Reasons suggested for the visit have been the political situation in Italy and
the landings in the south of France.

6. GERMANY

This week there has been considerable talk about the possibility of the Germans
making peace proposals before the Allies reach Germany, in order to prevent the
devastation of their country.

All but a very small minority feel most strongly that such trickery should not
be allowed – '1918 must not be repeated'. Some are very uneasy lest we be too
lenient and the Germans escape adequate punishment for 'all the misery, suffering
and devastation they have caused'.

PRESIDENT ROOSEVELT'S STATEMENT TO PRESS REPRESENTATIVES
(17TH AUGUST) about the need for complete Allied occupation of Germany has,
however, encouraged people; all comment is approving.

A few think the Nazis will never surrender but will go on fighting underground
even after Germany has collapsed.

7. RUSSIA

Though confidence and praise continue, there is very much less comment this week;
Russian news has been pushed into the background by events in France.

People are disappointed that the anticipated rush into Germany has not materialised, but they expect the advance will be resumed soon.

Hope continues, for the familiar reasons, that the Russians will reach Berlin first.

Some distrust of Russia, and apprehension as to her future attitude, however, continue.

7A. RUSSO-POLISH RELATIONS

Uneasiness about the position in Warsaw is widespread and people are disappointed that the Russians do not help the patriots. Many feel they have let them down deliberately and are suspicious of Russian motives. It is asked why supplies have to be flown all the way from Italy by the RAF; and it is rumoured the Russians have refused our planes fighter protection.

Disquiet continues about Russo-Polish relations generally; opinion is divided between sympathy for the Poles and pro-Russian sentiment – the latter predominating among working-class people. Likewise, people are divided in their attitude to the Polish government in London.

8. FAR EAST

People are pleased that the Japanese have at last been cleared from India. There is also some praise for the air attacks on the Japanese islands and people are looking forward to the bombing of the mainland.

Other comment is on familiar lines.

9. TURKEY

Turkey's break with Germany continues to be looked on simply as an attempt to be on the winning side and to get a share of the spoils. Some think, however, that the move will have favourable repercussions in the Balkans; others that Turkey still needs watching.

Some hope she will allow us airfields.

10. ALLIED AIR OFFENSIVE

The news of the heavy raids on Kiel and Stettin – particularly the low percentage of losses – has been welcomed.

11. NEWS PRESENTATION

The BBC *War Report* remains very popular; though a small minority find it repetitive. News bulletins are also liked; some people preferring unvarnished facts to 'racy reporting'.

Widespread dissatisfaction is, however, reported, particularly among ex-servicemen and relatives of serving men, at the lack of publicity in press, films, and on the radio about what British forces are doing. This is thought to apply in whatever field the British army is operating, but particularly to France ... 'Have we any troops in France, or is it a dream?' People say the Poles, French, Canadians and

Americans get all the headlines; it is felt particularly that our men's part suffers from lack of publicity in comparison with the Americans'.

Criticism otherwise is mostly of over-optimism and exaggeration; again, the press is thought a worse offender than the BBC. The manner in which the possibilities of the Falaise pocket were dealt with is quoted as an example of over-optimism – 'the first impression was that the whole German Seventh Army had been trapped, then it was daily softened down till only remnants were left'.

II. SPECIAL COMMENTS

BRIEF WEEKLY REVIEW

12. HOLIDAYS

People continue to feel the need for a real holiday away from home. Increasing numbers appear determined to put up with any travel difficulties to get away for a change of surroundings and air. However, some will not risk it, as accommodation is so crowded.

Complaints of overcrowded trains and buses continue, and workers, feeling entitled to a holiday, ask that more transport should be provided.

Holidays at home get some approval; but generally they appear to have little appeal for tired workers. Those who took holidays at home say they spent most of their time queuing for transport and food; they are discouraged to see the thousands who did go away.

BEACHES: People continue to press for more beaches to be opened, not only so that people can get a breath of sea air, but also as a means of easing travel difficulties; if local beaches near industrial areas were available, workers and their families say they would not travel so far afield. Great pleasure is reported at the opening of several beaches on the north-east coast.

13. THE BEER SHORTAGE

There are widespread complaints of the shortage of beer, thought particularly hard on harvesters. Holiday-makers complain about 'dry' holidays in the recent heat. It is thought that the hours of opening of public houses should be both curtailed and uniform. Some publicans, irrespective of licensing laws, are opening and closing when they like, and refusing to serve customers from opposition houses which have closed owing to the shortage.

14. THE WATER SHORTAGE

The water shortage, particularly in country districts, is making the sufferers ask if the Government can speed up its plans for rural water supplies.

Evacuees have added to the difficulties.

Complaints come particularly from the Newbury rural district, where some villagers are having to rely on water carts visiting them two or three times a week; from Enstone, Oxon; north-west Dorset; the Bath and Swindon districts; parts of

Nottinghamshire; and Northampton and district – here cups of tea are rationed in cafés, one of which has closed altogether; baths are 'a thing of the past'; and doctors are alarmed about unflushed lavatories. Some places have been without water for days; others have only an intermittent trickle.

There are, too, complaints of lack of official information as to when the water will be on or off.

III. PERIODICAL REVIEW

15. YOUTH AND MORALS

DURING THE PAST FOUR WEEKS comment has continued on familiar lines though in slightly less volume. Complaints have again been chiefly of:

(a) SEXUAL IMMORALITY – particularly of young girls with servicemen of various nationalities. The behaviour of young married women whose husbands are abroad also causes concern.

(b) JUVENILE AND ADOLESCENT DELINQUENCY, ROWDINESS AND DAMAGE TO PROPERTY: Their bad manners and lack of respect for their elders, and the general unruliness of children, are also criticised.

(c) DRINKING – again chiefly by young girls, and often by those under eighteen.

FACTORS BLAMED continue to be: lack of parental control; lack of harmless recreational facilities; too much money to spend – though low wages for young girls are also thought partly responsible for their running after servicemen; and the bad example set by older people.

MORE WOMEN POLICE and MORE WELFARE WORKERS are felt to be needed.

YOUTH CLUBS AND ORGANISATIONS continue on the whole to be praised. Some think they are the only solution to the problem of the behaviour of young people and urge that more of them be set up – particularly in places such as Liverpool.

There is some criticism, however, that they are not run on suitable lines; more discipline and less 'bribing' with entertainments are urged.

NO. 204: TUESDAY 22 AUGUST 1944 TO TUESDAY 29 AUGUST 1944

I. GENERAL COMMENTS

1. GENERAL

Spirits continue to soar higher than ever. People have been thrilled, and even bewildered, by the news, in particular the astonishing speed of Allied advances in

France, the liberation of Paris, and events in the Balkans. The past week is spoken of as 'one of the best ever'.

The wave of optimism grows. The great majority believe the war is nearly over. October remains the general guess; many think it only a matter of weeks now, some of days. People are laying bets, looking out flags, planning celebrations.

Some have, nevertheless, found it difficult to reconcile recent statements by Allied leaders (e.g. General Eisenhower's warning against wishful thinking, August 15; General Montgomery's 'the end is in sight', August 21; and Mr. Churchill's 'the enemy is still active and strong', August 23).

The only dark spots in the picture are: (i) the flying bomb; (ii) resentment that British troops are not receiving the publicity they are thought to merit; and (iii) anxiety about a post-war job – there is great fear of unemployment.

2. FRANCE

THE LIBERATION OF PARIS has been the great event of the week and was received with a gamut of emotions ranging from satisfaction to 'great joy, as on hearing of the recovery of a sick friend'.

Initial pleasure gave way for a time to confusion and disappointment, when it was learned that there was still German resistance in Paris. Many people felt the Parisians had been over-hasty in claiming the liberation of their city ... 'Strange goings on – rejoicing and fighting at the same time!' Their precipitance was variously put down to hysteria and excess of emotion, to over-eagerness to celebrate, or to a desire to take all the glory to themselves. It is thought that they would have done better to have cleared the enemy out before allowing vast crowds to assemble and risking large-scale slaughter. Some also criticise them for 'making an armistice with the Germans in the city and letting them remove their stock, without consulting the Allied High Command'.

Nevertheless, the great majority are pleased that the French liberated their own capital, and there is much admiration for their guts and initiative. People are glad of this proof that the French are wholeheartedly opposed to the Germans. Some are glad, too, because they feared Paris would be liberated by the Americans.

However, it is hoped that the French are not going to be in too much of a hurry to forget that they did not free their city quite unaided. There is some feeling that recent French utterances have appeared to give the Parisians all the credit, whereas the Allies are thought to have paid dearly in men and aircraft, having had 'to go in under the noses of the Germans to provide the liberators of Paris with arms and ammunition'.

The 'majestic deportment' of General de Gaulle during the Notre Dame shooting has been greatly admired and people are glad he has had a good reception from the French in liberated areas.

Mr. Eden's broadcast (August 24) was very well received.

NORTHERN FRANCE: The speed of Allied advances continues to give the utmost pleasure. People are saying they had never expected France would be 'such a walkover'. The general view seems to be that the Germans are finished in France and will be unable to make a stand until they reach their own frontier. Some think the whole country will be freed within a fortnight. It is widely hoped that the flying bomb sites will very soon be captured.

The generalship, strategy, and organisation are all highly praised. People are pleased at the lightness of casualties and the care taken of the wounded.

There continues to be a great deal of discussion of THE RELATIVE ROLES OF THE BRITISH AND AMERICAN FORCES. It is widely assumed that the job assigned to the British and Canadians has been tougher than that of the Americans, and it is widely regretted that it is less spectacular. A minority wonder if the Americans have got 'something which we haven't – either better organisation or more concerted push when required'; but they are not prepared to believe that they are better fighters. There is, however, plenty of admiration for the Americans' fighting qualities and 'lightning strategy'.

There continues to be widespread dissatisfaction on the grounds that more publicity is given to US than to British exploits (see Section 13, News Presentation).

GENERALS MONTGOMERY AND BRADLEY: Though the mistake has now been rectified, there continues to be annoyance that it should ever have been allowed to occur. 'Those to whom Monty is a hero consider that restitution has not been made in any satisfactory form.' (No reactions yet to statements in today's press, August 31.)

SOUTHERN FRANCE: Much less interest than in the northern fighting, but delight at the rapid advances and the capture of Marseilles. A minority still think the Pas de Calais would have been a much better place for a landing.

THE FRENCH are being 'welcomed back into the fold' and many people are experiencing a change of heart towards them. This is due in general to the work of the FFI and, in particular, to the part played by the French in the liberation of their own capital, which has done much to reduce distrust and scepticism.

A minority, however, remain obdurate, remembering Indo-China, Syria, Madagascar, North Africa and French political factions; feeling, too, that the French in France had not done a great deal before D-Day to help themselves or us.

3. FLYING BOMBS

THE COUNTRY AS A WHOLE

Apart from London, comment is again on a reduced scale. Concern about damage and casualties, and sympathy and admiration for the sufferers are again widely reported.

There continues to be some belief that damage and casualties are worse than official accounts make them out to be.

DEFENCES AND COUNTER-MEASURES: There is widespread hope and expectation that the sites will soon be captured and the menace finally overcome. A few, however, are pessimistic as to whether early relief can be hoped for, since they believe that the bombs are already being dispatched from the Netherlands or Germany. Some think, too, that a final 'all-out' attack is to be expected before the sites are given up.

Opinion remains divided as to the extent of our success in dealing with the bombs. Some are satisfied that everything possible is being done; others are critical that more successful measures have not been found.

FUTURE EXPECTATIONS: There is again considerable speculation and some apprehension. Gas or rockets are thought the most likely forms of attack.

REACTIONS IN TARGET AREAS

A. LONDON: Good news from all fronts, evacuation and the recent lull are all thought to have helped maintain people's calmness. Some expect the raids to stop in a few weeks. A weary minority are, however, fearful of the raids continuing into the winter.

EVACUATION: Criticism of the Government plan continues slightly to outweigh praise. Some think present evacuation is a preparation for V2 rather than a necessity because of V1.

A comprehensive scheme for getting old people away continues to be asked for.

Reception areas are again censured for their 'coldness'.

POST-RAID SERVICES: There are once more complaints of delay and inadequacy in house repairs; anxiety is reported lest repairs are not completed before winter sets in.

The work of the Civil Defence – particularly of volunteers from the provinces – is praised. The Assistance Board is also praised.

Sentences for looting are thought too light.

SIRENS: Planes flying about during alerts continue to be disliked. There is some criticism of delay in fixing imminent danger signals; fire-watchers regret their not being sounded at night.

B. SOUTH-EASTERN DISTRICT: It is felt that the attacks cannot continue much longer, and, while there is said to be some nervousness in the areas most affected, people are determined 'to see the matter through'.

EVACUATION: There is less discussion. Some satisfaction with the scheme is expressed.

Better facilities for the aged and infirm continue to be asked for; there is also some criticism of poor facilities for expectant mothers.

C. SOUTHERN REGION: People think the raids will soon be a thing of the past.

D. EASTERN REGION: It is widely assumed that the raids will only have to be endured for a few weeks longer. Some anxiety continues to be reported, but generally there is said to be less concern.

4. EVACUATION

Comment is again less, and again on familiar lines. On the whole the scheme is thought to be working well, and both householders and evacuees are believed for the most part to have settled down; some mothers with children remain the exception.

At the same time, the following criticisms have continued to be levelled against the Government's scheme: (a) communal and not private billeting should have been the rule; (b) the smaller and poorer home is the worse sufferer; and (c) the billeting allowance is too small.

General criticisms of the behaviour of evacuees have continued on familiar lines. There is some increase in complaints of their laziness and dirtiness, though it is said to be realised that only a minority are to blame. On the other hand, there are also complaints of the unhelpful behaviour of some householders. It is suggested that both sides could be helped by being given a clearer idea of what is expected of them.

Complaints have also continued of increased transport difficulties, food and shopping difficulties, and accommodation shortage resulting from the influx of evacuees.

Housewives' difficulties in making do with household linen and bedding have also continued the subject of complaint.

5. RUMANIA

People have welcomed Rumania's volte-face, though only a few show much enthusiasm. People are contemptuous of this German satellite 'leaving the sinking ship', though some feel more sympathy for Rumania than for Bulgaria.

There is some anxiety lest we forget Rumania's bolstering-up of the Nazi regime and accept her too readily as a co-belligerent; people want her to be made to work her passage home.

It is hoped the Germans will at last really feel the oil shortage. People expect, too, widespread repercussions among the other satellites, especially in the Balkans; it is thought all the Balkan countries will back out as soon as possible now.

6. BULGARIA

The news from Bulgaria has caused no great surprise or enthusiasm, though people are pleased that she should want to make peace.

No sympathy is reported for 'this perfidious, treacherous nation'. It is hoped other satellites will follow her example.

7. RUSSIA

Comment continues on a much-reduced scale, the Eastern front being overshadowed by events nearer home.

Though praise is less superlative, satisfaction and admiration continue, despite some conjecture and disappointment at 'the halt in the great non-stop offensive to Berlin'. Some think German resistance has stiffened, but the majority regard the lull as merely temporary, for regrouping purposes, and a big push is expected before long.

Some fear continues about Russia's future attitude; also a little talk about the possibility of war between Russia and this country.

7A. RUSSO-POLISH RELATIONS

Concern about the situation in Warsaw, and disappointment that the Russians have not yet captured the city, have increased and are now widespread. People feel great admiration for the Poles fighting in Warsaw and are anxious they should be helped, but there are amazement and bewilderment at our having to supply them from Italy when the Russians are only a few miles away.

A good many think the city could well have been captured by now and that the delay is political rather than military; they are suspicious of Russian motives. Some, however, think the resisters themselves made a tactical blunder by rising prematurely; a few blame the Polish government in London. Others think the Russians have suffered a military setback. Others, again, 'just don't know what to think'.

8. THE FUTURE OF GERMANY

There is now widespread discussion about what to do both with Germany as a whole, and with individual war criminals.

Hatred of Germany is growing and people believe that she must be treated harshly and 'made to pay to the full'. First, they are most anxious she should suffer complete military defeat … 'If Germany capitulates as soon as our troops invade that country and we call off the war before their army is crushed, we shall be making a serious mistake.' Second, they think drastic action must be taken to see that she never again has an army, navy, or air force … 'She will start another war, given the slightest chance.'

It is particularly felt that war criminals must not be allowed to get away unpunished.

Various suggestions are made for punishing the Germans and ensuring future peace, including (a) long-term military occupation; (b) splitting Germany up; (c) 'lopping off Prussia'; (d) death for all who have committed atrocities; (e) extermination of the whole nation; (f) sterilisation of all males. A more elaborate suggestion is that all children from 2 to 12 should be taken from Germany, together with all war orphans and illegitimate children, and distributed among the Colonies. They should be given different names and brought up as orphans of the war.

There are, however, many fears that we shall be too lenient with the Germans and that they will escape proper punishment.

9. ITALY

Satisfaction with progress continues, but comment is again limited. Some people are wondering how soon the armies in Italy and southern France will link up; others suggest the army in Italy will be content with a holding role, and that a landing will be made in the Balkans, to link up with Tito.

Praise continues for General Alexander.

MR. CHURCHILL'S VISIT continues to meet with approval, especially for its cheering effect on our troops. His prolonged absence was, however, beginning to worry some people, and anxiety had been felt for his safety. There is some regret that he should have visited the Pope, who 'all through the war has been on the side of our enemies'; it is hoped the Prime Minister was blunt with him. Mr. Churchill's meeting with Marshal Tito, on the other hand, caused pleasure; some think it will lead to an Allied landing in Yugo-Slavia.

10. FAR EAST

Confidence and satisfaction continue; there is a growing feeling that the Far Eastern war will not last long after Germany is defeated.

Lord Louis Mountbatten's report, though well received, aroused little interest.

11. TURKEY

Sarcastic comment continues about her 'sitting on the wall' till we were well on the road to victory, though a few recall that 'she stood by us in the bad days'.

A few also hope Turkey may make a definite move against Germany.

12. ALLIED AIR OFFENSIVE

People are pleased that, despite commitments in the field of battle, heavy attacks on Germany are still possible.

The work of the Typhoons is much admired.

12A. THE FRECKLETON DISASTER (AUGUST 23)

People are shocked at this 'horror of war'. In the North-East, it has resulted in some alarm about low-flying planes, particularly in crowded seaside resorts in the East Riding.

13. NEWS PRESENTATION

News presentation in general has been criticised on the following grounds:

(a) TOO LITTLE PUBLICITY GIVEN TO THE BRITISH AND CANADIANS IN FRANCE, AND TOO MUCH TO THE AMERICANS: Press and newsreels are particularly blamed ... 'Have we no army in France?' Forces' wives are specially bitter. Some people fear the 'capture of the limelight by the Americans' is a very bad augury for post-war relations.

(b) OVER-OPTIMISTIC AND MISLEADING STATEMENTS: The Falaise pocket is again cited ... 'far too much talk of 100,000 Germans facing annihilation; every day the number dwindled'.

(c) PREMATURE ANNOUNCEMENTS IN ADVANCE OF THE ACTUAL FACTS, e.g. the liberation of Paris. 'The Russian habit of announcing only faits accomplis' is preferred.

BBC: The BBC's presentation of the news is specially praised and is thought to be more accurate than that of the press. Particular reference is made to:

(a) WAR REPORTS: These remain very popular with the majority, though a few are getting tired of them and some relatives of fighting men dislike the battle noises.

The 'thrilling' *War Reports* on the liberation of Paris have been highly commended. Sunday night's, in particular, was considered 'the best thing they've done yet' ... 'just like the hunch-back of Notre Dame'. 'The shooting of Robert Dunnett' and the coolness of the girl with him were much admired.

(b) THE RESUMPTION OF WAR COMMENTARIES: The return of Major Lewis Hastings has given great pleasure.

(c) THE 'BOMB-WAYS TO LONDON' PROGRAMME: 'It was untrue to say that it was not so bad as 1940/41.'

(d) THE PRONUNCIATION OF FRENCH NAMES, which is said to confuse those who do not know French: 'Some place names are anglicised, like Paris and Lyons; others are given French pronunciation, like Caen and Versailles'.

II. SPECIAL COMMENTS

BRIEF WEEKLY REVIEW

14. HOLIDAYS

The longing for holidays away from home continues, and more transport is asked for. Those who have been away say they were badly in need of a change and were prepared to put up with inconvenience and crowded travel. Those stopping at home are indignant at the holiday-makers.

Holidays at home are both praised and criticised. Those who enjoyed them praise the arrangements but hope for a proper holiday next year. The main criticism is of lack of transport to and from places of enjoyment.

15. LIFTING OF THE COASTAL BAN

Opinion is divided.

Those living away from the coast and would-be holiday-makers express satisfaction; it is thought to be long overdue, and to show that the danger of invasion is past. People hope the beaches will be cleared of mines as soon as possible.

Those living in coastal towns fear it will cause evacuation difficulties, and an increase in food, shopping and transport problems. Isle of Wight people think they should have been warned, so that they might have prepared for visitors.

Some look on the lifting of the ban as an indication to the Germans that we do not intend to invade the Low Countries.

16. FOOD

BEER: The shortage continues to arouse widespread complaint. Evacuees and US troops are both blamed. In Birmingham, some night-shift workers come in late for work, saying they cannot get a drink in the morning, as the pubs do not open till mid-day when they are in bed; and do not re-open till 8 p.m. when they are supposed to be at work; they add they are used to getting a drink and will not do without it.

FRUIT: Shortage and bad distribution are complained of. Strong resentment is felt in the Northern Region and Scotland that English home-grown apples are not to come north.

WHISKY: Irate comments are reported from many parts of Scotland about the fluctuating prices of whisky ... 'When the pubs open it is 1/6 a half; then it goes up to 1/9; then 2/-; then 2/3 at closing time'. It is said English people do not appear to appreciate the immensity of this issue.

III. PERIODICAL REVIEW

17. US TROOPS IN THE COUNTRY

DURING THE PAST FOUR WEEKS comment has again considerably decreased, as a result both of the departure of many Americans, and of such distractions as the fighting in France and the flying bombs.

However, there are a number of references to the Americans becoming increasingly popular, mainly because of the fine job they are doing in Normandy, which has changed people's opinion of their fighting qualities. Getting to know them better has also helped; and it is believed they are better behaved and less noisy than formerly.

The Americans' generosity, especially to children, their cheerfulness and general bearing are all liked. The coloured troops are again singled out for praise; some think they are better behaved than the white troops.

Criticism is on the usual lines; again, their behaviour with young married women and with girls excites most censure. The troops and the girls come in for about equal criticism and people are afraid of trouble ahead when British servicemen return from overseas and find their wives have been unfaithful. The Americans' high pay, and consequent ability to give girls a good time, is chiefly blamed.

Also criticised are – wasting petrol on taking girls to dances in jeeps or in using taxis for short journeys; drunken, rowdy behaviour; dangerous driving; waste and destruction of food and equipment; and the white Americans' attitude to their coloured compatriots.

BRITISH AND AMERICAN TROOPS: Comment about differences of pay continues; also about the better food and cheaper tobacco available to the Americans. A few people think British and US servicemen are mixing better than in the past, but others comment about the 'coolness' between them.

SHORTAGES are thought in part to be due to the Americans. Beer, hotel accommodation, and food are all mentioned.

BRITISH CHILDREN'S BEGGING HABITS continue to be deplored.

PROFITEERING at the expense of the Americans is condemned, laundries, restaurants, and taxi-drivers being mentioned.

NO. 207: TUESDAY 12 SEPTEMBER 1944 TO TUESDAY 19 SEPTEMBER 1944

I. GENERAL COMMENTS

1. GENERAL

People continue delighted with Allied progress in western Europe and the fact that the Germans are now having a taste of war on their own soil; also with the relaxation of the blackout and other regulations.

Spirits remain at the same high level as last week; in London, however, they are slightly lower because of the renewal of flying bomb attacks; and the explosions, which are the subject of widespread rumours all over the country.

The end of the war in Europe is still expected within a week or two, or by Christmas at the latest; but optimism is said to be a little more subdued than it was.

POST-WAR problems loom large, particularly employment, housing and demobilisation.

2. THE BATTLE FOR GERMANY

There continues to be widespread amazement and enthusiasm at the 'breath-taking' speed of Allied advances ... 'We have out-blitzed Hitler at his own game.' The planning, organisation and execution of the campaign are all the object of profound admiration, and the lightness of the casualties is the subject of special relief.

Comment, which is seldom detailed, is chiefly about:

THE FIGHTING ON GERMAN TERRITORY: People are delighted that the Germans are now having a taste of war on their own soil. There is also pleasure and surprise that the Siegfried Line has been so quickly pierced. Two minority reactions are pleasure that the invasion of 'Germany proper' has been from the west and not from the east, and disappointment that the British were not the first in.

Opinions differ as to the strength of opposition likely to be encountered from now on. Those who think resistance will stiffen, now that the fatherland itself is being defended, appear to outnumber those who expect a speedy collapse. The prospect of tougher fighting on German soil – with corresponding devastation – causes no dismay, except at the possibility of heavier casualties.

THE AIRBORNE INVASION OF HOLLAND has caused pleased excitement, according to preliminary reports.

THE CAPTURE OF SOME OF THE CHANNEL PORTS was received with relief, particularly that of Le Havre; the small number of casualties there, compared with the number of prisoners, was favourably noted. There is said to be some confusion as to which ports have been taken and which are still holding out.

THE ROLES OF THE BRITISH AND AMERICAN TROOPS and the publicity accorded them continue to be discussed on familiar lines. Satisfaction at the British entering Brussels has been some compensation for the US march through Paris; increased publicity given to British achievements has, too, done something to quieten resentment at what was regarded as too much limelight for the Americans.

FIELD-MARSHAL MONTGOMERY: His address to the men under his command (September 17) was thought most inspiring. His promotion and the circumstances attending it still continue to cause familiar comment.

FFI: The exploits of the FFI have aroused admiration – even enthusiasm – and have removed much of the anti-French feeling which existed before D-Day. Some persist, however, in the belief that the French let us down in 1940 and are still not to be trusted.

General de Gaulle's thanks for British help are appreciated, but a few still consider that the FFI claimed too much credit for the liberation of Paris, 'which was, after all, made possible by British and American spadework'.

2A. CONDITIONS INSIDE FRANCE AND BELGIUM

Surprise and intense annoyance continue to be widely reported on the same lines as last week, though on a slightly reduced scale. People feel they have been misled about conditions in occupied countries and are beginning to think that, instead of our making sacrifices for starving Europe, perhaps something could now be done for 'the ordinary civilian in this country, who is considered to have had the rawest deal of all'. Particular reference is made to:

(a) CLOTHING: Women who have 'spent hours on make-do and mend' are infuriated when they see newsreels showing fashion displays in Paris and read of 'the smartness of the Parisians and their new perfumes'.
(b) FOOD: 'Soon the liberated countries will be feeding starving Britain', is the kind of comment caused by photographs of plump French and Belgians and accounts of ice-cream in Brussels.

3. ATTITUDE TO GERMANY AND THE GERMANS

Hatred of Germany, discussion of how to deal with her after the war, fear that we shall be too lenient and that war criminals will escape retribution – all these continue to be widely reported on the same lines as last week. People are determined that the Germans must have a thorough experience of war on their own soil: 'we must give them what we failed to give them in 1918', smash our way through Germany, and not stop till we reach Berlin.

There are two new points since last week, in connection with:

ALLIED TROOPS FRATERNISING WITH GERMAN CIVILIANS: There are strong objections to press photographs of American troops feeding German civilians (September 16). Satisfaction is, however, mentioned, that the Americans obliterated a German village.

THE GERMANS' FRIENDLY REACTIONS TO THE INVADING ARMIES: It is felt the press and BBC are over-doing this; the Germans, it is thought, can only be trying to curry favour ... 'too late for soft soap now'.

4. EXPLOSIONS IN THE LONDON AREA

Numerous widespread rumours of a new weapon being used against London, causing mysterious explosions, are this week reported from twelve Regions. The majority of people consider they are caused by V2 – an enemy rocket bomb. Explosions are thought by many people to have occurred at Chiswick, Kew and Dagenham; other places in or near London are also mentioned, as well as places as far afield as Nottingham, Newcastle and Belfast.

It is rumoured that the explosions are terrific and cause enormous damage, e.g. craters larger than the Houses of Parliament; blast carrying debris back across the Channel; everyone and everything blown to dust; one explosion killing 5,000 people.

The majority think an official statement should be made, to deter evacuees from returning and to stop rumours. A few appreciate that an announcement would help the Germans.

REACTIONS IN LONDON

The explosions have been a main topic of discussion. Here, too, the general view is that they are caused by V2. Rumours of damage are more moderate than in the rest of the country and are declining; there are still a few who attribute the explosions to sabotage; others say the rocket is covered in ice or that there is ice in the crater after the explosion.

The majority now accept official silence as a necessity.

There is little anxiety, though a few are worried by the lack of warning. Most people do not expect the nuisance to last for long.

Returned evacuees are annoyed to find what they have come back to.

4A. FURTHER ENEMY ACTION

Speculation continues and a number of people expect the Germans to launch yet another weapon against us. Gas is the most popular guess.

5. FLYING BOMBS

THE COUNTRY AS A WHOLE

Earlier in the week people were very relieved that the attacks had ceased and that people in London and the south-east were having some peace. There has been some concern at their renewal, and sympathy and admiration for those in target areas. Two suggestions are that London should be awarded the George Cross and Kent have the George Medal.

MR. DUNCAN SANDYS' STATEMENT (September 7) has caused continued interest; there is widespread admiration for our methods of defence. With the return of V1, and the new explosions, there is now some feeling that Mr. Sandys spoke too soon.

There is some suspicion that the official casualty figures are an understatement.

REACTIONS IN LONDON

At the beginning of the week, most people thought this particular menace was ended; renewed activity has correspondingly damped some spirits.

POST-RAID SERVICES: Complaints of slow and poor-quality repair work to damaged houses have increased. It is said that roofs are left with the rain still able to penetrate, and that the substitute window material gets detached from the frame by wind and rain in a few days.

It is thought more provincial labour should be drafted in, though drafted builders in Stepney complain of being put on to repair non-useful factories, and of being moved on to other jobs when one is only partly finished.

There is some confusion as to whether local authorities or private contractors are responsible for final repairs. Some traders are 'insisting on a firm order and a deposit' before giving estimates for submission to the War Damage Commission and Board of Trade.

RECEPTION AREAS: People now think they should receive more praise for their kindness.

6. EVACUATION

Discussion this week is largely confined to the wisdom – or otherwise – of evacuees returning home. A big majority think it very foolish, though this does not preclude relief and pleasure among billeters where evacuees do decide to return.

A number of people think the Government should forbid evacuees to return; others that they should be warned more precisely about the possibility of rocket bombs. The Government is criticised for causing confusion by contradictory official statements and policy. Mr. Sandys' statement and the end of official evacuation are contrasted with the 'stay put' advice to people already evacuated.

Chief factors in encouraging people to return home are thought to be: Mr. Sandys' statement; the easing of the blackout; evacuees' anxiety about their homes; the decrease in the number of raids; and the suspension of the evacuation scheme.

7. THE QUEBEC CONFERENCE

This has been overshadowed by news from the Western front. Nevertheless, people are pleased Mr. Churchill and Mr. Roosevelt have met again. Some, however, fear that all this travelling is too much for the Prime Minister and ask 'Why couldn't Roosevelt come here?'

People expect results – 'like after the last conference' – but they hope no modification has been made in the unconditional surrender terms for Germany.

M. STALIN'S ABSENCE is regretted. It is variously attributed to (a) Russia not being at war with Japan; (b) Stalin preparing a knock-out blow for Germany; (c) 'His stand-offishness'.

Marshal Chiang Kai-Shek's absence added, it is felt, to the incompleteness of the conference.

MR. EDEN'S FLYING VISIT caused speculation.

8. RUSSIA

Interest in the Eastern front continues overshadowed by events in the west, but admiration for Russia's progress in the Balkans remains widespread.

Some are surprised that Russian progress in East Prussia has been so slow; others think the Germans intend to hold the Russians off, possibly at the cost of letting us in, because 'we shall treat them less roughly'.

Others continue to speculate as to who will reach Berlin first.

FINLAND: Little interest is reported and no sympathy. People think she should have made peace long ago and that if she receives harsh terms now it is her own fault.

8A. RUSSO-POLISH RELATIONS

The Russian entry into Praga and intensification of activity on the Warsaw front have pleased and, to some extent, reassured people. Confusion, uneasiness and concern, however, continue to be widely reported.

The majority remain suspicious of Russia's attitude, for the familiar reasons. Criticism of the Poles – particularly of the government in London – also continues on the usual lines.

Sympathy for the patriots is widespread and people hope their ordeal will soon be over.

Fears of the possible repercussions of the situation on Allied unity also continue to be reported.

8B. BULGARIA AND RUMANIA

There is general admiration for the way Russia has handled Rumania and Bulgaria – particularly the latter. A few, however, think these countries are escaping too lightly and contrast this with Russia's attitude to Poland.

People remain contemptuous and distrustful of both countries.

9. ITALY

MILITARY: Although much overshadowed by events on the Western front, satisfaction with the steady progress of a very difficult campaign is reported. People appreciate the stiffness of the opposition and express sympathy for troops 'enduring bad conditions without much praise and glory'. They feel the campaign has not had its deserts either in the press or on the radio. A minority think 'big things may happen any moment' and hope that action from the south of France towards the Po Valley may relieve the weight on the forces near the Gothic Line.

A few, however, continue disappointed at the rate of progress and some wonder if the troops have adequate air support. Again, a few are puzzled by the heavy fighting on the Gothic Line ... 'Why don't we drop men behind?'

Faith in General Alexander is again reported.

POLITICAL: Anxiety about civil administration is reported. Some people fear we are showing weakness towards the Fascists and that 'Italy is being allowed to get away with it'. People cannot forget former treachery and ask if 'collaboration by Italy is a full remission of past sins'.

Criticism of the 'apparently pro-Nazi Pope' continues.

9A. ITALIAN PRISONERS OF WAR

Growing dissatisfaction about the increased privileges and lenient treatment accorded to Italian prisoners of war – and the results – is reported from seven Regions. There is indignation at the way girls and young women flirt and walk about arm-in-arm with them. People object also to their receiving bicycles when civilians have none; and to their being transported in special buses when workers have to queue or walk. It is thought that if they are admitted to Service canteens there will be serious trouble; quarry workers in Derbyshire object to their being served in their canteens, and they are said to be banned from WVS canteens.

People recall the cruelties which the Italians inflicted on our men in Africa, and on British prisoners of war. It is generally suggested that the best thing to do with them is to ship them back to Italy to fight for their country.

10. FAR EAST

This theatre of war continues to be eclipsed by events in Europe, and interest is slight.

Satisfaction is, however, reported at the news of the losses of Japanese planes and shipping during American attacks on the Philippines – regarded as a major disaster for the Japs.

Speculation continues as to how long the war against Japan will last after the finish of the European war. People hope servicemen who have been through many campaigns will not be sent out to the East.

The desire for more news of the Far Eastern war continues. Relatives of soldiers in the 14th Army are said to think their men have been forgotten by the powers-that-be.

There is support for the view that the pay of our men in India should be increased.

11. THE SHELLING OF DOVER AND FOLKESTONE

People in shelled areas complain of having a terrible time; they say they have suffered 'as much as should be expected'. There is, however, no sign of panic; they remain sustained by the hope that the Germans cannot hold the Channel ports much longer.

The *Folkestone Herald* is censured for printing in large headlines 'You can all come back.'

12. NEWS PRESENTATION

GENERAL: The majority regard the news as being well handled apart from the relative publicity given to US and British troops, complaints about which are now declining.

BBC: Continued praise for:

(a) WAR REPORTS, though a minority still consider there are too many US and Canadian speakers.
(b) MAJOR LEWIS HASTINGS.

THE PRESS is blamed for encouraging optimism and for publishing too many unconfirmed statements and premature announcements. The BBC, though considered slower in releasing news than the press, is regarded as more truthful.

II. SPECIAL COMMENTS

BRIEF WEEKLY REVIEW

13. RELAXATION OF BLACKOUT

Great pleasure continues. In many towns people went out just to see the lights; in Glasgow and Edinburgh, and elsewhere in Scotland, 'thousands paraded up and down the streets gazing at the lights'. People continue to interpret the relaxation as a sign the end of the war is in sight.

Some minority dissatisfaction is, however, expressed in connection with:

(a) The relaxation being premature: 'It's tempting Jerry.'
(b) Half measures having been taken: 'If the blackout is no longer necessary then full lighting should be allowed.'
(c) The confusing nature of the present position. Some people do not know:
    (i)   How much light is allowed: 'Is frosted glass sufficient?' 'The police state curtains must not be flimsy, but all curtains now are flimsy and replacements out of the question.' A few also wonder what is to be done about churches and permanently blacked-out factories.
    (ii) Where the relaxation does or does not apply. At Bridport, for instance, 'the streets were thronged with people on Sunday evening waiting to see the lights go up, but things are just as they have been and many people feel they have been badly let down and disappointed.'
(d) Alleged lack of timely instructions to local authorities, who have been unable to comply because of equipment difficulties. They point out that by the time they have adapted street lighting 'all need of a dim-out may have gone'.
(e) The continued restrictions in coastal areas. Disappointment is reported in the South-Western Region and Wales, and the preliminary announcement

is blamed for having raised false hopes. On the other hand, people on the east coast are pleased, as 'they feel safer with the blackout'.

(f) The failure to allow brighter headlamps on vehicles.

(g) The negligible improvement in street lighting in some places.

13A. HOME GUARD, FIRE GUARD AND CIVIL DEFENCE

General satisfaction continues at the easing of duties. Among paid Civil Defence workers and Fire Guards, however, there is some fear of unemployment.

III. PERIODICAL REVIEWS

14. THE LUBLIN ATROCITIES

DURING THE PAST THREE WEEKS little spontaneous comment has been received. People are believed to be loath to discuss or even to think of the stories – some are said to refuse to read them in the press.

The majority believe the stories and are deeply horrified and shocked at the disclosures. They find them almost incredible. Hatred of the Germans has been intensified ... 'such stories can never be forgiven nor forgotten'. They are insistent that the perpetrators and anyone in any way connected with these atrocities must be punished – some think the whole German people must be held responsible. In any case, they are thought added evidence of the need for a 'tough' peace and for the complete re-education of Germany.

Only minorities are sceptical of the stories' truth or believe them to be exaggeration or propaganda. Some of these quote last war atrocity stories – particularly 'corpse-factory' stories – afterwards found to be untrue. Others are chary because there has been no 'official' statement about them. Some find the stories incredible and 'foreign' and cannot possibly believe them. A few are suspicious because they come from Russian sources, but these are changing their minds as similar stories are received from France.

Another minority are 'keeping an open mind' and suspending judgment until there is more evidence.

15. SHAVING OF WOMEN COLLABORATORS' HEADS

DURING THE PAST THREE WEEKS there has been little spontaneous comment although, when the subject was mentioned, most people apparently knew quite clearly what they thought. It seems that, although opinion is divided, a definite majority disliked the practice and people are glad it has now ceased. On the whole men seem to have been more shocked than women.

THOSE WHO OBJECTED did so on the grounds that:

(a) It means a descent to mob or lynch law; it is the antithesis of all civilised ideas of punishing people only after trial.

(b) Sadistic methods of punishment are just what we are fighting against.

(c) It is crude and repulsive; it made people feel vaguely uneasy and distressed. Newsreels and photos in the papers shocked people particularly.

(d) It gives an opportunity for merely paying off private scores.

(e) Such methods are silly.

THE MINORITY WHO DID NOT OBJECT OR WHO APPROVED said:

(a) 'Serve them right, they deserve it.'

(b) It does no great harm.

(c) It is not our business and the French should be left to do as they think fit; local people are the best judges.

(d) They got off very lightly and deserved more severe punishment.

(e) It was 'rather a joke'.

(f) We should have done the same in similar circumstances. A few even say some of our own women could do with similar treatment.

16. YOUTH AND MORALS

During the past four weeks comment has continued on familiar lines, and complaints have again been chiefly of:

(a) SEXUAL IMMORALITY, with troops of all nationalities, particularly Americans, both black and white, on the part of young girls, including some in their early teens, and young married women whose husbands are abroad. People wonder what will happen when these husbands return.

In some areas there has been less comment since the departure of many Americans.

From two Regions there is criticism of the behaviour of young girls with Italian prisoners of war.

(b) THE DRINKING HABITS OF YOUNG GIRLS AND BOYS: This is thought to increase the immorality problem.

(c) HOOLIGANISM AND DELINQUENCY AMONG CHILDREN, ESPECIALLY BOYS: Wilful destruction of property, thieving and housebreaking are all commented on.

(d) GENERAL RUDENESS AND BAD BEHAVIOUR OF YOUNG PEOPLE OF BOTH SEXES.

It is also deplored that young people start their working lives with no ideals of service or communal responsibility, but only with thoughts of 'dance halls, pictures and dogs'.

FACTORS BLAMED ARE: (a) high wages paid to boys and girls (people wonder what will happen to these youths after the war); (b) lack of parental control and break-up of family life, through fathers being in the Services and mothers working; (c) lack of discipline at school; (d) the leniency of present-day parents; (e) the 'weak and sentimental' attitude of juvenile courts; (f) the preponderance of sensational and horror films, even at special children's showings.

REMEDIES SUGGESTED are very few. Again, it is thought there should be more women police and more counter-attractions to the pubs. In this latter connection there is considerable indignation in Scotland at the Glasgow Corporation's refusal to allow British Restaurants or other premises to remain open in the evenings.

YOUTH ORGANISATIONS: There is some approval of the work done, and people think they should be further developed and their number increased in rural areas. At the same time, a number of people criticise youth organisations for lax discipline and catering only for amusement. It is said they do not teach practical crafts such as cookery or woodwork; nor the responsibility of citizenship.

NO. 209: TUESDAY 26 SEPTEMBER 1944 TO
TUESDAY 3 OCTOBER 1944

I. GENERAL COMMENTS

1. GENERAL

Spirits have again declined owing to the sobering effect of:

(a) Our withdrawal from Arnhem, together with the loss of so many men there.
(b) Stiffening German resistance generally.
(c) The Prime Minister's reference to the possibility of the war continuing into 1945.

People have been jolted out of their optimism about a speedy end to the war, and the majority now speak of spring 1945 as the finishing date. A few, however, while no longer thinking in terms of days or weeks, still expect peace by Christmas.

The Government's White Paper on social insurance has on the whole had a good reception, although some points are the subject of considerable controversy. The demobilisation plan continues to be thought fair and reasonable.

Anxiety is still prevalent about housing and employment – present and future.

2. ARNHEM

The battle and subsequent withdrawal have in turn been the main interest of the past week. The news of how things were going at Arnhem was the 'most eagerly awaited since Dunkirk'. Anxiety over the position, already reported last week, increased daily and found confirmation in the ban on news. Nevertheless, after all the excitement and enthusiasm over the airborne landings, the withdrawal came as a great shock and caused widespread disappointment. The outcome is generally regarded as a serious setback, those who thought the war as good as won being particularly dismayed by this evidence of the strength and determination of German opposition. Comment chiefly centres round:

(a) THE OPERATION ITSELF: The majority view is that the undertaking represented a legitimate risk which did not come off. People believe that if it had succeeded it would have resulted in the turning of the Siegfried Line and the shortening of the war. This majority consider that the bad weather was the main factor against success, coupled with unexpectedly severe German resistance. They feel, too, that the venture was not entirely unsuccessful, though there is some reluctance to accept assurances that it was worth all the sacrifices involved. Field-Marshal Montgomery's words to General Urquhart – 'You did not fail' – are thought to have gone a little beyond the facts.

A minority criticise the operation as a serious blunder on the part of the High Command, who are accused of over-optimism and running undue risks. (The relatives of men involved are said in one report to be very bitter.) The Prime Minister's words have, however, reassured some of those who doubted the wisdom of the undertaking.

Once more it is asked why the British troops get the toughest jobs.

(b) THE MEN TAKING PART: There is unanimous admiration and praise for the heroism and endurance of those taking part, and great sorrow that so many brave men have been lost. Many people feel that the survivors should receive some special recognition, either in the form of an 'Arnhem medal' or immediate return home ... 'They've done their bit.'

There is praise, too, for those who attempted to fly supplies to Arnhem and for the war reporters who landed with the airborne troops.

(c) OPTIMISTIC FORECASTS: Some people consider that the first reports of the landings (particularly in the press) were too optimistic and flamboyant, giving the impression that they were bound to succeed.

2A. THE BATTLE FOR GERMANY

The 'epic of Arnhem' has left little attention for the rest of the fighting in the west. No reactions have yet been received to reports of the new offensive against the Siegfried Line, and the general impression during the past week has been that the Allied advance had come to a standstill in the face of strong German opposition; there was disappointment as a result. There is some realisation that we must pause to bring up supplies, but it is feared that the weather may soon be against us and that we may get 'bogged down for the winter, as in Italy'.

THE CAPTURE OF CALAIS has given great satisfaction, primarily as putting an end to the shelling of the Dover area, but also as promising us better port facilities for supplying our Forces.

There is, however, some regret that we had to direct so much of our bombing forces to bomb a French town, when 'most people would like to see it concentrated on Germany'.

2B. ATTITUDE TO GERMANY AND THE GERMANS

'What to do with Germany after the war' remains the subject of much discussion of a familiar kind. Feeling against the Germans continues strong, and proposals for dealing with them are extremely varied. Any suggestion of Nazi leaders escaping punishment causes an uproar, and surprise, indignation and suspicion are reported at the news that 'Hitler, Goering, Himmler and Co. are not listed as war criminals'. Some people do not believe that our Government really means to tackle this problem. (No reactions yet to Mr. Churchill's answer in the House on this question, October 4.)

Stories and photographs of Allied troops fraternising with Germans continue to cause resentment; it is hoped our men will not be taken in by 'smiling Fräuleins with bowls of plums'. The press is criticised for 'its neutral attitude in publishing such things', and also for 'poor dear Germans' propaganda and 'stories of Germans not wanting to fight but being driven to it by their officers'.

2C. CONDITIONS INSIDE FRANCE AND BELGIUM

Bitter comment continues on familiar lines and shows no signs of abating. Press reports and pictures of well-fed and well-dressed people in Paris and Brussels are 'killing people's readiness to make further sacrifices for starving Europe'. Pictures and accounts of Paris fashions have greatly annoyed and tantalised women. Some, too, are displeased at a rumour that 'luxury goods may be exported to the Continent, while our women must put up with poor-quality "utility" goods'. Any suggestion of sending supplies to Europe now causes resentment.

People say that if earlier reports of privations and ill-treatment under Nazi rule are now found to be exaggerated, it would be better to admit it frankly. They are asking for an explanation of the real position.

2D. AMERICAN BUSINESSMEN IN PARIS

Press stories of American businessmen visiting Paris have given rise to some criticism and concern ... 'People are nettled.' It is feared that others are getting ready to secure world markets, while we go on making war equipment.

There is welcome for the restrictions since imposed by General Eisenhower, but these are not thought to go far enough.

France's large order to the USA for railway equipment also upsets some ... 'Who gave France her first helping hand?'

3. GOVERNMENT WHITE PAPER ON SOCIAL INSURANCE

THE PLAN AS A WHOLE

The plan has had a widespread and very warm welcome, although there is still some caution and withholding of judgment, through people not yet having digested it in detail. A number call it 'a great advance' which should carry the nation a long way towards freedom from want; others say, however, that the value of the benefits will depend on the purchasing power of the pound. Many are surprised and pleased that the plan contains so much of Beveridge; a very few think it an improvement.

At the same time, while approving the plan, a considerable number, among whom workers and left-wing people are specified, are convinced it will never be implemented, or will be whittled away with excuses ... 'They made a start by postponing the raising of the school-leaving age.' Others, though not sceptical, are nevertheless depressed at the thought of 'the long time' it will take to put the provisions into practice. A few dismiss it as 'a political stunt to catch votes'.

A smaller number take it as a sign that the Government is 'at last getting down to it' and are said to feel more hopeful than for some time.

Opposition to the plan comes chiefly from, or is thought by workers to come from: (a) middle-class people, who are thought to be penalised by having to pay and get 'nothing out of it'; (b) friendly societies; and (c) employers and self-employed people.

Other reactions to the plan as a whole are:

(a) CONFUSION as to what will happen about insurance contributions already made to:
   (i)   APPROVED SOCIETIES: The whole position of these societies is also discussed, people on the whole thinking it is a good thing they are 'being done away with'; it will mean more and equal benefits for the insured. Some, however, regret their going. A few wonder what will happen to the societies' employees.
   (ii) SUPERANNUATION SCHEMES: One suggestion is that some extra voluntary payment might be arranged for people concerned, to bring the state pension up to the level of the pension for which they have been contributing in the past.
   (iii) PRIVATE INSURANCE COMPANIES: Will people be allowed to keep their policies on if they wish?

(b) FEAR OF THE POSSIBLE EFFECT ON PEOPLE'S CHARACTERS: Many people, the middle and professional classes and right-wing opinion being specified, are afraid the plan may 'make life too easy'; they think it will encourage improvidence and laziness among workers ... 'who will booze their money away' – or that it will in effect subsidise the unemployed who do not want to work.

(c) ALARM AS TO HOW THE PLAN WILL BE PAID FOR: This seems largely confined to right-wing people, those who do not expect to benefit, and 'financiers'. Some think we shall not be able to afford it; others that it can only be done by very heavy taxation or control of private enterprise.

SPECIFIC PROVISIONS

Specific provisions mainly discussed are:

(a) CONTRIBUTIONS: People like the idea of a single weekly contribution. At the same time, they feel that everyone pays in full for the benefits they are to receive: 'there are no rabbits out of the hat'.
   Those whose contributions are thought by themselves or others to be particularly onerous are:

    (i)   EMPLOYEES.

    (ii) EMPLOYERS, especially small ones. A few people wonder whether the cost will be passed on to the consumer. Some jobbing gardeners and charwomen are said to be apprehensive about getting work in the face of these higher contributions.

    (iii) SELF-EMPLOYED PERSONS.

    (iv) AN AVERAGE FAMILY.

(b) RETIREMENT PENSIONS: People think the rates are inadequate, although there is at the same time satisfaction that some security for all old people will be provided.

(c) FAMILY ALLOWANCES: The idea is generally welcomed, and only a very few oppose it on principle. However, there is a good deal of criticism of the exception of the first child from the cash allowance; and of this being only 5/- instead of the 8/- proposed by Beveridge.

    There is very little comment about the services in kind, although in one Region the workers discuss them favourably.

(d) UNEMPLOYMENT BENEFIT: The limitation to 30 weeks continues to be criticised. People also ask what happens at the expiry of this period, workers strongly opposing any means test.

    There is criticism of there being no provision for self-employed persons 'if they come a cropper, though they have to contribute just the same'.

3A. GOVERNMENT WHITE PAPER ON INDUSTRIAL INJURY INSURANCE

Comment is limited, but is largely approving, particularly among workers.
CHANGES PARTICULARLY LIKED ARE:

(a) The abolition of lump sum settlements.

(b) Setting up of tribunals, so that compensation will no longer be a disputable issue between employer and worker, with the former in a position to 'trip a man up'.

ADVERSE COMMENT IS CHIEFLY ABOUT:

(a) Office workers and others in relatively safe occupations, and their employers, having to pay heavily for benefits 'they will never require'. For instance, it is said that employers of gardeners or domestic servants who now pay a premium of 2/6d to 5/- a year, will have to pay 26/-, which, with the same amount paid by the workers, means 52/- a year.

(b) The proposed flat rate of compensation.

(c) The danger that employers will lose their fear of accidents and that protection against accident may consequently suffer.

4. GOVERNMENT WHITE PAPER ON DEMOBILISATION

Widespread approval continues. People think the plan is fair, though realising there are bound to be a lot of hard cases whatever scheme is adopted.

Approval is also again reported, particularly among servicemen's relatives, for the continued call-up, but a few think it is idiotic to apply it to men hitherto in reserved occupations.

People insist on the necessity of finding work for the demobilised men, even if, in order to do so, they have to be released more slowly.

Discussion about Scale B continues. It is thought that priority should be given not only to men in building trades, but also to teachers, key men in industry, youth leaders, those with jobs to return to or with businesses of their own, and those whose technical or professional training was interrupted.

It is feared there may be scope for favouritism in applying Scale B.

People think that more consideration should be given to:

(a) MEN WITH OVERSEAS SERVICE, particularly Far East troops. Some think they should have first priority. (A few fear that the demobilisation plan may not be applied in their case at all).

(b) MEN WITH FAMILY RESPONSIBILITIES, ESPECIALLY MARRIED MEN.

(c) THOSE WHO HAVE SERVED IN POSTS OF DANGER, e.g. air crews, 'front-line men', etc.

5. THE PRIME MINISTER'S STATEMENT IN THE HOUSE (SEPTEMBER 28)

Mr. Churchill's speech has been very well received. Some lack of comment is reported, but hardly a word of criticism. Most interest has been aroused by his references to:

THE POSSIBILITY OF THE WAR CONTINUING INTO 1945, which came as a great shock to many. A minority, however, think a word of caution was badly needed.

BRITAIN'S SHARE IN MILITARY OPERATIONS: People are delighted that he stressed this, both as regards the number of divisions involved and their achievements in the field. It is hoped that this will not pass unnoticed in the USA.

THE BURMA CAMPAIGN: This part of his speech was greatly appreciated, particularly his reference to its being the largest land operation yet undertaken against Japan, and his account of the many obstacles to be faced.

RUSSO-POLISH RELATIONS: Interest and mixed feelings are reported, but very little detailed comment. Russian sympathisers are said to be pleased, Polish sympathisers disappointed.

6. EXPLOSIONS

IN LONDON ITSELF, both discussion and apprehension are again less, though there is some fear lest the attacks become heavier.

Opinion is divided as to whether official silence is necessary.

IN THE REST OF THE COUNTRY discussion and rumours are widespread. The general belief continues to be that rockets are the cause of the explosions – they are described as dropping silently from the stratosphere.

There are several reports this week of them dropping outside London – some are said to have fallen as far afield as Ireland.

Opinion is evenly divided as to whether an official statement should be made. Some think it necessary to allay rumours and anxiety; others appreciate the need for silence.

6A. FLYING BOMBS

Some concern and disappointment have continued. The attacks are not expected to reach their former proportion, however. Sympathy is expressed for those who have to suffer them.

IN LONDON there is disappointment at the raids starting again but they are thought only to be a 'dying kick' and are said not to be upsetting people generally, though a few find them very trying.

POST-RAID HOUSING REPAIRS: Widespread anxiety and some discontent are reported though a few are said to be pleased that repairs to bombed houses have been given priority. It is thought that still more labour should be allocated; NFS, Civil Defence workers and Italian prisoners of war are suggested.

There is some complaint that repairs are often superficial or poorly done.

6B. EVACUATION

The 'premature' announcement that the Battle of London was over continues to be widely criticised, Mr. Duncan Sandys' statement again receiving most of the blame.

At the same time evacuees are criticised for returning – parents taking back children, especially. A firm direction from the Government to prevent this is felt to be necessary.

6C. THE DOVER SHELLING

'Jubilation' at the cessation of the shelling is reported. A few are still sleeping in shelters, however, 'fearing something else may come'.

There is some criticism of press exaggeration of the rejoicing that took place.

7. ITALY

MILITARY: Though still overshadowed by events on the western front, satisfaction with progress continues – especially with the breaking of the Gothic line and the capture of Rimini, and people hope the advance into northern Italy may now be more rapid.

Disappointment with the slow advance is, however, again reported, although the majority at the same time refer to the difficulties of the campaign with understanding and sympathy. Only a small minority feel 'the war there is lasting too long', or 'have lost interest until something really startling happens'.

Praise and admiration for General Alexander continue.

POLITICAL: People are still concerned and distrustful. Many feel that we are being too lenient and are apparently forgetting the Italians were our enemies and 'helped to bomb London' ... 'We are treating the country as if it were being liberated rather than as a hostile nation that has been defeated.' People wonder 'what constitutes the grounds for making Italy's passage easy'.

Distrust of Vatican policy continues, and any signs of intervention by the Pope are said to be resented.

7A. CARUSO'S TRIAL AND THE LYNCHING OF CARRETTA

Comment is very much less, but the outbreak of mob violence which resulted in the lynching of Carretta has made people feel that the Italians are not able to govern themselves and must be taken in hand for some time to come. Some think we should have taken measures to ensure against such a 'terrible happening'.

People were revolted by the publication of photographs of Caruso's execution and details of the lynching of Carretta.

7B. ITALIAN PRISONERS OF WAR

Resentment continues widespread at the privileges and freedom Italian prisoners of war enjoy; there is particular indignation in a few areas at their being allowed in cinemas 'where they crowd other people out'.

People still think they should be sent back to Italy to fight and to liberate their own country; in Bideford it is rumoured that this is to happen to Italians in that neighbourhood. At Didcot it is considered that the collaborators employed at the RAOC depot should be sent home to release our own men at the Italian front and to make room at the depot for our own ex-servicemen when demobilisation takes place.

Criticism is again made of the friendship shown to Italians, and especially the attitude of some English girls towards them.

8. RUSSIA

Though interest is still limited, there is satisfaction with Russian advances in the Baltic and Balkans. People are still wondering, however, why the Russians have halted outside East Prussia; some think they are consolidating their position there before starting a great offensive.

THE CAPITULATION OF BULGARIA, RUMANIA AND FINLAND has continued to give satisfaction, and Russia's handling of them is again praised.

8A. RUSSO-POLISH RELATIONS

Bewilderment and concern at the Russo-Polish tangle continue widespread: 'Discussion about this goes on and on.' Criticism of the behaviour of the Russians and of that of the Polish government in London continues on familiar lines.

Fears of the dispute prejudicing the post-war settlement and concern about Russia's future intentions also continue on familiar lines.

The situation of Warsaw and its inhabitants has been the subject of concern and sympathy, but no reactions have been received since its capitulation.

9. FAR EAST

Interest continues slight, though an increase is reported in three Regions. Comment is on familiar lines:

(a) Satisfaction with progress in the Pacific and appreciation of the part the Americans are playing.
(b) Criticism of the lack of news about our 'Forgotten Army' in Burma.

10. CAPTAIN RAMSAY'S RELEASE

Criticism and indignation are reported – his attendance at the House of Commons is particularly resented. People ask if he will be allowed to attend secret sessions.

Some sympathy is expressed for Mr. Gallacher's protest.

11. NEWS PRESENTATION

For Arnhem news, see Section 2.

People are glad to see 'a little more publicity given to the British soldier' and the handling of the Arnhem news has been commended in this connection.

Stories of local county regiments are particularly appreciated.

BBC: There is praise for war reports in general, and special praise for those relating to Arnhem, though some of the descriptions are thought to have been too violent and harrowing for people who had relatives in the airborne division. Johann Fabricius' tribute was much appreciated.

II. SPECIAL COMMENTS

BRIEF WEEKLY SUMMARY

12. RELAXATION OF REGULATIONS

BLACKOUT: Delight continues in the dim-out areas, particularly with 'the godsend of street lighting'. There is, however, considerable grumbling in the areas still blacked-out and a feeling that 'we ought to have been told from the beginning that there was to be no change, and no hopes would have been aroused'.

Other points mentioned are:

(a) The many people still blacking-out. Reasons for this are (i) lack of curtain material – housewives bitterly resent that 'only the rich can afford to buy curtains without surrendering coupons'; and (ii) in the Eastern, London, and Southern Regions – dislike of having to put up the blackout when the alert sounds.

(b) Difficulties of bus and private car drivers. They complain that night driving is very difficult now as the new form of lighting casts shadows between lamps. People feel brighter headlights should be allowed.

(c) The possibility of further enemy attack and consequent anxiety that easing of restrictions is premature.

(d) Alleged confused instructions.

(e) Failure of some local authorities to provide better street lighting.

HOME GUARD: Relief is still reported. The men are specially pleased that Sunday parades are not to continue. Comment among members has also again been about:

(a) The method of notification. Irritation continues.

(b) Their willingness to co-operate in the voluntary scheme.

(c) Their wish to be allowed to keep their boots and other clothing which would be useful in civil life. On the other hand, it is suggested that a watch should be kept on the uniforms as 'some are already finding their way into the market'.

(d) The regretted loss of camaraderie.

CIVIL DEFENCE: Reception continues to be mixed. Voluntary workers are relieved; some full-time workers are apprehensive about finding employment.

There is some speculation as to whether CD personnel will be allowed to retain or at least buy their uniforms.

13. SERVICEMEN'S PAY

The proposed increases in pay for 'prolonged service' and in respect of service in the Far East continue to be greatly welcomed, although some think them 'long overdue' or 'not enough'. It is also again pointed out that there will still be a big difference between the pay of British and US troops serving in the same theatre of war.

14. THE HEATING BAN

Complaints have continued of the hardship caused by the lack of central heating now that the cold weather has come. The ban is said to be responsible for an epidemic of colds and chills, and for the loss of a good number of working hours.

DATES OF REMOVAL OF RESTRICTIONS (announced September 29): The only reaction yet received comes from the North-Eastern Region. While appreciation is reported – October 8 is earlier than was expected – there is also some demand for the immediate lifting of the ban, as 'work for many people for a week or two has been most unpleasant owing to the cold'.

NO. 215: TUESDAY 7 NOVEMBER 1944 TO TUESDAY 14 NOVEMBER 1944

I. GENERAL COMMENTS

1. GENERAL

There is little change in spirits this week. People are now resigned to another winter of war – the onset of which, combined with bad weather, has had a depressing effect. War-weariness and lack of interest in the fighting continued widespread; but there has been a fair amount of comment about President Roosevelt's re-election, Mr. Churchill's visit to Paris, and the assassination of Lord Moyne.

ON THE HOME FRONT, employment, housing and industry continue main anxieties. Complaints remain widespread about clothing, and the freedom and privileges allowed to Italian prisoners of war.

2. WESTERN FRONT

There is not much detailed discussion. People continue pleased at the liberation of Antwerp and at the progress in the Scheldt estuary and Walcheren. There is, however, much sympathy and concern at the naval and military losses involved; a few strongly criticise the Walcheren landings, saying they should have been delayed until the RAF was able to provide full air cover.

Slowness of progress is attributed mainly to the weather and consequent terrible fighting conditions.

Opinion is divided as to whether or not there will soon be a big push now that Antwerp is clear for bringing in supplies.

There is little comment on the American fighting near Metz. It is not thought to be on a very large scale.

Much sympathy is reported for the plight of the DUTCH; and support for the proposal that they should be given some German territory as a recompense.

Friendliness towards BELGIUM is marked.

THE BOMBING OF GERMANY: Satisfaction – and amazement at the capacity of the German people to take it – continue. Some wonder why Cologne has had to receive so much treatment; a few suspect the bombing may be stiffening German morale.

2A. INSIDE GERMANY NOW

There is considerable speculation about Hitler's silence. Most people seem to regard it as a sign of confusion and lack of leadership inside Germany, rather than as an indication that something has happened to Hitler. In Scotland, apparently, most people hope he is not dead, having in mind for him 'lingering tortures'.

2B. WHAT TO DO WITH GERMANY

The official news of the arrival of V2 has strengthened demands for a hard peace for Germany. Suggested methods follow the usual lines.

Once again, the re-education of German youth is widely mentioned as perhaps the toughest job facing the Allies.

There is some comment on the vicar who offered to send rat poison to German prisoners of war. His attitude is condemned, particularly by relatives of our own prisoners of war, who fear it may have an adverse effect on them.

2C. SUPPLIES FOR LIBERATED COUNTRIES

Comment is less, but on the same lines as last week.

3. ROCKETS

THE PRIME MINISTER'S STATEMENT (November 10) was welcomed and has been well received on the whole, both in the areas affected and elsewhere. Most people wanted an announcement on the subject to allay the anxiety and uncertainty, which had been attributed partly to official silence. Prior to the statement, 'fantastic' rumours had been in circulation (e.g. 96 rockets on London alone in the last week of October); even now, it is feared the rumours may continue, since the statement did not reveal how much damage has been caused.

The statement was, however, not very favourably received by: (i) those who say that it was long overdue and merely confirmed what was already known or suspected; and (ii) those who had not heard the rumours and to whom the news came as a great shock – in Northern Ireland, particularly, it made a very deep impression and 'came near to unsteadying the public'.

Some people regret that the Germans were able to publish the story first; others are sorry the British announcement was made when it was, on the ground that it would serve to distract the Germans from their military reverses.

Other reactions to the announcement are:

(a) Discussion and speculation about the weapon's potentialities. Most people in areas not yet affected appear little concerned – at any rate as regards this war; however, in the Northern Region and Birmingham, a few fear the enemy may succeed in extending the range of the rockets, and some people question 'the wisdom of standing down the CD services'.

(b) Still further hardening of feeling against Germany; a desire for even harder peace terms and heavier bombing. Some resentment is reported in Scotland that we have not used similar weapons: our 'kid glove methods' are criticised.

(c) Concern or criticism at our inability to counter the weapon.

AREAS AFFECTED

IN LONDON, rockets are said to be the chief topic of conversation. Many people are worried and nervy, and apprehensive at the possibility of more frequent attacks. A considerable number, however, show little concern, some preferring rockets to flying bombs.

COUNTER-MEASURES are discussed, some thinking the launching bases should be bombed, others that only the threat of reprisals would be effective. A number 'realise that nothing can be done'. The rockets are thought to come from Holland.

THE LACK OF WARNING is found trying, but a few prefer not to know what is coming.

IN THE SOUTH-EASTERN DISTRICT, concern and apprehension continue, though here, too, some find rockets less disturbing than flying bombs.

IN THE EASTERN REGION, some nervousness continues to be reported, together with much anger against Germany. People are relieved to know that V2s can no longer be sent from the Scheldt area.

3A. FLYING BOMBS

IN LONDON (up to Monday, November 13) people continued thankful for the lessening of these attacks, said to be 'almost ignored'. A number were described as resigned to rocket and flying bomb attacks continuing till the end of the war.

IN THE SOUTH-EASTERN DISTRICT, people are dismayed – and some nervous – at the return of flying bombs, 'when we were led to believe they were over'.

IN THE COUNTRY AS A WHOLE, there is now said to be little reference to flying bombs, though in the Northern Region there is slight fear of attack by flying bombs launched from planes over the North Sea.

3B. REPAIRS TO BOMB-DAMAGED PROPERTY

IN LONDON, anxiety and dissatisfaction continue over the repair of damaged houses, particularly as winter is approaching. Many think progress is very slow and criticise the Government for 'its lack of action'. (Similar comment about London repairs is reported from the North Midland Region.)

Causes of slowness are variously thought to be: slacking on the part of the workmen; shortage of materials and labour; lack of method; and the weather. There is also criticism of the order in which repairs are carried out, e.g. churches repaired while the bombed-out live in shelters.

IN THE SOUTH-EASTERN DISTRICT, there is comment on the difficulty of getting damaged houses repaired. It is realised that there is a shortage of materials, but the Government are criticised for 'not doing their best'.

IN SCOTLAND, 'some alarm is shown at the combing out of plumbers, plasterers, slaters, etc. for the restoration of London. The fact that Scotland is already bare of such tradesman – and becoming barer – is leaking out, and more people are beginning to realise the position. While they have every sympathy for London, they see no reason why London should be dealt with at the expense of – say – Clydebank.'

4. THE PRIME MINISTER'S VISIT TO FRANCE

People are very pleased at Mr. Churchill's visit and at the warm welcome given him in Paris. They hope the visit may do much to re-establish French prestige and to assist France to build up a real fighting force. Some, however, still distrust France and do not want to see her on an equal footing with the great powers.

Other reactions have been:

(a) Anxiety about Mr. Churchill's safety.
(b) Surprise that his daughter should have been given leave from her ATS duties to accompany her father.

5. THE PRIME MINISTER'S MANSION HOUSE SPEECH

Most people seem to have been disappointed with Mr. Churchill's speech, on the grounds that he sounded very tired and was, on the whole, uninformative.

Appreciation is expressed of his tribute to General Alexander and our armies in Italy, and at his 'steadying words to over-optimists'. There has been some disappointment at his failure to refer to the campaign in Burma or to the late Archbishop of Canterbury.

6. US PRESIDENTIAL ELECTION

The re-election of President Roosevelt has given real pleasure everywhere. People are most relieved there will be no change in leadership at this stage of the war. They feel Mr. Roosevelt is a 'proved friend' and that good Anglo-American relations both now and in the post-war world are assured.

In Scotland, 'the fact that the House of Representatives also showed a Democrat increase is taken as meaning American public opinion is pretty solidly on the side of post-war co-operation'.

7. LORD MOYNE

Horror and indignation greeted the news of the assassination of Lord Moyne by Jewish terrorists. An increase in anti-Semitic feeling is reported, though some say 'thinking people will not associate this crime with Zionism as a whole'.

People regret Lord Moyne was not more closely guarded in spite of his wishes and hope the ringleaders will be brought to justice speedily.

8. ITALIAN PRISONERS OF WAR

People do not find much new to say about the soft treatment accorded to Italian collaborators, but the familiar complaints continue widespread ... 'The Government's rooted determination to pamper these men is hard to understand.'

8A. ITALY

Still little comment about the fighting. Progress is regarded as disappointingly slow, but many consider we are making the best of a difficult job, in view of the weather. A few, however, wonder if the weather is being used as an excuse; while some, having been led to believe that when the Gothic Line was broken our tanks could be used over the Lombardy plain, are puzzled that we still seem to be fighting in the mountains.

There is sympathy and praise for the men and warm regard for General Alexander; his review of the campaign (November 2) is again praised, but people still think more publicity for this campaign is necessary.

Many people's main interest is in the sufferings of our troops in rain and mud and of the wounded in our hospitals – 'so different from the palatial US hospitals'. There is dissatisfaction, too, over the 'lack of comforts for our troops in Italy' and 'the poor food and conditions'. Recent correspondence in the *Sunday Dispatch* (October 22 and 29) has attracted some attention.

9. RUSSIA

MARSHAL STALIN'S SPEECH, NOVEMBER 6: This has had a very favourable reception: people were pleased with the recognition of Allied successes in Western Europe and thought the speech most promising for future collaboration between Russia, Britain and the USA. However, Marshal Stalin's branding of Japan as an aggressor nation aroused most interest and much warm approval. It stimulated speculation as to what part Russia will play in the war against Japan after the defeat of Germany. Some think she will declare war on Japan, or at any rate grant us bases for bombing; but others think she will not undertake new commitments.

MILITARY: Satisfaction and confidence continue, though there is some disappointment at the slow progress in East Prussia. Some people, too, think the newspapers have been misleading about the position in Hungary; a week ago Budapest was said to have been reached by the Russians, whereas now the fighting is apparently some distance away.

RUSSO-POLISH RELATIONS: Disquiet continues.

PERSIAN OIL: Little comment, though some think Russia's attitude savours of power politics and ask whether she has not enough oil of her own.

10. FAR EAST

The increased interest in this theatre of war continues. People ask for more information and maps, and the tendency to regard the Far East as 'an American affair' is decreasing. Comment has been mainly about:

BURMA: The increased press and radio publicity has given pleasure, and people ask for 'still more stories'. Satisfaction with progress is reported, but the terrible conditions under which the 14th Army has to fight are causing much anxiety to relatives and friends. Great sympathy is felt for 'our gallant men', and some disquiet about lack of comforts for them. It is hoped Lord Munster's visit will do some good.

CHINA: People are concerned and mystified about the situation in China, especially about the circumstances leading to General Stilwell's recall. They find the news 'bewildering and disquieting' and ask for some authentic statement about what has been happening in China. There is some speculation about the attitude of General Chang Kai-Shek, who was rumoured to be 'more interested in getting rid of communism than Japs'; thus it is said that 'but for his stubbornness, the communist armies would be defeating the Japs now'. Concern that Allied supplies have been used for civil war is reported.

THE PACIFIC: The recent US naval victory gave much pleasure, though a minority feel the results were not so good as at first claimed by the press. Admiration for the work of the Americans in the Philippines is reported, but there is some bewilderment about stiff fighting on Leyte, as earlier reports gave the impression that resistance there was practically at an end.

10A. ARMY LEAVE

It is again strongly urged that men who have given several years' service overseas, particularly in Burma, should now be allowed home leave. Some suggest that the men in the army do not get the same 'humane consideration' as those in the RAF and the RN.

11. GENERAL ELECTION

Discussion is limited, though the majority continued to agree with the Prime Minister that an election should be postponed until the end of hostilities in Europe. However, some people's impatience has been increased by the US presidential election ... 'If they can have an election, why can't we?'

12. GREECE

Delight at the liberation of Greece, and sympathy for her sufferings, continue. People are glad that it was our troops who threw out the Germans.

13. SPAIN

There is great distrust of General Franco: his recent pronouncements are described as 'brazen effrontery'. There is some demand for the Government to take a stronger attitude and (prior to statement in the House, November 15) for Spain not to be invited to the peace settlement.

14. CIVIL AVIATION CONFERENCE

Very little comment, though there is some continued perturbation at Russia's refusal to participate, opinion as to the rights and wrongs being divided.

15. BROADCASTING AND NEWS PRESENTATION

There is considerable criticism of the press this week, for having encouraged false hopes by over-optimistic accounts of Allied progress; sensational headlines, in particular, are censured. Some feel that BBC news bulletins are not blameless in this respect, though most people appear satisfied that they are fair and honest.

War Commentaries, particularly those of Hastings, Strachey and Joubert, are widely praised; as also are *War Reports*, though some find them very difficult to hear.

There is increasing satisfaction with broadcast discussions and debates, particularly those dealing frankly with controversial subjects. Praise for the *Brains Trust* is considerable, though some still criticise trivial questions and wordy answers.

The Week in Westminster is popular.

II. SPECIAL COMMENTS

BRIEF WEEKLY REVIEW

16. STRIKES

Strikes are widely condemned by the majority as unpatriotic and selfish, and people feel that they should be more severely dealt with. The Manchester gas strikers are particularly condemned; and the use of the army and subsequent prosecution of the strikers approved.

Some sympathy is, however, reported from Tyneside shipyard workers towards the strikers in the Walker Naval Yard.

17. REINSTATEMENT OF MEN OF THE MERCHANT NAVY

Dissatisfaction continues at the Government's refusal to let merchant seamen rank as servicemen for reinstatement in civil employment. There has also been a good deal of bitter comment about the recent Hull case.

NO. 216: TUESDAY 14 NOVEMBER 1944 TO TUESDAY 21 NOVEMBER 1944

I. GENERAL COMMENTS

1. GENERAL

There is little change in spirits – or in comment – this week. The Western front offensive has revived a few hopes of a decision against Germany this year, but most people are resigned to the prospect of another war winter.

Comment on home front topics also shows little change.

2. WESTERN FRONT

The new offensive has heartened people. A few are hoping it marks the beginning of the end and that a victory this year is possible after all. However, there is little tendency to over-optimism; the majority expect hard fighting and heavy casualties. Admiration for the troops – particularly those in Holland – is unbounded.

Earlier, there had been much comment about the rate of progress. Though disappointed that this was not speedier, most people considered that in view of the terrible weather, supply difficulties, and the stiffness of enemy opposition, progress was as satisfactory as could be expected. Many thought the lull a necessary prelude to a big attack; the clearing of the port of Antwerp continued to be welcomed as helping to make this easier.

THE BOMBING OF GERMANY: Approval continues, as also does wonder at the Germans' capacity to stand it. A few, however, doubt the real effectiveness of heavy bombing, since by now they think German industry should have been obliterated.

THE DUTCH: Much sympathy continues. People hope that we will be able to do something to help those already freed before winter sets in properly, and that the part of the country still under German control will soon be liberated.

2A. INSIDE GERMANY NOW

Hitler's silence and disappearance continue the subject of much speculation; he is variously thought to be ill, dead, mad, in hiding, supplanted by Himmler, or to have flown the country.

Whatever its cause, however, Hitler's disappearance has not given rise to optimism. People do not think it will make much difference to the fighting. Himmler is now regarded as 'Nazi No. 1' and, even if Germany is beginning to 'crack up morally', it is thought that propaganda and the Gestapo will keep people going and that the military machine will fight to the very end.

A few wonder whether threats, heavy bombing, and unconditional surrender terms may not be provoking stiffer German resistance.

2B. WHAT TO DO WITH GERMANY

Demands for a hard peace have been strengthened by the news of rocket bombs and the devastation in Holland. Suggestions for preventing Germany ever being able to make war again are on familiar lines.

This week some criticism is reported of the clergyman who collected for comforts for German prisoners of war, and some approval of the 'rat-poison vicar'.

3. ARMY LEAVE

The Prime Minister's statement in the House (November 17) that a month's leave will be granted to a number of men with long service overseas, has given very great pleasure. But there is a little disappointment that men in the Middle East will not get home for Christmas.

4. ROCKETS

There is a good deal of rather miscellaneous discussion about V2; comment and concern are less than in the case of flying bombs. The Prime Minister's statement was welcomed as relieving uncertainty and discouraging rumours, though many people thought it came rather late in the day and merely confirmed what was already known. In affected areas, however, praise and appreciation greatly outweigh other sentiments.

People in so-called safe areas (e.g. the North-West and South-West) tend to be indifferent or to minimise the dangers. At the same time, in Wales and the Northern and North-Western Regions, there is speculation as to a possible extension of the rocket's range.

Some sympathy for sufferers is expressed.

There are very conflicting views as to the extent of the damage and the deadliness of the weapon. Some are relieved at the news of small damage and casualties, but others have difficulty in reconciling evacuees' reports of 'dire damage' with the Prime Minister's 'lighter dismissal of incidents'. In spite of his statement, there are a number of rumours, though on a more modest and restricted scale than was the case with flying bombs. The following examples are typical – 'Herne Bay is unrecognisable'; 'one landed in Norwich 10 weeks ago'; '50 landed in Ilford in one week'; 'Euston Station destroyed'; rockets are reported to have fallen in Scotland, Northern Ireland, Preston, Skipton, Nottingham, etc.

Some uneasiness is reported from the North-West Region and Scotland at 'the disbanding of so many CD services under present conditions' ... 'Because the forwards are scoring, you don't send home the half-backs'.

In places involved, some people are anxious we should start retaliation bombing 'with the gloves off'.

AREAS AFFECTED

IN LONDON, discussion continues widespread; many, particularly in areas where rockets have fallen, are increasingly nervous. A good many, however, though disliking these attacks, take them calmly.

Apart from the lack of warning – which is found very trying by most people – rockets are not thought so bad as flying bombs.

The rocket bomb is considered to have no military value and the wickedness of the Germans in using such a weapon is stressed.

COUNTER-MEASURES are not thought likely to do much good, and while most people seem resigned to the attacks continuing till the end of the war, many hope the occupation of the launching bases will soon stop the menace.

MR. CHURCHILL'S STATEMENT was welcomed by Londoners ... 'It's a relief to be able to talk about it' ... 'The rest of the world will know we're still taking it.' Some are critical, however, on the grounds that damage and casualties were played down, and that the statement may encourage the Germans.

Damage and casualties are much discussed and wild rumours are still said to be current, though Mr. Churchill's statement has helped to dispel them. There is some wish for local casualty lists to be published to prevent exaggeration.

IN THE SOUTH-EASTERN DISTRICT, anxiety and nervousness continue, increased in some cases by lack of information. But, on the whole, enemy attacks are 'stood up to very well'. Little is hoped from counter-measures ... 'The attacks must be endured.'

IN THE EASTERN REGION, it seems to be almost unanimously agreed in the areas affected that rockets are far less trying than flying bombs: 'No warning means no time for nervous apprehension' ... 'If anything does happen, you don't know anything about it.' The terrifying noise of flying bombs is thought far more disturbing than a sudden explosion. Though some nervousness is reported, most people seem to be fatalistic and resigned. It is hoped that advances in Holland will eventually clear the bases, or that the amount of oil used in launching will prohibit many of them being sent.

4A. REPAIRS TO BOMB-DAMAGED PROPERTY

IN LONDON, the delay in repairs to damaged houses continues to cause much grumbling, particularly as it is feared repairs may not be completed before winter really sets in. (Disgust about the slowness of the London repairs is also again reported from the North Midland Region.) There is dissatisfaction at the conditions under which many are living.

Shortage of materials, especially of ceiling board, is thought to be the main stumbling block, but there is criticism of the lack of supervision of the repairers. These men are said not only to be lazy and unskilled but also sometimes to damage the furniture in the houses they are repairing. There is also dissatisfaction at boys of 18 in the building trade being called up for work other than building.

The Government is blamed for 'not tackling the matter seriously'; the local authorities for 'not using the powers granted them'.

It is variously suggested that women could quickly be trained to help with some repairs, that the £10 limit should be extended to the rest of the country, and that men who stay away from work to do their own repairs should not be penalised by losing their pay.

IN THE SOUTH-EASTERN DISTRICT, 'muddle' and misuse of labour are criticised, but it is realised that there is a shortage of material and labour, and that some of the labour is unskilled. A little satisfaction with repair work is mentioned.

5. LIBERATED COUNTRIES

THE PRIME MINISTER'S VISIT TO FRANCE: People are very relieved at Mr. Churchill's safe return. Many, however, are worried he takes so many risks with his health; they feel he should be urged to reduce his journeys abroad, and that President Roosevelt and Marshal Stalin should come to Britain for the next three-power conference.

Nevertheless, pleasure continues with the ovation given him in Paris, and with his visit generally; it is believed to have done much to promote unity in France and to foster Anglo-French relations.

FRANCE: Many are glad that France will be taking her place among the Allies as a great power, and hope this will encourage her to pull her weight in the fighting and in the production of war materials. There is, however, a lingering distrust of the French, and a minority refer to her 'rottenness' and 'the way she let us down in 1940'.

BELGIUM: Uneasiness is reported at the present political situation there, though some, while regretting it, consider internal unrest inevitable.

SUPPLIES: Comment about the 'good-quality' knitting wool for European relief, though still bitter, is less.

BRITISH PROPAGANDA: People believe that the Belgians and French have no proper appreciation of 'our hard struggle in this war'.

6. NEUTRALS

PEACE SETTLEMENT: The Government's decision to exclude neutrals has been widely welcomed, particularly in the case of 'Franco's Spain'.

In Ulster, people feel that the Nationalist claim for Eire's presence at the peace conference – on the 'specious' grounds that considerable numbers of Eire men and women have fought on the side of the Allies – should be disregarded.

ASYLUM FOR WAR CRIMINALS: Some unfavourable comment on Eire's evasive note is reported. In Northern Ireland, discussion is bitter: 'The big Unionist majority are quick to point out that Eire has been able to maintain her neutrality only because of the protection of Britain.'

7. RUSSIA

MILITARY: Satisfaction, admiration and confidence are again reported, though some disappointment continues at the slow progress both in East Prussia and in Hungary; there is a little criticism of the 'lack of effort' to free Warsaw. People, however, believe the enemy's defence in both north and south to be very stubborn. At the same time, a major Russian offensive is anticipated shortly, and some still hope and expect the Red Army will reach Berlin first.

People would like more news about the position on the Eastern front; at present there is some confusion.

MARSHAL STALIN'S SPEECH (NOVEMBER 6): Warm appreciation continues, particularly of his references to British and US help, and to Japanese aggression.

POLITICAL: Some uneasiness continues about Russia's possible aspirations at the peace conference and afterwards. At the same time, a few praise her 'refusal to associate with fascism wherever it is found'.

8. FAR EAST

Increased interest has been maintained. Some satisfaction with general progress is reported; but many, who had expected Japan to 'cave in' after the defeat of Germany, now think there may be a long war ahead. Relatives of servicemen are greatly concerned to know if their men will be sent to the Far East after the defeat of Germany.

CHINA: Considerable anxiety about the situation in China continues. The news of the loss of American air bases has caused much consternation. Speculation and bewilderment continue over the recall of General Stilwell, General Chiang Kai-Shek's position, and the use of Allied supplies to wage civil war. People feel that China is disunited and would like to know what is going on ... 'Nothing is known about the fighting except that the Chinese are always withdrawing.' A minority fear China may collapse as a fighting force.

THE PACIFIC: There is again widespread praise for the recent US naval successes, and the destruction of Japanese shipping, though a minority still doubt American claims of Jap ships sunk. The Americans are thought to be doing a 'good job'.

BURMA: Appreciation of the greater publicity given to this campaign is again reported; still more is asked for. There is much concern over the welfare of the troops fighting under terrible conditions; it is thought more could be done to lighten their burden. Lack of canteen and recreational facilities are alleged; people ask why no NAAFI operates there, instead of matters being left in the hands of profiteers.

JAPANESE ATROCITIES AGAINST PRISONERS OF WAR: The Secretary of State for War's statement (November 17) has been greeted with indignation, horror and distress, and has increased hatred of the Japanese.

9. ITALIAN AND GERMAN PRISONERS OF WAR

ITALIAN: Resentment continues at the privileges and freedom allowed to Italian co-operators. Comment is detailed and familiar. Many continue to advocate repatriation: 'they take up homes, food, and also work, which might otherwise be given to the unemployed'.

Disgust is reported that some ATS are having to sleep in leaky tents (*Daily Herald*, November 16), 'while Italian prisoners of war live in mansions'.

GERMAN: German prisoners of war in England are also thought to be too well treated, and there is some indignant comment at the idea that 'oranges and milk are supplied to them while our own people go short'. In Warrington it is rumoured that German prisoners at a local camp are allowed to walk about outside the camp sucking oranges; in the Chester-le-Street (Co. Durham) neighbourhood, the rumour that wounded German prisoners in the local hospital are given a shell egg for breakfast every morning is causing indignation.

10. ITALY

MILITARY: What little comment there is about the fighting is on familiar lines. Though most people assume it is the weather which is holding things up, some are now saying that progress is being slowed down by the transfer of men to other fronts.

Discussion continues of the conditions in which our men are fighting; and there is again dissatisfaction at accounts of the hospital accommodation provided.

POLITICAL: Some people continue distrustful of Italy and think she is being too gently dealt with.

11. THE TIRPITZ

The sinking of the *Tirpitz* has given great satisfaction and there is much praise and admiration for the RAF. People are particularly pleased that a part of our fleet will now be released for duty elsewhere.

However, reports of earlier attacks on the *Tirpitz* have occasioned some minority comment about the 'toughness' of enemy ships, compared with some of our own famous vessels – particularly the *Prince of Wales*.

12. CIVIL AVIATION CONFERENCE

Comment is sparse and not detailed. On the whole, however, people seem pessimistic, both because of Russia's absence, which is regretted, and because they consider there is little chance of competing successfully against the USA or of coming to an agreement with her. Some think the Americans are only concerned with protecting their own interests.

A few, however, believe that our standards of production are such as to ensure us success.

Scottish people feel Prestwick should be the chief British air terminal after the war; some add that there are forces at work trying to prevent this.

13. AIR CHIEF MARSHAL SIR TRAFFORD LEIGH-MALLORY

There is much concern and regret at the loss of 'this valued leader'. A few wonder whether it would have occurred 'if his farewell party had not been reported in the press', adding that the approximate date of departure was well known to a number of people. Some feel the plane should have been escorted all the way.

14. LORD MOYNE'S ASSASSINATION

Horror and concern, with some increase in anti-Semitic feeling, continue. The Prime Minister's statement (November 17) warning the Jewish organisations is approved.

15. US PRESIDENTIAL ELECTION

The re-election of President Roosevelt for a fourth term is again referred to with great pleasure: 'a well-tried friend again in office'.

16. NEWS PRESENTATION

On the whole, news presentation is thought satisfactory; there are, however, a few complaints of people being treated like children and not given the full facts. There is again much praise for *War Commentaries* – particularly those of Hastings and Joubert – and, to a lesser extent, for *War Reports*.

There are continued complaints of poor reception.

II. SPECIAL COMMENTS

BRIEF WEEKLY NOTE

17. ICE-CREAM

The lifting of the ban on the manufacture of ice-cream has been greeted with mixed feelings – mainly critical. Though some say the idea is 'tempting', others ask 'who wants ice-cream in this weather?'

The main criticism, however, is that the ingredients could be put to better use if issued to householders.

III. PERIODICAL REVIEW

18. US TROOPS IN THIS COUNTRY

DURING THE PAST FOUR WEEKS there has been a further decline in comment, due mainly to the departure of US troops from many districts.

Relations have continued very cordial on the whole, and appreciation and tolerance have been enhanced by US military successes in the Far East and in Europe. The Americans here are praised for their help in air raids, their friendliness, and their 'homely ways'. People again say that criticism comes largely from those who do not know any Americans personally; at the same time, there is considerable relief in areas from which US troops have departed.

Comment otherwise has been about:

(a) BEHAVIOUR WITH WOMEN AND GIRLS: Comment is on familiar lines, some blaming the girls, who are chiefly attracted, it is said, by the amount of money the men are willing to spend on them.

(b) US PAY, COMPARED TO BRITISH: The disparity continues to cause resentment.

(c) DRIVING: Complaints are particularly about fast driving along narrow, winding country roads, and of blinding headlights. Some say road accidents in which US vehicles are involved have increased recently.

(d) GENERAL BEHAVIOUR: A small amount of criticism of boastfulness, drunkenness, and lack of discipline, and some comment about the number of Americans involved in recent murder cases.

(e) COLOURED TROOPS: There is praise for their quiet, considerate, well-mannered behaviour; though in the Southern Region there is some disapproval of the 'gangster-type' of negro recently drafted into camps formerly occupied by well-behaved coloured troops.

(f) GENERAL CONDITIONS: There is a feeling that US troops are better looked after over leisure, food and leave than our own men.

(g) HOSPITALITY: Some feel more should be done to provide for the men's leisure time and to encourage families to offer hospitality.

NO. 219: TUESDAY 5 DECEMBER 1944 TO TUESDAY 12 DECEMBER 1944

I. GENERAL COMMENTS

1. GENERAL

There has been a general drop in spirits this week, due chiefly to grave disquiet about the situation in Greece and Britain's part in it. Other dispiriting factors have been the slowness of progress on the fighting fronts, realisation that the war is going on for a long time yet, and the weather – depressing at home and a hardship and hindrance to our troops. War-weariness and strain continue.

ON THE HOME FRONT, the chief preoccupations continue to be present and post-war employment and housing, clothing difficulties, and – to a more limited extent – the price and shortage of toys. There is little Christmas feeling yet.

2. GREECE

Grave disquiet about the tragic situation is widespread. Everybody is unhappy that our men are having to fight our friends the Greeks, and that British blood is being shed in a civil war in an Allied country. There is also very general bewilderment as to the issues involved; 'moderate' people alone, on account of this, refraining from passing judgment. Others discuss the matter with great heat, and opinion is sharply divided between those who are against British policy and those who are for it:

(a) AGAINST GOVERNMENT POLICY: These are certainly the more vocal, possibly the more numerous, and consist mainly of left-wing people, including most industrial workers. (Only in Northern Ireland are the majority of workers said to be solidly behind Mr. Churchill.) These people are highly discontented with the following:

(i) Our military intervention being on the side of 'reaction'; some say 'If law and order had to be kept, then both sides should have been disarmed.' They feel our troops are fighting against progress, and against those who bore the brunt of German occupation and who fought for the liberation of their country. They also feel that we are trying to force an unwanted government on the Greeks, and that EAM and ELAS probably represent the wishes of the Greek people. Some take the general strike to prove the solidarity of the workers behind ELAS.

(ii) The way the issue was handled in the House, particularly its being made the subject of a vote of confidence.
(iii) Our having 'interfered too much'. The Greeks should be left a free hand to choose the government they like.

(b) FOR GOVERNMENT POLICY: These are mainly described as right-wing people, 'better informed people', and those convinced by Mr. Churchill's speech. Reasons for their support of the Government include the following:

(i) The need to establish law and order, as it is thought we must maintain our lines of communication and prevent any military hold-up.
(ii) Fear of communism. A few suspect Russia is behind the whole affair.

Three further points of view are expressed – neither specifically for nor against the Government:

(a) Fear that Allied relations may suffer, particularly our relations with the USA and Russia.
(b) Impatience with the Greeks 'squabbling' politically: 'after we have already sacrificed so much to liberate them, they are now hindering us in our war against Germany'. Many feel 'let us clear out and leave them to fight it out among themselves'.
(c) Belief that there should have been an Allied military occupation until elections could have taken place.

LIBERATED COUNTRIES IN GENERAL: Uneasiness and comment, though in a milder and more limited form, are similar to those about Greece. People particularly fear that these troubles will lead to dissension among the Allies and are a bad augury for the post-war world.

2A. THE POLITICAL SITUATION IN ITALY

People are concerned, but far less so than about Greece – 'as the Italians are our ex-enemies'. The vetoing of Sforza is not understood, and our Government is suspected of siding with reactionaries and royalists against the left.

MR. STETTINIUS' 'REBUKE': Opinion is divided between (a) the majority, who feel it was justified: 'We should have consulted America; in any case, it is ill-advised to place ourselves in a position where the US can criticise us'; (b) a minority, particularly right-wingers, who resent the rebuke.

3. WESTERN FRONT

In view of the weather and the stiffness of German resistance, progress is thought as satisfactory as can be expected. There is, nevertheless, increasing disappointment and, in some cases, depression at its slowness. Some find the 'hold-up' difficult to understand, in view of our 'vaunted' superiority in men and materials, and wonder if we have misjudged German strength – particularly since it has been found that they have more divisions available than we expected. A few are asking if something has gone wrong with our plans.

Most people now expect bitter and prolonged fighting and are fearful of heavy casualties. Some, however, continue to expect big moves at any moment.

Sympathy and admiration for the men are again reported.

THE AIR OFFENSIVE: There is considerable satisfaction with the 'stepped-up' offensive against Germany and continued amazement at the way the Germans are standing up to it.

4. ROCKETS

Little general comment. Rumours of damage and casualties continue; many people believe that things are much worse than they are led to suppose and ask for more facts and figures. The only reaction to the publication of casualty figures reported so far comes from Scotland, where the 'large death roll' has surprised people and increased their sympathy for Londoners.

Press diagrams and photographs of V2 have stimulated speculation as to the potentialities of this weapon, but only a very few people in areas so far safe are seriously concerned at the possibility of an extension of the rockets' range.

The bombing of V2 sites and stores is strongly approved, though it is generally felt that the menace will end only with the war.

AREAS AFFECTED

IN LONDON, though individual incidents are much discussed, nervousness appears to have lessened this week, except in areas where rockets have fallen. Otherwise, reactions are on familiar lines, with a slightly increased wish for reprisal bombing of German cities.

IN THE SOUTH-EASTERN DISTRICT, alarm and apprehension are reported and seem to be slightly increased – apparently as a result of rumours of devastation rather than actual experiences.

5. FAR EAST

Some satisfaction with general progress is reported and the demand for more news continues. While some feel the war with Japan will be long and hard, a few still hold Japan will not present serious difficulty once Germany is defeated.

There is pleasure that Whitehall has 'at long last' published the names of British regiments in the Far East; people regard this as an encouragement to our men, and also as a revelation to our Allies that 'they are not finding all the men for the Far Eastern struggle'.

Great anxiety continues among relatives of prisoners in Japanese hands.

CHINA: Much anxiety over the serious internal situation is reported. Some feel China is not pulling her weight in the war effort but is relying on the US and Great Britain to defeat Japan. They resent the use, in civil war against the Communists, of supplies sent by us to fight the Japanese.

BURMA: Pleasure at increased publicity, anxiety over 'appalling conditions', and some satisfaction with progress are again reported.

JAPAN AND THE PACIFIC: Again, great satisfaction over the bombing of Tokyo and the sinking of so many Japanese vessels. There is also pleasure that British vessels are now working with the Americans in the Pacific.

6. RUSSIA

MILITARY: Comment has declined. People are enthusiastic about progress in Hungary and are eagerly awaiting news of the fall of Budapest. Disappointment continues about the situation in the north, though this week a much smaller number mention the possibility of political motives behind the hold-up; others appreciate the difficulties presented by the weather. People continue to hope for a big general offensive soon.

POLITICAL: Fear of Russia's post-war political intentions and anxiety about Russo-Polish relations continue.

7. ITALY

MILITARY: Still little comment. It is thought that the disappointing slowness of our progress is due mainly to the weather and terrain, but also to 'numbers and equipment being now so depleted'. A few, however, were cheered by the capture of Ravenna; and there is some slight expectation of a big push when the weather improves.

7A. ITALIAN CO-OPERATORS

Familiar comment continues on a reduced scale. People persist in thinking the Italians ought to be sent back to their own country where 'they would probably be more appreciated'.

8. WAR AT SEA

News of the launching of the new battleship has given much pleasure. People think it 'a good augury for the war against Japan'.

9. THE WHITE PAPER ON THE UNITED KINGDOM WAR EFFORT

Appreciative comment continues on the same lines as last week.

10. NEWS PRESENTATION AND BBC PROGRAMMES

News presentation continues to be thought good on the whole, though interest is again said to be less. *War Reports* and *War Commentaries* – particularly by Hastings and Joubert – are again praised.

BBC PROGRAMMES: Debates and discussions continue popular. *Jobs for All* is particularly praised.

Treasure Island was liked, but there are some complaints that it was broadcast too late in the evening for children to listen.

II. SPECIAL COMMENTS

FULL WEEKLY REVIEW

11. POST-WAR

Apprehension is again widely reported about post-war jobs, industry, trade, and housing. Scepticism about Government promises, and the demand for definite plans and action, persist.

12. EMPLOYMENT, INDUSTRY AND TRADE – PRESENT AND POST-WAR

Comment continues on the same lines as last week, with the main preoccupations again:

(a) Unemployment. Fear both for the immediate and post-war future, because of present change-over difficulties, and reports of dismissals and redundancy.

(b) Export trade. People are worried we will be left behind by the USA.

13. HOUSING – PRESENT AND POST-WAR

Except for disappointment – and even shock – at Mr. Sandys' announcement on December 7 that production of steel houses cannot begin until the end of the European war, reactions to the housing situation are exactly the same as those described last week. Briefly these are: widespread and often bitter complaint about the shortage and high price of every kind of accommodation; disquiet and frustration at post-war housing prospects, and dissatisfaction with what is felt to be the Government's slowness in dealing with the situation ... 'If they don't get a move on soon, there'll be riots when the men get home'; dislike of the idea of temporary housing but grudging toleration of the Portal as being better than nothing, with much criticism of cost and detail.

14. HOME GUARD

HM the King's broadcast and the final parades have done a good deal to get rid of the previous ill-feeling about the stand-down, though familiar comment about this is still heard, as well as regrets at the disbanding.

Some criticism of 'the adulation and ceremony' accorded the Home Guard comes from those who feel that the CD and NFS services have done – and are still doing – more than the Home Guard, and who are also under the impression that the Home Guard is largely composed of men who in 1940 had not volunteered for the CD services, nor for any other form of national service.

15. SERVICE LEAVE

Delight over the leave arrangements for men serving overseas continues. There is, however, some criticism of the ballot system; thus it is said that men with three years' service have been passed over, in some cases, for men who have only two years' service. Some continue to think that men with long overseas service should come home for good.

The fear that when leave is over men may be drafted to the Far East is increasing.

16. CLOTHING

Comment is on familiar lines. Chief complaints are again of: the inadequacy of the coupon ration; the poor quality and shortage of footwear – particularly children's; the shortage and high price of bedding; the high price of clothing generally – particularly non-utility; and the shortage of children's clothing.

16A. TOYS

The price, poor quality, and shortage of toys are again the subject of much bitter comment. Telling people not to buy high-priced, shoddy toys, but to report the shopkeeper, is considered no adequate solution ... 'Parents have to get the children something, even if it does mean paying 12/6d for two bits of unplaned wood badly stuck together.'

17. FOOD, AND SHOPPING DIFFICULTIES

Comment continues on familiar lines, the extra Christmas rations being the chief topic.

The disclosures in the press (December 3) on the inequalities between our rations and those of the Americans and Canadians are said to have caused some indignation – it being thought that the time has come to 'equalise this burden'.

EXTRA CHRISTMAS RATIONS: Satisfaction continues. However, some people are disappointed at the non-appearance or shortage of the promised suet, dried fruit and turkeys.

WINES AND SPIRITS: Complaints are of shortage and high price. Whisky is said to be obtainable only at £3 to £4 a bottle.

18. DOMESTIC FUEL

Comment continues on familiar lines, with reference particularly to the irregularity of deliveries and to the poor quality of coal 'though it is sold at the maximum price'.

In mining areas in the North Midland Region there is growing irritation over the question of miners, including officials, receiving up to a ton of coal a month. The order which prevents a miner giving part of his monthly allowance away is regarded by the miners themselves as ridiculous.

18A. MINERS AND MINING

Comment is mostly on familiar lines, though there has been an increase in talk about the ballot. People do not like the scheme and once more suggest miners should be released from the army. The Bevin boys are again criticised for inefficiency and unwillingness to work.

19. NATIONAL INSURANCE

Comment is almost entirely confined to expressions of hope that the White Paper proposals will be made law with the least possible delay, coupled with scepticism as to this happening. The King's speech (November 29) and other recent official statements have increased fears that legislation will be delayed and the proposals whittled down.

20. TRANSPORT AND PETROL

The familiar comments continue on much the same lines as last week: complaints of inadequate and overcrowded bus services; discomfort increased by wet weather and lack of shelters; appreciation where services have improved; and criticism of late and overcrowded trains.

The reintroduction of the basic petrol ration remains the subject of hopes, demands and rumours.

21. THE DIM-OUT

Pleasure at the relaxations has been increased by the announcement that it is not necessary to black-out premises when the alert is sounded.

MOTORISTS continue to complain bitterly of increased difficulties; they want the masking of head lamps done away with, both to avoid accidents and to compete with the 'dazzling and powerful lights on US vehicles'.

22. AGRICULTURE

So far little comment has been received on Mr. Hudson's statement in the House (December 5) about farm prices. Many farmers continue anxious and fear a drift back to the old conditions, but a minority find in Mr. Hudson's speech a 'faint hope for agriculture after all'.

Adverse weather and labour shortage continue to be the main problems, both in the gathering of the potato and beet harvests and in the preparation of the land for next year ... 'a sodden countryside has brought agriculture to a standstill for the time being'.

23. HEALTH

Complaints of minor ailments and war-weariness, particularly among women, continue. People again criticise Government statements ... 'Does the Government really understand how weary people are?'

Concern about outbreaks of diphtheria is also reported. In one area there is some annoyance because 'the RDC has not yet carried out a sewage system for the district, despite the fact that a plan was got out seven years ago'.

23A. NATIONAL HEALTH SERVICE

The recent meetings of the British Medical Association have aroused some interest in the National Health Service, but there is little comment. In Scotland it is said the man-in-the-street is taking it for granted that a National Health Service is on the way.

There is some criticism of the 'narrow and clannish' attitude of the medical profession, but also some support for their 'resistance to lay control'. A few feel that doctors in the Services should have an equal say in the matter with their colleagues at home.

III. PERIODICAL REVIEW

24. YOUTH AND MORALS

DURING THE PAST THREE MONTHS complaints of the behaviour of young people and children have continued on familiar lines. Comment has been chiefly of:

IMMORALITY: The association of young girls and young married women with Italian prisoners of war and American troops is particularly deplored. People expect 'murder when our men get back'.

EXCESSIVE DRINKING – again chiefly by young girls.

THE 'HOOLIGANISM' of young and adolescent boys. 'Wanton' damage to property, and rowdiness, are the chief complaints.

GENERAL BAD MANNERS AND BEHAVIOUR.

JUVENILE DELINQUENCY: This is believed to be on the increase.

FACTORS BLAMED are:
  (a) LACK OF PARENTAL CONTROL as the result of fathers being in the Forces and mothers out working. Lack of interest on the part of some mothers is also blamed. Some people think an attempt should be made to educate parents in their responsibilities.
  (b) HIGH WAGES and 'nothing to spend them on'.
  (c) OVER-KIND AND 'SENTIMENTAL' TREATMENT BY COURTS AND MAGISTRATES: A few think more birchings would be in order.
  (d) THE SHORTCOMINGS OF PRESENT EDUCATION – for which the shortage of teachers is chiefly blamed.

(e) LACK OF 'HEALTHY' RECREATION FACILITIES – including lack of the
     'right kind' of films.
(f) THE DECLINE OF INTEREST IN RELIGION.

More women police, more powers for the police to take protective action, and more
recreational facilities are suggested.

YOUTH CLUBS: The need for more clubs and for more facilities for existing
ones are urged. The shortage of good youth leaders is deplored.

Some, however, feel that youth clubs provide too much entertainment and too
little discipline.

PRE-SERVICE ORGANISATIONS: There are many complaints of declining
attendance and lack of interest in the ATC as a result of the likelihood of the lads
being sent into the army or mines, 'however proficient'.

Discussion of the future of these organisations is reported. Some are anxious that
they should continue after the war; others are against 'regimentation.'

FINAL WEEKLY REPORT

NO. 221: TUESDAY 19 DECEMBER 1944 TO
WEDNESDAY 27 DECEMBER 1944

I. GENERAL COMMENTS

1. GENERAL

Spirits have continued to fall, in some cases considerably. This is said to be mainly
due to Rundstedt's offensive and the situation in Greece – though Mr. Churchill's
presence in Athens has given some hope of a solution. Other dispiriting factors have
once more been the housing and employment situations, and the prospect that the
war may not be over for a long time – even by next Christmas. Flying bomb attacks
have come as an unpleasant shock in areas hitherto immune.

Christmas has given some pleasure, rest and relief, but has been accompanied by
widespread and bitter complaint about the price, poor quality and scarcity of toys
and gifts, and much grumbling over unequal food distribution.

2. WESTERN FRONT

Shock and surprise continue at the success of the German counter-offensive. There
has been considerable anxiety, as well as depression that the war must now last much
longer than had been expected. The better news towards the weekend has, however,
reassured some people.

People cannot understand how we could have been taken so much by surprise. They wonder whether our intelligence was at fault and we misjudged German resources of men and material, or if something went wrong with our plans.

Some, however, have not been seriously perturbed by the offensive, thinking it to be Germany's last bid, and that by making it she has given us an opportunity to smash her completely and to finish the war west of the Rhine.

There is some comment – and some relief – that the breakthrough took place in a sector held by the Americans. A few fear their inexperience may have been responsible for their failure to hold the attack. Some think 'it may do good, by making the American people see the war in a different light'.

THE AIR OFFENSIVE: Satisfaction continues, but there is some surprise that our air superiority and the weight of our attacks have not made the launching of a German counter-offensive impossible.

A few express concern at the reappearance of the Luftwaffe on the Western front.

3. GREECE

Everyone hopes that the Prime Minister's visit may help to solve the problems. The presence of the Prime Minister and Mr. Eden in Greece came as a complete surprise, and people greatly admire Mr. Churchill's energy, determination and unselfishness: 'You have to hand it to him for going off suddenly at Christmas.' At the same time many are anxious about his health and safety.

Otherwise, discussion continues on familiar lines, with widespread concern about the whole situation in Greece and the use and loss of British troops there.

4. V BOMB ATTACKS

Comment mainly refers to the attacks during the twenty-four hours ending at dawn on December 24, and are as follows:

NORTHERN REGION: 'People could not believe their ears when they heard the sirens', their first thought being that it was one of our own planes in distress or a reconnaissance plane. There appears to be no fright, alarm or despondency and people seem to have taken the official announcement quietly, but the fact that flying bombs can reach the north has acted as 'a bit of a jolt' and there is some apprehension about further attacks. The greatest concern is felt for the safety of children in places where shelters have been given up.

Rumours as to the places in the Northern Region where bombs have fallen are many and varied.

NORTH-EASTERN REGION: The arrival of flying bombs in the north was a rude shock to complacency. People had got the impression that, so far as they were concerned, the danger of air attack was over. There is some criticism of the cutting down of Civil Defence Services and of the fact that, on the sounding of the siren, wardens, Fire Guards and other services were slow in getting on the job.

There are many and widely varying rumours about the number of bombs and casualties. Manchester is thought to be the place most seriously affected.

NORTH MIDLAND REGION: The weekend alerts and the announcement that northern England is now in the target area have increased discussion and rumours about V weapons and the damage and casualties caused.

LONDON AND SOUTH-EASTERN DISTRICT: Familiar reactions continue.

SOUTHERN REGION: The recrudescence of bombing attacks in the north as well as the south has shaken the complacent attitude of many people and has greatly increased the feeling that the war is far from finished.

MIDLAND REGION: There are many rumours about the raids in the north, mostly about places where bombs are thought to have dropped; one rumour is to the effect that 'one dropped every two minutes for half-an-hour'.

NORTH-WESTERN REGION: The explosions and the alert came as a great shock to many people, and some resentment has been expressed that the Civil Defence Services and the Home Guard should have been 'stood down' while there was still some likelihood of this type of incident. At the same time, where bombs have dropped it is reported that all past and present members of CD services turned out readily to give their assistance. There was some comment on the fact that the first explosion was heard before the siren, as it was felt that after the bomb had traversed so much land there should have been plenty of warning. It is rumoured in this connection that people in Sheffield heard the bombs launched from the plane. The incident only disturbed Christmas festivities to the extent that many people preferred to stay in their own homes for their entertainment.

5. FAR EAST

Some satisfaction with progress is reported, but this week there is little general interest.

BURMA: Comment mainly concerns the conditions under which our men are fighting. Lord Munster's report, and the steps being taken to implement it, are welcomed. People are full of praise and sympathy for the men and appreciate the improved news service. In the Northern Region, however, it is reported that 'letters from men themselves show, despite denials, that they do in fact consider themselves forgotten'.

JAPAN AND THE PACIFIC: There is continued satisfaction with the bombing of Japanese towns, progress in the Philippines, and the sinking of Japanese ships.

CHINA: Some relief over the apparent improvement in the military position, but also the feeling that China is sacrificing her war effort for political ends.

PRISONERS OF WAR IN JAPANESE HANDS: Anxiety continues; relatives are eagerly awaiting the promised cables.

6. RUSSIA

MILITARY: People are well pleased at Russian progress on the Budapest front but continue to wonder about the lull in East Prussia. Some suspect that the Russians are deliberately delaying a smashing blow on the Polish front, in the hope that continued German occupation will make the Poles more amenable.

6A. RUSSO-POLISH RELATIONS

The Prime Minister's speech is again commented on as emphasising the seriousness of the situation. This week, majority opinion appears to support the Government view that Russia should take over the country up to the Curzon line, some adding that, whatever anyone says, Russia will have her own way. A few are fearful lest we end up by fighting the Poles.

7. ITALY

Hardly any comment. Progress is thought slow, but not unreasonably so in view of the difficulties to be contended with. A little pleasure greeted the capture of Faenza.

8. GERMAN PRISONERS OF WAR IN NORTHERN IRELAND

The news that large numbers of German prisoners are being sent to camps in Northern Ireland is said to have caused a good deal of criticism there. Although the camps are in the northern part of the Region, people still fear that many prisoners will escape and seek sanctuary in Eire.

9. NEWS PRESENTATION

This week there is again increased criticism, particularly of over-optimistic and misleading statements ... 'The war has been reported through rose-coloured spectacles.'

War Commentaries and *War Reports* continue to be praised.

II. SPECIAL COMMENTS

FULL WEEKLY REVIEW

10. HOUSING – PRESENT AND POST-WAR

Comment remains unchanged. There are bitter complaints of the present shortage and high price of accommodation, and widespread anxiety about the future. Again this week there are references to 'the Portal fiasco causing a great slump of confidence among the thousands who had hoped for this kind of temporary accommodation'; the public is said to be growing 'more and more restless on account of Government delay'.

11. INDUSTRY – PRESENT AND POST-WAR

Workers continue anxious about redundancy in war factories, with consequent dismissals and transfers. They fear unemployment now and a return to mass unemployment after the war.

It is also felt that present wage reductions do not encourage hopes for the future. According to the report from the Northern Region, engineering workers are particularly sceptical about getting a square deal after the war. 'More and more firms are joining in a wage-cutting wangle under the cloak of redundancy – recognised as a new name for unemployment. Workers say, "We well remember the savage reductions we suffered after the last war and we are getting ready for the fight; we won't readily surrender any progress we have made during this war."'

11A. CALL-UP

The new call-up 'at this stage of the war' has surprised people. Many younger men in industry are somewhat bitter – particularly those who were not allowed to leave their essential jobs earlier on when they wanted to join the armed forces.

12. FOOD AND SHOPPING DIFFICULTIES

Comment has been mainly about the bad distribution or non-appearance of turkeys, nuts and oranges. Those who succeeded in getting Christmas extras rejoice.

TURKEYS: In addition to the shortage, a black market in turkeys and their high price are the subject of complaints.

NUTS: It is thought they should have been fairly distributed on ration books.

UNDER-THE-COUNTER SALES: There has been a revival of complaints about under-the-counter sales.

13. TOYS

The high price, poor quality and shortage of toys have continued the subject of much bitter comment.

14. CLOTHING

Complaints have again been on familiar lines; the chief topics being the inadequacy of the coupon allowance and the poor quality, shortage and high price of footwear – particularly children's.

15. TRANSPORT AND THE DIM-OUT

Transport complaints continue on familiar lines. While improved services in general are wanted, there is a particular wish for later evening bus services where these have not been introduced.

Preliminary reports suggest that motorists are overjoyed at the new order which permits the use of unmasked lamps on cars.

16. DOMESTIC FUEL

People continue anxious about the shortage, uncertain deliveries, poor quality and high cost of coal.

Reference is also made to a shortage of coke. In Scarborough, coke consumers are very concerned at a story that coke has been delivered to local premises requisitioned by the Services but empty for weeks.

16A. MINING

There is less comment this week, the two points most discussed being:

(a) NATIONALISATION OF THE COAL INDUSTRY, which some people feel is 'the only solution'.
(b) BEVIN BOYS: Criticism of the scheme continues.

17. HEALTH

Little comment. War-weariness and strain – said to be increasing in Scotland – continue to be reported. There is also minority complaint of colds and other small ailments.

18. SERVICE LEAVE

Pleasure continues over the leave arrangements for men serving overseas. There is, however, some fear that the German breakthrough in Belgium will cancel leave arrangements for our men on the Western front.

19. AGRICULTURE

Very little comment – but some anxiety continues about:

(a) THE POTATO HARVEST: Comment is made about the shortage of potatoes in the South, while fields in north Northumberland and Lincolnshire are said still to be unharvested owing to shortage of labour and bad weather.
(b) THE FUTURE OF AGRICULTURE IN THE POST-WAR PERIOD.

III. PERIODICAL REVIEWS

20. EDUCATION

DURING THE PAST THREE WEEKS there has again been some discussion of:

(a) THE BURNHAM COMMITTEE'S SUGGESTED SALARY SCALES FOR TEACHERS: Among the public there is some feeling that teachers are already paid quite enough without raising their pay any higher. Among the teaching profession most reported discussion has again centred round the failure to give sufficient recognition to a university degree ('an injustice which will lead to a deterioration of teaching standards in secondary schools') and the failure to differentiate between elementary and secondary school teachers.

(b) THE EDUCATION ACT: Miscellaneous and familiar comment: regret at lack of teachers and buildings, and at the postponement of the raising of the school-leaving age; approval of free entrance to secondary schools.

21. SERVICE PENSIONS AND ALLOWANCES

DURING THE PAST THREE WEEKS comment has been limited; it has been about:

(a) DISABLED SERVICEMEN'S PENSIONS: Discontent is reported that some servicemen are invalided out of the Services without pensions. It is felt that all men originally accepted as A.1 and discharged for health reasons should be pensioned; also that men with conditions 'aggravated by service' should get full pensions. Some feel that tribunals are too hard on servicemen.

(b) INADEQUACY OF SERVICEMEN'S PENSIONS AND DEPENDANTS' ALLOWANCES: It is felt these should be increased, and people still ask why war service grants have been decreased to match the increase in wives' allowances.

V

Special Reports

HOME INTELLIGENCE SPECIAL REPORT NO. 1

ANTI-SEMITISM

15 JANUARY 1942

1. GENERAL

The following summary on public feeling about Jews is based on special reports from all Regional Information Officers.

Seven RIOs report that there has been no appreciable change lately in public feeling. Anti-Semitism is reported to be latent, however, in most districts, and to become noticeable when it is 'stimulated by a report or rumour of some offence in which a Jew is implicated – as, for instance, black market prosecutions'. All the RIOs except those in the Northern and Northern Irish Regions refer to a general belief that black markets are largely run by Jews. It is said that Jews 'play a prominent part in all schemes to "get round" legislation restricting the sale of various commodities in short supply'.

There is, nevertheless, no indication of any feeling that as a nation we are 'Jew-led' on the lines suggested by enemy propaganda, though some people are said to have a 'sneaking feeling that by getting rid of the Jews, Hitler and those of like thought through the ages were right'.

Refugee Jews, however, seem to be regarded with sympathy and 'a few people appear genuinely sorry for their persecution'.

2. INCREASE AND PREVALENCE OF ANTI-SEMITISM

Anti-Semitism is said to be increasing in areas where Jews have evacuated themselves from danger spots, and in towns with a large percentage of Jews in their normal population. The following places are specifically mentioned: Oxford, Reading, Luton, Brighton (where 'anti-Jewish sentiment runs very high'), Camberley, Farnborough, Colwyn Bay, Llandudno, Glamorgan, and the south-west of Scotland. The situation in Glasgow has been described as 'a banked fire which could easily flare up if fanned'. At Sheffield and Leeds 'the close contact between Jews and the population has led to a continuous simmering of anti-Jewish feeling'.

In Northern Ireland, alone, there is said to be 'no Jewish problem'; out of a total population of a million and three quarters, there are only fourteen hundred Jews: 'So long as Protestants and Roman Catholics are so deeply concerned with their own quarrels and antipathies anti-Semitism is unlikely to thrive.'

3. REASONS GIVEN FOR ANTI-SEMITISM

BLACK MARKET ACTIVITIES: Typical comments are: 'Jews are almost always thought to be associated with black market dealings. Shopkeepers accuse Jews of cornering commodities, alleging that they pay high wholesale prices and pass the increased price to the customers. The honest trader is thus excluded from the market. It is also complained that Jewish wholesalers and retailers work together to exclude the ordinary trader' (North-Eastern).

'The Jews are considered very active in the black market business and are always able to pull a fast one across us' (Scotland). 'The tie-up between Jews and the black market is now well established in people's minds. When there are prosecutions there is usually at least one Jewish name in the list of directors.' Also: 'They are always willing to pay the extra price for things, so that under-the-counter trade is encouraged' (London). 'Jews are accused of being the prime offenders in all the black markets, both as vendors and purchasers' (Wales). In Brighton, it is said that when the ban on visitors was lifted 'Jews descended on the town like locusts, bought up all stocks of tobacco and drinks at higher prices than retail and returned to London to operate in the black market; they cleaned up the town within forty-eight hours of the removal of the ban.'

AVOIDANCE OF WAR OBLIGATIONS: Feeling runs high over the number of Jews said to be evading their war obligations. The following instances are given:

a) EVASION OF MILITARY SERVICE: From the North Midland, London, South-Western, Welsh and Scottish Regions come stories of young Jews avoiding their call-up for the Services. It is suggested that they manage this 'either through rich parents buying them smallholdings to farm, or through using their wits to find war work of a more congenial type than soldiering'. From Cardiff comes the question: 'Are Jews automatically exempt from military service or do they know a way of becoming temporarily unfit?'

b) EVASION OF CIVIL DEFENCE DUTIES: It has been alleged in the Southern Region that 'able-bodied Jews avoid Civil Defence service and allowed local women to fire-watch their houses'. In Sheffield, 'the most frequent comment about Jews concerns their unwillingness to take their part in Civil Defence duties'.

c) Young Jewish girls in the Luton district are said to be escaping war work. 'Caustic references are heard about the number of frail Jewish women, who, owing to their state of health, need to keep their daughters at home.'

BUSINESS METHODS AND EVASION OF REGULATIONS: 'One of the main difficulties appears to be that Jews continually prove themselves more than a match for Gentiles in business', says a report from the North Midland Region.

'Their capacity for money making leads to envy in the general population and abuse from those in competition.' The Midland Region, also, suggests that 'a lot of criticism might be described as "envious"'. Reports from other Regions say it is often alleged that 'Jews fail to follow Government requests and instructions'; they 'can be expected to be in any kind of "ramp" intended to mislead or defraud the public'. There seems to be suspicion that 'the Jews are not popular because they "do not play fair" over legislation'. In Cardiff it is said that 'Jews cannot help avoiding the law and finding ways round it. The way they play about with the bankruptcy laws is monstrous.' The RIO South-Eastern Region sums up the feeling in these words: 'Fundamentally the intense dislike for the Jews seems attributable to what are described as their low business morals and methods as compared with those of ordinary business-folk; methods and actions, which the majority of Gentiles regard as despicable, are considered to be the regular business practice of the Jews.'

EVACUATION TO SAFER AREAS: The RIO Southern Region reports 'constant complaints of wealthy Jews alleged to have taken an unfair advantage over other evacuees by offering exorbitant prices for house purchase and rents'. In Ayrshire many Jews are said to have evacuated themselves to the safer areas and to be 'monopolising transport'. The attitude of Jews to invasion is also said to have led to resentment in Llandudno and Brighton: 'At the first hint of danger they fled like rabbits to safer quarters, but they are now said to be "retaking possession" of the town.'

OSTENTATION AND THE SPENDING OF MONEY: A typical comment comes from the North-Eastern Region: 'Ostentatious spending by Jews, the apparent luxury of their dress, households and especially cars, cause many expressions of disgust.' There are also complaints that 'as they have the money and the time, they shop out of their districts and go from shop to shop for goods in short supply for which they will pay any price'. In the North-Eastern, London and Midland Regions, there is sarcastic comment on the number of Jews to be seen in the more expensive restaurants.

HOME INTELLIGENCE SPECIAL REPORT NO. 19

PUBLIC REACTION TO GERMAN PROPOSALS FOR A BOMBING TRUCE

15 MAY 1942

The following memorandum summarises reports from Regional Information Officers on the public's reactions to proposals recently made on the German wireless for a bombing truce. The general tone of these reports suggests that the British public's feeling of ruthlessness towards the German people is increasing.

NORTHERN REGION

Few people seem to be aware of any such proposals.

The majority appear to be delighted with the RAF's present Continental offensive and are convinced that the damage being inflicted upon Germany is 'more severe than anything they have been able to let us have in return. Consequently, the public is in no mood to welcome a bombing truce.'

None of the recent blitzes has affected towns in this Region. In Durham, however, during the week before last, 'many people had their bags packed' and were ready to evacuate in anticipation of their city being 'next on the list'. At the same time, 'it might also be said that people (there) are a little disappointed that their standing in Baedeker has not been confirmed'.

NORTH-EASTERN REGION

A 'considerable body of the public' are said not to have heard of the proposals for a truce. Among contacts who included businessmen, schoolmasters, university students and 'good-class working men', the feelings about such a truce are described as 'not merely negative but hostile. The feeling is strong that we should show no mercy now that we have the means to hit the enemy.' Indeed, it is suggested that 'any weakness on the part of the Air Ministry towards Germany might result in the Government being turned out of office'.

The proposals are said to be interpreted in two ways: either as an attempt to trade on the sentimentality of the British public; or as 'the first sign of Germans squealing, now that the tide is turning against them'. The photographs of damage at Rostock have been studied 'almost with gloating, and the destruction of non-military targets has evoked no protest'. Much as 'our historic buildings are prized', it is felt that it is better to lose them than to lose 'our own or our children's liberty'.

The only city in this Region which has recently suffered a heavy attack is York, and even here the truce proposals are said to have aroused 'very little interest'. Further raids were expected, and were 'awaited with determination'. (There were strong feelings, however, about the BBC's announcement of York Minster's escape, which was regarded, as such statements invariably are, as an invitation for the Luftwaffe to return.)

From Ripon, Beverley and Harrogate where no severe raids have yet been made, but might be expected, there is said to have been little interest in the proposed truce.

NORTH-MIDLAND REGION

There appears to be no knowledge among the public in this Region that any suggestion of a bombing truce had been made.

EASTERN REGION

Though there is reported to be 'a general assumption ... that the Germans might at this stage suggest a truce', owing to the superiority of our attacks over theirs, there seems to be no knowledge of such a proposal. The majority seem to be against any such idea, even though reprisals for the RAF's present heavy attacks are regarded as 'almost inevitable'. It is suggested that 'if the Germans agreed to a truce, it would mean that they believed they would stand to gain by it'.

In some historic towns, however, anxiety about the possibility of raids is said to be 'very apparent', and people have been 'sleeping with suitcases packed'. Librarians in Cambridge and King's Lynn report that numerous requests have been made for Baedeker; in these towns, as in Ipswich and Colchester, there are rumours that, according to Haw-Haw, each locality is 'number so-and-so on the list'.

With regard to our own raids on Germany, a point which is said to have aroused discussion is the legitimacy of 'working men's homes' as a target. There appears to be little realisation of how effective such bombing may be as a means of slowing down production. Consequently, and particularly among the working classes themselves, damage to workers' houses is regarded either as an attack upon morale or as an 'expression of spite'. The fact that such bombing did not destroy our morale leads 'the greater number to argue that it will not break the Germans' either'.

LONDON REGION

Only a very small number of people seem to be aware that any proposals for a bombing truce have been made and no discussion of the subject has been reported.

SOUTHERN REGION

'Few people have heard anything about the German proposals.' Among those who have, however, opinion against a truce is described as 'unanimous'. It is felt that such a proposal would not have been made had not the Germans felt 'they were now getting the worst of the bombing'. It is suggested that, despite the prospect of retaliation, 'there is an overwhelming demand for heavier and heavier bombing of Germany'. In towns such as Portsmouth and Southampton, which have already been heavily raided, 'this feeling is said to be even stronger than in towns so far immune from bombing ... people want no squeamishness in air action on account of Germany's retaliatory attacks'.

Though apprehension of raids is reported from both Oxford and Winchester, 'there is no evidence that this leads to a demand for a bombing truce'. On the contrary, the desire for our own attacks to be intensified is also apparent in these towns, 'partly because it is thought the German people cannot stand up to raids as well as our own people'.

SOUTH-WESTERN REGION

For the most part, the proposals for a truce seem to have gone unheard in this Region. Among the few, however, whom they have reached the reaction is said to have been 'clearly and immediately against giving (them) any consideration at all'. The proposals are regarded as 'the first positive evidence that the Germans are being hurt – they would not make these proposals if they were not to their own advantage.

They could certainly not be trusted to honour any such arrangement.' The views of the majority may be summed up in the phrase: 'Give them more and see who can stick it out the longest.'

Opinion in the raided towns of this Region is said to be 'vehemently in favour of intensifying our effort' against the Germans. In Exeter the desire to 'smash the enemy even harder' is reported to be 'quite remarkably strong', women being 'even more vigorous than men' in expressing this ambition.

In certain historic towns, hitherto un-raided, there is said to be 'a windy element', among whom there is some inclination to trek out of the town at night. But the general attitude in these districts seems to be: 'We've got to take it, and we must stand up to it like other places.'

In certain parts of this Region, notably the Forest of Dean, the Taunton-Yeovil area, and Bristol, a certain air of 'resignation to bombing attacks, rather than offensiveness' has been noticed since the Bath and Exeter raids, though no signs of defeatism are reported from these places.

WALES

Little seems to be known about the proposals in this Region. Generally speaking, opinion appears to be 'dead against' a truce, which is said to be regarded 'as an attempt ... to cancel the obvious advantage that the RAF now has over the Luftwaffe'. In most areas the public seem to be very glad that 'at last Germany is squealing under our bombing' and they are eager that she should continue to be 'thoroughly and systematically bombed'. The nearest approach to a solitary phrase of approval comes from a young woman who said that 'a bombing truce would be all right, if we could trust Hitler – but we certainly couldn't'.

In Cardiff, though some nervousness of reprisals is reported among women, it seems to be generally thought that we should continue to 'deliver the goods in larger quantities and with no half measures'.

From the cathedral town of Bangor, slight anxiety is reported as a result of the recent raids on similar towns in other Regions.

MIDLAND REGION

So far as is known, there have been no spontaneous references to the truce proposals in this Region.

NORTH-WESTERN REGION

Though the proposals have apparently not aroused 'much interest or discussion', it is thought that a large majority would be very strongly against them and might possibly 'throw the Government out' if it were thought to be giving them serious consideration. 'The furthest most people are prepared to go is to hope that we may try to avoid bombing cathedrals and hospitals.'

In areas where heavy bombing has already been experienced, such as Manchester and Merseyside, opinion is described as being '100% against any truce'.

In Chester [...] and Wigan, where there have so far been no serious raids, there does not appear to be any 'special fear or reaction' at the possibility of reprisals by the Germans.

Among a small minority – to be found mostly among women in un-raided areas – who favour a truce, the argument is usually the humanitarian one that 'we should not make war on women and children'.

SCOTLAND

Few people seem to be aware that proposals for a truce have been suggested; the attitude, however, of those who have heard of the idea is implicit in the comment: 'Not bloody likely!' It is assumed that such a truce 'would last only as long as Germany wanted it'. That the idea is now being propounded is taken to mean that she is being 'hard hit', and that 'Hitler is just playing on our humanitarian instincts.'

SOUTH-EASTERN REGION

Again in this Region, very few people have heard of the proposals and there seems to have been 'little or no discussion of the subject'. 'The idea of a truce commends itself to *no one*.'

Among the reasons given for its rejection is mistrust of the German Government 'who would merely use the truce to re-equip the Luftwaffe'; Germany must 'have a taste of what she has given us, and the bigger the dose, the better. We've gone through it before and, if necessary, can go through it again, especially if we know the RAF is hitting back with ever increasing strength.'

The belief that these proposals are a sign of the effect of our raids upon Germany is less marked here than in some other Regions.

Reactions from Canterbury, Guildford and Chichester indicate that though raids may be expected in these areas people are not unduly frightened at the prospect.

NORTHERN IRELAND

There has been little discussion of the proposals here. The general opinion seems to be that had the suggestion been widely heard it would have been 'treated with scant respect'. The raids on Rostock are said to have thrilled the workers in a large war-production factory, and there appears to be a very strong feeling that we should continue to bomb the Germans as heavily as possible.

CONCLUSIONS

Only a very few people appear to have heard of the German proposals and little discussion of them has been reported.

Among those who have heard of them, opinion in all classes is said to be very strongly against any such suggestions. This seems to apply equally to raided and un-raided areas. A small minority, however, in which women appear to predominate, is reported to favour a truce on humanitarian grounds.

Among reasons given for rejecting any such suggestion, the commonest seems to be that we should be throwing away a supreme advantage, the German proposals being interpreted as a sign of the RAF's superiority over the Luftwaffe.

Distrust of Germany's promises is quoted as another reason, and it is thought that a bombing 'truce' would merely serve as a respite for Germany while she recouped her losses.

Although natural anxiety exists in un-raided towns of historical or antiquarian interest, it is usually coupled with a determination to face boldly whatever may be in store rather than to accept it with resignation.

On the whole, the public, in both raided and un-raided areas, strongly favours the bombing of Germany on an ever-increasing scale, despite the possibility of reprisals. The RAF's destruction of workers' homes and 'non-military targets', whether by accident or design, seems to be regarded with resignation or indifference rather than with regret. A minority doubt the wisdom and ethics of such a policy.

PUBLIC FEELING ON POST-WAR RECONSTRUCTION

A REPORT BY HOME INTELLIGENCE

NOVEMBER 1942

I. INTRODUCTORY NOTE

On June 5th 1942 the Paymaster General asked the Minister of Information if the Home Intelligence Division would undertake an enquiry on public feeling in connection with:

i.   The nature, extent, and source of demands for reconstruction plans.
ii.   Any specific points strongly felt by the public as desirable in such plans.

The Minister replied that he would be glad to arrange for such an enquiry to be made. This report is presented in fulfilment of his undertaking.

II. THE METHOD OF INVESTIGATION

Most of the material used in this report was collected by the thirteen Intelligence Officers on the staffs of the Regional Information Officers in the Civil Defence Regions. Each Intelligence Officer was given two months in which to carry out enquiries – from August 5th to October 5th, 1942. Their enquiries were directed to members of the public in all walks of life, and in many cases their findings were checked against the views of members of Local Information Committees, who are themselves widely representative. The high degree of agreement between the reports from the different Regions (except on purely local matters) suggests that the method is valid.

Special reports were prepared by the Postal Censorship Department and the Listener Research Department of the BBC; a number of other sources were also drawn upon, and these additional checks confirmed the Intelligence Officers' findings.

Great stress was laid on the necessity for obtaining spontaneous and unprompted opinion, and it is thought that this report does, in fact, reflect such opinion. The amount of space devoted to each subject is not an index of the amount of interest it is arousing, but rather of the variety of views expressed.

No attempt was made to treat the material statistically, as the method of collection would have made such an attempt invalid.

Since the report summarises the opinions of a large number of people, it inevitably presents a more complete picture than is present in any one person's mind, and in reading it, this proviso should be remembered.

An attempt has been made to show not only the extent of public knowledge and expectation but also the extent of public ignorance.

USE OF QUOTATION MARKS

Members of the public do not express themselves in conventional or stereotyped English. If their feelings are to be adequately reflected, it is necessary on occasion to use their own words; wherever this has been done, quotation marks have been used.

III. GENERAL CONCLUSIONS

THE FEELINGS OF THE MAJORITY ABOUT RECONSTRUCTION

A great many people – and almost certainly a majority of women – think about the end of the war only in personal terms, of reunited families, normal domestic life, and freedom from many wartime worries and anxieties – particularly air raids and the blackout. For the rest, these feelings are coupled with a mixture of hopes, expectations and fears. Hopes are greater than expectations, and fears are greater than hopes.

The fears spring mainly from bitter memories of hard times after the last war, and from an inability to see any signs of determined post-war leadership. The expectations often take the form of catch-phrases: 'It will never be the same again'; 'they won't be able to fool us this time'; and 'capitalism is dead'. Hopes range from 'rather indefinite wishing for something better' to much more clear-cut proposals, usually for the practical reform of individual problems. There are a few whose hopes for the future rest in escape to the Dominions or Colonies, or 'to a chicken farm in the country'.

This majority includes many who express impatience with all talk or discussion about reconstruction. Their views will be considered in detail in a later section.

THE THINKING MINORITY

The major division of opinion is no longer along political lines. The cleavage is rather between those who think about the problems of the future and those who do not. This thinking minority is in some ways an artificial conception; everyone thinks to a certain extent about the future. The term, as used throughout this report, covers those who look beyond their immediate personal environment, and at least attempt to formulate the broader issues facing their section of the community. As thus defined, the thinking minority is found in all social classes, and in all parts of the country. Its numbers are greatest in the working classes, though it is proportionally bigger among the professional classes. It is by no means absent among industrialists and businessmen, and is probably smallest among the lower middle classes (small traders, clerks, etc.). Its size is estimated as being somewhere between 5% and 20% of the population. The views it holds are, with a few exceptions, held unanimously; they frequently reflect the opinions expressed by social reformers during the past twenty years. Their suggested solutions of post-war problems are practical and pragmatic, rather than theoretical; and their interest in abstract political or economic theory is very slight. Home affairs and domestic questions occupy their minds much more than international problems.

When clear views are expressed by the less thoughtful majority, these views coincide almost always with those of the thinking minority, though the emphasis may be slightly different. For example, both groups regard unemployment as the most vital of all post-war problems. While the majority place housing second and education third, the minority reverse this order. It is, then, not unreasonable to assume that when the uninformed majority crystallise their views, these will be very like those expressed by the more thoughtful.

THE MAIN TRENDS OF THOUGHT

Running through all hopes for the future are certain outstanding themes:

i. There must be work at a living wage for everyone who is capable of doing it.
ii. Private profit must cease to be the major incentive to work; everyone must work primarily for the good of the community.
iii. There must be financial security for everyone who is unable to work.
iv. There must be decent homes for everyone at a cost which will not reduce people to poverty.
v. The same education must be available to everyone so that all will have an equal chance.
vi. There must be no more wars, and we must remain strong in order to prevent them.

The war has brought about a great decline in concern about restrictions on personal liberty. If rationing and registration are the prices to be paid for a fair distribution of supplies, and a fair call-up, it is felt that the price is well worth while. Even high taxation, 'if it is necessary for the common good', causes remarkably little complaint. There is much evidence to suggest that if restrictions on liberty would lead to more equality in the post-war world, they would be readily accepted. This, however, does not extend to restriction on choice of occupation, which few people seem even to have considered.

ORGANISED OPINION

No attempt whatever has been made to study organised opinion, though the thinking minority includes many who belong either to informal discussion groups or specialised bodies concerned with one particular aspect of post-war planning: for example, education, health services, housing or town planning. But unorganised opinion is undoubtedly influenced to some extent by the views expressed by organised groups. The main formative factors, however, are personal experiences after the last war and during this.

THOSE WHO OPPOSE DISCUSSION ABOUT RECONSTRUCTION

Included in this group are a number who oppose discussion, but are not, in fact, opposed to post-war planning. Their opposition springs from the following sources:

i. They feel that the problems are too complicated for them, that they have too little basic knowledge, and that it is a job for the experts: 'It's up to the Government to produce plans, and then the public can say what it thinks of them.'

ii. They feel that at present all that discussion leads to is 'vague promises of a new and better world for the common man'. These are compared with the promises made in the last war, and their results, and are greeted with indifference, impatience, or cynicism. Such people profess themselves ready to listen either to 'concrete plans' or to 'something definite on the statute book'.

iii. They fear that discussion may divert much-needed energy from the war effort, particularly as 'the best brains are needed for both tasks, and winning the war must come first'.

Such opponents of public discussion nevertheless hope that when the time comes the Government will, in fact, have made the necessary preparations, and a factual statement of its plans would be welcomed at any time: 'We must not be caught napping again, as we were after the last war.'

It is noticeable that no one suggests that discussion should be postponed for fear of producing national disunity. This is presumably because, for most people, the issues have ceased to be controversial.

There remains a large number of people who oppose discussion, without expressing any views as to whether the Government should continue to prepare plans or not. The great majority of these people believe in the need for winning the war first and 'talking afterwards'. Other reasons are:

i. 'What right have we to be thinking about our comforts after the war, when the Russians are risking everything at Stalingrad?'

    ii. 'How can we know what things will be like at the end of the war, so what is the use of drawing up plans now?'

   iii. 'We should wait till the men in the Forces come home, so that they can express their opinions.'

Finally, there are those whose present conditions are so much better than they were in peacetime that they 'do not dare to look ahead', and those whose peacetime life was so comfortable and so satisfactory that 'looking ahead fills them with foreboding'.

FLUCTUATIONS IN OPINION

In the earlier days of the war, there was a tendency for thought and discussion about post-war reconstruction to increase whenever there was a lull in events on the battlefronts. Now, however, the situation is reversed. The outbreak of new fighting stimulates discussion, presumably because this is felt to be a sign that the end of the war is appreciably nearer.

REGIONAL DIFFERENCES

Regional differences of opinion were remarkably slight. In Scotland, expectations were considerably more gloomy than elsewhere, especially with regard to unemployment; and there was much less demand for educational reform, presumably because their existing system gives greater satisfaction than is the case elsewhere. In Wales, the most marked difference from the rest of the country is in the demand for greater autonomy.

OPINION IN THE FORCES

No attempt whatever was made to tap Forces' opinion. It is generally believed by the public, however, that interest in reconstruction is much stronger in the Forces than among the civilian population.

IV. UNEMPLOYMENT AND INDUSTRY

In all classes of the community unemployment is thought to be the outstanding post-war problem. It is, indeed, more than a problem: it is a personal and individual fear, which is constantly at the back – and often in the forefront – of the minds of servicemen's families, of workers in all the war industries, and of the many thousands who have temporarily entered Government service. Indirect evidence suggests that it exercises the minds of men and women in the Forces even more strongly than it does those in civilian occupations.

The major trends of public feeling are:

    i. Fear of unemployment. This is the strongest single emotion. It is based on 'bitter memories of conditions between the two wars'. The troubles and fears of parents have infected the younger generation.

ii.   Hope that it will not recur. This hope is far less strong than the fear: 'Generalised declarations, like the Atlantic Charter, carry little conviction.' Only when the Government announces a 'practical and positive post-war employment policy will most working people feel justified in looking forward hopefully'.

iii. Determination that it shall not recur. This is strongly expressed, particularly by younger workers. The possibility of violence is spoken of, if the post-war Government fails to solve the problem ... 'and many young men now know how to fight'.

iv.   Belief that it can be avoided: 'If we can get rid of unemployment by having a war, we can do it in peace; if we can spend thousands of millions on making arms, we can spend them on making all the things people need; the Government has dealt with selfish private interest in wartime, it can do the same, if necessary, in peacetime.'

v.   Belief that 'unemployment is necessary for industry in order to keep down wages'. This view is attributed to a limited number of employers.

THE IMMEDIATE POST-WAR PERIOD

It is generally realised that the demand for labour in the expanding peacetime industries will be very great; but it is even more generally feared that the numbers released from the Services and munition industries will exceed this demand. The thinking minority hope, and even expect, that the transition will, in fact, be carried out with planning and foresight.

SUGGESTED CURES FOR UNEMPLOYMENT

Consideration of what the public feel should be done to cure unemployment leads to the kind of picture they have in their minds of post-war industry. At this point only their proposals for immediate remedies will be considered. These fall into two groups: those which increase productive employment, and those which reduce the available labour force.

The main suggestions in the first group are:

i.   The initiation of a large post-war building programme, to rebuild blitzed areas, to provide homes for the many new family units, to improve school accommodation, and to continue the work of slum clearance.

ii.   State schemes of public works: in particular, for roads, water supply and drainage in rural areas, and for more electricity services.

iii. The training and retraining of workers. There is particular concern about untrained and partly trained men leaving the Forces, and those at present doing unskilled munitions work.

Suggestions for reducing the available labour force are:

i.   Continued conscription for a standing army, an army of occupation, and later an international police force.

ii.   An earlier retiring age with adequate pensions for all. The age of 60, or
      even 55, is suggested.
iii. Shorter hours of work for all.
iv.   Raising the school-leaving age.
v.   The return of industrially employed women to their homes.

While restrictive measures on industrial output for the maintenance of prices are
bitterly opposed, restriction of labour supply finds common support. It is true,
however, that the latter is only proposed when industry has failed to absorb available
labour. At the same time, not more than a small number of even the more intelligent
people understand the relationship between national production and a national
standard of living, or, for that matter, the relationship of standard of living to the
import and export trade.

THE GENERAL PICTURE OF THE FUTURE OF INDUSTRY

In peacetime, it was the general rule for the worker to feel that his employer was
working for profit, while he had to sell his abilities to the employer for as large a
slice of that profit as possible. Any idea that the product of his labour was of general
value to the community seldom if ever entered his head.

For the past three years, however, all the machinery of Government and
unofficial propaganda has been directed to convincing workpeople that their jobs,
no matter how humble or obscure, are integral parts of the national war effort.
This propaganda has been, on the whole, successful, and the majority of working
people now seem satisfied that even the 'non-obvious' jobs are primarily for national
service, and only secondarily for employers' profits.

As a result, the view has sprung up everywhere that 'as we work for the community
in war, why should we not do so in peace?' Feeling among the working classes,
as well as among 'the more intelligent management class', is now that 'the aim of
industry should no longer be the pursuit of profit but, instead, the service of the
people'.

In particular, there are two demands which are made of industry:

i.   It must provide 'guaranteed' jobs for all. There must be no more
      fluctuations of industrial activity, with the standing-off of employees during
      slack periods.
ii.   There must be no more deliberate restrictions on output to keep up prices,
      while the needs of any part of the community remain unsatisfied.

If any industry under private control cannot ensure these two essentials, then it must
be taken over by the state.

Opposition to state control on the grounds of inefficiency is now apparently
confined entirely to employers. The Post Office, the police and the highways are
cited as examples of 'things efficiently run for the service of the public and not for
profit'. Although the term 'nationalisation' is seldom used, except in connection
with the land, there are a number of industries which, it is generally felt, should be
controlled by the state:

i. All monopolies. There is a widespread suspicion that monopolies offer an opportunity to the unscrupulous to 'bolster up prices by keeping down production'.
ii. All public utility services, including transport, electricity, gas, water supply and drainage.
iii. The armament industry in all its various branches.
iv. Certain major industries, where fluctuations of conditions have been particularly severe: e.g. coal mining, cotton, etc.

Direct Civil Service control finds few advocates; the only alternative suggestion is the establishment of National Boards, with representatives of the employers, managers and workers under an independent chairman representing the Government and the consumers.

GOVERNMENT CONTROLS

The wartime controls which have affected the lives of the general public have been of two kinds, economic and social. Broadly speaking, the social controls, such as the blackout, the restrictions on travel, and the setting up of defence areas, are intensely unpopular, and everyone is hoping to see the last of them at the earliest possible moment.

The attitude towards economic controls is very different. They are no longer looked upon as an interference with personal liberty, but rather as a guarantee of fairness and equality. Memories of the food situation in the last war are contrasted with what has happened this time, and the credit balance which accrues to the Ministry of Food spreads over to approval for rationing and price control in general.

CONTROL OF RAW MATERIALS

The public, as a whole, knows little or nothing of this subject. Among those who consider the problem, it is assumed that raw materials will have to be controlled for a time after the war, and that if a stable world economic system is to be built up, such control may have to be continued indefinitely. Even 'businessmen, most of whom are impatient with controls and opposed to them in principle, think they will be necessary in the immediate post-war period'.

RATIONING

A minority – and it is quite a large one – expect rationing to stop when the war ends. The majority, however, think it should continue, and expect that it will do so, for a considerable time. The longest period mentioned is ten years. Rationing, as such, is not unpopular though details of the machinery are often criticised. Indeed, for all goods and services in short supply it is generally looked upon as the only fair method of distribution.

One aspect of rationing which is particularly praised is the award of priorities to those who have special needs. It is hoped that the following facilities will continue indefinitely: extra, cheap and free milk for children and pregnant women and nursing mothers; extra clothes for heavy workers; canteens for factory workers; and British Restaurants for 'many who never took a meal out before'.

PRICE FIXING

In the early days of the war it was generally believed that price fixing always led to the disappearance of goods from the market. That belief has now disappeared, and price fixing is one of the most popular war-time measures. A large majority hope that it will continue for an indefinite period. Of the subsidies and other machinery behind price fixing the public knows little or nothing.

RESTRICTION OF PURCHASING POWER

The high rate of wartime taxation is accepted, for the most part, with remarkable philosophy, even by the many who have never paid income tax before. It is generally expected that 'money will be pretty tight after the war, and that high taxation will continue'. Though this prospect is naturally disliked, it is increasingly believed that if high taxation is the price that must be paid for good schools, good social services and the abolition of unemployment, then it is well worth while.

The public, as a whole, do not believe they will ever receive their post-war credits. Similar scepticism exists about National Savings, yet even those who speak of the scheme as a 'swindle' continue to put money into it. There would be little surprise if 'something went wrong and the money disappeared'. It seems, however, that National Savings have become a habit for those who cannot spend their money otherwise.

RESTRICTION ON THE CHOICE OF OCCUPATION

Those provisions of the Essential Work Order which help the employee are popular with workers. In particular, it is hoped that the days will never return when notice of dismissal is suddenly discovered in the weekly pay-packet. Some employers, too, welcome the stability it gives in a limited labour market. But the idea that direction into employment should continue after the war seems to have been neither discussed nor considered.

At the same time it is realised that unless care is taken, workers may find that they are no longer near the factories and there are urgent pleas, particularly from the pre-war distressed areas, that the Government should 'firmly and ruthlessly plan the location of future industry'.

V. CONDITIONS OF WORK AND INDUSTRIAL RELATIONS

Linked with the growth of the feeling that all work should be for the service of the community, there is also growing up an increased demand that all workers should 'have their say' in the management of industry, that we should try to build up an 'industrial democracy', and that 'masters and men should get together'. It is felt that administrative skill, technical skill, and manual skill are equally important, and each should have a real share in management and responsibility.

JOINT PRODUCTION COMMITTEES

It is widely felt that, in spite of many failures, Production Committees in factories and mines point the way to the future, and that they should continue after the war.

Some managements are still said to be opposed to them on principle, while others complain that the worker members are 'not truly representative'.

Workers on the other hand complain that managements are under no obligation to carry out Committees' recommendations.

WAGES

There is a considerable demand for a standard minimum wage in all industries. The satisfaction of the dockers with the decasualisation scheme, which guarantees them a regular minimum wage, is cited as an example of what can be done.

There is some fear of unrest when those who have been earning very high wartime wages – in particular juveniles – have to return to the general level.

HOURS OF WORK

There is little discussion about reduction in hours of work, except as a suggested means of reducing unemployment. But it is believed that in the more distant future, hours of work will be reduced as a result of 'increased efficiency and scientific invention'.

WORKERS' AMENITIES

It is generally hoped that such services as works' canteens, factory welfare, workers' travel arrangements and priorities will continue and be extended after the war.

TRAINING AND APPRENTICESHIP

It is generally agreed that blind-alley employment for young people should not be permitted. The remedy suggested is a big extension of the apprenticeship system, with 'something on scholarship lines to help parents who cannot afford a delay in earning power'. It is felt that apprenticeship produces 'a better type of citizen, a craftsman with skill and pride in his work'. It is felt also that something should be done to vary the work of young employees on monotonous jobs.

TRADE UNIONS

It appears that among many workers the prestige of the trade unions has declined; first because of their inevitably closer connection with both Government and employers, and secondly because of suggestions that they are 'conservative bodies, thinking only about benefiting their own members, rather than the community as a whole'.

Large numbers of 'industrial dilutees' resent their temporary membership of trade unions. They are anxious about their post-war status and fear that the unions will jettison them as soon as the war ends; they believe that, thanks to their experience, they will in fact be equal to regular tradesmen.

Apart from these points, the future of the Unions is little discussed – in marked contrast to that of Joint Production Committees.

WOMEN IN INDUSTRY

Many women, particularly servicemen's wives, are anxious to return to the home as quickly as possible after the war. Many, however, for whom home life represents only 'household drudgery', hope to continue in industry. A minority of women of both types feel strongly that their sex should, in future, play a much greater part in national and local government.

Men who fear post-war unemployment frequently advocate the compulsory return of the married woman to the home.

There is almost universal support for the view that women should receive equal pay for equal work after the war. Many men support this, though less for altruistic reasons than because they fear 'unfair competition'.

VI. SOCIAL SECURITY

Three years ago, the term social security was almost unknown to the public as a whole. It now appears to be generally accepted as an urgent post-war need. It is commonly defined as 'a decent minimum standard of living for all'. The level of war expenditure has led the great majority to believe that finance cannot, in future, be regarded as a barrier to achieving this, and 'even if it involves the continuation of high taxation, it is well worth the price'.

The proposals suggested for bringing it about are:

i.   Work for all who are physically and mentally able to work, with a standard minimum wage based on the cost of living.
ii. Family allowances to parents, both in order to encourage an increase in the birth rate, and to enable parents to prolong their children's education. Interest in family allowances has been greatly stimulated by the problems of Service dependants.
iii. Really adequate pensions 'above the poverty line' for widows and orphans. In this connection, the necessity for the RAF Benevolent Fund is regarded as a national disgrace.
iv. Adequate unemployment allowances, 'without the taint of charity' – though it is hoped that these will seldom be needed.
v.   Adequate sickness allowances, so that financial anxiety shall not be added to the inevitable worry which ill health brings.
vi. Adequate and earlier old-age pensions for all.

The general view is that the cost of these proposals is such that no contributory scheme could meet them, even though 'higher contributions would cheerfully be paid'. It is also generally agreed that the state must run the huge national organisation which is necessary, if administration is to be economical and benefits equal for all. Graded contribution, based on earnings or income, would be willingly accepted.

The continuance of anything in the nature of a means test is generally condemned. It is felt that no poor person should be 'penalised for thrift'. Measures penalising thrift among the wealthy are, however, less widely resented.

Lastly, it is generally agreed that social security should cover everyone in every class, regardless of income.

VII. HEALTH AND MEDICAL SERVICES

Public interest in health matters is generally described as increasing. This is attributed to the following factors:

i. Evacuation revealed to many people for the first time the effect of a slum environment on health. Lice, scabies, and malnutrition, which had previously meant nothing to many upper- and middle-class people, were seen in their immediate neighbourhood, or even in their own homes.

ii. The greatly increased amount of health publicity in the press, in the cinema and on the radio, and by posters, has aroused public interest in matters about which it was largely ignorant. In particular, publicity about diphtheria is apparently becoming more and more effective. The Ministry of Food's publicity about nutrition has also played a big part.

iii. Though much of the wartime health legislation has not been specifically noticed by the public, the measures taken, or to be taken, against diphtheria and tuberculosis have been widely commented on.

iv. The heavier burdens of wartime taxation on the upper and middle classes have made them far more unpleasantly conscious of the size of doctors', surgeons', and nursing home bills.

v. The proposals of the British Medical Association for reforming the health services have aroused considerable interest among the more intelligent.

There are a number of points on which feeling is very strong and, in some cases, unanimous:

i. In the future, the best possible medical, surgical and hospital treatment should be available to everyone, and 'without the stigma of charity'.

ii. The panel as run at present is strongly and widely disliked, primarily because of the discrimination which doctors are thought to show between panel and private patients; and secondly because no provision is made for dependants.

iii. There is growing feeling in favour of regular periodical medical examination.

iv. There should be much more prevention of disease: tuberculosis, diphtheria
     and cancer being particularly mentioned. The school of thought which
     favours 'the payment of doctors as long as they keep you well' has many
     supporters. It is pointed out that prevention saves the community not only
     ill health but also the cost of treating it.
v.   A majority appear to favour the national ownership and control of
     hospitals.

THE DOCTOR IN THE HOME AND NATIONAL HEALTH INSURANCE

It is widely felt that the doctor is not always what he should be – the servant of his
patients. The medical profession is repeatedly described as being 'in bad odour',
'not too popular', and 'mainly concerned about fees'. In particular, there is intense
feeling against any form of discrimination, which is thought to be greatly encouraged
by the panel as it now exists.

It is generally thought that a state insurance system is the only practical method
of arranging medical care. This insurance system must cover the dependants of all
insured people, the middle classes, and the independent worker and small trader.
There is strong feeling in favour of a free choice of doctor. The insurance must
supply not only the home doctor service, but also dental and eye services, a specialist
service and hospital treatment.

On the financial side, there appears to be unanimous feeling against the approved
societies. It is thought that they are more concerned about their profits than the
needs of their members. The touts entering working-class homes are strongly
resented. The greatest odium is, however, reserved for their handling of 'workmen's
compensation'. It is felt that sickness benefit must be adequate to meet family needs
without public assistance, so that the worker is 'not afraid to take his illness early,
and so nip it in the bud'. Lastly, it is felt that there must be some form of death
benefit to cover funeral expenses.

CLINICS, HOSPITALS, AND THE NURSING SERVICES

There is evidence of the growing popularity of clinics. In rural areas there are many
complaints about the lack of clinics and the distances which have to be travelled in
order to get to those which exist.

On the subject of hospitals, there is a small body of opinion which favours the
retention of the voluntary system 'because it links up with local feeling'; those who
hold this view favour state subsidy. The majority, however, are for state ownership
and control of hospitals. It is thought that this is the only way of getting rid of
inequalities of treatment, and of supplying remote and rural areas with an adequate
service. Among the more intelligent, regional planning is regarded as essential.
Particular points about the existing system which are strongly criticised are: the
long waits in out-patient departments; the long delay before non-urgent cases are
admitted to voluntary hospitals; lack of accommodation for maternity cases in many
areas; and the conditions of life in many public mental hospitals. In country places

the mental hospital is often regarded with horror, as being as bad as or worse than a poor-law institution.

The abolition of private nursing homes is advocated by both the majority who object to 'discrimination' and the minority who have to pay their bills.

The need for many more workers' convalescent homes is strongly emphasised. It is widely felt that many people return to work far too soon because of this lack.

Another matter, on which feeling is apparently unanimous, is that rates of pay in the nursing profession should be drastically increased.

PREVENTION, RESEARCH, AND HEALTH EDUCATION

As has already been mentioned, there is growing feeling that more should be done to prevent disease. There appears to be little knowledge of how much can be done in this direction, but a large and increasing number of people are advocating regular routine medical examination.

On the subject of medical research, it is felt that more state money should be available, especially for research on cancer and tuberculosis.

It is hoped that the increase in health education which has occurred during the war will continue in peacetime 'on a still wider scale'. In particular, it is hoped that education about tuberculosis and venereal diseases will be extended, so that people will be able 'to catch them quickly, and in time, and not be ashamed of them'.

It is hoped, too, that the work of the Ministry of Food in connection with the supply of milk, vitamins and other 'health foods', the control of 'synthetic foods and substitutes', and education about diet and cooking, will continue.

VIII. EDUCATION

Among 'thinking people of all classes', the need for post-war educational reform is placed second only to the need for preventing unemployment. By the majority of the public it is placed third in importance, housing ranking with unemployment as a more vital problem. In both groups, however, the details of feeling are much the same; and, for both, the outstanding question is that of greater equality.

EDUCATIONAL EQUALITY

It is generally thought that the present system pushes children into 'watertight compartments', from which most of them will never be able to escape. These compartments depend partly on parents' income and partly on the county in which a child happens to live. Lack of money excludes poor children completely from boarding schools, often from secondary schools and universities (because parents cannot afford to keep them or to be without their earnings), and almost completely from professions which have very long training periods.

Two solutions of this problem find general backing:

i.   Schools, whether day or boarding establishments, should be 'the same for everyone'. The public schools should be converted into 'schools for the public'; and parents should be able to choose whether to send their children to boarding or day schools. It appears that the great majority of the working class prefer day schools and do not want their children to leave home. But only when all schools are open to everyone will all children start life with an equal chance.

ii.   Every child with ability should have a proper chance to go to a university and follow the career of his choice. If parental poverty stands in the way, this must be overcome by state allowance.

The need for 'more free education' is strongly stressed, particularly by those who are themselves well educated, presumably because it is on them that the present high cost of boarding schools and universities falls heaviest.

THE SCHOOL-LEAVING AGE AND CONTINUATION TRAINING

There is general approval for the idea of raising the school-leaving age to fifteen or sixteen, but this must be combined with financial allowances to parents who need their children's earning capacity. The only opposition comes from those who fear a consequent shortage of juvenile labour, especially for the land and the mines. Those who advocate sixteen as the leaving age stipulate that the last few years at school should be increasingly concerned with technical training.

There is also general agreement that some form of education is needed after the leaving age is reached. It is felt that this should be largely technical and should include, if necessary, the free use of books and instruments. For such a scheme to be really effective, however, the working hours of young people will have to be shortened, as the present system of evening classes deprives them of much of their leisure.

There appears to be considerable support for the idea that psychological tests, to help young people to choose the most suitable jobs, should be generally available.

TEACHERS

It is widely felt that the status and salaries of teachers should be raised, so that the most suitable people are attracted to the profession. Standards of qualification should be higher, and no more uncertificated teachers should be admitted.

TEACHING AND THE CURRICULUM

There would be general approval of a drastic reduction in the size of classes, as well as for compulsory secondary education, with equal facilities in both town and country. It is felt that 'teaching for exams' has gone too far, and that records of work and individual interviews should be just as important as examination results in deciding school promotions. This should apply also to the awarding of scholarships, which should not be limited in number, according to the wealth of the education authority, but by the ability of those competing for them.

The general view about what should be taught may be summed up under two headings:

i.   Education should consist not of cramming in facts, but in the development of 'initiative, powers of analysis, individual thought, and constructive criticism'.
ii.   It should be much more practical, in the sense that it should aim at fitting the child for the world in which he has to live. It should include 'the principles of democracy', the duties of a citizen, politics and economics. In elementary schools, it might well be linked up with the local industry. At secondary schools it should be increasingly vocational, with more instruction for girls in home management.

SCHOOL BUILDINGS

There is increasing interest in school buildings. The need is frequently emphasised for 'modern well-designed buildings, attractive to children'; they should be 'warm, well-lit, and well-ventilated'.

NURSERY AND SPECIAL SCHOOLS

Such interest as there is in nursery schools appears to be favourable. Hope is expressed that special schools for the mentally backward and physically unfit will be generally developed.

YOUTH MOVEMENTS

There is comparatively little discussion about youth movements. While it is generally felt that every young person should have somewhere better to go than the street corner, compulsory youth movements of any sort are felt to 'smack too much of Hitlerite Germany'. There is also some fear that these movements may be given a 'political slant'. 'The state may have to interfere with our work, but at least our leisure and our private lives should still be free.' Organised country holiday camps are, however, universally praised. It is also hoped that if conscription continues after the war, training will include instruction in the duties and responsibilities of citizenship, and that advanced educational courses will also be provided.

IX. PHYSICAL RECONSTRUCTION

Among the general public the problem of post-war housing looms almost as large, if not, in fact, as large, as the possibility of post-war unemployment. Among the more intelligent, education is regarded as a more vital matter, but housing is next in order of interest. Land ownership and town planning, on the other hand, are much less mentioned by the general public, except in badly blitzed areas. Even among the intelligent they are not discussed very widely.

The widespread interest in post-war housing is stimulated by the following factors:

i.   The housing shortage after the last war is still vividly remembered by many people.
ii.   Since so much property was destroyed in the blitz, it is expected that the shortage will be even more severe than it was last time.
iii. Many young people who have married since the war have not set up homes of their own. The husbands have been in, or have joined, the Forces and the wives have continued to live with their own families or have joined those of their husbands. Couples such as these are most anxious to set up homes at the earliest possible moment.

The points about which there appears to be a high degree of unanimity are:

i.   There must be no more 'jerry-building' and speculation in land or houses, against which feeling is said to be very strong.
ii.   Women must have a far greater say in the design and planning of houses in the future. Not only must their advice be sought, but they ought to have some real control over the building of houses; though how this is to be attained is not stated.
iii. Among the poorer and middle-income groups, the dislike of flats is intense. The demand is for detached houses for all families, though flats are considered reasonable for old and unmarried people. Even among old people, however, the preference is for 'cottage homes'.

HOUSING

Because the fear of a post-war shortage is so acute, there are considerable demands for the Government to get its plans ready now. It is widely feared that unless these are complete before the war ends, the situation will be chaotic, the door will open for the speculative 'jerry-builder', and there will be great increases in the cost of land and houses and in rents.

Little positive thought is given to the kind of machinery the Government should use to solve the housing problem. It is generally agreed that it is the Government's job, but it is assumed that the municipalities will also play a large part. The most generally favoured solution is 'government control, and if necessary inspection, of all building and repairs'. The general feeling is that 'houses should be built for the occupier and not for someone else to make money out of'. Feeling against speculative builders is very strong; there must be no 'jerry-building' and no use of shoddy materials.

If discussion about the organisation of post-war building is vague, this does not extend to the nature of the housing people want. Among all except a small group, there is an overwhelming demand for detached houses, each in 'its own bit of ground'. There should be much more privacy for gardens. The house is looked upon as the basis of the family unit, a position which can never be occupied by a flat. Every house should have three bedrooms at least, an indoor lavatory, a bathroom which is not combined with the scullery or kitchen (feeling against such combined rooms is particularly intense), adequate clothes washing and drying facilities, constant hot water, electric light, built-in cupboards, and 'all labour-saving devices'. Larders should not be cupboards but small rooms, with windows which do not catch the sun. Living rooms and bedrooms should not be 'poky little affairs' and should have big windows. There is a considerable demand, in towns and even more in country areas, for an outside shed in which to keep prams, bicycles and garden tools, and which should be big enough for the man of the house to do his odd jobs in.

There is some fear of too much uniformity in the appearance of houses. There are still said to be 'many uneducated people' who want 'desirable villa residences or bungalows', though 'even they do not want them to be jerry-built'. Among younger people, 'a surprising number – even in the working classes' appreciate good design and workmanship as well as useful simplicity 'when they can find it'. Control of building by architects is advocated among the educated but is thought to be feared by builders; yet even they are said to appreciate an introduction to new methods and materials.

The feeling against 'working men's flats' is intense; though the need for flats for spinsters and bachelors is appreciated. In such flats, there should be restaurants and hair-dressing facilities. For old people, one-floor cottages with partial service are advocated.

The interest of women in the future of housing is a most striking feature. They demand not only to be allowed to advise but also to play their part in the actual control of building. From a geographical standpoint, interest is greatest in large towns and cities, and in rural areas. In small towns it is much less marked. In rural areas the demand for adequate water supplies and drainage has been greatly stimulated by the sight of Service camps and aerodromes getting these facilities within a few months.

The need for still more slum clearance was brought home to many people in the earlier part of the war by the conditions revealed through evacuation. It is assumed that the work of slum clearance will go on, and should, in fact, go on much faster. The view that the slum dweller automatically turns a good house into a slum is no longer widespread. In areas where back to back houses still exist there is strong feeling that they must be got rid of.

On the subject of rent or ownership feeling is divided. There is, however, a wide demand that both rents and prices should be controlled, and some feeling that ground rents for leasehold property should be abolished.

THE LAND AND ITS OWNERSHIP

Feeling is unanimous that land speculation should at all costs be prohibited. A majority appear to favour nationalisation; this majority includes 'many who are opposed to nationalisation in other spheres'. Nationalisation should be accompanied by compensation of the present owners. The only alternative suggestion is 'strict government control', with, as a subsidiary plan, a general development of smallholdings. It is felt that local authorities should never have to hold up their plans because private interests stand in their way. They should have stronger powers to take what they need at a reasonable price.

The Scott and Uthwatt Reports are entirely unknown to the general public.

For many people, land means only agricultural land. It is noticeable that townspeople are increasingly interested in the countryside, first as a result of evacuation, and secondly because they are linking their own larders much more closely with British agriculture. It is widely hoped that these links between town and country will be greatly extended in the future, and that both town and country dwellers will come to know and understand each other better. 'Amenities in rural areas' to prevent the drift to the town are generally supported.

Among more intelligent people there appears to be unanimity of feeling in favour of national parks, green belts, and an extension of the work of the National Trust. Among all classes there is a demand for 'free access to beauty spots', and for planned and organised holiday camps – 'not bungalows and caravans scattered everywhere'.

TOWN PLANNING

This is a subject of strong feeling only among an educated minority, and among the inhabitants of blitzed cities who feel that 'this great opportunity must not be missed'. Once again, the main trend of feeling is: 'The Government must at all costs stop the exploitation of the community by private interests.' It is felt that the hands of local authorities must be greatly strengthened, but that even they must submit to higher control on a regional or national basis. It is thought that the cost of town planning should be borne nationally.

There is some fear of 'over-planning': that the result will be too much standardisation, regularity and uniformity. 'But uncontrolled building is thought to be the greater evil.' Need is felt for the control of shop and cinema facades 'to avoid shoddiness and freaks' – but without rigid standardisation.

On the question of distance of home from work, opinion is divided. This division is even reported in places where industry is particularly dirty. On the one hand, people say they are used to the dirt, they always have been near their work, and they want to go on. On the other hand, there are many who are quite prepared to travel long distances rather than live near their work.

Again, opinion is divided as to whether it is better to provide more 'communal land' in the form of parks and playgrounds, or to use available land for bigger back gardens. In London, the feeling in favour of more parks is stronger than elsewhere.

Even in the grimiest areas, there appears to be little interest in smoke abatement.

There is general feeling, though it is not very vocal, against ribbon development and in favour of road by-passes for all large towns and 'sensible traffic planning', and the provision of 'recreational facilities' close to 'residential areas'. An 'easy outlet to the country for everybody' is also generally supported. 'Community centres' for housing estates, containing clinics, libraries, nurseries, shops and entertainment centres, are favoured by the more imaginative of those who have not got them.

X. AGRICULTURE

The present conditions of agriculture are such that most farmers and farm workers ask only that they should continue, complete with controls and subsidies. The public's interest in agriculture has been stimulated by the story of wartime farm production and by personal experience through evacuation. But generally speaking, knowledge of agricultural matters is still slight.

Both town and country support the thesis that 'agriculture must not be allowed to slip back to where it was before the war'. But, 'in view of our experience after the last war', there is some scepticism about Government promises. It is also generally thought that for strategic reasons we should never again rely too much on overseas sources for essential foodstuffs.

Two practical points are raised, the first very strongly:

i. The need for improved rural amenities to prevent 'the drift from the land'.
ii. The need for more farming research and more training in scientific farming, in which young workers are said to show a growing interest.

Farmers in general are said to be 'too busy for much thinking ahead'.

XI. RETAIL TRADE

It is widely believed that the process of 'squeezing out' the small trader has Government support and that it may well continue after the war. Though large stores and multiple shops are popular, both for the variety of their wares and because they keep down prices, the small trader gets a great deal of support from the general public for the following reasons:

i. Personal service is preferred to 'the impersonality of the big stores', particularly where children are of necessity sent out to do shopping.
ii. Poorer people cannot afford to travel to shops and cannot spend much time away from their domestic duties. They must, therefore, go to shops which are near their homes.
iii. The one-man business is 'a stepping stone out of the rut for the artisan', and is a symbol of 'individual achievement and personal responsibility'.

XII. LOCAL ADMINISTRATION

LOCAL AUTHORITIES

Interest in local authorities has increased as a result of their many new or enlarged wartime activities, such as the wardens' service, shelter marshals, fire-watching, British Restaurants, salvage, etc. But many people are still without any interest in, or knowledge of, the work done by local authorities: 'They know their own council exists, but nothing more.' Local authorities are perhaps less criticised than Parliament, but criticism of them is more detailed. The councillors are too old and often represent only the tradespeople. Overlapping between different authorities results in waste. In some councils there is much 'jobbery and corruption'. The standards achieved by different authorities vary far too widely.

These are suggestions made to improve matters:

i.   There should be more young men and more women among councillors.
ii. The small expenses of local elections are beyond the means of the working man – and 'this should be overcome'.
iii. The smaller authorities should be amalgamated.
iv. The public's interest in local politics should be stimulated. Everyone should be educated in civics and citizenship; this would make for 'less short-sighted and ignorant councillors, and a more responsible public'.
v.   The national government should demand a 'minimum standard of achievement' from all local authorities and should compel rather than permit them to do things. It should also adopt special powers to prevent 'graft' among local authorities.
vi. These authorities should be 'more democratic in the real sense of the word'. The public should be encouraged in every way to attend council meetings. The link between public and council, which has been to some extent provided by Civil Defence, should be strengthened.

REGIONALISATION

Only a very small minority of the public is interested in the pros and cons of regionalisation. Its opponents are vociferous and are described as being largely 'local government officials and others closely affected'. In fact, a 'strong vested interest in the continuation of the present local authorities' is apparent.

The case against regionalisation is described thus: 'Local authorities must not lose their prestige …'; 'We don't want any extension of bureaucracy …'; 'Departmental jurisdiction over local affairs is cumbersome and undemocratic …'; 'Local people understand local sentiment and are therefore best able to deal with local affairs.' In some regions, animosity between local and regional authorities impedes logical and unbiased thought.

Those who support regionalisation see it as having two main functions:

i.   To 'ginger up' local government; prevent local corruption; check isolation and narrowness in small authorities; and to provide a useful link between individual authorities and the central government.
ii. To take over certain services which need to be run on a big scale. Those named include health, education, housing, transport, water supply and drainage, electricity and gas.

In general, it is thought that an elected regional authority would get wide support; whereas a continuation of regional control in its present form would not be so popular. Though it might be convenient for the central government to have offices in the regions, they should only be there to advise and help local authorities and the public.

WALES

There is a strong demand from Wales for greater self-government inside the present Parliamentary framework. This is crystallised in the request that a Secretary of State for Wales should be appointed.

XIII. INTERNATIONAL AFFAIRS

No essential problem of the post-war world arouses less interest among the general public than that of international affairs. Only on the treatment of Germany is feeling strongly and emphatically expressed. Among more intelligent people, however, the need for an international authority to maintain peace ranks fourth in interest (after unemployment, education, and housing). With the exception of the sections on the treatment of Germany and on British diplomacy, what follows may be taken to represent the views of the intelligent minority which, of course, exists in all social classes.

BRITISH DIPLOMACY

The diplomatic service is regarded by many people as 'the apotheosis of the old school tie'. It is thought that our diplomats know practically nothing of the life and work of the ordinary people in countries to which they are sent; that they are more concerned with 'protecting British interests' than with doing their best for general peace and prosperity; and that they are chosen for 'cleverness' rather than 'honest ability'. It is thought that the exclusiveness of the diplomatic service should be broken down: it should no longer be 'a closed preserve for the public schools', and in future, 'we should send ordinary people as diplomats'. The day-to-day work of the diplomatic service is unknown to the general public.

POST-WAR CO-OPERATION WITH THE USA AND THE USSR

The continued co-operation of the three main Allies is looked on as 'a first necessity for a stable world'. Among working people, interest in co-operation with the USSR is the greater. Among the 'better educated', it is thought that co-operation with the USA will be easier, because our ways of life are more similar.

On the other hand, there are some slight fears of 'US financial domination' and a wish that Russia would allow 'more internal civil liberty'.

TREATMENT OF GERMANY

'Germany must never again be allowed to plunge the world into war'; on this, there is universal agreement. In the future of Italy and Japan there is no interest. Roughly two-thirds of the general public think only in terms of punishment, while one-third have some longer-term views. But both groups are prepared for drastic measures: 'The weakness of 1918 must not be repeated.'

There is a fairly widespread fear that 'we might be too lenient'. For this reason, there are many who feel that 'things might well be left to the people of the occupied countries'.

After this 'preliminary blood-bath', the Nazi leaders should be punished. It is assumed that Germany will be completely disarmed and must be kept disarmed by armies of occupation or international police. The slightest sign of Nazism or Prussianism must be sternly nipped in the bud. A few people speak of the complete extermination or sterilisation of the German people, but this is generally dismissed as 'impossible'. There is, however, little hope of reforming them: 'they must be kept peaceful by force'. There appears to be little desire, however, to victimise the German people economically.

WORLD FEDERATION AND THE LEAGUE OF NATIONS

The belief that there will have to be some form of world organisation after the war is fairly general, but ideas about what form it should take are few. A small number of people favour reviving the League of Nations, but a majority are against this 'because it failed to stop wars last time'. There is more support for a federation having its nucleus in the United Nations. Only a very small minority are concerned about 'the possible loss of freedom by sovereign states'. The relation of the Axis powers to such a federation is not discussed.

INTERNATIONAL POLICE

It is generally assumed that any form of world federation must be able to back up its decisions by force: 'The League failed last time because it had no powers of coercion.' There are two views about the nature of the proposed force:

i.   It should be composed of the armed forces of the Empire, the USA and Russia.
ii. It should include also the smaller nations.

Some people think it should be primarily an air force.
   Three practical points are raised:

i.   It should be composed of men of the highest integrity, and for this reason a volunteer force is suggested, with good pay and conditions of service.
ii. The manufacture of armaments, particularly warplanes and submarines, should be limited to meet the needs of this force.
iii. The force should be used not only to stop wars, but should also have 'positive social functions' in controlling drug traffic, white slaving, etc.

A small minority oppose an international police force because they fear 'it will cause continuous wars'; they believe also that 'we have no right to inflict ourselves on others'.

WORLD ECONOMIC PLANNING AND CO-OPERATION

The general view appears to be that there must be some kind of world economic planning. Completely free international competition has few advocates; but even these often favour strong government action to help them to recover lost markets overseas.

The form of organisation needed for the task is not at all clear in people's minds. Some see it as part of a world federation, or as an 'international parliament'. Others favour economic treaties 'on the lines of the Anglo-Soviet treaty'. Others again think it will 'spring up automatically from the job of feeding Europe and restoring it to order after the war'.

About the objects of international economic planning there is more certainty. Raw materials should be allotted to the nations of the world according to their needs: 'The days of imperialistic policy are over, and the world's natural wealth should be made available to all.' Manufacture and distribution should also be planned to meet needs rather than furnish profits. Improved standards of living abroad will mean more work at home. There are some advocates of 'an international system of barter controlled by a central body'.

'International bankers and capitalists' are looked on with suspicion by the general public. They are thought to be closely linked with arms manufacturers 'in having a vested interest in making wars'.

Businessmen are said to be 'increasingly inclined to look at the problem on a world scale'. 'The more enlightened ones seem ready to accept some kind of international control.' Only small minorities advocate imperial preference, or similar 'restrictive arrangements'.

THE BRITISH EMPIRE

While the war has strengthened the 'sense of kinship' with the Dominions, there is no speculation or discussion about their future.

Interest in the future of the Colonies is also slight. The loss of Malaya and Burma aroused the public 'conscience' for a while: it was felt that 'something must have been very wrong with our administration'. But this temporary concern has subsided.

Interest in the future of India is almost equally limited. It is assumed that she will get self-government after the war but that, for the present, defence needs must come first.

THE ATLANTIC CHARTER

This excites neither interest nor discussion. It is thought to be 'too nebulous' and 'in danger of becoming a catch-phrase similar to the "Covenant of the League"'.

XIV. DEMOBILISATION

There is a sharp division of opinion on this subject. In all social classes people of the more thoughtful kind consider that demobilisation will be, and ought to be, slow. But a very large number – perhaps the majority – and particularly the poorer classes are concerned mainly with the questions:

i.   'How soon can our men get home again?'
ii. 'If they don't get out at once, all the best jobs will have gone before they are demobilised.'

Many mothers of servicemen have bitter memories of their own husbands' experiences after the last war. They forget the initial prosperity after the last war and remember only the years of depression and unemployment. They picture the future as a scramble for jobs, in which the devil will take the hindmost, and they expect immediate and rapid demobilisation; paradoxically enough, this is also what they hope for.

The points made by more thoughtful people everywhere are these:

i.   Demobilisation must be slow and carefully regulated, if only to prevent men leaving the Services while there are no jobs for them. At all costs, 'the plight of the out-of-work ex-service man' must not be allowed to recur.

ii. A large standing army will certainly be needed for some years after the war: first for the purpose of occupation, and later as part of an international police force; both these factors will help to slow down demobilisation.

iii. Since this is bound to be a gradual process, there ought to be 'priority classes' for early release; this is desirable from a social rather than an economic standpoint. The classes particularly mentioned are:

> Men now overseas
> Men of long service
> Those who joined up first
> Family men
> Married men
> Younger men conscripted during their apprenticeship or training.

There is no discussion, and little realisation, of the problem of women's demobilisation.

XV. THE CONTINUATION OF CONSCRIPTION

The general view among all classes appears to be that, however much it is disliked, conscription must go on after the war for a considerable time if peace is to be maintained: 'We must never again get back to the state we were in in 1939.' Apart from the natural objection to conscription as a breaker-up of families, the following points are made:

i.   The physical training and discipline are good for young men. But more ought to be done for their minds.

ii. Conscription is 'anti-democratic' and 'fosters a militant spirit'; it should therefore go on not a moment longer than is absolutely necessary.

iii. At all costs it must be fair, and should allow no exemption to anyone, except on purely medical grounds – or, a few people add, 'on proved grounds of conscience'.

The general dislike of conscription makes some people favour a volunteer international police force, 'provided enough men could be raised by this means'.

XVI. RELIGION

No special efforts were directed towards assessing the public's feelings about religion in the post-war world. Some evidence of opinion on the subject was, however, received, and from this the following tentative conclusions may be drawn.

i.   Many of those who give thought to the subject hope for a 'religious revival' and 'a more spiritual way of national and international life'; but generally speaking they do not expect their hopes to be fulfilled.

ii. Clergy should be men of a better type and should be better trained for their work.

iii. The Church has responsibilities and duties – which are left undefined – in connection with social justice and social reform.

iv. A minority feel that 'the Church should not meddle in politics'.

v.   Nazi educational methods have awakened many people to 'the need for better religious teaching' in schools.

vi. At the same time, denominational schools receive no great support, and some people would like to see them abolished. Among the great majority of the public, however, such schools arouse neither interest nor strong feeling.

HOME INTELLIGENCE SPECIAL REPORT NO. 34

HONDURASIAN LUMBERMEN IN SCOTLAND

3 DECEMBER 1942

This report on conditions under which men from British Honduras are living in Scotland is based on the experiences of Ministry of Information film projectionists and on the personal observations of one of the Ministry's Scottish Intelligence Officers.

For over two years Hondurasian lumbermen have been working at timber camps in outlying parts of Scotland, mainly at Duns, Kirkpatrick Fleming, and East Linton. The MOI's first contact with these men arose through an anonymous letter signed 'British Hondurasians', which struggled bravely with the complexities of the English syntax to express a general grievance against living conditions.

This letter was forwarded to the Ministry of Supply's Edinburgh Office, and our Intelligence Officer was later told that on investigation the alleged grievances were found to be largely unjustified. Our Officer suggested, however, that by providing films and speakers the MOI might help to break the monotony of life for the Hondurasians. This idea was agreed to, and as an experiment films and speakers are now being sent to the camps.

The following account by our Intelligence Officer of a personal visit to the camps gives a picture of conditions which, particularly in view of the attention being paid to American negroes in this country, will be of interest.

CAMP CONDITIONS: According to our standards of camp life, conditions are bad. The roadways, after rain, are like quagmires, and duck boards have only recently been laid down. A few weeks ago an MOI film van had to be pulled into one of the camps by tractor as it was impossible to drive in. There is no electric light – although it would appear that this could easily be installed from nearby villages – and inside the huts there is chaos, dirt and confusion. Though there is a building called 'the canteen', this supplies only cigarettes and aerated waters. The men have apparently asked frequently for hot drinks, but at Duns they were told last time that 'Kirkpatrick Fleming is bigger and must be looked after first. We hope that hot drinks will be served there *after the winter*. Your turn will come after that.' There is a piano, a dart board, some boxing gloves, and a supply of books, but little use seems to be made of any of these.

Many complaints are made about the food, and that sampled by the Intelligence Officer was said to be ill-cooked, unappetising and 'difficult to analyse'.

ATTITUDE TO WORK: The men are largely engaged on piece work and the results, according to the manager at Kirkpatrick Fleming, are '300 per cent better' than when the work is done on time rates. If, however, the manager decides that weather conditions prevent work (e.g. during periods of heavy snowfall) a time rate is given. One of the worst problems is absenteeism. 'They want to lie off for the most trivial reasons', the manager said. 'Back home, if they have a cut finger or a headache, they don't stay off. They are exploiting the new situation here.' The men particularly dislike the cold weather and use this as an excuse for staying off work.

DISCIPLINE: This is a most difficult question as the men appear greatly to resent attempts to keep them in order. The authority of camp managers seems to be very limited, and the managers themselves would like their powers to be better defined and extended. The men recognise the manager's right of authority only during working hours, and at Kirkpatrick Fleming he has twice been assaulted when trying to promote order and decency. At East Linton the manager is a very strict disciplinarian, and though the men dislike this and have complained, the camp appears to be run on very good lines and there are few complaints from the public.

RELATIONS WITH THE PUBLIC: At the beginning of their stay the Hondurasians appeared to be great favourites with the public, and at Brora, for instance, where a camp has just been established, the local people seem so far to like them very well. But though this was at first true of Duns and Kirkpatrick Fleming, subsequent happenings appear to have modified local feeling. The men themselves often ask people: 'What do you think of the coloured boys?' and are delighted when told that they are very well liked. The local barber in Kirkpatrick Fleming said that the Hondurasians seemed annoyed because he kept special implements for them; but as he explained, 'their hair is so hard to cut, and they are so hard to shave' that he had to keep special articles for them. The men enjoy mixing with white people in pubs, at meetings, and at dances, and in Duns some are even attending evening classes.

ENTERTAINMENT: The Hondurasians love entertainment, and would, if possible, 'go to the pictures every night in the week – they walk or cycle miles' to do so. Local people say 'the men are dancing mad'. Many have their own musical instruments, and in Kirkpatrick Fleming they have a dance band which undertakes paid engagements. The sound of a guitar or trumpet, accompanied by the rhythmic beating of feet, is almost constantly heard in the camps. The men love bright clothes. They usually wear a navy blue uniform for working, but on their off-hours they appear in brilliant yellow waistcoats and bright blue pullovers with flashing rings and tie pins.

THE DRINK PROBLEM: The men become very excitable under the influence of drink, and are themselves aware of this; one intelligent Hondurasian in Duns said 'We were well liked until we started drinking.' So many disturbances have occurred here that certain hotels and pubs now refuse to admit them. They are 'mad on soft drinks', which, they say, are a substitute for the fruit juices they were accustomed to at home, and shopkeepers say that as soon as their quota of lemonade comes in 'the Hondurasians snap it up'. There are many rumours about wild scenes in pubs when the Hondurasians have had a few drinks, and reports have appeared in the local press of Police Court cases following disturbances. It would seem, however, that the Hondurasians are not always to blame for these scenes and apparently our own troops 'egg them on occasionally' with remarks such as 'Let's see your knife.'

THE SEX PROBLEM: This is probably the most serious one. The Hondurasians' attitude to sex is much more simple and direct than ours, and their conversation and behaviour show that they have few inhibitions. Everywhere stories are told of prostitutes from Newcastle, South Shields and Berwick arriving regularly, and especially on pay nights. There are also rumours of local girls becoming pregnant, and many stories are told of village women, some with husbands in the Forces, harbouring Hondurasians in their homes. Four married women in Duns are said to have been 'thrown out by their husbands' because of their liking for the coloured men, and are now said to be living in the camps. Some women are undoubtedly doing so, and in Duns and Kirkpatrick Fleming the situation seems to be almost out of hand. Our Intelligence Officer was present when the manager warned a girl of about fourteen out of the camp. It was useless, he said, to speak to the girl's mother, since she 'welcomes the Hondurasians into her own home'. This problem has excited a great deal of public interest and steps have been taken in some cases to protect the welfare of young children whose mothers are associating with Hondurasians. The powers of the police under defence regulations are also being urgently considered.

The Hondurasians' attitude to our women is, of course, influenced by experience in their own country. At the same time, the more intelligent of them are surprised at the readiness of our women to associate with them. Among the young men themselves a common complaint is that British girls 'only love you for one minute'. They seem delighted, therefore, when friendship is offered as well as commercial 'love'.

In view of what was seen in these camps the Intelligence Officer has put forward the following suggestions:

(1)   Greater attention to camp conditions seems necessary. Electric light, better food and canteen facilities, more opportunities for indulging the men's love of music and dancing, and a supply of illustrated papers and picture books should be provided. The men have shown an interest in dramatic work but their poor powers of concentration might be a bar to this.

(2)   A resident Welfare Officer, preferably a Hondurasian who understands conditions 'back home', and also conditions here, would go a long way towards improving the camps.

(3)   The men seem passionately devoted to the cinema. MOI film shows are invariably received with almost pathetic gratitude. Remarks such as 'This makes me feel better' – 'I am more anxious now to help Britain' were, according to the projectionists, often made after these shows.

(4)   Many of the men expressed their interest in, and enjoyment of, the religious services arranged locally; they particularly liked the hymn singing, arrangements for which might perhaps be developed.

(5)   Possibly their love of display, dressing up, and uniforms could be used as an inducement for their joining the Home Guard. Some are already members but their attendance seems to be dropping, possibly because of the colder weather. If short, simple talks were given on the necessity and value of Home Guard training, and if patriotic reasons were given for joining, the response might be greater and the men's interest more lasting.

(6)   The sex problem is much more difficult to deal with. In the opinion of the camp manager at Kirkpatrick Fleming, powers should be obtained to keep women out of the camps, especially at night. This question is being looked into.

(7)   The men complain that many 'official people have been round' and have promised reforms which never happen. For example, one camp doctor asked in March for linoleum to cover the floor of the sick bay. So far as he knows, this was agreed to, but the order for the linoleum was put forward only last week. A speeding up in simple matters of this sort seems to be called for.

HOME INTELLIGENCE SPECIAL REPORT NO. 36

THE SOVIET YOUTH DELEGATION

9 DECEMBER 1942

At the request of the Soviet Relations Branch of Foreign Division (A), Intelligence Officers were asked to report on the impressions made upon the public by the recent tour of the Soviet Youth Delegation.

During the tour, which lasted from 17th to 27th November, visits were made to eight Regions. But so brief was the delegates' stay in each place, and so congested the programmes arranged for them, that there was apparently not 'much opportunity for the general public to receive an impression of them'. This, it seems, was the main criticism of the arrangements that had been made.

Where the delegates attended meetings and visited factories, they appear to have been 'warmly welcomed', particularly by working-class people. An enthusiastic welcome was also given by students and members of youth organisations, and the delegates, especially Lieut. Pavlichenko, were said to be greatly admired for 'their undoubted bravery' and as representatives of a gallant ally.

Although in four Regions it is reported that the 'delegates were not particularly noted by the general public', some instances are given of friendly demonstrations towards them. In Birmingham a procession was formed in the streets to welcome them, and outside the Council House, where they were presented to the Mayor, the square was 'practically filled'. During their visit to Bermondsey news of their presence 'got round very fast and an enthusiastic crowd gathered – even the police were enthusiastic'. In the Midland Hotel at Manchester the staff, who are described as 'extremely blasé', are reported to have spared no efforts to oblige the delegates, and to have gone 'to unusual lengths ... to collect autographs'.

THEIR RECEPTION IN FACTORIES

In the North-Western and Midland Regions 'considerable enthusiasm from the workers was noted at all the works visited'. In Manchester the 'delegation was mobbed in the factories', and in the Midland Region the workers gave them a 'rousing reception by banging on the benches'. The manager of an aircraft factory in this Region said that 'the workers have got so blasé over distinguished visitors that even the King wouldn't raise a cheer – but the Russians did'.

THEIR RECEPTION BY MINERS

At a meeting of the Durham Miners' Association 'there was noticeably a louder and more prolonged burst of cheering for Lieut. Pchelintsev than for Dr. Beneš or any other speaker at Durham conferences'. During a visit to a Welsh colliery 'questions were asked which indicated a keen interest in all that pertained to Russia and its industrial background, and a friendly conversation extracted the promise to speed up production'.

THEIR RECEPTION AT STUDENT AND YOUTH MEETINGS

The delegates appear to have been 'warmly received' at all such meetings. In Birmingham the gathering was reported to be unusually large and the applause 'vociferous'; while the youth of Glasgow is said to have 'taken the entire delegation to their hearts and to have greatly admired them for their valour'. Certain criticisms have, however, been reported:

(a) Manchester students were said to be dissatisfied because 'they thought that the Russians were here to study conditions of youth in this country', and wondered, somewhat illogically, 'why they wasted time having a look at the war effort'.

(b) In Wales the students are reported to have felt that the delegates were inclined to 'harangue' them, though they were 'not unfavourably received by the general body of students'. 'Intimate talks' between the delegates and students at Aberdare Hall are described as having been 'most successful'. 'Here', it is said, 'all political differences were forgotten, and a very genuine attempt made to effect a common understanding. Some four or five students had a heart-to-heart discussion with Lieut. Pavlichenko on the position of the church in Russia.'

(c) At youth meetings in Glasgow and Birmingham it is reported that 'Left-wing elements captured the meeting.' In Birmingham some people took exception to the sale of 'red literature' in the foyer of the hall; no criticisms of the delegates were reported, however, though it was said that 'there was a good deal of disappointment that the Russians did not say more about Russian youth'.

THE PERSONALITIES OF THE DELEGATES

Widespread admiration of the delegates is reported from six Regions – 'the direct, charming and straightforward attitude of the visitors appealed greatly to everyone who came into contact with them. Not unnaturally, interest centred in the personality of Lieut. Pavlichenko', and the men, 'though well received, were less easy and did not compete for interest'. 'Special enthusiasm' for Lieut. Pavlichenko is reported from women and 'younger intellectuals'. As is remarked in the report from Wales, 'Here was a young woman who had proved herself capable of playing a man's part in the greatest struggle of all ages, and who through it all had preserved the natural charms of womanhood.'

On the other hand, a minority of people in four Regions are said to have been 'horrified' by what is described as the 'blood lust' of the Russians, and to have deplored 'the savagery of applauding a monster whose only claim to fame is that she shot three hundred men'. Some older people in the Southern Region are also said to have considered Lieut. Pavlichenko's character to be 'quite alien to our womanhood'. In Birmingham it was doubted if 'any sniper could last long enough to kill three hundred men', and it was rumoured that 'she was a fraud and did not know how to hold a gun'.

THE DELEGATES' SPEECHES

The delegates' speeches are said to have been applauded everywhere. In Scotland they were voted 'excellent' and were listened to 'with rapt attention, even though they were in Russian'. Their interpretation of the speeches was highly praised in Manchester, but was criticised in the Midland Region for being 'rather flat.'

THE PURPOSE OF THE VISIT

So brief were the delegates' visits, and so full their programmes, that some people found it difficult to believe that a serious attempt was being made 'to study the war effort'. Indeed, apart from Manchester students, few people seem to have regarded this as the purpose of the delegates' tour. In three Regions there appears to have been little 'knowledge of why they came'. In others various suppositions were made, two reports suggesting they were here to 'harangue' rather than to study conditions; other reports suggested that they came to promote Anglo-Soviet relations and to help to increase production. In Scotland they were simply regarded as 'distinguished visitors with a first-hand story to tell'.

THE ARRANGEMENTS FOR THE TOUR

In the Midland, North-Western and Scottish Regions, the chief criticism of the tour was 'that the programme was far too heavy'; on their arrival in Glasgow the delegates were reported to have been 'tired out', and 'their weariness was unnecessarily increased' by attending at least five press conferences during their twenty-four hours' stay. There were also complaints of incomplete travelling arrangements, and about the organisation of the Youth Meeting at Glasgow.

The representatives of youth organisations were apparently not invited to this meeting until the afternoon of the day on which it took place; 'many of them did not know what was expected of them until they arrived at the hall'. In Birmingham, people 'concerned with local government deplored the fact that the visit was not properly organised by one body, like the Ministry of Information'.

HOME INTELLIGENCE SPECIAL REPORT NO. 39

PUBLIC FEELING ABOUT HOUSING

11 MARCH 1943

A note submitted by Mass Observation, but not sponsored by Home Intelligence.

Of late, housing has become a prominent subject of discussion amongst all those concerned with post-war reconstruction. What are the homes built after the war going to look like? What sort of homes do the people want? During the last two years, Mass Observation has been making an intensive study of housing problems, collecting facts about people's attitudes to their present homes, and probing their wishes about houses built after the war.

People were visited in their homes in several parts of England in flats, garden cities, housing estates and old houses, comparative data being collected for each type of home. Asked whether they liked or disliked their home, they answered as follows:

80% on housing estates liked their home
79% in garden cities liked their home
78% in flats liked their home
62% in old houses liked their home

Definite single factors influencing people in their attitude to the house or flat in which they live can be traced.

People who have lived in their homes for more than ten years liked them more (74%) than people who had lived in them for less than three years (68%).

People who owned their homes liked them more (76%) than people who rented them (70%).

People possessing bathrooms liked their homes significantly more (81%) than those without (61%).

THE KITCHEN

Perhaps the most important single factor influencing people's likes and dislikes of their home was the kitchen. 82% of those who liked their kitchens liked their houses, while only 43% who disliked their kitchens liked their houses.

The kitchen is the most used room in the average working-class home, and the place where the housewife spends most of her waking hours. Yet, it is often the Cinderella of rooms in the home; it is sometimes dark and usually small. Here is a description of a kitchen in a modern block of flats; nearly everyone owning a kitchen of this type liked it, the only complaints coming from a few people who would have liked it a little larger in size:

Each flat is fitted with a very modern kitchenette, containing electric cooker, copper, sink with two draining boards, built-in larders, and built-in cupboards. Water is heated by an efficient stove in the living room.

These kitchens contained almost everything a housewife could want; they were labour-saving and convenient to run, requiring only a minimum amount of cleaning, since all cupboards are built in.

Features found in many other, especially older kitchens, and much disliked, were open dressers, small sinks with tiny or no draining boards, dirty stoves and coppers heated by coal. In several instances, kitchens with three or more doors leading into them were found, making the kitchen cold and draughty. Having to store coal in the kitchen constituted a major grumble and was strongly resented. Instances of badly arranged artificial lighting were often met with.

THE BATHROOM

Baths, bathrooms and lavatories figure prominently in people's housing wants and criticisms. Even the poorer working-class section of the population today feel that they have a right to a bathroom; the question of a bath has become one of the major social dividing lines. Since the last war, the need for a bath even in the more modest types of home has been recognised, and few homes have been built without a bath in the last twenty years. Architects have tried to solve this problem in various ways. In some houses in garden cities, a bath was installed in the kitchen, or more rarely, a bath was put into the third bedroom. In a few houses on housing estates, a sliding wall separates the bathroom from the kitchen, but in the majority of houses the bathroom is upstairs, usually combined with the lavatory. Nearly all these arrangements are unpopular; what people want is a bathroom containing the bath and a sink with hot and cold water laid on to both. (At present in the majority of working-class homes, the only sink found in the house is situated in the scullery, so that the family has to wash and shave there. This is strongly disliked.) But even more disliked is the lavatory-bathroom combination, many asking that these two should be separated, or that there should be a second lavatory in the house, preferably downstairs. Having to heat the bathwater in the copper and pumping it upstairs proved also unpopular, and people constantly asked for an efficient hot water stove.

GARDENS

Possession of a garden is a very important focal point in the whole housing set-up. The average Englishman and Englishwoman dreams of his or her own *home and garden*. When people are asked whether they would like a garden nearly all answer in the affirmative, though there was less demand for gardens in areas where only some of the houses had them.

Gardenless people gave many different reasons for wanting gardens. They are in order of importance:

> Growing vegetables,
> Growing flowers,
> Growing things generally,
> Keeping chickens,
> Relaxation,
> Children to play in,
> Drying, washing.

In fact, people who already had gardens put them to the following uses:

> Growing vegetables,
> Drying washing,
> Growing flowers,
> Nothing.

The majority of people with gardens took pride in them and kept them well, particularly in garden cities where only 9% of neglected gardens were found. In the whole sample, 18% had neglected gardens, often people with children or very old people, who found difficulty in properly cultivating a garden.

OWNING AND RENTING

At present, only a small fraction of the population own their homes; the majority rent them. In this sample, though 24% would have liked to own a house only 7% in fact did so. There was thus a considerable margin of unfulfilled desire to own. A large number of people rented their homes because they either never had the money or opportunity to buy them; in some cases where people lived in flats or housing estates, the home could, in any case, not be bought. A great many people were deterred from owning by the feeling of being tied, once they possessed a house. As some put it, they wanted to be free to retire to the seaside or country, after retiring from work. A few were afraid of the expenses, such as repairs, incurred when owning a house.

On the other hand, a fairly large number of people regretted never having bought a house, many remarking that they might have bought the house in which they lived several times over, had they paid instalments instead of rent. Yet many, though they saw no immediate prospect of owning a home, would like one day to buy their house and settle down.

PRIVACY

Another important, but often overlooked, factor in the whole housing set-up is the strong feeling in favour of privacy in the home. Anything interfering with this privacy is deplored. Living in rooms, sharing a house, sharing a porch or gate (common in housing estates), having a garden that is overlooked, are all disliked; once people are in their own homes, they liked to exclude the rest of the world as much as possible. This is what home means to a young, married girl, who for wartime reasons has not been able to set up a home of her own:

> Home means somewhere that belongs to me. Something that I can call my own. Preferably it should have someone there who shares my life and home and books and wireless set. But primarily it is somewhere where I have the right to refuse others admission. Somewhere that belongs to ME.

The old phrase that 'the Englishman's home is his castle' dies hard. The home means to people the place where they reign, where nothing and nobody is allowed to intrude. They like their home to be part of a larger community, but once inside their home, people want to exclude everything and everyone except their own family.

HOME INTELLIGENCE SPECIAL REPORT NO. 40

AN AMERICAN LOOKS AT AMERICAN TROOPS IN BRITAIN

11 MARCH 1943

The following report was prepared by an American civilian, working in Cambridge and Huntingdon during the first half of March 1943. It is presented as submitted.

SUBJECT OF INVESTIGATION

The state of mind of American troops stationed in England, with particular reference to:

(a) Their attitude toward the English people among whom they are living.
(b) Their attitude toward the coloured American troops with whom they have been sent here.

METHOD OF INVESTIGATION

The investigator, himself an American, wandered about the streets, entered the pubs, the restaurants, the cinema, the barber shop, the bank, the dance hall, the hotels, the shops, the market place, the cafés of the community at all hours of the day and evening. He struck up conversations with American soldiers about matters far afield and, gradually and he trusts imperceptibly, led them around to the subject of the investigation. At no time were the soldiers told an investigation was in progress. The investigator attempted always to conceal his real interests behind a cloak of idle bar-room gossip. He thinks, based on his intimate knowledge of Americans and their habits, that in this process of concealment he was sufficiently successful to justify the statement that the material gathered is at least uncoloured by the self-consciousness, and probably lacks most of the inaccuracies, that usually accompany evidence given for publication.

QUALIFYING NOTES

It should be noted that, although the investigator was wearing civilian clothes, most of the soldiers interrogated did not ask the reason for his presence in the district. In three instances, when the question *was* asked, the investigator replied that he was in England on a writing assignment for a New York magazine. The explanation did not result in a noticeable diminution of the desire to impart information. On the contrary. There was an immediate increase in loquacity and variety of information. The investigator attempted to take this artificial increase into consideration in assessing the facts thus divulged.

The conclusions in this report are based exclusively on information extracted, either by direct statement or by eavesdropping, from men in the ranks and non-commissioned officers. Although the investigator was successful in drawing several commissioned officers into conversation, he found that their statements were far from spontaneous. These officers were friendly enough, but guarded in their comment and so generally noncommittal in their opinions that the investigator decided to dismiss their evidence completely rather than run the risk of weighting his conclusions by what appeared to be deliberately, although not maliciously, jaundiced evidence.

In all, 23 American soldiers were talked to at some length, about 30 contributed evidence by joining conversations to agree or disagree or in some way add to a discussion already underway, and about 40 soldiers were eavesdropped upon in the midst of discussions among themselves. No Negro soldiers were talked to or eavesdropped upon.

To avoid the cumbersome process of documenting each conclusion with a statistical table of the number of conversations on which it is based, the investigator has decided to employ the device of a hypothetical spokesman who shall be known, in this report, as 'the American soldier in England'. At the risk of being tedious, the investigator would like to point out that, so far as he knows, the individual he has labelled 'the American soldier' does not exist. He is an artificial mouthpiece, a composite portrait, a mosaic constructed of bits culled from various sources, a blending of opinions that run all the way from vigorous statements to indifferent shoulder shrugs. Similarly, the words 'in England' actually mean 'in Cambridge and Huntingdon'.

FINDINGS

A. GENERAL

The American soldier in England is not completely at ease. Although attempts have been and are constantly being undertaken, by his own morale units and by the English people around him, to make him comfortable and welcome, he does not feel thoroughly at home. He appreciates the attempts, and is in fact surprised by their intensity, but he cannot help feeling that they are doomed inevitably to fall short of their ultimate goal. He is, against his wishes, a stranger in a foreign land. He would prefer to be in the only place where he feels really comfortable, namely, at home in America. He realises, however, that the necessities of war make this, for the moment, impossible. He considers himself fortunate, therefore, to be stationed in a foreign land where the people are friendly and, apparently of tremendous importance, speak his language or, as he thinks of it, a sufficiently close variation of his language to serve most practical purposes.

The excitement of coming to a new country (none of the men who contributed evidence had ever been to England before and only one had ever been outside the United States: a two-day business trip to Montreal, Canada) has worn off. This novelty did not last very long. The excitement aroused by the exotic quality of a foreign land visited for the first time, to which he had looked forward, proved disappointing. The points of difference between American and English life, although many, proved to be differences of degree rather than of kind. There was, therefore, not enough excitement to outweigh the discomforts, which he hastens to add were minor. It would not be inaccurate to wonder whether he *really* considers them minor.

The American soldier in England wonders a trifle wistfully how it would be if he were stationed in Australia where, he has heard, and this is somewhat paradoxical in view of the original desire for exotic experience, the people and their customs are closer to America. He says (about half the soldiers interviewed raised this point themselves) that he thinks he would prefer to be stationed in a totally foreign land, North Africa, for example, because there he would know he couldn't possibly expect even remote similarities with the life he knew at home. (Several soldiers added, however, that they knew the grass always seemed greener in another pasture and they stated, with wry grins, that if they were transferred to North Africa they would probably regret the change in a short time.)

On the whole, therefore, the American soldier in England is not happy, but it is also true that he is not unhappy. He is, in short, a human being transplanted from his home against his will.

(Whenever the opportunity arose the investigator asked if they, the soldiers, thought their feelings would be different if they had come to England of their own free will, as tourists, rather than as soldiers. Most of the men answered in the affirmative. Some shrugged and said they didn't know. None made a negative reply.)

The American soldier in England has gone through a period of adjustment that, although it has not resulted in the ideal Anglo-American relationship, nevertheless has borne comparatively happy fruit. He admits himself that it could have ended in a fashion far worse than the situation that exists at present.

He arrived in a fairly eager, almost zealous, frame of mind. He is neither an intense student of politics and international affairs nor is he even an analytical newspaper reader, but he had the impression that England was in a difficult position, that she needed help, that she had asked her traditional friend, ally, and comrade-in-arms, America, to give her that help. The American soldier in England arrived with the expectation that he would be welcomed with open arms. He was welcomed, of course, but the open arms were more in the nature of a gesture than a spontaneous movement prompted by the heart. The American soldier in England, knowing nothing in the beginning of British reserve or the Englishman's true feelings toward America in this particular conflict, but highly sensitive to variations from the open-handed, loud, cheery, easy-going camaraderie to which he has been accustomed since infancy, was rocked back on his heels and flung into a period of bewilderment not unmixed with resentment.

(Only one of the soldiers interviewed still harboured this resentment and he, at the time of the interview, was much the worse for liquor. The investigator considers it an open question, as well as a reflection on his ability as an observer, whether the soldier in his cups, with all his unconscious censors out of action, was not closer to the truth than his more sober fellows.)

The American soldier in England is not quite certain (perhaps it would be more accurate to say the investigator was unable to discover) precisely what it was that brought him through this dangerous period of bewildered resentment to what he considers the present state of reasonably good relations with the British people. He is inclined to attribute it to a gradual and perhaps fortuitous muddling through to an approximate understanding of the two things previously mentioned, about which originally he knew nothing: British reserve and the Englishman's true, as differentiated from the editorial writer's, feeling toward America in this particular conflict.

Unfortunately, the American soldier in England is unable to state clearly the nature of his new understanding of these two things, although he is able to give many examples of how he, the American soldier in England, has learned to combat, or rather live harmoniously with, them. Many of these examples are frankly cynical. More are unconsciously cynical. Some, however, by far in the minority, are the products of unalloyed sincerity. The balance of this report is devoted to a statement and, wherever possible, explanation of as many of these samples as the investigator was able to discover.

B. SPECIFIC

The American soldier in England has learned that the violently adjectival, frequently brutal, criticism that Americans in high spirits are accustomed to indulge in about their native cities and states is not the blueprint for a successful relationship with

English people. Regardless of what he may feel about England, the American soldier in England has learned not to express himself openly except to his fellows: 'If you want to get along with them, don't knock their country because they can't take it. Just tell them you think everything here is great.'

The American soldier in England, however, does not think everything here is 'great'.

He thinks the country is inexcusably old-fashioned. He concedes that there is something to be said for tradition, but he will not admit that you can say enough in this direction to counter-balance the agonisingly leisurely shopkeepers, the uncomfortable hotels, the outmoded lavatory equipment, the funny trains, the cut of the women's clothes, the style of men's haircuts, the left-hand drive, the slovenly business offices, and the dozens of other things that visiting Americans have, with a singular lack of either originality or effect, been mentioning for years.

He thinks the monetary system is an example of carrying a national joke a bit too far. He doesn't take pounds and shillings really seriously and, knowing very little or almost nothing about the workings of international rates of exchange, he is convinced they are part of an elaborately contrived device for extracting dollars from the pockets of visiting Americans as quickly as possible.

He prefers the English civilian to the English soldier. He gets along better with the Englishman and the Englishwoman of middle and later years than with the young people, except the girls. He feels that the English soldier is jealous of him because he earns more money and resents him because it looks as though he has come over here to win a war that the English soldier has been fighting desperately but without conspicuous success for three- and-a-half years. This is where the American soldier in England grows bewildered. He realises that the British soldier earns less money but he says, with inexorable logic if unnecessary frankness, that he can't do anything about that. He therefore resents the British soldier's resentment. He admits, though he may not sincerely believe, that the British soldier is a great fighter, worthy of respect and admiration, but he cannot escape the incontrovertible fact that here he is, at Britain's request, in uniform and under arms, to *help* the British soldier fight. He does not understand the Englishman's feeling that America is not really helping Britain, that this is as much America's war as it is Britain's war, that Britain stood alone in the gap for a long time, holding the common fort against overwhelming odds, while America dawdled and shirked her responsibility. When this is explained to the American soldier in Britain he nods and says he agrees, but he does not really believe it. He sees, however, that the British soldier *does* believe it. This confuses him. Therefore, as much as possible, he avoids the British soldier.

The American soldier in England has a faintly patronising attitude toward the British civilian. Because he has always been taught to respect older people, he does not himself realise how much real contempt is mixed in with this apparently only faint patronising attitude. He thinks the lower and middle-class Englishman is docile: satisfied, because of timidity, with far less than the American of similar station in life.

He does not understand the deep, sincere, unshakeable, and universal loyalty to the Crown and the royal hierarchy. He says it is undemocratic, without himself understanding, save vaguely, the true meaning of the word. In spite of himself he is, however, awed by the Crown and the respect it commands. He does not like this involuntary awe. He feels that somehow it is an unfair attack, hitting below the belt, on his principles which, by the way, he cannot define with clarity.

The Englishman's good manners embarrass him. He realises it is better to have good manners than bad, and he wishes half-heartedly that his own manners were better in the Englishman's sense, but he prefers to believe that this universal good breeding is 'sissy' and merely another sign of the Englishman's unmanly docility: 'You'd think they'd say nuts to the politeness and yell their heads off once in a while to get a little more dough for their wives and kids.'

The Englishman's precision of speech, the clarity of his enunciation, embarrass the American soldier in England. The fact that even an English waitress seems to talk 'better' than he does makes the American soldier in England feel uncouth. This manner of talking is associated, erroneously but firmly, in his mind with the upper classes. He thinks of it as a sort of national Harvard accent, put on deliberately by an entire nation instead of a small snobbish group in his own country, to make the outlander feel inferior, to 'ritz' him. It *does* make him feel inferior and, as a result, he is derisive about other things: 'They ought to lay off this cheerio stuff and learn how to eat right.'

He thinks English food is abominable, English cooking inexcusable, English coffee atrocious, English restaurants unclean, English waitresses untrained, English dietary habits unhealthy. When he is asked to remember that he is talking about, and living in, an island nation, dependent almost entirely on ocean commerce for its produce, a nation that has been totally at war in many theatres all over the world for three-and-a-half years, he stops carping, seems embarrassed for several moments, as though he has been caught berating a child for its inability to get a man's work done, then shrugs truculently and says 'I hear it wasn't a hell of a lot better in peacetime.'

The American soldier in England realises he is drinking too much, far more than he drinks at home, and he admits it, but says 'What else is there to do?' The alternatives suggested do not strike him as convincing.

He prefers the English girl to the English young man. He feels an English young man will be nice to you when you are facing him, but the moment your back is turned he will 'do' you. He attributes this to jealousy and is secretly proud of it.

He has very little sincere respect for English girls. By and large, he is convinced they are all inferior to American girls, in beauty, in intelligence, in knowledge of the world, in smartness of clothes, in traditional submission to men, in the use of make-up, in the ability to dance, in independence of spirit, in verve. His attitude toward them is that they are all that is available and will have to do until he gets back to God's country. He considers them all fair game. He is convinced he can sleep with all of them and, without much prompting, will substantiate his statement with a variety of detailed and colourful examples out of his allegedly personal experience. He says they live dull, stodgy, drab existences, work far too long hours for too little pay, and didn't know what a good time meant until the Americans came along. He says he can cut out any Englishman, soldier or civilian, with any girl and admits freely that this is due in large measure to his novelty as a visitor from a country where beautiful clothes are ridiculously inexpensive and the world's best dance bands grow on trees, and the fact that even on the pay of a soldier he has more money to spend than any Englishman these girls are accustomed to going out with. He realises this is not contributing toward his popularity with Englishmen, particularly English soldiers, and he admits this is unfortunate, but he has no intention of voluntarily giving up his concrete advantage for so nebulous a thing as better Anglo-American relations.

The Negro question makes him angry.

(On this point the investigator would like to depart somewhat from his device of an artificially created mouthpiece. It is the one subject on which the investigation proved most unsuccessful. The moment the question was raised, however obliquely, the soldier to whom it was addressed seemed to become suspicious. The investigator received the impression, perhaps erroneous, that the soldiers he was interrogating had been either badgered in this respect to the point of distraction or they had been warned, perhaps by other American soldiers or their officers, to avoid discussing it. Some facts, very few, were brought to the surface of several conversations and others were gleaned from such unreliable things as facial expressions and pregnant shrugs. On the whole, the investigator would not regard his findings in this connection as anything more than contributory evidence toward a later and more thoroughly documented conclusion.)

If he comes from a southern state, the American soldier in England is angry with the American authorities for putting the Negro into the army, with the Negro for daring to don the same uniform he wears, and with the English people for not sharing his views about the Negro. If the American soldier in England comes from a northern or, as the phrase goes, more enlightened state, he is angry with the southern soldier for bringing his bigotry into a war and into a foreign country where enough misunderstandings exist already, with the American authorities for not having enough sense to work out some discreet system of segregation similar to that which operates in the northern cities of the United States, and with the English people, who have never had to face the problem, for daring to take sides in a dispute about which they know nothing and in which the dictates of pure reason, elementary liberalism, and simple decency do not, unfortunately and according to all past experience, point the way to a solution. Aside from the southern white soldier, who has never been able to think straight or see anything but red on the Negro question, this particular problem to the American soldier in England arouses feelings similar to those that, let us say, Job might have experienced if, after all the sufferings he bore with so much patience, he found that someone had stolen his last razor blade. It is the last straw.

For all these points of difference with the English people (there are undoubtedly others not revealed by this rather cursory investigation, just as there are a great many other points of identity and harmony), England, to the American soldier stationed in it, is the traditional ally, the homeland of the mother tongue, the country of Dickens and Shakespeare and Keats, the fountainhead of much of spiritual beauty and worth that was hammered into him by his parents, his teachers, his school books, his childhood songs, even some of his games. He does not use these words to express this feeling, but he comes fairly close. (Even the most illiterate soldiers interrogated spoke respectfully of 'this guy Shakespeare.' During the height of one soldier's vitriolic and not unfunny comments about the filthy towels in the barber shop where he had had his hair cut that morning and the long, infuriatingly patient queue in front of the cinema where he had spent the afternoon, the investigator asked if the speaker thought these sufficient reasons for refusing to fight by England's side in this war or for fighting on the side of the Axis where, with the assistance of America's genius for laundry equipment and her talent for efficiency, the barber shop towels in Berlin would soon be spotless and the queues in front of Rome's cinema theatres would disappear overnight, the caustic and critical soldier almost started a brawl before the investigator could complete his hasty assurance that he was speaking in jest.)

CONCLUSION

The American soldier in England is, first and foremost, fortunately or unfortunately, an American. This means that, along with many other and better things, he thinks his country is the best and only place in all the world, that every other country, ally or enemy, will fall short of this to him faultless standard, and that, for better or for worse, he will insist, against all advice, pleas, or orders to the contrary, on his right to say so vociferously and often.

Precisely what can be done to change this is not, happily for this investigator, the subject of this investigation.

FINAL NOTE

Most of the findings in this report are on the negative side. This does not mean that relations between the American soldier in England and the British people are hopelessly bad. It is merely a lack of balance in the report due to the fact that the investigator, conscious of friction between American troops and their hosts, was more interested in the points of difference than the points of affinity. Also, it seemed easier to get the soldiers to talk about the things that irked them than the things that pleased them. It is interesting, and highly significant, that in almost every instance, where a grievance was aired exhaustively, the speaker invariably added a comment couched in a variation of these words: 'But don't get the idea I'm kicking. They're (the English people) okay and I'm for them and we'll win this war. It's only that, well, you know …' The unfinished sentence would be completed with a rueful grin, a bewildered shrug, and a suggestion that we all have another. We did.

HOME INTELLIGENCE SPECIAL REPORT NO. 51

COMPLACENCY IN FACTORIES

24 SEPTEMBER 1943

1. ORIGIN, SCOPE AND LIMITATIONS OF ENQUIRY

The enquiry was undertaken at the request of the Ministry of Production, to discover the extent to which complacency exists among workers at present, and the main causes of it.

The following summary is based on reports received from all Regions except the Southern, the South-Eastern and Northern Ireland. Care was taken to discount the fear often expressed by anxious people that complacency will develop as a result of the general good news, and Intelligence Officers were asked to secure evidence about the state of mind of the workers themselves, though no direct investigations were undertaken in factories. Non-factory workers, such as miners and transport workers, have not been included in the enquiry. More than one Intelligence Officer stressed that it had not been possible to make more than a superficial investigation because the time allowed – a fortnight – was too short and also because a number of their contacts were then on holiday. Even so, the reports received show a high measure of agreement on the causes of complacency.

It should be noted that, though some of their reports were not completed till later, Intelligence Officers finished their investigation by September 1, before the Allied landings on the Italian mainland and Italy's capitulation.

2. WHAT IS COMPLACENCY?

Complacency is not the best word to describe the state of mind revealed by this enquiry. One report points out that 'possibly no two correspondents would agree exactly as to the characteristics of a complacent worker'. Not many people are reported to be complacent, in the dictionary meaning of 'self-satisfied, in pleasant mood', but if complacency is taken to mean the lack of a sense of urgency, then it appears to be the mood of a large minority. Indeed, in so far as a sense of urgency is dependent on a sense of extreme crisis – as at the time of Dunkirk – its decline may be regarded as widespread, though not necessarily affecting the workers' output. For the purpose of this report, then, complacency is taken to mean a lack of the sense of urgency which does adversely affect the worker's output. It should, however, be borne in mind that this lack of urgency may take different forms according to the causes underlying it: it may show itself as over-optimism, light-heartedness, contentment with present conditions, lethargy, apathy, boredom, indifference, grumbling, uneasiness, cynicism or frustration. All these are mentioned in reports, frequently as better describing people's mood than does complacency.

3. HOW WIDESPREAD IS COMPLACENCY?

It is not possible to say to what extent a lack of urgency exists among workers at present, to such a degree as adversely to affect their output. It undoubtedly exists, but reports do not agree as to its extent. The long list of causes (Section 5) given to account for it, however, covers a far wider field than is indicated by the types specifically said to be affected, and is probably a more reliable indication of its extent.

4. WHAT TYPES OF WORKERS ARE PRINCIPALLY AFFECTED?

The following are particularly mentioned:

(a) WORKERS IN OCCUPATIONS NOT DIRECTLY, OR NOT OBVIOUSLY, CONNECTED WITH THE WAR EFFORT, such as workers in the clothing, boot and shoe, and chemical trades. Among some iron and steel workers there is said to be 'a strong feeling that, because they are only making billets, pig iron, joists, plates, etc., they are not doing any actual war work'. Even shipyard workers are not quite exempt from this feeling: 'their work differs so little from that of peace that there is not the same feeling as if they had switched over to war work'. The type of occupation is said to be a more important factor than the grade of the worker.

(b) YOUNG WORKERS, particularly young unmarried workers – women especially – with good pay and no relatives in the Forces; also young men who would rather be in the Forces.

(c) TRANSFERRED WORKERS: This includes workers transferred to another part of the country, often with a resultant sense of grievance, as well as workers transferred from one factory or one workshop to another, without understanding the reason for the change.

(d) DIRECTED LABOUR, particularly people directed into occupations for which they have no liking. Thus, a contact in a shipyard attributes an increase of slacking there since the war to the larger proportion of non-regular shipyard workers, i.e., the casual and directed labour, who have no interest in the work and are anxious to get out of it as quickly as possible.

(e) TIME WORKERS: Those on piece work and bonus schemes are more enthusiastic than those paid by the hour.

(f) THOSE ON MONOTONOUS AND UNSKILLED WORK.

5. WHAT ARE THE CAUSES OF COMPLACENCY AND RELAXED EFFORT?

(These are arranged in order of the frequency with which they were mentioned in reports. The first four – a, b, c & d – appear to be widespread.)

(a) CERTAINTY OF ALLIED VICTORY appears to be the most widespread cause: 'The sense of danger has passed, never to return, and with it has passed the sense of urgency.' The apparent impotence of the Luftwaffe, the absence of heavy raids, the belief that we shall not be invaded and that the Battle of the Atlantic is won, or nearly won — all these have added to the sense of security.

'RECENT GOOD NEWS': It is generally agreed that 'the sense of urgency is being progressively lost as the war situation improves', but it is by no means certain that recent events have greatly hastened the process. Some consider that 'recent good news, by improving people's spirits, has improved health and encouraged people to greater effort and has done much to counter-balance the widespread feeling of fatigue and strain'; it is even thought that it has 'increased the workers' will to finish off the job'. Many people, on the other hand, do not regard the present situation as particularly cheering – in view of 'the delay in opening the second front' and 'doubt as to our relations with Russia' – and compare the present period with that of 'the phoney war'.

(b) DESIRE FOR A SECOND FRONT: For most people, the invasion of Italy seems not to qualify and many of them 'feel the war hasn't started, and won't start till we land in France'. It is considered that the launching of the awaited second front would have a most noticeably bracing effect and would increase output in all types of industry, both by using up the large stocks of arms which are thought to be greatly in excess of present needs, and by involving a larger number of British troops than are actively engaged at present. In the meantime, many are weary or cynical because they feel that: (i) 'We are letting Russia win the war for us' and are not doing our share; (ii) 'Many higher-ups in this country are pleased at the thought of a weakened Russia'; (iii) the Government's handling of the war on the battlefront is too leisurely. Few now believe 'the excuse of lack of arms for a major offensive'.

(c) THE BELIEF THAT POST-WAR CONDITIONS WILL BE WORSE THAN THE PRESENT: There seems to be fairly widespread fear of unemployment and a slump after the war. Many are cynical about post-war plans and ask: 'Why hurry to end the war with the prospect of dole queues instead of good wages?' For many, the war means increased wages and comparative security with the result that they are well satisfied with present conditions. It is thought that if workers could feel some sort of security for the post-war period, there would be more energy put into their war effort.

(d) FATIGUE, STRAIN AND REDUCED VITALITY, both mental and physical. These are attributed to: (i) all the restrictions and difficulties on the home front, such as the blackout, transport, shopping, queuing, etc.; (ii) wartime diet, whether its lack of variety or – for heavy workers – its insubstantiality; (iii) Home Guard and Civil Defence duties added to already long hours. The length of the war and monotony of wartime life are both thought to contribute.

The public's determination to have a holiday away from home at all costs this year has been attributed far more to the physical and mental need

for it than to the feeling that the war is as good as won – though this has
seemed to justify a holiday.

(e) 'THE GULF BETWEEN WORKERS AND MANAGEMENTS' and the
workers' distrust of the managements. There is a feeling among workers
that 'the mainspring of industry is still profit for the employer'.

Managements and foremen are accused of indifference and are
variously blamed for 'failing to provide an incentive to work', particularly
in not explaining the reason for hold-ups, etc.; for 'bad supervision'; for
'failing to take Production Committees seriously'. Examples are given
of the good results when managements try to increase workers' interest,
either in overcoming their boredom by putting them on a different type of
machine, or by publicising the success of their products in the fighting line.

(f) INCOME TAX, particularly in connection with overtime, as workers
'don't see why they should work extra, just to pay the money back to the
Government'. The method of deduction, too, means that 'some workers do
not like to earn too much money in the summer when working hours are
longer, as the tax on these earnings will have to be paid in the winter, when
earnings are least'.

(g) HIGH WAGES, with little opportunity for spending, tend to make some
people work only the minimum number of hours necessary to earn a
livelihood.

(h) THE BELIEF THAT WE HAVE PILED UP ENORMOUS QUANTITIES
OF WAR MATERIAL WHICH IS NOT BEING USED: This belief has
been confirmed by:

(1) The present change-over in industry. Staff reductions in munition
factories; transfers of labour; the closing down of some factories
and the partial operation of the full capacity in others; rumours
of cancelled contracts – all these give workers the impression that
'things are slackening off' and that there is less need for effort.
Insufficient work, resulting in enforced idleness, may be interpreted
either as evidence of surplus production or merely as 'just another
example of mismanagement'.

(2) Press reports and 'speeches of prominent men extolling the enormous
production of Britain and America'. For example, 'workers in Singers,
Dalmuir, say that Sir Andrew Duncan told them some time ago that
we have as many small arms as will last us for the next 18 months'.

(i) SUSPICION OR DISTRUST OF THE GOVERNMENT, particularly over:

(1) The second front and co-operation with Russia.
(2) The Beveridge Plan and post-war conditions.
(3) Muddle or inefficiency – whether on the part of industrial
managements or in the administration of the home front – which
the Government is thought to cause or condone.

Thus, Government officials, inspecting industrial plants, are
considered to be either 'stupid or inside the racket, when machines

that have been idle for years are set going, or models – produced perhaps years before – are laid out as if just off the bench'.

Transferred workers – especially those transferred to England from Scotland and Wales – are said to be bitter about the Government for what they consider lack of planning and disregard of workers.

(j) INABILITY TO RELATE THE PRODUCT OF THEIR LABOUR TO THE NEEDS OF THE WAR EFFORT (See Section 4 (a)).

(k) RESENTMENT AT INEQUALITIES, particularly:

    (1) Inequality of wages, especially between skilled and unskilled: 'Men do not like to find their daughters bringing home pay packets that are as big and in some cases bigger than their own, for work that they regard as being much lighter and less arduous.'

    (2) Inequality of sacrifice, such as: 'restricted holidays for the workers while the wealthy go away; overcrowded transport for the workers while the wealthy use taxis; the combing of shops by the leisured while the workers have no time for shopping; preferential treatment of the "better-to-do" in shops; discrimination in the call-up'.

(l) THE BAD INFLUENCE OF PARTICULAR WORKERS: 'One grouser, or one man who has "not had a fair deal", will effectively distract work in one workshop, outweighing any effects of news or appeals.' So, too, will 'the idle youth or the flashy girl, who ought not to continue in such employment', but are sometimes protected from dismissal by their Union or the Essential Work Order.

HOME INTELLIGENCE SPECIAL REPORT

THE PRESENT STATE OF FEELING ON THE SUBJECT OF THE BEVERIDGE REPORT AND THE GOVERNMENT'S FORTHCOMING PROPOSALS ON SOCIAL SECURITY

21 APRIL 1944

This summary is based on reports from all Regions except Northern Ireland. Intelligence Officers were asked particularly for details of the public's expectations, hopes and fears in connection with:

1. The Beveridge proposals as a whole.
2. The rates of benefit. Are people thinking of definite figures or of figures related to cost of living? Have they any definite figures in mind?
3. The future of industrial insurance and the approved societies.
4. The date of starting any scheme which may be introduced.

The enquiry was limited by time and by the need for a confidential approach to contacts and the avoidance of direct questions. The results, except under the first general heading, are extremely meagre; they may be summarised as follows:

1. THE BEVERIDGE PROPOSALS AS A WHOLE

A. ARE PEOPLE TALKING ABOUT THEM?

The proposals are little mentioned by the public at the present time, though they continue to be discussed by those specially interested in social reforms and post-war reconstruction, and by discussion groups.

The scheme is not forgotten, however, and a general underlying interest in it continues, though the details have largely faded from people's minds.

Reasons given to account for the present absence of general discussion are:

(i)   A feeling of CYNICISM or DISILLUSIONMENT about post-war conditions in general and, in particular, the Government's intentions regarding them.

(ii) The COMPETING CLAIMS of (a) more immediately urgent matters such as the impending second front, the need to win the war first, and present housing difficulties; (b) positive Government plans announced since the publication of the Beveridge Report, such as the Education Bill and, to a lesser extent, the National Health Scheme. The application of PAYE has also distracted attention from other financial proposals affecting personal earnings.

(iii) WAR-WEARINESS and over-work.

B. WHAT IS THE PUBLIC'S ATTITUDE TO THE BEVERIDGE PROPOSALS?

The public as a whole appears to be as strongly in favour of the Beveridge Plan – or a scheme on similar lines – as they were when it first appeared. The working and poorer classes especially look on it as capable of 'turning the country into a paradise'.

Nevertheless, people seem to be very hazy as to its provisions; to the majority it simply means security and greater benefits in times of need.

Objection to the scheme comes, as before, from a minority who wonder who is to pay for it all and whether the country can afford it. Some middle- and upper-class people, in particular, object to 'having to foot the bill to provide for those who are too idle to provide for themselves'. Other objections come from those, especially older people, who think it will kill initiative and enterprise, and from employers who fear the reduced incentive to work which may result from the scheme.

C. WHAT DOES THE PUBLIC THINK IS THE GOVERNMENT'S ATTITUDE TO THE PROPOSALS?

There is widespread suspicion of the Government's attitude to the Beveridge Plan. A great many, perhaps the majority, are convinced that it will be either shelved, mutilated or whittled away, or else an inferior substitute put forward instead. It is frequently referred to as 'the carrot in front of the donkey to keep us going during the war'. It is not understood why the Government should get Beveridge to compile such a comprehensive report and then hold it up.

The Government's claim to be able to improve on Beveridge (the Minister of Health, February 26) is regarded cynically by those who mention it: 'Let's have the report first; improve on it afterwards.'

A number of people regard the National Health Service Scheme as a substitute for the Beveridge Plan; workers in particular saying that it is a way of fobbing them off with an inferior Beveridge Plan.

A minority, however, are hopeful that the Government will either implement the Beveridge proposals or come out with a social security scheme of their own in due course.

2. THE RATES OF BENEFIT

The rates of benefit are little discussed and rarely in any detail. The present rates are regarded as inadequate and there is strong objection to any means test.

People do not seem to be thinking in terms of specific figures. Isolated – and somewhat contradictory – comments of this kind only are mentioned, e.g. workers wanting benefits to be at least three-quarters of their present wage; future benefits should be double the present figure; benefits should be inclusive, covering health, unemployment, and a pension of £2 a week for man and wife, with some allowance for general expenses.

Among the few who make spontaneous comment, opinion is divided as to whether benefits should relate to the cost of living or should be fixed. Those in favour of fixing a constant amount feel that the cost of living figures are rather artificial and illusory; and that if the worst came to the worst, pressure could always be brought to bear on the Government to raise the fixed amount.

Some objection is reported that a weekly contribution of 4/- (which some people have in mind as a premium) is too high. As it is, many working people grumble at the deductions from their pay. It is even suggested, in one report, that there may be a demand for increased wages to cover the outgoings, 'if and when the Beveridge Plan is put into execution'.

3. THE FUTURE OF INDUSTRIAL INSURANCE AND
THE APPROVED SOCIETIES

This is also little discussed. Many workers believe that these societies, and in particular the Prudential Assurance Co., are 'the powerful interests which are preventing the Government from passing the scheme'.

What evidence there is suggests that the public would like to see the disappearance of the Prudential and other large assurance companies, their functions being replaced by state insurance; though reasons for this are not usually given. Some people feel that a reduction in the number of organisations now disbursing relief would be an advantage; there is criticism, too, of the difference in cash and other benefits (dental and medical) given by various approved societies. Many feel that a big national scheme would make for uniformity in benefits. There is also some feeling that 'the less reputable insurance societies need cleaning up' and that if a national Beveridge scheme were to supplant them, 'unprotected, trustful and exploited people would get a fair deal'. According to the North-Western Region report, 'the reputations of certain companies (particularly the Prudential) are far from good in this part of the country'.

4. THE DATE FOR STARTING ANY SCHEME WHICH MAY BE INTRODUCED

No definite date is suggested. Many profess to doubt whether a Government social security scheme will ever materialise; or say 'only when doctors and insurance companies are assured that it will be a good thing for them as well as the working class'.

Those who do expect a Government scheme variously suggest 'when the war in Europe is over'; 'immediately the war ends'; or vaguely 'sometime after the war'.

On this point, as on all other points of detail, hopes and expectations are vague.

5. CONCLUSIONS

The public as a whole wants the Government to implement the Beveridge Report. The detailed contents of the Report – even the simpler financial details – are not generally known. The Report is seen as offering security against unemployment, ill health, and old age; but even more is it seen as a touchstone of the Government's intentions for the post-war world.

It is widely – if not generally – believed that the Report has been shelved; or that the public will in due course be offered a watered-down version.

It would appear, therefore, important that if the Government proposals are to be accepted willingly, they should neither deviate, nor appear to deviate, fundamentally, except where they are more generous, from those of the Beveridge Report. Furthermore, the more closely they can be linked with the name Beveridge the more likely are they to be welcomed.

ABBREVIATIONS

AA	anti-aircraft
AEF	American Expeditionary Force
AMGOT	Allied Military Government of Occupied Territory
ARP	Air Raid Precautions
ATC	Air Training Corps
ATS	Auxiliary Territorial Service
BBC	British Broadcasting Corporation
BEF	British Expeditionary Force
BMA	British Medical Association
CAB	Citizens' Advice Bureau
CD	Civil Defence
COs	conscientious objectors
EAM	Greek National Liberation Front
ELAS	Greek People's Liberation Army (military wing of EAM)
EPT	excess profits tax
EWO	Essential Work Order
FFI	French Forces of the Interior (French resistance)
GATC	[possibly] Girls' Auxiliary or Girls' Training Corps
GCB	Knight Grand Cross of the Order of the Bath
GFP	General Forces Programme
GTC	Girls' Training Corps
HE	high explosive
HG	Home Guard
HP	horsepower
ICI	Imperial Chemical Industries

IRA	Irish Republican Army
KO	knockout
LMS	London, Midland and Scottish Railway Company
MO	medical officer
MOI	Ministry of Information
NAAFI	Navy, Army and Air Force Institutes
NCO	non-commissioned officer
NFS	National Fire Service
PAC	pilotless aircraft
PAYE	pay-as-you-earn
PPC	prospective parliamentary candidate
RA	Royal Artillery
RAF	Royal Air Force
RDC	Rural District Council
RIO	Regional Information Officer of the Ministry of Information
RAOC	Royal Army Ordnance Corps
RN	Royal Navy
ROF	Royal Ordnance Factory
SHAEF	Supreme Headquarters Allied Expeditionary Force
TU	trade union
TUC	Trades Union Congress
USAAF	United States Army Air Forces
VAD	Voluntary Aid Detachment
VC	Victoria Cross
VD	venereal disease
WAAF	Women's Auxiliary Air Force
WAEC	War Agricultural Executive Committee
WLA	Women's Land Army
WRNS	Women's Royal Naval Service
WVS	Women's Voluntary Services
WX	women's extra

GLOSSARY

A.1: medical category.

Abbot of Downside: in February 1944 the Rt. Rev. Sigebert Trafford, abbot of the Benedictine monastery of Downside, justified the bombing of Monte Cassino abbey as a vital military necessity.

ABCA pamphlet: in December 1942 a briefing pamphlet on the Beveridge report, prepared by the Army Bureau of Current Affairs for discussion in the army, was withdrawn by the War Office. This was on the grounds that ABCA discussions of the report ought to be postponed until parliament had had a chance to debate the report, and that the impression might be given that the report was already settled government policy when in fact no decisions had yet been reached on its recommendations.

Aberdare Hall: university residence in Cardiff.

access to coastal areas: in April 1943 new regulations came into force which meant that along the east and south coasts, from the Humber to Penzance, and up to a depth of ten miles inland, access to visitors could be either restricted or completely barred without prior notice by the military authorities. It was stated that this was not just connected to the risk of invasion but also to the use of the country as a base for offensive operations.

Agar, Lieutenant Commander Herbert: special assistant to the US Ambassador in London, John Winant.

Alexander, A. V.: First Lord of the Admiralty.

Alexander, General Sir Harold: from August 1942, commander-in-chief in the Middle East; from February 1943, deputy Allied commander-in-chief (under Eisenhower) in North Africa, and subsequently the Mediterranean theatre, with command over all the forces actually fighting the enemy; from January 1944, Allied commander-in-chief in Italy.

American battle schools: areas allotted to the US army as battle training grounds.

Amery, Leo: Secretary of State for India and for Burma.

ammunition train incident: in June 1944 the driver of an ammunition train, Benjamin Gimbert, noticed that a fire had broken out in the front wagon of his train whilst approaching Soham station in Cambridgeshire. Rather than leaving the train, Gimbert instructed the train fireman, James Nightall, to uncouple the burning wagon, which contained ten tons of bombs, from the other fifty ammunition wagons with a view to using the engine to tow it to the safety of open country. However, whilst the leading wagon was being moved away from the station it exploded with great force. Nightall was killed, as was a signalman, Frank Bridges. Gimbert was seriously injured. For their gallantry in preventing an even greater catastrophe at Soham, Gimbert and Nightall were awarded the George Cross.

Anderson, Sir John: from September 1943, Chancellor of the Exchequer.

Anderson shelter: outdoor domestic air-raid shelter named after Sir John Anderson who, as Lord Privy Seal in 1938, initiated its development.

Angell, Sir Norman: writer and foreign policy commentator. He was awarded the Nobel Peace Prize for 1933.

Anglo-Russian agreement: in July 1941 Britain and the Soviet Union signed an accord under which they agreed to assist each another in the war against Germany and refrain from making any separate peace with Hitler.

Anglo-Soviet Treaty: a treaty of May 1942 that formalized and amplified the Anglo-Russian agreement, and committed the two parties to work together after the war to secure peace and prosperity in Europe.

animus: hostility.

approved societies: private insurance companies and other agencies approved to administer social benefits under the National Insurance Act of 1911.

Archbishop of Canterbury: the Archbishop, Dr William Temple, died in October 1944.

Ark Royal: Royal Navy aircraft carrier sunk by a U-boat off Gibraltar in November 1941. One crew member was lost. A rumour circulated that the ship had been re-floated.

Armstrong, John: Labour Director at the Ministry of Fuel and Power and former vice-president of the National Union of Scottish Mineworkers.

Arnim, General Hans-Jürgen von: German commander in Tunisia who succeeded Rommel when the latter left North Africa in March 1943. Von Arnim was captured in May.

Assistance Board: provided public assistance to those in financial distress.

Astor, Lady: Conservative MP for Plymouth Sutton.

Atlantic Charter: declaration drawn up by Britain and the United States in August 1941 that set out a series of 'common principles' for a 'better future for the world'.

ATS hostel victims: in May 1943 a hostel in Great Yarmouth, Norfolk, used by members of the ATS, was bombed during a German air raid. Twenty-six female auxiliaries were killed.

Attlee, Clement: leader of the Labour party and, from February 1942, Deputy Prime Minister in the coalition government.

Auchinleck, General Sir Claude: from July 1941 to August 1942, commander-in-chief in the Middle East; he was also briefly commander of the Eighth Army from June to August 1942; from June 1943, commander-in-chief in India.

Axis: the powers – principally Germany, Italy and Japan – that opposed the Allied powers.

Badoglio, Marshal Pietro: appointed prime minister of Italy after the fall of Mussolini in July 1943. He had commanded Italian forces in Abyssinia in 1935–36. He resigned in June 1944.

Baedeker raids: the targets of these bombing raids were reputedly selected from the German Baedeker travel guide to Britain and met the criterion of having been awarded a three-star rating in the handbook.

bait: packed lunch.

balloon barrage: large balloons, tethered with metal cables, to defend against low-flying enemy aircraft.

ballot system: owing to a shortage of manpower in the coal industry it was decided that thousands of young men, who would otherwise be called up for the armed forces, would instead be required to serve in the mines. In December 1943 Ernest Bevin announced that ballots would be held to select randomly those conscripts who were to be sent to the mines. The draftees became known as 'Bevin boys'.

ban on travel: in March 1944 it was announced that all travel (with very few exceptions) between Britain, on the one hand, and Northern Ireland and *Éire,* on the other, would be suspended for military reasons until further notice. This was reported to be as a result of the refusal of the government of neutral *Éire* to remove Axis consular and diplomatic representatives from *Éire*. In addition to the restrictions on travel to Ireland, in April 1944 travel from Britain to all overseas destinations was suspended. The only exceptions were those who needed to travel overseas on urgent business of national importance.

Barham: Royal Navy battleship sunk by a U-boat off the coast of North Africa in November 1941 with the loss of 868 lives.

Barkers: London department store.

Barlow report: report of a royal commission, under the chairmanship of Sir Montague Barlow, appointed to advise on the distribution of the industrial population. It was published in January 1940.

Barr, Robert: BBC war correspondent.

Bartlett, Vernon: journalist, broadcaster and Independent Progressive MP for Bridgwater.

Basic English: a simplified English, limited to about 850 selected words, intended as a form of international language.

Battle of the Atlantic: long-running naval battle, at its height between 1940 and 1943, during which German U-boats attacked Allied convoys traversing the North Atlantic in an effort to cut Britain's North American supply lines.

Beaverbrook, Lord: from June 1941, Minister of Supply; from 4 February 1942 to 19 February 1942, Minister of Production; from September 1943, Lord Privy Seal.

Beneš, Dr Edvard: head of the Czechoslovak government-in-exile.

Bevan, Aneurin: Labour MP for Ebbw Vale.

Beveridge, Sir William: economist and social reformer. In April 1942, he produced a report for the Board of Trade on domestic fuel rationing. In November 1942, he completed a further report for the Paymaster General on social insurance and allied services.

Bevin, Ernest: prominent trade unionist who served as Minister of Labour and National Service.

Big Ben: nickname for the great bell in the clock tower of the Houses of Parliament in London. Its chimes were broadcast by the BBC before the 9.00 pm news.

billeting: finding temporary accommodation for people, including evacuees, in private households.

Bishop of Chichester: in February 1944 the bishop of this Anglican diocese, Dr George Bell, stated in the House of Lords that while he recognized the legitimacy of concentrated Allied bombing raids on military and industrial targets, and the inevitable loss of civilian life this would entail, the obliteration of German towns and cities was not a justifiable act of war.

Bismarck: German battleship sunk some 600 miles west of Brest in May 1941 after a pursuit by the Royal Navy.

black-coated workers: clerical workers.

black market: illegal trade in officially controlled commodities.

blackout: in September 1939 it was ordered that lights inside buildings had to be obscured during the hours of darkness, and lights outside buildings extinguished (subject to certain exemptions in the case of external lighting for vital war work), in order to prevent them being seen by enemy aircraft during air raids. In September 1944, it was announced that some easing of restrictions would be permitted, except in a few coastal areas. These 'dim-out' concessions included a relaxation of the blacking-out of windows and improved street lighting.

Blitzkrieg: a term, literally meaning 'lightning war', generally used to denote the rapid German military victories in Europe in 1939–41.

Boche: nickname for Germans.

bogey: something that causes alarm.

Bolsheviks: Russian revolutionaries.

bombing of the school: on 20 January 1943, Sandhurst Road School in Catford, London, was bombed by the Luftwaffe. Thirty-eight children and six members of staff were killed.

Bonomi, Ivanoe: anti-fascist politician appointed prime minister of Italy in June 1944.

Boots: drug company and chain of chemist shops.

Boris III, King: king of Bulgaria.

Borstal: a custodial institution for young offenders.

Bracken, Brendan: Minister of Information.

Bradley, General Omar: commander of the US First Army, and then the US Twelfth Army Group, in Normandy.

braggart: boastful.

Brains Trust: BBC discussion programme during which a panel of experts (originally, C. E. M. Joad, Julian Huxley and A. B. Campbell were the main panellists) answered questions submitted by listeners. One such question was 'How does a fly land on the ceiling?'.

British Institute of Public Opinion: British affiliate of George Gallup's American Institute of Public Opinion.

British Israelites: those who advocated that the British people were directly descended from the ten lost tribes of Israel.

British Restaurants: a network of communal feeding centres, run by local authorities, which were intended to provide nutritious meals at affordable prices.

Broch, Theodor: exiled mayor of Narvik, Norway.

Brockington, Leonard: Canadian lawyer and adviser to the Empire Division of the Ministry of Information.

Brown, W. J.: General Secretary of the Civil Service Clerical Association.

browned-off: fed up.

Burma Road: supply route from Burma to south-west China.

Burnham committee: in November 1944 the standing committee that negotiated teachers' pay (which continued to bear the name of its late chairman, Lord Burnham) recommended new salary scales for teachers in publicly maintained schools.

byres: cowsheds.

ca canny: deliberately limiting output.

Cairo conference: Allied conference in Egypt in November 1943 which was attended by Churchill, Roosevelt and Chiang Kai-Shek. It was announced that Japan would be stripped of all the islands in the Pacific it had seized since 1914 and all the territories taken from China restored to the latter. A second Cairo conference was held in December attended by Churchill, Roosevelt and the president of Turkey.

Carretta, Donato: at the trial of Pietro Caruso in September 1944, Carretta, former governor of Rome's Regina Coeli prison, and a prosecution witness, was seized by a mob at the courthouse in Rome and beaten to death. His corpse was hung outside the prison.

carrying of gas masks: in July 1942 the government advised that the public no longer needed to carry gas masks on a daily basis.

Caruso, Pietro: former fascist police chief in Rome who was tried and executed by the Italian authorities in September 1944.

Casey, Richard: Australian politician and diplomat who served as Minister of State in the Middle East from March 1942 to December 1943.

Cassandra: pen name of William Connor, a *Daily Mirror* columnist. In a BBC *Postscript* in July 1941, he launched a vituperative attack on P. G. Wodehouse for consenting to broadcast for the Nazis.

Cassidy, Henry: American journalist who represented the Associated Press in Moscow. In October 1942 Stalin replied to a set of questions put to him by Cassidy about the importance of a second front, the effectiveness of Allied aid to the Soviet Union, and the Soviet capacity for resistance.

catch crops: crops sown between the plantings of the main crop.

Catering Bill: in January 1943 a Catering Wages Bill to regulate pay and conditions in the catering industry was presented to the House of Commons. The bill was passed but over 100 Conservatives voted against.

Catroux, General Georges: Free French commander in the Levant.

Cazalet, Colonel Victor: Conservative MP for Chippenham. In 1940 he was appointed as a British liaison officer to the Free Poles and in July 1943 perished in the plane crash that killed General Sikorski.

Cecil, Lord: president of the League of Nations Union.

cereal zoning: a scheme that limited the range of breakfast cereals available within designated zones in order to reduce transport and ensure an even distribution across the country.

chain stores: a series of shops owned by one company and selling the same goods.

chaining of prisoners of war: in October 1942 it was reported that the Germans had manacled British and Canadian troops who had been captured at Dieppe two months previously. This was said to be a reprisal for the treatment of German soldiers apprehended during the Dieppe raid who were alleged to have had their hands tied, as well as similar instances during the raid on Sark. In retaliation, the British government announced its intention to manacle an equal number of German prisoners.

charwoman: a woman employed to clean a house or premises.

chary: cautious.

Chiang Kai-Shek, General: Chinese nationalist leader.

Churchill, Winston: Prime Minister and Minister of Defence. He succeeded Neville Chamberlain as leader of the Conservative party in October 1940.

Citrine, Sir Walter: General Secretary of the Trades Union Congress.

civil aviation conference: a conference of fifty-four nations held in Chicago in November–December 1944. A convention governing international civil aviation was agreed.

Civil Defence: services to protect the public against the effects of air attack. They included such personnel as air-raid wardens, firefighters, first-aid parties, heavy rescue squads and decontamination teams.

Clayton, Rifleman William: in March 1943, this soldier, who was suffering from tuberculosis, died at an army detention centre at Fort Darland in Gillingham, Kent, after allegedly being struck by a regimental sergeant major and a quartermaster sergeant. The assailants were sent for trial and found guilty of manslaughter. One was sentenced to eighteen months' imprisonment, the other to twelve months'. The competence of the centre medical officer was also called into question.

coastal ban: from 1 April 1944 it was announced that, for reasons of operational security, a coastal belt, roughly ten miles in depth, running from the Wash along the east and south coasts to Land's End, together with some coastal strips around the Firth of Forth, would become protected areas. Only persons who resided in these areas, or who had special reason to enter them, would be permitted access. In July 1944, it was notified that the restrictions would be lifted in the south-west; and in August in other coastal areas of England.

cobblers: those who mend shoes.

colliers: coal miners.

Cologne Cathedral: in June 1943 it was reported that this German cathedral had been damaged during an Allied air raid. Nazi propagandists spoke of an 'intentional assault on a sacred and venerable monument of European art'.

Colonel Blimp: David Low's cartoon character which appeared in the *Evening Standard* in the 1930s. It depicted an irascible and reactionary old army officer.

colour bar: racial discrimination and segregation.

commando raid on Boulogne: in April 1942 a British–Canadian force mounted a reconnaissance raid at Hardelot near Boulogne in France. It was reported that during the raid one of the British officers, a former police inspector, had worn carpet slippers. 'I intend to invade France in comfort', he had quipped.

Comintern: Moscow-backed international communist organization.

Common Wealth party: formed in 1942, and led by Sir Richard Acland, it has been described as a 'middle-class socialist party'. It fielded parliamentary candidates in defiance of the wartime electoral truce and gained a handful of MPs, including John Loverseed who won the Eddisbury by-election.

conchies: conscientious objectors.

Constantine, Learie: Celebrated West Indian cricketer. During the war he was employed by the Ministry of Labour as a welfare officer on Merseyside to assist West Indians who arrived in Britain to work in munitions factories. In July 1943, whilst in London to play for a Dominions' XI against England at Lord's, Constantine and his family were refused accommodation at the Imperial Hotel in Russell Square on racial grounds. In 1944 he was awarded nominal damages of five guineas against the hotel for refusing 'to receive and lodge him'.

Cooke, Alistair: US-based journalist and broadcaster. British born and raised, he was granted US citizenship in 1941.

Cooper, Alfred Duff: from July 1941 to November 1943, Chancellor of the Duchy of Lancaster; briefly Resident Minister at Singapore for Far Eastern Affairs between December 1941 and January 1942.

co-ops: cooperative societies.

corpse-factory stories: during the First World War it was rumoured that the Germans were rendering fat from the bodies of their fallen soldiers to make such commodities as glycerine.

cost plus: a system under which government contracts were awarded on the basis that contractors would be paid reasonable costs plus a specified payment to allow for a profit. This payment could either be a percentage of costs or a fee fixed in advance which did not vary with the costs of the work.

cotes: shelters for birds.

County of London plan: a plan for the post-war reconstruction of the capital produced for the London County Council in 1943 by Patrick Abercrombie, Professor of Town Planning at University College, London, and J. H. Forshaw, architect to the LCC.

coupons: ration books were issued to all members of a household. These books contained coupons, and when rationed commodities were purchased the retailer extracted or crossed off the appropriate coupons.

Coward, Noël: playwright, composer, actor, film maker and wit.

crêpe de chine: a silky fabric.

Cripps, Sir Stafford: Independent MP for East Bristol. From June 1940, British Ambassador in Moscow; from February 1942, Lord Privy Seal and Leader of the House of Commons; from November 1942, Minister of Aircraft Production.

Croft, Lord: Parliamentary Under-Secretary of State for War.

Crowther, Geoffrey: editor of *The Economist*.

Cunningham, Lieutenant-General Sir Alan: from September to November 1941, commander of the Eighth Army. Brother of Admiral Sir Andrew Cunningham.

Cunningham-Reid, Captain Alec: Independent MP for Marylebone. He had the Conservative whip withdrawn in 1942.

Curtin, John: prime minster of Australia.

Curzon line: a proposed demarcation line between Poland and the Soviet Union that came to be associated with Lord Curzon, the British Secretary of State for Foreign Affairs during the Polish-Soviet war of 1919–20.

cwt: abbreviation of hundredweight, a unit of weight equivalent to 112 pounds.

Daily Worker: communist newspaper. In January 1941 it was banned on the grounds of 'systematic publication of matter calculated to foment opposition to the prosecution of the war to a successful issue'. The ban was lifted in 1942.

Dakar: Vichy-controlled West African port.

Dalton, Dr Hugh: from May 1940, Minister of Economic Warfare; from February 1942, President of the Board of Trade.

Darlan, Admiral François: commander-in-chief of the Vichy armed forces who had held prominent roles in the Vichy government. By chance, he was in French North Africa when American and British forces landed there in November 1942, and he threw in his lot with the Allies. Controversially, he was recognized as High Commissioner for French North Africa. In December 1942 he was assassinated in Algiers by Fernand Bonnier de la Chapelle, a young French royalist.

Davis, Elmer: Director of the US Office of War Information.

Dawson, Lord: physician-in-ordinary to the King.

debutante: a well-to-do young woman introduced into fashionable society.

defence areas: designated areas of restricted access.

demobilisation: the process of returning servicemen and women to civilian life at the end of the war. Various priorities for release were proposed, but in the end the government settled on a scheme based mainly on a combination of age and length of war service.

Desoutter: a north London engineering company. Its status as a scheduled firm under the Essential Work Order was cancelled by the government after it failed to reinstate one of its employees.

De Valera, Éamon: the Taoiseach – head of the Irish government.

Devonshire: Royal Navy heavy cruiser.

Dill, Field Marshal Sir John: Chief of the Imperial General Staff, 1940–41. After stepping down from his role as CIGS, it was intended that Dill would become Governor of Bombay, but instead he became head of the British joint staff mission in Washington.

dilly-dallying: wasting time through indecision.

Dimbleby, Richard: BBC war correspondent.

diplomatic victory in the Azores: reference to a British–Portuguese agreement of October 1943 to permit British forces to establish bases in the Azores to assist them in their task of protecting merchant ships crossing the Atlantic from the threat of U-boats. In announcing the agreement, Churchill made reference to a 600-year alliance between the two nations, the basis of which was a treaty signed in 1373.

Dobbie, Lieutenant-General Sir William: Governor of Malta, 1940–42.

Dominion troops: a term generally associated with troops from Canada, Australia, New Zealand and South Africa.

doodlebugs: nickname for the German V1 flying bombs.

double summer time: policy of setting the clocks two hours ahead of Greenwich Mean Time over the summer months.

Downing Street: the official residence of the UK prime minister.

drones: people who do no useful work.

Drummond, Professor Sir Jack: nutritional biochemist and scientific adviser to the Ministry of Food.

dual control: system under which both the state and the churches provided school education.

Duke of York: Royal Navy battleship.

Duncan, Sir Andrew: from February 1942, Minister of Supply.

Dunkirk: French port from which the British Expeditionary Force was evacuated back to the UK in May–June 1940.

dunning: making persistent demands for money.

East Grinstead raid: during a German bombing raid on this Sussex town in July 1943, 108 people were killed. Many of the victims, including children, were watching a 'Hopalong Cassidy' film at the local Whitehall cinema.

E-boats: high-speed German naval craft armed with torpedoes.

Eden, Anthony: Secretary of State for Foreign Affairs.

Edwards, Anne: journalist for *Woman* magazine.

egg distribution scheme: in June 1941 it was announced that the supply of home-produced eggs would be controlled and producers would be required to sell their output to licensed packers or approved buyers.

Egyptian crisis: in February 1942 Sir Miles Lampson, the British Ambassador in Cairo, surrounded the royal palace with tanks and King Farouk was forced to appoint *Muṣṭafā al-Naḥḥās Pasha* to head a pro-British government.

Éire: Irish word for Ireland.

Eisenhower, General Dwight D.: US general who was appointed commander-in-chief of the Allied expeditionary force in French North Africa. Before the landings in North Africa, he had not heard a shot fired in anger. He was subsequently supreme Allied commander in the Mediterranean theatre and then supreme Allied commander of the invasion forces for north-west Europe.

electoral truce: in September 1939 the main political parties in the House of Commons agreed that there would be no contests between them in parliamentary by-elections during the war. The political party that held a seat which became vacant was to be allowed to nominate a new candidate without opposition. This, however, still left open the opportunity for independents and minor party candidates to contest vacant seats.

Emmanuel III, Victor: king of Italy. In June 1944, his royal powers were transferred to his son.

Essential Work (Coalmining Industry) (Amendment) Order: under this order of September 1942, it was an offence for anyone employed in a scheduled coal mining undertaking to absent himself from work without reasonable excuse, be persistently late for work, fail to comply with any lawful and reasonable orders given to him, or persistently behave in such a manner as to impede the effective production of the undertaking. Contraventions of the order were to be reported to investigating officers of the Ministry of Fuel and Power, who could recommend that a National Service Officer of the Ministry of Labour and National Service take proceedings.

Essential Work Order: under this order of March 1941, certain industries were classified as essential to the defence of the realm, the efficient prosecution of the war effort and the life of the community. In these scheduled undertakings the right of the management to sack employees, and of the employees to leave of their own volition, was strictly controlled and in general subject to the special permission of the Ministry of Labour and National Service.

Evans, Admiral Sir Edward: a regional commissioner for London under the civil defence scheme.

Evatt, Dr H. V.: Australian Attorney-General and Minister for External Affairs.

excess profits tax: a tax on the wartime profits of trades and businesses in excess of the profits made at a specified pre-war level.

execution of the merchant seaman for treachery: in November 1942, Duncan Scott-Ford, a British merchant seaman, was executed at Wandsworth prison for treachery. He was alleged to have passed details about the movement of convoys to a German agent in neutral Lisbon and to have toured public houses in the UK to 'pump' fellow merchant seamen for information.

extension of conscription: under the National Service (No 2) Act of December 1941, military conscription was extended to unmarried women between the ages of twenty and thirty who were not employed in vital war work. However, those who did not wish to join one of the women's auxiliary services (the ATS, WAAF or WRNS) had the right to opt for a job in war industry or civil defence. The act also raised the upper age limit for the conscription of men into the armed forces from forty-one to fifty-one. In January 1943 it was announced that single women of nineteen would henceforth be liable for call-up.

Fabricius, Johan: Dutch writer and journalist.

Faenza: town in north-east Italy.

Farm Sunday: a designated day to celebrate the wartime farming community and encourage non-agricultural volunteers to help bring in the harvest.

fascist camp disturbances: in September 1941 three Nazi sympathizers escaped from Peveril internment camp on the Isle of Man. They were quickly apprehended, but their recapture and a misunderstanding over whether they had been fed sparked a riot at the camp.

Ferguson, Mary: journalist and wartime broadcaster.

Fifth Column: term originating from the Spanish Civil War to denote those within a country who were thought to be sympathetic to, or working for, the enemy.

Fighting French: in July 1942 de Gaulle's Free French movement changed its name to Fighting France.

Fire Guard: in August 1941 it was announced that men between the ages of eighteen and sixty in all residential areas vulnerable to bombing were to be made liable for compulsory fire-watching duties with the Fire Guard.

fishing zone scheme: in October 1942 the country was divided into zones for the distribution of white fish from the port of landing to fishmongers and fish fryers. Supplies were to be allocated so as to provide an equal allowance to all areas based on population.

'fit for service, fit for pension': slogan implying that if service personnel were deemed fit enough to serve, and then discharged as unfit, they should be entitled to a war pension.

five American senators: in October 1943 it was reported that, after a tour of the war fronts, a party of US senators had, among other things, criticized Britain for dilatoriness in launching an attack on Burma and deriving improper advantage from Lend-Lease.

flapdoodle: nonsense.

Fleet Air Arm: aviation branch of the Royal Navy.

Fleming report: report of a committee, under the chairmanship of Lord Fleming, appointed to look into the ways in which the association between the public schools and the general educational system might be developed and extended. It was published in July 1944.

Flit: a brand of insecticide.

flower scheme: in January 1943 it was announced that, as a special measure, the government would compensate smaller flower growers who had converted their land from the cultivation of flowers to that of food.

Flying Fortress: American bomber aircraft.

fly papers: sticky strips of paper designed to trap flies.

Food and Drugs (Milk and Dairies) Bill: under this legislation, which was passed in July 1944, the Ministry of Agriculture assumed powers for controlling the conditions under which milk was produced on farms.

food offices: local offices of the Ministry of Food.

food shortage in Bengal: in 1943 there was a devastating famine in Bengal in north-east India. It has been estimated that there were three million famine-related deaths.

footling: trivial and irritating.

four-year plan: in April 1944 a new national four-year wages pact for the coal mining industry was agreed. This sought to introduce greater rationality into the wage system and restore the financial incentive to production.

Franco, General Francisco: Spanish dictator.

Fraser, Sir Ian: Conservative MP for Lonsdale and a governor of the BBC.

Freckleton disaster: in August 1944 a US Liberator bomber crashed on the village of Freckleton in Lancashire during a thunderstorm. Along with the crew, fifty-eight people were killed, including thirty-eight infants at the village school.

French Committee for National Liberation: a central French authority set up in Algiers in June 1943, under the chairmanship of Generals de Gaulle and Giraud, which acted as a de facto government-in-exile. De Gaulle came to dominate the committee. In November 1943 Giraud resigned from this governmental body and in April 1944 was removed from the post of commander-in-chief.

French fleet at Alexandria: in May 1943 a French naval squadron, which had been anchored at the Egyptian port with skeleton crews since the 1940 armistice, came over to the Allies.

French village and Hungarian Jew massacres: in July 1944 it was reported that German troops of an SS division had massacred hundreds of French civilians at Oradour-sur-Glane near Limoges. In the same month it was reported that the German occupation forces in Hungary, in tandem with the collaborating Hungarian government, were deporting Jews to concentration camps in Poland where they were being put to death in gas chambers.

friendly societies: mutual insurance organizations of working-class origin.

Front Line: an official pamphlet, published in 1942, telling the story of civil defence 1940–41.

fuel flashes: public information broadcasts by Freddie Grisewood designed to encourage fuel economy.

Gallacher, William: Communist MP for West Fife.

Gallagher, O. D.: South African–Irish journalist and war correspondent.

Gammans, Captain David: Conservative MP for Hornsey.

Gandhi, Mohandas Karamchand (known as Mahatma Gandhi): Indian nationalist leader. In February 1943 he began a twenty-one-day fast at the Aga Khan's palace in Poona, where he was under detention. During his fast he was reported to have consumed water flavoured with lime juice. He apparently ended it by sipping a tumbler of orange juice.

Garbett, Dr Cyril: Archbishop of York.

Garro-Jones, George: Parliamentary Secretary to the Ministry of Production.

Gaulle, General Charles de: leader of the Free French.

Gaumont-British: film and cinema company.

General Forces Programme: a BBC radio service launched in February 1944.

general post: a party game involving the swopping of seats.

general practitioners: family doctors.

gentile: a person who is not Jewish.

George Cross/Medal: decorations intended primarily for civilian gallantry. The George Cross was ranked next to the Victoria Cross, the George Medal more widely distributed.

German proposals for a bombing truce: in May 1942 it was reported that the New British Broadcasting Station, a German radio station broadcasting black propaganda to Britain, had advocated negotiations for a bombing truce.

German shooting of air force officers: in May 1944 it was announced that forty-seven officers from the RAF, Dominion and Allied air forces had been shot dead by the Germans after a mass escape from the German prisoner-of-war camp Stalag Luft III in March. Some were said by the Germans to have been shot 'while resisting arrest'; others during 'a new attempt to escape after capture'. In fact, fifty of the seventy-three captured escapees had been selected for summary execution by the Gestapo on Hitler's orders. This episode later became immortalized in the film *The Great Escape* (1963).

Gert and Daisy: female comedy duo, played by sisters Elsie and Doris Waters, who featured on the BBC radio programme *The Kitchen Front*.

Gestapo: German secret police.

Gilbertian: ludicrous and comical.

Gillard, Frank: BBC war correspondent.

Giraud, General Henri Honoré: succeeded Admiral Darlan as High Commissioner for French North Africa after the latter's assassination in December 1942. He was a rival to de Gaulle for leadership of the French forces opposing Germany.

glass house: slang for military prison.

gleaning: gathering left-over grain, or other crops, after the harvest.

Gloucester, Duke of: third son of King George V.

Goebbels, Joseph: Nazi propaganda minister.

Goering, Hermann: commander-in-chief of the Luftwaffe.

Gordon Highlanders: Scottish infantry regiment.

Gordon, John: editor of the *Sunday Express*.

Gothic line: a series of German defences running through the Apennine mountains in north-central Italy.

government water scheme: in April 1944 the government issued a White paper on a national water policy. A Rural Water Supplies and Sewerage Act of July 1944 obliged local authorities to improve piped water supplies to rural communities.

graft: corrupt practices.

Greek mutiny: in April 1944, units of the Greek army and navy in Egypt sympathetic to the communist-dominated National Liberation Front (EAM) in occupied Greece mutinied against the Greek government-in-exile based in Cairo. British forces intervened to quell the mutiny.

Green Line coaches: bus company.

Greene, Lord: Master of the Rolls. In June 1942, he chaired a board of investigation to inquire into the coal miners' wages claim. In April 1943, his board announced a comprehensive conciliation scheme for the coal mining industry.

Greene, Roger: war correspondent for the US news agency Associated Press.

Grigg, Sir James: from February 1942, Secretary of State for War.

Grisewood, Freddie: BBC broadcaster.

grouse: complaint.

half: a measure of whisky.

Halifax, Lord: British Ambassador in Washington.

Hamm: railway centre in north-west Germany.

hammer and sickle: communist symbol.

Handley, Tommy: comedian.

Harris, Air Marshal Sir Arthur: appointed commander-in-chief of RAF Bomber Command in February 1942.

Harrods: London department store.

Hastings, Major Lewis: BBC military commentator.

Haw-Haw, Lord: nickname given to William Joyce, former member of the British Union of Fascists, who broadcast German propaganda to Britain.

hawkers: those who travel around selling easily transportable goods.

heating ban: in order to conserve fuel, various restrictions on the use of central heating were put in place. In April 1944, for example, it was prohibited in public premises, offices, shops and blocks of flats, until the autumn. Restrictions on other forms of heating were also instituted over these months for these premises.

Helmore, Group Captain William: technical adviser to the Ministry of Aircraft Production and broadcaster.

Henderson, Arthur: Financial Secretary to the War Office.

Henderson, W. Craig: prominent lawyer and Leader of the Parliamentary Bar.

Herbert, A. P.: author and Independent MP for Oxford University.

Hereford case: in October 1943 the High Court heard an appeal against the conviction of Dennis Craddock who, along with another boy, had been found guilty some months earlier by the magistrates at Hereford Juvenile Court of theft and malicious damage. Eleven-year-old Craddick had been ordered to be placed under the care of the local education authority for seven years and receive four strokes of the birch. It was alleged that various procedural irregularities had taken place at the hearing and this was upheld by the High Court. A writ was then issued by the Craddock family against the magistrates for assault and false imprisonment. However, the Home Secretary and the Lord Chancellor ordered a public inquiry into the case. In November this concluded that there was no wrongful conviction and the High Court had been misinformed.

Hess, Rudolf: Hitler's deputy who undertook an abortive freelance peace mission to Scotland in May 1941. He was swiftly captured and incarcerated in Britain for the rest of the war. In August 1943 it was reported that at a press conference in New York, Brendan Bracken, the Minister of Information, disclosed that Hess had travelled to Britain to identify 'quislings' to overthrow the Churchill government and give Hitler a free hand against the Soviet Union. In his comments, Bracken described Hess as an 'overgrown Boy Scout'. He subsequently sent a telegram of apology to Lord Somers, the Chief Scout.

hewers: miners who cut coal from the seams.

Heydrich, Reinhard: Nazi governor of occupied Bohemia and Moravia and a leading architect of the 'final solution'. In May 1942 he was fatally wounded in Prague by Free Czech agents who had been trained in the UK by the Special Operations Executive (SOE).

Hilton, Professor John: social scientist and broadcaster.

Himmler, Heinrich: head of the SS, chief of the German police and, from August 1943, Nazi Minister of the Interior.

Hitler, Adolf: leader of Nazi Germany.

Hoare, Sir Samuel: British ambassador in Madrid.

Hogg, Quintin: Conservative MP for Oxford City.

holidays at home: a government campaign to encourage workers to take their holidays close to home in order to reduce wartime travel. Local authorities and voluntary bodies were to provide amusements and entertainments for holidaymakers.

hollowware: hollow utensils such as pots and jugs.

Holmfirth flood: on Whit Monday, May 1944, a storm swept over the north of England, and Holmfirth in Yorkshire was badly flooded. Three people were drowned and much damage done to the town. Geoffrey Riley, a local fourteen-year-old schoolboy, was awarded the Albert Medal (later superseded by the George Cross) for his bravery in trying to save the life of one of the victims. His father, Donald, died in the rescue attempt.

Home Guard: local part-time defence force composed of those who were ineligible for call-up to the armed forces, often as a result of age. Affectionally nicknamed 'Dad's Army'.

homogenised milk: milk which has been subjected to a process which prevents the cream from separating.

Hondurasian lumbermen: some 900 lumbermen from British Honduras were employed in forestry units in Scotland.

Hong Kong atrocities: in March 1942 Anthony Eden, the Foreign Secretary, announced in the House of Commons that Japanese forces in Hong Kong had perpetrated against prisoners of war and civilians 'the same kind of barbarities which aroused the horror of the civilized world at the time of the Nanking massacre of 1937'.

Hopkins, Harry: close adviser to President Roosevelt and coordinator of the USA's Lend-Lease programme.

Houghton, Douglas: general secretary of the Inland Revenue Staff Federation.

howitzer: artillery gun with a short barrel.

Hudson, Robert: Minister of Agriculture.

Hull bill: reference to the Kingston-upon-Hull Corporation (Development) Bill. This private bill, which included the granting of powers to Hull to purchase and develop land in and around the city, was defeated in the House of Commons in April 1944.

Hull case: in October 1944 Michael Giles, a former joiner who had been discharged from the wartime merchant navy on the grounds of ill health, applied to a tribunal in Hull to be reinstated in his former employment under the Reinstatement in Civil Employment Act. His application was, however, rejected on the grounds that the act applied to those who had served in the armed forces of the crown and the merchant navy was not classed as an armed force. He appealed against this decision, but the judgement was upheld.

Hull, Cordell: US Secretary of State until November 1944.

'human torpedoes': Royal Navy torpedo-shaped submersibles known as chariots. The crews sat astride these craft in diving suits and could propel them either along the surface or at periscope depth in order to attach explosive charges to enemy vessels. In April 1944 news was released of a British attack on the Italian naval base at Palermo in Sicily in January 1943 during which these craft penetrated the harbour defences, sank an Italian cruiser and badly damaged a transport ship.

Hun: nickname for Germans.

Hurricane: British fighter aircraft.

husbandmen: farmers.

ICI offices in Glasgow: in January 1944 six youths, described as members of an organization known as Fianna na h-Alba, were sentenced to a period of imprisonment for wrecking the ICI board room in Blythswood Square in Glasgow by throwing hand grenades into the premises.

industrial 'dilutees': less skilled workers who undertook work previously done by those of greater skill.

industrial ten: ten extra clothing coupons issued to a wide range of manual workers.

Inge, Dean William: former Dean of St Paul's Cathedral in London.

Inter-Allied conference: meeting of representatives of the Allied governments in London in September 1941.

'Internationale': national anthem of the Soviet Union until 1944. In July 1941 it was announced that the Sunday evening broadcast of the Allies' national anthems would cease. Instead, the national music, songs and airs of each of these nations would be played in turn each week.

iron ration: a grant of clothing coupons, additional to the 'industrial ten', to those in exceptionally heavy industries.

Ironside, Field Marshal Lord: Chief of the Imperial General Staff, 1939–40.

Italian co-operators: prisoners of war who volunteered to work for the Allied war effort and were granted certain freedoms and privileges.

ITMA: *It's That Man Again*, BBC comedy programme starring Tommy Handley. The fifth series of the programme ended in January 1943.

Jameson, Sir (William) Wilson: chief medical officer at the Ministry of Health and Board of Education.

jam scheme: in March 1941 it was announced that no extra sugar allowance would be given to housewives for making their own jam from soft fruit. Instead, they were urged to sell their spare fruit to a common pool from which jam would be produced by such organizations as the National Federation of Women's Institutes. In June some sugar concession was made for the making of jam out of the stone fruit crop.

Japanese atrocities: in January 1944 Anthony Eden reported to the House of Commons that evidence was now clear of the brutal treatment of British prisoners of war and civilian internees at the hands of Japanese. Their captors, he noted, had 'violated not only the principles of international law but all canons of decent and civilised conduct'.

Jarman, Charles: general secretary of the National Union of Seamen.

Jehovah's Witnesses: Christian religious movement associated with the American pastor Charles Taze Russell.

Jerry: nickname for Germans.

jerry-builder: builder who badly or hastily builds using poor-quality materials.

Joad, Dr Cyril: philosopher.

Job: biblical figure who exemplified patience in the face of provocation.

jobbery: using public office for personal gain.

jobbing: occasional work.

joint production committees: committees of management and workers' representatives to maximize war production.

Jones, Thomas: philanthropist, educationalist and former civil servant.

Joubert de la Ferté, Air Chief Marshal Sir Philip: Inspector General of the RAF. In November 1943 he retired, but he was shortly thereafter redeployed as Deputy Chief of Staff in South East Asia Command.

Keeling, G. V.: a managing director of engineering factories and foundries; previously a miner.

Kendall, Denis: Independent MP for Grantham.

Kent, Duke of: fourth son of George V. He was killed in an RAF plane crash in Scotland in August 1942.

Kesselring, Field Marshal Albert: German commander in Italy.

Kimmins, Commander Anthony: naval officer, playwright and film maker.

King, the: George VI.

King George V: Royal Navy battleship.

King, W. L. Mackenzie: prime minister of Canada.

King-Hall, Commander Stephen: Independent National MP for Ormskirk and Chairman of the Fuel Economy Publicity Committee.

Klopper, Major-General Hendrik: South African commander of the British and Commonwealth garrison at Tobruk when it surrendered to Axis forces in June 1942.

knavery: roguery.

Knox, Chief Controller Jean: Director of the Auxiliary Territorial Service.

Knox, Colonel Frank: US Secretary of the Navy.

kowtowing: excessive subservience.

Krupp: German armament manufacturer.

'L' drivers: learner drivers.

Lancaster: British bomber aircraft.

Land bill: in June 1944 the government presented a Town and Country Planning Bill to the House of Commons.

Laskier, Frank: merchant seaman gunner. In 1941 his ship was sunk by a German merchant raider off the coast of West Africa and he lost a foot in the action. He was rescued from a life raft by a passing Spanish steamer.

lasts: foot moulds for making shoes.

laundry zoning scheme: in May 1943 a laundry zoning scheme was introduced in Oxford which tied customers to certain laundries.

Laurie, Major-General Sir Percy: in April 1943 Laurie, the Provost Marshal of the United Kingdom and a former Assistant Commissioner of the Metropolitan Police, appeared at Bow Street Police Court charged with making a false statement to obtain a new ration book, unlawfully using the book and failing to deliver it to the Minister of Food. He was fined a total of £550 and ordered to pay 35 guineas in costs. Laurie successfully appealed against the conviction but retired shortly thereafter.

Laval, Pierre: from 1942, head of the Vichy government under Marshal Pétain.

Layton, Sir Walter: economist and newspaper proprietor. He was director-general of programmes at the Ministry of Supply, 1940–42.

Lease-Lend: under a bill signed into law by President Roosevelt in March 1941, the United States, which was still neutral, was able to lease or lend war materials to countries whose defence was deemed vital to the US. The terms and conditions of such aid were to be those that the president deemed 'satisfactory'.

Lebanon: in November 1943 the government of Lebanon, which was a French-controlled territory under a League of Nations mandate, unilaterally revised the country's constitution in order to abolish the mandate. In response, the Fighting French authorities, who in 1941 had seemingly promised the country progress towards independence, arrested the Lebanese president and prime minister. In the face of international pressure, the French released the government officials and reiterated the pledge of Lebanese independence.

Leese, Lieutenant-General Sir Oliver: from January 1944, commander of the Eighth Army.

Leigh, Vivien: Oscar-winning film star.

Leigh-Mallory, Air Marshal Sir Trafford: from November 1942, commander-in-chief of RAF Fighter Command; from November 1943, commander of the Allied Expeditionary Air Force. In November 1944, while en route to India to take up a new post as Allied Air Commander-in-Chief, South East Asia Command, he was killed in an air crash near Grenoble in south-east France.

Lewis, John L.: President of the United Mine Workers of America.

Lidell, Alvar: BBC announcer. In February 1943 he left the BBC to join the RAF, but he returned to the corporation a year later.

limerick: a humorous rhyming verse.

Lindbergh, Charles: prominent American aviator who, up until the Japanese attack on Pearl Harbor, was an outspoken advocate of the USA staying out of the war.

Lippmann, Walter: American journalist and author.

Lisbon air-liner disaster: In June 1943 an unescorted passenger aircraft was shot down by the Luftwaffe over the Bay of Biscay. The actor and film director, Leslie Howard, who was returning from a visit to Spain and Portugal under the auspices of the British Council, was among the seventeen passengers and crew killed, as was Alfred Chenhalls, a chartered accountant and business associate of Howard.

lisle: a smooth cotton fabric.

Litvinov, Maxim: Soviet Ambassador to the United States.

Lloyd George, David: Prime Minister from 1916 to 1922.

Lloyd George, Major Gwilym: Minister of Fuel and Power.

Lofoten: in March 1941 these German-occupied Norwegian islands were raided by British commandos in order to destroy fish oil factories (the glycerine from which was used in munitions production).

Longland, Jack: mountaineer and county education officer for Dorset.

Lord Winster's Bill: in May 1944 Lord Winster sponsored a Reinstatement in Retail Business Premises Bill designed to assist small traders who had been discharged from war service. The government declined to back the bill.

Lublin atrocities: in August 1944 it was reported that when Soviet forces captured Lublin in Poland they discovered a German 'annihilation camp' where thousands of inmates had been murdered in gas chambers and their bodies burnt in incinerators. It was alleged that the ashes had been mixed with manure and used as fertilizer for SS farms.

Luftwaffe: German air force.

Lyndoe, Edward: astrologer.

Lyttelton, Oliver: from March 1942, Minister of Production. In July 1942, at a speech in Aldershot to mark Anglo-Soviet week, he described the coming eighty days as 'some of the gravest that we have ever faced'. In June 1944 he was reported to have claimed at an American Chamber of Commerce lunch in London that the US had provoked Japan to such an extent that 'the Japanese were forced to attack the Americans at Pearl Harbour'. He subsequently apologized and sought to clarify his remarks.

MacArthur, General Douglas: from July 1941, commander of US forces in the Far East; from April 1942, supreme Allied commander in the south-west Pacific area.

Mafeking: British-held town in South Africa besieged by the Boers from October 1899 to May 1900 during the South African War. When the siege was lifted there was great public rejoicing in Britain.

Maisky, Ivan: Soviet Ambassador in London.

Malaya: Royal Navy battleship.

Mallon, Dr J. J.: Warden of Toynbee Hall and a governor of the BBC.

Margesson, Captain David: from December 1940 to February 1942, Secretary of State for War.

Marshall, Howard: BBC war correspondent.

Masefield, Peter: aviation journalist and war correspondent.

Mauretania: Cunard-White Star liner converted to a troopship.

McCullough, Donald: first question master of the BBC programme *Brains Trust.*

means test: an intrusive official investigation into a person's financial circumstances to determine eligibility for welfare payments and other state benefits.

Mediterranean convoy battle: running battle in August 1942 between Axis forces and a Royal Navy convoy of merchant ships attempting to resupply besieged Malta. Only five of the original fourteen merchant ships reached the island. Captain Dudley Mason, Master of the SS *Ohio,* was awarded the George Cross for his gallantry during the operation.

Men of Munich: politicians associated with the appeasement of Hitler at the Munich conference of 1938.

Mihailović, General Draža: royalist resistance leader of the Yugoslav 'Chetniks'.

mobile women: women regarded as being available for employment away from their home areas.

Montgomery, Lieutenant-General (later Field Marshal) Bernard: from August 1942, commander of the Eighth Army; from January 1944, commander-in-chief of 21st Army Group with command of all Allied ground forces in the first phase of Operation Overlord.

Moorehead, Alan: Australian-born journalist and war correspondent.

mor: US canned meat.

Morris, John: repatriated Professor of English Literature at Keio University, Tokyo.

Morrison, Herbert: Home Secretary and Minister of Home Security.

Morrison shelter: indoor domestic air-raid shelter named after Herbert Morrison.

Moscow agreement: in October 1943 the British, Soviet and US foreign ministers attended a conference in Moscow at which agreement was reached on, among other things, the establishment of a three-power European Advisory Commission to begin work on the problems that would arise in Germany and the wider continent when the Nazi regime collapsed.

Mosley, Sir Oswald: leader of the British Union of Fascists. In May 1940 he was arrested and interned as a security risk. His wife, Diana, was interned a few weeks later. In November 1943 a flare-up of phlebitis in Mosley's leg, which he had injured during the First World War, persuaded Herbert Morrison, the Home Secretary, to sanction their release from Holloway prison.

Mosquito: British fighter-bomber aircraft.

Mountbatten, Lord Louis: naval officer who was chief of combined operations from 1942 to 1943. He was appointed Supreme Allied Commander, South-East Asia, in August 1943.

Moyne, Lord: from January 1944, Minister Resident in the Middle East. Regarded as being anti-Jewish by some Zionist groups, Moyne was assassinated in Cairo in November 1944 by members of the Fighters for the Freedom of Israel (the Stern gang).

Mrs and Miss Churchill: there was some public comment about Churchill's wife and daughter Mary (who was an officer in the ATS) accompanying him to the Quebec conference in August 1943. This included speculation about whether their journey 'was really necessary' and 'how Miss Churchill could get away from her duties'.

Mullins, Claud: lawyer, writer and police court magistrate. In December 1942 a woman described as a 'housekeeper' appeared before Mullins on a charge of stealing a book. Mullins was said to have cast aspersions on the morality of housekeepers by insinuating from the bench that those who described themselves as such were often not 'real' housekeepers but mistresses.

Munda: Japanese air base in the Solomon islands.

Munster, Lord: from January 1943, Parliamentary Under-Secretary of State at the India Office; from October 1944, Parliamentary Under-Secretary of State at the Home Office. In September 1944 he was asked to investigate the welfare conditions for British forces in India and South East Asia.

Murrow, Edward: American broadcaster and war correspondent.

Mussolini, Benito: Italian dictator.

mutiny of Japanese prisoners: in February 1943, Japanese prisoners of war at Featherston Camp in New Zealand rioted after a dispute over working parties. The camp guards opened fire. Forty-eight prisoners were killed, as well as one guard.

napkins: babies' nappies.

Nasmith, Matthew: in March 1944 it was reported that a court case in Leeds had revealed that Matthew Nasmith, an ex-soldier employed on munitions work in Leicestershire, had been unable to find accommodation for his wife and children in the area where he worked so he had sought shelter for them in a public assistance institution and offered to pay for it. Yet by seeking such poor relief he had had to give up his war work and he and his family became paupers.

national conference of women: in September 1943 a government-sponsored conference of women was held at the Albert Hall in London.

national loaf: a government-approved wheatmeal loaf.

National Service Bill 1942: under this legislation of December 1942, young men became liable to be enrolled for military service as soon as they turned eighteen, rather than having to wait (as had been the practice) until they were at least eighteen years and four months.

National Trust: statutory organization for the preservation of places of historic interest or natural beauty.

Nelson: Royal Navy battleship.

nettled: irritated.

Neutrality Act: US isolationist legislation of the 1930s designed to prevent the USA becoming embroiled in foreign wars.

Newcastle enquiry: in February 1944 the Home Office launched an inquiry into the administration of the fire, police and civil defence services in Newcastle-upon-Tyne after allegations of corruption. The inquiry found this not to be the case, but unearthed evidence of irregularities and the mixing up of public and personal affairs.

new Fire-Guard Orders: in September 1943 new regulations came into force which, among other things, extended the maximum age of liability for men to undertake these duties to sixty-three and reduced the onus on women to undertake such duties. They also closed the loophole whereby men employed in prescribed premises that required Fire Guards escaped these duties because they lived in areas where there was no compulsory enrolment. This was the so-called 'funk express'.

new strike regulations: in April 1944 the government issued a new defence regulation (1AA) which included severe penalties for those who incited strikes or lockouts in essential services, whether or not the cause of the stoppage came within the legal definition of a 'trade dispute'. The penalties included a maximum of five years' penal servitude, or a fine of £500, or both.

Norwegian fiasco: in April 1940 British and French troops had landed in Norway in order to assist the Norwegians after the German invasion. The campaign ended in failure and a few weeks later the British and French were forced to withdraw.

notifiable disease: a serious infectious disease that must be reported to the appropriate authorities.

Notre Dame shooting: on 26 August 1944, shooting broke out inside Notre Dame cathedral as de Gaulle arrived for a service of thanksgiving for the liberation of Paris. He was said to have stridden defiantly up the central aisle, with bullets whistling all around him, and inspired by his example the congregation rose to sing the Te Deum with the general at the head of them. Robert Reid, the maternal grandfather of the editor of this volume, was a BBC war correspondent with the US First Army and he broadcast a dramatic eye-witness account of the events in Notre Dame for *War Report*.

Nottinghamshire strike: in September 1943 the imprisonment of an eighteen-year-old surface mine worker, Sidney Page, who refused to work underground, led to a strike in the Nottinghamshire coalfields. Page was released a week into his one-month sentence after agreeing to work underground.

Nuremberg: Bavarian city that was the site of pre-war Nazi party rallies.

open-cast coal: a method of mining by which coal is extracted at, or from a level close to, the earth's surface.

open city: a city declared to be undefended and thus exempt from bombardment.

Orangemen: members of the Orange Order, a Protestant unionist organization based primarily in Northern Ireland.

Osborn, F. J.: town planner and writer.

Otley case: in May 1944 Sam Higson from Rawdon in Yorkshire was fined £1, and ordered to pay two guineas in costs, at Otley police court for borrowing coal from a personal friend. This coal, it was argued, was in excess of the five cwt permitted and was not supplied by a licensed coal merchant.

Ovaltine: a drink mixture made from malt, milk and eggs.

Oxford County Court decision: in May 1943 this court ruled that the law did not entitle Mrs Dorothy Blackwell, who was separated from her husband, to the savings she had accumulated with the Oxford Cooperative Society whilst married. It was argued that the money in her account derived from savings from the housekeeping money that her husband had provided whilst they were living together, and that such savings remained the property of the husband.

Oxford Group: Christian religious movement founded by the American minister Dr Frank Buchman.

oz: abbreviation for ounce, a unit of weight equal to one-sixteenth of a pound.

panel doctors: doctors who provided treatment for patients under the National Insurance Act of 1911.

paraffin priority scheme: in May 1943 it was announced that priority of paraffin supplies would be given to those who were wholly dependent on this fuel for lighting, heating or cooking.

pasteurisation: a process of heat treatment to eradicate harmful bacteria.

Patulin: a drug regarded as a possible cure for colds.

Pavlichenko, Lieutenant Lyudmila: Soviet sniper.

Pchelintsev, Lieutenant Vladimir: Soviet sniper.

perambulator: a baby's pram.

Peyrouton, Marcel: former Vichy Minister of the Interior appointed Governor-General of Algeria by General Giraud in January 1943.

Pickles, Wilfred: BBC broadcaster.

piecework: work paid according to the amount produced.

Player's: a make of cigarette.

ploughing out: ploughing up grassland in order to increase the production of crops.

points rationing scheme: under the basic rationing scheme, coupons entitled consumers to fixed quantities of a specific rationed item and a consumer had to register with a retailer to purchase such an item. The points rationing scheme, which was first introduced in 1941 for clothing and non-perishable goods such as canned foods, differed in that the coupons covered a range of different rationed items to which points values were allocated and the consumer could 'spend' these points at any retailer where the items were available.

Poor Law: system of poor relief, dating back to Elizabethan times, that came to be associated with the workhouse.

Pope, the: Pius XII.

Portal, Lord: from February 1942 to November 1944, Minister of Works.

Portal house: a government prefabricated house named after Lord Portal. It was to be made of steel and designed to last ten years.

Porter committee: in September 1943 an independent tribunal headed by Lord Porter, set up under the coal mining industry conciliation scheme, laid down a scale of minimum wages for juveniles working as miners. In January 1944 the tribunal increased miners' minimum pay for both adult and juvenile workers.

Postscript: series of talks broadcast on the BBC, usually after the 9.00 pm news on a Sunday night.

post-war credit scheme: a scheme in which the extra income tax that was to be paid through the reduction of personal allowances and earned income allowance was to be offset by a credit given to taxpayers, after the war, in the Post Office Savings Bank.

potato clamp: method of storing potatoes outside using a pyramid structure of straw and soil.

poultry restrictions: in June 1942 it was announced that during the coming winter there would be a reduction of balancer meal for domestic poultry. It was suggested that poultry keepers could obtain additional meal if neighbours surrendered their shell egg ration coupons, the resulting extra eggs being shared among households.

Pound, Admiral Sir Dudley: First Sea Lord and Chief of the Naval Staff. He died in October 1943.

Praga: district of Warsaw on the eastern side of the Vistula river.

prating: endless foolish talk.

Pravda: newspaper of the Communist party of the Soviet Union.

prefabricated houses: factory-produced homes to enable quick and easy assembly on site.

press gang: forcibly enlist.

Priestley, J. B.: novelist, playwright and wartime broadcaster.

Priory pit: in July 1943 the Ministry of Fuel and Power took over the management of the Priory colliery in Blantyre, Lanarkshire. It was reported that this pit's output had been unsatisfactory for some time and it was facing an ongoing industrial dispute.

Prudential: life assurance company.

Prussian attitude: militaristic attitude.

public houses: pubs.

putters: miners who transported coal away from the coal face.

Queen, the: Elizabeth, consort of George VI. Later styled Queen Elizabeth, the Queen Mother.

Queen Elizabeth: Cunard-White Star liner converted to a troopship.

Queen Mary: Cunard-White Star liner converted to a troopship.

Rabaul: naval and air base in New Guinea captured by the Japanese in 1942.

Radio Doctor: BBC radio programme in which Charles Hill, a medical doctor and administrator at the British Medical Association, gave health advice.

radiolocation: radar.

Radio Padre: BBC radio programme in which Ronald Selby Wright, a Church of Scotland minister and army chaplain, broadcast on religious themes.

Ramillies: Royal Navy battleship.

ramp: a swindle.

Ramsay, Captain Archibald: Unionist MP for Peebles who founded a secret society known as the Right Club which distributed anti-war and anti-Jewish literature. He was detained in 1940 under regulation 18B but released in September 1944.

Rathbone, Eleanor: Independent MP for the Combined English Universities.

'rat-poison' vicar: in October 1944 it was reported that Rev. Harold Green, vicar of St Nicholas, Ipswich, had sent a tin of rat poison to Rev. J. C. S. Chamberlain, vicar of Christ Church, Shooters Hill, London, when the latter appealed for donations of 'comforts' for German prisoners of war in hospital. Green was rebuked by the Bishop of Ipswich.

rayon: textile fibre used as a substitute for silk.

reception areas: areas of the country that were believed to be less vulnerable to air attack and to which those from the evacuation areas were sent to escape the bombing.

recrudescence: recurrence.

Red Army: the army of the Soviet Union.

red tape: unnecessary bureaucracy.

Regional Commissioners: officials who coordinated civil defence measures across the various regions of the country.

registration of women: under the Registration for Employment Order of March 1941, married and single women of specified ages (which eventually came to include those born between 1893 and 1926) were required to register at local offices of the Ministry of Labour and National Service and make themselves available for interview by a ministry official. If their circumstances permitted, they could be 'directed' to undertake appropriate war work.

Regulation 18B: defence regulation under which the government could detain any person it believed posed a threat to public safety or the defence of the realm. Oswald Mosley was taken into custody under this regulation.

Regulation 33B: defence regulation under which any person named as a source of venereal disease infection by at least two patients could be compelled to undergo medical examination and receive any necessary treatment.

Reichenau, Field Marshal Walter von: German army commander in the Soviet Union who died in January 1942, apparently of a stroke compounded by injuries sustained in an air crash while returning to Germany for treatment. He was, however, rumoured to have been shot by the Gestapo or to have taken his own life.

Reichstag: German parliament. Under the Nazis, it had merely a ceremonial role.

rentier: those who lived on income from investments.

repairs to bomb-damaged property: in October 1944 it was announced that licences for building work costing over £10 would be required in the London area in order to prioritize the repair of bomb damage.

reserved occupations: under a Schedule of Reserved Occupations, workers deemed vital to the war effort on the home front had their call-up to the armed forces deferred.

Reuters: international news agency.

Reynolds, Quentin: American journalist and war correspondent.

rig-out: outfit of clothes.

ringing of bells: on 15 November 1942 church bells were rung across the country to celebrate victory at El Alamein.

Ritchie, Major-General Neil: from November 1941 to June 1942, commander of the Eighth Army.

'Road to Mandalay': sentimental song, featuring lyrics by Rudyard Kipling, about colonial military service in South East Asia.

Roatta, General Mario: appointed chief of staff of the Italian army under Mussolini in June 1943, and retained by Badoglio's government, he was accused of war crimes whilst commanding Italian occupation forces in Yugoslavia.

Robson, H.: most likely R. W. Robson: New Zealand-born journalist and founding editor of the *Pacific Islands Monthly*.

rocket gun: in December 1943 it was rumoured that the Germans had large rocket guns stationed on the French coast capable of bombarding London.

Rommel, General Erwin: commander of German–Italian forces in North Africa and the Western Desert; subsequently commander of German Army Group B in northern France which opposed the Allied landings. In July 1944, he was badly wounded in an air attack and removed to hospital.

Roosevelt, Franklin D: president of the USA.

Rostock: Baltic coast port in northern Germany.

roundsmen: those who took orders for, and delivered, such items as milk.

Rundstedt, Field Marshal Gert von: German commander-in-chief in the West during the Ardennes offensive in December 1944.

Russia and Finland: in 1941 Finland had joined Germany in the war against the Soviet Union, but as the conflict turned against Germany peace feelers were put out and in February 1944 the Soviet Union issued armistice terms to the Finns. These were not accepted, but in the face of Soviet military pressure the Finns sued for peace in September 1944.

Russo-Polish dispute: in April 1943, the Soviet Union severed its diplomatic relations with the Polish government-in-exile in the wake of the German discovery of the graves of thousands of Polish officers executed by the Soviets at Katyn near Smolensk in 1940. It was claimed by the Soviet Union that the Germans had committed this atrocity and that the Poles were exploiting the episode to extract territorial concessions from Moscow.

'Salute the Soldier' weeks: a week of army-related national savings activities.

salvage: superfluous or waste materials useful to the war effort.

Sam Browne belt: a leather belt worn by army officers.

Sandys, Duncan: from February 1943, Parliamentary Secretary to the Ministry of Supply. He was also chairman of the Flying Bomb Counter-Measures Committee. From November 1944, he was Minister of Works.

scabies: contagious skin condition.

Scale B: under demobilization plans announced in September 1944, some service personnel (designated 'Class B') would be released out of turn if they belonged to occupational groups needed for urgent reconstruction work.

Scott, Lieutenant Commander Peter: son of the Antarctic explorer, he served as a wartime naval officer in light coastal craft and was decorated for bravery.

Scott report: report of a committee, under the chairmanship of Lord Justice Scott, appointed to advise on land utilization in rural areas. It was published in August 1942.

Scharnhorst: German battlecruiser sunk by the Royal Navy (with assistance from the Royal Norwegian Navy) off northern Norway in December 1943. Some 2,000 crew members were lost.

school feeding scheme: in late 1941 it was announced that steps were being taken to expand the provision of school meals and milk.

scuttling of the French fleet: in November 1942 the French fleet at Toulon was scuttled on the orders of the Vichy navy in order to avoid it falling into German hands when the latter occupied Vichy France.

Sforza, Count: Anti-fascist Italian politician who was in exile during the Mussolini era. In November 1944 the British government objected to the Count's appointment as Italian foreign minister on the grounds that he had been working against the post-liberation Italian government.

sheep scab: contagious parasitic disease of sheep.

shelling incident at Steyning: in May 1944, in an incident of 'friendly fire', British army shells accidentally landed in and around the town of Steyning during military exercises on the Sussex Downs. Two people were killed.

Shelter enquiry: an investigation by Laurence Dunne, a police court magistrate, into the circumstances of the Bethnal Green tube shelter disaster of March 1943. His report was eventually published in 1945 and concluded that the disaster was caused by a mixture of psychological and physical factors. The allegations of a Jewish panic were said to be 'demonstrably false'.

shilly-shallying: failure to act decisively.

Shinwell, Emanuel: Labour MP for Seaham.

shop stewards: local trade union officials who represent their members in discussions with management.

Shvernik, Nikolai: leader of the Soviet trade union delegation at the Trades Union Congress in September 1943.

Siegfried line: a line of German fortifications along the western border of Germany between the Netherlands and Switzerland.

Sikorski, General Władysław: prime minister of the Polish government-in-exile and commander-in-chief of the Polish armed forces. In July 1943, whilst returning to Britain from an inspection of Polish troops in the Middle East, he was killed when his aircraft crashed shortly after take-off from Gibraltar. German propagandists claimed that Sikorski had been murdered by the British, but a court of inquiry found no evidence of sabotage.

Sinclair, Sir Archibald: Secretary of State for Air.

Sinclair, W. A.: Lecturer in Philosophy at the University of Edinburgh and wartime broadcaster.

slush: overly sentimental songs.

Smuts, General Jan: prime minister of the Union of South Africa.

soldier's bus: to help mitigate the effects of a strike by bus workers in London in April 1944, soldiers drove buses, and army lorries were deployed on the bus routes.

Sollum: harbour on the Egyptian-Libyan border.

spam: US canned meat.

Spitfire: British fighter aircraft.

'Squander bug': a bug-like cartoon character to discourage frivolous spending.

Stalin, Joseph: leader of the Soviet Union.

Stanley, Colonel Oliver: from November 1942, Secretary of State for the Colonies.

starlit: modified street lighting of low intensity.

Stettinius, Edward: US Secretary of State from December 1944. He disassociated himself from British opposition to the appointment of Count Sforza as Italian Foreign Minister and pointed to the State Department's view that the Italians should work out problems of government along democratic lines without external influence.

Stilwell, General Joseph: US army officer who served as Chiang Kai-Shek's chief of staff and commanded American forces in the China–Burma–India theatre. He was subsequently made Deputy Supreme Allied Commander, South-East Asia, under Mountbatten.

Strachey, Squadron Leader John: socialist theorist and former Labour MP who served in the wartime RAF as a public relations officer.

stymied: prevented or hindered.

suspension of diplomatic rights: as a security measure, in April 1944 the government informed all diplomatic missions in Britain that, until further notice, they were not permitted to transmit or receive telegrams that were not in plain language, and neither were they to despatch or accept delivery of diplomatic bags that had not been censored. In addition, no diplomats, couriers, or members of diplomatic staffs were permitted to leave the country.

Swing, Raymond Gram: American journalist and broadcaster.

Sydney: Royal Australian Navy light cruiser. She sank off the coast of Western Australia after a clash with the German merchant raider *Kormoran* in November 1941. The entire crew of 645 were lost.

Talbot, Godfrey: BBC war correspondent.

Tarran house: a type of prefabricated house designed by Tarran Industries of Hull.

Tate, Mavis: Conservative MP for Frome.

Tempest: British fighter aircraft.

Tenth Army: British formation created in Persia and Iraq in 1942.

terror raids: bombing raids aimed at centres of civilian population to break morale.

Thoma, General Wilhelm Ritter von: commander of the German Afrika Korps during the battle of El Alamein in October–November 1942. He was captured and taken to General Montgomery's headquarters, where he was entertained to dinner.

Thomas, Howard: BBC producer of, among other programmes, the *Brains Trust*. In December 1943 it was announced that Thomas had decided to resign from the corporation on the grounds that the BBC did not sufficiently encourage new ideas for programmes. Thomas was to be released by the corporation in February 1944, but when the *Brains Trust* was broadcast in January his name was omitted from the credits even though he was still producing the programme at this time. Thomas was reported to have claimed that this was 'the BBC's childish revenge on someone who has dared to leave'.

tied cottage: cottage typically rented by an employee from an employer.

Timoshenko, Marshal Semyon: Soviet military commander.

Tirpitz: German battleship.

Tito (Broz, Josip), Marshal: communist resistance leader of the Yugoslav partisans.

Tōjō, General Hideki: Japanese prime minister. He resigned in July 1944.

treating: buying a round of alcoholic drinks in a pub.

trekking: in some urban areas vulnerable to bombing residents would 'trek' out of their cities each evening in order to find safe havens from the bombs.

Trent, Lord: chairman of Boots Pure Drug Company.

trippers: those who go on a pleasure trip or excursion.

Trotskyites: those who adhered to the revolutionary theories of Leon Trotsky.

Truk: Japanese naval and air base in the Caroline Islands.

TT milk: Tuberculin-tested milk.

Tyneside strike: in October 1942, Tyneside shipyard workers went on strike. This was reported to be in protest over changes in arrangements for the payment of wages.

Typhoon: British fighter-bomber aircraft.

U-boat: German naval submarine.

Udet, Ernst: Luftwaffe general and First World War fighter ace. He took his own life in November 1941.

under-the-water bridge: in December 1942 it was reported that Soviet troops had secretly constructed a bridge some two feet below the surface of the water at a river crossing and were able to drive tanks across it.

Unionists: those who believed in preserving the place of Northern Ireland within the United Kingdom.

Urquhart, James: BBC news reader.

Urquhart, Major-General Roy: commander of the British First Airborne Division during the Arnhem operation in September 1944.

'Usherette' murder: in November 1943 the court of criminal appeal quashed the conviction of Gunner Dennis Leckey for the murder of Mrs Caroline Trayler, an usherette at a Folkestone cinema. It was argued that, whilst there was evidence to convict Leckey, the judge had misdirected the jury at the trial.

Uthwatt Report: report of a committee, under the chairmanship of Mr Justice Uthwatt, appointed to examine the payment of compensation and recovery of betterment in respect of the public control of the use of land, and advise on how best to prevent the work of reconstruction from being prejudiced by land speculation. It was published in September 1942.

Utility: a range of civilian goods, such as clothes and furniture, designed to standard government specifications so as to save materials and labour, as well as ensure sound quality at reasonable prices.

V1: German jet-propelled cruise missile with a range of approximately 150 miles.

V2: German rocket-propelled ballistic missile with a range of approximately 220 miles.

Vansittart, Lord: Permanent Under-Secretary at the Foreign Office, 1930–38, and chief diplomatic adviser to the Foreign Secretary, 1938–41. He was associated with strong anti-Germanism.

'V' campaign: a BBC propaganda campaign, launched in 1941, which encouraged the people of occupied Europe to mobilize themselves as a 'V army' against the Germans and adopt the 'V' symbol (for victory and freedom) as a rallying emblem.

Vichy: term for the French collaborationist regime based in the city of that name.

Vickers: armaments firm.

Victoria Cross: the UK's highest decoration for military gallantry.

voluntary hospitals: self-governing institutions, funded principally by philanthropy or contributory schemes, which generally provided treatment for acute medical conditions.

wages doctrine: in July 1941, Ernest Bevin stated that he was not opposed to high wartime wages as long as they were matched by production.

Wakefield, W. W.: Conservative MP for Swindon and Director of the Air Training Corps.

Wakes weeks: traditional holiday periods (originally a religious celebration), generally associated with factories and mills in the industrialized north and midlands.

War Agricultural Executive Committees: a network of committees established by the Ministry of Agriculture across the counties, composed of landowners, farmers and other land-related members, to help increase food production. They enjoyed extensive powers over the farming world.

war criminals: in September 1944 it was reported that the names of Hitler, Himmler and Goering had been omitted from a list of war criminals prepared by the United Nations War Crimes Commission.

wardens: air-raid wardens.

Wardlaw-Milne, Sir John: Conservative MP for Kidderminster and Chairman of the House of Commons Select Committee on National Expenditure. He tabled the motion that led to the vote of censure on the government in July 1942.

War Report: BBC radio programme that broadcast eye-witness despatches from Normandy and north-west Europe after the 9.00 pm news.

war service grants: grants to supplement the ordinary allowances paid to families and dependents of those serving in the armed forces in order to prevent serious financial hardship.

Warspite: Royal Navy battleship.

Wasp: US aircraft carrier. In the spring of 1942, it transported Spitfires to Malta to help defend the island against Axis air attack.

Waste of Fuel Order: from June 1942, the unnecessary or uneconomic use of coal, gas, electricity, paraffin and liquid fuel was prohibited.

Wavell, General Sir Archibald: from July 1941 to June 1943, commander-in-chief in India; from October 1943, Viceroy and Governor-General of India.

Weir house: a type of prefabricated house designed by G. & J. Weir of Glasgow.

Welcome Club: British Welcome Clubs, promoted by the Women's Voluntary Services, provided home comforts for American and other Allied service personnel.

wellingtons: rubber boots.

Werth, Alexander: Russian-born journalist and commentator for the BBC.

West Derbyshire by-election: in February 1944 Alderman Charles White, standing as an Independent Labour candidate, defeated the Conservative candidate, Lord Hartingdon.

Weygand, General Maxime: Vichy's Delegate-General in French North Africa until November 1941.

Whitehall: a street in central London, comprising many government offices, used as a metonym for the British government and civil service.

white paper: a British government policy document.

Whittle, Group Captain Frank: RAF aeronautical engineer and pioneer of the jet engine.

Wilkinson, Ellen: Parliamentary Secretary to the Ministry of Home Security.

Williams, Emlyn: actor and playwright.

Willkie, Wendell: defeated Republican candidate in the 1940 US presidential election. He subsequently travelled to the Middle East, the Soviet Union and China as Roosevelt's personal envoy.

Wilson, General Sir Henry Maitland: from August 1942, commander-in-chief, Persia–Iraq Command; from February 1943, commander-in-chief in the Middle East; from January 1944, supreme Allied commander in the Mediterranean.

Wilson, Woodrow: President of the USA from 1913 to 1921.

windy: frightened.

'Wings for Victory' weeks: a week of air-force-related national savings activities.

Winster, Lord: formerly the Labour MP, Reginald Fletcher, and parliamentary private secretary to A. V. Alexander, 1940–41.

Winter War: Soviet-Finnish war fought over the winter of 1939–40.

wireworm: wormlike larva.

Wodehouse, P. G.: British comic author who was living in France at the outbreak of war and was interned by the Germans. In June 1941 he was freed and taken to

Berlin where he made a series of humorous broadcasts on German radio to the United States, which was then neutral, about his experiences as a prisoner. In Britain he was widely condemned as a collaborator, but an MI5 investigation in 1944 found no evidence of treachery.

Women's Fire-Guard Order: in August 1942, owing to a shortage of Fire Guards in target areas, women between the ages of twenty and forty-five were made liable for compulsory fire-guard duties in areas where compulsion was in force for men. Those exempt included expectant mothers, those with a child under fourteen living with them, and those who worked a fifty-five-hour week or longer at business premises.

Women's Land Army: a civilian organization which undertook agricultural work.

women's services committee: a committee appointed in January 1942 to inquire into amenities in the ATS, WAAF and WRNS.

women snipers: in June 1944 it was reported that a German civilian woman sniper named Myra had been captured in Normandy and had been brought back to Britain where she was interned. It was also reported that some French women, who were married to German soldiers, had been sniping at Allied troops. However, the Allied military authorities claimed that no authenticated cases of French civilians acting as snipers had been found.

Woolworth: retail chain.

Woolton, Lord: from April 1940, Minister of Food; from November 1943, Minister of Reconstruction.

'your fuel target': government campaign under which householders in different parts of the country were encouraged to calculate their recommended yearly fuel units and keep within these in order to win the 'Battle for Fuel'.

youth registration: under the Registration of Boys and Girls Order of December 1941, young people between the ages of sixteen and eighteen were required to register at a local office of the Ministry of Labour and National Service and, if called upon to do so, attend an interview with the local education authority. If their circumstances permitted, they could be encouraged to join a youth organization or junior Service unit in order to undertake some form of national service in their leisure time.

Yugoslav patriots: those fighting the Axis occupying forces.

INDEX

Page references in *italics* indicate a figure and glossary terms are shown in **bold**.